The VINEYARDS of FRANCE

DON PHILPOTT

MPC

British Library Cataloguing in Publication Data

Philpott, Don
  The Vineyards of France.
  1. Wine and wine making — France
  2. France — Description and travel —
  1975- —Guide-books
  I. Title
  914.4'04'38   DC29.3

ISBN 0 86190 162 2 (paperback)

ISBN 0 86190 179 7 (hardback)

For Pam

Published by:
Moorland Publishing Co Ltd,
Moor Farm Road, Airfield Estate,
Ashbourne, Derbys
DE 61HD, England

Printed in the UK by:
Redwood Burn Ltd,
Trowbridge, Wiltshire

Contents

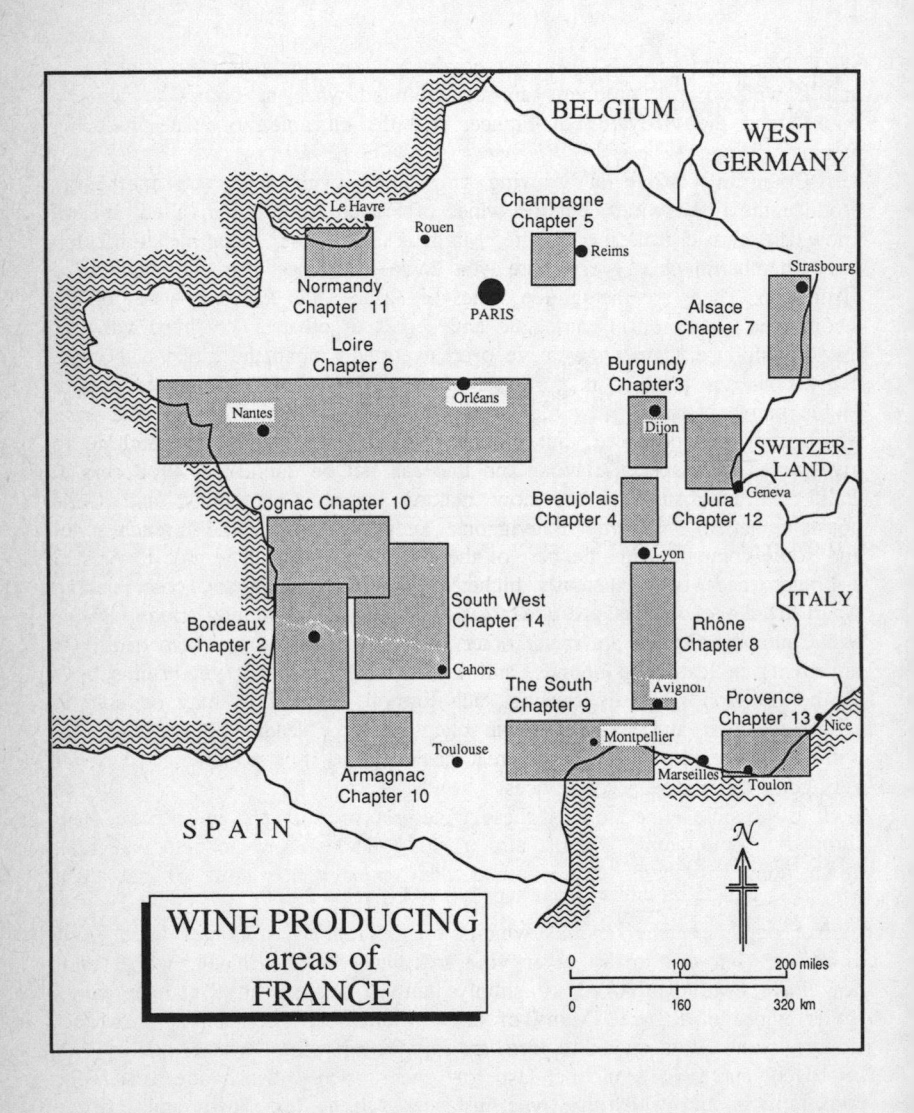

BELGIUM

WEST GERMANY

Le Havre

Rouen

Champagne
Chapter 5

Reims

Strasbourg

Normandy
Chapter 11

PARIS

Alsace
Chapter 7

Loire
Chapter 6

Burgundy
Chapter 3

Orléans

Nantes

Dijon

SWITZER-
LAND

Cognac Chapter 10

Beaujolais
Chapter 4

Jura
Chapter 12

Geneva

Lyon

ITALY

South West
Chapter 14

Bordeaux
Chapter 2

Rhône
Chapter 8

Cahors

The South
Chapter 9

Avignon

Provence
Chapter 13

Nice

Armagnac
Chapter 10

Toulouse

Montpellier

Marseilles

Toulon

SPAIN

N

**WINE PRODUCING
areas of
FRANCE**

| 0 | 100 | 200 miles |
| 0 | 160 | 320 km |

Preface

WRITING about wine is always a good deal less satisfying than drinking it, and a wine-writer's problems are compounded when he comes to write a book about the vineyards of France, still the champion of wine-producing nations.

Countries capable of growing grapes are vying with one another to produce the finest wines, but the wines of France are still unrivalled. We all know the classic names of Lafite, Margaux and Latour, Montrachet, Corton and Chambertin, but everywhere you look in France there are wines of distinction. There are the unique wines of Alsace, the powerful wines of the Rhône, the classics of Champagne and scores of others. The grape varieties used to produce these wines have been exported around the globe and while many countries produce magnificent wines, they are not strictly comparable to the native product. They may possess the characteristics of the vine from which they are produced, but climate, soil and geography all combine to give wines their special flavour and this can not be duplicated. Producers in California and Australia are now making superb Chardonnay, and Chile boasts remarkable Cabernet Sauvignons. They are made in the 'French style' and some compare with the best of the French, but France is able to present a bigger range of consistently higher quality wines than any other nation. Apart from the obvious prestige areas of Bordeaux, Burgundy, Loire, Rhône and Champagne, there are many other areas worth exploring where quality is improving in leaps and bounds, and whose wines have not yet been subject to the inflation which is causing such turmoil. Few of us may be able to afford the first and second growth clarets, or the leading Burgundies, but with a little exploration, and a great deal of fun, it is possible to discover very good wines at very good prices.

It is possible either to buy these wines on your travels, or to have them shipped to your home, and the aim of this guide is to try to help you track down some of these bargains, and then explain how best to get them delivered to your cellar.

Not only have the obvious wine-producing regions of France been given a chapter, but also many other vineyards have been included, which until now have been overlooked, or simply jumbled together in a chapter called 'other wines of France'. Many of these smaller regions, such as Provence, Cahors, Roussillon and the Jura are producing wines whose quality has improved enormously in the last few years, wines which are ready for consumption, and which in some instances can be laid down and left for maybe twenty years. They are often wines that have been overlooked by the experts, or dismissed by the large wine stores and buyers because production is too small.

The format of this book includes a brief description of the history of each region, its culture, geography and cuisine, and an itinerary to allow you to explore, but above all it concentrates on its wines. I have tried to gather together the most comprehensive list of vineyards open to the public ever published, although it is not a complete list of every such vineyard. Details of how best to travel to them, and where to stay and eat nearby, have also been included.

The aim of this book is to encourage you to go to the vineyards of France, to taste the wine which they produce, and to buy those which please you most. Tastes in wine differ widely; a wine which gives pleasure to some may be regarded with distaste by others. Additionally, the quality of the vintage can suffer wide variations from year to year, and so of course can prices. The task of recommending 'best buys' which will suit everyone has, therefore, been set aside: it is hoped that you will go out and find your own.

I am indebted to Food and Wine from France, the UK marketing organisation for French agricultural produce, for their invaluable help and generous assistance in this task.

Note on the Listings:
The larger producers frequently have many properties in several villages and all their holdings are listed, often with a common name, address and telephone number to contact for visting, tasting and buying. Some of the larger companies have separate numbers for their different estates, even though contact names and addresses remain the same.

Many vineyards in very small villages and hamlets do not carry a full postal address as there is no difficulty in finding them. In most cases they are usually well signposted. Some of the very small producers do not have a telephone and many are cooperatives with no named owner or manager.

Many of the hotels and restaurants are likewise in small villages and carry no full postal address, but they are usually well signposted and easy to locate. Most have been visited by the author or have been personally recommended by his colleagues.

Chapter 1

<u>FRANCE</u>
A General Background

Bergerac

Geography

FRANCE is a large country and it is impossible to visit all of it in one trip unless you have many months to spare. Indeed, it is possible to spend several weeks just exploring the vineyards of Bordeaux. This guide should encourage you to return to France time and time again, each visit holding out the possibility of discovering another wine, making new friends and seeing and doing many different things.

France is a republic and after Russia, the second largest country in Europe. It is bounded on the north by the English Channel, on the west by the Atlantic and in the south by the Mediterranean. It stretches from 42° 20' to 51° 5' North latitude, and from 7° 85' East to 4° 45' West longitude. It has a land and sea border of about 3,000 miles, and is divided into 95 *départements* including the island of Corsica off the Italian coast. It covers an area of 211,207 sq miles (547,026 sq km) and has a population of about 54 million. Its chief cities are the capital Paris, followed by Marseille, Lyon and Toulouse.

Because of the size of the country there are many geographical areas and great climatic differences, and all these contribute to the special characteristics of particular wine growing regions. To the north and west, France is mostly low-lying, with mountains in the south and east. The Paris Basin, in the centre of the country, occupies a third of France's land area, and is one of the finest agricultural regions in Europe. The Loire with its magnificent châteaux and fairy-tale castles, is the longest river in France, rising in the Massif Central and flowing 634 miles to the sea, past the sprawling industrial town of Nantes. The Massif Central, with peaks rising to over 5,000ft, contains many old volcanic cones, and covers about a seventh of the country. The highest mountains, however, are the French Alps in the south east, and Europe's tallest peak, Mont Blanc, is to be found here towering 15,781ft into the sky. It is a breathtaking sight as you follow the autoroute south down past Lyon to Avignon, and on a fine day you can see it on your left for mile after mile. The other great range of mountains is to be found in the south-west, separating Spain and France. The Pyrénées afford all-year skiing and provide shelter for the vineyards to the east, protecting them from the Atlantic weather.

Climate

France is the only country in Europe with the continent's three distinct European climates — maritime, continental and Mediterranean.

In the west and north-west, especially Brittany and Normandy, there is a maritime climate similar to that of southern England; mild winters and warmish summers with most of the rainfall in the spring and autumn. Eastern France and the Massif Central both share a moderate continental climate with cold winters and wet, warm summers. The south enjoys a Mediterranean climate of mild winters and dry, very hot summers, although vulnerable to occasional cold winds such as the Mistral in Provence, coming off the Alps. The high mountains, such as the Alps and Pyrénées, experience extremes of weather with very heavy falls of snow in winter and high summer temperatures.

As you travel east from the Atlantic there is a change in rainfall patterns. On the Atlantic coast, most rain falls during the winter, and this changes to summer rainfall in the east of France.

The great climatic advantage France has, however, is the number of regions and even sub-regions which have their own micro-climates, because they are surrounded by mountains, forests, or other geographical features. These micro-climates are responsible for the special growing conditions which favour many of the vineyards.

Although the summer is the main holiday period in France, the best time for the visitor interested in wine is during the spring or autumn. It is interesting to see how the harvest is gathered, but you will be the last person a *vigneron* wants to see as he struggles to get his grapes to his winery unless of course you have already written to him and offered your services in gathering the grapes. It is an exhausting but very rewarding way of getting involved in winemaking.

The Land

Almost 90 per cent of land in France is productive, a third of it being cultivated, a quarter permanent pasture and a further quarter forest. Deciduous woodland covers much of the north and west, and the marvellous forests of Fontainebleau and Compiègne have been planted with broadleaved trees. The Ardennes, ravaged by two World Wars, have been planted with conifers, and the forests are considered to be the best managed in Europe. Huge conifer forests have also been planted in the Low Vosges and in the sands of the Landes. In Provence there are extensive oak forests mingled with Mediterranean pine; and under the oaks, exquisite truffles are sniffed out by pigs and dogs. Towards the southern coast, the vegetation becomes scrubby, consisting mainly of wild olive trees, myrtle, laurel, stunted evergreens and herbs, such as lavender and thyme.

More than 10 per cent of the country's work-force is employed on the land, mostly on small farms, a relic of the Napoleonic Code which insisted that estates must be divided equally between all children. The constant breaking down of farm size which resulted has now been reversed because the units were becoming uneconomic, and while there were more than four million farming units in 1930, there are less than 1½ million today. While cereal farming dominates, accounting for almost half the arable land, wine is the most prestigious product. France is the second largest wine producer in the world, after Italy, and the leader in both quality and variety. Vineyards account for something like 2½ per cent of agricultural land, and they produce about 1,300 million gallons of wine a year.

In the north there are orchards of apples, both for eating and making cider and Calvados, the fiery apple spirit of Normandy. In the south and south-west there are thousands of acres of fruit, ranging from peaches to plums, kiwi fruit to nectarines. There are also orchards of almonds, chestnuts and olives. France tops the production league in many agricultural products, producing more butter than any other country in Western Europe, more rice, grown in the Camargue, more sugar beet, and more speciality soft cheeses. Food is never in short supply in France and the French pride themselves, rightly so, on the excellence of their cuisine.

The People

The population of France is 54 million. Paris, and its suburbs which make up Greater Paris, account for just over 9 million people, while only four other cities have populations in excess of 300,000. The people originate from three main type of early settlers, Alpine, Mediterranean and Nordic, but throughout its history, France has frequently been invaded and subjected to a wide range of influences and cultures.

It is possible to get by without speaking French, but in country areas it may be difficult to find people speaking English, and making the effort to speak the local language, no matter how badly, is appreciated. There are still some areas, however, notably in the north in Brittany and in the south, where language can be a barrier. In many parts of Brittany they still speak Breton, a Celtic language similar to that spoken for centuries in Cornwall. In Alsace, the language is Alsacien, which reflects the region's frequent domination by neighbouring Germany, while in the Camargue and Roussillon, they speak a form of Catalan because of their strong Spanish links. Near the Italian border, and especially in Nice, the locals have an Italian patois, while in Corsica they speak their own language of Corse. Many of the bigger vineyards and wineries do have English speaking guides and this has been marked, where possible, in the text.

History

This guide is not meant to be a comprehensive study of France, but some impression of its history and culture does help to explain why the country has such a long tradition of producing the finest wines.

The French language is derived from Latin, which was introduced in about 200BC when the Roman legions marched into what they called Gallia (later to become Gaul). Before then the country had been inhabited by Celts and other tribes. Between 58 and 51BC the Roman armies under Julius Caesar conquered the various kingdoms within Gallia and the people were persuaded to adopt the customs and language of the victors. During the next 500 years, the Romans transformed France. They built roads, bridges, and aqueducts; introduced a more sophisticated agriculture and more vines (the first vines could have been introduced by the Greeks around Marseille, or might even have been native); and with them came a new culture with theatres, arenas and galleries. Roman influence predominated for a long time, and while many of the other appendages of Roman life were subsequently to disappear, they left a legacy of a love of the arts and civilised living.

In about the fifth century AD the Roman Empire began to decline, and the legions were pulled back to defend Rome. The borders of Gallia became vulnerable to attack from other warfaring tribes. It was the Franks, one of the fiercest of the German tribes under their King Clovis, who in AD481 defeated the remnants of the Roman army at Soissons. He established the Merovingian dynasty, and to gain support from other parts of the country he adopted Christianity. Provence, in the south, had already converted to Christianity and the alliance of Provence and the Franks was formed to drive out the Visigoths who had captured Aquitaine. It was the Franks who gave France its name, although the Merovingian dynasty died out in 752.

Charles Martel 'The Hammer', became ruler of virtually all the territory which forms part of present day France in the 730s. Charlemagne, Charles Martel's grandson, who ruled from 771-814, championed the Roman Catholic cause and greatly expanded the frontiers of the country. He was crowned Emperor of the Romans in 800 by Pope Leo III, which gave him control over the whole of Western Christendom, for his services to the Church. Learning and culture flourished under Charlemagne, but his empire collapsed after his death, and even the partition of the country among his three grandsons in 843 could not stop the decline.

France had now become part of the kingdom of Carolingia under Charles the Bald and was constantly being attacked by Viking raiding parties. The Norsemen sacked Paris four times and sailed up the estuaries pillaging and looting. The king was powerless to stop these attacks, and the local people looked to their feudal lords for protection. Thus started the age of the powerful dukes but even they had to concede land to the Vikings to put an end to further attacks; they were given land on the lower Seine and they called their kingdom Normandy, the land of the Norsemen.

The Kings of France started to re-exert their authority in 987 when Hugh Capet, Duke of Francia, was crowned King of all France. For the next 400 years they gradually increased their authority. Philip Augustus, who reigned from 1180-1223, re-established the cultural heritage of the nation. With Paris as his capital, he built the Louvre, established the Sorbonne University and ordered work on Notre Dame Cathedral to commence. It was one of sixteen cathedrals started in his reign. The monarchy gradually established its authority over the various Dukedoms, often only after long and bloody wars, but the process led to the establishment of a system of administration and justice which was the envy of most of its neighbours.

The Hundred Years' War between England and France was a bitter struggle which devastated much of France. The English claim to the French throne, together with their overlordship of the Angevin dominions, were finally overthrown at great cost, and the names of Joan of Arc and the Burghers of Calais have passed into the history and legend of the period. One beneficial result of the Hundred Years' War was that the feudal nobility had exhausted itself in the international and internecine strife, and were forced to submit to the authority of the king.

The end of the war did not, however, see the end of religious and political strife, which was having such a damaging effect on the country. Henry IV, himself a Calvinist, issued the edict of Nantes in 1589 which allowed freedom of worship (until its revocation by Louis XIV); this ended religious strife, and his encouragement of trade, industry and agriculture gave a firm foundation to French expansion as a great power.

Richelieu and Mazarin, the statesmen-cardinals, greatly improved the efficiency of the French government, and laid the foundation of the Golden Age of Louis XIV. He was the first king of France with the power to rule and the state organisation to make the rule effective. It was indeed a great and glorious age. The 'Sun King' built Versailles, and the brilliance of his court was dazzling, as indeed was the immense intellectual and artistic flowering which occurred at this time. However, a major policy of Louis XIV and his grandson, Louis XV, was the waging of aggressive war in attempts to assert France as the major country in Europe. An unfortunate corollary of this policy was a failure to continue to improve industry, agriculture and trade, and increasing, and increasingly unfair, burden of taxation.

In 1789 the first events of the French Revolution took place; the First Republic was established, after much bitter fighting, in 1792. The 'Reign of Terror' instituted by the Jacobins saw the execution of many of the nobility, but their new order, with a new state, new religion and even new Calendar, proved increasingly vulnerable to the attacks mounted on it by neighbouring countries. The resultant wars saw the dramatic rise to power of Napoléon Bonaparte, whose facility at gaining victories assured his prominence. The overthrow of the Jacobins in 1794 led to a series of increasingly dictatorial governments in France, and Napoléon's proclamation as First Consul in 1799 and his coronation as Emperor in 1804 was the logical outcome of this process. Napoléon's new state, with its internal reforms and its new legal system provided the basis for the modern French state, and some of his innovations are still in force today.

Napoléon's skill in waging war achieved the mastery of Continental Europe of which Louis XIV had dreamed. However, England's naval supremacy and Russia's unlimited reserves of manpower and territory eventually resulted in his defeat and exile.

The Bourbon restoration, with the attempt by Charles X in 1830 to restore the old order, was short-lived; Louis Philippe was installed on the throne in 1830 to govern 'by the will of the People'. His reign was almost as brief, for in the 'year of revolutions', 1848, he was overthrown by Louis Napoléon, nephew of the Emperor, who proclaimed himself president of the Second Republic.

The Second Republic was fated not to last long; in 1852 Louis Napoléon seized power as Emperor Napoléon III. The Second Empire saw the second great intellectual and artistic blossoming of France commence, symbolised by the creation of Paris as we know it today by Hausmann, with its boulevards and spacious planning. However, governmental frivolity and corruption, and the failure to prepare France adequately for the modern age, led to its speedy defeat in 1870 by the Germans at Sedan, and the occupation of Paris. Napoléon ended his life in exile.

The Third Republic, established in 1870, lasted until 1940. Its early years saw perhaps the apogee of French artistic achievement, and the foundation of a colonial empire. The traditional policy of hostility to England was surprisingly reversed by the Triple Alliance (Russia was the third party). However, the division during the early years of the twentieth century, of Europe into two hostile camps culminated in World War I. Some of the bloodiest battles were fought on French soil, which was partially occupied by the Germans. Although France emerged as one of the victorious powers from this conflict, the damage inflicted on her territory, manpower and social fabric was immense. To give but one example: 10 per cent of the workforce, or 1.3 million men, were killed in the war. This weakness, and the internal strife evident in many European countries during the inter-war years, helped to ensure the rapid defeat of the Third Republic by Germany in 1940, when France was again partially occupied.

France was liberated in 1944, and General de Gaulle, leader of the Free French Government in London, took control in France in the name of the Fourth Republic. In 1945, however, he resigned when the new constitution failed to award him the executive power he required. In his absence, the Fourth Republic was beset by the many problems of a country recovering from the ravages of war; perhaps the most obvious problems, however, were the wars taking place in the colonies. In Indochina, fighting between France and the indigenous population continued until 1954 when the French withdrew. In that year, the troubles with Algeria began. The difficulties besetting the administration can be assessed by the fact that twenty-six cabinets fell during the fourteen years of the Republic. Perhaps the major achievement of those years was the formation, with five other European countries, of the EEC in 1957.

In 1959, de Gaulle assumed Presidency of the Fifth Republic, after obtaining the power he required. France withdrew from Algeria in 1962, and de Gaulle resigned in 1969. Since the start of the Fifth Republic, France has reasserted its international position and its economy has flourished. Helping this recovery, have been the nation's wines, which are some of the best ambassadors one could wish to find.

Travelling in France

Travel in France could not be easier, whether by air or sea. There are regular international flights from North America and Britain, and a very comprehensive network of ferry crossings from a number of Channel ports. Flying is obviously the fastest method of travel, and not only can Paris be reached quickly, there are regular, scheduled internal services to almost all the wine regions. Although this internal air service is efficient and relatively cheap and there is a very good main-line railway network, local travel can be difficult. The vineyards, for obvious reasons, are in the countryside, and are not always regularly served by buses. A car is therefore the best way of visiting the vineyards; one must always be conscious, however, of the drinking and driving laws which are vigorously enforced in France.

Those driving to France from Britain will use a ferry or hovercraft out of any of the ports right along the Channel. Ferry crossings from Kent and Sussex — Dover, Folkestone and Newhaven — take a couple of hours or less, while the routes from Portsmouth, Southampton and Plymouth can take eight or nine hours, but land in the Brittany peninsula, much nearer to the wine producing areas of the Loire and *en route* to Bordeaux and the Dordogne. Hovercraft services from Dover take only thirty minutes.

The length of time it takes to cross the Channel is an important consideration, and choice of port depends partly from which area of Britain you travel. People living in the west and Midlands will find it easier to drive down to Portsmouth or Plymouth. Although these routes take much longer than those further east, you can always take a berth overnight, and arrive in France early in the morning, fresh for the day's drive ahead. For many people, the actual ferry crossing is an important part of the holiday, when it is possible to enjoy a pleasant meal and drink. There is just about enough time to do this on the Dover and Folkestone crossings, and this is the best route if you want to travel down to Champagne country, or beyond to Burgundy and the Rhône.

Although in the summer months there are literally scores of ferries and operators to choose from, it is essential to book well ahead. At other times of the year, in the spring and autumn particularly, it is still sensible to book but if for some reason you arrive at the port very early or late, it is usually possible to get a place on board.

To drive in France, under French law, you must have your driving licence, suitable insurance, a green card, a red warning triangle (although this is not necessary if the car is fitted with hazard warning lights), and spare bulbs for headlights, side lights and rear lights. National identity plates must be carried, and it is advisable to take the car's registration documents. Headlights should also be adjusted so that they dip to the right, and covered so that they appear yellow to other traffic. This can be done by simply applying paint, sold by most auto parts shops, or by fitting a yellow-coloured lens over the headlight glass. The former is cheaper, but the paint can be washed off in very wet weather. If you do not take any action, you will find yourself constantly being flashed by motorists at night.

The wearing of seat belts in front seats of vehicles is compulsory. Newly-qualified drivers, with less than a year's full licence, are restricted to 90km (or 56mph). Other speed limits are:

motorways (with tolls)	130km/h (81mph)
(when wet)	110km/h (68mph)
dual carriageways/toll free motorways	110km/h (68mph)
(when wet)	100km/h (62mph)
other roads	90km/h (56mph)
(when wet)	80km/h (50mph)

The toll autoroutes can prove expensive, but they are the fastest way of travelling, and are often not too busy because most people prefer the free dual carriageways, which run parallel to the most used routes. These alternative routes do usually run through the villages and so can slow you down. If time is not important, however, why bother to pay? It is much nicer to be able to travel at your own speed, and to be able to stop and explore.

Traffic regulations are strictly enforced and there can be on-the-spot fines for driving on a provisional licence; driving under the age of eighteen; allowing children under ten years of age to travel in the front; stopping on an open road, except in the case of breakdown, and even then you are expected to push the car off the road if possible; failing to stop at a STOP sign (a complete stop is necessary, not simply slowing down); failing to observe 'no overtaking' signs, and crossing continuous white lines; speeding; drunken driving.

The laws relating to drinking and driving are the same as in the UK, and random checks operate with heavy fines or worse. The minimum on-the-spot fine for speeding is 1,300F, and for driving when under the influence of drink 2,500F, although in bad cases, arrest and detention will apply. It is not worth the risk. On the motorways there are petrol stations every 20km (12 miles) and emergency telephones every 2km (1.2 miles) French motorail provides a range of overnight services for those who prefer to avoid a long drive. At Boulogne, Calais or Dieppe you can check straight into the Motorail terminal, where there are English-speaking staff on hand. Luggage stays securely in the car, and a small overnight bag is the only necessity. There is a wide range of accommodation: single and double sleepers, family sleepers with three beds, and couchettes, four or six to a cabin. Breakfast is included in the ticket price. For those who prefer to fly in, there are flights from all major airports in Britain, the US and Canada to France, and an efficient internal service by Air Inter. Car hire is available at all major airports, or can be arranged once you arrive at your hotel and have had a chance to work out an itinerary. It is possible in some areas, in Alsace and parts of Burgundy for example, to do all your exploring on foot. There are local bus services but they can be erratic, and there are also local taxis which avoids the problem of drinking and driving. Taxis become a better idea if you are travelling as part of a group and can share the cost, especially if you hire a mini-bus. The car, especially your own, is however, generally the best way of travelling around, and it has the advantage that there is somewhere to stow your purchases of wine.

The Vineyards

Vineyards in France have occupied the same site for centuries and the tough wine laws in the best growing areas strictly control all new plantings. Methods of cultivation and grape varieties are laid down by the *appellation* regulations, and most growers are quite content to abide by them because they are based on proven results. The experimentation took place perhaps hundreds of years ago, and people now know which areas produce the best grapes, the best methods of pruning and so on.

The variety of grape grown, methods of training, pruning, yields and picking are also regulated under the AC (*Appellation Contrôlée*) laws, and even in areas previously noted for quantity rather than quality, strong efforts are being made to boost controls to raise quality in the face of increasing competition from other wine-producing countries. The AC system was created to govern the growing of grapes and production of wine in those areas making the best wines. The French insist that the AC is a guarantee of quality because the wines have to undergo tasting and laboratory examination to ensure a minimum standard. If the wines do not meet this standard, they are rejected and cannot carry the AC label. There is a growing body of opinion, however, mostly outside France, which would like to see some other quality rating instead of the AC, which is simply no more than a guarantee of where the wine comes from, the grapes used and the methods used to vinify it. It seems a nonsense to many that there are some magnificent *Crus Bourgeois* which are better than some Fourth and Fifth Growths; this cannot be argued away.

The French consider soil to be the most important factor in the vineyard, and there is no doubt that the type of soil can impart special characteristics. in a wine. The soil can even affect the colour of the wine. It is important to retain heat in the soil, so in areas subject to cool weather, vineyard owners have gathered together stones, slates or rocks to act as storage heaters, absorbing the heat of the sun during the day and slowly releasing it at night. Drainage is also important and it is better if the vines have to put down deep roots in search of moisture because this anchors them into the ground, and makes them less susceptible to damage in storms and wind. Chemicals absorbed through the roots can also influence the wine.

Because of the weight of grapes in some areas, or their value in others, it is necessary to train the vines. In some areas, where the wind is strong off the Atlantic, the vines are kept squat, and supported by a single pole. In the south of France, where quantity is sometimes more important than quality, the vines are grown on high trellises. The system of vine training varies throughout France.

Having chosen the variety, planted the vine and started its training, it is necessary to prune it. The aim of pruning is to control growth to get the best yields of grapes, not necessarily the largest. Shoots are not needed because they simply use up energy which should be going to the fruit.

It is also a fact that vines grow better on slopes, and on some slopes better than others. The French words *côte* and *coteau* mean slope. A slope facing the sun means the plant will get more warmth, there will be better photosynthesis, and less risk of frosts. It does not always follow, however, that a south-facing slope is best, because a great deal depends on local conditions. In Burgundy, many of the estates prefer east-facing slopes so that the ground can absorb the morning sunshine and release it during the rest of the day. This is also preferred in Alsace, where the Vosges Mountains in the west cast a rain shadow, and there is a very sunny local microclimate. In other areas the slope will be preferred which gives protection against sea mists which may roll in, especially off the Atlantic.

The vines need all the protection they can get, because they have to stand everything the elements can throw at them. In the *appellation* areas of France irrigation is absolutely forbidden, so the vines have to withstand drought; another benefit of encouraging long root growth. The vines have to withstand frost, and two very cold spells in Bordeaux in January and April, 1985 (the coldest nights for fifty years) set the grapes back many days. In Champagne some growers reported 60 per cent of their vines damaged by frost. The vines also have to withstand summer storms, wind and the worst of the weather conditions, hail. In 1984 a freak storm cut a swathe just a few yards wide in St-Emilion, wiping out the entire crops of some vineyards, while growers just a yard or two either side suffered no damage at all.

Having taken so much trouble to plant the vines in the proper position, establish them and train them, imagine the heartbreak when a year's, and sometimes a lifetime's, work can be wiped out in just a few minutes by the weather.

The work in the vineyard never really ends. In January each vine has to be pruned and this is a backbreaking, demanding job. In February cuttings are usually taken for grafting later on in the year. Although some vines last as long as a man, most have to be replaced after a much shorter period, and because of phylloxera, the disease which devastated Europe's vineyards in the late nineteenth century, these cuttings have to be grafted on to New World phylloxera-resistant root stock. In March the sap starts to rise. This is a critical time, one during which the owners pray that frost will not strike. In April, and sometimes earlier, the soil is turned over to aerate it, the vines are trimmed back and the first application of spray is used. May is the month for weeding and keeping the vines tidy, and in June the flowers should appear, the first real indication of the vintage that lies ahead. There is more spraying and tying up of vines, and weeds are cut back or sprayed so they do not take valuable nutrients from the soil.

With the period of maximum growth approaching, July is spent weeding and clearing away unwanted vine shoots to ensure the young grapes have room and the right conditions to grow. August is holiday time in France but work in the vineyard continues. It is illegal to spray after early July in some regions, but an eye has to be kept on the grapes, weeds need to be controlled and so on. During August and September the grapes continue to swell and change colour, and picking starts in some areas in September. It continues in other regions in October depending on the ripeness required by the grower. As the grapes are picked, the vineyards are tidied up and for the next two months, earth is piled up against the roots of the vines to protect them from the cold, they are trimmed, and then it is January again — and the process starts all over again.

The Winery

The winery of today is a far cry from that of just a decade or two ago.

Science and stainless steel have made their mark, computers are often used to control the various stages of vinification, and laboratories constantly check to ensure that everything is going well. A modern winery is a huge investment, and for many estate owners it is only in use for a few weeks after the vintage. But, as in all the stages in the winemaking chain, what happens in the winery determines whether you have a good wine at the end of the day or a bad one, a fine wine or an outstanding one.

Wine at its simplest involves the picked grapes being crushed and the juice fermented, using yeast and natural sugar to produce alcohol. When the required level of alcohol, or sweetness, has been achieved, the process is stopped and the wine is filtered and bottled. All grape juice is white, and the colour of the wine depends on how long the juice lies on the grapes, and sometimes the stalks. A wine will spend more time on the grapes and stalks to make a red wine than it would to make a rosé. The techniques for making white, red, rosé, sparkling and fortified wines are all different, and this is the briefest of descriptions to give some idea of the processes involved.

The first necessity is to pick the grapes. In the very best areas, the Bordeaux and Burgundy *appellations* for instance, grape yields are restricted to about two tons an acre or less. The growers can produce more grapes, but they must not go into the principal wine of the vineyard. Thus Mouton Cadet was created to use up the extra grapes not allowed to go into the production of the Baron's first growth, or when the vintage was not good enough to declare a first growth. Alas, the wine has become so popular around the world, that the present Mouton Cadet is a blend including wines both from the Médoc and outside.

The picking of grapes is in itself an art. In the very best vineyards, the pickers may take only one or two grapes from a bunch at a time depending on their ripeness, and it may take many passes up and down the rows over a day or two before all the grapes are gathered in. The timing of the picking is also critical, and usually follows the rule that it takes place 100 days after the flowering. Some vineyards prefer to pick early so the grapes still have a high acid content, while others specialise in sweet wines, so try to pick as late as possible to increase the sugar content of the grapes. This can be a gamble because the rains are always threatening around harvest time and a delay can often prove disastrous. It is necessary, once the decision to pick has been made, to gather the grapes in as quickly as possible. Many estate owners now use expensive grape-picking machines, but the best estates still tend to use skilled handpickers so that individual selection of the grapes can be made. Some vineyards are so keen to gather their grapes in quickly that they even work through the night, and the pickers have miner-type helmets with torches fitted, and the tractors have spotlights so the work can continue.

Once the grapes are picked they are put into baskets and transported to the winery. The less damage caused to the grapes at this stage, the better. The best vineyards use small baskets or plastic boxes to carry the grapes because there is less risk of them being crushed. The bigger cooperatives, or those concerned with producing wine for distillation, will often receive their grapes by the trailer-load, and you can see the juice run out because the pressure of grapes has started the crushing process prematurely. It is essential to get the grapes to the winery quickly, because if they are allowed to stand about in the sun, fermentation can begin and this can create problems. It is also usually advisable to get the grapes to the winery as cool as possible. The organisation needed to arrange deliveries of grapes to a winery during the vintage is also quite spectacular and every grower must stick to a carefully arranged schedule telling him exactly when to pick and when to deliver to the winery.

The quality of the grapes is determined when they arrive at the winery; it is assessed by the laboratory from a sample, usually taken as the grapes are weighed on arrival. This is particularly important when a winery is buying in grapes from a number of vineyards. Not only is it important to be able to identify the higher-quality grapes and press them separately, but also the growers of these grapes can expect a premium payment. This rewards them for the trouble taken and acts as an incentive to others to do better next time.

The grapes are then crushed to extract the juice. The traditional method of crushing using the human foot is rapidly dying out, although it is still practised by at least one vineyard in northern Rhône, and at least one Burgundy producer claims to use it for part of his harvest. A number of different 'crushing' techniques are used depending on the style of wine that is being made. Almost all the crushing equipment now used is ultra-modern and very delicate, able to extract just the amount of juice required.

The juice is extracted by putting the grapes into a press which also separates out the skin, pips, stalks and any stem. Red wine gets its colour by allowing the juice to stay in contact with the skins, and it can absorb tannin (for long life) from contact with the stalk and pips. The longer the juice, or 'must', remains in contact with the skins, the darker will be the colour of the wine. For white wine, there is no need for contact with skins, so the grapes are normally destalked on arrival at the winery and a special press is used to extract the juice. Only big, powerful whites are allowed some contact with the skins, not to gain colour but to acquire 'body'.

A horizontal press is normally used for white wines. The grapes are put into the cylindrical container until it is full, and it then revolves. As it rotates, chains inside the container thrash the grapes, and the juice is allowed to run off either to fermenting vats or barrels. A second type of horizontal press contains a bag which is slowly inflated once the grapes have been loaded. The inflating bag presses the grapes against the side of the container and the juice is released and allowed to run off for collection. Not all the juice is extracted at the first press, but the quantity of juice collected is up to the winemaker. The juice from the first pressing is always considered to make the best wine.

In wineries where large quantities of wine are made, the pressing may be done by a huge Archimedes screw. The grapes are simply poured into a well, and then transported along by the Archimedes screw which crushes them on the way. The rate of the turn of the screw can be controlled to regulate the amount of juice released. The fewer the revolutions, the less pressure on the grape and the smaller the quantity of juice released.

Usually, different grape varieties are pressed separately and the 'must' kept apart to see how it develops before blending takes place. There are some vineyards, however, which throw everything in together, and there must be some winemakers who then sit back with their fingers crossed wondering what the result will be. Others have perfected the art, and there is a red Burgundy wine called Passe-Tout-Grain, literally meaning 'processed all at the same time'.

Red wine, or rosé, gets its colour from contact with the skins, as has been mentioned. A rosé spends less time in contact than a red, and even the smallest contact is often enough to give a wine a faintly pinkish hue. Once the juice has been extracted and has spent its time in contact with the skin, if necessary, it is piped into fermentation vats where it begins its conversion into wine.

Wine is produced when yeast, which occurs naturally, attacks the sugar in the grape juice, breaking it down to release energy in the form of heat, which increases the yeast's working rate. The action of yeast on sugar produces a number of by-products which include carbon dioxide, and most important of all, alcohol. The yeast goes on working until it has used up all the sugar in the juice, until the alcohol reaches a certain level above which it cannot function, or until the fermentation is stopped artificially. Yeasts can only operate within certain temperature levels. If the temperature falls, they go into a state of suspension; if the temperature rises too high, they are killed. It is clear, therefore, why such huge sums are now being invested in modern fermentation vats which can be cooled or warmed as necessary. Controlled temperature fermentation is one of the biggest advances in winemaking in the last hundred years, and has enabled many areas, especially those with hot climates, to improve the quality of their wines enormously. The fermentation vats are normally double-skinned, allowing a cooling agent between skins to keep the temperature constant. Another method used is to allow cold water to run down over the tanks.

In the past, because of temperature fluctuations, the aim was to complete the fermentation process as quickly as possible to avoid problems of sudden temperature variations. Today, using sophisticated controls, the fermentation period has been lengthened and the wine is allowed to remain much longer in the tanks. One advantage is that this enhances the flavour of the wine, and avoids 'baking' the juice. However, a wine that has been fermented too long under a controlled cool environment can sometimes develop a 'pear drop' flavour, and this is a problem most winemakers try to avoid. Each winemaker knows the temperature at which his wine develops best during fermentation and this varies according to the character and style of the wine.

After fermentation, the white wine is usually allowed to settle for a few hours and then it is filtered. The new horizontal presses are very efficient at extracting juice, but they also allow small particles of skin to enter the must. This is one reason why the fermented wine has such a cloudy, milky appearance, and the particles must be removed. At this stage, the winemaker is allowed to 'adjust' the wine. In parts of France sugar can be added, a process called *chaptalisation*. This reduces the acidity of the wine but in the south of France, sugar is not allowed, and concentrated must has to be used which raises both the alcohol content and the acidity level. The winemaker may also add small quantities of chalk to reduce acidity levels, if necessary.

A lot of the mystique of wineries is being shattered nowadays, as concrete vats and stainless steel tanks take over from the traditional oak barrels. The latter may look marvellous in a cellar, but generally they are not as efficient as the modern storage containers. Stainless steel tanks have the added advantage that they can be used for both fermenting and storage or blending, while wood is difficult to clean and hugely expensive.

Only occasionally is white wine allowed to ferment a second time — malolactic fermentation — to reduce acidity levels. It does still happen, however, in parts of Chablis, the Loire and Burgundy, and occurs in the spring when the warmer weather stimulates dormant yeasts. If the wine is not to have secondary fermentation it must be removed from the vats, and this process is known as racking. Before this happens the winemaker must decide the style of wine he wants. If it is to be a completely dry wine, all the sugar must naturally be fermented out. If it is to be medium or sweet, the fermentation will have to be stopped artificially using filters. The wine is passed through very fine screens which extract all the yeasts so there can be no more fermentation. In some areas, for example, Germany, sweet juice is then added to increase the residual sugar content of the wine.

The wine is racked — that is, drawn off the lees (the sediment at the bottom of the fermenting tanks) — using filters or a centrifuge. The next stage is stabilizing the wine to prevent the formation of tartaric acid crystals, a totally harmless substance which occurs naturally in wine but which must be responsible for more complaints to wine waiters than any other problem. To prevent these crystals forming, the wine is cooled to just below freezing point and held like this for several days before its final bottling, labelling and dispatch.

The red winemaking method is different from the beginning. In Burgundy some winemakers keep the stems on for pressing, while others remove them. In the Rhône and Beaujolais, they are always included, in Bordeaux rarely, and in the Loire they are left on to assist the pressing and reduce the acidity of the resulting wine. During fermentation of red wine, the skins, stems and so on, float to the surface of the vats, and because this cap or *chapeau* is vulnerable to attack from bacteria, it has to be constantly mixed. Men are employed with long poles or paddles to keep it mixed, but the modern method is simply to pump fermenting juice over the cap at regular intervals.

After fermentation, the first wine to run off is the *vin de goutte*, literally the free run. The rest of the wine is still absorbed in the pulp of stems etc, and is known as the *marc*. It has to be pressed to release extra juices. These are held separately. The first press from the *marc* can produce good quality wine, but subsequent pressings are usually destined for distillation. The liquid is then 'fined' and filtered to extract any solids still remaining before being piped off to barrels or tanks. Most red wine undergoes secondary fermentation during this last stage.

As the wine develops, it is up to the winemaker to decide whether individual varietal wine should be made, or a blend. If the wine is not to be aged for long periods, it is usually pasteurised, to kill off any bacteria, and then it can be bottled. If it is to be aged, it will usually go deep into the vineyard's cellars and be kept in oak barrels, the size of which varies depending on which part of France you are in. Wine can age in the bottle as well, and the finest wines are those which have a combination of both barrel and bottle ageing.

The Quality Classifications of French Wine

There are four main categories of French wine, two for table wines and two for quality wines. The position is then further complicated, because various regions have introduced quality bands within the top categories, some of which are legally binding, and others which are followed voluntarily. The four main categories, however, are strictly enforced both by the wine authorities and the French government, and are now incorporated into Common Market wine legislation.

Table Wines

Vin de Pays, literally 'country wine', used to mean the *Vin Ordinaire* which tourists consumed by the litre. In the last few years, there have been great strides forward in quality and the *Vin de Pays* now represents the top end of the everyday table-wine market even though quality still varies considerably.

The category was instituted in 1973, and covers wines made from approved grape varieties from a designated area, which can vary from a single village to an entire region. The wines must have a minimum alcoholic strength, which varies from region to region. In the Mediterranean, for instance, the wines must have a minimum strength of 10°, while in the Loire it need be only 9°. The other major innovation of the *Vin de Pays* has been to limit the production to about 29,500 bottles an acre. By reducing quantity, the vines yield higher quality grapes (the surplus bunches can be discarded well before picking) and ensure high-quality wine, especially with improved vinification techniques. The *Vin de Pays* while not achieving the quality necessary to move them into the highest quality categories, are still policed by the *Office National Interprofessionnel des Vins de Table*.

Vin de Table is the lowest category of wine, and includes all blended wines, often sold under brand names, which do not meet the standards necessary to become a *Vin de Pays*. These wines can be produced by blending the produce of one or several regions. The wine is sold according to its alcoholic strength, which must be declared on the label. These wines are the *Vin Ordinaire* that most ordinary Frenchmen and women have with their weekday meals.

Quality Wines

The two quality categories are *Vins Délimités de Qualité* Supérieure (VDQS) and *Appellation d'Origine Contrôlée* (AOC) or as we know them, simply *Appellation Controlée* (AC) wines. The VDQS category was introduced in 1945. It applies to wines which come from a particular area, have already established a name for themselves and are striving to get full AC status. VDQS wines are serving an apprenticeship, and once they have proved their consistent quality, they are promoted to AC status. Eventually the category should die out as all VDQS wines achieve AC status.

Appellation Contrôlée is the top category of wine, the finest produced from a specific area, using approved grape varieties and laid-down methods of vineyard cultivation and winemaking. Everything is controlled by the *Institut National des Appellations d'Origine* (INAO), who are responsible for monitoring the VDQS wines as well. The AC category regulates how much wine can be produced from each acre of vineyards; on average, about 13,200 bottles per acre. Each region, however, has agreed different AC regulations. In Bordeaux, for example, the yield for red AC Bordeaux is restricted to 2,700 gallons per acre, while the AC Haut-Médoc stipulates 2,350 gallons.

Because of the concentration of good producers in the more famous winegrowing regions, especially Bordeaux, Burgundy and Champagne, attempts have been made to classify the wines into a hierarchy, and thus we have the various *crus*, or classes.

The first classification of red wine was for claret, in 1855, when the best sixty-two châteaux of the Médoc were placed in five classes. That classification has remained virtually unchanged ever since. In the original classification there were four first class wines, or *Premiers Crus* — Château Lafite-Rothschild, Château Margaux, Château Latour and Château Haut-Brion. Château Mouton-Rothschild, in Pauillac, was originally classified as a second class, or second growth wine, but after petitioning it was elevated to *Premier Cru* status in 1973, the only one ever to win promotion.

The red wines of Graves were officially classified in 1953, and those of St-Emilion the following year. In St-Emilion the classification consists of the *Grands Crus Classés*, or First Great Growths, of which there were twelve, followed by seventy Great Growths.

In 1855 the white wines of Sauternes and Barsac were also classified, with Château d'Yquem being ruled the only First Great Growth. There were then eleven First Growths and a dozen Second Growths. In 1953 the white Graves were also classified and eight were given *cru* status. The rest can call themselves either *Crus Bourgeois* or *Crus Exceptionnels*.

As you go through the various regional sections, you will discover the various peculiarities as far as the AC laws are concerned. Beaujolais for instance has its *Nouveau* wines as well as the *Beaujolais Villages* from about forty named communes, and nine *crus*. In Champagne there is also a hierarchy of producers, even though the AC covers the entire producing region. These top growers and producers are known as the *Grandes Marques*.

The AC system is not really complicated, and will be come clearer as you read on.

Chapter 2

<u>BORDEAUX</u>

The Château of Monbazillac
Bordeaux

THE links between Britain and Bordeaux have been forged over the centuries, and it was the English who coined the word claret. Although wine has certainly been produced in Bordeaux since Roman times, it was the marriage between Henry II of England and Eleanor of Aquitaine in 1152 which brought it to the attention of the English. Eleanor, who was thirty (eleven years older than Henry) had most of Western France including Gascony as her dowry, and all her territories came under English rule. This rule lasted for just over 300 years, with ups and downs, until General Talbot, the Earl of Shrewsbury, was defeated by the French. General Talbot was defeated at Castillon, near St-Emilion, and the scene was later to be immortalised by Shakespeare in Henry VI. His name still lives on in Château Talbot, the marvellous Fourth Growth from St-Julien.

The English connection allowed a flourishing trade to develop between England and Bordeaux, and many historians believe that this trade had a significant influence on England's development as a great maritime nation.

At this stage in the trade, most of the wine being shipped to England did not actually come from Bordeaux but from surrounding regions, such as Bergerac and Cahors. There is a record of the 'Black wine of Cahors' being traded on the London Stock Exchange in 1225. The vineyards of Bordeaux were being developed and expanded but the English taste was for young wines and for hundreds of years there was no thought of producing fine, aged wines.

During the middle of the seventeenth century, the first serious disruption in trade with Bordeaux occurred. In 1652 the first coffee house was opened in London and wine sales were hit. There were also diplomatic problems between England and France because of the aggressive foreign policy being pursued by Louis XIV. As a protest the English levied high taxes on the import of French wines in 1697 and these stayed in force for almost the next 100 years. Although wine was still shipped to England, for a time the quantities fell dramatically from the pre-1697 levels. At that time, up to 200 ships used to take part in the convoys bringing the wines back to England just after the New Year. The wine was carried in large barrels called tonnes or tuns, each one holding 252 gallons, and it was the ship's capacity to carry so many tonnes that led to the term tonnage which is still used to determine the capacity of a vessel. The merchant ships carrying the wine used to race for home because apart from the rough seas, they also had to confront pirates who operated at various points along the French coast, especially off Brittany. Because of this they started to carry weapons, and the armed merchantman was created.

Because of the heavy taxation, cheaper wines from other parts of Europe had gained popularity in England, so the people of Bordeaux began to change the style of their wine to try to woo back their traditional customers. The vineyards became much more organised, and laws were created to control various factors in the winemaking process, such as when the grapes should be picked. Bordeaux also started to build up its own fleet to carry wines to England, as the English fleet declined to make the journey.

Despite the troubles between England and France, many English wine merchants had established themselves in Bordeaux and they remained there. During the French Revolution, and the ensuing Reign of Terror, the English merchants and their families were imprisoned, but none were executed, unlike 300 of the top Bordeaux aristocracy who lost their lives at the guillotine erected in what is now place Gambetta.

By 1721 a record 34,138 tuns of wine was shipped from the booming port of Bordeaux, the highest level for more than 200 years, but most was going to Germany and the Low Countries, being too expensive in England for all except the very rich. Because the rich continued to drink the wine but had rather better palates, they no longer wanted to drink the wine of the last vintage. Estates started to produce wines which were aged and which commanded much higher prices, and so the first signs of the new order of *crus* began to emerge.

Even the Napoleonic Wars did not stop the Bordeaux trade with England, although most of the wine reaching the country was brought in by smugglers, but Napoléon's defeat at Waterloo brought a new influx of English *émigrés* to the region, the most notable of whom was the soldier, Sir Charles Palmer, who had served in the Peninsular War. He bought Château de Gasq in the Médoc, changed the name to Château Palmer and established another link between Britain and Bordeaux which still survives. Unfortunately, his success as a vineyard owner was short lived; he ran out of money and was forced to sell in 1843, but the vineyard still bears the general's name.

Other outsiders also saw the potential of Bordeaux at this time and began to invest in its vineyards, the Rothschilds from Paris, and the Péreires who took over Palmer. As more money was invested and standards improved, the idea of a classification of the best wines grew, and in 1855 the list was produced. Wine-lovers and vineyard owners have argued about it ever since.

Just as all this effort was being made, however, the vineyards of Bordeaux and the rest of Europe were about to suffer their greatest tragedy, the ravages of phylloxera which swept the area in the late 1870s and 1880s. Phylloxera is a plant-louse which travels through most soils destroying the vines. Its spread through Bordeaux was slow because of the nature of the soils, but there was no cure. Despite frantic searches for a treatment, the scientists could only come up with two solutions — to flood the vineyards, which would destroy the lice, but perhaps not permanently, or to replant everywhere using rootstock which was phylloxera-resistant. It was discovered that the phylloxera originated in America, but that American vines were not attacked by it, so a programme which was to last for twenty years was started to replant all the vineyards of Bordeaux. The only other protection against phylloxera was sand because the lice could not, or would not, travel through it. There are still, in some parts of France, vines growing on their original rootstock dating back to pre-phylloxera times. Now, all new vines planted in France, and throughout Europe, are cuttings taken from European stock, and grafted on to American root stock.

As if the phylloxera outbreak was not bad enough, the Bordeaux vines were then attacked by fungi. One fungal disease, Oidium, had attacked before phylloxera but was quickly overcome by applying sulphur. At the height of the phylloxera outbreak, however, another fungal disease appeared: mildew. Scientists developed a cure, a copper sulphate spray now universally known as Bordeaux Mixture. The other sort of rot to be found in the vineyards is the Noble Rot, used to prepare the grapes for the luscious wines of Sauternes and Barsac.

After the period of replanting, the Bordeaux winemakers had to wait for the new vines to develop. Between 1900 and 1920 there were no great vintages, and then France had to struggle through and recover from the effects of two World Wars. Despite all these problems, Bordeaux remains the world's top wine-producing region with more fine wines than anywhere else.

Geography and Climate

Bordeaux enjoys a temperate climate, similar to that of the south of England but with warmer summers and milder winters. The summers are hot enough to ripen the grapes, but not hot enough to scorch them. There is usually enough rainfall in the summer to maintain growth, but not enough to cause disease and rot, and generally the winters are wet but not cold. The bitter frosts in January and April of 1985 were the worst for fifty years in some parts of Bordeaux. Within the region, however, there are many micro-climates, and these transform the great wines of one estate into the outstanding wines of a neighbouring property.

The landscape of Bordeaux is best described as very gently undulating, although there are great expanses where it is flat for as far as the eye can see. As you drive through the Médoc, to the east of the Gironde and Garonne, it is easy to imagine the area as it was thousands of years ago, when it was a huge bog thrown up by the sea.

Vines will grow almost anywhere, but it is a fact that the best grapes come from those vines which have to struggle for existence. They do not like rich, loamy soil, preferring well-drained earth in which they can force down their roots in search of moisture.

The price of land in Bordeaux and its surrounding country is high because it is so good for the production of quality grapes. Very few other crops would do well here, although there are plenty of flowers growing. It is still possible to see roses planted at the end of the lines of vines on some estates. The locals tell two stories about why this is done. It was said that the scent of the roses attracted the insects which helped pollinate the vines; but a nicer tale is that in the olden days the horses always knew when it was time to turn round, as they caught the flowers' fragrance. In that way, the horses would work steadily all day going up and down between the vines, turning every time they reached the roses.

The siting of the vine is critical, and the best vineyards are those planted on slopes. If the vines are planted on flat ground there may be problems with drainage, and if they are at or near the summit of a slope, they may be more prone to wind and weather damage, lacking the protection of vines lower down. Vines on the flat and those at the top of slopes rarely produce grapes which make great wine.

Much of the Bordeaux area covered by vines has the added protection of the huge forests which were planted between the Atlantic coast and the Garonne in an attempt to bind the sand dunes together. The forests of the Landes are now some of the largest in Europe, and the pine trees not only yield valuable resin which is collected in pots or plastic bags strapped to the trunks, they also act as a barrier preventing the worst of the Atlantic weather penetrating inland.

There are about 2,000 properties in Bordeaux, of which about 200 stand out as the producers of the finest wines. The vines cover an area of more than 500 sq miles, split evenly between the production of grapes for red and white wines. The majority of the wine produced in the Bordeaux region has *appellation* status, and there is nowhere else in the world with such a wealth of different wines within such a small area.

The Districts of Bordeaux

THE MEDOC

The Médoc is normally divided into two areas: the Médoc in the north and the Haut-Médoc in the south. The land is slightly rolling and there are plenty of trees and forests. The northern area runs from St-Germain d'Esteuil to Talais and Soulac and the Atlantic coast at the mouth of the Gironde estuary. The Haut-Médoc, from La Jalle de Blanquefort to St-Seurin-de-Cadourne, has the greatest concentration of fine vineyards anywhere in Bordeaux. Within this district are many parishes, many of which have their own *appellation* status. Each produces wine which can differ enormously from that of its neighbours, but all are noted for their finesse, and generally they take longer to mature than wines from other parts of Bordeaux. All the vineyards are within two miles of the estuary, and the soil is predominantly gravel, sand and clay. The gravel decreases towards the south and clay takes over in the Haut-Médoc.

Margaux and Cantenac

These two parishes tend to have stone and gravel soils and the subsoils, into which the probing roots push, account for the different styles of wines. Margaux as an *appellation* covers 778 acres, Cantenac 962 acres, and neighbouring villages include Arsac (217 acres), Soussans (340 acres), Labarde (282 acres), Arcins and Avensan. Margaux has a wine information centre, a *Maison du Vin*, and boasts the most gravelly land in the Médoc; also the finest and most fragrant wines. The wines of Cantenac are thought to have a little more body. The wines of Margaux are light and full of flavour when young, but they mature into rounded, complex creations still retaining that original mouth-filling fragrance.

Moulis

The land here consists of a mixture of many soils; there is sand and gravel, gravel and limey clay, and chalk and clay. The wide variety of both top soils and subsoils accounts for the wide range of styles, but all Moulis wines are noted for their lightness, delicacy and bouquet. There are 860 acres under vine and some fine *Crus Bourgeois*.

Listrac

This commune covers 1,324 acres, and the wines generally are not considered to be as fine as those of Moulis. The land is more undulating and the soil consists mostly of gravel, although there are areas of clay and chalk. The wines are sturdy and astringent, have less body and fruit than the wines of Moulis, but are nevertheless, very much worth drinking.

St-Julien

One of the great names of Bordeaux, but the smallest of the best *appellations* in the Médoc, covering just 1,820 acres. The undulating countryside is also gravelly and contains more clay than in Margaux. The gravel is thought to impart finesse into the wine and the clay helps to produce a pronounced bouquet. There are only about 450 acres producing wines of *Cru Bourgeois* or *Cru Artisan* designation, all the rest are producing classified growths. For many, the wines of St-Julien typify all that is best in claret. The vineyards near the river produce the most pronounced wines, and the wine tends to become more full-bodied, deeper in colour and richer as one moves inland towards the plateau of St-Laurent.

Pauillac

Pauillac is, in fact, a small town rather than a village, and it commands an area which includes many of the great names of Bordeaux. Three of the First Growths are to be found here — Château Lafite, Château Latour and Château Mouton-Rothschild. The town itself is on the river, but the days when the ships used to call to take the wine have long since gone, and there is now a sleepy atmosphere. There is also a *Maison du Vin,* which houses an interesting wine museum as well as offering advice to visitors.

Latour is at the southern end of the commune and Lafite in the north, and they produce totally different wines. The soil of Pauillac is generally stony on a subsoil of sandstone. Again, it is this subsoil which imparts so much to the wine, and this particular sandstone, or *alios*, is reputed to give the wines of Pauillac their great qualities; powerful, elegant long-lasting wines, bursting with flavour. A young Pauillac often appears harsh, but it should not be drunk young because the wines age magnificently and are among the longest-lasting of the clarets. The Pauillac vineyards extend to 2,336 acres.

St-Estèphe

This commune consists of six hamlets covering 2,660 acres on hilly and wooded land. Most of the wine is *Cru Bourgeois*, produced from grapes grown on the gravelly soil with *alios* beneath. They need time to develop, lack the finesse of the Great Growths, and make good, strong robust wines, full of fruit and flavour. Some of the lesser wines can be harsh, and these may be discouraging to a drinker discovering claret for the first time; but persevere, there are some marvellous up-and-coming wines in St-Estèphe.

Ludon

This is a small parish by the river famous above all as the home of Château La Lagune. The first vineyard was planted in 1794, and it is the first import-ant château arrived at after leaving Bordeaux. There is a gravelly, sandy soil and the wines are subtle, with great finesse and a wonderful nose.

Macau

The style of this parish is a little more austere than Ludon, although the soils are similar, comprising gravel and sand, with a subsoil of *alios* and gravel. Château Cantemerle is the most famous property, set in its own wooded gardens. A good percentage of Merlot is used to give fine wines of great fruitiness, elegance and long life.

Lamarque and Cussac

Neighbouring regions making fragrant, medium-bodied wines on sand and gravel soils. Both communes lie along the river and are low-lying, but Cussac has some small areas of gravel producing high quality wines. The fourteenth-century Château de Lamarque was used by the King of England.

St-Laurent

A very varied parish in both landscape and geology. It has stony, sandy soil making fine wines, and also limestone and clay. Next to St-Julien.

St-Sauveur, Cissac and Vertheuil

Parishes to be found in Pauillac producing their own style of distinguished clarets, with fine colour and refreshing flavour.

St-Seurin-de-Cadourne, St-Germain d'Esteuil, St-Yzans, St-Christoly and Bégadan

These are all wine parishes at the top of the Médoc, producing good, and sometimes fine wine. The land here is also used for market gardening, and there are forests on the hilly slopes. The wines are characterised by their robustness, and fresh and fragrant style.

GRAVES

This is one of the oldest wine regions in Bordeaux, and it used to stretch for about forty miles up the Garonne from the city to beyond Léognan, and west, towards the Atlantic and the huge pine forests of the Landes. Just over half of the 3,735 acres produce red wine, the best of which comes from the area nearest to Bordeaux in the north. The wines often lack the delicacy of the best Médocs, but make up for it in body, depth of flavour and original style. The most famous Graves come from Château Haut-Brion, La Mission Haut-Brion and Pape-Clément in the commune of Pessac, and from the Domaine de Chevalier and Château Haut-Bailly in the commune of Léognan. The soil, as one might guess, is mainly gravel and stony, and the subsoil contains ironstone clay and limestone, but there are many local variations.

White Graves tend to be dry or medium-dry with good body and flavour. The higher qualities are usually dry, and possess a subtle bouquet and lingering flavour. The finest white Graves wine is, according to Hugh Johnson, comparable to the very best Burgundies. Some producers make it with just the Sémillon, others prefer to use only Sauvignon, while others choose a blend. The wine is made in a variety of ways, too, with some producers using stainless steel tanks and bottling in the early spring, while others make and mature it in new oak barrels. The latter producers create the finest white Graves. Hugh Johnson has called for the creation of a Haut-Graves *appellation* because the contrast between the north and south of the area is so marked. In his excellent *Wine Companion*, he lists the communes he would like to see in the new Haut-Graves area as Pessac, Talence, Gradignan and Villenave-d'Ornon, Léognan, Cadaujac and Martillac in the north, and Portets in the south.

The wines of Graves were classified in 1953, and the list was revised in 1959. Château Haut-Brion has always been first. In fact, it is the first growth mentioned in English literature because Pepys referred to it in 1663, although he spelled it 'Ho Bryen'.

Sauternes and Barsac

Sauternes is a small district just seven miles long by four miles wide, yet known the entire world as the producer of the very best sweet white wines. Barsac is a parish within Sauternes, and both are within the Graves area, although Sauternes and Barsac each have their own *appellation*. There are five parishes in the Sauternes region; Sauternes, Barsac, Bommes, Fargues and Preignac. They are towards the south of the Bordeaux region where production of white wines has taken over from that of red. White wine is produced because the climate here tends to be slightly cooler than farther north, and because the flinty, limey soil is perfect for producing the great qualities of white wine — body and vitality.

The vineyards of Sauternes nestle on a small river, the Ciron, which is a tributary of the Gironde. To the south of the river the five villages lie in a much hillier landscape, while Barsac on the opposite bank is on much flatter land. The presence of the Ciron and the influence of the Gironde are responsible for producing these luscious wines. The grapes are not picked when ripe but allowed to stay on the vines well into autumn, and they are harvested by experienced pickers. They are allowed to remain on the vines to attract a mould, *botrytis cinerea*, which develops in the autumn mists created from the moisture of the nearby rivers and streams. This becomes the so-called 'Noble Rot'. If the weather is fine and sunny, the mould attacks the grapes, and the sun shrivels them. As water is evaporated, the grapes become smaller but their sugar content intensifies. This natural sweetness is essential for making these wines. Pickers are sent into the vineyards to select individual grapes, rather than whole bunches, and the picking can take several days to complete, with several sweeps having to be made of the same row before all the best grapes are gathered in. This very special method of gathering is not only expensive, it depends a great deal on the weather. A sudden spell of wet weather can destroy the harvest. Because only the best grapes are used, the production is small and the yield is only about 300 bottles an acre. The very best Sauternes are enormously expensive, not only because of the winemaking techniques used, but also because the weather frequently affects the quality, and top quality wine may only be produced one year in every three.

Because the yields per acre are small, the estates in Sauternes tend to be larger than elsewhere in Graves, and it is to be hoped they will be able to survive despite the enormous economic disadvantages they face. Producers in other parts of the world are producing sweet wines using modern vinification techniques, and often simply adding sugar. These wines are much cheaper than Sauternes but lack their quality, and with any luck there will always be people who appreciate the difference.

The reason why 'Noble Rot' wines were first made is not known, but there are records of sweet wines dating back to Greek times. Certainly, the Hungarians were using 'Noble Rot' to produce the great wines of Tokay as far back as 1650 and it was 100 years or more before the technique caught on in France and Germany. The first records of Sauternes occur in 1845. The most likely reason for the development of sweet wines is that in former times, the vineyard owner was compelled to obtain permission from his feudal ruler, a duke or archbishop, or even the king, before he could pick the grapes and start the vintage. Legend has it that the messenger returning with the go-ahead to pick was delayed, the grapes started to rot and the resulting wine was not dry, as was the style of the day, but sweet.

At Château d'Yquem, producer of the supreme Sauternes, the grapes are pressed and then fermented at about 68°F, until the wine has an alcohol content of between 13° and 14°. When it reaches this level, the fermentation stops naturally because an antibiotic produced by the rot prevents the yeast working. The wine is then put into casks and allowed to develop. The best wines have enormous staying power and continue to improve for decades, and much spends at least three years in cask before bottling. The best Sauternes are beautifully-balanced, honeyed wines with a long-lasting sweet finish. Barsacs are often less rich but more intense, and the initial sweetness is replaced by a subtle hint of dryness at the finish.

In France it is quite normal to offer a Sauternes to a guest before a meal. The wine may also accompany first courses such as *pâté de foie gras*, will go with strong cheeses, such as Roquefort, and can complement many a dessert. The difficulty created by serving it at the beginning of a meal is to decide what best to follow it with.

Dry white wines are also made in Sauternes although they are not allowed to carry the *appellation*, because this only applies to sweet wines. The dry whites tend to be firm, full wines, with a hint of sweetness on the nose.

ST-EMILION

The district of St-Emilion produces soft, velvety clarets, quicker-maturing and slightly heavier than the clarets of the Médoc. Production is huge, but of varying qualities; almost all good, some excellent and some outstanding.

The St-Emilion area has been under the vine for centuries; King John had links with the town of Libourne in 1199 when he granted its charter. For many years before that it was an English outpost. The town was over-shadowed, however, by the faster development of Bordeaux, and its wines were not considered as good as those from the Médoc. In 1855 they were not considered worthy of display at the Paris Exhibition, and it was not until the beginning of this century that the wines began to attract the attention they deserved. It is only in the last thirty or forty years that they have really come into their own, and in many countries they still do not command the high prices of their comparable cousins from the Médoc.

The town of St-Emilion nestles into a hill with vineyards on all sides. The hill has been quarried to provide limestone for building, and caves in which to store the wine, and the vineyards almost touch the ancient city walls. The area is hilly and rocky, and there are still many relics of its former Roman occupation. The best wines come from quite steep hillside vineyards, or *côtes*, from the escarpment running round the town and from a small area of gravelly soil about two miles away, near the border with Pomerol, and producing the St-Emilion Graves wines. The valley of the Dordogne has sandy soil, and this produces yet another style of St-Emilion — heavier, firmer and with less finesse than those of the Côtes, or Graves. The main difference between St-Emilion together with its neighbour Pomerol and the other areas of Bordeaux producing fine wines, is the predominance of Merlot as the favoured grape variety, rather than Cabernet Sauvignon. There is also more Malbec grown here than in other parts of the Médoc, although the variety is known as Pressac in St-Emilion. The use of Merlot produces wonderfully balanced wines, full of fruit and warmth. They have more alcohol than the Médoc wines but less tannin, and this combination gives rise to their velvety softness. The wines mature more quickly than those of Médoc or Graves and can be ready for drinking in two years, but they also have wonderful ageing ability. The main villages of St-Emilion are Sables, Lussac, Montagne, St-Georges, Puisseguin and Parsac.

The wines were classified in 1955 and there are plans to introduce a new classification shortly which will simply list *Grands Crus*. Estates will apply each year for the right to call their wines *Grand Cru* and if it fails this tasting, it will simply carry the name St-Emilion. At present the two out-standing wines of St-Emilion are Château Cheval-Blanc and Château Ausone.

POMEROL

Pomerol is the smallest fine wine-producing district of Bordeaux, and many would argue that it contains the finest producer — the magnificent Château Pétrus. It has never been officially put into a classification, but is univer-sally recognised as having *Premier Cru* status, even though its reputation and subsequent massive increase in price is largely a postwar phenomenon. For years it was simply listed as part of St-Emilion. Although Château Pétrus dominates the wines of Pomerol, there are many other fine producers in this district, which can trace winemaking back to pre-Roman times.

Pomerol is another deceptive area where at first sight the landscape appears to be flat, but on closer inspection you can see that the vineyards are planted on slight slopes on a soil consisting mostly of clay, with gravel and sand. Much of the subsoil is gravel too, and this gives the wines of Pomerol their elegance and charm. There are about 180 producers in Pomerol with just over 1,800 acres between them, and every year about 300,000 cases of wine are produced; hence the high prices. The emergence of Pomerol as a serious wine producing district in its own right came in 1878 when Château Pétrus gained a Gold Medal at the Paris Exhibition, but any chance of making enormous profits as a result of this was dashed because of the small annual production from Pomerol. The wines were, and are, destined to be delicacies, commanding the sort of price one normally has to pay for luxuries.

As in St-Emilion, the Merlot is the most important grape variety and Cabernet Franc, known in Pomerol as Bouchet, is more popular than Cabernet Sauvignon. At Château Pétrus, 95 per cent of the vineyard is planted with Merlot and the grapes are only picked in the afternoon, so that the morning dew does not dilute the juice. It is this sort of meticulous detail, both to the picking and to the wine making, that makes Château Pétrus one of the great wines of the world.

BOURG AND BLAYE

The Côtes de Bourg is on the right-hand bank of the Gironde, and the vineyards cover the steeply-rising slopes which rise about 200ft from the water's edge. The district has been making wine for centuries, and has long associations with the English crown. To the north is the Côtes de Blaye. Both Bourg and Blaye were medieval ports, and there is a fortress at the former which was pre-eminent during the time when the English crown ruled the area thanks to the acquisition of Aquitaine through marriage. Bourg makes more red wine than white, and Blaye more white than red. The best reds of Bourg are superior to the best of Blaye. Both Bourg and Blaye lie on the other side of the river Médoc but they have a totally different landscape. Bourg produces its best wines nearest the river, mostly from Merlot and Cabernet Franc. The reds are full-bodied and rounded with fine noses, and are best between three and five years old, although the best vintages can go on for a few more years. Blaye is the most northerly vineyard on the right bank, producing good red wine. The wines tend to be lighter and less full-bodied than the Bourgs, but are much fruitier. As with Bourg, the majority of the production is now in the hands of cooperatives.

FRONSAC

The hilly, wooded district of Fronsac lies 2½ miles to the west of Libourne, and the village which bears its name is found at the junction of the Dordogne and its most northern tributary, the Isle. It is a medieval town, surrounded by hills up to 300ft high, which affords it special protection from frosts during severe winters. There are about 1,500 acres of vineyards in Fronsac, and a further 750 acres in the adjoining Côtes de Canon Fronsac, which carries a separate *appellation*. The wines have a very special character, especially when young, because of the Cabernet Franc which is the main grape variety used. Generally the wine produced in the lower slopes of the hills carries the Fronsac *appellation* while the wine from the higher slopes is Canon Fronsac. The wines have a quality and elegance that has been overlooked in the past. They age well, and because they tend to be overshadowed by the 'big name' neighbours, they are still excellent value.

ENTRE-DEUX-MERS

The region produces both red and white wines, but the *appellation* only covers dry white wines which have been gaining ground in terms of quality in the last few years. The red wine is usually sold under the name of Bordeaux Supérieur.

The south of the region is split between vines, woodland and agriculture, but the north is concerned only with the grape, and there are some massive producers. The largest cooperative at Rauzan produces well over one million cases of wine a year. In the north the soil is composed of sand, silica and limestone, all suited to growing grapes for white wine, and the preferred variety is now Sauvignon. The region rarely produces great wines, but specialises in honest, dry, refreshing, light, crisp wines, which are bottled young and need to be drunk young.

PREMIERES COTES DE BORDEAUX

This district is a long, narrow strip along the east bank of the Garonne, stretching from Carbon-Blanc to just beyond Macaire. It lies opposite Graves, and inland is Entre-Deux-Mers territory. In the north, red wines are made, but the further you travel south, the more white wine predominates, and the sweeter it gets. The communes in the far south of the district can produce sweet wines comparable to those of Sauternes, but generally the wines are lighter and lack the true honeyed character of the 'Noble Rot'. The reds bearing the name Premières Côtes are better than Bordeaux Supérieur wines and some growers are making efforts to improve quality by new vinification techniques. These producers are making the light, fruity-style clarets that have become so popular recently in both Britain and the United States.

A Tour of the Bordeaux Region

Bordeaux is the world capital of wine. Simply driving through the Médoc for a few miles will cause a certain amount of strain in the attempt not to miss any of the great names. While wine must be the great attraction, there are plenty of other things to see and do in the area, and Bordeaux itself is a great city in which to make a base. There are regular flights to Bordeaux from London and Paris, and very many from other airports in France. There is a special shuttle service from the airport to the centre of Bordeaux which runs every thirty minutes from Monday to Saturday (less frequently on Sunday). The journey takes between twenty and thirty minutes depending on the traffic. There are trains to Bordeaux from all the main line stations, and it is possible to see something of the Gironde by train. For Arcachon the SNCF runs an hourly service from St-Jean Station. Other train services do not really go to the most popular wine areas, and although there is a bus network, this may entail long waits for connections. The best way to see the area is either by car or by bicycle. There are fast routes from the Channel ports and Paris to Bordeaux, but the best way of exploring the city is on foot. The streets can be packed, and there are strict parking laws, so use one of the many cheap car parks. If you travel to Bordeaux by plane or train, you can hire cars or bicycles if you wish.

For travelling in and close to Bordeaux the bus is more than adequate and there are fare reductions if you buy a block of tickets in advance.

Tour of Bordeaux

Any visit to the region should begin with an exploration of the delightful town of Bordeaux. Strolling through old Bordeaux it is easy to recall the grace and elegance of bygone years. Today the streets can often be blocked with traffic and people. A hundred or more years ago it had no such problem, with the three majestic avenues of cours Victor Hugo, cours d'Alsace et Lorraine, and cours du Chapeau-Rouge running down to the river, fronted with elegant mansions and buildings. Along this frontage today there are still marvellous sixteenth-century houses with their inner courtyards, and the magnificent place de la Bourse, formerly the place Royal. This area is best explored on foot, with a good street map, because it is easy to get lost in the warren of side streets.

A suggested route, which can take two or three hours (or a whole day if you wish), can start near the tourist information Centre in the cours du xxx Juillet. Just down the road to the east is the monument to the Girondins erected at the turn of the century. The tourist office itself is housed in an early nineteenth-century building, and this is a good place to start because a free guide to this route is available here.

Opposite the tourist office is the Hôtel Gobineau, started in 1786 from drawings made by Victor Louis. He also designed the Grand Theatre on the corner of place de la Comédie and the cours du Chapeau-Rouge. Built in 1773, it resembles a Greek temple with twelve Corinthian columns crowned by muses and goddesses. Inside is a marvellous Italian-style theatre. Turn right into cours de l'Intendance, where the Hôtel de Roly, built in 1780, the Hôtel Acquart built in 1785, and Hôtel Pichon, started in 1610 and not completed until 1900 can be seen. After visiting the seventeenth-century church of Notre-Dame, return to the Grand Theatre. Opposite is the Hôtel

Bonnafé, built in 1782 by architect Etienne Laclotte. Continue down the cours du Chapeau-Rouge, where there are many fine old buildings, including the Hôtel Laubardemont, 1608; Hôtel Louis, designed by Victor Louis in 1774–80; and another of his works, the Hôtel Boyer Fonfrède, built in 1775–6.

A quick detour through the lanes opposite leads you to the sixteenth-century church of St Rémy; after visiting this, take the road back to the river, and stroll round the splendours of the place de la Bourse. Take rue F. Philippart to the place du Parlement, formerly the place de Marché Royal, with its fine mid-eighteenth-century mansions and buildings, and fountains. Leave by the bottom left-hand corner of the square for the church of St Pierre dating from the fifteenth century, and then take the rue des Argentiers into the conservation area. All around you will see the results of careful conservation and preservation work. Just to the north there is the area of the Tours de Grassies, where many projects are now being carried out; in the nearby headquarters for the Centre for Architectural Aid, information and maps showing what projects are in hand are available.

At the corner of the road, turn left towards the river again and visit the Porte Cailhau, dating from 1495, built to commemorate the return of the French to Bordeaux. Cut through from here to the cours d'Alsace and Lorraine, opened in 1869, and then into the rue de la Rousselle and the mansion where Michel Montaigne lived in the sixteenth century.

Running almost parallel to this street, to the north, is rue Neuve with some very old buildings, including the Maison Noble from the fourteenth century. Some other properties of the same age have, unfortunately, been altered and their façades have been changed. From here, cut through into cours Victor Hugo. This boulevard follows the path of the old moat that was used for the western defence of the city. A little way up and on the left is the rue Pilet, which should be explored for its half-timbered fifteenth-century houses, and then it is down to the fifteenth-century church of St Michel with its magnificent steeple. The church is reached by cutting through the rue des Faures. After visiting the church, walk down to the river and stroll back along it until you reach the allées d'Orléans, which will lead back to the tourist office.

This is only a fraction of things to see in the old city, but the route does cover many of the most interesting sights. Other things of interest to see in Bordeaux include the place Camille-Jullian, with its Gallo-Roman remains and sixteenth-century church of St Simon and the seventeenth-century church of St Paul built between 1663 and 1676 by Mathurin Biziou. There is the Porte de la Grosse Cloche, dating from the fourteenth century, and the former alarm tower. There are the ruins of the Palais Gallien, the Roman amphitheatre dating from the third century which could seat 15,000 people. There is also a superb collection of statues from this period in the Museum of Aquitaine. Also, visit the early Christian site of St Sernin.

The church of St Sernin dates from the eleventh century, but stands over a much older crypt containing third- and fourth-century sarcophagi. The church of Ste Croix has one of the finest examples of a Romanesque portal, and the eleventh-century cathedral of St André and the fifteenth-century bell tower next door should also be visited.

Bordeaux boasts many fine gardens, including the English style *Jardin Public*, and the Botanic Garden and Orangerie just north of it.

Museums to visit include the customs and excise museum; the museum of fine arts with works from the fifteenth to twentieth centuries; Galerie des Beaux-Arts with its collection of paintings, sculptures and tapestries; and the Museum of Aquitaine which traces the history of the region from the earliest times. There is also a natural history museum; a museum of contemporary art; the Centre National Jean Moulin; a military museum; a museum for the decorative arts; and the Casa de Goya, where the Spanish painter lived during his exile and died.

There are hotels and restaurants in Bordeaux to suit all tastes and pockets, and a wine-tasting centre where some idea of the produce of the surrounding countryside can be gained.

While Bordeaux has a wealth of architectural treasures, museums and other places of interest, this cannot be said for the region surrounding it. There are many fine old houses, fortified farms and the like, but these are often hidden behind trees or large walls. Many of the larger estates taking visitors have created their own museums devoted to the history of wine, cooperage and so on. The itineraries given below suggest routes or one day's travel, all based on Bordeaux.

Tour of Blaye and Bourg

This is an interesting region to explore because the countryside is more hilly than elsewhere in the region, thus its nickname 'the Switzerland of Bordeaux'. It is a good area to start a tour of Bordeaux because although the wines can be very good, they are not comparable to those produced just a few hundred yards away across the Garonne. Both Bourg and Blaye produce pleasing reds and whites, and as this is the first day of the tour, it is a good idea to taste the wines in the morning, find a nice spot for a picnic and then, in the afternoon, relax beside the river, sampling some more of the wine. If it is raining, explore the towns of Blaye and Bourg and enjoy the hospitality of some of the village cafés. Blaye is noted for its citadel, and has always been important because of its strategic position dominating the Garonne. Louis XIV commissioned the great architect, Vauban, to build a large castle at Blaye to protect Bordeaux. In fact the fortress had two functions; to stop invaders coming in and to stop smugglers getting out. There was at that time much illicit trade, which robbed the city of revenue. The citadel still stands today and can be visited, and there are marvellous views of the Médoc, just across the river, from its ramparts.

Blaye is an attractive, unhurried little town and both its wines and winemaking techniques have made enormous strides in recent years. Less than thirty years ago the grapes were still taken to the wineries by ox and cart, but these were replaced when a number of Algerian French moved into the area and introduced mechanisation. Blaye produces both white and red wine and the latter is better quality and remarkably good value. There is a tasting centre at Blaye at the allées Marine, open from Easter to 30 September.

The red wine of Bourg is better, however, than that of Blaye and it is interesting to compare the two. Bourg is a small village almost exclusively devoted to wine and surrounded by vineyards. There is a tasting centre at the Hôtel de la Jurade. To drive to Blaye, take the N10 from Bordeaux to St-André-de-Cubzac, and then the N137. On the return journey follow the N699 to Bourg, passing through Plassac, and then on down to St-André, and the N10 back to Bordeaux.

Tour of St-Emilion and Pomerol

Between Bordeaux and Libourne are the wine areas of Fronsac, Pomerol and St-Emilion. It is possible, but exhausting and inadvisable, to tour them in a single day.

At Libourne, the heart of Pomerol, the vineyards grow almost up to the houses. It is an attractive town, a small river port, built at the point where the Isle river joins the Dordogne. The town was founded in 1270 by an English knight, Roger of Leybourne. The towers by the Grand Port are part of his medieval fortifications, and there are still quite a few old houses. The square, with its arcades, is the town's most charming feature. There are also some good hotels and restaurants. However, after a quick visit to the town, you should see the unimposing Château Pétrus, producer of the most expensive wine of Bordeaux and arguably the best wine in the world. There are other excellent vineyards to visit in the tiny Pomerol area, especially Gazin, La Pointe, Clos-René, Vieux-Château-Certan, La Conseillante and L'Evangile.

A short detour to Fronsac can be made by following the N670 just before Libourne. The Fronsac vineyards are on the hill, a rarity in Bordeaux, and a visit is worthwhile because again, you can compare the red wines and note how three distinct producing areas, almost on top of each other, can produce wines of such different character and quality. The best of the Fronsac wines are very good, and good value for money. The best of the Pomerols are exquisite, but alas too expensive for most occasions.

St-Emilion is a charming town, with the houses built on a small level ridge of land overlooking the river. It is named after a holy man from Brittany, who arrived in the district in the eighth century. He established a monastery and the nearby village became known as St-Aemilianus, which in the local dialect was pronounced St-Emilion. Because of its popularity with tourists, there are now many craft shops, but it is still a delight to walk through the narrow, cobbled and often steep streets. There is a wine museum, catacombs and the cave where St Emilion once lived. The collegiate church is a mixture of architectural styles, which have grown together to make a unique and surprisingly splendid building. There are the ruins of the abbey cloisters, a huge church carved into the rock, and the remains of a Gothic church abandoned 500 years ago.

At nearby Castillon-la-Bataille there is a memorial to the Earl of Talbot, who fell in battle in 1453 when the English were defeated by the French at the Battle of Castillon; also worth a visit is St-Michel-de-Montaigne. The great essayist and former Mayor of Bordeaux retired here in 1570, and his tower can still be visited.

The St-Emilion region is world-famous for its wines. There are said to be more than 1,000 châteaux making wine, and the most famous by far is Cheval Blanc, just across the border from Pomerol and Château Pétrus. Many of these vineyards, especially near St-Emilion, accept visitors and the car may be left in the town as they are mostly within walking distance. Two are of special importance, Clos Fourtet because the caves, hewn from the rock, extend to several galleries, and Château Ausone, which is said to have been built on the site of a Roman villa owned by Ausonius, the poet and tutor to the Emperor Gratian.

Tour of Entre-Deux-Mers

Although only the white wines of Entre-Deux-Mers are allowed to call themselves that, the region produces an enormous amount of wine, red, white and rosé, and is well worth a day's visit. The area encompasses all the land to the east of Bordeaux between the Dordogne and the Garonne. 'Entre-deux-Mers' literally means 'between two seas', the seas in this case being the rivers Dordogne and Garonne. This area produces most of the red wine for Bordeaux and Bordeaux Supérieur AC wines, and it makes reds, rosés, and dry and semi-sweet whites.

There are a number of ruins of abbeys and other religious institutions throughout the area, and there is a well-signposted 'Tour of the Abbeys' which, in its 75 miles, takes you through the region.

Places to see must include Langoiran, south-east of Bordeaux on the Garonne, and Cadillac, just up the river from Langoiran: the former for its wine-tasting, and the latter for its wine and its history. Cadillac is a village with many medieval and Renaissance remains, including the Château d'Epernon, built by King Henri III's High Admiral of France. The village also gave its name to the famous limousine. Antoine de la Mothe Cadillac was a colonial administrator in Canada in 1701, and started to build a fort near the Great Lakes. The fort was to defend a strait between Lake Huron and Lake Ontario. The French for strait is *étroit*, the village was *ville d'étroit* which eventually became Detroit. When the car company wanted a name for their new limousine, they chose the name of the man who had founded their city. There are Maisons du Vin at Beychac and Caillau, and Cadillac in the château of the Dukes of Epernon. The different *appellations* to look out for are Cadillac (semi-sweet and sweet whites) Côtes de Bordeaux St-Macaire (semi-sweet and sweet whites), Entre-Deux-Mers (dry white), Graves de Vayres (red and dry and semi-sweet whites), Loupiac (semi-sweet and sweet whites). Premières Côtes de Bordeaux (reds, semi-sweet and sweet whites), Ste-Croix-du-Mont (semi-sweet and sweet whites), and Ste-Foy-Bordeaux (reds, semi-sweet and sweet whites).

Tour of Sauternes and Barsac

This is the area producing the luscious honeyed sweet white wines. There is a signposted 'Tour of Sauternais', which visits most of the great names, and Barsac and Sauternes can be reached in less than half an hour of leaving Bordeaux. The region is compact but hilly, and the route weaves back and forth through the lanes to pack in as much as possible.

The most famous name of Sauternes is Château d'Yquem, and it stands imposingly on the hill just to the north of the small village of Sauternes. Château d'Yquem was built in the thirteenth century, and was originally named Eichem after its owner. Work on the château continued for 200 years and the name gradually evolved to Yquem. Stop to look at Château de Malle, although it is not open to the public, and drive through the grounds of Château Filhot, which is.

Five towns make up the Sauternes *appellation*, and you can see them all from the battlements of Château d'Yquem — Fargues to the east, Preignac and Barsac to the north, Sauternes to the south, and Bommes, less than a mile away to the west. At Preignac there is the first growth Château Suduiraut. The seventeenth-century château lies in a park designed by Le Nôtre, who was also responsible for the gardens at Versailles.

The area of Sauternes and Barsac is small and it is not full of great historic interest, although many of the châteaux date from the seventeenth century or earlier; but it does have its wines. That is enough.

Tour of Graves

Graves is the area south of Bordeaux and to the west of the Garonne, a strip about five miles wide and thirty-five miles long. It produces both white and red wine, and both can be tremendous. There is a well-marked tourist route through the classified growths of Graves, signposted by arrows, and this runs through Léognan, Cadaujac and Martillac.

By travelling out of Bordeaux on the N650, Pessac and Talence, almost suburbs of the city, are soon reached. They contain some of the most famous classified growths such as Haut-Brion and Pape-Clément. A little further on is Léognan with Haut-Bailly, Carbonnieux, Domaine de Chevalier, Fieuzal and Olivier.

Château Haut-Brion dates from the sixteenth century and is set in beautiful gardens. Château Pape-Clément is one of Bordeaux's oldest vineyards; in the thirteenth century it was owned by the Bishops of Bordeaux, one of whom later became Pope Clément V in 1305. It was Clément who moved the Papacy from Rome to Avignon.

Château Carbonnieux can also trace its winemaking history to the thirteenth century although the château dates from the fifteenth. For many years it was a sanctuary for pilgrims. Château Oliver dates back to the thirteenth century and has turrets, buttresses and a moat. Well worth visiting is Château de Labrède, a moated fifteenth-century mansion, and birthplace of Montesquieu. The house with its library, and the grounds, are open to the public.

There are many delightful and old châteaux throughout this area, and because it is so compact you can explore it at leisure. The most famous wines, all with interesting houses, are to be found to the immediate south-west of Bordeaux, but it is also worth exploring further south.

Tour of the Médoc and Haut-Médoc

The Médoc, including Haut-Médoc, is the area running northwards from Bordeaux, hugging the western banks of the Gironde. The area is home of many of the world's greatest wines, and a day trip can only scratch the surface of what is on offer. Even experts on wine, who return to the Médoc year after year, have still to see it all.

There are a number of tourist routes created so that different parts of the Médoc and Haut-Médoc can be seen. All are clearly signposted and take in separate sections of the area. Any tour, however, must try to take in the most famous parishes of St-Estèphe, Pauillac, St-Julien, Moulis, Listrac and Margaux. In addition to these, Cantenac, St-Christoly and St-Yzans are also worth visiting.

Many of the châteaux are hidden behind high stone walls and trees and most are very attractive old buildings, although sadly some have seen better days and are in need of repair. Château Margaux, however, is not one of these; it is a marvellous building, designed by Combes, a pupil of Victor Louis, and the pillared *chais* are worth a visit. Opposite is Château Palmer, which often has three flags flying to denote its joint English, French and Dutch ownership. Nearby is Château Lascombes, owned by UK brewers Bass Charrington, which is also worth a visit.

In St-Julien is Château Beychevelle with its fine gardens, which was owned by the Grand Admiral of France in 1587. He gave the château his name. Château Langoa dates from 1759 and can be studied from the road, and look also at Château Léoville-Lascases, famous for its massive gates.

Château Latour in Pauillac used to be owned by the Marquis de Ségur who also owned Latour, Lafite, Mouton and Calon-Ségur. (His dinner parties must have been wonderful!). Today it is owned by Harveys of Bristol. For many centuries the château was an observation post to alert people up river of the approach of unfriendly ships.

Also in Pauillac are the châteaux of Pichon Contesse, Pichon Baron and Lynch-Bages. In the town itself, on the quay, is a wine museum and tasting centre. There are also tasting centres at Margaux and St-Estèphe.

Just outside Le Pouyalet is Château Lafite, and nearby are Mouton Rothschild and Pontet-Canet. At Mouton there is a museum of art which has wine as its theme, and you can visit the *chais*.

St-Estèphe is home of Cos d'Estournel, a strange building with an Eastern flavour. The Germans built a gun emplacement on the top of the mansion during World War II because of its commanding position.

Other communes to see include Ludon, with Château La Lagune, designed by Victor Louis. This is but the briefest thumbnail sketch of Bordeaux, but for the first-time visitor, it is an introduction. Having visited it once, you are certain to return time after time.

Gastronomy of Bordeaux

The food of the Gironde matches perfectly the excellence of its wines. The Bordelais have a huge supply of local food to call on, whether this be from the sea, from the forests of the Landes or the neighbouring farms. The dishes of the region tend to be less ornate than in other areas of France, but this is intentional, because it shows the wine to best advantage. That is not to say, however, that you cannot eat excellent food as you travel through the region.

There is a local caviare (although in the past much was shipped to Russia); there are oysters to be washed down with excellent dry white, or very light red wine; lampreys which were once reserved for royalty; and the famous local lamb. There is game and *foie gras* from the Landes, and fresh local fruit and vegetables. To the British and American visitor, the best restaurants in Bordeaux and surrounding towns are those serving reasonably-priced meals made from local ingredients. These meals are great value, the portions are normally over-generous and there is none of the pretension of *nouvelle cuisine*, thankfully. Each area has its speciality — gigot of lamb in the Médoc, snails in the Graves, fresh duck liver in Sauternes, shad in Entre-Deux-Mers, and lamprey in St-Emilion. Fronsac creates marvellous dishes of *pibales*, baby eels caught in the various branches of the Gironde, and there is the original *entrecôte Bordelaise* from Blaye.

What better way can there be to start a meal than with a plateful of oysters? The Arcachon Basin is one of France's major suppliers. There are a number of different types of oysters cultivated in the special rafts in the Basin, but the two most common are *gravette* and Portuguese. The *gravette* is a variety of flat oyster, farmed in the Gironde for at least 2,000 years. In the 1920s the oyster beds were attacked by disease and since then Portuguese oysters have been cultivated to boost supplies. The first Portuguese oysters are thought to have come from India on the hulls of ships, and there is a story that an English vessel carrying a cargo of Portuguese oysters found the smell so offensive that they threw them all overboard in the Gironde, thus helping to start the first colony. You may see oysters advertised as *vertes de marennes* and these are naturally green from the algae and sea weed on which they feed in the basin. *Belons* are the finest oysters, at least three years old, and considered so special they even have their own *appellation*. Oysters are classified by size from 00 the largest, to 6 the smallest.

All other shellfish are available, and caviare is produced from the female sturgeon which is to be found in the Gironde. The sturgeon is now protected, but mysteriously supplies of caviare do still appear from time to time!

The lamprey is another speciality of the region, especially *lamproie à la Bordelaise*. The lamprey is an eel-like fish caught in the estuaries. It is sometimes known as the sucker-fish because it has a sucker on its head with which it attaches itself to other fish. The lamprey does not have a backbone, but it does have a poisonous vein running down the length of its back which must be carefully removed. It used to be so rare that it was reserved for royalty, and legend has it that King John of England died from eating too many lampreys while in Normandy. It is much more likely that he died from food-poisoning, however. The traditional Bordelais way of cooking lamprey is to slice it and cook it with leeks, red wine and garlic and to bind the sauce with blood. The flesh of the lamprey is creamy and it does not have a very fishy taste, especially when cooked as above.

Pibales, or baby eels, are another delicacy. They are boiled for a few minutes, seasoned and then eaten with your fingers and a glass of Entre-Deux-Mers. They can be served cold with a vinaigrette sauce, or fried. The sardines caught locally are excellent, and you can buy magnificent ones on the quays in Bordeaux. Known as *petits royans,* they are sold either salted or unsalted. Shad is the speciality fish of the region, where it is known as *alose*. It is a delicate fish with many small bones, and it can be grilled over vine twigs, or baked with a sorrel sauce. It can also be served cold with a variety of sauces. Other fish specialities to look out for are *anguilles aux pruneaux* (eels stewed in red wine and prunes), *anguilles au verjus* (eels soaked in grape juice and grilled), *chaudrée rochelaise* (a fish soup with white wine), and *pain de brochet d'Angoulême* (a fish terrine made from pike).

Lamb is plentiful and good, especially the *agneau de prés-salés*, which is specially reared on the salt marshes of the Gironde. It is mouth wateringly tender, but the French prefer all their meat pink, so you must tell the waiter if you prefer it cooked a little longer. Many meats are grilled over vine cuttings (*aux sarments*), especially beef. There are marvellous small pork sausages with truffles (*crépinettes truffées*) which are sometimes sliced and served with oysters, and the local snails (*cagouilles*) cooked in white wine, parsley and shallots.

The local mushrooms, *cèpes*, are also worth trying. They are very fleshy, and normally they are sautéed in oil with parsley and shallots; they make an excellent course by themselves. Other specialities are *entrecôte à la Bordelaise* (a steak in wine, shallot and beef marrow sauce), *gratons de Lormont* (a pork and meat paste), *foie de canard aux raisins*, flambéed duck's livers (or goose) cooked with grapes, *cèpes* and sometimes with added liqueurs — a very rich dish. From the forests of Landes comes a variety of game, and there is duck from the marshes. The Bordelais also eat many small birds, mostly buntings, which are captured, fattened and then roasted whole. The diner is expected to eat the lot, head and beak, and everyone overlooks the dreadful crunching noise as you try to accomplish this.

The local vegetables are always fresh and *soupe des vendanges,* a mixture of meat and vegetables, is a treat in itself. Traditionally, it has been served to the grape pickers during the harvest.

The Bordelais do not much favour desserts, and usually fruit, fruit in syrup or liqueurs and cheeses from outside the region are offered. In St-Emilion they make mouth-watering macaroons, and a special chocolate mousse laced with rum.

HOTELS AND RESTAURANTS OF THE BORDEAUX REGION

CITY OF BORDEAUX

Frantel
15 rue Robert-Lateulade
☎ (56) 90 92 37
Not central but a modern air-conditioned hotel, with 196 rooms, good restaurant. English spoken.

Grand Hôtel de Bordeaux
2 place de la Comédie
☎ (56) 90 93 44
Opposite the Opera House. Nearby parking. Good restaurant. 98 modern comfortable rooms.

Normandie
7 cours 30–Juillet
☎ (56) 52 16 80
Very central comfortable hotel with 100 rooms. No restaurant but breakfast served. English spoken.

Royal Médoc
3 rue de Sèze
☎ (56) 81 72 42
A small centrally located hotel with 45 rooms, no restaurant but breakfast available. English spoken.

Majestic
2 rue Condé
☎ (56) 52 60 44
Small, comfortable 50-room hotel, conveniently situated. Parking facilities, no restaurant but breakfast available.

Sèze
23 allées de Tourny
☎ (56) 52 65 54
A very central, very comfortable 25-room hotel. No restaurant, but breakfast available.

Arcade
Gare St-Jean
60 rue Eugène Le Roy
☎ (56) 90 92 40
Opposite the railway station, a very modern 140-roomed hotel, ideal for families. Shuttle service to airport 7 miles away, restaurant.

Français
12 rue Temple
☎ (56) 48 10 35
Small, very comfortable 36-room hotel, conveniently situated. No restaurant, but breakfast served.

Novotel Mérignac
At airport, 11km west on D106
☎ (56) 34 10 25
Modern,well-equipped, sound-proofed hotel, less than a mile from airport.

Le Bistrot de Bordeaux
10 rue des Piliers-de-Tutelle
☎ (56) 52 92 32
Closed weekends and mid-August. Excellent fixed-price menu with local specialities; includes wine and the *à la carte* is worth exploring.

La Chamade
20 rue des Piliers-de-Tutelle
☎ (56) 48 13 74
Closed second and third week of August. An innovative restaurant. Dishes such as tournedos in Graves wine, or crayfish fried with julienne of fennel.

Clavel
44 rue Charles-Domercq
☎ (56) 92 91 52
Closed Sunday evenings and 3 weeks in July. Garcia is another talented, creative chef who maintains the highest standards, a delightful combination of the best Bordelais and Spanish cuisine, but in his personal style.

Dubern
42 allées de Tourny
☎ (56) 48 03 44
Closed Sundays and holidays. Christian Clément has transformed this restaurant into one of the finest in Bordeaux. Very good value fixed-price menu, and exciting à la carte. Superb wine cellar. English spoken. Best to reserve.

Au Comestible
10 rue Porte-de-la-Monnaie
☎ (56) 92 99 00
Closed weekends. One of the best restaurants offering Bordelais food such as blood sausage, cabbage *tarte* and chicken liver *bouchées*. Very reasonable fixed price menu.

Le Grande Café
16 rue Montesquieu
☎ (56) 52 87 40
Spend a delightful evening in this busy, bustling recently re-opened bar. A limited but good menu includes cheek of beef and tripe in white wine.

Le Rouzic
35 cours du Chapeau-
Rouge
☎ 44 39 11
In front of the Grand
Theatre and under the control of patron chef Michel
Gautier. His menus concentrate on regional dishes.
The 'surprise menu'
consists of seven dishes
and depends on what is
available that day. Good
wine list. Excellent value.

Périgord St Jean
202 cours de la Marne
☎ (56) 91 42 80
Closed weekends and last
3 weeks of August. A
small establishment run
by Jacques Biard. Advis-
able to book if you want
to try the seafood specialities or regional dishes,
especially from the
Landes. Dishes include
stuffed mussels, eels in
wine, fricaséed lobster,
duck and goose.

Chez Philippe
1 place du Parlement
☎ (56) 81 83 15
Unfortunately closed for
most of the summer, but
worth a visit at other
times to sample the exquisite seafood in this inti-
mate bistro. Very expens-
ive, but worth the treat.

La Tupina
6 rue Porte-de-la-Monnaie
☎ (56) 91 56 37
Closed weekends. A
charming place for a late
meal down on the quays.
Very friendly, good menu
specialising in sea food

and local dishes grilled
over vine cuttings. Take a
look at the wine list, and
ask why more restaurants
in Britain and the US cannot follow this example.

Le Vieux Bordeaux
27 rue Buhan
☎ (56) 52 94 36
Closed Saturday
lunchtime, Sundays and all
of August. Young patron
chef Michel Bordage has
created a new style of
superbly light cuisine that
has become so popular
that it is essential to
book well in advance.
Marvellous fish dishes,
especially salmon and
lobster, and steamed sea
bass with broad beans and
cucumber.

Restaurant St James
place Camille-Hostein
☎ (56) 20 52 19
Closed on Mondays and in
February. Owned by Jean-
Marie Amat, the man
credited with bringing
good food back to
Bordeaux. He has moved
out of the city to a white
villa overlooking the
Garonne. Even the experts
use words like 'sublime',
'exquisite' and
'breathtaking', to describe
the marvellous cuisine.

**Near the Bordeaux
Exhibition Centre**

Sofitel
Bordeaux-le-Lac
☎ (56) 50 90 14
A modern, air-conditioned
100-room hotel, ideal for

the exhibition centre and
congress halls. Excellent
restaurant (La Pinasse)
noted for its seafood.

Sofitel Aquitania
Parc des Expositions
☎ (56) 50 83 80
Another big conference
hotel. The 210 rooms are
well-equipped, air-condi-
ioned and there is a pub,
pool, nightclub and
restaurant (Les Acanthes).
Useful for visiting both
the Médoc and St-Emilion.

Novotel
Bordeaux-le-Lac
☎ (56) 50 99 70
A modern air-conditioned
hotel with 173 rooms.
Transport is advised, as it
is well out of the centre.

Mercure
Bordeaux-le-Lac
☎ (56) 50 90 30
A large, modern air-
conditioned hotel with
108 rooms, pool,
restaurant and normally,
an exhibition of wines
from the region.

L'Alouette-Pessac

La Réserve
ave. de Bourgailh
L'Alouette-Pessac
☎ (56) 07 13 28
A 20-room hotel run by
the Flourens, who also
own Dubern in the centre
of Bordeaux. The food and
wine is excellent. Ideal for
visiting the Graves
vineyards and very close
to Haut-Brion.

MEDOC AREA

Blanquefort
(33290 Gironde)

Auberge des Criquets
on the D108
☎ (56) 35 09 24
Good regional cooking.
English spoken.

Margaux
(33460 Gironde)

Relais de Margaux
☎ (56) 88 38 30
Very comfortable hotel
with 18 rooms and good
restaurant.

Larigaudière
Soussans-Margaux
☎ (56) 88 74 02
Closed 12 November-12
December and Mondays in
winter. A former wine
château, now run by
Dominic Pradet who
specialises in seafood and
regional dishes.

Le Savoie
place Tremoille
☎ (56) 88 31 76

Closed December-22
January, and on Sundays.
A very reasonably-priced
restaurant offering
excellent local cuisine.

Lamarque
(33460 Gironde)

Relais du Médoc
on the D2 between
  Margaux and St-Julien
☎ (56) 58 92 27
A good value restaurant.

Salunes
(33160 Gironde)

Domaine des Ardillières
on the D105
☎ (56) 05 20 70
A small country hotel
with 24 rooms, ideal for
visiting the vineyards, the
forests of the Landes or
the sandy Atlantic coast.
It has a modest restaurant.

Listrac
(33480 Gironde)

Hôtel de France
☎ (56) 58 03 68
A small, friendly hotel
with 7 rooms, simple
good food.

St-Laurent-et-Benon
(33112 Gironde)

La Renaissance
☎ (56) 59 40 29
Good country cooking.

Lion d'Or
☎ (56) 59 40 21
Closed 5–22 April and13
December-6 January.
10 comfortable rooms
and restaurant.

Lesparre
(33340 Gironde)

Le Mare aux Grenouilles
☎ (56) 41 03 46
Closed Sundays from 1
October-1 March. A very
good restaurant just a
short drive from many of
the great châteaux of
Pauillac and St-Estèphe.

ST-EMILION AND POMEROL

St-Emilion
(33330 Gironde)

Hostellerie de Plaisance
place du Clocher
☎ (57) 24 72 32
A 12-room hotel built
above a ninth-century
church. Has a fine
restaurant.

Auberge de la
  Commanderie
Rue des Cordeliers
☎ (57) 24 70 19
An ideal place for people

on a small budget. Good
simple fare and 14 pleas-
ant, inexpensive rooms.
Closed November to
beginning of June. Now
has a brasserie-crêperie.

Chez Germaine
place du Clocher
☎ (57) 24 70 88
A convenient restaurant in
the centre of town.

Logis de la Cadène
place du Marché-au-Bois
☎ (57) 24 71 40

Closed 15–30 June, 1–15
September. A good value
restaurant run by Mme
Mouliérac, open for lunch
only. Lampreys are a
speciality and there is a
good wine list.

St-Jean-de-Blaignac
(33420 Gironde)

Auberge St-Jean
☎ (57) 84 51 08
A small restaurant over-
looking the Dordogne;
excellent cuisine.

Libourne
(33500 Gironde)

Loubat
32 rue de Chanzy
☎ (57) 51 17 58
A traditional hotel near
the railway station, with a
good and improving
restaurant.

L'Etrier
20 place Decazes
☎ (57) 51 13 59

Closed Sunday evenings
and Mondays, and from 15-
28 February and 1-15
July. A wood-panelled,
cosy restaurant watched
over by Jean-Paul Marion.
The warm lobster salad,
grilled shad and veal
kidneys are among the
magnificent specialities.
There is also an excellent
but expensive wine list.

Hôtel Parc
109 ave. Galliéni
☎ (57) 51 18 42
12 rooms, light meals and
breakfast.

Hôtel Gare
43 rue de Chanzy
☎ (57) 51 06 86
Modest hotel and
restaurant, 10 rooms.

SAUTERNES AND BARSAC

Sauternes
(33210 Gironde)

Auberge des Vignes
place de l'Eglise
☎ (56) 63 60 06
Closed Mondays and in
February. A very simple
auberge with just two
rooms, but a good
restaurant and some
impressive wines. Try the
speciality, *magret* (breast
of duck fatted for *foie
gras*) cooked over vine
cuttings.

Restaurant de la Forge
☎ (56) 63 60 69
A new restaurant which
has started very well.

Barsac
(33720 Gironde)

Hostellerie du Château de
  Rolland
☎ (56) 27 15 75
Closed Wednesdays in the
off-season. Telephone
booking advisable. A 7-

room hotel, formerly a
fifteenth-century Carthusian monastery. Ideal spot
for visiting the vineyards.
Good comfortable rooms
and pleasant restaurant.

Langon
(33110 Gironde)

Claude Darroze
95 cours du Gén. Leclerc
☎ (56) 63 00 48
Closed Mondays in the off-
season; 10 October-5
November and 15-28
February. A small, very
comfortable hotel run by
Claude Darroze, son of the
famous chef Jean Darroze,
well worthy of the two
stars from Michelin.

Bazas
(33430 Gironde)

Relais de Fompeyre
on the Mont-de-Marsan
  road
☎ (56) 25 04 60

Closed 5 October to 15
March. A magnificent
hotel with 35 rooms set
in a lovely park. Chef
Paul Morais's food is
regional, rich and
expensive.

Hostellerie St-Sauveur
cours Gén. de Gaulle
☎ (56) 25 12 18
A 10-room hotel, no
restaurant but breakfast
served.

Hôtel France
cours Gén. de Gaulle
☎ (56) 25 02 37
Closed in January. 13
rooms and restaurant.

Blaye
(33390 Gironde)

La Citadelle
Blaye
☎ (57) 42 17 10
A comfortable hotel with
21 rooms and fine views
over the estuary. A good
restaurant.

THE VINEYARDS OF BORDEAUX

MEDOC

Many of the larger producers have many properties in various villages, but with one address for appointments, hence they have more than one entry.

Jau Dignac et Loirac
*(Appellation Médoc
Contrôlée)*
(33590 St-Vivien-de-Médoc)

Château Moulin
de Ferregrave   TRE
(Cru Artisan)
Le Broustéra
M. Francis Ducos
☎ (56) 41 42 37
Open daily 8am-8pm.
Make an appointment for
English speaking guide.

Château Sestignan   TRE
(Cru Bourgeois)
☎ (56) 41 43 06
M. Bertrand de Rozières
Open daily 8am-8pm.

Vensac
*(Appellation Médoc
Contrôlée)*
(33590 St-Vivien-de-Médoc)

- Château David   TR
(Cru Artisan)
David
☎ (56) 41 44 62
M. and Mme Henry Coutreau
Open Monday to Friday
normal working hours,
and by appointment on
Saturday.

Valeyrac
*(Appellation Médoc
Contrôlée)*
(33340 Lesparre)

Château Bellerive   TR
(Cru Bourgeois)
☎ (56) 41 52 13
M. Guy Perrin

1 July-1 September,
Monday to Saturday 11am-
1pm and 3-7pm. Sunday
and rest of year by
appointment.

Château Bellevue   TR
(Cru Bourgeois)
Au Bourg
☎ (56) 41 52 17
M. Yves Lassalle and son
1 June-10 September
Monday to Friday 9.30am-
7pm. Saturday to Sunday
10am-7pm. Rest of year,
Monday to Friday 9am-
7pm only.

Château Roquegrave   TRE
(Cru Bourgeois)
☎ (56) 41 52 02
MM. Joannon and Lleu
Monday to Friday 8am-
noon and 2-6pm. Saturday
8am-noon.

Queyrac
*(Appellation Médoc
Controlée)*
(33340 Lesparre)

Cave St-Roch   TR
(Cave Coopérative)
Le Sable
☎ (56) 41 07 36
or (56) 59 83 36
M. Rémy, M. Taudin
   (President)
Monday 2.30-6.30pm;
Tuesday to Friday 8.30am-
12.30pm and 2.30-6.30pm
Saturday 8.30am-noon.

Bégadan
*(Appellation Médoc
Controlée)*
(33340 Lesparre)

Château Le Tréhon   TRE
Courbian
☎ (56) 44 21 45
or (56) 41 52 79
M. Alain Monge
Tasting and English guided tours by appointment.

Château Vieux Robin   TR
(Cru Bourgeois)
Les Anguilleys
☎ (56) 41 50 64
M. François Dufau
1 June-15 September,
Monday to Friday 9am-
noon, 2-6pm; Saturday
10am-noon. Sunday am by
appointment. Rest of
year, Monday to Friday
9am-noon, 2-5pm.
Saturdays by appointment.

Château La Clare   TRE
(Cru Bourgeois)
Condissas
☎ (56) 41 50 61
M. Paul de Rozières
Open daily 8am-6pm.

Château La Tour de By
Société Viticole du Médoc
(Cru Bourgeois)   TREG
☎ (56) 41 50 03
M. Marc Pages (Dir.Adm.)
1 July-31 August, Monday
to Friday 8am-noon, 2-
6pm; Saturday 8am-noon.
1 September-30 June,
Monday to Friday 8am-
noon, 2-6pm.Tour of
vineyards and cellars by
appointment.

Château du Monthil   TR
(Cru Bourgeois)
☎ (56) 41 50 73
M. Jean Gabas
1 July-30 September,

T=tasting   E=English spoken   G=guided tours   C=château/building to visit

Monday to Friday 9am-
noon, 2-6pm or by
appointment. Rest of year
by appointment.

Château de By   TR
(Cru Bourgeois)
By
☎ (56) 41 51 53
M. Baudon
15 June-15 September
Monday to Saturday 10am-
noon and 2.30-6pm or by
appointment. Rest of the
year by appointment.

Château Greysac   TR
(Cru Grand Bourgeois)
☎ (56) 41 50 29
M. Coudoin
(Maître de Chai)
By appointment.

Château Rollan de By   TR
(Cru Artisan)
By
☎ (56) 41 57 21
M. Malcor
15 June-15 September
every day 3-8pm. Rest of
the year, 9am-6pm or by
appointment.

Château Laujac   R
(Cru Bourgeois)
☎ (56) 41 50 12
M. Bernard Cruse
By appointment.

Cave St-Jean   TR
*(Société Coopérative de
Vinification)*
☎ (56) 41 50 13
M. René Chaumont
Monday to Friday 9am-
noon, 2-7pm. Saturday
9am-noon.

Château Patache d'Aux   TR
(Cru Grand Bourgeois)
☎ (56) 41 50 18
M. Lapalu
Monday to Thursday 8am-
noon and 2-5pm. Friday
8am-noon and 2-4pm.

Château St-Saturnin   TR
(Cru Bourgeois)
☎ (56) 41 50 82
M. Adrien Tramier
15 June-25 September,
Monday to Saturday 9am-
noon and 2-7pm. Rest of
year, Monday to Saturday
9am-12.30pm and 2-7pm.

Vieux Château Landon
(Cru Bourgeois)   TRC
☎ (56) 41 50 42
M. Gillet (Prop.) and M.
Ballanger (Maître de Chai)
1 June-15 September,
Monday to Friday 9am-
12.30pm and 2.30-
6.30pm. Weekends by
appointment. Rest of
year, Monday to Friday
9am-12.30pm, 3-6pm.
Weekends by appoint-
ment. Inspect the
beautifully carved barrels
in the cellar.

St-Christoly
*(Appellation Médoc
Contrôlée)*
(St-Christoly-de-Médoc
33340 Lesparre)

**Château Moulin de
Castillon**   TR
Le Bourg
☎ (56) 41 53 01
M. Pierre Moriau
Visiting and tasting by
appointment.

Château St-Christoly   TR
(Cru Bourgeois)
☎ (56) 41 52 95
M. Hervé Héraud
1 July-15 September,
Monday to Friday 10am-
noon and 3-6pm. Saturday
3-6pm. Saturday am,
Sunday and rest of year by
appointment.

Château Moulin Taffard
Castillon   TRC
☎ (56) 41 54 98
M. Pierre Peyruse
Monday to Saturday 10am-
7pm. Site of a thirteenth-
century English fortifi-
cation.

Couquèques
*(Appellation Médoc
Contrôlée)*
(33340 Lesparre)

Château Les Ormes   TREC
Sorbet
(Cru Grand Bourgeois)
Le Bourg
☎ (56) 41 53 78
M. Jean Boivert
(Vigneron-Récoltant)
Monday to Friday 9am-
noon and 2-6pm. Week-
ends by appointment.
Inspect the cellars and
note the traditional way of
making the wine in
barriques (large barrels).

Civrac
*(Appellation Médoc
Contrôlée)*
(Civrac-en-Médoc
3340 Lesparre)

Château Panigon   TR
(Cru Bourgeois)
☎ (56) 41 50 31
M. Gérard Lamolière
1 June-15 August,
Saturday 9-11.30am and
2.30-5pm. Sunday 10-
11.30am. Monday to
Friday and rest of year,
by appointment.

R=red wine   W=white wine   P=rosé wine   S=sparkling wine

Château Bournac **TR**
(Cru Bourgeois)
Bournac
☎ (56) 41 51 24
M. Pierre Secret
18 June-15 September,
Monday to Saturday 9am-
noon, 3-6pm. Sundays by
appointment. Rest of
year, Monday to Friday
10am-noon and 2-6pm.
Weekends by appoint-
ment.

Gaillan
*(Appellation Médoc
Contrôlée)*
(Gaillan-en-Médoc 33340
Lesparre)

Uni-Médoc **TRE**
*(Union de Caves
Coopératives)*
☎ (56) 41 03 12
MM. Bailly and Caulet
15 June-31 August, Mon-
day-Saturday 8.30am-
12.30pm and 2-6pm. Sun-
day evenings after 6pm.
Rest of year Monday to
Thursday 8.30am-12.30pm
and 2-6pm. Friday 8.30am-
12.30pm and 2-5pm.

Prignac
*(Appellation Médoc
Contrôlee)*
(Prignac-en-Médoc 33340
Lesparre)

Les Vieux Colombiers **TRG**
(Cave Coopérative)
Lafon
☎ (56) 41 01 02
M. André Bérard
Monday to Saturday
8.30am-12.30pm and 2-
6pm.

Château Haut-Garin **TR**
(Cru Bourgeois)
Lafon
☎ (56) 41 05 42
MM. Georges and Gilles
Hué
Monday to Saturday 9am-
noon and 2-7pm. Sunday
by appointment.

Château Tour Prignac **TRG**
(Cru Bourgeois)
☎ (56) 41 02 19
Monday to Friday 9-
11.30am and 2-5.30pm.
Appointment necessary
for groups.

Blaignan
*(Appellation Médoc
Contrôlée)*
(33340 Lesparre)

Château Les Granges **TRE**
d'Or
(Cru Bourgeois)
Les Granges d'Or
☎ (56) 41 57 71
or (56) 41 52 02
MM. Joannon and Lleu
Monday to Friday 8am-
noon and 2-6pm. Saturday
8am-noon.

Château des Tourelles **TR**
(Cru Bourgeois)
☎ (56) 41 14 88
M. Miquau (proprietor)
Monday to Friday 9am-
noon and 2-5pm

Château La Tour Haut-
Caussan **TRC**
(Cru Bourgeois)
☎ (56) 41 04 77
M. Philippe Courrian
Monday to Friday 9am-
noon and 2-5pm.
Weekends by
appointment. Eighteenth-
century windmill.

Château La Gorce **TRE**
(Cru Bourgeois)
☎ (56) 41 21 42
M. Henri Fabre
Monday to Friday 8am-
noon and 2-6pm or by
appointment.

St-Yzans
*(Appellation Médoc
Contrôlée)*
(St-Yzans-de-Médoc
33340 Lesparre)

Château Sigognac **TRE**
(Cru Grand Bourgeois)
☎ (56) 41 15 04
Mme C. Bonny
15 June-30 September
Monday to Friday 9.30am-
noon and 2-5.30pm.
Closed October.
1 November to 14 June
9.30-noon and 2-5.30pm.

St-Brice **TR**
(Cave Coopérative)
M. Paul Mottes
Monday to Saturday
8am-noon and 2-6pm.

Château Bois de Roc **TR**
(Cru Artisan)
☎ (56) 41 09 79
M. Philippe Cazenave
Tasting and visits by
appointment.

Château Lestruelle **TR**
(Cru Bourgeois)
☎ (56) 41 15 01
or (56) 41 14 16
M. Ladra
Monday to Saturday 9am-
noon and 2-7pm. Sunday
by appointment.

Château Haut-Maurac **TRC**
(Société Civile Fermière)
Queyzans
☎ (56) 41 15 37
MM. Manizan

T=tasting   E=English spoken   G=guided tours   C=château/building to visit

15 June-15 September,
Monday to Friday 2-8pm;
Saturday 10am-noon and 2-
8pm. Special cellar visits
on Saturdays.

Château Loudenne   TREC
(Cru Bourgeois)
☎ (56) 41 15 03
or (56) 41 15 23
M. Gabriel Fay
Monday to Friday 9.30am-
noon, 2-4.30pm.There is
an interesting museum of
early winemaking and
vineyard tools, and a
collection of old bottles.

Château des Brousteras TR
(Cru Artisan)
Queyzans
☎ (56) 41 15 44
Monday to Saturday 8am-
8pm, Sunday 8am-noon.

Lesparre
*(Appellation Médoc
    Contrôlée)*
(33340 Lesparre)

Maison du Médoc
Artisanat-Vin-Tourisme
place du Tribunal
☎ (56) 41 85 65
Information centre for
wine, tourism and crafts-
men's exhibition.

Château Preuillac   TREC
(Cru Bourgeois)
☎ (56) 41 03 47
Mme and Mlle Bouet
1 July-1 August, Monday
to Friday 8.30am-noon
and 2-6pm. Weekends by
appointment. Cellars have
traditional old barrels

Ordonnac
*(Appellation Médoc
    Contrôlée)*
(33340 Lesparre)

Domaine de la Croix   TR
Plautignan
☎ (56) 41 14 14
or (56) 41 82 42
MM. Francisco
1 June-30 September,
Monday to Saturday 9am-
12.30pm and 3-8pm.
Sunday by appointment.
Rest of year 9am-noon
and 3-8pm.

Pavillon de Bellevue   TR
(Cave Coopérative)
Plautignan
☎ (56) 41 14 13
M. Guy Prevosteau
    (President)
1 July-31 August, Monday
to Saturday 8am-11.50am
and 2-5.50pm. 1 Septem-
ber-30 June, Tuesday to
Saturday 8am-11.50am and
2-5.50pm or by
appointment.

St-Germain d'Esteuil
*(Appellation Médoc
    Contrôlée)*
(33340 Lesparre)

Château Livran   TRE
(Cru Bourgeois)
☎ (56) 41 12 05
or (56) 41 81 76
M. Godfrin, M. Roba
    (Maître de Chai)
15 June-31 August,
Monday to Friday 10am-
noon and 3-6pm. Sunday
by appointment. Rest of
year, Monday to Friday
10 am-noon and 2-5pm.
Sundays by appointment.

**St-Seurin-de-
Cadourne**
*(Appellation Haut-Médoc
    Contrôlée)*
(33250 Pauillac)

Château Coufran   TREGC
(Cru Bourgeois)
☎ (56) 44 90 84
M. Eric Miailhe
1 July-31 August, Monday
to Friday 10am-12.30pm
and 2-6.30pm. 1 Septem-
ber-6 June, Monday to
Friday 8.30am-noon and 2-
5.30pm. Wine shop.

**Châteaux La Mothe et
    Grand Moulin   TRE**
(Société Civile)
(Cru Bourgeois)
☎ (56) 59 35 95
1 June-31 August, Monday
to Friday 8am-noon and 2-
6pm; Saturday 8am-noon.
Saturday pm and Sunday
by appointment.
1 September-31 May
Monday to Friday 8am-
12noon and 2-6pm.

Château Bel Orme   TR
Tronquoy de Lalande
(Cru Bourgeois)
☎ (56) 59 31 09
M. Sou (Maître de Chai)
15 June-19 August, Mon-
day to Friday 8am-
12.30pm and 2-6pm. Satur-
day 9am-12.30pm. Rest of
year by appointment.

Château Lestage Simon TR
(Cru Bourgeois)
☎ (56) 59 31 83
M. Charles Simon
Monday to Saturday 9am-
6pm. Sunday by
appointment.

Château Bonneau Livran
(Cru Bourgeois)   **TR**
Livran
☎ (56) 59 31 26
Mmes Micalaudy and
    Millon
1 June-30 September,
Monday to Saturday 9am-
noon and 2-7pm.

R=red wine   W=white wine   P=rosé wine   S=sparkling wine

Château Senilhac TR
(Cru Bourgeois)
☎ (56) 59 31 41
MM. Michel and Jean-Luc
Grassin
Monday to Saturday 9am-
6pm. Sunday by
appointment.

La Paroisse TR
(Cave Coopérative)
☎ (56) 59 31 28
M. André Verges (Presi-
dent) or M. Jean Roi
Monday to Friday 9.30am-
12.30pm and 3-5pm.
Saturday 10am-noon or by
appointment.

**Château Pontoisc
Cabarrus** TRC
(Cru Grand Bourgeois)
Au Bourg
☎ (56) 59 34 92
M. Francois Tereygeol
Visiting and tasting by
appointment. Studio
specialising in painting
on silk.

**Château Sociando
Mallet** TRC
(Cru Grand Bourgeois)
Baleyron
☎ (56) 59 36 57
M. Jean Gautreau
1 June-30 September,
Monday to Friday 9am-
noon. 1 October to 31
May, Monday to Friday
9am-noon and 2-5pm.
Important collection of
large barrels, and fine
views of the Gironde.

**Châteaux Verdus and
Bardis** TREC
(Cru Bourgeois)
☎ (56) 59 31 59
MM. Dailledouze
15 June-30 September,
Tuesday and Wednesday
9am-8pm. Rest of year by
appointment. Dovecote.

Château St-Paul TR
(Cru Bourgeois)
☎ (56) 59 34 72 (office)
or (56) 59 33 63
M. Robert Boudaud
Visiting and tasting by
appointment.

St-Estèphe
*(Appellation St-Estèphe
Contrôlée)*
(33250 Pauillac)

Maison du Vin de St-
Estèphe TRE
place de l'Eglise
☎ (56) 59 30 59
1 July-15 September,
Monday to Saturday 10am-
noon and 2-6pm. 16
September-31 December,
Monday to Saturday 10am-
12 noon and 2-6pm.
The whole range of St-
Estèphe wines on sale
here. Information.

Château Le Boscq TR
(Cru Bourgeois)
☎ (56) 59 38 44
M. Philippe Durand
1 June-30 September,
Monday to Friday 8am-
noon, and 2-6pm. Rest of
year by appointment.

Château Tour des Termes
(Cru Bourgeois) TR
☎ (56) 28 30 52
M. Jean Anney
Monday to Friday 9am-
noon and 2-5pm. Saturday
9am-noon or by
appointment. Closed July.

Château Phélan-Segur
*(Cru Bourgeois
Exceptionnel)*
☎ (56) 59 30 09
M. Roger Delon
Monday to Friday 9am-
noon and 2-6pm. Closed
August. Spectacular views.

**Château Lafitte
Carcasset** TR
(Cru Bourgeois Supérieur)
☎ (56) 59 32 29
or (56) 59 34 32
M. Philippe de Padirac
1 June-30 September,
Monday to Friday 10am-
noon and 3-5.30pm. Rest
of year by appointment.

Marquis de St-Estèphe TR
(Cave Coopérative)
☎ (56) 59 32 05
M. Hélie
Monday to Friday 9am-
noon and 2.30-6pm;
Saturday 9am-noon and
2.30-5.30pm.

Château Brame-le-Tours TR
Leyssac
M. le Vicomte Aimery de
Foulhiac de Padirac
M. Duprat (Maître de Chai)
Monday to Saturday
8.30am-noon and 2-7pm.

**Châteaux St-Estèphe and
Pomys** TR
(Cru Bourgeois)
Leyssac
☎ (56) 59 32 26
M. François Arnaud
15 May-15 September,
Monday to Friday 10am-
noon and 2.30-7pm. 1
November-15 May,
Monday to Friday 2-7pm
or by appointment.

Château Haut-Marbuzet TR
*(Cru Grand Bourgeois
Exceptionnel)*
Marbuzet
☎ (56) 59 30 54
M. Henri Duboscq
Monday to Saturday 8am-
noon and 2-5pm.

Château Le Crock TR
(Cru Bourgeois Supérieur)
☎ (56) 59 30 33

T=tasting E=English spoken G=guided tours C=château/building to visit

M. Cuvelier, M. Garrigou
1 July-15 September,
Monday to Friday 8am-
noon and 2-6pm. Rest of
year, Monday to Friday
8am-noon and by
appointment 2-6pm.

Château MacCarthy
(Cru Bourgeois)
Marbuzet
☎ (56) 59 30 25
M. J. Raymond
Visits and tasting by
appointment.

Château Cos Labory   TRE
(Grand Cru Classé)
☎ (56) 59 30 22
MM. François and Bernard
  Audoy
Visits and tasting by
appointment.

Château Cos d'Estournel
(Cru Classé)   TRE
☎ (56) 44 11 37
1 August-15 September,
Tuesday to Saturday 12-
6pm. Rest of year, Mon-
day to Friday 10am-noon
and 3-5pm. Saturday and
Sunday by appointment.

Château Lafon Rochet TR
(Cru Classé)
☎ (56) 59 32 06
or (56) 52 15 71
MM. Paul Bussier and
  Alfred Tesseron
1 July-15 September,
Monday to Friday 9am-
noon and 2-5pm. Rest of
year, Monday to Friday
9am-noon and 2-5pm by
appointment.

Vertheuil
*(Appellation Haut-Médoc
  Contrôlée)*
(33250 Pauillac)

Château Le Meynieu   TR
(Cru Grand Bourgeois)
☎ (56) 41 98 17
M. Jacques Pedro
1 June-30 September
(closed 3-18 August),
Monday to Friday 10am-
noon and 2-6pm by
appointment.

Château Le Souley Ste-
Croix   TR
(Cru Bourgeois)
☎ (56) 41 98 54
M. Riffaud
15 June-30 September,
Monday to Friday 9.30am-
noon and 2.30-6.30pm.
Saturday 9.30am-noon. 1
October-15 June, Monday
to Friday 9.30am-noon
and 2.30-6.30pm. Satur-
day 9.30-noon and 2-6pm.

Château Le Bourdieu TRE
  and Château Victoria
(Cru Bourgeois)
☎ (56) 41 98 01
Mlle Monique Barbe
1 June-15 September,
Monday to Friday 10am-
noon and 2.30-6pm.
Saturday 10am-noon. Rest
of year, Monday to Friday
10am-noon and 2.30-4pm.

Châtellenie   TREC
(Cave Coopérative)
☎ (56) 41 98 16
M. Berger
1 June-15 September,
Monday to Saturday
8.30am-12.30pm and 2-
6pm. Rest of year, Tues-
day to Saturday same
hours. Visit caves and
abbey.

Cissac
*(Appellation Haut-Médoc
  Contrôlée)*
(33250 Pauillac)

Château Hanteillan   TRC
(Cru Grand Bourgeois)
Hanteillan
☎ (56) 59 35 31
Mme Blasco
Monday to Friday 8am-
noon and 1.30-5.30pm.
Collection of amphora,
museum.

Château Vieux
  Braneyre   TRE
(Cru Bourgeois)
Aux Gunes
☎ (56) 59 54 03
M. Georges Guges
1 June-30 September,
Monday to Friday 8am-
noon and 2-6pm. Saturday
and Sunday by appoint-
ment. Rest of year by
appointment. Visit the
chai and tasting room.

Château Larrivaux   TRE
(Cru Bourgeois)
☎ (56) 59 58 15
M. Carlsberg
Tasting and visits by
appointment.

Château Puy Castera   TRE
(Cru Bourgeois)
Le Castera
☎ (56) 59 58 80
or (56) 41 43 06
M. Mares
Monday to Saturday 8am-
8pm.

Château Lamothe-
  Cissac   TRE
(Cru Grand Bourgeois)
Lamothe
☎ (56) 59 58 16
M. Fabre
Monday to Friday 8am-
noon and 2-6pm.

Château du Breuil   TREC
(Cru Bourgeois)
Le Breuil
☎ (56) 59 58 22
M. Gérard Germain

R=red wine   W=white wine   P=rosé wine   S=sparkling wine

1 July-15 September, Monday to Saturday 2-8pm. Rest of year by appointment. Visit eighteenth-century château.

St-Sauveur
(Appellation Haut-Médoc Contrôlée)
(St-Sauveur
33250 Pauillac)

Château Fontesteau TR
(Cru Bourgeois)
Fontesteau
☎ (56) 59 57 08
M. Leglise and M. Fouin
1 July-30 September,
Monday to Friday 9am-noon and 3-6pm; Saturday 10am-noon and 2-5pm. Rest of year by appointment.

Château du Junca TR
Lescarjean
☎ (56) 59 56 35
M. Serge Tiffon
15 June-15 September, Monday to Friday 2-6pm; Saturday 9am-noon and 2-6pm. Sunday 9am-noon or by appointment. Rest of year, Saturday 9am-noon and 2-6pm and Sunday 9-11am, or by appointment.

Château Ramage
La Batisse TRE
(Cru Bourgeois)
☎ (57) 40 62 90
M. Picamoles
Visits and tasting by appointment.

Cantcrayne TR
(Cave Coopérative)
☎ (56) 59 57 11
M. Guy Martin
Monday to Saturday 8am-noon and 2-6pm.

Château Liversan TRE
(Cru Grand Bourgeois)
☎ (56) 59 57 07
Prince and Princesse Guy de Polignac
Monday to Friday 9am-noon and 2-5.30pm.

Château Peyrabon TR
(Cru Bourgeois)
☎ (56) 59 57 10
M. Jacques Babeau
Monday to Friday 9am-noon and 2-5pm. Closed October and November.

Château Lieujan TRE
(Cru Bourgeois)
Lieujan
☎ (56) 59 57 23
M. Jean-Louis Audoin
Monday to Friday 9am-noon and 2-5pm. Saturday and Sunday by appointment.

Pauillac
(Appellation Pauillac Contrôlée)
(33250 Pauillac)

Maison du Tourisme et du Vin de Médoc (Tourist Office) TRE
La Verrerie
☎ (56) 59 03 08
M. Fabrice Fatin
1 May-30 June, Monday to Saturday 9.30am-12.30pm and 2-7pm. 1 July-30 September, Monday to Saturday 9am-7pm. 1-31 October, Monday to Saturday 9.30am-12.30pm and 2-7pm. 1 November-30 April, Monday to Saturday 9.30am-12.30pm and 2-6pm. Sale of wines of all *appellations* of the Médoc.

Château Lafite TRE
Rothschild
(1er Grand Cru Classé)
☎ (56) 59 01 74
M. Rokvam
Monday to Friday 9-11am and 3-5pm or by appointment. Closed 16 September-31 October.

Château Mouton TRE
Rothschild
(1er Grand Cru Classé en 1973)
Le Pouyalet
☎ (56) 59 22 22
Mlle Martine Courtiade
By appointment, Monday to Friday 9.30-11.30am and 2-7pm

Château Pontet Canet TRE
(Cru Classé)
☎ (56) 59 04 04
or (56) 52 15 71 (office)
M. Alfred Tesseron and M. Geffier
1 July-15 September, Monday to Friday 9am-12 noon and 2-7pm. Rest of year by appointment.

Château Colombier TREC
Monpelou
(Cru Bourgeois)
☎ (56) 59 01 48
M. Bernard Jugla
15 June-8 August, Monday to Friday 9am-noon and 2-5.30pm. Exhibition of cooperage tools.

La Rose Pauillac TRE
(Cave Coopérative)
☎ (56) 59 26 00
rue Maréchal-Joffre
M. Lafforgue and M. Ribeaux
1 June-30 August, Monday to Sunday 8am-noon and 2-6pm. Rest of year, Monday to Saturday 8am-noon and 2-6pm.

T=tasting E=English spoken G=guided tours C=château/building to visit

Château Lynch-Bages TRE
(Cru Classé)
☎ (56) 59 19 19
or (56) 59 25 59
M. Daniel Llose
Monday to Friday 9-
11.30am and 2-5pm.

Château Croizet-Bages TR
(Cru Classé)
Hameau de Bages
☎ (56) 59 01 62
M. Claude Ribeaux (Maître
de Chai)
15 June-19 August,
Monday to Friday 8am-
12.30pm and 2-6pm;
Saturday 9am-12.30pm.
Rest of year by
appointment.

Château Batailley TREC
(Cru Classé)
☎ (56) 59 01 13
or (56) 48 57 57
M. Casteia
1 March-30 September,
Monday to Friday 8am-
noon and 2-6pm. Saturday
and Sunday by appoint-
ment. 1 October-27 Feb-
ruary, Monday to Friday
9am-noon and 2-6pm.
Saturday 10am-noon and 2-
6pm; Sunday 2-6pm.Visit
the *chais* and gardens.

Château Pichon- TR
Longueville Baron
(2er Cru Classé)
St-Lambert
☎ (56) 58 91 01
M. Bertrand Bouteiller
Monday to Friday 9.30am-
noon and 2-5pm.

Château Pichon-
Longueville de Comtesse
Lalande TREC
(2e Cru Classé)
St-Lambert
☎ (56) 59 19 40

Mme de Lencquesaing
Monday to Friday 9.30-
11.30am and 3-5pm.
Closed August.
Spectacular views.

Château Latour TRE
(Société Civile)
(1er Cru Classé)
St-Lambert
☎ (56) 59 00 51
M. Jean-Louis Mandrau
Visits and tasting by
appointment.

Château Lynch-
Moussas TREC
(Cru Classé)
☎ (56) 59 57 14
M. Casteja
1 June-15 September,
Monday to Friday 9am-
noon and 2-6pm. Sunday
and holidays by
appointment. 10 October-
31 May, Monday to
Friday 9am-noon and 2-
6pm; Saturday 9am-noon.
Saturday pm and Sunday
by appointment. Beautiful
château and gardens.

St-Julien-Beychevelle
*(Appellation St-Julien
Contrôlée)*
(33250 Pauillac)

Château Léoville Poyferre
(2e Cru Classé) TR
☎ (56) 59 08 30
M. Dourthe
1 July-15 September,
Monday to Friday 8am-
noon and 2-6pm. Rest of
year same hours but by
appointment.

Château Langoa-Léoville
Barton TRE
(Grand Cru Classé)
☎ (56) 59 06 05

or (56) 59 06 03
M. André Leclerc and M.
Michel Raoul
Visits and tasting by
appointment.

Château Terrey-Gros-
Cailloux TR
(Cru Bourgeois)
☎ (56) 59 06 27
MM. Fort and Pradère
Monday to Friday 9am-
noon and 2-6pm; Saturday
9am-noon.

Château Moulin
de la Rose TR
(Cru Bourgeois)
☎ (56) 59 08 45
M. Guy Delon
Monday to Saturday 9am-
noon and 2-6pm; Sunday
9am-noon.

Château Lagrange TR
(Cru Classé)
☎ (56) 59 23 63
M. Ducasse
Visits and tasting by
appointment.

Château Beychevelle TR
(Cru Classé)
☎ (56) 59 23 00
M. Ruelle
Monday to Friday 10am-
noon and 2-5.30pm.

St-Laurent-et-Benon
*(Appellation Haut-Médoc
Contrôlée)*
(33112 St-Laurent-et-
Benon)

Château de Cach TRE
(Cru Bourgeois)
☎ (56) 59 45 91
M. Musso
1 June-30 September,
Monday to Sunday 9am-
12.30pm and 2-6.30pm.
Rest of year, Monday to
Saturday 10am-12.30pm
and 2-6.30pm.

R=red wine   W=white wine   P=rosé wine   S=sparkling wine

Château Balac TREC
(Cru Bourgeois)
☎ (56) 59 41 76
M. Luc Touchais
1 June-30 September,
Monday to Friday 9am-
noon and 2-7pm; Saturday
9am-noon. 1 October-31
May, Monday to Friday
9am-noon and 2-6pm.
Sunday and August by
appointment. Eighteenth-
century château.

Château Larose- TRE
Trintaudonn
(Cru Bourgeois)
☎ (56) 59 41 72
or (56) 59 49 23
Visits and tasting by
appointment. Nineteenth-
century château.

Château Barateau TR
(Cru Bourgeois Supérieur)
☎ (56) 59 40 25
or (56) 59 42 07
M. Pla
Monday to Friday 9am-
noon and 2-5pm. Week-
ends by appointment.

Château La Tour Carnet
*(Grand Cru Classé en
1855)* TRC
☎ (56) 59 40 13
Mme Pelegrin
Monday to Friday 8am-
noon and 2-4pm. Closed
August. Thirteenth-century
tower.

Château de Camensac TREC
(Cru Classé)
☎ (56) 59 41 69
or (56) 59 44 23
Visits and tasting by
appointment. Nineteenth-
century château.

Château Belgrave TRE
(Cru Classé)
☎ (56) 59 40 20
or (56) 59 90 82
M. Patrick Atteret
1 June-15 September,
Monday to Friday 9am-12
noon and 2-5pm. Week-
ends by appointment. 16
September-31 May,
Monday to Friday 9am-
noon and 3-5pm. Week-
ends by appointment.

Cussac-Fort-Médoc
*(Appellation Haut-Médoc
Contrôlée)*
(33460 Margaux)

Château Lanessan TREC
(Member of *l'Académie des
Vins de Bordeaux*)
☎ (56) 58 91 01
M. Hubert Bouteiller
31 March-11 November,
Monday to Sunday 9-
11.30am and 2-6pm. 12
November-20 March,
Monday to Saturday 9-
11.30am and 2-6pm. Visit
Museum and Château
Lachesnaye.

Les Chevaliers du Roi
Soleil TR
Les Capérans
☎ (56) 58 95 48
(President)
or (56) 58 92 85
M. Denis Fedieu
15 June-15 September,
Monday to Sunday 3-6pm
or by appointment. Rest
of year by appointment.

Château du Moulin Rouge
(Cru Bourgeois) TRE
☎ (56) 58 91 13
Mme Pelon
1 June-30 September,
Monday to Saturday 8am-
noon and 1-8pm. Rest of
year, Monday to Saturday
9am-noon and 1-8pm.

Château Aney TREC
G.F.A.d'Arnaussan
(Cru Bourgeois)
☎ (56) 58 94 89 (office)
or (56) 58 91 21 (home)
MM. or Mmes Raimond
1 June-30 September,
Monday to Saturday 8am-
noon and 2-7pm; Sunday
8am-noon. Rest of year,
Monday to Saturday 8am-
noon and 2-6pm. Sunday
8am-noon and by appoint-
ment. Collection of agri-
cultural and winemaking
artefacts.

Château Beaumont TREC
(Cru Bourgeois)
☎ (56) 58 92 29
or (56) 28 15 53
M. Bernard Soulas
Monday to Friday 9am-
noon and 3-6pm. Saturday
and Sunday by
appointment.

Château du Retour TRC
(Cru Bourgeois)
☎ (56) 58 90 34
or (56) 58 90 14
M. Gérard Kopp
Visits and tasting by ap-
pointment. Old windmill.

Château Tour du Haut TR
Moulin
(Cru Grand Bourgeois)
Cussac le Vieux
☎ (56) 58 91 10
M. Laurent Poitou
15 June-15 September,
Monday to Saturday 10am-
noon and 1-8pm; Sunday
10am-noon and 2-7pm.
Rest of year, Monday to
Friday 10am-noon and 2-
6pm. Weekends by
appointment.

T=tasting E=English spoken G=guided tours C=château/building to visit

Lamarque
*(Appellation Haut-Médoc
Contrôlée)*
(33460 Margaux)

Château de Lamarque TRC
(Cru Grand Bourgeois)
☎ (56) 58 90 03
or (56) 58 94 71
M. Gromand and Mme
Coulary
Monday to Friday 9am-
noon and 2-6pm or by
appointment. Closed 16
September-31 October.
Twelfth-century château.

Château Malescasse TR
(Cru Bourgeois)
☎ (56) 58 90 09
or (56) 52 15 71 (office)
M. Dufau or M. Alfred
Tesseron
Monday to Friday 9am-
noon and 2-5pm.

Listrac
*(Appellation Listrac
Contrôlée)*
(33480 Castelnau-de-
Médoc)

Château Cap Leon Veyrin
(Cru Bourgeois) TREC
Donissan
☎ (56) 58 17 28
or (56) 58 20 44
M. or Mme Meyre
Monday to Saturday 9am-
noon and 2-8pm. Sunday
by appointment.
Collection of winemaking
equipment.

Château Moulin de Laborde
(Cru Artisan) TR
☎ (56) 58 03 83
M. and Mme Michel
Hostens
Monday to Friday 8am-
7pm.

Château Fourcas Dupré TR
*(Cru Grand Bourgeois
Exceptionnel)*
☎ (56) 58 21 07
M. Guy Pages
Monday to Saturday 8am-
noon and 2-6pm

Château Fourcas Hosten TR
*(Cru Bourgeois
Exceptionnel)*
☎ (56) 58 21 15
M. Patrice Pages
Monday to Friday 8-
11.30am and 2-5.30pm.

Château Liouner TR
(Cru Bourgeois)
☎ (56) 58 14 38
M. Pierre Bosq
Monday to Saturday 8am-
noon and 2-8pm. Sunday
by appointment.

Château Peyredon-
Lagravette TRC
(Cru Bourgeois)
☎ (56) 58 17 75
M. Paul Hostein
1 June to 15 September
Saturday 9am-1pm and 2-
8pm. Sunday 9-10.30am
and by appointment. Rest
of year Sunday 9am-8pm.
Collection of winery
tools.

Grand Listrac TRE
(Cave Coopérative)
☎ (56) 58 23 19
or (56) 58 03 19
M. Maurice Meyre
Monday to Sunday 9-
11am and 2-5pm.

Château Clarke TREC
☎ (56) 88 88 00
or (56) 88 84 29
Baron Edmond de
Rothschild

6 June-30 September,
Monday-Saturday 10am-
7pm; Sunday 11am-6pm.
Tours and tasting 11am,
2.30 and 4pm. Rest of
year, Monday to Friday
9am-noon and 2-5pm.
Exhibition of history of
winemaking at the
château.

Châteaux Fonreaud and
Lestage TREC
*(Crus Bourgeois
Supérieurs)*
☎ (56) 58 14 43
Mme Chanfreau and M.
Jean Chanfreau
Monday to Friday 8am-
noon and 2-6pm. Saturday
and Sunday by appoint-
ment. Collection of
ancient winery tools.

Clos des Demoiselles TRE
(Cru Artisan)
☎ (56) 58 25 12
or (56) 58 22 72
Mme Micheline Augeau
15 May-15 September,
Monday to Saturday 8am-
noon and 2-9pm; Sunday
9-11am and 4-9pm. Rest
of year, Monday to
Saturday 8am-noon and 2-
6pm; Sunday 9-11am and
2-6pm.

Château Lalande TR
(Cru Bourgeois)
Mayne de Lalande
☎ (56) 58 19 45
Mme Darriet
Monday to Saturday 9am-
noon and 2-7pm. Sunday
by appointment.

Château Semeillan-
Mazeau TR
(Cru Bourgeois Supérieur)
☎ (56) 58 01 12
M. Chambaud
By appointment. Closed
15 September-31 October.

R=red wine   W=white wine   P=rosé wine   S=sparkling wine

Arcins
*(Appellation Haut-Médoc
Contrôlée)*
(33460 Margaux)

Château Barreyres
(Cru Bourgeois)
☎ (56) 58 91 29
Mlle Castel
Visits and tasting by
appointment.

Château Arnaud   TR
(Cru Bourgeois)
☎ (56) 58 90 17
Mme Maurice Roggy
Monday to Saturday 9am-
noon and 2-7pm, or by
appointment.

Château Tour du Roc   TR
(Cru Bourgeois)
☎ (56) 58 90 25
M. Philippe Robert
1 June-30 September,
Monday to Saturday 9am-
1pm and 2-6pm or by
appointment. 1 October-
31 May, Monday to
Saturday 9am-noon and 2-
6pm, or by appointment.

Château Arcins   TR
(Cru Bourgeois)
☎ (56) 58 91 29
Mlle Castel
Monday to Friday 10am-
7pm.

Moulis
*(Appellation Moulis
Contrôlée)*

(33480 Castelnau-de-
  Médoc)

Château Maucaillou   TRE
(Member of *l'Union des
  Grands Crus de Bordeaux*)
Grand Poujeaux
☎ (56) 58 17 92
M. Philippe Dourthe
Monday to Friday 10am-
noon and 3-5pm.
Weekends by
appointment.

Château Poujeaux   TREC
*(Cru Bourgeois
Exceptionnel)*
Grand Poujeaux
☎ (56) 58 22 70
or (56) 58 23 69
MM. Fr. and Ph. Theil
Monday to Friday 9am-
12.30pm and 2-6pm.
Collection of cellar
equipment.

Château Lestage
  Darquier   TR
(Cru Bourgeois)
Grand Poujeaux
☎ (56) 58 96 86
M. François Bernard
1 July-27 August, Thurs-
day and Friday 2-7pm,
Saturday 8am-noon. Sun-
day 8am-noon and 2-7pm.
Rest of year, Monday to
Thursday 8am-7pm. Week-
ends by appointment.

Château Tour Granins   TR
(Cru Bourgeois)
Grand Poujeaux
☎ (56) 58 22 59
M. André Batailley
Monday to Saturday 9am-
noon and 2-6pm, or by
appointment.

Château Bel-Air
  Lagrave   TRE
(Cru Bourgeois Supérieur)
Grand Poujeaux
☎ (56) 58 17 51
M. and Mme Bacquey
Monday to Saturday 8am-
9pm or by appointment.

Château Gressier-Grand-
  Poujeaux   TRC
(Cru Bourgeois)
☎ (56) 58 17 74
M. Bertrand de Marcellus
Monday to Friday 9-
11.30am and 2-4.30pm.
Visit the new oak vats.

Château Chasse-Spleen
*(Cru Bourgeois
Exceptionnel)*   TREC
Grand Poujeaux
☎ (56) 58 17 54
or (56) 58 17 68
M. Michel Conroy
Visits and tasting by
appointment. Visit the
underground *chai* — rare in
Bordeaux.

Château Franquet Grand-
  Poujeaux   TR
Grand Poujeaux
☎ (56) 59 04 94
M. Pierre Lambert
15 June-15 September,
Monday to Friday 10am-
noon and 3-6pm. Rest of
year same hours but by
appointment.

Château Brillette   TRE
(Cru Bourgeois Supérieur)
☎ (56) 58 22 09
Mme Berthault
1 May-30 September,
Monday to Saturday 9am-
12.30pm and 2-6pm. Rest
of year by appointment.

Château Biston-Brillette TR
(Cru Bourgeois)
Petit-Poujeaux
☎ (56) 58 22 86
M. Michel Barbarin
Monday to Friday 9am-
noon and 2-6pm; Saturday
9am-noon, or by
appointment.

Château La Mouline   TR
(Cru Bourgeois)
La Mouline
☎ (56) 45 07 89
M. Jean-Louis Coubris
Visits by appointment.

T=tasting   E=English spoken   G=guided tours   C=château/building to visit

Château Moulin à Vent TRE
(Cru Bourgeois Supérieur)
Bouqueyran
☎ (56) 58 15 79
M. Dominique Hessel
1 June-30 September,
Monday to Friday 8am-
noon and 1.30-6pm. Rest
of year, Monday to Friday
8am-noon and 2-5pm.

Soussans
*(Appellation Margaux
Contrôlée)*
(33460 Margaux)

Château Tayac TR
(Cru Bourgeois)
Tayac
☎ (56) 88 33 06
M. or Mme André Favin
  or Mme Nadine Portet
Monday to Friday 10am-
noon and 2-6pm.

Château Haut-Breton
  Larigaudière TR
(Cru Bourgeois)
☎ (56) 88 74 02
MM. Marc Raymond or
  Dominique Pradet
Visits by appointment.

Château La Tour de TRC
  Mons
(Cru Bourgeois Supérieur)
☎ (56) 88 33 03
MM. Bertrand or Christian
  Clauzel
Monday to Friday 9am-
noon and 2-5pm or by
appointment. Visit ruins.

Margaux
*(Appellation Margaux
Contrôlée)*
(33460 Margaux)

Maison du Vin de
  Margaux TRG
place La Trémoille
☎ (56) 88 70 82
Monday 2-6pm; Tuesday
to Saturday 9am-noon and
2-6pm. Full range of
Margaux wines on sale.

Château Lascombes TRE
(2 e
☎ (56) 88 70 66
or (56) 88 76 15 (château)
M. Gobineau
1 June-30 July and 20
August-30 September,
Monday to Friday 9.30am-
noon and 2-5pm. Rest of
year, Monday to Friday
10am noon and 2-5pm.
Closed 1-19 August.

Château Margaux TRE
(1 er
1855)
☎ (56) 88 70 28
M. Paul Pontallier
Monday to Friday 10am-
12.30pm and 2-5.30pm.
Groups by appointment.
Closed during August and
wine-making.

Château Canuet TRE
(Cru Bourgeois)
☎ (56) 88 70 21
Mme Sabine Rooryck
Monday to Friday 10am-
noon and 3-5pm. Saturday
3-5pm by appointment.
Rest of year by
appointment.

Château Durfort-
  Vivens TREC
(2e
☎ (56) 88 70 20

M. Lucien Lurton
Group visiting by
appointment, at least 4
days notice required.
Closed August. Otherwise
Monday to Friday 9am-
noon and 2-5pm.
Collection of winemaking
and vineyard equipment.

Château Marquis de Term
(Cru Classé) TRE
☎ (56) 88 30 01
M. Jean-Pierre Hugon
Monday to Friday 9am-
noon and 2-5pm.

Château Rausan Ségala TRE
(2e Cru Classé en 1855)
☎ (56) 88 70 30
or (56) 52 11 82 (office)
M. René Baffert
15 June-15 September,
Monday to Friday 9am-
noon and 2-6pm.
Weekends and rest of year
by appointment.

Château Rauzan Gassies
(Société Civile) TRE
(2eGrand Cru Classé)
☎ (56) 88 71 88
M. Jean-Marc Espagnet
  (Maître de Chai)
Monday to Friday 8.30am-
noon and 2-5.30pm.
Saturday by appointment.

Avensan
*(Appellation Haut-Médoc
Contrôlée)*
(33480 Castelnau-de-
Médoc)

Château Villegeorge TRE
*(Cru Bourgeois
  Exceptionnel)*
☎ (56) 88 70 20
M. Lucien Lurton
Monday to Friday 9am-
noon and 2-5pm.

R=red wine   W=white wine   P=rosé wine   S=sparkling wine

Château Tour Carelot TRC
(Cru Artisan)
Le Bourg
☎ (56) 58 71 39
M. Christian Braquessac
15 June-15 September,
Tuesday to Saturday 9am-
noon and 2-7pm. Sunday
10am-1pm or by appoint-
ment. Rest of year, Tues-
day to Friday 10am-noon
and 4-7pm. Saturday 9am-
noon and 4-7pm, Sunday
10am-1pm or by appoint-
ment. Audiovisual on the
work of the vineyard.

Château Citran   TRE
(Cru Bourgeois)
☎ (56) 58 21 01
Visits and tasting by
appointment.

Cantenac
*(Appellation Margaux
   Contrôlée)*
(33460 Margaux)

Château Martinens   TRC
(Cru Bourgeois Supérieur)
☎ (56) 88 71 37
M. Jean-Pierre Seynat-
Dulos
Monday to Friday 9am-
noon and 2-6pm. Visit
eighteenth-century
château.

Château Palmer
(3e
☎ (56) 88 72 72
M. Bouteiller (Adm.),
M. Chardon (Maître de
Chai)
Monday to Friday 9-
11.30am and 2.30-5pm

**Château Brane-
Cantenac   TRE**
☎ (56) 88 70 20
M. Lucien Lurton
Monday to Friday 9am-
noon and 2-5pm. Closed
August. Groups, 4 days
notice.

Château Prieuré-Lichine
(Grand Cru Classé) TREC
☎ (56) 88 36 28
M. Jean-Yves Cristien
Monday to Saturday 9am-
7pm. Collection of
plaques.

Château Desmirail   TRE
(3e Cru Classé en 1855)
☎ (56) 88 70 20
M. Lucien Lurton
Monday to Friday 9am-
noon and 2-5pm. Closed
August. Groups by
appointment only.

Château Boyd-Cantenac TR
(3e Cru Classé en 1855)
☎ (56) 88 30 58
M. Pierre Guillemet
1 June-31 August, Monday
to Friday 10am-noon and
3-7pm, or by appoint-
ment. Rest of year,
Monday to Friday 10am-
noon and 3-6pm.

Château Pouget   TR
(4e Cru Classé en 1855)
☎ (56) 88 30 58
M. Pierre Guillemet
1 June-31 August, Monday
to Friday 10am-noon and
3-7pm, or by
appointment. Rest of
year, Monday to Friday
10am-noon and 3-6pm, or
by appointment.

Château d'Angludet   TRE
(Cru Bourgeois)
☎ (56) 88 71 41
M. Peter A. Sichel
Monday to Friday 9am-
noon and 2-5pm.

Labarde
*(Appellation Margaux
   Contrôlée)*
(33460 Margaux)

Château Siran   TREC
(Grand Cru Exceptionnel)
☎ (56) 88 34 04
or (56) 81 35 01 (office)
M. Miailhe or M. Daney
15 June-30 September,
Monday to Friday 9am-
noon and 2.30-6pm.
Weekends 9am-5pm. 1
October-14 June, Monday
to Friday 9am-noon and 2-
6pm. Weekends by
appointment. Collection
of China and fine gardens.

Château Danzac   TRE
*(Grand Cru Classé en
   1855)*
☎ (56) 88 32 10
M. Dufaure
Monday to Friday 9-11am
and 2-5pm.

Château Giscours   TRE
(Cru Classé)
☎ (56) 88 34 02
M. Lucien Guillemet
Monday to Friday 8am-
noon and 2-6pm. Closed
August. Groups by
appointment.

Arsac
*(Appellation Margaux
   Contrôlée)*
(33460 Margaux)

Château Ligondras   TR
Ligondras
☎ (56) 88 31 43
M. Pierre Augeau
Monday to Sunday 8am-
8pm.

Château Mongravey   TR
(Cru Artisan)
☎ (56) 88 74 45
M. Régis Bemaleau
Visits and tasting by
appointment.

T=tasting   E=English spoken   G=guided tours   C=château/building to visit

Château Monbrison   TRE
(Cru Bourgeois)
☎ (56) 88 34 52
or (56) 88 37 61
Mme Davis
Monday to Friday 9am-
noon and 3-7pm. Week-
ends by appointment.

Ludon
*(Appellation Haut-Médoc
   Contrôlée)*
(33290 Blanquefort)

Château La Lagune   TR
(3ᵉ Cru Classé)
☎ (56) 30 44 07
Mme Boyrie
Monday-Friday 9am-noon
and 2-6 pm.

Blanquefort
*(Appellation Haut-Médoc
   Contrôlée)*
(33290 Blanquefort)

Château Dillon   TR
(Cru Bourgeois)
☎ (56) 35 02 27
M. Navarre
1 July-31 August, Monday
to Friday 9-11.30am and 2-
5.30pm. Rest of year,
Monday to Friday 8.30-
11.30am and 2-5.30pm.

Château du Grand   TR
   Clapeau
(Cru Bourgeois)
Le Grand Clapeau
☎ (56) 95 00 89
or (56) 35 06 27
M. Pierre Baudinière
1 May-15 September.
Tasting by appointment.

Château Magnol   TRE
(Cru Bourgeois)
☎ (56) 35 03 07
or (56) 35 84 41

M. Michel Fouchaux
Visits and tasting by
appointment with
Madeleine Croteau.

Le Taillan Médoc
*(Appellation Haut-Médoc
   Contrôlée)*
(33320 Eysines)

Château du Taillan   TREC
et la Dame Blanche
(Cru Bourgeois)
☎ M. Cruse (56) 35 14 26
(home)
or (56) 39 63 94 (office)
M. Bozzo
☎ (56) 35 16 41)
Monday to Friday 8am-
noon and 2-6pm. Saturday
8am-noon, or by
appointment. Visit
historic *chais*.

GRAVES

Many growers have both
red and white wine, but
not always both each
year.

Pessac
(33600 Pessac)

Château Pape Clément   TR
(Grand Cru Classé)
☎ (56) 07 04 77
Montagne
Every day except Saturday
8am-noon and 2-5pm.
Groups must give notice.
Closed August.

Cadaujac
(33140 Pont-de-la-Maye)

Château Bouscaut   TREC
(Grand Cru Classé)
☎ (56) 30 72 40

Monday to Friday 9am-
noon and 2-5pm. Closed
weekends and August.
Groups must give notice.
Very old. Wine aged in
barriques.

Martillac
(33650 Labrède)

Château Lafargue   TR
☎ (56) 23 72 30
J.P. Leymarie
Open daily for visits and
tasting. Groups must give
notice.

Domaine de la Solitude TE
☎ (56) 23 74 08
or (56) 23 72 67

*Association du Domaine
de la Solitude* (proprietor)
Rolland Belloc (manager)
Open daily for visits and
tasting. Very old.

Léognan
(33850 Léognan)

Château Haut-Bailly   TRE
(Grand Cru Classé)
☎ (56) 21 75 11
or (56) 27 16 07
*(Société Civile Château
   Haut-Bailly et Le Mayne)*
Jean Sanders (manager)
Monday to Friday for
tasting and visits. Closed
at weekends, unless by
appointment. Wine aged
in *barriques*.

R=red wine	W=white wine	P=rosé wine	S=sparkling wine

Domaine de Grand
Maison   TE
☎ (56) 21 75 37
Jean Bouquier
Monday to Friday 9am-
noon and 2-7pm. Week-
ends and holidays by
appointment. Groups must
give notice.

Labrède
(33650 Labrède)

Château Magneau   TE
Château Guirauton
☎ (56) 20 20 57
Henri Ardurats and son
Open daily from 2-6pm by
appointment. Groups must
give notice. Wine aged in
barriques.

Château Lassalle   T
☎ (56) 20 20 19
Louis l'Abbé
Tasting and visits by
appointment, between
Monday to Saturday 8am-
noon and 2-7pm.

Château La Blancherie   T
☎ (56) 20 20 39
Françoise Braud
Visits and tasting by
appointment.

Château Meric   TC
☎ (56) 20 20 53
or (56) 23 78 04
Pierre Barron
Visits and tasting by
appointment any day.
Wine aged in *barriques*.

Château Bichon-
Cassignols   TE
Le Baradey
☎ (56) 20 28 20
Jean-François Lespinasse
Monday to Saturday 9am-

7pm. Groups must give
notice. Wine aged in
barriques.

St-Selve
(33650 Labrède)

Château Bonnat-Jeansotte T
☎ (56) 20 25 11
Françoise Camus
Visits and tasting any
day, by appointment.
Wine aged in *barriques*.

St-Morillon
(33650 Labrède)

Château Claron   TE
☎ (56) 20 25 75
GAEC Ardurats
Visits and tasting any
day, by appointment.
Wine aged in *barriques*.

Château Belon   TE
☎ (56) 20 30 35
Jean Depiot
Monday to Saturday 8am-
7pm. Sundays and
holidays by appointment.
Very old house.

Château Piron   TE
☎ (56) 20 25 61
Paul Boyreau
Open for visits and
tasting Monday to Satur-
day 9am-noon and 2-5pm.

Castres
(33640 Portets)

Château St-Hilaire   TE
Clos de la Périchère
☎ (56) 67 12 12
Gabriel Guérin
Open daily from 8am-
8pm. Wine aged in
barriques.

Château de Haut-   T
Pommarede
☎ (56) 67 01 34
Mmes Delguel and Larrue
Visits and tasting by
appointment. Closed in
July.

Domaine Périn de   T
Naudine
*(Société Civile du Domaine
Périn de Naudine)*
Visits and tasting by
appointment.

Beautiran
(33640 Portets)

Château Le Tuquet   T
☎ (56) 20 21 23
or (56) 20 30 23
Paul Ragon (proprietor)
Monday to Friday 8am-
noon and 2-6pm. Wine
aged in *barriques*.

Portets
(Portets 33640)

Domaine Château
Millet   TE
☎ (56) 67 18 18
Henri de la Mette
Monday to Saturday 9am-
noon and 2-5pm.

Château Pessan (Portets) TC
Château Boyrein (Roaillan)
☎ (56) 27 03 51
J. Medeville and son
Monday to Friday normal
opening hours for visits
and tasting. Wine
Museum.

Château Cheret-Pitres   TC
☎ (56) 67 06 26
J. Boulanger
Visits and tasting by
appointment. Very old
château.

T=tasting   E=English spoken   G=guided tours   C=château/building to visit

Clos Lamothe TE
☎ (56) 67 23 12
SCE Clos Lamothe
Louis Rouanet (proprietor)
Monday to Saturday 8am-
12.30pm and 2-7pm.
Open on public holidays.
Wine aged in *barriques*.

Château Madelis T
☎ (56) 67 22 03
Jean Courbin
Visits and tastings by
appointment.

Domaine de Lucques TEC
☎ (56) 67 11 52
Louis Haverlan
Open daily 8am-6pm, by
appointment for tasting to
buy. Museum.

Château Cheret Lamothe T
☎ (56) 67 32 23
or (56) 67 36 21
Bernard Labat
Monday to Friday 9am-
8pm. Saturday and Sunday
morning by appointment.

Château du Grand
Abord TE
☎ (56) 67 22 79
Marc Dugoua
Visits and tasting by
appointment.

Budos
(33720 Podensac)

Château Pouyanne T
☎ (56) 62 51 73
E. Zausa
Visits and tasting by
appointment.

Domaine de l'Hermitage T
☎ (56) 62 51 58
Michel Courbin
Monday to Saturday 10am-
12 noon and 3-6pm.
Wine aged in *barriques*.

Arbanats
(33640 Portets)

Château Lagrange TC
☎ (56) 67 21 35
Hubert Dozier
Visits and tastings by
appointment

Podensac
(33720 Podensac)

Maison des Graves T
☎ (56) 27 09 25
Reception and tasting
facilities. Open daily.

Château de Mauves T
25 rue François-Mauriac
☎ (56) 27 17 05
Monday to Saturday
9am-6pm. Closed August.

Château Mayne TEC
d'Imbert
23 rue François-Mauriac
☎ (56) 27 08 80
Visits and tasting by
appointment. Very modern
chais.

Château de TEC
Chantegrive
☎ (56) 27 17 38
H. F. Leveque
Monday to Friday 8am-
noon and 2-6pm. Saturday
mornings only, or by ap-
pointment. Visit the *chais*.

Virelade
(33720 Podensac)

Domaine de Lugey T
☎ (56) 27 04 32
Joseph Faubet
Visits and tasting by
appointment.

Landiras
(33720 Podensac)

Château St-Agrèves TE
Artigues
☎ (56) 62 50 85
Marie-Christiane and
Claude Landry
Monday to Friday 9am-
noon and 3-6pm. Open on
public holidays.

Domaine du Moulin-à-
Vent TEC
☎ (56) 62 50 66
Pierre & Paulette Labuzan
Open daily 8am-7pm.
Wine produced by organic
farming methods.

Château d'Arricaud TE
☎ (56) 62 51 29
M. and Mme A.J. Bouyx
Monday to Friday 9am-
noon and 2.30-6pm. Satur-
days, Sundays and public
holidays by appointment.

Château Carbon
d'Artigues TE
Artigues
☎ (56) 62 53 24
Joseph Turroques
(proprietor)
Open daily 9am-noon and
2-5pm. Wine aged in
barriques.

Château Le Druc TE
de Perran
☎ (56) 62 40 37
Gérard Labuzan
Visits and tasting daily
but by appointment. Wine
aged in *barriques*.

Illats
(33720 Podensac)

Château de Navarro T
☎ (56) 27 20 27
Biarnes and son
Monday to Friday 9am-
6pm by appointment.

R=red wine W=white wine P=rosé wine S=sparkling wine

Château d'Ardennes   TEC
Château La Tuilerie
☎ (56) 62 53 80
or (56) 62 53 66
F. and B. Dubrey
Monday to Friday 8-
11.30am and 3-5pm, by
appointment. Closed 15-
30 August and 15 Sep-
tember-15 October. Visit
the winery and vineyard.

St-Michel-de-Rieufret
(33720 Podensac)

Château Lugaud   TE
☎ (56) 62 52 94
Jean Laty
Visits and tasting by
appointment.

Preignac
(33720 Podensac)

Château Respide-   TE
Medeville
Domaine des Justices
☎ (56) 63 27 59
Christian Medeville
Visits and tasting Monday
to Friday by appointment.
Very old château.

Toulenne
(33210 Langon)

Château de Courbon   TE
Jean Sanders
☎ (56) 63 19 54
Visits and tasting by
appointment.

Langon
(33210 Langon)

Château Fernon   T
☎ (56) 63 38 93
Girard de Langlade
Monday to Friday 9am-

noon and 2-5pm.
Weekends and public
holidays by appointment.

Domaine de Roland   T
route de Bazas
☎ (56) 63 25 69
J. Duperrieux-Pin
Visits and tasting by
appointment.

Château Camus   T
route d'Auros
☎ (56) 63 13 29
Larriaut and son
Visits and tasting by
appointment.

Domaine du Teigney   T
route d'Auros
☎ (56) 63 17 15
Visits and tasting daily
9am-7pm, by
appointment.

Domaine de Moleon   TEC
rue des Chênes
☎ (56) 63 11 45
Jean Pierre Reglat
Visits and tasting at any
time by appointment.
Wine display.

Château Le Maine   TE
route d'Auros
☎ (56) 63 52 26
Jean-Pierre Duprat
Tuesday to Saturday 9am-
noon and 3-7pm, by
appointment. Wine aged
in *barriques*.

Château Lehoul   TE
route d'Auros
☎ (56) 63 17 74
Serge Fonta
Visits and tasting by
appointment.

Château Brondelle   TEC
☎ (56) 63 05 73
Roland Belloc

Visits and tasting by
appointment. Very old
château.

Roaillan
(33210 Langon)

Château de Respide
Château Le Pavillon-de-
 Boyrein
☎ (56) 63 24 24
Bonnet and son
Visits and tasting by
appointment.

St-Pierre-de-Mons
(33210 Langon)

Château Magence   TE
☎ (56) 63 19 34
or (56) 63 07 05
D. Guillot de Suduiraut
Visits and tasting daily
8am-noon and 2-6pm, by
appointment.

Château Toumilon   T
Château Cabanes
☎ (56) 63 07 24
Jean Sevenet
Visits and tasting by
appointment.

Château de St-Pierre   T
☎ (56) 63 08 40
Henri Dulac
Visits and tasting daily
9am-6pm, by
appointment.

Mazères
(33210 Langon)

Château de Roquetailla
 -Grange   TEC
☎ (56) 63 24 23
Pierre and Jean Guignard
Visits and tasting daily
9am-noon and 2-6pm.
Nearby château and
pleasant shaded picnic
sites.

T=tasting   E=English spoken   G=guided tours   C=château/building to visit

LES VINS BLANCS LIQUOREUX DE BORDEAUX (SWEET WINES)
Sauternes, Barsac, Cérons, Graves, Supérieures (many growers also produce red wines)

Area between Ste-Croix-du-Mont and St-Genès-de-Lombaud

Most vineyards are open on weekdays unless stated otherwise.

Château La Rame   TWR
Ste-Croix-du-Mont
33410 Cadillac
Claude Armand
☎ (56) 63 20 33

Clos de Crabitan   TWR
Ste-Croix-du-Mont
33410 Cadillac
Bernard Solanne
☎ (56) 63 20 36

Château La Clyde   TWR
Tabanac
33550 Langoiran
J. Marie Cathala
☎ (56) 87 11 78

Château Loupiac-
   Gaudiel   TWR
Loupiac
33410 Cadillac
Marc Ducau
☎ (56) 27 13 05
Visits by appointment

Château Le Tarey   TWRP
Loupiac
33410 Cadillac
Robert Gillet
☎ (56) 27 03 13

Château Fayau   TRW
33410 Cadillac
M. Medeville and son
☎ (56) 27 03 51
Open: 10am-noon, 3-6pm

Château Le Thys   TWE
Béguey
33410 Cadillac
Pierre Segonnes
☎ (56) 27 03 68

Château Rondillon   TRWE
Clos Jean
Loupiac
33410 Cadillac
Henry Bord
☎ (56) 27 03 11

Domaine de Maillard   TRW
St-André-du-Bois
33490 St-Macaire
Jean Dubourg
☎ (56) 62 20 04

Château de Damis   TRW
Ste-Foy-la-Longue
33490 St-Macaire
Michel Bergey
☎ (56) 62 21 42

Château Labatut   TRWE
St-Maixant
33490 St-Macaire
Michel Bouchard
☎ (56) 62 25 22

Château Barakan   TRW
Capian
33550 Langoiran
Pierre Moysson
☎ (56) 67 20 01

Château du Peyrat   TRWP
Capian
33550 Langoiran
M. Lambert
☎ (56) 23 95 03

Château Genisson   TRWE
St-Germain-des-Graves
33490 St-Macaire
Jeanne Arrive and Cauboue
(no telephone)

Château Brethous   TR
Camblanes
33360 Latresne
François Verdier
☎ (56) 20 77 76

Château du Biac   TWRE
Haut-Langoiran
33550 Langoiran
Mme Nicole Ducatez
☎ (56) 67 19 92

Domaine de la Grave TRWE
St-André-du-Bois
33490 St-Macaire
Jean François Massieu
☎ (56) 62 20 31

Cave Coopérative
   Vinicole   TRW
Quinsac
33360 Latresne
☎ (56) 20 86 09

Clos de Garras   TRWP
Béguey
33410 Cadillac
Porta and Marche
☎ (56) 27 13 61

Château Bel-Air   TRW
Ste-Croix-du-Mont
33410 Cadillac
Michel Meric
☎ (56) 63 19 06

Château Couillac   TRW
Ste-Croix-du-Mont
33410 Cadillac
Gérard Despujols
☎ (56) 63 45 30

Château Arnaud-
   Jouan   TRWP
Ste-Croix-du-Mont
33410 Cadillac
Michel Darriet
☎ (56) 27 13 78

West of the River Garonne

Clos La Maurasse   TRW
route de Bazas
33210 Langon
Jean Despujols
☎ (56) 62 61 22

R=red wine   W=white wine   P=rosé wine   S=sparkling wine

Château Navarro   TWR
Château Suau
Barsac
33720 Podensac
Roger Biarnes
☎ (56) 27 12 85

Château Bastor-   TW
  Lamontagne
Preignac
33210 Langon
Jean Baup
☎ (56) 63 27 66
Open: weekends by
appointment.

Domaine du Moulin-
  à-Vent   TWRE
Landiras
33720 Podensac
Robert Labuzan
☎ (56) 62 50 66

Château Hillot   TWRE
Illats
33720 Podensac
Bernard Leppert
☎ (56) 62 53 38

Château Rieussec   TW
Fargues
33210 Langon
Albert Vuillier
☎ (56) 63 31 02

Château Bechereau   TWR
Bommes
33210 Langon
M. Benquet-Deloubes
☎ (56) 62 61 73

Clos Haut-Peyraguey   TW
Château Haut-Bommes
Bommes
33210 Langon
Jacques Pauly
☎ (56) 62 61 53

Château Filhot   TWE
Sauternes
33210 Langon
Henri de Vaucelles
☎ (56) 62 61 09

Château Simon   TWRE
Barsac
33720 Podensac
Jean Dufour
☎ (56) 27 15 35

Area around Cadillac

Château La Rame   TWR
Ste-Croix-du-Mont
33410 Cadillac
Claude Armand
☎ (56) 63 20 33

Château La Prioulette TWR
St-Maixant
33490 St-Macaire
François Bord
☎ (56) 63 23 03

Château Balot   TWRE
Montprimblanc
33410 Cadillac
Yvan Réglat
☎ (56) 27 06 03

Domaine de Chasse-
  Pierre   TWRPE
33410 Cadillac
André Lejeune
☎ (56) 21 12 72

Domaine des Deux-
  Lions   TRWP
Ste-Croix-du-Mont
33410 Cadillac
Gérard Despujols
☎ (56) 63 45 30

Château Lange   TWR
Clos Sahuc-Bommes
33210 Langon
M. Picot and son
☎ (56) 63 61 69

Château La
  Bertrande   TRWE
Omet
33410 Cadillac
Mme Henri Gillet
☎ (56) 27 06 (57)

Domaine du Mourcat TRWE
Cardan
33410 Cadillac
André Lagayette
☎ (56) 27 04 95

Château Haut-Bardin TRWP
St-Martial
33490 St-Macaire
Yves Cathérineau
☎ (56) 63 71 52

Château Vertheuil   TWRE
Ste-Croix-du-Mont
33410 Cadillac
Philippe Noël
☎ (56) 63 25 71

Barsac

Château Broustet   TW
33210 Barsac
☎ (56) 24 70 79
Open: by appointment.

Château Caillou   TW
Joseph Bravo
Barsac
33720 Podensac
☎ (56) 56 27 63
Open: by appointment.

Château Cantegril   TW
M. Dubourdieu
33210 Sauternes
☎ (56) 27 15 84
Open: by appointment.

Château Coutet   TW
(*Société Civile du Château
  Coutet*)
Barsac
33720 Podensac
☎ (56) 27 15 46
Open: Monday to Friday
9am-noon and 2-6pm.

Château Doisy-Daene   TW
M. Dubourdieu
Ch. Cantegril
33210 Sauternes
☎ (56) 26 15 84
Open: by appointment.

T=tasting E=English spoken G=guided tours C=château/building to visit

Château Farluret   TW
Robert Lamothe
Haut-Bergeron
Preignac
33720 Langon
☎ (56) 56 63 24
Open: by appointment
only.

Château Liot   TW
M. David
Barsac
33720 Podensac
☎ (56) 27 15 31
Open: by appointment
only.

Château Menota   TW
SCEA du Château Menota
Barsac
33720 Podensac
☎ (56) 27 15 80
Open: by appointment
only.

Château Mont-Joie   TW
Franck Glaunés
Cassoil Barsac
33720 Podensac
☎ (56) 71 12 73
Open: by appointment.

Château Nairac   TW
Thomas Heeter-Tari
Barsac
33720 Podensac
☎ (56) 27 16 16
Open: by appointment
only.

Château Piada   TW
Jean Lalande
Barsac
33720 Podensac
☎ (56) 27 16 13
Open: by appointment
only.

Château Piot-David   TW
Domaine de Poncet
Jean-Luc-David
33410 Omet
☎ (56) 62 97 30
Open: by appointment
only.

Château St-Marc   TW
André Laulan
Barsac
33720 Podensac
☎ (56) 27 16 18
Open: by appointment
only.

Château Suau   TW
Roger Biarnes
Illats
33720 Podensac
☎ (56) 27 20 27
Open: by appointment
only.

Château Tucau   TW
Bernard Leppert
Illats
33720 Podensac
☎ (56) 62 53 38
Open: by appointment
only.

Sauternes

Château d'Arche   TW
Pierre Perromat
Gornac
33540 Sauveterre-de-
Guyenne
☎ (56) 61 97 64
Open: by appointment
only

Baron Philippe   TW
Baron Philippe de
  Rothschild
La Baronnie
33250 Pauillac
☎ (56) 59 20 20
Open: Monday to
Thursday 9.30-11.30am
and 2.30-5.30pm; Friday
2.30-3pm only.

Château Bergeron   TW
M. Laurans
Bommes
33210 Langon
☎ (56) 63 60 17
Open: by appointment
only.

Château Bouyot   TW
Bertrand Jammy-Fonbeney
Le Bouyot
33210 Barsac
☎ (56) 27 19 46
Open: by appointment.

Château Cameron   TW
Pierre Guinabert
Bommes
33210 Langon
☎ (56) 27 16 39
Open: by appointment.

Château Climens   TW
Lucien Lurton
Ch. Brane-Cantenac
33460 Margaux
☎ (56) 88 70 20
Open: by appointment.

Château Boisy-Vedrines TW
Pierre Casteja
Barsac
33720 Podensac
☎ (56) 27 15 13
Open: by appointment.

Château Gilette   TW
Château Les Justices
Christian Medeville
Preignac
33210 Langon
☎ (56) 63 27 59
Open: by appointment
only.

Château Gravas   TW
Bernard Perre
Barsac
33720 Podensac
☎ (56) 27 15 20
Open: by appointment.

Château Lafaurie
  Peyraguey   TW
Domaine Cordier
33210 Bommes
☎ (56) 63 60 54
Open: Monday to Friday
8am-noon and 2-6pm;
closed end of August and
beginning of September.

R=red wine   W=white wine   P=rosé wine   S=sparkling wine

Château Lafon TW
M. Jean-Pierre Dufour
Sauternes
33210 Langon
☎ (56) 63 30 82
Open: daily 8.30am-1pm
and 2-7pm, closed mid-
August and last half of
September and October.

Château Latrezotte TW
Marie-Pierre Badoures
Barsac
33720 Podensac
☎ (56) 27 16 50
Open: by appointment.

Château Rabaud-Promis TW
Mme Dejeans
Bommes

33210 Langon
☎ (56) 63 60 52
Open: by appointment.

Château Romer-
du-Hayot TW
André du Hayot
Bommes
33210 Langon
☎ (56) 27 15 37
Open: by appointment,
(closed August).

Château St-Amand TW
Louis Ricard
Preignac
33210 Langon
☎ (56) 63 27 28
Open: by appointment.

Château Siglas-Rabaud TW
Mme de Lambert des
Granges
Bommes
33210 Langon
☎ (56) 63 60 62
Open: by appointment.

Château La Tour BlancheTW
Bommes
33210 Langon
☎ (56) 63 61 55
Open: by appointment.

Château d'Yquem TW
Comté de Lur-Saluces
Sauternes
33210 Langon
☎ (56) 63 21 05
Open: by appointment.

ST-EMILION

St-Emilion
(33330 St-Emilion)

All are open to the public
for tasting and buying.
All produce red wines
only. English spoken in
most cases.

Château Angelus TR
De Bouard de Laforest
brothers
☎ (57) 24 71 39

Château Ausone TR
Vauthier and Mme Dubois-
Challon
☎ (57) 24 70 94
or (57) 24 70 26

Château Badette TR
Daniel Arraud
☎ (57) 74 42 13

Château Badon-Fleurus TR
Mazière
☎ (57) 24 70 42

Château Bagnols TR
Lafaye
☎ (57) 40 18 28

Château Baleau TR
*(Sté civile des Grandes
Murailles)*
☎ (57) 24 71 09

Château Balestard-La-
Tonnelle TR
Jacques Capdemourlin
☎ (57) 24 74 35

Château Barbeyron TR
Jean-Claude Bassilieaux
☎ (57) 40 06 71

Château Barrail-Les-
Graves TR
Christian and Gérard
Descrambes
☎ (57) 84 51 54

Château Barraud TR
Edgard Valadier
☎ (57) 51 52 72

Château Beard TR
R. Goudichaud
☎ (57) 24 72 96

Château Beard-La
-Chapelle TR
Richard Moureau
☎ (57) 52 21 46
or (57) 74 44 13

Château Beauregard TR
Louis-Robert Pendary
☎ (57) 24 75 29

Château Beausejour TR
Héritiers Duffau-Lagarrosse
☎ (57) 24 71 61

Château Beusejour-
Bécot TR
Michel Bécot
☎ (57) 74 46 87

Château Bel-Air TR
Mme J. Dubois-Challon
☎ (57) 24 70 94

Château Bel-Air-Ouy TR
Gellie U. de P.
☎ (57) 24 70 71

Château Belle-Assise-
Coureau TR
Yvan Brun
☎ (57) 24 61 62

Château Bellefont-
Belcier TR
J. Labusquière
☎ (57) 24 72 16

T=tasting E=English spoken G=guided tours C=château/building to visit

Château Bellefont-Belcier-
Guillier TR
Philippe Guillier
☎ (57) 24 72 41

Château Bellegrave TR
Pierre Dangin and son
☎ (57) 84 53 01

Château Bellevue TR
L. Horeau, Mme de Lavaux,
de Coninck
☎ (57) 24 14 12

Château Bergat TR
Bertin
☎ (57) 24 71 32

Château Berliquet TR
Vte and Vtesse de Lesquen
☎ (57) 24 70 48

Château Bigaroux TR
B. Dizier
☎ (57) 24 71 97

Château Bonnet TR
Roger Bonnet and son
☎ (57) 40 15 23

Château Boutisse TR
Jean-François Carrille
☎ (57) 24 74 46

Château Bragard TR
Jean Bernard
☎ (57) 51 03 61

Château Brun-
Beauvallon TR
G.F.A. Brun
☎ (57) 24 77 06

Château Cadet-Bon TR
F. Gratadour
☎ (57) 24 71 29

Château Cadet-Piola TR
M. Jabiol
☎ (57) 24 70 67

Château Cadet-Pontet TR
M. Mérias
☎ (57) 24 72 66

Château Canon TR
S.V. Château Canon
☎ (57) 24 70 79

Château Canon-La-
Gaffelière TR
Comte de Neipperg
☎ (57) 24 71 33

Château Cantenac TR
J.B. Brunot
☎ (57) 51 35 22

Château Canterane TR
Trabut-Cussac
☎ (57) 40 18 14

Château Cap-de-Mourlin TR
Mme Jean Capdemourlin
☎ (57) 24 70 83

Château Cap-de-Mourlin TR
Jacques Capdemourlin
☎ (57) 24 74 35

Château Capet TR
Marne & Champagne
☎ (26) 54 21 66

Château Capet-Guillier TR
Mme Bouzerand, Mme
Galinou
☎ (57) 24 70 21

Château Cardinal-
Villemaurine TR
Pierre Carrille
☎ (57) 24 71 04

Château Carillon TR
Roger Visage
☎ (57) 24 78 22

Château-Côtes-Daugay TR
Bertrand and son
(57) 24 73 94

Château-Carteau-Matras TR
Claude Bion
☎ (57) 24 72 35

Château Champion TR
Jean Bourrigaud
☎ (57) 74 43 98

Château Chapelle-
Madeleine TR
Mme Dubois-Challon
☎ (57) 24 70 94

Château Chauvin TR
Ondet
☎ (57) 51 33 76

Château Cheval-Blanc TR
*(Sté Civile du Cheval-
Blanc)*
☎ (57) 24 70 70

Château Cheval-Noir TR
Malher-Besse
☎ (57) 29 16 75

Château Clos Badon TR
Philippe Dugos
☎ (57) 24 71 03

Château Clos Belle-
Rose TR
Jean Faurie
☎ (57) 74 07 03

Château Clos de la Curé-
Milon TR
Arteau-Bouyer
☎ (57) 24 77 18

Château Clos de
l'Oratoire TR
(Sté civile du Château)
Peyreau
☎ (57) 24 77 86

Château Clos des
Ghildes TR
Gérard Faisandier
☎ (57) 51 20 79

Château Clos des
Jacobins TR
Cordier

Château Clos du Bon-
Pasteur TR
Pierre Delage
☎ (57) 51 13 18

Château Clos Doumayne TR
Roland Bel
☎ (57) 51 00 88

R=red wine   W=white wine   P=rosé wine   S=sparkling wine

Château Clos Fongaban TR
Guy d'Arfeuille
☎ (57) 24 70 52

Château Clos Fourtet TR
F. Lurton
☎ (57) 24 70 90

Château Clos
Grand-Gontey TR
Jean-Robert Mestadier
☎ (57) 51 42 87

Château Clos Labarde TR
Jacques Bailly
☎ (57) 24 71 31

Château Clos La
Madeleine TR
Pistouley
☎ (57) 24 71 50

Château Clos des
Menuts TR
Pierre Rivière
☎ (57) 24 70 59

Château Clos St-Julien TR
J.J. Nouvel
☎ (57) 24 72 05

Château Clos St-Martin TR
*(Sté Civile des Grandes
Murailles)*
☎ (57) 24 71 09

Château Clos St-Valery TR
Pierre Berjal
☎ (57) 24 70 97

Château Clos Trimoulet TR
Guy Appollot
☎ (57) 24 71 96

Château Corbin TR
*(Sté civile des Domaines
Giraud)*
☎ (57) 24 70 62

Château Corbin-Michotte
Jean-Noël Boidron
☎ (57) 96 28 57

Château Cormey-Figeac
R. Moreaud
☎ (57) 24 70 53

Château Côtes Bernateau TR
Régis Lavau
☎ (57) 40 18 19

Côte de la Mouleyre TR
Emile and Pierre Roques
☎ (57) 40 16 48

Château Côte Puy-
Blanquet TR
Daniel Bertoni and son
☎ (57) 40 18 35

Château Côtes
Rocheuses TR
Union de Producteurs
de St-Emilion
☎ (57) 24 70 71

Château Coudert TR
Jean-Claude Carles
☎ (57) 24 78 92

Château Coudert-
Pelletan TR
Jean-André Lavau
☎ (57) 24 77 30

Château Coutet TR
David Beaulieu
☎ (57) 24 72 27

Château Cravignac TR
Jay-Beaupertuis
(57) 28 09 96

Château Croix-de-
Bertinat TR
Christian Lafaye
☎ (57) 24 74 36

Château Croix-Simard TR
Claude Mazière
☎ (57) 24 70 42

Château Croque-MichotteTR
Mme Rigal-Geoffrion
☎ (57) 24 13 64

Château Cros-Figeac TR
Christian Cassagne
☎ (57) 24 76 32

Château Cruzeau TR
Luqot
☎ (57) 51 18 95

Château Curé-Bon-La-
Madeleine TR
Hubert Lande
☎ (57) 51 20 36

Château d'Arcie TR
J.A. Baugier U. de P.
☎ (57) 24 70 71

Château Dassault TR
Dassault
☎ (57) 24 71 30

Château de Candale TR
Jean Dugos
☎ (57) 24 72 97

Château de l'Epinette TR
Domaines Dubourg
☎ (57) 63 23 06

Château de Ferrand TR
Bich
☎ (57) 24 77 07

Château de Lescours TR
SA d'Exploitation
☎ (57) 24 74 75

Château de Lisse TR
Jean Petit
☎ (57) 40 18 23

Château de Pressac TR
Héritiers de André Pouey
☎ (57) 40 18 02

Château de Rol TR
Jean Sautereau
☎ (57) 24 70 38

Château de St-Pey TR
J.P. and Ph. Musset
☎ (57) 40 15 01

Château des Places TR
Claude Fritegotto
☎ (57) 40 18 27

Château des Templiers TR
*(Sté des vignobles
Meneret-Capdemourlin)*
(57) 24 71 41

Château Destieux TR
G.F.A. du château
☎ (57) 24 77 44

Château Destieux-BergerTR
A. Cazenave U. de P.
☎ (57) 24 70 71

T=tasting   E=English spoken   G=guided tours   C=château/building to visit

Château Domaine Chante-
l'Alouette TR
Pierre Berjal
☎ (57) 24 70 97

Château Domaine de la
Gaffelière TR
Claude Mazière
☎ (57) 24 70 42

Château Domaine de
Peyrelongue TR
Pierre Cassat
☎ (57) 24 72 36

Château Doumayne TR
Francis Robin
☎ (57) 51 03 65

Château du Barry TR
Noël Mouty
☎ (57) 84 52 80

Château du Calvaire TR
Jean-Pierre Cisterne
☎ (57) 40 18 06

Château du Cauze TR
(Société Civile)
☎ (57) 24 77 01

Château du Marquis-de-
Mons TR
Micheau-Maillou and
Palatin
☎ (57) 24 77 48

Château du Paradis TR
Raby
☎ (57) 84 53 27

Château du Pontet TR
Paul Fomperier
☎ (57) 24 71 56

Château du Rocher TR
Stanislas de Montfort
☎ (57) 40 18 20

Château du Sème TR
Philippe and Nicole
Rivière
☎ (57) 24 73 01

Château du Val-d'Or TR
Roger Bardet
☎ (57) 84 53 16

Château Faleyrens TR
J. Brisson
☎ (57) 24 72 (57)

Château Faugères TR
Jean Esquissaud
☎ (57) 40 18 22

Château Faurie-de-
Souchard TR
M. Jabiol
☎ (57) 24 70 67

Château Ferrandat TR
SA d'Exploitation Ch. de
Lescours
☎ (57) 51 70 67

Château Figeac TR
Thierry Manoncourt
☎ (57) 24 72 26

Château Flouquet TR
Christian Bernard
☎ (57) 24 72 48

Château Fombrauge TR
Bygodt
☎ (57) 24 77 12

Château Fomplegade TR
*(Sté des Vignobles A.
Moueix)*
☎ (57) 24 71 60

Château Fonrazade TR
Guy Balotte
☎ (57) 24 71 58

Château Fonroque TR
Mme J. Moueix
☎ (57) 24 70 82

Château Fontenelle TR
Bigarette brothers
☎ (57) 40 08 86

Château Fougueyrat TR
Daniel Nicoux
☎ (57) 24 70 64

Château Fouquet TR
SCA du Château
☎ (57) 24 70 42

Château Fourney TR
J.-P. Rollet
☎ (57) 40 15 13

Château Franc-Bigaroux TR
Yves Blanc
☎ (57) 51 54 73

Château Franc-Capet TR
Jean-Jaime Chambret
☎ (57) 51 06 51

Château Franc-Lartigue TR
Ch. Lafourcade U. de P.
☎ (57) 24 70 71

Château Franc-Patarabet TR
Barraud and Faure
☎ (57) 24 70 36

Château Franc-Pineuilh TR
Jean-Paul Deson
☎ (57) 24 77 40

Château Franc-Pipeau TR
Mme Bertrand Jacqueline
☎ (57) 24 73 94

Château Franc-Pourret TR
Ouzoulias
☎ (57) 51 07 55

Château Gaillard TR
J.-J. Nouvel
☎ (57) 24 72 05

Château Gaillard-de-la-
Gorce TR
J.-P. Rollet
☎ (57) 40 15 13

Château Gaubert TR
Jean Ménager
☎ (57) 24 70 55

Château Gessan TR
B. Gonzalez
☎ (57) 74 44 04

R=red wine   W=white wine   P=rosé wine   S=sparkling wine

Château Grand-Barrail-
Lamarzelle-Figeac   TR
Association carrière
☎ (57) 24 71 43

Château Grand-Bert   TR
Philippe Lavigne
☎ (57) 40 60 09

Château Grand-Bigaroux TR
Jean-Louis Fayard
☎ (57) 24 75 18

Château Grands-Champs TR
Jean Blanc
☎ (57) 40 07 59

Château Grand-Corbin   TR
Alain Giraud
☎ (57) 24 70 62

Château Grand-Corbin-
Manuel   TR
P. Manuel
☎ (57) 51 12 47

Château Grand-Destieu TR
R.-C. Thibaud
☎ (57) 24 73 48

Château Grangey   TR
F. Arroz U. de P.
☎ (57) 24 70 71

Château Grandes-
Murailles   TR
*(Sté Civile des Grandes
Murailles)*
☎ (57) 24 71 09

Château Grand-Mayne   TR
Jean-Pierre Nony
☎ (57) 74 42 50

Château Grand-Mirande TR
Raymond Junet
☎ (57) 51 31 39

Château Grand-Pey-de-
Lescours   TR
Escure
☎ (57) 51 07 59

Château Grand-Pontet   TR
S.C.A. Grand-Pontet
☎ (57) 24 72 14

Château Gravet   TR
Jean Faure
☎ (57) 24 75 68

Château Gravet-
Renaissance   TR
Pierre Gagnaire
☎ (57) 24 73 91

Château Gros-Caillou-
Boulerne   TR
Paul Lafaye
☎ (57) 24 75 75

Château Guadet-St-JulienTR
Robert Lignac
☎ (57) 24 70 89

Château Guadet-Le-Franc-
La-Grace-Dieu   TR
Siloret
☎ (57) 51 17 13

Château Gueyrosse   TR
Yves Delot
☎ (57) 51 02 63

Château Gueyrot   TR
Fayet brothers
☎ (57) 24 72 08

Château Guillemin-La-
Gaffelière   TR
Paul Fomperier
☎ (57) 24 71 56

Château Guinot   TR
Mme Tauziac
☎ (57) 40 18 24

Château Haut-Boutisse TR
Gérard and Bernard Fretier
☎ (57) 24 74 81

Château Haut-Brisson   TR
Yves Blanc
☎ (57) 84 53 19

Château Haut-Cadet   TR
Jean Bernard
☎ (57) 51 03 61

Château Haut-Corbin   TR
Edward Guinaudie
☎ (57) 51 05 74

Château Haute-Nauve   TR
R. and A. Reynier U. de P.
☎ (57) 24 70 71

Château Hautes-Graves-
d'Artus   TR
J.G. Musset
☎ (57) 84 55 66

Château Haut-Fonrazade TR
Jean-Claude Carles
☎ (57) 24 78 92

Château Haut-Grand-
Faurie   TR
J.F. Capdemourlin-
Meneret
☎ (57) 24 71 41

Château Haut-Gravet   TR
M. and Mme Alain Aubert
☎ (57) 40 06 93

Château Haut-Gueyrot   TR
Jean-Marcel Gombeau
☎ (57) 24 60 53

Château Haut-Lavallade TR
Jean-Pierre Chagneau
☎ (57) 24 77 47

Château Haut-Mazerat   TR
Héritiers Gouteyron
☎ (57) 24 71 15

Château Haut-Patarabet TR
Ouzoulias
☎ (57) 51 07 55

Château Haut-Peyroutas TR
Labécot and son
☎ (57) 84 53 31

Château Haut-Plantey   TR
Michel Boutet
☎ (57) 24 70 86

Château Haut-Quercus   TR
U. de P.
☎ (57) 24 70 71

Château Haut-
Renaissance   TR
D. Barraud-Mouty
☎ (57) 84 54 73

T=tasting   E=English spoken   G=guided tours   C=château/building to visit

Château Haut-Rocher
de Monteil   TR
☎ (57) 40 18 09

Château Haut-Sarpe   TR
Joseph Janoueix
☎ (57) 24 70 98

Château Haut-Segottes   TR
D. André
☎ (57) 24 60 82

Château Haut-Simard   TR
Claude Mazière
☎ (57) 24 70 42

Château Haut-Vachon-La-
Rose   TR
André Quenouille
☎ (57) 24 78 93

Château Jacques-Blanc   TR
G.F.A. du Ch. Jacques-
Blanc
☎ (57) 40 18 01

Château Jacques-Noir   TR
Rémy Daut
☎ (57) 40 11 88

Château Jean-Blanc   TR
Yvonne Brette
☎ (57) 40 15 21

Château Jean-Faure   TR
Michel Amart
☎ (57) 51 49 36

Château Jean-Voisin   TR
Raby-Saugeon
☎ (57) 84 53 27

Château Jupile   TR
Roger Visage
☎ (57) 24 78 22

Château La Boisserie   TR
La Boisserie U. de P.
☎ (57) 24 70 71

Château La Bonnelle   TR
R. Sulzer U. de P.
☎ (57) 24 70 71

Château La Clotte   TR
Héritiers Chailleau
☎ (57) 24 72 52

Château La Clusière   TR
Valette family
☎ (57) 24 72 02

Château La
Commanderie   TR
Pierre Brasseur
☎ (57) 24 60 44

Château La Couspaude   TR
Vignobles Aubert
☎ (57) 40 01 15

Château La Croix-
Chantecaille   TR
M. Angle
☎ (57) 51 11 51

Château La Croix-Fourche-
Mallard   TR
Jean-Marie Mallard
☎ (57) 23 93 04

Château La Croix-
Fourney   TR
Alain Bonneau
☎ (57) 84 50 01

Château La Dominique   TR
Fayat
☎ (57) 51 69 74

Château La Fagnouse   TR
Anne-Marie Coutant
☎ (57) 40 00 08

Château La Fleur   TR
Mme Lacoste
☎ (57) 49 60 03

Château La Fleur-Cauzin TR
Raynal-Demur
☎ (57) 24 77 58

Château La Fleur-Pourret TR
*(Société des domaines
Prats)*
☎ (57) 44 11 37

Château La Fleur-Vachon
Tapon
☎ (57) 24 71 20

Château La Gaffelière   TR
Comte Léo de Malet de
Roquefort
☎ (57) 24 72 15

Château La Gomerie   TR
Marcel Lescure
☎ (57) 24 71 35

Château La Grace-Dieu TR
Maurice Pauty
☎ (57) 24 71 10

Château La Grace-Dieu-des-
Prieurs   TR
Laubie
☎ (57) 51 07 87

Château La Grace-Dieu-Les-
Menuts   TR
Xans Pilotte
☎ (57) 24 73 10

Château La Grange-de-
Lescure   TR
(Sté Marne et Champagne)
☎ (26) 54 21 66

Château Lamartre   TR
Vialard U. de P.
☎ (57) 24 70 71

Château Lamarzelle   TR
Association Carrière
☎ (57) 24 71 43

Château Lamarzelle-
Cormey   TR
Robert Moreaud
☎ (57) 51 06 57

Château La Melissière   TR
Jeanne Bernard
☎ (57) 24 73 87

Château La Mondotte   TR
Comte de Neipperg
☎ (57) 24 71 33

Château La Mondotte-
Belisle   TR
René Chaput
☎ (57) 24 72 84

R=red wine   W=white wine   P=rosé wine   S=sparkling wine

Château l'Ancien-
Moulin TR
Gilbert Favrie
☎ (57) 51 29 02

Château Langranne TR
Musset Branche
☎ (57) 40 15 01

Château Laniote TR
Héritiers Freymond
☎ (57) 24 70 80

Château Lapelleterie TR
Pierre Jean
☎ (57) 24 77 54

Château La Petite-Fuie TR
Jean Faure
☎ (57) 40 06 93

Château Lapeyre TR
Mme Tauziac
☎ (57) 40 18 24

Château La Pignonne TR
Denis Pueyo
☎ (57) 51 13 26

Château Laplagnotte-
Bellevue TR
Biais
☎ (57) 08 03 17

Château Larcis-Ducasse TR
H. Gratiot-Alphandery
☎ (57) 24 70 84

Château Larmande TR
J.F. Meneret-
Capdemourlin
☎ (57) 24 71 61

Château La Rocaille TR
François Florit
☎ (57) 51 01 23

Château Laroque TR
SCA Gérant Roger Droin
☎ (57) 24 77 28

Château La Rose TR
Jean-Claude Carles
☎ (57) 24 77 36

Château La Rose-Côtes-
Rol TR
Yves Mirande
☎ (57) 24 71 28

Château La Rose-Pourret TR
Bertrand Warion
☎ (57) 24 71 13

Château La Rose-Puy-
Blanquet TR
J. Robert Bellanger
☎ (57) 40 18 37

Château La Rose-
Trimoulet TR
J.C. Brisson
☎ (57) 24 73 24

Château Laroze TR
*(Sté Civile du Château
Laroze)*
☎ (57) 24 72 10

Château La Sablière TR
Robert Avezou
☎ (57) 24 73 04

Château La Sablonnerie TR
Lavigne and son
☎ (57) 24 75 35

Château Lassègue TR
Jean-Pierre Freylon
☎ (57) 24 72 83

Château La Serre TR
B. d'Arfeuille
☎ (57) 24 71 38

Château La Tour-du-Pin-
Figeac TR
Vignobles Moueix
☎ (57) 51 50 53

Château La Tour-du-Pin-
Figeac TR
Micheline Giraud
☎ (57) 51 06 10

Château Lavallade TR
Pierre Gaury
☎ (57) 24 77 49

Château Le Basque TR
E. Lafaye U. de P.
☎ (57) 24 70 71

Château Le Bois-de-l'Or TR
M. and Mme Lenne
☎ (57) 40 07 87

Château Le Bois-du-Loup TR
M. and Mme Lenne
☎ (57) 40 07 87

Château L'Eglise-Pontet TR
Lespine
☎ (57) 84 50 06

Château Le Castelot TR
Jean-François Janoueix
☎ (57) 51 41 86

Château Le Châtelet TR
Pierre Berjal
☎ (57) 24 70 97

Château Le Chevalier TR
Musset Branche
☎ (57) 40 15 01

Château Le Couvent TR
(Sté Marne et Champagne)
☎ 26 54 21 66

Château Le Freyche TR
Henri Domezil
☎ (57) 40 21 61

Château L'Eglise-Pontet TR
Lespine
☎ (57) 84 50 06

Château Le Jurat TR
Edward Guinaudie
☎ (57) 51 05 74

Château Le Loup TR
P. Garrigue U. de P.
☎ (57) 24 70 71

Château Le Mayne TR
Jean-Claude Dupuy
☎ (57) 58 17 41

Château Le Prieuré TR
Baronne Guichard
☎ (57) 51 18 62

T=tasting E=English spoken G=guided tours C=château/building to visit

Château Lenoir TR
Léopold Couderc
☎ (57) 51 19 84

Château Lespinasse TR
P. Orens Bentenat & son
☎ (57) 40 15 08

Château L'Epine TR
Jean Ardoin
☎ (57) 51 07 75

Château L'Hermitage TR
Association Brunot
☎ (57) 51 35 22

Château Magdelaine TR
J.P. Moueix
☎ (57) 51 75 55

Château Magnan-La-
Gaffelière TR
Pistouley
☎ (57) 24 71 50

Château Martinet TR
De Lavaux
☎ (57) 51 17 29

Château Matignon TR
Henri Matignon
☎ (57) 51 12 86

Château Matras TR
Mme Gaboriaud
☎ (57) 51 03 61

Château Maurens TR
Bygodt
☎ (57) 24 77 12

Château Mauvezin TR
Pierre Cassat
☎ (57) 24 72 36

Château Mauvinon TR
Tribaudeau and son
☎ (57) 24 75 05

Château Mayne-Figeac TR
Jean-Jaime Chambret
☎ (57) 51 06 51

Château Melin TR
René Debacque
☎ (57) 51 00 66

Château Millaud-
Montlabert TR
Mme Brieux and son
☎ (57) 24 71 85

Château Moine-Vieux TR
Arthur Pigeon
☎ (57) 24 73 29

Château Monbousquet TR
Alain Querre
☎ (57) 24 75 24

Château Mont-Bel-Air TR
Fernand Denamiel
☎ (57) 40 18 03

Château Monte-Christo TR
Philibert Rousselot
☎ (57) 74 06 71

Château Montlabert TR
Barrière
☎ (57) 24 70 75

Château Monlot-Capet TR
Mme Ichon
☎ (57) 24 72 98

Château Moulin-
Bellegrave TR
Max Périer
☎ (57) 84 53 28

Château Moulin-du-Cadet TR
Moulièrac-J.-P. Moueix
☎ (57) 51 75 55

Château Moulin-de-
Pierrefitte TR
Jean-Louis Fayard
☎ (57) 24 75 18

Château Moulin-St-
Georges TR
Alain Vauthier
☎ (57) 24 70 26

Château Nardon TR
Raymond Rufat
☎ (57) 24 77 08

Château Naude TR
Alain Bonneau
☎ (57) 84 50 01

Château Pailhas TR
Robin Lafugie
☎ (57) 24 71 83

Château Palais-Cardinal-
Lafue TR
Gérard Fretier and son
☎ (57) 24 75 91

Château Panet TR
Jean-Claude Carles
☎ (57) 40 00 52

Château Patris TR
Michel Querre
☎ (57) 51 73 37

Château Pavie TR
Valette family
☎ (57) 24 72 02

Château Pavie-Decesse TR
Valette family
☎ (57) 24 72 02

Château Pavie-Macquin TR
A. Corre
☎ (57) 24 74 23

Château Pavillon-Cadet TR
Anne Llammas
☎ (45) 92 77 20

Château Petit-Faurie-
Desoutard TR
F. Aberlen
☎ (57) 24 72 31

Château Perey-Grouley TR
Rémy Xans
☎ (57) 24 73 17

Château Petit-Figeac TR
Domaines Prats
☎ (57) 44 11 37

Château Petit-Garderose TR
Jacques Hénocque
☎ (57) 51 58 84

Château Petit-Gravet TR
Mme Nouvel
☎ (57) 24 72 34

R=red wine   W=white wine   P=rosé wine   S=sparkling wine

Château Petit-Mangot TR
Decamps and son
☎ (57) 40 18 33

Château Petit-Val TR
Michel Boutet
☎ (57) 24 70 86

Château Peyreau TR
(Sté Civile du Château)
Peyreau
☎ (57) 24 70 86

Château Peyrelongue TR
Jean-Jacques Bouquey
☎ (57) 24 71 17

Château Peyrouquet TR
Maurice Cheminade
☎ (57) 40 15 39

Château Pindefleurs TR
Mme Dior
☎ (57) 24 72 04

Château Piney TR
Jean Catusseau
☎ (57) 24 70 22

Château Pipeau TR
Pierre Mestreguilhem
☎ (57) 24 72 95

Château Pontet-Clauzure TR
(Sté Marne et Champagne)
☎ (26) 54 21 66

Château Puy-Blanquet TR
Jacquet
☎ (57) 40 18 18

Château Puy-Blanquet-
Carrille TR
Jean-François Carrille
☎ (57) 24 74 46

Château Puy-Razac TR
Guy Thoiliez
☎ (57) 24 73 32

Château Quentin TR
De Coninck
☎ (57) 24 77 43

Château Queyron TR
Louis Goujou
☎ (57) 24 74 62

Château Quinault TR
Henri Maleret
☎ (57) 51 13 39

Château Reynaud TR
Terras
☎ (57) 24 70 31

Château Ripeau TR
Janoueix/De Wilde
☎ (57) 51 41 24

Château Robin TR
Buzet
☎ (57) 24 77 64

Château Rochebrune TR
Alfred Chal
☎ (57) 51 10 46

Château Rocher-Bellevue-
Figeac TR
R. Pagnac U. de P.
☎ (57) 24 70 71

Château Roc-St-Michel TR
J.P. Rollet
☎ (57) 40 15 13

Château Rol-de-
Fombrauge TR
A. Bonnet
☎ (57) 24 77 67

Château Rolland-Maillet TR
Geneviève Rolland
☎ (57) 51 10 84

Château Royal TR
U. de P.
☎ (57) 24 70 71

Château Rozier TR
J.B. Saby
☎ (57) 24 73 03

Château St-Christophe TR
G. Richard
☎ (57) 24 77 17

Château St-Georges-Côtes
Pavie TR
R. Masson
☎ (57) 24 71 08

Château St-Hubert TR
Etienne Aubert
☎ (57) 40 01 15

Château St-Lo TR
Tabouy
☎ (57) 40 15 22

Château St-Pey TR
M. Musset
☎ (57) 40 15 25

Château Sansonnet TR
Francis Robin
☎ (57) 51 03 65

Château Simard TR
Claude Mazière
☎ (57) 24 70 42

Château Soutard TR
Cte and Ctesse des
Ligneris
☎ (57) 24 72 23

Château Tarreyre TR
Brissaud-Peyrebrune
☎ (57) 24 74 30

Château Tertre-Daugay TR
Comte de Malet-Roquefort
☎ (57) 24 72 15

Château Tertre-Rôte-
Bœuf TR
François Mitjavile
☎ (57) 24 70 57

Château Teyssier TR
Gérard Colin
☎ (57) 84 53 25

Château Tonneret TR
Albino Gresta
☎ (57) 24 60 01

Château Touran TR
Geens Rudiger
☎ (57) 40 08 88

T=tasting   E=English spoken   G=guided tours   C=château/building to visit

Château Tour-Baladoz TR
De Schepper
☎ (57) 24 41 03

Château Tour-
Beauregard TR
Fritegotto Illario
☎ (57) 24 73 15

Château Tour-Blanche TR
Emile and Pierre Roques
☎ (57) 40 16 48

Château Tour-des-
Combes TR
Jean Darribehaude
☎ (57) 24 70 04

Château Tour-Carre TR
Henri Gulter
☎ (57) 24 77 15

Château Tour-Grand-
Faurie TR
Jean Feytit
☎ (57) 24 73 75

Château Tour-Puy-
Blanquet TR
Lapoterie and son
☎ (57) 40 18 32

Château Tour-St-
Christophe TR
Henri Gulter
☎ (57) 24 77 15

Château Tour-St-Pierre TR
J. Goudineau
☎ (57) 24 70 23

Château Tour-Vachon TR
René Rebinguet
☎ (57) 24 70 27

Château Touzinat TR
Marcelle Nérac
☎ (57) 40 15 32

Château Trapaud TR
André Larribère
☎ (57) 40 18 08

Château Trapeau TR
Claude Mazière
☎ (57) 24 70 42

Château Trianon TR
Mme Lecointre
☎ (57) 51 42 63

Château Trimoulet TR
Pierre Jean
☎ (57) 24 77 54

Château Troplong-
Mondot TR
Claude Valette
☎ (57) 24 70 72

Château Trottevieille TR
Héritiers Borie
☎ (57) 24 71 34

Union des Producteurs TR
☎ (57) 24 70 71

Château Verdet TR
Edmond Beaugier
☎ (57) 51 71 56

Château Veyrac TR
J. Robert Bellanger
☎ (57) 40 18 37

Château Vieille-Tour-
La-Rose TR
Ybert and son
☎ (57) 24 73 41

Château Vieux-Castel-
Haut-Lavallade TR
Denis and J.P. Chagneau
☎ (57) 24 77 47

Château-Vieux-Château-
Doumayne TR
François P. Janoueix
☎ (57) 51 05 44

Château Vieux-Château-
Pelletan TR
M. Magnaudeix
☎ (57) 24 77 55

Château Vieux-Château-
Peymouton Hecquet-
Milon TR
☎ (57) 74 42 42

Château Vieux-Clos-St-
Emilion TR
Michel Terras
☎ (57) 24 60 91

Château Vieux Fortin TR
M. T. Tomasina
☎ (1) 46 07 85 40

Château Vieux-Grand-
Faurie TR
Jean Bourrigaud
☎ (57) 74 43 98

Château Vieux-Guinot TR
Rollet
☎ (57) 40 15 13

Château Vieux-
Larmande TR
M. Magnaudeix
☎ (57) 24 77 55

Château Vieux-Lartigue TR
Claude Mazière
☎ (57) 24 70 42

Château Vieux-Moulin-
Du-Cadet TR
G. Gombeau
☎ (57) 24 72 13

Château Vieux-Pourret TR
Mazière-Halamoda
☎ (57) 24 71 72

Château Vieux-Rivallon TR
Charles Bouquey
☎ (57) 51 35 27

Château Villemaurine TR
Robert Giraud
☎ (57) 24 71 57

Château Viramon TR
Lafaye
☎ (57) 40 18 28

Château Yon-Figeac TR
Lussier
☎ (57) 24 70 08

Château Yon-La-Fleur TR
Jean Menozzi
☎ (57) 24 78 60

R=red wine   W=white wine   P=rosé wine   S=sparkling wine

POMEROL

(33500 Libourne)
All vineyards are open for tasting. All produce red wines only.

Château Beauregard   TR
Clauzel Héritiers
Pomerol
☎ (57) 51 13 36
Open: By appointment only, closed July.

Château Belle-Brise   TR
Michel Lafage
Ch. Belle-Brise
Pomerol
☎ (57) 51 16 82
Open: by appointment.

Château Bonalgue   TR
Pierre Bourotte
rue Trocard
Pomerol
☎ (57) 51 20 56
Open: by appointment.
Closed last two weeks July-first two weeks August.

Château Le Bon Pasteur   TR
Mme Geneviève Rolland
Pomerol
☎ (57) 51 10 94
Open: by appointment.

Château La Cabanne   TR
Jean-Pierre Estager
rue de Montaudon
Pomerol
☎ (57) 51 04 09
Open: by appointment only; closed August.

Château Certan   TR
Mme Barreau-Badar
Pomerol
☎ (57) 51 41 53
Open: by appointment.

Château Gombaude-
   Guillot   TR
Laval and daughters
Pomerol
☎ (57) 51 17 40

Open: Monday to Wednesday only, 10.30am-4.30pm.

Château Clos-René   TR
Pierre Lasserre
Pomerol
☎ (57) 51 10 41
Open: by appointment.

Château La Conseillante   TR
Nicolas Héritiers
Pomerol
☎ (57) 51 15 32
Open: by appointment only.

Château La Croix
   Toulifaut   TR
Jean-François Janoueix
Pomerol
☎ (57) 51 19 05
Open: by appointment only.

Château La Croix-de-
   Gay   TR
M. Raynaud
Pomerol
☎ (57) 51 19 05
Open: by appointment.

Château L'Enclos   TR
(Société du Ch. L'Enclos)
Pomerol
☎ (57) 51 04 62
Open: by appointment.

Château L'Evangile   TR
(Société du Ch. L'Evangile)
Pomerol
☎ (57) 51 15 30
Open: by appointment.

Château La Fleur-Pétrus   TR
(Société Ch. La Fleur-Pétrus)
Pomerol
☎ (57) 51 17 96
Open: by appointment.

Château La Ganne   TR
Lachaud Dubois
222 ave. Foch
Pomerol
☎ (57) 51 18 24
Open: Monday to Saturday 8.30am-noon and 2.30-7pm; closed August.

Château Gazin   TR
Etienne de Baillencourt
Pomerol
☎ (57) 51 88 66
Open: by appointment.

Château Les Graves-
   Guillot   TR
Paul Clauzel
Pomerol
☎ (57) 51 13 36
Open: by appointment only.

Château La Grave-Trignan-
   de-Boisse   TR
Christian Moueix
Pomerol
☎ (57) 51 78 96
Open: by appointment only.

Château Mazeyres   TR
M. Querre
Pomerol
☎ (57) 51 00 40
Open: Monday to Friday 9am-noon and 2-6pm.

Château Moulinet   TR
Société Civile
☎ (57) 51 50 63
Open: Saturday and Sunday 8am-noon and 2-6pm.

Château Petit-Village   TR
Bruno Prats
Pomerol
☎ (57) 44 11 37
Open: by appointment.

Château Pétrus   TR
Mme Lacoste-Loubat
Pomerol
☎ (57) 51 17 96
Open: by appointment.

Château Plincette   TR
Jean-Pierre Estager
rue de Montaudon
Pomerol

T=tasting   E=English spoken   G=guided tours   C=château/building to visit

☎ (57) 51 04 09
Open: by appointment.

Château La Pointe TR
M. d'Arfeuille
Pomerol
☎ (57) 51 02 11
Open: by appointment.

Château La Renaissance TR
François de Lavaux
Ch. Martinet
Pomerol
☎ (57) 91 17 29
Open: by appointment.

Château Rêve d'Or TR
M. Vigier
Pomerol
☎ (57) 51 11 92
Open: by appointment.

Château Rocher-
Beauregard TR

Max Tournier
Pomerol
☎ (57) 51 36 49
Open: by appointment.

Château de Sales TR
Bruno de Lambert
Pomerol
☎ (57) 51 04 92
Open: by appointment.

Château Les Grands-
Sillons-Gabachot TR
François Janoueix
20 quai du Priourat
Pomerol
☎ (57) 51 55 44
Open: by appointment.

Château Taillefer TR
Marcel Moueix
Pomerol
☎ (57) 51 50 63

Open: Saturday and Sunday
8am-noon and 2-6pm.

Château Trotanoy TR
(Société Civile du Ch.
Trotanoy)
Pomerol
Open: by appointment.

Château Valois TR
(Société des Vignobles
Leydet)
Pomerol
☎ (57) 51 19 77
Open: Monday to Saturday
9am-noon and 2-7pm.

Château Vieux-Certan TR
Pomerol
(Société du Ch. Vieux-
Certan)
☎ (57) 51 17 33
Open: daily 9am-noon and
2-7pm.

THE COTES DE BOURG

Area between St-
André-de-Cubzac
& Prignac/Marcamps
(33710 Bourg-sur-Gironde)

Châteaux Croûte-Terrasse
& Fond-de-l'Ile TR
☎ (57) 68 40 07
Open: Monday to
Saturday.

Château Croûte Courpon TR
☎ (57) 68 42 81
Open: by appointment.

Château Lagrange TR
Christian Sicard
☎(57) 68 43 11
Open: by appointment.

Château de Lidonne TR
Roger Audoire
☎ (57) 68 47 52
Open: daily.

Château Moulin
d'Yquem TR

Robert Seurin
☎ (57) 68 44 26
Open: Saturday afternoon.

Château Brulesécaille TR
Jacques Rodet
☎ (57) 68 40 31
Open: Monday to
Saturday.

Château Cave Vinicole de
Tauriac TRWP
route de Bourg
Tauriac
☎ (57) 68 19 12
Open: daily except
Monday.

Château Haut-Macô TR
Bernard & Jean Mallet
Tauriac
☎ (57) 68 81 26
Open: Monday to
Saturday.

Château Soulignac
de Robert TR
M. and Mme Cebals
Tauriac
☎ (57) 68 41 17
Open: daily.
Cave Coopérative Vinicole
de St-Gervais TR
☎ (57) 43 03 04
Open: Tuesday to
Saturday.

Area between Pugnac
and St-Mariens
(33710 Bourg-sur-Gironde)

Château Camponac TW
Jean José Rios and Annie
Margoteau
☎ (57) 68 40 26
Open: daily.

Château Guionne TW
Richard Porcher

R=red wine   W=white wine   P=rosé wine   S=sparkling wine

Lansac
☎ (57) 68 42 17
Open: daily except August

Château Canterane   TR
Bernard Micas
Lansac
☎ (57) 68 43 28
Open: daily.

Château du Moulin
  Vieux   TR
Jean Gorphe
Tauriac
☎ (57) 68 44 65
Open: daily.

Cave de Vinification
  de Lansac   TRWP
☎ (57) 68 41 01
Open: Tuesday to
Saturday.

Château Les Vieilles
  Tuileries   TR
Serge Rabotin
Lansac
☎ (57) 68 44 32
Open: daily.

Cave Coopérative Vinicole
  de Pugnac   TRW
Bellevue
Pugnac
☎ (57) 68 81 01
Open: by appointment.

Château Denis   TR
Michael Bertin
Lansac
☎ (57) 68 41 04
Open: daily.

Château Lamothe   TR
Pierre Pessonnier
Lansac
☎ (57) 68 41 07
Open: by appointment.

**Area between
Teuillac and
Montendre**
(33710 Bourg-sur-Gironde)

Château Begot   TR
Alain Gracia
Lansac
☎ (57) 68 42 14
Open: daily.

Château Les Hauts de
  Terrefort   TRW
Pierre Landreau
Mombrier
Open: by appointment.

Château Le Pont
  de la Tonnelle   TRWP
Gérard Juin
Teuillac
☎ (57) 42 19 29
Open: daily.

Château Moulin des
  Graves   TRW
Robert Bost
Le Poteau de Teuillac
☎ (57) 42 09 41
Open: daily.

Château Peychaud   TR
J. & B. Germain
Teuillac
☎ (57) 42 19 63
Open: Monday to
Saturday.

**Area between Bel-
Air and Le Pontet**
(33710 Bourg-sur-Gironde)

Château La Croix-de-
  Bel-Air   TR
Marcel Arnaud
St-Seurin-de-Bourg
☎ (57) 68 40 41
Open: daily.

Château de Laurensanne TR
Francis Levraud
Open: daily.

Château Colbert   TR
Mme André Humbert
Comps
☎ (57) 42 14 32
Open: daily.

Château Beaulieu   TRE
Frank Groneman
Samonac
☎ (57) 68 43 93
Open: by appointment.

Château Rousset   TR
M. and Mme Teisseire
Samonac
☎ (57) 68 46 34
Open: by appointment.

Château Maray   TR
Serge Latouche
Samonac
☎ (57) 68 41 50
Open: daily.

Château du Castenet   TR
R. and J. Marcon
Samonac
☎ (57) 42 15 50
Open: daily

Château La Tour Birol TR
Gérard Roy
Samonac
Open: by appointment.

Château Haut-Castenet TR
Pierre Audouin
Samonac
☎ (57) 42 16 15
Open: daily. Has also a
gîte rural.

Château Montaigut   TR
François de Pardieu
Nodeau-St-Ciers-de-
  Canesse
☎ (57) 42 17 49
Open: daily.

Domaine Les Graves   TR
  de Méteau
André Gilbert
St-Trojan
☎ (57) 42 12 39
Open: daily.

**Area between Blaye
and La Côte**
(33710 Bourg-sur-Gironde)

Château Le Clos du
  Notaire   TR

T=tasting   E=English spoken   G=guided tours   C=château/building to visit

Roland Charbonnier
Bourg
☎ (57) 68 44 36
Open: daily.

Château Caruel   TR
Francis Auduteau
Bourg
☎ (57) 68 43 07
Open: daily.

Château La Plantonne   TR
Jacques and Jeanne
  Fougnet
Bourg
☎ (57) 68 41 52
Open: daily.

Château La Croix de
  Millerit   TR
M. and Mme Amédée
Jaubert
Bayon
☎ (57) 41 14 13
Open: daily.

Château Les Rocques   TR
Pierre Feillon and son
St-Seurin-de-Bourg
☎ (57) 68 47 66
or (57) 68 42 82
Open: daily.

Château les Cailloux   TRW
Robert and Raymond Roy
St-Seurin-de-Bourg
Open: daily.

Château Falfas   TR
Château La Joncarde
Mme M. Jaubert
Bayon
☎ (57) 42 14 04
Open: daily.

Château Le Breuil   TR
Henri Doyen
Bayon
Gauriac
☎ (57) 68 42 79
or (57) 42 14 10
Open: daily.

Domaine de Loudenat TRW
Cave du Bourgeais Gauriac
☎ (57) 42 06 45
Open: Tuesday to Saturday.

Château Haut-Lacouture TR
Serge Roy, Christiane Sou
Gauriac
Open: daily.

Château de Thau   TR
Léopold Schweitzer
Gauriac
☎ (57) 42 01 27
Open: daily.

Château Peyrer   TR
Michel Jaubert
Gauriac
☎ (57) 42 19 28
Open: daily

Château de Barbe   TR
Savary de Beauregard
Villeneuve-de-Blaye
☎ (57) 42 16 51
Open: daily.

Château Sauman   TR
Dominique Braud
Villeneuve-de-Blaye
☎ (57) 42 16 64
Open: by appointment.

Château Pey-Chaud   TR
  Bourdieu
Marc Roy
Villeneuve-de-Blaye
Open: by appointment.

Château de Mendoce   TR
Philippe Darricarrère
Villeneuve-de-Blaye
☎ (57) 42 25 95
Open: daily.

Château Rouselle   TR
St-Ciers-de-Canesse
☎ (57) 42 16 62
Open: daily.

Château Plaisance   TRP
Alibert Belougne
Villeneuve-de-Blaye
Open: daily.

**Area between
Villeneuve and
Teuillac**
(33710 Bourg-sur-Gironde)

Château La Croix
Davids   TR
André Birot
Lansac
☎ (57) 68 40 05
Tasting at 57 rue Valentin
Bernard, Bourg.

Château Cayac   TR
Pierre Saturny
St-Seurin-de-Bourg
☎ 68 40 60
Open: weekends.

Château D'Yquem   TR
SA de Vignobles Bayle-
  Carreau
Bayon
☎ (57) 42 02 43
Open: daily.

Château Bel-Air-Coubet TR
Alain Faure
St-Ciers-de-Canesse
☎ (57) 42 17 06
Open: daily .

Château Les Heaumes   TR
Max Robin
St-Ciers-de-Canesse
☎ (57) 42 17 11
Open: daily .

Château Bélias   TR
Mexant Morin
St-Ciers-de-Canesse
☎ (57) 42 03 25
Open: daily .

Château Mercier   TRWP
Philippe and Martine
Chety
St-Trojan
☎ (57) 42 17 34
Open: daily. Also *gîte*
accommodation.

R=red wine   W=white wine   P=rosé wine   S=sparkling wine

Château Haut-Guiraud TR
Jean Bonnet
St-Ciers-de-Canesse
☎ (57) 42 17 39
Open: Tuesday to
Saturday. Closed August.

Château Haut-Launay TR
André Noailles
Teuillac
☎ (57) 42 09 44
Open: daily.

Château Haut-Rousset TR
Joël Grellier
St-Ciers-de-Canesse
☎ (57) 42 17 45
Open: daily.

ENTRE-DEUX-MERS

All vineyards produce
white wines and have
tasting.

Château Les Arromans TW
Jean Duffau
Moulon
33420 Branne
☎ (57) 84 50 87
Open: by appointment.

Château Baron d'Espiet TW
Coopérative d'Espiet
33420 Branne
☎ (57) 24 24 08
Open: Monday to Friday
8.30am-12.30pm and
2.30-6.30pm.

Château Bauduc TW
Véronique Thomas
33670 Créon
☎ (56) 23 23 58
Open: by appointment.

Château Bellevie TW
Bruno de Ponton
d'Amercourt
33540 Sauveterre-de-
Guyenne
☎(56) 71 54 56
Open: by appointment.

Château Bernot TW
Union Coopérative
Agricole Blasimon
33540 Sauveterre-de-
Guyenne
☎ (56) 71 55 28
Open: by appointment.

Château Bonnet TW
André Lurton
Grézillac
33420 Branne
☎ (57) 84 52 07
Open: by appointment.

Château Busqueyron TW
René Maugey
33750 St-Germain-du-Puch
☎ (57) 24 55 34
Open: by appointment.

Domaine des Cailloux TW
Nicole Lagrand
Romagne
33760 Targon
☎ (56) 23 09 47
Open: by appointment.

Château Candeley TW
Henri Devillaire
St-Antoine-du-Queyret
33790 Pellegrue
☎ (56) 61 31 46
Open: by appointment.

Château Canet TW
Bernard and Jacques Large
Guillac
33420 Branne
☎ (57) 84 52 08
Open: by appointment.

Château de Chardavoine TW
Claude Paillet
Soulignac
33760 Targon
☎ (56) 23 94 09
Open: by appointment.

Château de Crain TW
SCA de Crain
33750 St-Germain-du-Puch
☎ (57) 24 50 66
Open: by appointment.

Domaine La Croix
de Miaille TW
J. Cailleux
Escoussans

33760 Targon
☎ (56) 23 63 23
Open: by appointment.

Château Fillon TW
Serge Laguens
Cazaugitat
33790 Felleme
☎ (56) 61 32 40
Open: by appointment.

Château Fongrave TW
Pierre Perromat
Gornac
33540 Sauveterre-de-
Guyenne
☎ (56) 61 97 64
Open: by appointment.

Château Gabachot TW
Roger Fernandez
33450 Sauveterre-de-
Guyenne
☎ (56) 71 51 24
Open: by appointment.

La Gamage Union
St-Vincent TW
St-Vincent-de-Pertignas
33420 Branne
☎ (57) 84 13 66
Open: by appointment.

Château Gaury-Balette TW
Yvon Bernard
33540 Mauriac
☎ (57) 40 52 82
Open: by appointment.

Château Grand-Monteil TW
(Société Civile Ch. Grand
Monteil)
Salleboeuf
33370 Tresses

T=tasting   E=English spoken   G=guided tours   C=château/building to visit

85

☎ (57) 21 29 70
Open: daily 8am-noon and
2-6pm.

Château Haut-
 Brousquet   TW
Robert Giraud
33240 St-André-de-Cubzac
☎ (57) 43 01 44
Open: by appointment only.

Château Les Haut-de-
 Fontaneau   TW
Coopérative de Grange-
 Neuve
Ramagne
33760 Targon
☎ (56) 23 94 62
Open: by appointment
only.

Les Hauts-de-Ste-Marie TW
M. Mondon-Dupuch
33760 Targon
☎ (56) 23 64 30
Open: by appointment
only.

Coopérative de Juillac-
 Flaujagues   TW
Flaujagues
33350 Castillon-la-
 Bataille
☎ 40 08 06
Open: by appointment
only.

Château de Lagarde   TW
Norbert Raymond .
St-Laurent-du-Bois 33540
☎ (56) 63 73 63
Open: by appointment
only.

Château Launay   TW
SCEA Claude-Bernard
Greffier
Soussac
33790 Pellegrue
☎ (56) 61 31 51
Open: daily 9am-noon and
2.30-7pm.

Château Mougneaux   TW
Jean Bocquet
Ste-Ferme
33580 Monségur
☎ (56) 61 62 02
Open: by appointment
only.

Château La Nardique-la-
 Gravière   TW
GAEC Thérèse and son
St-Genès-de-Lombaud
33570 Créon
☎ (56) 23 01 37
Open: by appointment
only.

Cave de Nérigean   TW
Cave Coopérative de
 Nérigean
Nérigean
33750 St-Germain-du-Puch
☎ (57) 24 50 64
Open: by appointment
only.

Château Petit-Freylon TW
Jean-Michel Lagrange
St-Génis-du-Bois
33119 Frontenac
☎ (56) 71 54 79
Open: by appointment
only.

Château du Petit-Puch TW
33750 St-Germain-du-Puch
☎ 24 52 36
Open: by appointment
only.

Château Peyrebon   TW
Jean-André Robineau
Grézillac
33420 Branne
☎ (57) 84 52 26
Open: by appointment.

Domaine de Pourquey   TW
Roger Fouilhac and son
Castelviel
33540 Sauveterre-de-
 Guyenne

☎ (56) 61 97 62
Open: by appointment
only.

Château Pudris   TW
François Dupeyron
Casseuil
33190 La Réole
☎ (56) 71 11 99
Open: by appointment
only.

Château Les Ram-
 beauds   TW
Jean Cazade
Fosses-et-Baleyssac
33190 La Réole
☎ (56) 61 72 72
Open: by appointment
only.

Château Rebullide   TW
Jacqueline Grasset
Guillac
33420 Branne
☎ (57) 84 52 23
Open: by appointment
only.

Château Tour-de-
 Mirambeau   TW
M. Despagne
Naujan-et-Postiac
33420 Branne
☎ (57) 84 52 58
Open: by appointment
only.

Château Turcaud   TW
Maurice Robert
La Sauve Majeure
33670 Créon
☎ 23 04 41
Open: Monday to Saturday
9am-noon and 2-7pm.

Château Turon-La-CroixTW
Saric and son
Lugasson
33119 Frontenac
☎ (56) 24 05 55
Open: by appointment only.

R=red wine   W=white wine   P=rosé wine   S=sparkling wine

COTES DE BLAYE AND PREMIERES COTES DE BLAYE

All vineyards offer tasting and produce only white wine.

Château Domaine
  Arnaud   TW
Dominique Arnaud
St-Christoly-de-Blaye
33920 St-Savin
☏ (57) 42 48 24
Open: by appointment only.

Château Barbe   TW
Château Eyqueau
Bayon
33710 Bourg-sur-Gironde
☏ (57) 64 32 43
Open: Monday to Friday
8am-noon and 2-6pm.

Château Berthenon   TW
Henri Fonz
33390 St-Paul-de-Blaye
☏ (57) 42 52 24
Open: by appointment only.

Château Bertinerie   TW
Daniel Bantignies
Cubnezais
33620 Cavignac
☏ (57) 68 70 74
Open: by appointment only.

Château La Botte   TW
René Blanchard
33920 St-Savin-de-Blaye
☏ (57) 58 90 03
Open: by appointment.

Château Cap-St-Martin TW
Laurent Ardoin
St-Martin-Lacaussade
33390 Blaye
☏ (57) 42 13 92
Open: Monday to Friday
9am-noon and 3-5pm;
closed end September to
middle October.

Château Capville   TW
Mme Janick Bénéteau
Cars
33390 Blaye
☏ (57) 42 80 84
Open: Tuesday to Friday

Château Les Chaumes TW
Robert Parmentier
Fours
33390 Blaye
☏ (57) 42 18 44
Open: by appointment only.

Domaine du Chay   TW
Guy Bénéteau
Cars
33390 Blaye
☏ (57) 41 15 24
Open: daily 8am-8pm.

Château Cone-Taillason TW
Sabourin brothers
Château Crusquet-Sabourin
Cars
33390 Blaye
Open: Monday to Friday
9am-noon and 2-7pm.

Château Crusquet de la
  Garcie   TW
Lagarcie
33390 Blaye
☏ (57) 42 15 21
Open: by appointment.

Château Crusquet-
  Sabourin   TW
Société Sabourin brothers
Cars
33390 Blaye
☏ (57) 42 15 27
Open: Monday to Friday
9am-noon and 2-7pm.

Château l'Escadre   TW
Société G. Garreau and son
Cars
33390 Blaye
☏ (57) 42 15 18

Open: Monday to Saturday
8am-noon and 2.30-
7.30pm.

Château Fouche   TW
Jean Bonnet
Ch. Haut-Guiraud
St-Ciers-de-Caresse
33710 Bourg-sur-Gironde
☏ (57) 42 17 39
Open: by appointment.

Château Gardut-Haut-
  Cluzeau   TW
M. Revaire
Cars
33390 Blaye
☏ (57) 42 30 35
Open: by appointment.

Château Gardut   TW
M. Revaire
Cars
33390 Blaye
☏ (57) 42 30 35
Open: daily 8am-1pm and
2-8pm.

Château Le Grand
  Mazerolles   TW
Claude Rigal
Cars
33390 Blaye
☏ (57) 42 86 68
Open: by appointment .

Château Grillet-
  Beausejour   TW
Jean-Jacques Jullion
Berson
33390 Blaye
☏ (57) 42 52 16
Open: by appointment.

Château Lardière   TW
Réné Bernard
Marcillac
33860 Reignac
☏ (57) 32 41 38
Open: by appointment only.

T=tasting E=English spoken G=guided tours C=château/building to visit

Château Loumede TW
Louis Raynaud
33390 Blaye
☎ (57) 42 16 39
Open: by appointment.

Château Marinier TW
Thierry Cotet
Cézac
33620 Cavignac
☎ (57) 68 63 13
Open: by appointment.

Château des Moines TW
Jean and Alain Carreau
33390 Blaye
☎ (57) 42 12 91
Open: by appointment.

Château Penaud TW
Sergé Penaud
La Lande
St-Aubin-de-Blaye
33820 St-Ciers-sur-
  Gironde
☎ (57) 64 71 70
Open: by appointment.

Château Perenne
  Oudinot TW
M. Oudinot
St-Genès-de-Blaye
33390 Blaye
☎ (57) 42 118 25
Open: by appointment.

Domaine des Petits TW
M. Chapard-Truffeau
Cars
33390 Blaye
☎ (57) 42 19 09
Open: by appointment
only.

Château Les Petits
  Arnauds TW
Société G. Carreau and son
Cars
33390 Blaye
☎ (57) 42 15 18
Open: Monday to Saturday
8am-12.30pm and
2.30-7.30pm; closed last
two weeks of August.

Château Peyreyre TW
Michel Trinque
St-Martin-Lacaussade
33390 Blaye
☎ (57) 41 18 57
Open: Monday to Friday
9am-noon and 2-6pm.

Château de Rebouquet-la-
  Rouquette TW
M. Braud
Berson
33390 Blaye
☎ (57) 64 35 06
Open: Monday to Saturday
9am-noon and 2-7pm.

Château La Rivalérie TW
SCEA La Rivalérie
St-Paul
33390 Blaye
☎ (57) 42 18 84
Open: by appointment.

Château Roland La
  Garde TW
Olivier Martin
St-Seurin-de-Cursac
33390 Blaye
☎ (57) 42 18 04
Open: daily 9am-7pm.

Château Sociondo TW
Michel Ellie
ave. de Ferrard
Berson
33390 Blaye
☎ (57) 64 33 61
Open: by appointment
only.

Château Tayat TW
Guy and Bernard Favereaud
Cézac
33620 Cavignac
☎ (57) 68 62 10
Open: Monday to Saturday
9am-7pm.

R=red wine   W=white wine   P=rosé wine   S=sparkling wine

88

Chapter 3

<u>BURGUNDY</u>

Beaune
Bourgogne
(Burgundy).

EVERYBODY has heard of the wines of Burgundy, from Chablis to Beaune, Beaujolais to Mâcon. The region has always produced great wines, but in the last few years, they have achieved an almost cult-like following, and prices are already out of the reach of many ordinary wine drinkers.

The tradition of making fine wines stretches back for centuries, and the growers have long been famed for their dry whites and powerful reds.

The old Kingdom of Burgundy is in the east of France, lying between Chablis in the north to beyond Villefranche-en-Beaujolais in the south. The region can trace its history back for thousands of years. Man was certainly hunting in the area 12,000 years before Christ, and works of art from the sixth century BC have been discovered.

When the Romans invaded Gaul, it took six years before they finally overcame the tribes of what is now Burgundy in 52BC. The first vines had been introduced by the Greeks, but the Romans brought order to the area, replanting the vineyards and improving the quality. In AD312, the Emperor Constantine received a speech praising the wines of the Côte de Nuits and Côte de Beaune, and thanking him for reducing the taxes. Because of its nearness to the border, the region now known as Burgundy was constantly under attack from the warring German tribes. Many Roman buildings were destroyed, and the locals built fortified sites for protection. The remains of one of these sites can still be seen above Beaune on the Mont-St-Désiré.

The Roman Empire collapsed in 410, and its provinces fell victim to further attacks. Burgundy was invaded by the Goths and Vandals, who pillaged and then left the countryside. The Franks and Burgundians took over, and the Burgundians from Germany gave their name, Burgundia, to their new kingdom. They and the Franks ruled for almost a thousand years. Charlemagne was King of the Franks, and a great champion of Burgundian wines. He owned his own vineyards in the region and passed laws to improve the quality of the wines. There is still a vineyard bearing his name — Corton Charlemagne — which produces marvellous white wines. Another innovation for which Charlemagne was famous was his edict banning the pressing of grapes in the traditional method — by foot — because he considered it unhygienic.

After Charlemagne's death in 814, his family were unable to agree on a successor, and the kingdom was eventually divided into three, between his grandsons. Charles the Bald received the western part of the territory, and this became the Dukedom of Burgundy. For the next six hundred years the Duchy prospered, thanks not only to the power and influence of the Dukes but also to the support they received from a powerful Church, and the many religious orders in Burgundy. In AD587 there is a record of a parcel of land being presented by the King of Burgundy, Gontran, to the Abbey of St Benigne in Dijon. The land contained vineyards, and the Church's involvement in vines and wine has continued ever since. It became fashionable for the lords and members of the court to make gifts of land to the Church, and the wine produced as a result was sought after throughout Europe. There are records of wine being produced at Aloxe in 696, Fixey in 733, Santenay in 858, Chassagne in 886, Savigny in 930 and Pommard in 1005.

In 910 the Duke of Aquitaine established the religious order of Cluny, which on many occasions proved itself more powerful than the King. At one stage the order controlled 1,450 monasteries and 10,000 monks. They established hospices for travellers, and rapidly gained great wealth and power. The other powerful religious order of that time was Cîteaux, established in 1098. It was started by three former monks from Cluny who wished to return to the austere style of monastic life. They lived in the marshes, among the water holes and reeds opposite the Côte de Nuits. The wells were called cisterns and this led to the monks becoming known as Cistercians.

Both monastic orders prospered during the Crusades, obtaining more vineyards and winning acclaim for the quality of their wines. The Cistercians planted vines when they created a new chapter at Clos de Vougeot, and nuns from the order from the Abbey of Notre-Dame du Tart bought a vineyard in Morey, the now world-famous Clos de Tart.

Although Burgundy is in what is now France, it was for many hundreds of years a separate kingdom and was constantly feuding with the French king. During the Hundred Years' War, Burgundy was allied to England. Between the eleventh and fifteenth centuries, the Burgundian dukes increased their 'empire', usually by marriage, but occasionally by war, until it covered much of what is now northern France, Belgium, Holland and Luxembourg.

In 1363 the King of France put his son Philip on the Burgundian throne and the reign of the four succeeding royal Valois dukes, which lasted until the death of Charles the Bold in 1477, saw the heyday of Burgundy's political and artistic achievements. Charles the Bold died in 1477 while laying siege to Nancy during an ill-fated bid to recapture Lorraine. He had no male heir and so the Duchy was reclaimed by King Louis XI of France.

Apart from the international reputation of their wines, the Burgundians were famous for the lavishness of their hospitality, and gargantuan feasts were not uncommon. Burgundy is also reputed to be the first place to use a menu, so that guests could know in advance what they were eating. The menu is said to be the creation of Queen Isabeau of Bavaria, wife of Charles VI, the King of France, who was a frequent visitor to Dijon.

The Valois dukes entertained lavishly and decorated their courts accordingly. Artists like van Eyck and Roger van der Weyden were employed, as were sculptors like Claus Sluter, and illuminators who produced a magnificent library of manuscripts. The region still shows much of the splendour, especially Dijon.

Burgundy continued to wield enormous influence, even after the French king resumed authority over it; the dukes exerted enormous power until the French Revolution. Throughout this time, they controlled every aspect of wine production, banning the planting of some varieties, controlling the acreage under vines, and ordering poor vineyards to be uprooted. Many of the wines have not changed their style since that time. During the French revolution, however, many of the lords and large landowners were executed, and the power of the religious orders was curbed. Instead of a handful of powerful owners, the land was divided into thousands of small plots, which still exist today.

Geology, Climate, and Geography

Burgundy stretches from Chablis, which is 114 miles south-east of Paris, southwards almost to Lyon. The vineyards are on the slopes of the Morvan hills, on the right hand bank of the River Saône. The area is not one long stretch of vineyard, but rather a number of clearly-defined separate areas, which include many of the great names in wine. From the north you travel from Chablis and the Auxerrois, to the Côte de Nuits, the Côte de Beaune, the Côte Chalonnaise, the Mâconnais and then finally Beaujolais, which is dealt with separately in a further chapter.

Although for hundreds of years it was a Dukedom, and therefore a region in its own right, Burgundy was divided after the French Revolution and now forms a part of the *départements* of the Yonne, Côte d'Or and the Saône-et-Loire.

The vineyards of Chablis, less than two hours' drive from Paris, lie in the Yonne *département*. Chablis produces only dry white wines from the vineyards on the slopes of the hills. The soil is mostly limestone, and the chief grape is Chardonnay, which produces all the finest Burgundian wines. Nearby is the Auxerrois, which also grows Sauvignon and Aligoté and produces the sparkling wine of Burgundy, the Crémant de Bourgogne.

The Côte d'Or, or Golden Slope, is divided into two areas, the Côte de Nuits in the north and the Côte de Beaune in the south. The area is believed to have got its name from the golden colour of the vine leaves in the autumn just before they fall. Both areas stretch for just under forty miles from Dijon to Santenay. Almost all the vineyards are east-facing, but the soils and subsoils vary considerably as you travel through the region, which is why the wines differ so much from one area to the next. Throughout the Côte d'Or, the vineyard strip is narrow, nowhere more than a mile wide. In the Côte de Nuits, the vines are planted on the hillsides almost up to the tree-lined summits. The vineyards face east or south-east, and get many hours of sunshine without the grapes being scorched. The Côte de Beaune is flatter and the soil is richer and thicker, but the vineyard belt is again restricted to quite a narrow strip, never more than two miles wide. The best wines come from grapes grown on the slopes.

The Côte Chalonnaise is another centre for sparkling wine, and efforts are being made to revitalise the still wine industry with new vineyards. Some excellent white wines are made, and because they are overshadowed by their neighbour to the north they tend to be cheaper.

The Mâconnais is a large producer of white wines, notably Pouilly-Fuissé, Bourgogne red and white, Bourgogne Aligoté and Mâcon, both red and white. The area is very hilly, and the vineyards fill the slopes leaving the fertile valleys free for other agricultural enterprises.

Burgundy has unpredictable weather. The summers can be very hot and the winters very cold. Severe frosts in 1956 destroyed thousands of vines in Chablis. Hail is another problem, and a severe hailstorm can cause very severe damage to harvest prospects in minutes. It rains in Burgundy on 155 days a year, on average. Even in summer there can be heavy rainfalls and travellers are advised to have waterproof garments or an umbrella with them. June and October are the wettest months. Summer rains tend to be light and constant, rather than torrential downpours, but cloudbursts are common. There is a record of more than two inches of rain falling in just one hour on 16 July 1947. Heavy rainfall in June can be a problem because it is the time when the vines are in flower. The rains can damage the flowers; they can affect fertilization; and they can cause the onset of various diseases, especially rot. Most of the rain comes up from the south, and thus the rainfall is heaviest in the southern part of Burgundy. It decreases as you travel northwards through the Côte d'Or. The hillsides afford the vines some protection and do assist drainage. July is normally the hottest month of the year with temperatures of about 70-75°F, December, January and February are the coldest months. They are the time of the frosts, which around Dijon occur on about sixty days of the year. The vines bud late, and this protects them from frost damage (unless the temperatures fall below 0°F, but a late spring frost, during the time when the vines are shaking themselves back into growth and the sap starts to rise, can be disastrous.

Considering its inland location, and its situation in the hills, Burgundy gets a surprising amount of annual sunshine — an average 2,000 hours — and temperatures can, occasionally, rocket. There are records of temperatures of 85°F and more in May, but these most often occur in midsummer. The high sunshine readings are part of a typical continental climate of long hot summers as high pressure areas are trapped over the land masses. The sunshine is nature's compensation for the high rainfall, much of which falls at the wrong time for most vineyard owners. The sunshine helps to dry out the vines, ripen the grapes and a combination of warmth and wind can prove an effective natural deterrent to the development of rot after rain.

Burgundy is one of the best places to study the geology of a wine-growing area, because the contrast of soils is clear to see as you travel through the region. The rocks in the hills of Burgundy were resculptured during the age when the Alps were formed. They were subjected to enormous pressures, which accounts for the many rifts and valleys. For millions of years, the whole of the area now known as Burgundy was part of a massive inland sea, and this explains why so many seashell fossils are to be found in the rocks and subsoils, and why the ground is so rich in minerals. When the inland sea drained away, the mountain-building which was to create the Alps, the Pyrénées and the Atlas mountains in North Africa began.

Most of the vineyards are now on limestone, but there are isolated areas of gravel and marl, a limey clay. The limestone ridges extend as far south as the Mâconnais, where they merge into granite, the main feature of the Beaujolais area. The colour of the soil changes as you travel south through Burgundy, because while the covering is predominantly limestone, it consists of a large number of different varieties. It is quite easy to see where the variety changes as the earth changes from a red to a sandy colour.

The best grapes come from vines on the first part of the slopes, which have soils containing a high proportion of silts and clay. The stony, chalky tops of the slopes are best suited for white wines, while the flat land at the foot of the hills is often turned over to other agriculture.

Many of the vineyards have stony soils which act as storage heaters, trapping the sun's heat during the day and releasing it slowly during the night. Stones and pebbles in the soil also aid drainage, which as we have seen can be a particular problem in Burgundy. Grape varieties in Burgundy are Pinot Noir and Gamay for reds, and Chardonnay, Pinot Blanc, Pinot Gris and Aligoté for whites. The Pinot Noir produces all the classic red wines of Burgundy, while the Gamay, which is believed to have originated in the Côte d'Or, is now the grape of Beaujolais. It is still planted, however, in parts of northern Burgundy where it is blended with Pinot Noir to make Bourgogne Mousseaux and Bourgogne Passe-Tout-Grain.

Chardonnay, likewise, produces all the great white wines of Burgundy and it is interesting that the two — Chardonnay and Pinot Noir — when blended, produce the 'queen of wines', Champagne. Aligoté is an important variety in Burgundy, producing highly acidic, refreshing white wines which are best drunk young. Its advantage is that it is a sturdy vine, which produces good yields and can be planted on ground not suitable for Chardonnay. The Pinot Blanc and Pinot Gris are both planted, but their acreage is declining, and they are being used less for blending.

The Districts of Burgundy

CHABLIS

The twenty communes of Chablis sit among the limestone hills in the most northerly part of Burgundy, and produce a white wine which is famous the world over. Certainly Chablis is the most-ordered white wine in restaurants, perhaps because the name is easy to say, but also because it drinks so well. The wines are light-coloured, pale and dry but balance masks the high acidity. They are superb with seafood, oysters in particular.

The district of Chablis is just under two hours' drive from Paris, down the A6, the main autoroute south. You leave the autoroute at Auxerre and head for the town of Chablis, which is well worth a visit in its own right. Formerly owned by the Crown, the town of Chablis and surrounding land was one of those areas which was presented to the Church. It was a gift from Charles the Bald in AD867 to the monks of St-Martin-de-Tours in the Loire. It stayed in the hands of the Church until the French Revolution in 1789, when the lands were again distributed among the peasants.

The town lies in the valley of the river Serein, and in Roman times there was a ferry here. The cluster of stone houses now looks out over the limestone slopes to the east, where the grapes for the seven Great Growth Chablis are grown. Chablis has had a troubled history, being so close to the border. Although part of Burgundy, it was captured several times by the French during the Hundred Years' War and then retaken by the English and their allies. Its greatest disaster, however, occurred during World War II when in June 1940 Mussolini's airforce bombed the town. Why Chablis was chosen, no-one knows, but the centre of the town was destroyed and fires raged for three days.

Much of the prestige of the area comes from the religious orders, especially the Cistercians, who gained permission to plant vines around Chablis from the monks of the Order of St Martin. They selected the best sites for the vines, improved the quality of the wine, and established a tradition that has continued for centuries.

The seven *Grand Cru* growths are Vaudésir, Preuses, Les Clos, Grenouilles, Bougros, Valmur, and Blanchots, and their popularity was enhanced because the vineyards were so close to Paris.

Chardonnay has always been the dominant grape here, and is known locally as the Beaunois, because it was introduced to Chablis by the Cistercians from Beaune in the Côte d'Or. It is not a heavy producer, but the soft, northern sunshine, the soil and the slopes all combine to produce a magnificent wine. The best Chablis vines are all grown on a chalky clay, littered with pebbles and stone overlying the limestone rock. Obviously quality does vary, and a lot of the production is actually bottled further south in Beaune and Nuits-St-Georges.

The other major problem of producing wine in this area is frost, which seems to linger for days. In the worst years, and there have been several since the end of World War II, entire vintages have been wiped out. In the 1950s, half the vintages of the decade were totally lost.

There are four categories of Chablis: Chablis *Grand Cru*, *Premier Cru*, Chablis and Petit Chablis. The best growths are obviously the *Grands Crus*, seven in all, on the hills above the River Serein, a tributary of the Yonne, which gives its name to the *département*. Only in the best years are wines labelled under their *Grand Cru* title. If they do not meet all the strict criteria needed for a *Grand Cru* they will be downgraded to *Premier Cru,* or simply Chablis. The *Grands Crus* must contain 11 per cent natural alcohol, and be made only from the Chardonnay grape. The vines are carefully manicured, and only the best grapes are kept for harvesting. If a *Grand Cru* is made, the output is only about 1,800 bottles an acre. In the best vintages the seven *Grands Crus* will produce between them only about five thousand cases, which is reflected in their subsequent high price. The wines are bottled about a year after the vintage, and then spend up to four years in cellars before being sold. The classic Chablis has a pale colour with a green tinge on the rim. It is dry but with a mouth-filling flavour, which lingers on long after the last sip.

Chablis *Premier Cru* is the next quality category. These wines must have an alcohol content of at least 10 per cent natural alcohol, and production is limited to about 2,080 bottles an acre. There used to be about two dozen vineyards allowed to use the title *Premier Cru*, but in 1967 the list was reduced to eleven, for the sake of simplicity, and these vineyards are: Beauroy, Côte de Lechet, Vaillons, Melinots, Montmains, Vosgros (all on the south side of the Serein); and Fourchaume, Montée de Tonnerre, Mont de Milieu, Vaucoupin, and Les Fourneaux (on the north side of the river).

One of the problems of Chablis is the small size of the vineyards. After the Revolution the great estates were split up, and since then, on the death of the vineyard owner, the land has been subdivided between all the members of the family. This continual division has led to thousands of small vineyards, which would be totally uneconomic if they were left to produce wine themselves. They survive by pooling their grapes and producing wine under one or other of the vineyard names allowed under the *Premier Cru appellation.*

The Chablis *appellation* yields up to 1,250,000 bottles in a reasonable year, and the vineyards extend away from the town of Chablis towards Auxerre in the west. The wine must have a minimum of 10° natural alcohol, and must comply with all the other rules laid down for the cultivation and vinification of Chablis. Again the smallness of the individual vineyards means that the wine is always blended, and because it can come from a wider area than allowed for *Premier* or *Grand Cru*, problems in one village can be overcome by blending with grapes from another. The best *appellation* Chablis is produced in and around the villages of Maligny, Beine, Lignorelles, Chemilly and Bertu. They are bone dry, and best drunk young.

Petit Chablis is not widely known outside France, and some growers are campaigning to have the *appellation* changed to Chablis Villages to make it more meaningful. The *appellation* covers a score of villages circling the town of Chablis. The wine must reach a minimum of $9^1/2°$ of natural alcohol, and volume is restricted to that of the Chablis *appellation*. A lot of vineyard replanting is now taking place in the Petit Chablis area, as growers try to cash in on the world popularity of the wine.

Although the Chardonnay is the only grape allowed in Chablis, wine producers do grow some Aligoté, which is used to produce Bourgogne Aligoté, a very crisp, dry wine for everyday drinking. Also made is the sparkling Crémant de Bourgogne which comes from the area around Auxerrois. It is made in the *méthode Champenoise*, using the Sacy grape, which is high yielding, high in acidity and reasonably low in alcohol — all ideal for the production of sparkling wines.

COTE DE NUITS

The Côte de Nuits is the northern half of the Côte d'Or, and is to Burgundy what the Médoc is to Bordeaux. Just travelling through the villages of the district is like flipping through an atlas of the world's best wines. There are names such as Chambertin, Clos St-Jacques, Clos de la Roche, Clos St-Denis and Gevrey-Chambertin. In the south of the area there is Musigny, Clos de Vougeot, Clos de Tart, Nuits-St-Georges and many others.

The Côte de Nuits, which gets its name from Nuits-St-Georges, starts at Dijon in the north and runs south for just over twelve miles to Corgoloin in the south. The vineyards are rarely more than half a mile deep, and in places less than a quarter of a mile wide, as they hug the south-east facing slopes of the continuous range of small hills making up the Côte d'Or. There are three main areas of excellence in the Côte de Nuits, around Chambertin, Musigny and Romanée-Conti, and the vineyards here constitute some of the most expensive agricultural land in the world. Not all the land is devoted to vines, and the best wines come from the vineyards in the middle of the predominantly clay and chalk soil. Here, the combination of slope, soil and Pinot Noir, the only grape allowed, is magnificent.

As in Chablis, the growers have to contend with very difficult weather. Heavy rains and hail in the late summer can often do great damage, and sunshine in September is essential to finish off the ripening.

The most fascinating thing about the wines of the Côte de Nuits is how much they can vary, the wine of one great vineyard being very different to that of its closest neighbour. This is even more surprising when one sees the very small size of these vineyards. One word frequently heard in Burgundy, especially in the Côte de Nuits, is *climat*. Each vineyard can have its own microclimate because of the slope of the hill, the way the vineyard faces into the soil, the composition of the soil and so on. All these factors combine to give the wine its character, and the combination varies from vineyard to vineyard.

The wines of the Côte de Nuits are characterised by softness. They are smooth and velvety. They have acidity for backbone and long life. The northern sun is not strong enough to convert all the sugar to alcohol, so additional sugar frequently has to be added. This is a legal process, called *chaptalisation*. The wines also have very complex noses and scents of truffles, violets and raspberries can often be detected. They age magnificently, and many of the great Côte de Nuits need ten to twenty years to reach their peak.

Larrey

Larrey is the most northerly village in the Côte de Nuits and can also be included in the Côte de Dijon. Many of the vineyards have been swallowed up over the last hundred years or so by the spread of Dijon and the best known is now Les Marcs d'Or, which is unusual in that it has a north-east aspect.

Chenôve

This village has also seen better days, and once boasted of some fine vineyards with an international reputation. There is a story that the village got its name from *chanvre*, or cannabis, which was reputedly grown there. Today it is worth a visit to see the massive presses dating back to the fifteenth century. The wines from the villages are sold under the Bourgogne Rouge label.

Marsannay-la-Côte

Marsannay-la-Côte is five miles south of Dijon, and the first major producer encountered after leaving the city. Its claim to fame lies in the marvellous rosé produced from the Pinot Noir grapes. The majority of the production comes from the *Cave Coopérative* and *Clair-Dau*. Vines have been grown here for at least 1200 years (and probably much longer), and with neighbouring Couchey, many of the vineyards were turned over to Gamay to satisfy the demands of Dijon which doubled in size in the eighteenth century. Since the last war, plantings of Pinot Noir have increased and growers are now striving to win the right to call their wines *Appellation Contrôlée Côte de Nuits*.

Fixin

Fixin is two miles south of Marsannay-la-Côte, off the N74, and the first village south of Dijon to have AC status. For many years the wines of Fixin were used for blending with those of Chambertin, but it gained AC status in 1936 and many new vineyards are now producing wine with great depth of colour and robustness. A tiny amount of white Fixin is also produced.

Brochon

This is the next village south and its wines are used for blending. The northern vineyards are used to produce wine for blending with Côte de Nuits Villages, while those in the south are often used for blending with Gevrey-Chambertin.

Gevrey-Chambertin

This village has given its name to some of the finest wines in the world. It is the home of Chambertin, the favourite red wine of Napoléon, and other classic vineyards such as Latricières-Chambertin, Chambertin-Clos-de-Bèze, Mazis-Chambertin, Ruchottes-Chambertin, Charmes-Chambertin, Mazoyères-Chambertin, Griottes-Chambertin and Chapelle-Chambertin. The Gevrey-Chambertin AC is the largest village AC in the Côte de Nuits and has again been producing wine since Roman times, but the Church had the biggest influence on wine production.

In AD630 the Duke of Amalgaire donated a plot of land to the Abbey of Bèze and the vines planted started the long and illustrious history of Clos de Bèze. The name Chambertin is supposed to have come from the name of a peasant farmer who owned land next to the Abbey's vineyard. He was called Bertin, and his vineyard was known first as *Campus Bertini*, then *Champ de Bertin* (the field of Bertin) and eventually, simply Chambertin. The Abbey of Cluny acquired its first land in the area in 895, a gift from the Duke of Burgundy, and it continued to expand, buying land whenever possible. In 1257 work started on the château on the orders of Abbot Yves de Poissey. The fortified château was used for centuries to protect the villages when attacked, and parts of it still remain and can be visited free of charge. Gevrey-Chambertin has more *Grands Crus* to its name than any other village of Burgundy and more than a score of *Premiers Crus*. The Gevrey-Chambertin vineyards cover almost 1,250 acres, and average annual production is about 1,900,000 bottles.

Morey-St-Denis

Morey-St-Denis is the home of the famous Clos de Tart vineyard mentioned earlier, in the hands of the Mommessin family of Mâcon. In 1120 part of the village, then known as Mirriacum Villa, was given to the Abbey of Cîteaux, and in 1171 another parcel of the village was donated to the Abbey of Bussières by Guillaume de Marigny, the High Constable of Burgundy. The effort put into the vineyards by the monks, and especially the Cistercians, helped create the magnificent wines of today. There are four *Grands Crus* of Morey-St-Denis: Bonnes Mares (although much of this vineyard is in neighbouring Chambolle-Musigny), Clos St-Denis, Clos de Tart and Clos de la Roche.

The Clos St-Denis property can trace its history back to College of St-Denis de Vergy which was established in 1203. The title of Morey was extended in 1927, when St-Denis was added to the name. Clos de Tart was owned by the nuns of Notre Dame de Tart. They bought it in 1141 and the sale was ratified by a Papal Bull signed by Lucius III in 1184.

Chambolle-Musigny

This village was known by the Romans as *Campus Ebulliens*, the boiling field, not because of heat but because of the turbulence of the stream which runs down the hillside during the floods following the spring rains. The wines of the commune have been noted for many years for their delicacy, and while this may still not be the case, they command very high prices. There are two *Grands Crus* here, Musigny and Bonnes Mares. Musigny is near the Clos de Vougeot and is first mentioned in 1110. Pierre Cros, the Canon of St-Denis de Vergy, is recorded as having given a parcel of land known as Musigné to the Abbey of Cîteaux. The exact origin of Bonnes Mares is not known. There are two schools of thought: the first is that the name comes from the pools of water from which the animals used to drink, and the second, is that it comes from an old French verb *marer* which means to tend or care for the land. A small quantity of Musigny white wine is also made.

The *Premier Cru* vineyards include Les Amoureuses (the first vineyard as you approach from the north), Les Charmes, Les Cras, Les Borniques, Les Baudes, Les Plantes, Les Hauts Doix, Les Châtelots, Les Gruenchers, Les Groseilles, Les Fuées, Les Lavrottes, Derrière la Grange, Les Noirots, Les Sentiers, Les Fousselottes, Aux Beaux-Bruns, Les Combottes and Aux Combottes. The two best-known are Les Amoureuses and Les Charmes. The wines of the commune are fine and elegant, and unlike many of the big, powerful red Burgundies which are clearly masculine, the wines of Musigny can best be described as feminine.

Vougeot

Vougeot plays host to the *Confrérie des Chevaliers du Tastevin* which holds its dinners, with suitable pomp and ceremony, elaborate robes, trumpet blasts and drum rolls, in the medieval château, the Clos de Vougeot. This is one of the most important buildings in Burgundy and a sight which should not be missed. The château was built by the Cistercians in the sixteenth century, although there had been a building on the site for at least 500 years before that. The building has very low walls so that the high sloping wall could trap as much water as possible whenever it rained. This water was then stored in huge wells.

The *Confrérie* was founded in 1934 in order to promote the wines of Burgundy. They bought the Clos in 1944 and have since painstakingly restored it, thanks to donations from all over the world. Every year the *Confrérie* meets about twenty times and up to 500 people sit down in the banqueting hall for a superb dinner. The *Confrérie* has a more serious role, however, which is to maintain and improve quality. In 1950 all growers and wine merchants were invited to submit their wine to the *Chevaliers* for tasting. Those that met with their approval were allowed to carry the *Tastevinage* label and all the bottles were numbered. This continued a tradition started by the Cistercian monks, centuries before. The monks had three categories of wine, and the best were not for sale, but were reserved as gifts for the hierarchy of the Church, the nobility and royalty. There is no doubt that this grading stimulated interest and the monks had little trouble selling both the other categories. After the French Revolution, the vineyards of the Clos were confiscated and auctioned. For a time they were in the hands of a single owner, M. Focard, but in 1889 they were divided and are now owned by about eighty different growers. A share in the Clos de Vougeot vineyard is still much sought after.

There are some other vineyards in the commune which are worth attention; Clos de la Perrière, Le Clos Blanc, Les Petits-Vougeots, Les Cras, and Clos du Prieuré.

Flagey-Echézeaux

This is a village lying on the flat plain opposite the Côte de Nuits, on the other side of the N74 highway. In 1188 it belonged to the Abbey of St Vivant, and it now has two of Burgundy's most famous vineyards, both *Grands Crus*: Grands Echézeaux and Echézeaux. Les Grands Echézeaux extends to 22.5 acres and Les Echézeaux covers just over 74 acres and comprises 11 vineyards. Between them they produce about 12,500 bottles in an average harvest.

Vosne-Romanée

This village, about a mile north of Nuits-St-Georges, is reached by one of three turnings off the N74. There are so many famous vineyards bunched together around the stone houses of the village, that it is easy to pass a great name without knowing it. The best way to explore the village and its vineyards is on foot and there are various wine maps available to help you; the best is the Larmat map of the Côte de Nuits which is available locally.

Over two centuries ago, the Abbé Courtépée declared that only fine wines were made in the village, and while this is not strictly true today, the majority of the wine can be considered as such. There are five *Grands Crus*, hugging the hillsides above the town; they are: Richebourg, Romanée, Romanée-St-Vivant, La Tâche, and lastly, perhaps the finest red wine of Burgundy, Romanée-Conti.

The village gets its name from the Romans and their vineyards, which were already famous in the fourth century. Not surprisingly, the church again had an influence on the development of the vineyards, and for a time, the vineyard of Romanée-Conti was owned by the Priory of St-Vivant, who simply called it *Le Cloux*, which meant 'the best'. The vineyards of Romanée--Conti have an interesting history; a feud between Louis François, the Bourbon Prince of Conti, and Madame de Pompadour led to them both bidding for it in 1760. Louis François was successful in his bid and became the new owner, adding his name to the vineyard, but he lost his prestige at court and had to relinquish his position as chief minister. He died in 1776; during the French Revolution the land was taken over, and it changed hands a number of times between then and 1869, when it was purchased by Monsieur Duvault-Blochet. It has been in the family ever since. The present part-owner, M. de Villaine, is the great-grandson of M. Duvault-Blochet. He owns the vineyard with Henri Le Roy, and between them they created the *Société Civile du Domaine de la Romanée-Conti*, which now controls all or parts of six of the greatest vineyards in the area — perhaps the finest collection of Burgundian red wine. The Romanée-Conti wines are magnificent, round and velvety, full of fruit and bouquet, and long lived. They are the classic Burgundies, and unless bought young and laid down, their prices are staggeringly high. *Premiers Crus* are Aux Malconsorts, Les Beaumonts, Les Suchots, La Grande Rue, Les Gaudichots, Aux Brûlées, Les Chaumes, Les Reignots, Les Clos des Réas and Les Petits Monts.

Nuits-St-Georges

The town of Nuits-St-Georges gives its name to the wines of the region and is surrounded by vineyards, but there is not a single *Grand Cru* in the immediate area. There are, however, twenty-eight *Premiers Crus* from the Nuits-St-Georges commune, and a further ten from the commune of neighbouring Prémeaux. Needless to say, the town is the centre of the wine industry and not only houses the shippers, *négociants* and brokers, but all the other associated businesses necessary to keep the industry going; the label-makers for instance. Much of the fruit is grown locally and in the town there are fruit-juice factories and wineries producing sparkling wine.

It is interesting to note that as you travel to Nuits-St-Georges southwards, all the vineyards on the right are the ones producing the best wines and those entitled to the village *appellation* status. The vineyards on the left, between the road and the river, are generally providing grapes for AC wines.

Nuits-St-Georges is surrounded by vineyards, trees, and a number of quarries which have provided stone for the houses in the area. The best vineyards lie to the south of the town along the road to Beaune. The small village of Prémeaux, just to the south, is allowed to carry the Nuits-St-Georges *appellation*. There are just over 900 acres of vineyards in the *appellation*, and only one *Premier Cru* is on the 'wrong' side of the road, Clos des Grandes Vignes, which skirts the northern boundary of Prémeaux.

Prémeaux

The vineyards here are at least 700 years old, and they hug the narrow strip of land between the main road and the hilltop. They only produce *Premier Cru*, and Clos de la Maréchale, its southernmost vineyard, is the last wine allowed to call itself Nuits-St-Georges.

A small quantity of white wine is produced in the commune, mostly from La Perrière and Clos Arlots in Prémeaux. The vineyard of La Perrière is worth a visit for curiosity's sake, as well as for the quality of the wines. By a freak of nature, a part of the vineyard planted with Pinot Noir produces white grapes. Part of the vineyard has been replanted using grafts from these vines, and a small quantity of remarkable white wine is now produced every year. Even in a good year, only about 2,500 bottles are made and so the wine is both rare and expensive. It is much more like a Rhône white than a Burgundy. It is straw-coloured, full, fruity and marvellously balanced, and a treat to drink.

Prissey, Comblanchien and Corgoloin

These are the last villages of the Côte de Nuits on the southern boundary, before the transition to the Côte de Beaune. The three villages in the commune sell their wines under the Côte de Nuits Villages *appellation*, as do the two most northerly villages, Brochon and Fixin. The limestone that is so treasured in the vineyards to the north has here been quarried to provide the grand homes of the nobility in Paris. The pink limestone, known as *Rose de Prémeaux*, was excavated for many years, as was the marble which runs in strata above it. This granite was used in the construction of the Paris Opera House, and it is to be seen as flooring in many of the more elegant residences of the Côte d'Or.

The red wines of the Côte de Nuits villages are more robust than their cousins to the north and south, but full of colour and fruit. They have fragrant noses with a hint of burnt oak, and they age well, often better than the other wines of the Côte de Nuits.

COTE DE BEAUNE

The Côte de Beaune is the southern end of the Côte d'Or; the division is marked by a dramatic change in scenery. After Corgoloin the vineyards suddenly end, and you enter an area of old quarries and huge piles of discarded stone. Between the stone-workings, there are a number of small farms, but hardly a vineyard to be seen.

The vineyards start again at Ladoix-Sérrigny and then for the next fifteen miles they follow the N74 south. The northern vineyards of the Côte de Beaune are all on the west of the main road, hugging the many small hills that make up the Côte d'Or's southern tail. Only at its southernmost tip, around Volnay, do the vineyards switch to the left-hand side of the road.

The Côte de Beaune takes us from Ladoix, through Aloxe-Corton to Beaune (after a small detour west to Savigny), and then on to Pommard and finally Volnay. In this area, covering about 7,500 acres of vineyards (twice the growing area of the Côte de Nuits), are to be found some of Burgundy's greatest wines, and some of the world's finest dry white wines. There are the *Grands Crus* all bearing the Corton *appellation* and these include the magnificent white Burgundy, Corton Charlemagne. There are almost thirty *Premiers Crus* under the *appellations* of Corton, Pernand, Beaune, Pommard and Volnay.

The town of Beaune is the most important one in Burgundy, and it is the capital of the wine trade. It is therefore an excellent place to stay, and to make a base for a visit to the vineyards. It is quite possible to park your car and explore many of the vineyards on foot. The commune of Aloxe-Corton to the north is just over two miles away, Savigny to the north-west is about two and a half miles, and all the vineyards of Meursault are within three miles of Beaune. If the weather is fine, and your legs are strong there is no better way of visiting the vineyards, stopping for a picnic and a glass of wine along the way.

Apart from the annual vintage, the most important event in the wine calendar is the annual auction of wines at the Hospices de Beaune, the magnificent Hôtel Dieu, founded in the fifteenth century to look after the poor and the sick. It is always held on the third Sunday of November, during a weekend of eating and drinking. The prices paid are always high but in the last couple of years they have started to become astronomical. In a way this is commendable, because the proceeds go to charity, but it also indicates the way other Burgundies will be priced when they are made available to the trade, and many of the greatest wines are no longer within the reach of the ordinary wine drinker.

Ladoix-Sérrigny
This is the first wine-producing village of the Côte de Beaune. Although allowed to produce wines under its own name, they are usually used in the production of Corton, Aloxe-Corton *Premier Cru* and Côte de Beaune Villages.

Pernand-Vergelesses
This village is also allowed to carry its own name on the label, although some of the wine from its vineyards go towards Corton. It has a fine *Premier Cru*, Ile des Vergelesses. It has many of the qualities of its much more expensive neighbour to the south, and is usually a sound investment. Grapes for the Corton-Charlemagne are also produced here.

Aloxe-Corton
Aloxe-Corton has been making wine certainly since Roman times and it is associated with many of the great names in French history. Several kings of France have owned vineyards here, the most famous being Charlemagne, whose name is now used for the best white wine of the region. In AD858 the Bishop of Autun presented his vineyards to the cathedral. Other famous owners included The Knights Templar and the French kings Henri II and Louis XIV. Charlemagne made a donation of some of his vineyards to the Abbey of Saulieu in 775 which is why the village still carries an eagle on its coat of arms — Charlemagne's own symbol. The vineyards of Corton-Charlemagne are now owned jointly by shippers Louis Jadot and Louis Latour and a handful of local growers. Many of the vineyards producing grapes for this white wine are westerly-facing, so that they get less sunshine which keeps the sugar content down, and the alcohol levels up — both necessary for making great white wines. In the village itself there are two

tasting cellars worth visiting, although they are well advertised and can get very crowded. One is owned by the Château Corton-Andé, and the other by a consortium of local growers. The second cellar is owned by the village and the wines offered by the growers can be superb.

Altogether there are only about 580 acres of vineyards in Aloxe-Corton. Chardonnay is planted on the limestone near the top of the hills which rise to about 1,275ft. The red wine all comes from Pinot Noir, planted lower down where the soil is reddened because of the iron present below.

Savigny-lès-Beaune
This village lies between Pernand-Vergelesses and Beaune. It is an important wine producer with about 950 acres of vineyards, and well worth a visit, not only because of the spectacular views over the surrounding countryside but also because the village itself is interesting. There is a lovely old church; the tower dates back to the twelfth century and there is a fine fifteenth-century fresco. One of the novelties of the village is the number of houses which have delightful inscriptions carved into the stone lintels over the doors. There are also two châteaux, one large and one small.

Savigny is also important in the history of viticulture. Vineyards were first planted in straight rows here, and Guyot developed a new system for pruning, now widely used and still bearing his name. The first 'mechanised' vineyard cultivator was also made here. Horse drawn, the cart with wooden wheels was pulled along straddling the vines.

There are no *Grands Crus* in the commune, but almost two dozen *Premiers Crus* from all or parts of vineyards on either side of a stream which splits the area. The stream, which has the rather grand name of the River Rhoin, splits the commune into two very distinct areas of production. The vineyards to the north produce fuller wines from the clay soils, while those south of the stream, on gravelly soil, give rise to much lighter wines. The grape in the southern vineyards also ripen at least a week before those to the north.

Chorey-lès-Beaune
This is a small commune to the east of Savigny with about 300 acres of vineyards, mostly producing red wine sold under the Côte de Beaune Villages *appellation*. It does have the right to use its own village *appellation*. Almost all the vineyards are sited on the plains, and because of this, it produces a firm wine that is perfect for blending although not outstanding.

Beaune
The most famous town of Burgundy, its capital city and the commercial and trading centre for the whole Côte d'Or is Beaune. The origin of its name is unknown, although there are many theories. It is known, however, that Julius Caesar camped with his legions here about fifty years before the birth of Christ.

Beaune is now similar to many French towns, a mixture of old and new buildings. It is possible to overlook the city and see the ramparts which circle the old town, and then see the surburban spread encroaching on the vineyards. Beaune is also a huge wine-producing commune, and vineyards cover 1,400 acres. Again, there are no *Grands Crus* but thirty or so *Premiers Crus*. A very small amount of elegant, light white Côte de Beaune is produced.

The most famous building in Beaune is the Charitable Hospices de Beaune, and over the years the vineyards, donated by benefactors, have funded the work of the Hospices and the sale of wine still contributes a significant proportion of its income. Wines from the 140 acres or so of vineyards now owned by the Hospices are blended into special *cuvées*, and these are offered for sale on the third Sunday in November. The wines do not only come from Beaune itself; the Hospices now have plots of land in Meursault, Aloxe-Corton, Savigny-lès-Beaune, Pommard, Volnay, Gevrey-Chambertin, Monthélie, Auxey-Duresses, and Pernand-Vergelesses. With names such as these, one can see why the wine commands such high prices. All the wine is sold as *Premiers Crus* of the Côte de Beaune.

The vineyards are each under the control of one man, and in addition to a regular wage, he also receives a share of the proceeds from the annual auction, an incentive which helps to guarantee the high quality of the wine, year after year. The wines have been sold at public auction since 1859 and only in the very worst years is this cancelled. All the wines are vinified at the winery behind the Hôtel Dieu and today there are twenty-three red *cuvées* and nine white, together with some distilled wine.

The Sunday sale is always preceded by a dinner in the Château Clos de Vougeot. Thousands of people cram into Beaune for the auction; which is by invitation only and the preceding two days of tasting, and the sale itself, which takes place in the market, is followed by another magnificent dinner in the Hospices. It is an honour to be invited to either. The celebrations continue on the Monday with a lunch for the growers, and the three days of celebrations are rightly known as *Les Trois Glorieuses*.

Pommard

This is another ancient town, and there was once a Gallic temple here. Now, you can look instead at the square bell tower on the church and explore the narrow little lanes which mix incongruously with the wider modern thoroughfares. Pommard used to be an important fording point across the river Vandaine, which still floods, and inns sprung up to cater for the passengers from the stagecoaches. The wines were a favourite of Victor Hugo, and to many people the wines of Pommard are the epitome of fine red Burgundy. There are now 850 acres of vineyards in the commune and twenty-six *Premiers Crus*. Alas, the reputation of the wine has pushed up prices and demand, and while Pommard can produce extraordinary wines in good years, the ease with which growers can sell has led to a relaxation of standards by some. The best producers still make great wines, however, and these are universally acclaimed as Les Epenots, (also called Epeneaux) and Les Rugiens. Other fine producers are Clos de la Commaraine (with its château dating back to the twelfth century), Les Jarollières, Château de Pommard, Les Pézerolles, Clos Micot and Les Arvelets.

Pommards age well and should never be drunk until they are three years old, and for the *Premiers Crus* at least double this. If you stick to the *Premiers Crus* you will avoid disappointment.

Volnay

The village of Volnay is up on the hill just beyond Pommard but nearer still to Meursault. It is the last major vineyard area supplying grapes for the Côte de Beaune reds. From here on we move into white wine country. Because it is on the boundary, both whites and red are produced. Volnay is a small village with a big reputation, and there are magnificent views from the square across to the Jura. Because neighbouring Meursault is famed for its whites, the two villages have reached an understanding. White wine from Volnay is sold as Meursault, while Meursault's reds are sold as Volnay. There used to be a château at Volnay built by the Dukes of Burgundy, but this was totally destroyed nearly 250 years ago. The village was also famous for a company of crossbowmen who served first the Burgundian Dukes and then the Kings of France. The champion bowman, decided at an annual competition, was given a whole year off from working in the vineyards.

Because the vineyards of Volnay are higher than its neighbours, frost is a danger and so the visitor might see pots scattered amongst the vines. These are known as smudge pots and are filled with charcoal which is ignited when the temperature falls too much.

The red wines of Volnay are light and elegant, fruity and velvety and quality shines through. There are about 525 acres of vineyards and two dozen *Premiers Crus*. The rest of the red is sold as AC Volnay.

Monthélie

This village is also on a hill, but the vineyards are sheltered and the grapes are said to get more sun than any other vineyards in the Côte d'Or. Only grapes could survive on the very poor soil, and they have been grown here since the fourteenth century. There are now ten *Premiers Crus*, 325 acres of vineyards and all but 6,000 bottles of the production is red. The wines are very fine, well balanced and fragrant, and can be drunk quite young. They are always good value, but because of their limited production, they are difficult to find.

Auxey-Duresses

This is another commune on the border between red and white production. About 70 per cent of the production is red, and the remainder white. The red wines are good, similar to those of Volnay; the whites can be great, rivalling those of Meursault, although they are not so long-lived. There are nine *Premiers Crus*, including Les Duresses, 2$\frac{1}{2}$ acres of which are owned by the Hospices de Beaune.

St-Romain

St-Romain is surrounded by steep gorges, and while it is in the Côte de Beaune, it is really part of the Hautes-Côtes. It has the highest vineyards in the Côte d'Or, and the Chardonnay grapes planted on the higher ground tend to do better than the Pinot Noir lower down. The views from the hillsides are superb. There are no first growths here, and about a third of the production is white wine.

Meursault

The largest white wine producer in the Côte d'Or is Meursault. The twisting streets and the church with its fifteenth-century tower, which is one of the tallest in the region at 187ft, are a delight; and there is much to see and do; but everywhere one is reminded that this is a wine centre. There is a campsite just outside the town which is truly international in the summer with visitors from almost every country in Europe, and many from further afield. After Beaune, Meursault attracts more visitors than anywhere else on the Côte d'Or, mostly to drink the white wines as this is the capital of the Côte des Blancs.

The main festival in Meursault takes place the day after the auction at the Hospices de Beaune, when 400 people sit down to an enormous banquet with the very best wines.

There are three types of Meursault red; Meursault Rouge Tout Court, Volnay-Santenots and Blagny, a small hamlet next to the renowned vineyard of Les Perrières. Almost all the production of the commune is white wine; annual production is about 170,000 dozen bottles of white and only 8-9,000 cases of red.

The red wines are fruity and robust while the whites are soft, round and fresh. They should never be kept too long. The colour changes from a pale lemon when young to a glorious golden colour after four or five years, and the nose and taste can have hints of peaches and nuttiness. They are marvellous full wines and they retain their youthfulness for five or six years, but should really be drunk by then.

The most famous vineyards of Meursault are Meursault-Perrières and Meursault-Charmes, both bordering Blagny and Puligny-Montrachet. Between them Meursault and Blagny have nineteen *Premiers Crus*.

Puligny-Montrachet

This village produces the best white wines of Burgundy, and among the finest whites anywhere in the world. Founded in Gallo-Roman times, the village is said to get its name from the Latin for a bare hillside, because the soil is so poor it can only support vines. The French equivalent is *mont rasé*, and over the years this has become Montrachet. There are others who say the word derives from the Latin for a bunch of grapes, and if this were true, it would mean a history of winemaking in the commune dating back almost two thousand years.

There is little to see in Puligny-Montrachet, and there is no tasting centre. There is a château in its own parkland but this is not open to the public, although there is a good hotel in the centre of the village which makes an ideal base from which to explore.

Almost all the production is white wine, although about 3,500 cases of red are produced. Last century there was a lot of Gamay grown here, to satisfy the thirst of the travellers and to cope with the needs of the rapidly increasing population of Dijon. Blackcurrants have also been grown here traditionally, but both the Gamay and the blackcurrants have been replaced with the Chardonnay which now reigns supreme in the commune.

About 100,000 cases of white wine are produced in a good year, of which about 60 per cent comes from the four *Grands Crus* and the eleven *Premiers Crus*. The vineyards are considered so important that the French government even made extra money available in the early 1960s so that a proposed motorway could be re-routed away from the Le Montrachet vineyard. The *Grands Crus* vineyards of Puligny-Montrachet are probably the most expensive parcels of agricultural land anywhere in the world and an acre is estimated to be worth at least £2 million. The four *Grands Crus* are Le Montrachet (first mentioned in 1482, and now owned by about a dozen people), Chevalier-Montrachet, Bâtard-Montrachet, and Bienvenues-Bâtard-Montrachet. Many of the *Premiers Crus* are also magnificent and include Les Caillerets, Les Combettes, Clavoillons, Les Pucelles, Les Folatières, Le Champ-Canet, Les Chalumeaux, Les Referts, Sous le Puits, La Garenne and Hameau de Blagny.

Chassagne-Montrachet

This is a sprawling village on the other side of the A6 autoroute, and it has about eleven acres of vineyards contributing to the *Grands Crus* of Puligny. There is a fine banqueting hall, opened by the commune in 1967, which is used for tastings and local celebrations. Although peaceful now, the village has had a troubled past. In 1478 Swiss mercenaries in the pay of the King of France wreaked a terrible revenge on the villagers for their support of the Duke of Burgundy's daughter Mary, who was at odds with Louis XI. She enlisted the support of Jean de Chalon, Prince of Orange and he took refuge in Chassagne. When the Swiss advanced, he fled but the village was put to the torch and most of the inhabitants were killed. To this day, the villagers are referred to as 'the bruised ones'.

As with Puligny, the commune used to make more red wine than white, and it was only towards the end of the eighteenth century that white wines started to take hold. Some fine reds are still made and the best come from Clos St-Jean, Boudriotte, Morgeot and La Maltroie. The reds are firm and rounded, mellow with age and have glorious colour and bouquet. They can be drunk young but are at their best after about five years.

There are three *Grands Crus* producing white wines: Montrachet, Bâtard-Montrachet, Criots-Bâtard-Montrachet; and eighteen *Premiers Crus*, making white or red, or both.

Two other features worth mentioning in Chassagne are quarries and truffles. Stone has been quarried here for centuries and many of the houses in the village were built from it. A pink limestone, which polishes very well, has been used for at least the last 500 years and abandoned quarries still dot the landscape. The neighbouring churches have altars made from this stone and most date back to the fourteenth and fifteenth centuries.

Truffles are a local speciality, although not so common now. Twenty-five years ago there was a harvest in the woods surrounding the village, and 100lbs of truffles were gathered. The woods are still full of different fungi, of which the locals take advantage, yet visitors risk poisoning and perhaps death, if they are not sure just what they are picking.

St-Aubin and Gamay

St-Aubin borders Chassagne, but is higher up the hills and suffers a much harsher climate. There is less rainfall throughout the year, and often snow during the winter. The commune includes the village of Gamay which gives its name to the grape variety which used to be so common throughout the Côte d'Or. It is a typical Côte d'Or village with old stone houses, narrow twisting streets and a church which is being restored and is worth a visit, because skeletons of plague victims were discovered here.

Everyone in the village is concerned with growing or making wine. About two thirds of the production is red and the rest white. Despite its height, there are some sheltered vineyards and these include the eight First Growths: La Chatenière, En Remilly, Les Murgers-des-Dents-de-Chien, Les Frionnes, Sur-le-Sentier-du-Clou, Sur Gamay, Les Combes, and Champlot. The reds are rarely outstanding, but they have a rarity value as they are not widely known outside France. Much of the other red wine production goes towards Côte de Beaune Villages. There have been significant strides forward in the quality of the white wines, thanks to the introduction of new vinification techniques, and this is an area to watch.

Santenay

This is the last wine-producing commune of any importance at the southern end of the Côte de Beaune. Unlike the other towns in the Côte d'Or, however, Santenay has strings to its bow other than wine. There is a spa famed for its therapeutic properties, but like all spas in Europe, it is only a shadow of its former elegant self. There is also a casino which is very popular during the summer months, and efforts are now being made to improve both.

Santenay makes almost exclusively red wine which is strong and deep-coloured, and there are seven *Premiers Crus*: Les Gravières, Le Clos-de-Tavannes, La Comme, Beauregard, Le Passe-Temps, Beaurepaire and La Maladière. The white wines are easily overshadowed by their northern neighbours.

Décize-lès-Maranges, Cheilly-lès-Maranges and Sampigny-lès-Maranges

These three red wine villages sell their production as Côte de Beaune Villages. They are at the southernmost tip of the Côte de Beaune, and make strong, fine wines, which age well. Best drunk after five years, they will go on for some years after.

COTE DE BEAUNE VILLAGES AND COTE DE BEAUNE

The Côte de Beaune *appellation* carries more weight than Côte de Beaune Villages, and denotes a wine from within the boundaries of Beaune itself, or from a score of neighbouring properties that have been judged worthy of the name. You will also see Côte de Beaune used before the name of a particular commune such as Décize, Cheilly, Sampigny, Chassagne, Puligny, Meursault, Auxey and Chorey, and this upgrades the wine over that of just the village *appellation*.

The *appellation* Côte de Beaune Villages can be used by sixteen villages and any two or more of these can blend their wines to produce reds, or they can sell under their own village name. Quality can vary enormously, but the commune of Chorey-lès-Beaune, which sells its wine under the Côte de Beaune Villages *appellation* is an exception because the standard is consistently high. All the forty or so producers strive constantly to improve their wines and they are now much sought-after.

CHALONNAISE

After travelling south through the Côte d'Or, the next area of Burgundy reached is the Chalonnaise. The area has been overshadowed by the Côte de Beaune, and for many years the wines of the five villages that make up the Chalonnaise were sold as Côte de Beaune. Recently the vineyards have come into their own and fine wines are now produced; red, white and sparkling.

There is a marvellous restaurant at Hôtel Lameloise in Chagny, and there are a number of hotels and pensions here and in Chalon-sur-Saône which make a good base for touring the Chalonnaise. The museum at Chalon, the Musée Denon, is well worth a visit, and there are a number of good restaurants.

Pinot Noir still provides the grapes for the red wine, and Chardonnay and Pinot Blanc are used for the white. The Aligoté also does well and is used for the acclaimed Bourgogne Aligoté de Bouzeron. The vineyards of the Chalonnaise are fragmented, scattered along a twenty-mile-long stretch from Chagny in the north to Montagny in the south.

Rully

Rully is the first village one comes across entering the Chalonnaise from the north. For more that 150 years it has been making a sparkling Burgundy from a blend of Aligoté and Chardonnay. The still whites are dry and full-bodied, fruity and fresh, and should be drunk young, say after three years. They are excellent as an apéritif or with shellfish. Only white wine made from the Chardonnay can carry the Rully *appellation*. There are nineteen *Premiers Crus*.

Mercurey

This is perhaps the most famous village of the Chalonnaise, and its popularity has increased enormously in the last few years. Almost all the production is red wine from the Pinot Noir, which does well on the poor soil, similar as it is in composition to that of the Côte d'Or. Only the best red wine from three communes can carry the label Mercurey — St-Martin-sous-Montaigu, Bourgneuf-Val-d'Or and Mercurey. There are five *Premiers Crus* and the growers have formed their own *Confrérie* to promote their wines. The

Confrérie-St-Vincent et des Disciples de la Chante Flûté de Mercurey meet once a year to taste the wines, and only the very best are allowed to carry the special label *Chante Flûté*, a guarantee of high quality.

Givry

Wine from here has been praised ever since the sixth century and used to be supplied to the courts of the French kings, where it was a firm favourite. Perhaps this popularity led the building of the massive cellars which are worth visiting. Givry does not have any *Premiers Crus*, and the red wine is no longer a match for those of Mercurey. It is still a good wine, light, rounded and velvety, with a very distinctive nose; best drunk within five years.

The big threat to these vineyards comes from the attractive offers of property developers, ever anxious to grub up the vines and replace them with houses for the continually-spreading Chalon-sur-Saône.

Montagny

Montagny produces only white wines from the Chardonnay. There are only about 750 acres of vineyards and the wines are crisp and fresh, exceptionally dry, and some can have a slight earthiness that is in no way unpleasant. Others can be remarkably soft and they develop a golden colour with greenish tinges. They are best drunk young, between two and four years old. Montagny, as the name suggests, gets its name from the surrounding hillsides which rise to about 1,300ft. Nearby is the commune of Buxy, famous for its *Cave Coopérative*, which is now a major exporter.

Bouzeron

The fifth village is Bouzeron which has its own *appellation* because of the Aligoté which is used in the Bourgogne Aligoté. Apart from the *Village appellations*, the Chalonnaise also produces a lot of very drinkable wine, marketed under the Bourgogne Rouge label.

THE MACONNAIS

The area between the Chalonnaise and the Beaujolais; it produces wines that have become world famous — Pouilly-Fuissé in particular. The Mâconnais is trapped between two rivers; the Saône, on which Mâcon stands, which flows along the eastern side of the region, and the Grosne which meanders its way round the other three sides. Tournus is the first town of any size in the Mâconnais and the vineyards then run south for less than thirty miles to the west of the A6 and D103.

The Chardonnay grape produces pleasing whites, clearly Burgundies but a fraction of the price of their cousins from the Côte d'Or. In the past most of the wine produced was red made from the Gamay, the vineyards dotted on the slopes of the many small hills. The region has a mixed agriculture and Charollais cattle, named after the hills to the west, graze in the water meadows. There are woods and groves of sweet chestnuts and the area is rich in game, the hunting of which is a favourite pastime after the vintage is over.

Mâcon is the capital of the region, built in a strategic position dominating the Saône. The area was covered in woodlands, but the Romans planted the vineyards and there are early records of vines being grown around Tournus and Mâcon. There are also traces of the weapons made in Mâcon, arrow heads and spears, used for hunting game in the surrounding forests.

Today, the Mâconnais produces both red and white wines and while the reputation of the whites is already established, that of the reds is growing quickly. Much of the wine is now made by *coopératives*, and enormous investments have been made in new technology and equipment, which has clearly resulted in an improvement in quality.

The various *appellations* of Mâconnais are:

Mâcon Blanc is generally made from Chardonnay, must come from delimited areas and have a natural alcohol content of 10°. If the alcohol content increases to 11° the wine has the right to the *appellation* Mâcon Supérieur.

Mâcon Villages *appellation* can be used by the forty-three villages which are considered the best producers in the Mâconnais. They are generally to be found in the eastern part of the region.

St-Véran comes from eight communes in the south, some of which overlap into Beaujolais. The wine can be sold under the village name, or as Beaujolais Blanc, Mâcon Villages, or Bourgogne Blanc.

Mâcon Rouge is made from the Gamay and must have 9° alcohol. It is also made as Mâcon rosé.

Mâcon Supérieur Rouge must have a minimum 10° alcohol and must come from a delimited area. It also has the right to carry its particular *Villages* after the title Mâcon.

Pouilly-Fuissé comes from the communes of Pouilly, Fuissé, Solutré, Vergisson and Chaintré. It must have 11° of natural alcohol, and 12° if it also carries the vineyard's name.

Pouilly-Vinzelles has to follow the same rules as Pouilly-Fuissé except that the grapes must come from the communes of Vinzelles and Loché. It is not quite up to Pouilly-Fuissé standards but costs a lot less.

A Tour of the Burgundy Region

The best way of touring Burgundy is simply to drive through from north to south, and stop off where you please. Here, a six-day tour is offered which allows time to explore and taste the different styles of wine, but the trip can be extended almost indefinitely. Indeed, it is possible to spend several months in Burgundy and still not taste all the magnificent wines available.

Tour of Dijon

Dijon is an ideal place to begin the tour, and well worth visiting, thanks to its wealth of treasures and architectural heritage. It is also close to the Côte

de Nuits, the most northerly section of vineyards that make up the Côte
d'Or. The first day can take in the communes of Marsannay-la-Côte,
Couchey, Fixin, Brochon, Gevrey-Chambertin, Morey-St-Denis, Chambolle-
Musigny, Vougeot and Vosne-Romaneé. It is obviously impossible to visit
all these villages, but Fixin and the area south of Gevrey-Chambertin is the
most rewarding to the wine lover. Almost everywhere there are the famous
names of Burgundy, wines everyone has read about but few are able to afford.
There are wines like Les Hervelets, Les Perrières and Clos du Chapitre, all
famous *Premiers Crus* from vineyards to the west of Fixin, and *Grands Crus*
such as Chambertin, Chambertin-Clos-de-Bèze, Clos St-Jacques, Chapelle-
Chambertin, Clos de la Roche and Clos St-Denis below Gevrey-Chambertin.

This small area of vineyard, from Marsannay-la-Côte to Vosne-Romanée,
is only about ten miles long, but every signpost is full of famous names.

Dijon is now a busy commercial centre for the entire range of wines, as
well as being world-famous for its mustard, gingerbread, and blackcurrant
drink, *cassis*. For centuries it was the home of the Dukes of Burgundy, and
this is reflected in the splendour of many of the buildings. There is the
Ducal Palace dating back to the fourteenth century, and the cathedral, dating
from the thirteenth century, with its Romanesque crypt. There are many fine
churches reflecting wide-ranging styles of architecture. The church of Notre-
Dame is Burgundian Gothic, while the church of St Michael is pure
Renaissance. Other things to see are the Charterhouse of Champmol, which
contains Claus Sluter's 'Well of Moses', the Law Courts and the fine arts
museum, one of the finest in France. There are many other museums and
scores of fine private buildings which once housed the courtiers, scholars
and musicians attracted to the Burgundian Court.

Marsannay to Nuits-St-Georges

From Dijon, head south through the small village of Marsannay-la-Côte to
Fixin, which contains half a dozen excellent vineyards, and Chez Jeanette,
where a fine lunch is offered. The restaurant also has a number of
inexpensive rooms should the exertions of the day prove too much. Also in
Fixin is the famous statue, the 'Awakening of Napoléon', sculpted by Rudé
and commissioned by Claude-Charles Noisot, a veteran of the Napoleonic
wars. The statue is in the park founded by Noisot in 1846. His dying wish
was to be buried in the park, upright, sword in hand, so that he could
continue to serve and defend Napoléon. There is also a small museum
devoted to the imperial campaigns.

Just to the south is the village of Gevrey-Chambertin, which has been
the centre of a vineyard area since Roman times, and today produces two of
the world's most famous red wines — Chambertin and Clos-de-Bèze. Like
many other famous wines of the region, the latter owes its dominance to the
Benedictine monks who nurtured the vineyards, while the former achieved
international fame because it was the chosen wine of Napoléon, and is said
to have first sustained him, and then comforted him during his calamitous
invasion of Russia. Gevrey-Chambertin boasts three hotels and two fine
restaurants, La Rôtisserie du Chambertin and Les Millésimes. The Rôtisserie

has an incredible wine list and food to match. The sights to see are in the old part of the village. You can visit the château, parts of which date back to the tenth century, although it was mostly rebuilt in the thirteenth century. From here, travel to Morey-St-Denis, famous for its Clos de Tart vineyard; many of the vineyards were formerly owned by Cistercian monasteries.

Other vineyards worth visiting are those of Clos de la Roche and Clos St-Denis. Then down the road again to Chambolle-Musigny and Vougeot, and another clutch of *Grands Crus*; there are the vineyards of Clos de Vougeot, Vignes Blanches de Clos de Vougeot, Musigny, Echézeaux.

In Chambolle, visit the church which has some fine religious paintings, and there are good views across the vineyards. There is also some marvellous countryside just a stone's throw away from the vineyards, with bubbling rivers rushing through wooded gorges, a marvellous place for a picnic lunch.

Vougeot is of interest, apart from its wines, because of the Clos de Vougeot, built by the Cistercian monks and now the headquarters of the Brotherhood of the Knights of the Wine Taster, which is well worth a visit. The roof of the building was constructed in such a way to trap as much rainwater as possible, which was then stored in vats. The building dates from the twelfth century, when it was enclosed by a wall. The Clos was rebuilt by the monks in the sixteenth century but the original wine cellars, thirteenth-century dormitories, winemaking equipment and giant press remain. The next port of call should be Vosne-Romanée, with its narrow streets and granite houses. The village is surrounded by world-famous vineyards such as Richebourg, Romanée-St-Vivant, La Romanée and La Tâche. The most famous of all, and the only *Premier Grand Cru*, is La Romanée-Conti.

Most of the vineyards are older than the houses in the attractive village which has often seen troubled times. The wines of Romanée were first mentioned in a poem written in AD312 in honour of the Emperor Constantine. The vineyard of Romanée-Conti features in a feud between Madame de Pompadour, mistress of Louis XV, and Louis François de Bourbon, Prince of Conti. She wanted the vineyard but he managed to buy it in 1760 and immediately lost favour at court. The vineyard, still bearing his name, survives and produces one of the supreme Burgundies.

Nuits-St-Georges is an ideal place for the first overnight stop. It is a small town, and another bustling commercial centre, housing the cellars of many world-famous shippers. Before visiting the surrounding vineyards and cellars, have a look at the twelfth-century church of St Symphorien, and the Gallo-Roman and Merovingian excavations. Because of the narrow streets and busy traffic, it is best to park and explore the town on foot. The Hospice de Nuits-St-Georges, founded in 1692, is well worth visiting. After the Revolution, the Augustinian monks were deprived of control of the Hospice, which was handed over to the local Mayor. He appointed two nuns to look after the thirty-six patients. The Hospice originally had twelve beds and now has 166; it has changed its role during the years. In the nineteenth century, it concentrated on caring for tuberculosis victims; now it specialises in treating the poor and the old.

Many of the local vineyard owners are benefactors, and in 1938 the first auction of wines donated to the Hospice took place. The war halted the practice and it was not resumed until 1962 but is now firmly established.

Tour of Beaune

From Nuits-St-Georges, continue south to Beaune, a medieval fortified town famous for its hospice, museums, works of art and fine old buildings. To many it is the true capital of Burgundy, and some hours exploring the town is a very rewarding experience. Beaune, too, can trace its origins back to at least Roman times, when it was called *Belna*. It has always been a successful trading and commercial town, receiving city status in 1203, and therefore subject to attack from its enemies which is why the ramparts were built in the reign of Louis XI (these now house the cellars of many of Beaune's growers and shippers). Today, the town has spread, and the sprawling suburbs now house many of the wineries and bottling plants formerly to be found in the heart of the old town.

For centuries the town and its surrounding land has changed hands at regular intervals. It was the seat of the Burgundian Parliament, and home of the Dukes of Burgundy until the fourteenth century. At different times it has been owned by the Church, the monarchy, the Knights of Malta, and then after the Revolution, private ownership following the splitting up of the estates and a massive auction.

Many of the vineyards are now owned by the shippers who operate from the town, and the battlements which used to house the troops are now used for storing the wine. There are many buildings surviving from this period in the town's history. The Musée de Vin was formerly one of the town houses of the Duke of Burgundy. There are the church of Notre-Dame, dating back to the eleventh and twelfth centuries, and containing fifteenth-century tapestries illustrating the Life of the Virgin, and the church of St Nicholas. A few miles outside the town is the Archaeodrome, off the A6 motorway, which contains life-size models depicting the history of the region from the earliest times.

Beaune's most famous building is, however, the Hospices de Beaune. It comprises the Hôtel Dieu and the Hospice de la Charité, and was founded in 1441 by Nicholas Rolin, then Chancellor of Burgundy. He and his wife, Guigonne de Salins, decreed that all their worldly goods should be endowed to allow a hospice to be built to care for the poor and sick. It took eight years to build the Hôtel Dieu. The result is one of the finest examples of Flemish-Burgundian architecture; the Flemish craftsmen commissioned to aid the work built the patterned roof, one of the most notable features of the building.

A Flemish nursing order, the Dames Hospitalières, still runs the Hospices; naturally, conditions have improved over the centuries. When the Hôtel Dieu was opened, patients used to lie two or more to a bed. The beds were larger than those used today, and all were arranged in such a way that every patient could see into the chapel. The beds were still in use until 1948.

The building has been beautifully looked after, and apart from the original beds which can be seen in the Salle des Pauvres (which is 170ft long) there is a magnificent art gallery, housing priceless exhibits such as Roger van der Weiden's masterpiece, 'The Last Judgement', and also a museum, full of interesting exhibits, and the kitchen and dispensary containing original artefacts. A guided tour of the Hospices is available, and lasts about an hour.

The Hospices, like the one in Nuits, benefit from the patronage of local wine growers and merchants, and more than 100 acres of vineyards have now been donated to the Hospices to help maintain them. Every year since 1859 special *cuvées* from these vineyards have been sold at public auction, and even though the event is for charitable purposes, the prices now being offered are ridiculously high, because few people can afford their subsequent re-sale price. The auction is held during the third weekend in November and attracts buyers from all over the world. Today, twenty-three *cuvées* of red wine are offered, nine of white together with some brandies and *marc*. Although Beaune is famous for its red wines, it is usually the whites which command the highest prices at the auction, especially Corton-Charlemagne, Cuvée François de Salins. While the three days of the auction, the *Trois Glorieuses*, are exhilarating, the town is so packed with buyers and others, that it is not a good time to visit unless you have a ticket for the sales.

From Beaune you can visit the vineyards of many *Premier* and *Grand Cru* wines. To the west of Ladoix, just north of Beaune, and surrounding the village of Aloxe-Corton are the vineyards of Corton Renardes, Corton Clos du Roi and ten or more other *Grands Crus* reds. Just to the west of Aloxe-Corton is the vineyard producing the Corton-Charlemagne *Grand Cru* white, while south of the road to Savigny, are the vineyards of *Premiers Crus* reds such as Les Marconnets, Les Perrières, Aigrots, Vignes Franches and Clos des Mouches.

Pommard to Santenay

From Beaune, travel still further south to Pommard, famous as a Protestant centre and home, in the time of Louis XIV, to the Huguenots. They were forced to flee the town when the King revoked the Edict of Nantes, but the name they gave to their wine still lives on, and it is one of the most famous of all Burgundian reds. There have been problems in the past with the name Pommard — the wine was so popular that its consumption around the world apparently exceeded its production! Now the wine is either bottled locally or under licence in Burgundy, and most of the abuses, which usually occurred because the wine was shipped in bulk and bottled abroad, have now been stamped out. There is no doubt, however, that while Pommard produces some of the greatest Burgundian wines, it also produces a wide range of quality which which can cause problems. The most famous vineyards, and quite magnificent, are Les Rugiens Bas, Les Rugiens Hauts, Les Epenots, Clos de la Commaraine, Clos Blanc, Les Arvelets, Les Charmots, Les Argillières, Les Pézerolles, Les Boucherottes, Les Saucilles, Les Croix Noires, Les Chaponières, Les Fremiers, Les Bertins, Les Jarollières, Les Poutures, Clos Micot,

La Refêne, Clos de Verger, Derrière-St-Jean, La Platière, Les Chanlins Bas, Les Combes Dessus and La Chanière.

Just to the south of Pommard is Volnay. The village is a steady uphill climb and most of the vineyards are on the left below you. On a fine day, this is another ideal place for a picnic lunch and a chance to appreciate the Burgundian countryside, sipping a glass of Volnay, considered by many to be the finest wine from the Côte de Beaune. Wine has been produced here for centuries and many of the names have remained unchanged for 700 years. Then, many of the vineyards were owned by the Order of Malta. Since then they have changed hands from the Crown, to the Dukes of Burgundy, through the Revolution and so on, but the tradition of the very finest winemaking has never been lost. The best vineyards today are En Cailleret, Cailleret, Dessus, Champans, En Chevret, Fremiet, Bousse d'Or, La Barre, Clos des Chênes, Les Angles, Les Mitans, En l'Ormeau, Taille-Pieds, En Verseuil, Carelle sous la Chapelle, Ronceret, Les Aussy, Les Brouillards, Clos des Ducs, Pitures Dessus, Chanlin, Les Santenots, Les Petures and Village-de-Volnay.

Monthélie, the next village on the route, also produces fine wines, which until recently used to be sold as Pommard. The tiny village hidden in the hills is a natural sun trap; since it received *appellation* in 1937 it has produced consistently good, fragrant, delicate wine. Although most of the production is red, there is some very good white and this should be tried either in the village café, or the *coopérative* cellars at Les Caves de Monthélie.

Continue to cut through the hills heading south past the village of La Rochepot, with its ancient château, through Auxey-Duresses which has a fine restaurant, La Cremaillère, to St-Romain. This commune received its *appellation* in 1967 and has the highest vineyards in the Côte d'Or. It produces very good wines, both red and white, and has magnificent views from the vantage point up a steep path from the village. From Volnay, travel down the hill to Meursault, home of some of the world's most famous white wines. The small town is capital of the Côte de Blancs, which includes other such famous names as Blagny, Puligny-Montrachet and Chassagne-Montrachet. The houses are granite-built and typically Burgundian. Although it has a long history, little remains of that today although there is still an attractive fourteenth-century church with a steeple that guides you to the town.

Its most famous vineyards are those of Les Perrières and Les Charmes, but there are many others of importance — Genevrières, Blagny, Goutte d'Or, Bouchères, Les Santenots, Les Caillerets, Les Petures, Les Cras, La Jennelotte, La Pièce-sous-le-Bois and Le Poruzot. The tiny village of Blagny, up on the hill, is also noted for its white wines but it produces a fine, delicate red which should be tried.

A galaxy of famous names are passed on the route south via Puligny-Montrachet and Chassagne-Montrachet. Almost all deserve a stop, but the amount of time devoted to this area must depend on the flexibility of your timetable.

Santenay is also worth a visit both for its casino and its spa waters. The Source Carnot is a spring which is said to produce water helpful in the treatment of gout and rheumatism. The springs were already well-known in Roman times. Over the years, the original wells were polluted and new ones had to be drilled, and now there are a number drawing up water from several hundred feet below ground, each claiming to have different properties. A modern hotel has now been opened and this, with the Casino de Santenay (a popular attraction at weekends) should help to boost the town's prosperity.

Santenay really consists of three villages, Santenay-le-Haut which houses the hotel, spa and casino; Santenay-le-Bas (or Bains) where the villagers live and wine is made; and St-Jean, which boasts a fine thirteenth-century Romanesque-Gothic church.

From Chagny and Chalon to Mâcon

Just outside Santenay, on top of the hill, is a statue of winged horses, placed there to commemorate three lovers of Burgundy wine who died in the Paris air crash of 1974. And then it is on to Chalon-sur-Saône. Chalon is the commercial heart of the Côte Chalonnaise, and another bustling industrial town. It has a twelfth-century cathedral, many other fine churches and buildings, and museums worth a visit. The drive from Beaune to Chalon takes less than half-an-hour, but as you can see, it is quite easy to spend several days wandering through the magnificent vineyards along the way.

Chagny is the first village of the Chalonnaise although its neighbour to the south, Rully is the first to have its appellation. The Côte Chalonnaise runs along the hillsides for about twenty miles south from Chagny, which marks the dividing line between it and the Côte d'Or to the north.

Rully produces some fine white wines, and for more than 150 years has been making sparkling Burgundy, but its products are overshadowed by the wines of Mercurey just to the south.

Mercurey which, it is claimed, is named after a Roman temple to Mercury, has wine charters going back to AD557. It is the most important commune of the Chalonnaise and there are five vineyards with *Premiers Crus* status — Clos du Roi, Clos Les Voyens, Clos-Marcilly, Clos des Fourneaux, and Clos des Montaigus.

To the west of Chalon is Givry, which is now striving to retain its former glory. It once supplied wines to the best places in Paris, but between the wars, other wines became more popular. Givry received its *appellation* for good, full-bodied, almost sharp reds which are ready for drinking much earlier than those of its neighbours.

Chalon itself has much to attract the visitor, including fine hotels and restaurants. It has good shops and wide streets. Places of interest to visit include the twelfth-century cathedral, the seventeenth-century church of St Peter, and many sixteenth and seventeenth-century houses. There is an archaeological museum, the Musée Denon, including a photography museum, housing the works of Joseph Nicephore Niepce, who took the first photograph — a view of Chalon. He later teamed up with Daguerre, whose part in the development of photography is much better known.

The last port of call in the Chalonnaise is Montagny, just over five miles south of Givry, which produces clean, pleasant, refreshing white wines.

From Montagny, continue south just a couple of miles into the Mâconnais, a region trapped between two rivers: the Saône in the east, and the Grosne which wriggles its way in a wide sweep to the west from north to south. The Mâconnais combines agriculture and viticulture, and is an excellent place to end our tour of the region because both fine wines and tremendous food can be enjoyed. Although the town of Mâcon is the largest, it is Tournus that we reach first. It has a wonderful abbey church, and has always been a place of pilgrimage. In AD179 St-Valerian was martyred here, and many buildings still remain from the Middle Ages. The abbey church was started in the ninth century, but there are architectural gems to be seen everywhere and two local museums. The Mâconnais produces both red and white wine, but the whites have the edge, and the Pouilly-Fuissé is known everywhere. The reds tend to be light and fruity, similar in style to the Beaujolais, but less fruity, although the best can be very good indeed. The vineyards around Tournus produce mostly red wines, while the white production is concentrated to the west and south of Mâcon around Pouilly and St-Véran.

If time permits, it is worth the detour to Cluny, about ten miles from Mâcon. It is noted for its Benedictine abbey, founded in AD910, which was once the largest in all Christendom. Cluny also boasts Romanesque houses and a Renaissance palace.

Mâcon is a pleasing town, home of the poet Lamartine, full of the red-tiled buildings which become ever more numerous as you journey on towards the Mediterranean. The town is surrounded by hills which provide pleasant walking, and there are many Romanesque churches scattered about. There is good food to be had in the restaurants in and around Mâcon, and the remains of the twelfth-century church of St Vincent to explore.

The advantage of the Burgundian vineyards is that they run conveniently in a line that is easy to follow. A week could be spent exploring just one village, but this brief itinerary does allow flexibility to visit all the important areas but at a pace that suits you best.

THINGS TO SEE AND DO IN BURGUNDY

Alise-Ste-Reine
Fortified town where Caesar defeated Vercingetorix in 52BC. Interesting Gallo-Roman excavations, museum.

Ancy-le-France
Renaissance château of the sixteenth century. Apartments decorated by artists of School of Fontainebleau.

Anzy-le-Duc
Eleventh-century church with octagonal bell tower.

Arcy-sur-Cure
Series of caves, open to the public.

Arnay-le-Duc
Ancient town with fifteenth-century tower. Regional museum.

Autun
Roman town *Augustodunum*; two giant gateways dating from Gallo-Roman period; temple to Janus, and remains of the biggest theatre in Roman Gaul. Medieval town walls and cathedral dating

from twelfth century, with fine
Romanesque sculpture. Many fine
buildings and museums.

Auxerre
Medieval city with many historic
buildings. Twelfth-century cathedral, with
fine stained glass windows, carved door-
ways, crypt and frescoes. Abbey church
of St Germain (twelfth to fourteenth-
centuries), Carolingian crypt with earliest-
known (ninth-century) French frescoes,
sixteenth-century church of St Peter and
many fine buildings dating from the
fifteenth century.

Auxonne
Bonaparte museum.

Avallon
Ancient fortified town. Church of St
Lazarus, eleventh-century, belfry fifteenth-
century, old house, ramparts, museum.

Azé
Underground caves.

Beaune
Hospices founded 1441, famed for their
architecture, paintings, tapestries, museum. Winemaking museum, collegiate
church of Notre-Dame (eleventh-century),
church of St Nicholas, ramparts, and
many fine houses.

Berzé-la-Ville
Priory chapel with many fine paintings.

Berzé-le-Chatel
Feudal castle.

Beuvray
Site of the Gaulish capital of Bibracte.

Bèze
Subterranean lakes and caves.

Blanot
Romanesque church, Cluniac priory,
underground caves.

Bourbon-Lancy
Spa town with many old houses.

Boutissaint
Wildlife park of St Hubert, open to the
public.

Brancion
Feudal fortress town, Romanesque church,
magnificent views.

Buffon
Series of forges built in 1768, open to
the public.

Bussy-le-Grand
Sixteenth-century château with portrait
collection, Romanesque church.

Chalon-sur-Saône
Industrial and trading town. Twelfth-
century cathedral, seventeenth-century
church of St Peter, Musée Denon and
photography museum, many fine houses.

La Charité-sur-Loire
Church of Notre-Dame (eleventh-century),
with five naves (can hold 5,000)
sixteenth-century stone bridge and
archaeological museum.

Château Chinon
Magnificent views, museums of local
costumes and folk art.

Châteauneuf-en-Auxois
Eleventh-century castle and medieval
village overlooking the Canal de
Bourgogne.

Châtillon-sur-Seine
Archaeological museum in sixteenth-
century mansion. Church of St Vorles.

Cîteaux
Remains of St Nicolas-de-Cîteaux abbey,
founded in 1098, the cradle of the
Cistercian order.

Clamency
Thirteenth-century collegiate church of St
Martin, museum, old houses.

La Clayette
Castle and well-preserved fourteenth-
century outbuildings.

Cluny
Benedictine abbey founded in 910. The
abbey church, started in 1088, was the
largest in all Christendom. Parts still
remain and are open to the public. Other
fine churches, museum, palace and
Romanesque houses.

Commarin
Moated castle with heraldic tapestries.

Cormatin
Seventeenth-century Renaissance château, open to visitors.

Cosne-sur-Loire
Twelfth-century church of St Angan, museum illustrating the work of the Loire lightermen.

Couches
Castle built between twelfth and sixteenth centuries, open to public.

Le Creusot
Château de la Verrerie.

Cuiseaux
Renaissance houses with sixteenth-century arcading, church with fine carved choir stalls.

Décize
Home of St Just, church, convent and listed beauty spot.

Dijon
Many historic buildings, ducal palace and palace of the States General (fourteenth to seventeenth centuries), thirteenth-century cathedral, many fine churches, the Charterhouse with its works of art, many museums and galleries.

Flavingy-sur-Ozerain
Medieval village, well-preserved, ramparts, fortified gateway, abbey and thirteenth-century church.

Fleurigny
Château with fourteenth-century façade and courtyard, open to the public.

Fontenay
Fontenay Abbey founded 1118, well-preserved and open to the public.

Givry
Many fine eighteenth-century buildings.

Guérigny
Industrial archaeology museum.

Joigny
Ancient city, narrow lanes, many sixteenth-century houses.

Mâcon
Home of soldier poet Lamartine, many fine churches in the area.

Montbard
Museum of local history, housed in 170ft tower.

Montceaux l'Etoile
Twelfth-century church.

Montréal
Medieval country town with Gothic church and sixteenth-century choir stalls.

Mont-St-Vincent
Gothic church and magnificent views.

Nevers
Julius Caesar's *Noviodunum*; cathedral and tenth-century church, convent contains the tomb of Ste Bernadette of Lourdes, fifteenth-century ducal palace, museums.

Nolay
Fourteenth-century covered market, castle and archaeological sites.

Nuits-St-Georges
Twelfth-century church and Gallo-Roman excavations nearby.

Paray-le-Monial
Pilgrimage centre, sixteenth-century town hall, priory church modelled on the abbey church of Cluny.

Perrecy-les-Forges
Eleventh-century church with carved porch.

Pierre-de-Bresse
Seventeenth-century château, fine grounds and ecological museum.

Pontigny
Twelfth-century abbey church.

Prémery
Fourteenth-century castle, former home of the Bishops of Nevers, thirteenth-century church.

Ratilly
Thirteenth-century castle, craft centre.

St-Fargeau
Castle started in twelfth century, open to the public.

St-Florentin
Renaissance church with sixteenth-century stained glass windows.

St-Père-sous-Vézelay
Thirteenth-century church, archaeology museum, Gallo-Roman excavations.

St-Pierre-le-Moutier
Many fine churches.

St-Point
Castle remodelled in the nineteenth century by Lamartine; Romanesque church.

St-Révérien
Twelfth-century church.

St-Seine-l'Abbaye
One of the oldest Gothic churches in Burgundy.

St-Thibault
Thirteenth-century church, fine doorway.

Santenay
Spa town with thirteenth-century church.

Semur-en-Brionnais
Twelfth-century Romanesque church.

Sens
Twelfth-century cathedral with original stained glass windows, thirteenth-century synodal palace, museums of history and religious ornaments and relics.

Solutré
Prehistoric site above Pouilly-Fuissé vineyards.

Sully
Magnificent sixteenth-century château.

Talmay
Thirteenth-century keep, eighteenth-century château with formal French garden.

Ternant
Church with fine fifteenth-century gilt Flemish triptychs.

Tonnerre
Thirteenth-century hospital with panelled ceiling, fine chapel.

Tournus
Abbey church, tenth-century crypt.

Varzy
Church with collection of relics, museum.

Vézelay
Fortified medieval town and place of pilgrimage. Famous church of Ste Madeleine, noted for its architecture and sculpture.

Vic-sous-Thil
Ruins of ninth-century castle, fourteenth-century church above town.

Villeneuve-sur-Yonne
Thirteenth-century fortified town, original gateways, Gothic church.

Villiers-St-Benoît
Regional museum famed for its sculptures and earthenware.

Vougeot
Château du Clos de Vougeot, thirteenth-century wine cellar, dormitory and wine presses.

Gastronomy of Burgundy

The Burgundians eat well, and it is generally true that the best meals are to be had as a guest of a family rather than as a diner in a restaurant. Because of the thousands of tourists who visit the region every day, the restaurants and hotels have tended to become more international than Burgundian in their style, although there are still some who stick faithfully to the local cuisine.

Again, as a general rule, it is wise to avoid menus advertised as *touristique* or *gastronomique*, unless you know the establishment well. They are likely to cost the earth and the high price is unlikely to be matched by a similar culinary excellence.

The Burgundians do not go in for extremely elaborate cooking, but they work hard and eat well. Quality counts, but quantity is more important. They have always gone in for large scale entertaining and the banquets of some of the dukes of Burgundy are legendary. Up to 500 people would sit down to a gargantuan feast of a dozen or more courses, and the eating and drinking lasted well into the night.

The region benefits from its strong mix of wine and agriculture. In the south, the woodlands and forests of the Mâconnais provide excellent game, there is first class beef from the Charollais, truffles and mushrooms, good vegetables and hams. The finest food is generally found in the Côte d'Or, but there are good restaurants throughout Burgundy, and distinct styles of regional cooking as you travel from Chablis, through the Côte de Nuits, Côte de Beaune, and into the Chalonnaise and Mâconnais.

Dijon is still known for its mustard, and *crème de cassis*, made from blackcurrants. Try the gingerbread with honey, known as *pain d'épices*, which can also be made with spices. Regional specialities include *andouille* and *andouillette*. The first is a very rich sausage made from pig tripe, usually already cooked and served cold as a starter, the second is another pork sausage but usually grilled and served hot with mustard. Perhaps the region's most famous dish is *boeuf à la Bourguignonne*, a rich stew of beef cooked in red wine with onions, mushrooms and cubes of bacon. A Savigny-lès-Beaune is an ideal accompaniment.

Other first courses can be *jambon persillé*, ham flavoured with parsley in jelly, or *jambon de Morvan*, delicious raw ham from the area to the west of the Côte d'Or. *Jambon en saupiquet* is ham braised in wine and served with a piquant sauce (it is also known as *à la crème*, or *à la Morvandelle*). There is a very light cheese-flavoured choux pastry ring called *la gougère*, which is normally served cold, and *fouée*, which is a cream and bacon flan with walnut oil, which comes from the walnuts which grow in abundance in the Mâconnais.

You will see *morilles* on the menu either by themselves or as an accompaniment to other dishes. They are the field mushrooms picked locally in the spring and are highly regarded.

Beef is served in many forms, as simply Charollais steaks, or *boeuf à la mode*, which is beef stewed in red wine with vegetables and herbs and served either hot, or cold in its own jelly.

Coq au vin is also a speciality, and Chambertin should be used, but the recipe varies through the region. The chicken is cooked in the red wine together with vegetables, mushrooms and onions. Chicken also figures in many other regional dishes. *Poulet demi-deuil* is breast of chicken cooked with slices of black truffle; and there is *poulet en matelote*, chicken cooked in red wine with sliced eels, bacon and onions.

Escargots à la Bourguignonne are snails served in a hot garlic and parsley butter sauce.

A lot of game appears on the menus. *Rable de lièvre* is saddle of hare cooked in red wine. A variation of this is *lièvre à la Piron*, which is saddle of hare marinated in *marc*, the spirit distilled from the grape juice, and then cooked with shallots and grapes and served with a pepper and cream sauce. It is a speciality of Dijon.

Boudin is Burgundian black pudding, made with blood, and *quenelles de volaille* are finely-minced balls of chicken meat, moulded into a sausage shape and served with a sauce. Sausage also figures in *saucisse en brioche*, a large sausage in some form of pastry or dough. *Marcassin farci au saucisson* is young wild boar, from the Mâconnais, stuffed with sausage, and *meurettes* describes a sort of red wine sauce which can be served with fish, eggs or meat.

Pouchouse is a stew of freshwater fish from the Saône. Usually pike, perch, eel and tench are used, although carp is sometimes added. They are all cooked in a white wine to which cream and garlic is added. The secret is to use a very good wine. *Matelote* is another freshwater fish dish, usually eel, pike or trout cooked in red wine.

Salade à la Bourguignonne is made from a curly lettuce, liberal quantities of garlic, and diced bacon. *Haricots au vin rouge* speaks for itself, and *jambon à la lie-de-vin* is a meal in itself and quite delicious. It is ham which has been braised in the red wine left in the barrels after the bottling — the lees. Liberal quantities of bread are essential to mop up every drop of the sauce. *Queue de boeuf des vignerons* is oxtail stewed with white grapes.

The Burgundians prefer cheese to desserts, but you are likely to be offered *rigodon* or *tartouillat*. The first is a brioche flan with nuts and fruit, and the second is apple tart. Check the *rigodon* carefully because it is sometimes served with bacon as a savoury.

The hills of Morvan and Nivernais to the west of the Côte d'Or also have some speciality dishes including *sansiot*, calf's head, served with onions and mushrooms; *rapée Morvandelle*, grated potato baked with cream, eggs and cheese; and *potée Bourguignonne*, a vegetable stew to which one or several meats can be added, mostly pork, but chicken, beef or garlic sausage can be used. An *omelette au sang* has a sauce filling thickened with blood, and blood is also used to thicken a rich sauce in which a chicken is cooked for *du poulet au sang*. Pig's offal, cooked in red wine, is also popular, and served on the menu as *fressure*: it can sometimes be calf's offal, and it is cooked with onions, and eaten cold.

There are about a dozen regional cheeses, both from cow's milk and goat's milk, and they are worth seeking out because it is unlikely you will come across them outside Burgundy. They are always served after the main course to allow you to finish off the last of the red wine. The goat cheeses include *Charollais*, made around the town of Charolles, to the west of the Mâconnais. It is rolled into the shape of a log, has a blue rind and a firm, nutty tang. *Claquebitou*, made with added herbs and garlic, is only available from June to October. *Chévreton de Mâcon* again has a nutty taste when a little mature, but can be creamy when young. *Montrachet* is also log-shaped and wrapped in a vine leaf. It is creamy and mild. The cow's milk cheeses include *Aisy-cendré*, which can be served in a variety of shapes but is always covered in wood ashes. It is a firm, fruity cheese with a strong smell and sometimes cured in *marc*. *Cîteaux* is a tangy cheese made in the monastery, and *Epoisses* is a soft, tangy cheese in a distinctive orange-red rind. *Les Laumes* is made on farms. It has a strong flavour and a dark brown rind which arises from it being dyed with coffee. The monastery gives its name to *Pierre-Qui-Vire*, a strong cheese always sold on a mat of straw, but it can be eaten fresh when it is much milder. *St-Florentin* is a flat round cheese, with a spicy smell and shiny rind; *Soumaint-rain* is similar, but can be eaten young when creamy.

HOTELS AND RESTAURANTS OF THE BURGUNDY REGION

CHABLIS

Avallon
(89200 Yonne)

Hostellerie de la Poste
place Vauban
☎ (86) 34 06 12
A luxury hotel with 30 magnificent rooms; an old coaching inn with a cobblestone courtyard and a good restaurant. Some dishes have to be booked a day in advance. Closed in December and January, and the restaurant is closed Wednesday and Thursday lunchtime.

Hostellerie du Moulin des Ruats
Vallée du Cousin, 2³/₄ miles southwest of Avallon on the D427
☎ (86) 34 07 14
A very comfortable hotel, formerly a mill, with good restaurant and fine wine list. Closed from November to end of February.

Le Relais Fleuri
route de Saulieu, 3 miles east of Avallon on the N6
☎ (86) 34 02 85

A modern hotel with 48 chalet-style rooms, and restaurant.

Vauban
53 rue de Paris
☎ (86) 34 36 99
A comfortable 25-roomed hotel, without restaurant but breakfast served.

Moulin des Templiers
Vallée du Cousin
2¹/₂ miles south-west of Avallon on the D427
☎ (86) 34 10 80
A comfortable 14-roomed hotel, no restaurant but breakfast served. Open from April to 1 November, but closed Saturdays.

Le Morvan
7 route de Paris
☎ (86) 34 18 20
Run by M. Breton, this is a charming restaurant in a rustic setting, offering many local specialities, including smoked duck, oxtail stew and veal smoked with sorrel. It is advisable to book and to check opening times.

Les Capucins
6 ave Paul-Doumer
☎ (86) 34 06 52
Run by Daniel Aublanc, this is one of the best, yet most reasonable restaurants in Avallon. There are also 16 rooms.

Auxerre
(89000 Yonne)

Hôtel Le Maxime
2 quai Marine
☎ (86) 52 14 19
A comfortable hotel overlooking the River Yonne. 25 rooms and a reasonable restaurant.

Parc des Maréchaux
6 ave. Foch
☎ (86) 51 43 77
A 22-roomed hotel, without restaurant, but breakfast served.

Normandie
41 blvd Vauban
☎ (86) 52 57 80
47 rooms, parking, no restaurant but breakfast served.

Jardin Gourmand
56 blvd Vauban
☎ (86) 51 53 52
An elegant restaurant with
many specialities.

Chablis
(89800 Yonne)

Hôtel L'Etoile-Bergerand
4 rue des Moulins
☎ (86) 42 10 50
A modest 15-room hotel
with reasonable restaurant.
Ideal for those on a
budget.

Joigny
(89300 Yonne)

Modem'H Frères Godard
17 ave. Robert Petit
(close to the railway
   station)
☎ (86) 62 16 28
A very comfortable, well-
equipped and soundproofed
21-room hotel with small
swimming pool. The
restaurant, Le Mailler d'Or,
has a deserved reputation.

A la Côte St-Jacques
14 Faubourg de Paris
☎ (86) 62 09 70
A superb restaurant and a
very comfortable 18 room
hotel. Run by Michel

Lorain and his wife
Jacqueline. It deserves its
Michelin two stars. There
is a heated swimming
pool.

Saulieu
(21210 Côte d'Or)

Hôtel La Poste
1 rue Grillot
☎ (80) 64 05 67
A former post-house, now
a very comfortable 48-
room hotel run by M. and
Mme Virlouvet.

La Côte d'Or
2 rue d'Argentine
☎ (80) 64 07 66
Bernard Loiseau continues
to breathe life into this
establishment made
famous in former times by
Alexandre Dumaine. The
restaurant specialises in
nouvelle cuisine which has
earned M. Loiseau two
Michelin stars. The food
can be outstanding, and is
always innovative and
ingenious. The 17 rooms
are comfortable but do
not match the standards
set in the restaurant.

Sens
(89100 Yonne)

Hôtel Paris et Poste
97 rue de la République
☎ (86) 65 17 43
A 37-room, very
comfortable, smart hotel
with heated covered
swimming pool and
marvellous restaurant
under the guidance of
Charles Godard (one of the
Joigny Godards).

Tonnerre
(89700 Yonne)

Hôtel Centre
63 rue de l'Hôpital
☎ 55 10 56
A comfortable 30-room
hotel with restaurant.

L'Abbaye St-Michel
Montée de St-Michel
☎ (86) 55 05 99
A tenth-century
Benedictine abbey in its
own parklands on the
Tonnerre heights. A
luxurious base from which
to tour Chablis. There are
only 7 rooms and 3
apartments, very comfort-
able and well furnished,
and quite expensive. The
young chef, Christian
Coudrette, who studied in
Avallon at Le Morvan has
created a classical menu.

COTE DE NUITS

Dijon
(21006 Dijon)

Les Caves de la Cloche
1 rue Devosge
☎ (80) 30 12 32
The exciting restaurant of
the totally refurbished
Hôtel de la Cloche.
Entrance in place d'Arcy.
The hotel has 80 very
comfortable, tasteful

rooms, and the restaurant
under chef Yves Jury is
already re-making a name
for itself.

Hôtel le Chapeau Rouge
5 rue Michelet
☎ (80) 30 28 10
Right in the centre of
town, but soundproofing
keeps out the noise. The
hotel has 33 rooms and

the service is excellent.
The restaurant of the same
name is a delight, and
possibly the finest eating-
place in Dijon.

Hôtel Frantel
22 blvd de la Marne
☎ (80)72 31 13
A modem 124-room air-
conditioned hotel
opposite the exhibition

centre. It has a pleasant garden, swimming pool and the restaurant Château Bourgogne, under chef René Villard, provides exciting and near perfect cuisine. The wine list is breathtaking.

Hôtel Central-Ibis
3 place Grangier
☎ (80) 30 44 00
In the centre of town; a comfortable 90-room hotel, with a fair to good restaurant.

Hôtel le Chambellan
92 rue Vannerie
☎ (80) 67 12 67
or (80) 32 28 37
A completely renovated hotel in the centre of town near the church of St Michael. It has 20 very comfortable rooms but no restaurant.

Grésill-Hôtel
16 ave. Raymond Poincaré
☎ (80) 71 10 56
A modern comfortable hotel with 49 sound-proofed rooms. It is near the exhibition centre, a short walk from the town centre, and has an English 'pub' and restaurant.

Le Chabrot
36 rue Monge
☎ (80) 30 69 61
A small wine-bar serving excellent fish dishes in its bistro-style restaurant. There is a wider menu if you wish, but available at lunchtime only.

La Chouette
1 rue de la Chouette
☎ (80) 30 18 10
In Old Dijon near the Duke's Palace. Very good

food and a menu which changes with the season to guarantee freshness of produce.

Le Pré aux Clercs et Trois Faisans
13 place de la Libération
☎ (80) 67 11 33
Run by the indomitable Mme Françoise Colin, this elegant restaurant can scale culinary heights, but it occasionally slips back to being just good.

Le Rallye
39 rue Chabot-Charny
☎ (80) 67 11 55
Run by Roger and Yvette Roncin, this offers the very best in restaurant philosophy, the best possible food at the most reasonable price possible. Very friendly.

Le Vinarium
23 place Bossuet
☎ (80) 30 36 23
Entered by a courtyard, this thirteenth-century cellar offers very good regional specialities, under the arches. An interesting wine list.

Restaurant Thibert
10 place Wilson
☎ (80) 67 74 64
A small restaurant in old Dijon. Typically Burgundian-size meals and the excellence of the quality shines through.

Les Gourmets
8 rue du Puits-de-Têt Marsannay-la-Côte, about 5 miles south-west of Dijon on the D122
☎ (80) 52 16 32
The 10-minute drive from Dijon is worth it, to try the very special dishes

created by Joel Pérreaut, accompanied by an excellent wine list.

Fixin
(21110 Côte d'Or)

Chez Jeannette
☎ (80) 52 45 49
In this tiny village two miles south of Marsannay is a delightful restaurant with 11 rooms.

Marsannay-la-Côte
(21160 Côte d'Or)

Novotel
☎ (80) 52 14 22
A modern, comfortable 124-room air-conditioned hotel on the N74. Simple restaurant for quick meals, and a good touring base.

Vosne-Romanée
(21220 Côte d'Or)

La Toute Petite Auberge
☎ (80) 61 02 03
On the N74; a striking roadside restaurant (it is painted red) offering very good food at very reasonable prices, and a fine wine list.

Gevrey-Chambertin
(21220 Côte d'Or)

Hôtel Grands Crus
routes des Grands Crus
☎ (80) 34 34 15
Quite a new hotel among the vineyards. It has 24 rooms and breakfast service, but no restaurant.

Les Terroirs
route Dijon
☎ 34 30 76
A very attractive, well-furbished 15-room hotel. No restaurant.

La Rôtisserie du
  Chambertin
rue de Chambertin
☎ (80) 34 33 20
A magnificent restaurant
run by Mme Céline Menne-
veau, reputed to be Bur-
gundy's top woman chef.
Her husband Pierre looks
after the guests while his
wife creates the most
remarkable dishes. It is
expensive but deservedly
so. The wines are good
and it is worth exploring

the house, if given the
chance, because it is a
mini-museum of
Burgundian wine-lore.

Nuits-St-George
(21700 Côte d'Or)

Hostellerie
Gentilhommière
  de Meuilley
(1¼ miles north-west of
  the town)
☎ (80) 61 12 06
A modernised 20-room

hotel, which makes a
good centre for touring.

Côte d'Or
1 rue Thurot
☎ (80) 61 06 10
A very comfortable 7-
room hotel and a res-
taurant which owner Jean
Crotet is much prouder of.
He smokes his own
salmon, his *magret* is excellent and he has a wine
list of local fine wines to
match.

COTE DE BEAUNE

Beaune
(21200 Côte d'Or)

Hôtel de la Poste
No.1 blvd Clémenceau
☎ (80) 22 08 11
A recently renovated hotel
with 21 rooms and 4
apartments, and very
attentive service. Owner
Marc Chevillot also
oversees the kitchens of
the La Poste restaurant
which have won a
deservedly high
reputation.

Hôtel Le Cep
27 rue Maufoux
☎ (80) 22 35 48
A luxurious seventeenth-
century 21-room hotel but
no restaurant.

Hôtel La Closerie
61 route d'Autun
☎ (80) 22 15 07
No restaurant but a
delightful 30-room hotel
to the south of Beaune on
the D973.

Hôtel de Bourgogne
ave. Charles de Gaulle
☎ (80) 22 22 00

A modern, attractive 120-
room hotel with heated
swimming pool, near the
main road on the outskirts
of the town.

Hôtel de la Cloche
42 place Madeleine
☎ (80) 22 22 75
Comfortable and friendly
16-room hotel with good,
but inexpensive
restaurant.

Hôtel Samotel
on the route d'Autun, a
  mile out of town to the
  south on the D793.
☎ (80) 22 35 55
A modern 62-room hotel
with 4 apartments,
comfortable and friendly,
and a tolerable restaurant.

Au Raisin de Bourgogne
164 Route de Dijon
☎ (80) 22 31 13
A restaurant away from the
centre which boasts
almost anything on its
menus except Burgundian
cuisine. The food is
creative and good, and
worth a visit just to try to

discover why the Gault
Millau entry is so critical!
There are also 12
reasonably-priced rooms.

Rôtisserie de la Paix
47 Faubourg Madeleine
☎ (80) 22 33 33
A former barn on the edge
of Beaune, in the capable
hands of young chef Jean-
Luc Dauphin whose
creations include many
memorable dishes. Very
good value for money, and
delicious desserts.

Chorey-lès-Beaune
(21200 Côte d'Or)

L'Ermitage de Corton
☎ (80) 22 05 28
Easy to find, 2½ miles
north-east of Beaune on
the N74 and 2222, and
signposted. Run by André
Parra and his wife
Monique. He is in the
kitchens and she
welcomes guests. A
perfect combination;
excellent food, generous
helpings and not too
expensive.

Savigny-lès-Beaune
(21420 Côte d'Or)

L'Ouvrée
☎ (80) 21 51 52
A comfortable 22-room
hotel set amongst the
vineyards, 3 miles from
Beaune on the D2. A
reasonable restaurant.

Bouilland
(21420 Côte d'Or)

Le Vieux Moulin
☎ (80) 21 51 16
A delightful setting, 9
miles north of Beaune on
the D2. The inn has 8
charming rooms, and it is
fair to say that patron
chef Jean Pierre Silva
shows considerable style
with his cuisine, but has
yet to find a consistency.

Chagny
(71150 Saône-et-Loire)

Hôtel Lameloise
36 place d'Armes
☎ (85) 87 08 85
A very elegant and com-
fortable 25-room hotel; it
is advisable to reserve to
avoid disappointment.
Excellent base for touring,
and a warm welcome
assured from Jean Lam-
eloise and son Jacques,
who runs the kitchen.
Many people, including
Alexis Liching consider
this the finest restaurant
in Burgundy.

Meursault
(21190 Côte d'Or)

Le Relais de la Diligence
☎ (80) 21 21 32
Close to the station, a
convenient lunch stop-
over, good food and
reasonable prices.

Auxey-Duresses
(21190 Côte d'Or)

La Crémaillère
☎ (80) 21 22 60
A very popular restaurant
5 miles south of Beaune;
worth making the effort to
visit. Specialities include
quenelles Dijonnaise, trout
in cream and *jambon
persillé*. M. Clerc serves a
host of other Burgundian
specialities with a spectacular wine list.

Vignolles
(21200 Côte d'Or)

Au Petit Truc
☎ 22 01 76
2^{1}/2 miles north east of
Beaune. Book a table and
enjoy the elegance of
both the surroundings and
the food. There is a terrace
for summer dining.

THE CHALONNAISE

Chalon-sur-Saône
(71100 Saône-et-Loire)

Royal Hôtel-Mapotel
8 rue du Port-Villiers
☎ (85) 48 15 86
A very comfortable hotel
with 43 rooms and 8 apartments in the centre of the
town. Good restaurant.

Hôtel St-Georges
32 ave. Jean-Jaurès
☎ (85) 48 27 05
Very handy, and close to
the station. 48 comfort-
able rooms and a fine restaurant run by Gérard
Choux, with chef Jean
Bouthenet. An exciting
menu utilizing the best
regional produce.

Hôtel St-Regis
22 blvd de la République
☎ (85) 48 07 28
Comfortable hotel with 40
soundproofed rooms and
good restaurant.

Hôtel St-Jean
24 quai Gambetta
☎ (85) 48 45 65
An attractive hotel beside
the Saône. There are 25
rooms, adequate rather
than comfortable, no
restaurant but breakfast
served.

Le Bourgogne
28 rue de Strasbourg
☎ (85) 48 89 18
One of the finest restaurants of the region run by

chef Yves Choux. The
very reasonable prices
make a detour worthwhile.

Givry
(71640 Saône-et-Loire)

La Halle
place Halle
☎ (85) 44 32 45
A very reasonable, family-
run, 10-room hotel with
good regional cooking.

Mercurey
(71640 Saône-et-Loire)

Le Val d'Or
Grande Rue
☎ (85) 47 13 70
A village hotel with 12
rooms and a restaurant

that has won widespread acclaim. Chef Jean-Claude Cogny has created his own dishes as well as offering the specialities of the region; rabbit, salmon and lamb are all excellent, as is the local Mercurey wine.

Rully
(71150 Saône-et-Loire)

Hôtel du Commerce
place Ste-Marie
☎ (85) 87 20 09
A cheap but comfortable village hotel with 16

rooms and a restaurant serving good, honest regional fare.

Tournus
(71700 Saône-et-Loire)

Le Rempart
ave. Gambetta, on the N6
☎ (85) 51 10 56
A new hotel with 30 attractive rooms, air conditioned, some with fine views. The restaurant is already firmly established and famed for its elegance, charm and food prepared by Christian Guichard.

Le Sauvage
place du Champ-de-Mars
☎ (85) 51 14 45
32 comfortable, reasonably-priced rooms and a good restaurant striving to do better.

Greuze
4 rue Albert-Thibaudet
☎ (85) 51 13 52
Jean Cucloux is a master chef and one of the finest in Burgundy. His cooking is modern, exciting and always excellent. Pricey but worth it.

THE MACONNAIS

Crêches-sur-Saône
(71680 Saône-et-Loire)

Hostellerie du Château de la Barge
☎ (85) 37 12 04
An interesting 28-room hotel in parkland, owned by M. Edelli who also makes his own wines. Good restaurant and a chance to sample the *patron vigneron's* skill.

Cluny
(71250 Saône-et-Loire)

Hôtel Moderne
Pont-de l'Etang
☎ (85) 59 05 65
A very attractive, refurbished hotel on the river. The 15 rooms are comfortable, the service attentive and the restaurant, under young Patrick Deschamps, an increasing delight.

Bourgogne
place Abbaye
☎ (85) 59 00 58

A fine 18-room hotel with lovely views to the abbey, and a very good restaurant.

Abbaye
ave. de la Gare
☎ (85) 59 11 14
Another very comfortable 18-room hotel, prices reasonable and with a good restaurant.

Fuissé
(71960 Saône-et-Loire)

Château d'Igé
☎ (85) 33 33 99
A luxurious hotel converted from an ancient château. The fortifications were added in the thirteenth century. It stands imposingly among the vineyards at the junctions of the D85 and D134. 11 massive, very comfortable rooms, fair restaurant.

Mâcon
(71000 Saône-et-Loire)

Frantel
26 rue de Coubertin
☎ (85) 38 28 06
A modern 63-room hotel, by the river but close to the town centre. Its restaurant, Le St Vincent, is very good in the capable hands of Michel Thévenet.

Sofitel
Aire de St-Alban
8¹/2 miles to the north and reached by either the A6 or N6.
☎ (85) 33 19 00
A modern 96-room hotel with air conditioning, heated pool and a fair restaurant. Very close to the motorway so suitable for an overnight stay if you are in a hurry, but well soundproofed.

Hôtel Bellevue
416 quai Lamartine
☎ (85) 38 05 07
A very comfortable 31-room soundproofed hotel

on the river, with a restaurant noted for its flair and creativity.

Hôtel Terminus
91 rue Victor Hugo
☎ (85) 39 17 11
A comfortable medium range hotel with 41 rooms and reasonable restaurant.

Hôtel Genève
1 rue Bigonnet
☎ (85) 38 18 10
A conveniently-sited 63-room hotel with good restaurant.

Replonges
(01750 Ain)

La Huchette
☎ (85) 31 03 55

A very attractive restaurant and small 12-room hotel, run by Mme Marie-Yolande Gualdière. Set in its own grounds with a heated pool; everything about the establishment, service, food, and welcome is delightful.

St-Amour-Bellevue
(71570 Saône-et-Loire)

Chez Jean Pierre
☎ (85) 37 41 26
A very attractive restaurant, 7 1/2 miles from Mâcon.

Auberge du Paradis
☎ (85) 37 10 26

A small, reasonably-priced inn with fair restaurant.

Solutré-Pouilly
(71960 Saône-et-Loire)

Le Relais de Solutré
☎ (85) 35 80 81
A comfortable 30-room hotel with fine restaurant.

Thoissey
(01140 Thoissey)

Au Chapon Fin
rue du Champ-de-Foire
☎ (85) 04 04 74
A very agreeable restaurant with terrace, and an old hotel with modern annexe to give 25 comfortable rooms overlooking attractive gardens.

The Vineyards of Burgundy

Note: all these vineyards are very well signposted; there should be no difficulty in finding them. Many are open by appointment only, so telephone before departing.

YONNE

Beines
(89800 Chablis)

Louis Bellet   TW
☎ (86) 42 41 66

Robert Francelet   TW
☎ (86) 41 42 84

Alain Geoffrey   TW
☎ (86) 42 43 76

Sylvain Mosnier   TW
☎ (86) 42 43 96

Robert & Jean-Marie
Naulin   TW
☎ (86) 42 40 47

Daniel Roblot   TW
☎ (86) 42 43 00

Béru
(89700 Tonnerre)

Denis Bégue   TW
☎ (86) 75 90 58

Jacques Bégue   TW
☎ (86) 75 92 28

Bleigny-le-Carreau
(89230 Pontigny)

Michel Callement   TW
☎ (86) 41 81 52

Brienon (89210)

J. Sourdillat   TW
☎ (86) 56 12 63

Chablis (89800)

Josselin Bacheroy   TW
☎ (86) 42 14 30

Felix Besson and son   TW
☎ (86) 42 11 00

Simon Billaud   TW
☎ (86) 42 10 33

Domaine Pascal
Bouchard   TW
☎ (86) 42 18 64

Domaine Jean Collet
and son   TW
☎ (86) 42 11 93

Marius Collet   TW
☎ (86) 42 18 24

Coopérative de Chablis TW
La Chablisienne
☎ (86) 42 11 24

René and Vincent
Dauvissat   TW
☎ (86) 42 11 58

Domaine La Moutonne TW
A. Long Depaquit
☎ (86) 42 11 13

Paul Droin-Baudoin   TW
☎ (86) 42 12 83

Marcel Droin-Mary   TW
☎ (86) 42 10 74

Droin and son   TW
☎ (86) 42 16 78

Marcel Duplessis   TW
☎ (86) 42 10 35

William Fèvre   TW
Domaine de la Maladière
☎ (86) 42 12 51

Maurice Fèvre   TW
☎ (86) 42 11 21

Raoul Gautherin   TW
☎ (86) 42 11 86

Domaine Laroche   TW
☎ (86) 42 14 30

Jukes Lavens   TW
☎ (86) 42 10 24

Louis Michel and son   TW
☎ (86) 42 10 24

Maurice Michel   TW
☎ (86) 42 14 37

Christian Mignard   TW
☎ (86) 42 12 27

Jean Moreau and son   TW
☎ (86) 42 40 70

Roger Moreau   TW
☎ (86) 42 14 83

Louis Pinson   TW
☎ (86) 42 10 26

Denis Race   TW
☎ (86) 42 45 87

François & J-Marie
Raveneau   TW
☎ (86) 42 11 80

Guy Robin   TW
☎ (86) 42 12 63

Michel Robin   TW
☎ (86) 42 17 40

André Rogie   TW
☎ (86) 42 12 20

Domaine Rottiers-   TW
Clotilde
☎ (86) 42 41 37

Domaine Marcel Servin TW
☎ (86) 42 12 94

Jean-Pierre Tricon   TW
☎ (86) 42 11 60

R=red wine   W=white wine   P=rosé wine   S=sparkling wine

Domaine de Varoux   TW
☎ (86) 42 10 37

Domaine Robert
   Vocoret and son   TW
☎ (86) 42 12 53

Chitry
(89530 St-Bris-le-Vineux)

(All white wines)

Noël Aubron   TW
☎ (86) 41 41 90

Léon Berthelot   TW
☎ (86) 41 04 14

Jean-Claude Biot   TW
☎ (86) 41 42 79

Robert Bourrat   TW
☎ (86) 41 42 24

Aimé Chalmeau   TW
☎ (86) 41 40 17

Edmond Chalmeau   TW
☎ (86) 41 42 09

Marcel Chalmeau   TW
☎ (86) 41 42 41

Michel Colbois   TW
☎ (86) 41 40 23

Paul Colbois   TW
☎ (86) 41 40 87

Jean Demeaux   TW
☎ (86) 41 40 14

Gilbert Giraudon   TW
☎ (86) 41 40 03

Joel Griffe   TW
☎ (86) 41 41 06

Noël Joudelat   TW
☎ (86) 41 42 03

Michel Morin   TW
☎ (86) 41 41 61

Marcel Pichon   TW
☎ (86) 41 42 51

Roger Race   TW
☎ (86) 41 41 32

Régis Richoux   TW
☎ (86) 41 40 47

Henri Total   TW
☎ (86) 41 40 89

Roland Vire   TW
☎ (86) 41 42 74

Coulanges-la-Vineuse
(89580)

(All red wines)

Maxime August   TR
☎ (86) 42 22 70

Michel Bernard   TR
☎ (86) 42 25 72

Debaix brothers   TR
☎ (86) 42 20 97

Henri Dupuis   TR
☎ (86) 42 22 77

Raymond Dupuis   TR
☎ (86) 42 25 20

Henri Hervin   TR
☎ (86) 42 28 49

Christian Hervin   TR
☎ (86) 42 27 22

Serge Hugot   TR
☎ (86) 42 21 95

Maurice Ledoux   TR

Pierre Ledoux   TR
☎ (86) 42 30 09

André Martin and son   TR
☎ (86) 42 22 73

Pierre Vigreux   TR
☎ (86) 42 22 39

Courgis
(89800 Chablis)

(Chablis wines)

Gilbert Race   TW
☎ (86) 41 41 09

Jean Race   TW
☎ (86) 41 42 78

Irancy
(89290 Champs-sur-
Yonne)

(All vineyards produce red
wine but some also
produce a little rosé.)

Léon Bienvenu   TR
☎ (86) 42 26 10

Jack Bourguignat   TR
☎ (86) 42 26 92

Bernard Cantin   TR
☎ (86) 42 21 96

René Charriat   TR
☎ (86) 42 22 21

Robert Colinot   TR
☎ (86) 42 20 76

Germain Darles   TR
☎ (86) 42 20 94

Gabriel Delaloge   TR
☎ (86) 42 21 99

Michel Garlan   TR
☎ (86) 42 24 68

François Givaudin   TR
☎ (86) 42 20 67

Lucien Joudelat   TR
☎ (86) 42 31 46

André Melou   TR
☎ (86) 42 20 11

Lionel Meslin   TR
☎ (86) 42 31 62

René Meslin   TR
☎ (86) 42 20 75

Robert Meslin   TR
☎ (86) 42 31 43

T=tasting   E=English spoken   G=guided tours   C=château/building to visit

Yves Navarre TR
☎ (86) 42 31 00

Jean Podor TR
☎ (86) 42 26 85

Patrick Podor TR
☎ (86) 42 26 82

Daniel Quintard TR
☎ (86) 42 22 92

Daniel Renaud TR
☎ (86) 42 27 39

Jean Renaud TR
☎ (86) 42 22 67

Pierre Rey TR
☎ (86) 42 22 71

Jean-Claude Richoux TR
☎ (86) 42 21 60

Maligny
(89800 Chablis)

(Chablis producer)

Domaine de l'Eglantière TR
☎ (86) 47 44 49

St-Bris-le-Vineux
(89530)

GAEC Bersan TW
20 rue de l'Eglise
☎ (86) 53 33 73

Yvon Daudier TW
3 rue Bienvenu-Martin
☎ (86) 53 30 39

Robert Defrance TW
5 rue du Four
☎ (86) 53 33 82

Michel Esclavy TW
13 rue de Grisy
☎ (86) 53 31 14

Hughes Goisot TW
30 rue Bienvenu-Martin
☎ (86) 53 32 72

Serge Goisot TW
8 rue de Gouaix
☎ (86) 53 32 15

Jean Guimot TW
5 route de Champs
☎ (86) 53 32 84

Maurice Jouby TW
5 rue Dorée
☎ (86) 53 30 76

Bernard Marmagne TW
11 rue Haute
☎ (86) 53 31 24

Jacques Mazeau TW
4 rue de la Croix
☎ (86) 53 31 19

Marcel Persenot TW
1 rue des Orfèvres
☎ (86) 53 53 77

Guy Persenot TW
8 rue de la Croix
☎ (86) 53 33 27

Pierre et Jean Persenot TW
☎ (86) 53 30 52

Emile Petit TW
15 rue de Gouaix
☎ (86) 53 33 27

William Pinon TW
2 rue des Bougeilles
☎ (86) 53 31 88

Claude Seguin TW
rue Haute
☎ (86) 53 37 39

SICA du Vignoble TW
Auxerrois
5 quai de l'Yonne
Bailly-St-Bris
☎ (86) 53 34 00
Open: weekdays and
public holidays 2-5.30pm

André Sorin and son TW
7-8 route des Champs
☎ (86) 53 33 59

Michel Sorin TW
rue de Paris
☎ (86) 53 33 67

Luc Sorin TW
rue de Paris
☎ (86) 53 36 87

Jean-Paul Tabit TW
2 rue Dorée
☎ (86) 53 83 83

COTE DE BEAUNE

Aloxe-Corton
(21920)

Château de Corton-André
P.A. André TRW
☎ (80) 26 40 00

Domaine Lequin- TRW
Roussot
☎ (80) 20 61 46

Mestre and son
☎ (80) 20 60 11

Société d'Elévage TRW
et de Diffusion des
Grands Vins
☎ (80) 26 41 82

Auxey-Duresses
(21190 Meursault)

Domaine Bernard TRW
Delagrange
☎ (80) 21 22 72

Beaune
(21200)

Bidot-Bourgogne TR
☎ (80) 22 25 46

R=red wine   W=white wine   P=rosé wine   S=sparkling wine

Maison Bouchard
and son — TR
36 rue Ste-Marguérite
☎ (80) 22 07 67

Maison Bouchard
and son — TR
(at the Château)
☎ (80) 22 14 41

Calvet — TR
blvd Perpreuil
☎ (80) 22 06 32

Cauvard and son — TR
route de Savigny
☎ (80) 22 29 77

Caves des Batisines — TR
place Madeleine
☎ (80) 22 09 05

Caves des Hautes-Côtes — TR
route de Pommard
☎ (80) 24 63 12

Chanson and son — TR
10 rue Paul Chanson
☎ (80) 22 33 00

Domaine du Château
de Meursault — TR
☎ (80) 21 22 98

Bertrand Darviot — TR
☎ (80) 21 22 83

Bernard Delagrange — TR
☎ (80) 21 22 72

Jaboulet Vercherre — TR
5 rue Colbert
☎ (80) 22 25 22
Closed weekends.

Jaffelin Brothers — TR
2 rue Paradis
☎ (80) 22 12 49
Closed weekends.

Joliot and son — TR
☎ (80) 22 37 98

Gaulin Mallard — TR
28 rue S. Chauvelot
☎ (80) 22 18 34

Pierre Menard — TR
6 rue de l'Hôtel Dieu
☎ (80) 22 14 25

Albert Morot — TR
12 rue Poissonerie
☎ (80) 22 51 56

Patriarche and son — TR
☎ (80) 26 01 73

Domaine Jacques Prieur — TR
☎ (80) 21 23 85

Rebourgeon-Mignotte — TR
☎ (80) 22 29 33

Rebourgeon-Muré — TR
☎ (80) 22 75 39

Reine Pedauque — TR
☎ (80) 22 33 11

**Chassagne-
Montrachet**
(21190 Meursault)

Jacques and Vincent
Girardin — TRW
☎ (80) 20 61 95

Domaine Lequin-
Roussot — TRW
☎ (80) 20 61 46

Domaine Jacques
Prieur — TRW
☎ (80) 21 23 85

Prieur-Brunet — TRW
☎ (80) 20 62 39
Closed weekends.

Chorey-lès-Beaune
(21200 Beaune)

Arnoux and son — TR
☎ (80) 22 30 72

Domaine Goud de
Beaupuis — TR
☎ (80) 22 20 63

Jean-Ernest Maldant — TR
☎ (80) 22 11 94

Corpeau
(21190 Meursault)

Bernard Fagot — TR
☎ (80) 21 30 24

Echevronne
(21240 Savigny-lès-
Beaune)

Jean Ferry — TRW
☎ (80) 21 52 51

Bernard Jacob — TRW
☎ (80) 21 52 98

Dominique Jacob — TRW
☎ (80) 21 55 58

Hubert Jacob — TRW
☎ (80) 21 50 04

Domaine Lucien
Jacob — TRW
☎ (80) 21 52 15

Jacob-Lambert and
son — TRW
☎ (80) 21 50 04

Ladoix-Sérrigny
(21550)

P. A. André — TRW
☎ (80) 21 41 10

Bouchard and son — TRW
☎ (80) 22 14 41

Capitain-Gagnerot — TRW
☎ (80) 21 41 36

Edmond Cornu — TRW
☎ (80) 21 40 79

Michel Mallard and
son — TRW
☎ (80) 21 40 64

André Nudant and son — TRW
☎ (80) 21 40 82

La Rochepot
(21340 Nolay)

T=tasting   E=English spoken   G=guided tours   C=château/building to visit

Jean-Noel Bazin   TRW
☎ (80) 21 75 49

Michel Billard   TRW
☎ (80) 21 71 84

Centre Coopérative
de Diffusion   TRW
Château de la Rochepot
Open: daily 15 September-
1 July.

René Chevillard   TRW
☎ (80) 21 72 46

Denis Fouquerand   TRW
☎ (80) 21 71 59

Marc Fouquerand   TRW
☎ (80) 21 72 80

Charles Labry   TRW
☎ (80) 21 71 17

Maurice Masson   TRW
☎ (80) 21 72 42

Michel Serveau   TRW
☎ (80) 21 70 24

Domaine Rondot   TRW
☎ (80) 21 70 24

Meloisey
(21950)

NB: Many of the phone
numbers for these
vineyards are the same.
This is because a central
information service for
appointments operates.

Denis Carré   TRW
☎ (80) 26 02 21
Open: by appointment.

Alexandre Devaux   TRW
☎ (80) 26 00 58
Open: by appointment.

Léon Gérard   TRW
☎ (80) 26 02 19
Open: by appointment.

Guillemard-Dupont
and son   TRW
☎ (80) 26 01 11
Open: by appointment.

Guillemard-Pothier   TRW
☎ (80) 26 01 11
Open: by appointment.

Mazilly and son   TRW
☎ (80) 26 01 34
Open: by appointment.

Georges Parigot
and son   TRW
☎ (80) 26 01 73
Open: by appointment.

Phillippe Trenet   TRW
☎ (80) 26 01 11
Open: by appointment.

Meursault
(21190)

Bouchard and son   TW
☎ (80) 21 14 41

Domaine du Château
de Meursault   TW
☎ (80) 21 22 98

Bertrand Darviot   TW
☎ (80) 21 22 83

Domaine Delagrange
Bernard   TW
☎ (80) 21 22 72

Guillemard-Dupont
and son   TW
☎ (80) 22 49 19
Open: by appointment.

Guillemard-Pothier   TW
☎ (80) 26 01 11
Open: by appointment.

Le Manoir
Meursaultien   TW
☎ (80) 21 21 83

Mazilly and son   TW
☎ (80) 26 01 34
Open: by appointment.

Comte de Moucheron   TW
Château de Meursault
☎ (80) 21 22 98

Georges Parigot and
son   TW
☎ (80) 26 01 73
Open: by appointment.

Prieur-Brunet   TW
☎ (80) 20 62 39
Closed weekdays.

Domaine Jacques-
Prieur   TW
☎ (80) 21 35 85

Monthélie
(21190 Meursault)

Denis Boussey   TR
☎ (80) 21 21 23

Les Caves de Monthélie TR
☎ (80) 21 22 63

Paul Garaudet   TR
☎ (80) 21 18 78

Nantoux
(21190 Meursault)

Joliot and son   TRW
☎ (80) 26 00 30
or (80) 26 01 44
Open: by appointment.

Pernand-Vergelesses
(21420 Savigny-lès
Beaunes)

Chanson and son   TRW
10 rue Paul Chanson
Beaune
☎ (80) 22 33 00

Pommard
(21630)

Michel Arcelain   TR
☎ (80) 22 13 50

Jean Allexant   TR
☎ (80) 26 60 77

R=red wine   W=white wine   P=rosé wine   S=sparkling wine

Bidot-Bourgogne TR
☎ (80) 22 25 46

Billard-Gonnet TR
☎ (80) 22 17 33

Domaine Bernard
Delagrange TR
☎ (80) 21 22 72

Alexandre Devaux TR
☎ (80) 26 00 58
Open: by appointment.

Frotey-Poifol TR
☎ (80) 22 47 59

Domaine Gaunoux TR
☎ (80) 22 18 52

Guillemard-Dupont
and son TR
☎ (80) 26 00 47
Open: by appointment.

Lahaye and son TR
☎ (80) 22 04 01

Domaine Laplanche TR
Château de Pommard
☎ (80) 22 07 99

Domaine R. Launay TR
☎ (80) 22 12 23

Domaine Lequin-
Roussot TR
☎ (80) 20 61 46

Jacques Parent TR
☎ (80) 22 15 08

Domaine Pothier-
Rieusset TR
☎ (80) 22 00 27

Domaine Prieur-Brunet TR
☎ (80) 20 62 39
Closed weekends.

Rebourgeon-Mignotte TR
☎ (80) 22 29 33

Rebourgeon-Muré TR
☎ (80) 22 75 39

Virely-Arcelain TR
☎ (80) 22 19 71

Virely-Rougeot TR
☎ (80) 22 34 34

Puligny-Montrachet
(21190 Meursault)

NB All vineyards open to
visits by appointment.

Bernard Belicard TW
☎ (80) 21 31 25

Stanislas Bizkot TW
☎ (80) 21 33 39

Société Carillon TW
Louis and son
☎ (80) 21 30 34

Robert Carillon TW
☎ (80) 21 30 75

Christian Chavy TW
☎ (80) 21 33 99

Gérard Chavy TW
☎ (80) 21 31 47

Louis Chavy TW
☎ (80) 21 31 39

Domaine Henry Clerc TW
☎ (80) 21 32 74

David Comille TW
☎ (80) 21 30 18

Dupard the eldest TW
☎ (80) 21 32 85

Phillippe Garaudet TW
☎ (80) 21 13 18

Gérard Guérin TW
☎ (80) 21 30 90

Marc Jomain TW
☎ (80) 21 30 48

Domaine Leflaive TW
☎ (80) 21 30 13

Roland Maroslavac TW
☎ (80) 21 31 23

Stephan Maroslavac TW
☎ (80) 21 33 01

Georges Meney TW
☎ (80) 21 33 21

Henri Moroni TW
☎ (80) 21 30 48

Jean Pascal TW
☎ (80) 21 32 07

GAEC Paul Pernot TW
☎ (80) 21 32 35

Domaine Jacques Prieur TW
☎ (80) 21 23 85

Jacky Riger TW
☎ (80) 21 31 16

Domaine Sauzet TW
☎ (80) 21 32 10

St-Aubin
(21190 Meursault)

Jean-Claude Bachelet TRW
☎ (80) 21 31 01

Marc Colin TRW
☎ (80) 21 30 43

Jean Lamy and sons TRW
☎ (80) 21 30 97

SCE André Moingeon TRW
and son
☎ (80) 21 30 67

Henri Prudhon and
son TRW
☎ (80) 21 31 33

Domaine Roux Père
and son TRW
☎ (80) 21 32 92
or (80) 21 34 09

Gérard Thomas TRW
☎ (80) 21 32 57
or (80) 21 31 98

Michel Lamanthe TRW
☎ (80) 21 33 23

T=tasting E=English spoken G=guided tours C=château/building to visit

St-Romain
(21190 Meursault)

Barolet-Pernot TRW
☎ (80) 21 20 88

Henri Buisson TRW
☎ (80) 21 22 22

Domaine de Carran
Naudin Grivelet TRW
☎ (80) 21 21 36

Domaine Bernard
Delagrange TRW
☎ (80) 21 22 72

Bernard Fèvre TRW
☎ (80) 21 23 04

Charles Rapet TRW
☎ (80) 21 22 93

René Thevenin TRW
☎ (80) 21 23 63

Santenay
(21590)

Domaine de l'Abbaye TRW
Louis Clair
☎ (80) 20 61 68

Bardollet-Terret TRW
☎ (80) 20 60 61

Jean Battault TRW
☎ (80) 87 06 64

Adrien Belland TRW
☎ (80) 20 61 90

Domaine Belland
Joseph TRW
☎ (80) 20 61 13

Chapelle and son TRW
☎ (80) 20 60 09

Château de la
Charrière TRW
Domaine Jean Girardin
☎ (80) 20 61 95

André Cherrier TRW
☎ (80) 20 63 71

Michel and Denis
Clair TRW
☎ (80) 20 62 55

Michel Delorme TRW
☎ (80) 20 63 41

Michel Drain TRW
☎ (80) 20 63 12

René Fleurot TRW
☎ (80) 20 61 15

Jacques Girardin TRW
☎ (80) 20 61 95

Vincent Girardin TRW
☎ (80) 20 61 95

Jesiaume and son TRW
☎ (80) 20 60 03

Joly and son TRW
☎ (80) 20 60 07

Hervé de Lavoreille TRW
☎ (80) 20 61 57

Domaine Lequin-
Roussot TRW
☎ (80) 20 61 46

Mestre and son TRW
☎ (80) 20 60 11

Jean Moreau TRW
☎ (80) 20 61 79

Lucien Muzard TRW
☎ (80) 20 61 85

Hervé Olivier TRW
☎ (80) 20 61 35

Domaine Guy Prieur TRW
☎ (80) 21 23 92
Closed weekends.

Domaine St-Michel TRW
☎ (80) 20 60 27

Savigny-lès-Beaune
(21420)

P.A. André TRW
Château d'Aloxe-Corton
☎ (80) 21 40 10

Bouchard and son TRW
☎ (80) 22 14 41

Chanson and son TRW
☎ (80) 22 33 00

Domaine du Château
de Meursault TRW
☎ (80) 21 22 98

Laurent-Gauthier TRW
☎ (80) 21 52 62

Albert Morot TRW
☎ (80) 22 35 39

Pierre Petit Jean
and son TRW
☎ (80) 21 51 85

Réserve des Caves de
la Reine Pedauque TRW
☎ (80) 21 42 98

Volnay
(21190 Meursault)

Bidot-Bourgogne TR
☎ (80) 22 25 46

Bitouzet and son TR
☎ (80) 22 21 20

Henri Boillot TR
☎ (80) 22 01 40

Pierre Boillot and son TR
☎ (80) 22 18 26

Emile Bouley TR
☎ (80) 22 25 74

Jean-Marc Bouley TR
☎ (80) 22 59 79

Pierre Bouley and son TR
☎ (80) 22 34 22

Domaine François
Buffet TR
☎ (80) 22 18 96

R=red wine   W=white wine   P=rosé wine   S=sparkling wine

Valéry Carre TR	Bernard Glantenay TR
☎ (80) 22 30 61	☎ (80) 22 23 25

Valéry Carre TR
☎ (80) 22 30 61

Domaine Bernard TR
Delagrange
☎ 21 (80) 22 72

Henri Delagrange TR
☎ (80) 22 14 84

Domaine du Château TR
de Meursault
☎ (80) 21 22 98

Domaine de la TR
Pousse d'Or
☎ (80) 22 10 73

Domaine Prieur-Brunet TR
☎ (80) 20 62 39
Closed weekends.

Bernard Glantenay TR
☎ (80) 22 23 25

Georges Glantenay TR
☎ (80) 22 04 70

Michel Lafarge TR
☎ (80) 22 04 70

François Muré TR
☎ (80) 22 33 12

Michel Pont TR
☎ (80) 22 06 61

Domaine Jacques Prieur TR
☎ (80) 21 23 85

Rebourgeon-Mignotte TR
☎ (80) 22 29 33

Rebourgeon-Muré TR
☎ (80) 22 75 39

Rossignol brothers TR
☎ (80) 22 30 41

Roger Rossignol TR
☎ (80) 22 19 47

Régis Rossignol TR
☎ (80) 22 24 71

Bernard Vaudoisey TR
☎ (80) 22 21 69

Jean Vaudoisey TR
☎ (80) 22 16 39

Pierre Vaudoisey TR
☎ (80) 22 56 73

M. and J. Voillot TR
☎ (80) 22 34 30

THE PLAIN OF BEAUNE

Montagny-lès-Beaune

Michel Bouzereau TR
☎ (80) 22 20 56

Ste-Marie-la-Blanche
(21200 Beaune)

Jean Allexant TR
☎ (80) 26 60 77

Cave Coopérative TR
Viticole de Ste-Marie
☎ (80) 26 60 60

Merceuil
(21190 Meursault)

Allexant and son TW
☎ (80) 21 46 86

COTE DE NUITS

Arcenant
(21700 Nuits-St-Georges)

André Hudelot TRW
☎ (80) 61 07 61

Jean-Louis Joannet TRW
☎ (80) 61 13 07

Gustave Trapet TRW
☎ (80) 61 02 37

Jean-Claude Trapet TRW
☎ (80) 61 25 05

Alain Verdet TRW
☎ (80) 61 08 10

Chambolle-Musigny
(21770)

Bouchard and son TR
☎ (80) 22 14 41

Pierre Julien-Hudelot TR
☎ (80) 62 86 87

Domaine Jacques Prieur TR
☎ (80) 21 23 85

Comblanchien (21830)

A. Clavelier TR
☎ (80) 62 94 11

Armand Julien TR
☎ (80) 62 94 08

Roger Trapet TR
☎ (80) 62 94 40

Corgoloin
(21700 Nuits-St-Georges)

Domaine Fribourg TR
Marcel and Bernard
Fribourg
☎ (80) 62 91 74

Domaine de la Poulette TR
☎ (80) 62 98 02

Couchey
(21160 Marsannay-la-
Côte)

Clemancey brothers TRW
☎ (80) 52 23 62

Derey brothers TRW
☎ (80) 52 15 04

Daniel Fournier TRW
☎ (80) 52 18 38

T=tasting E=English spoken G=guided tours C=château/building to visit

Roger Fournier TRW
☎ (80) 52 24 75

Jacques Kohut TRW
☎ (80) 52 44 50

Michel Robert TRW
☎ (80) 52 44 27

Siruge and son TRW
☎ (80) 52 12 25

Jean Tardy TRW
☎ (80) 34 35 28

Fixin
(21220 Gevrey-
Chambertin)

André Bart TR
☎ (80) 52 12 09

Henri Bergerot TR
☎ (80) 52 47 28

Maison Berthaut TR
☎ (80) 52 45 48

Robert Bordet TR
☎ (80) 52 84 53

Ernest Bourgeot TR
☎ (80) 52 45 95

René Bouvier TR
☎ (80) 52 21 37

Jean Charlopin TR
☎ (80) 52 29 43

Michel Charlopin TR
☎ (80) 52 34 30

Roger Charlopin TR
☎ (80) 52 16 04

Clemencey brothers TR
☎ (80) 52 23 62

André Coillot TR
☎ (80) 52 12 51

Bernard Coillot TR
☎ (80) 52 17 59

Camille Crusserey TR
☎ (80) 52 45 54

Paul Debruyère TR
☎ (80) 52 84 50

René Defrance and son TR
☎ (80) 52 47 21

Derey brothers TR
☎ (80) 52 15 04

Jacques Durand TR
☎ (80) 52 45 28

Daniel Fournier TR
☎ (80) 52 18 38

Roger Fournier TR
☎ (80) 52 24 75

Jean-Pierre Guyard TR
☎ (80) 52 12 43

Lucien Guyard TR
☎ (80) 52 14 46

Huguenot and son TR
☎ (80) 52 35 38

Charles Quillardet TR
☎ (80) 34 10 26

Société Civile du Clos TR
St Louis
☎ (80) 34 31 11
or (80) 52 45 51

Gevrey-Chambertin
(21220)

Pierre Bernollin TR
☎ (80) 34 36 12

Bouchard and son TR
☎ (80) 22 14 41

André Chanceaux TR
☎ (80) 34 32 36

Derey brothers TR
☎ (80) 52 15 04

Phillippe Leclerc TR
☎ (80) 34 30 72

Naigeon-Chauveau
and son TR
☎ (80) 34 30 30

Domaine Jacques Prieur TR
☎ (80) 21 23 85

Charles Quillardet TR
☎ (80) 34 10 26

Gérard Quivy TR
☎ (80) 34 31 02

Siruge and son TR
☎ (80) 52 12 25

Société Civile du Domaine
de la Romanée-Conti TR
☎ (80) 61 04 57

Marsannay-la-Côte
(21160)

Charles Audoin TRP
7 rue de la Boulotte
☎ (80) 52 34 24

André Bart TRP
24 rue de Mazy
☎ (80) 52 12 09

Régis Bouvier TRP
☎ (80) 52 31 37

Cave Coopérative des TRP
Grands Vins Rosés
21 rue de Mazy
Closed Sunday.
☎ (80) 52 15 14

Bruno Clair TRP
3 rue de la Maladière
☎ (80) 52 28 95

Domaine Claire-Dau TRP
5 rue du Vieux Collège
☎ (80) 52 15 58

André Coillot TRP
14 rue de la Boulotte
☎ (80) 52 12 51

Bernard Coillot TRP
31 rue du Château
☎ (80) 52 17 59

Jean Collottee TRP
44 rue de Mazy
☎ (80) 52 24 34

Derey brothers TRP
☎ (80) 52 15 04

R=red wine W=white wine P=rosé wine S=sparkling wine

Bernard Drouin TRP
12 rue Paul Bert
(at Chenove)
☎ (80) 52 31 58

J.-L. Fougeray TRP
44 rue de Mazy
☎ (80) 52 21 12

Jean Fournier TRP
39 rue du Château
☎ (80) 52 24 38

Daniel Gallois TRP
83 route de Beaune
☎ (80) 52 26 66

Alain Guyard TRP
10-12 rue du Puits de Têt
☎ (80) 52 14 46

Jean-Pierre Guyard TRP
2 rue du Vieux College
☎ (80) 52 12 43

Lucien Guyard TRP
10 rue du Puits de Tét
☎ (80) 52 14 46

Albert Guyot TRP
39 rue de Mazy
☎ (80) 52 20 53

Olivier Guyot TRP
39 rue de Mazy
☎ (80) 52 20 53

Huguenot and son TRP
16 ruelle du Caron
☎ (80) 52 35 38

Charles Quillardet TRP
route Nationale at Gevrey-
Chambertin
☎ (80) 34 10 26

Morey-St-Denis
(21740)

Domaine Arlaud TRW
☎ (80) 34 32 65

Alain Michelot TRW
☎ (80) 61 14 46

Jean Taupenot TRW
☎ (80) 34 35 24

Nuits-St-Georges
(21700)

Jean Chauvenet TRW
☎ (80) 61 00 72

Marcel & Hubert TRW
Chauvenet
☎ (80) 61 09 65

Georges Chevillon TRW
and son
☎ (80) 61 12 66

Maurice and Robert TRW
Chevillon
☎ (80) 61 06 25

Georges Chicotot TRW
☎ (80) 61 19 33

André Chopin TRW
☎ (80) 61 87 36

Guy Deufouleur TRW
☎ (80) 61 07 07

Durieux and son TRW
☎ (80) 61 14 24

Joseph Faiveley TRW
☎ (80) 61 14 55
Closed Sundays.

Louis Fleurot TRW
☎ (80) 61 15 86

Christian Gavignet TRW
☎ (80) 61 16 04

Michel Gavignet TRW
☎ (80) 61 12 78

Domaine H. Gouges TRW
☎ (80) 61 04 40

Rémy and Albert TRW
Jafflin
☎ (80) 61 12 98

Domaine Machard TRW
de Gramont
☎ (80) 61 16 79

Henri Lamy TRW
☎ (80) 61 10 21

Domaine Lequin- TRW
Roussot
☎ (80) 20 61 46

Paul Henri Magnien TRW
☎ (80) 61 06 07

Alain Michelot TRW
☎ (80) 61 14 46

Morin and son TRW
☎ (80) 61 05 11

Henri and Gilles TRW
Remoriquet
☎ (80) 61 08 17

Réne Tardy and son TRW
☎ (80) 61 20 50

Prémeaux-Prissey
(21700 Nuits-St-Georges)

Bertrand Ambroise TR
☎ (80) 62 30 19

Jules Belin TR
☎ (80) 62 30 98

Bernard Chezeaux TR
☎ (80) 62 30 63

Jean-Jacques Confuron TR
☎ (80) 62 31 08

Robert Dubois and son TR
☎ (80) 62 30 61

Michel Dupasquier TR
☎ (80) 62 30 62

Roger Dupasquier
and son TR
☎ (80) 52 31 19

André Gros TR
☎ (80) 62 31 06

Bernard Mugneret TR
☎ (80) 62 31 12

Alain Pelletier and son TR
☎ (80) 62 30 24

T=tasting   E=English spoken   G=guided tours   C=château/building to visit

Daniel Rion and son   TR
☎ (80) 62 31 10

Villers-la-Faye
(21700 Nuits-St-Georges)

Domaine Fribourg   TRW
Marcel and Bernard
Fribourg
☎ (80) 62 91 74

Vosne-Romanée
(21670)

Robert Arnoux   TR
☎ (80) 61 09 85

Jacques Cacheaux   TR
☎ (80) 61 05 61

René Cacheaux   TR
☎ (80) 61 05 61

Caveau St-Martin   TR
Open: weekends and
public holidays from
Easter to September.

Confuron-Cotetidot   TR
☎ (80) 61 03 39

Marie-Andrée Gerbet   TR
☎ (80) 62 38 18

Domaine Gros François TR
☎ (80) 61 04 69

Domaine Gros brothers
and sisters   TR
☎ (80) 61 04 69

Domaine Jean Gros   TR
☎ (80) 61 04 69

Pierre Guyon   TR
☎ (80) 61 02 46

Jean Mongeard-   TR
Mugneret
☎ (80) 61 11 95

Denis Mugneret and son TR
☎ (80) 61 00 97

Jean-Pierre Mugneret   TR
☎ (80) 61 00 20

Domaine Charles
Noëllat   TR
☎ (80) 61 10 82

Rion and son   TR
☎ (80) 61 05 31

Robert Siruge   TR
☎ (80) 61 00 64

Vougeot (21640)

Domaine Bertagna   TR
☎ (80) 62 86 04

Château de la Tour   TR
☎ (80) 62 86 13

SGVV La Grande Cave TR
☎ (80) 61 11 23

Domaine Jacques Prieur TR
☎ (80) 21 23 85

Germain Tardy and sons TR
☎ (80) 62 85 82

CHALONNAISE

Rully

Thomas Bassot   TR
5 quai Dumorey
21700 Nuits-St-Georges
☎ (85) 62 31 05
Open: by appointment.

Domaine Belleville   TW
Belleville and son
rue de la Loppe
71150 Chagny
☎ (85) 91 22 19
Open: by appointment.

Château St-Nicolas   TW
Emile Chandesais
Fontaines
71150 Chagny
☎ (85) 91 41 77
Open: by appointment.

Guyot-Verdiot   TW
Hubert Guyot

rue du Château Rully
71150 Chagny
☎ (85) 87 04 48
Open: by appointment.

André L'Héritier   TWR
4 blvd de la Liberté
71150 Chagny
☎ (85) 87 00 09
Open: by appointment.

Domaine de l'Hermitage TR
Chanzy brothers
Bouzeron
71150 Chagny
☎ (85) 87 23 69
Open: by appointment.

Jacqueson   TR
place Ste-Marie
71150 Chagny
☎ (85) 87 07 88
Open: by appointment.

Domaine de Prieuré   TRW
Armand Monassier
71150 Chagny
☎ (85) 87 13 57
Open: by appointment.

Domaine Ninot Rigaud TR
71150 Chagny
☎ (85) 87 07 79
Open: by appointment.

Domaine de la Renarde TW
Jean-François Delorme
rue de la République
71150 Chagny
☎ (85) 87 10 12
Open: by appointment.

Château de Rully   TR
71150 Chagny
☎ (85) 87 20 42
Open: by appointment.

R=red wine   W=white wine   P=rosé wine   S=sparkling wine

Clos St-Jacques TW
Domaine de la Folie
71150 Chagny
☎ (85) 87 18 59
Open: Monday to Saturday
8am-noon, l.30-6.30pm.

Charles Vienot TR
quai Dumorey
21700 Nuits-St-Georges
☎ (85) 62 31 05
Open: by appointment.

Montagny

Coopérative des
   Vignerons de Buxy TW
Les Vignes de la Croix
71390 Buxy
☎ (85) 92 03 03
Open: by appointment.

Denizot and son TW
Les Moirots
Bissey-sous-Cruchaud
71390 Buxy
☎ (85) 42 16 93
Open: by appointment.

Château de la Saule TW
Alain Roy-Thévenin
Montagny-lès-Buxy
71390 Buxy
☎ (85) 42 11 83
Open: by appointment.

Jean Vachet TW
St-Vallerin
71390 Buxy
Open: by appointment.

Charles Vienot TW
5 quai Dumorey
21700 Nuits-St-Georges
☎ (85) 62 31 05
Open: by appointment.

Givry

Château St-Nicolas TR
Émile Chandesais
Fontaines
71150 Chagny

☎ (85) 91 41 77
Open: by appointment.

Jean Chofflet TR
Russilly
71640 Givry
☎ (85) 44 34 78
Open: by appointment.

Jean Cleau TR
rue des Berges
Poncey
71640 Givry
☎ (85) 44 31 35
Open: by appointment.

Domaine Joblot TR
71640 Givry
☎ (85) 44 30 77
Open: by appointment.

Yves Marceau TR
Grande Rue
Mercurey
71640 Givry
☎ (85) 47 13 21
Open: by appointment.

Jean Morin TR
Poncey
71640 Givry
☎ (85) 44 51 38
Open: by appointment.

Gérard Mouton TW
Poncey
71640 Givry
☎ (85) 44 37 99
Open: by appointment.

Domaine Ragot TR
Poncey
71640 Givry
☎ (85) 44 37 99
Open: by appointment.

Clos Salomon TR
M. Dugardin
71640 Givry
☎ (85) 44 32 24
Open: by appointment.

La Sauleraie TRW
Gérard Parize

rue des Faussillons
Poncey
71640 Givry
☎ (85) 44 38 60
Open: by appointment.

Mercurey

Domaine Brintet TR
Grande Rue
71640 Givry
☎ (85) 47 14 50
Open: by appointment.

Domaine de Chamerose TR
Louis Modrin
71640 Givry
☎ (85) 47 13 94
Open: by appointment.

Domaine du Château
   de Chamilly TR
Louis Desfontaine
Chamilly
71510 St-Léger-sur-
Dheune
☎ (85) 87 22 24
Open: by appointment.

Château de Chamirey TRW
Marquis de Jouennes
71640 Givry
☎ (85) 45 22 22
Open: by appointment.

Château St-Nicholas TRW
Emile Chandesais
Fontaines
71150 Chagny
☎ (85) 91 41 77
Open: by appointment.

Maison Faivelay TRW
rue du Tribourg
21700 Nuits-St-Georges
☎ (85) 61 04 55
Open: by appointment.

Chanzy brothers TW
Bouzeron
71150 Chagny
☎ (85) 87 23 69
Open: by appointment.

T=tasting   E=English spoken   G=guided tours   C=château/building to visit

Michael Juillot — TR
71640 Givry
☎ (85) 45 27 27
Open: by appointment.

Robert Landre — TW
71640 Givry
☎ (85) 47 13 84
Open: by appointment.

Antonin Rodet — TR
71640 Givry
☎ (85) 45 22 22
Open: by appointment.

Domaine Saier — TR
rue Valmy
94220 Charenton
☎ (01) 37 59 20
Open: by appointment.

Yves de Suremain — TR
71640 Givry
☎ (85) 47 20 87
Open: by appointment.

Emile Voarick
Le Bourg
St-Martin-sous-Montaigu
71640 Givry
☎ (85) 45 23 23
Open: Monday to Saturday
8am-noon and 2-6pm.

THE MACONNAIS

Adrien Arcelin — TW
La Roche-Vineuse
71960 Pierreclos
☎ (85) 36 61 38
Open: by appointment.

Thomas Bassot — TRW
quai Dumorey
21700 Nuits-St-Georges
☎ (85) 62 31 05
Open: by appointment.

Paul Beaudet — TW
Pontanevaux
71570 La Chapelle-de-
 Guinchay
☎ (85) 36 72 76
Open: Monday to Friday
8am-noon and 2-5pm

Bénas brothers — TRW
71960 Pierreclos
Serrières
☎ (85) 35 71 95
Open: by appointment.

Bernard — TW
Sologny
71960 Pierreclos
☎ (85) 36 60 38
Open: by appointment.

Château des Bois — TW
Philibert Moreau
rue Georges Lecomte
71000 Mâcon
☎ (85) 38 42 87
Open: by appointment.

Domaine de la
 Bon Gran — TW
Jean-Claude Thevenet
Le Bourg
71960 Pierreclos
☎ (85) 35 72 21
Open: by appointment.

André Bonhomme — TW
71260 Viré
☎ (85) 33 11 86
Open: by appointment.

Robert Bridon — TW
Montbellet
71260 Lugny
☎ (85) 33 13 23
Open: by appointment.

Domaine des Carmes — TW
Les Caves Rippe
Le Prieuré
Bissy-la-Mâconnaise
71260 Lugny
☎ (85) 33 23 22
Open: by appointment.

Coopérative Vinicole
 de Chaintré — TW
Chaintré
71570 La Chapelle-de
 Guinchay
☎ (85) 35 61 61
Open: by appointment.

Cave Coopérative de — TW
 Chardonnay

Chardonnay
71700 Tournus
☎ (85) 51 06 49
Open: by appointment.

Cave Coopérative de — TW
 Charnay
Charnay-lès-Mâcon
71000 Mâcon
☎ (85) 34 54 24
Open: by appointment.

Domaine de Chazelles — TW
Jean-Noël Chaland
Viré
71260 Lugny
☎ (85) 33 11 18
Open: by appointment.

Domaine de la — TW
 Condemine
Véronique and Pierre
 Janny
Péronne
71260 Lugny
☎ (85) 36 97 03
Open: by appointment.

Domaine des Granges — TW
Jean-François Cognard
71570 La Chapelle-de-
 Guinchay
☎ (85) 37 16 20
Open: by appointment.

Château de la Greffière — TW
Henri and Vincent
 Greuzard

R=red wine   W=white wine   P=rosé wine   S=sparkling wine

144

La Roche-Vineuse
71960 Pierreclos
☎ (85) 37 79 11
Open: by appointment.

Domaine Guillot-Broux TW
Cruzille
71260 Lugny
☎ (85) 33 21 89
Open: by appointment.

Cave Coopérative d'Igé TW
Igé
71960 Pierreclos
☎ (85) 33 33 65
Open: by appointment.

Henri Lafarge   TW
Bray
71250 Cluny
☎ (85) 59 21 11
Open: by appointment.

Producteurs de Lugny-
   St-Gengoux   TRW
71260 Lugny
☎ (85) 33 22 85
Open: by appointment.

Lycée Agricole de
   Mâcon-Davayé   TR
Davayé
71960 Pierreclos
☎ (85) 37 80 66
Open: by appointment.

Maison Mâconnaise
   des Vins   TRW
ave. de Lattre-de-Tassigny
71000 Mâcon
☎ (85) 38 36 70
Open: 8am-9pm.

Pierre Mahuet   TR
La Roche-Vineuse
71960 Pierreclos
☎ (85) 37 70 82
Open: by appointment.

Cave de Vignerons
   de Mancey   TR
Mancey
71240 Sennecey-le-Grand

☎ (85) 51 00 83
Open: by appointment.

Claude Manciat   TW
Lévigny-Charnay
71000 Mâcon
☎ (85) 34 18 77
Open: by appointment.

Réné Michel   TW
Clessé
71260 Lugny
☎ (85) 36 94 27
Open: by appointment.

Gilbert Mornand   TW
Clessé
71260 Lugny
☎ (85) 36 94 90
Open: by appointment.

Producteurs de Prissé   TW
Prissé
71960 Pierreclos
☎ (85) 37 82 53
Open: by appointment.

Domaine Les   TR
   Provenchères
Maurice Gonon
Serrières
71960 Pierreclos
☎ (85) 35 71 96
Open: by appointment.

Domaine de Roally   TW
Henri Goyard
Viré
71260 Lugny
☎ (85) 33 10 31
Open: by appointment.

Claudius Rongier   TW
Clessé
71260 Lugny
☎ (85) 36 94 05
Open: by appointment.

Des Vieux St-Sorcin   TR
René Gaillard
La Roche-Vineuse
71960 Pierreclos
☎ (85) 37 72 49
Open: by appointment.

Pierre Santé   TRW
La Roche-Vineuse
71960 Pierreclos
☎ (85) 37 80 57
Open: by appointment.

Jean Signoret   TP
Clessé
71260 Lugny
☎ (85) 36 93 74
Open: by appointment.

Paul and Philibert
   Talmard   TW
Uchizy
71700 Tournus
☎ (85) 51 10 37
Open: by appointment.

Jean-Claude Thevenet   TR
Le Bourg
71960 Pierreclos
☎ (85) 35 72 21
Open: Monday to Saturday
7.30am-noon, 1.30-7pm.

Le Tournons   TW
Charnay-lès-Mâcons
71000 Mâcon
☎ (85) 34 26 74
Open: by appointment.

Château de Verneuil   TW
Charnay-les-Macons
71000 Macons
☎ (85) 34 26 74
Open: by appointment.

Cave Coopérative de
   Verzé   TRW
Verzé
71960 Pierreclos
☎ (85) 33 30 76
Open: by appointment.

Charles Vienot   TRW
21700 Nuits-St-Georges
☎ (80) 62 31 05
Open: by appointment.

Cave Coopérative   TW
   de Viré
Viré

T=tasting   E=English spoken   G=guided tours   C=château/building to visit

71260 Lugny
☎ (85) 33 12 64
Open: Monday to Friday
8.30am-noon, 2-6.30pm.

Michel Bernard   TR
rue André-Vildieu
89580 Coulanges-la-
Vineuse
☎ (86) 42 25 72
Open: by appointment.

Pierre Bernollon   TR
Jully-lès-Buxy
71390 Buxy
☎ (85) 42 12 19
Open: by appointment.

Alain Berthault   TR
Cercot-Moroges
71390 Buxy
☎ (85) 47 91 03
Open: by appointment.

Léonce Bocquet   TRW
blvd Clémenceau
21200 Beaune
☎ (80) 22 28 49
Open: Monday to Friday
9.30-11.30am, 2-5.30pm.

Gérard Borgnat
rue d'Eglise
Escolives-Ste-Camille
89290 Champs-sur-Yonne
☎ (86) 53 35 28
Open: Monday to Saturday
9am-noon and 2-8pm.

Domaine Pierre   TWP
  Bouthenet
La Creuse
71490 Couches
☎ (85) 49 63 72
Open: by appointment.

Georges Bouthenet   TR
Eguilly
71490 Couches
☎ (85) 49 66 65
Open: daily 9am-6pm.

Clos de la Carbonnade TR
André l'Héritier
blvd de la Liberté
71150 Chagny
☎ (85) 87 00 09
Open: by appointment.

Michel Champion   TR
Cercot-Moroges
71390 Buxy
☎ (85) 47 90 94
Open: by appointment.

Guy Chaumont   TW
Le Treuil
St-Désert
71390 Buxy
☎ (86) 47 92 31
Open: by appointment.

Michel Colbois   TW
route de Montalery
Chitry-le-Fort
89530 St-Bris-le-Vineux
☎ (86) 41 40 23
Open: by appointment.

Château Corton André   TR
Pierre André
Aloxe-Corton
21420 Savigny-lès-Beaune
☎ (80) 26 44 25
Open: by appointment.

Bernard and Odile Cros TR
Cercot-Moroges
71390 Buxy
☎ (85) 47 92 52
Open: by appointment.

Lucien Denizot   TW
Les Moirots
Bissey-sous-Cruchaud
71390 Buxy
☎ (85) 42 16 93
Open: by appointment.

Jean Derain   TRW
Bissey-sous-Cruchaud
71390 Buxy
☎ (85) 42 10 94
Open: by appointment.

Bernard Désertaux   TRW
Corgoloin
21700 Nuits-St-Georges
☎ (80) 62 98 40
Open: by appointment.

Jean-Claude Desrayaud TW
Solutré
71960 Pierreclos
☎ (85) 37 84 60
Open: by appointment.

Roger Dessendre   TRP
St-Maurice-lès-Couches
71490 Couches
☎ (85) 49 67 60
Open: by appointment.

Louis Dussort   TR
rue Charles-Giraud
21190 Meursault
☎ (80) 21 21 21
Open: daily 9am-6pm.

Jean-Hughes-Goisot   TRP
rue Bienvenu-Martin
89530 St-Bris-le-Vineux
☎ (86) 53 35 15
Open: Monday to Saturday
8am-8pm.

Michel Goubard   TRP
St-Désert
71390 Buxy
☎ (86) 47 91 06
Open: daily 8am-7pm

Louis Jadot   TRW
rue Samuel-Legay
21200 Beaune
☎ (80) 22 10 57
Open: by appointment.

Jean-Noël Jeannet   TR
Mazenay
71510 St-Léger-sur-
Dhuene
☎ (85) 49 63 51
Open: by appointment.

Henri Joussier   TR
St-Denis-de-Vaux
71640 Givry
☎ (85) 44 32 42
Open: by appointment.

R=red wine   W=white wine   P=rosé wine   S=sparkling wine

Marc Laborde TR
St-Jean-de-Vaux
71640 Givry
☎ (85) 47 20 10
Open: by appointment.

François Laugerotte TR
St-Denis-de-Vaux
71640 Givry
☎ (85) 44 36 35
Open: by appointment.

Leroy TRW
Vosne-Romanée
21700 Nuits-St-Georges
☎ (80) 61 04 57
Open: by appointment.

Michel Martin TR
89580 Coulanges-la-
Vineuse
☎ (86) 42 22 73
Open: by appointment.

Réné Martin TW
Cheilly-lès-Maranges
71150 Chagny
☎ (86) 87 04 37
Open: by appointment.

Alain Mellenotte TR
Mellecey
71640 Givry
☎ (85) 47 10 98
Open: by appointment.

Coteaux de Montbogre TR
place Romaine
St-Désert
71390 Buxy
☎ (86) 47 91 41
Open: by appointment.

Michel Morin TW
rue du Ruisseau
Chitry-le-Fort
89530 St-Bris-le-Vineux
☎ (86) 41 41 61
Open: by appointment.

Noël Perrin TR
Culles-lès-Roches
71460 St-Gengoux-le-
National
☎ (85) 44 04 25
Open: by appointment.

Robert Perrin and son TR
Dennevy
71510 St-Léger-sur-
Dhuene
☎ (85) 43 35 58
Open: by appointment.

Antonin Rodet TRW
Mercurey
71340 Givry
☎ (85) 45 22 22
Open: by appointment.

Domaine Rougeot TR
rue André-Ropiteau
21190 Meursault
☎ (80) 21 02 59
Open: by appointment.

Gérard Thomas TR
St-Aubin
21190 Meursault
☎ (80) 21 32 57
Open: by appointment.

Les Toques Gourmandes TR
route de Versailles
78560 Port-Marly
☎ (01) 91 61 17
Open: by appointment.

Charles Vienot TRW
21700 Nuits-St-Georges
☎ (80) 62 31 05
Open: by appointment.

Jacques Vignot TP
22 Chemin Gravons
Paroy-sur-Tholon
89300 Joigny
☎ (86) 62 23 73
Open: by appointment.

Bourgogne Aligoté

Domaine Goud de TW
Beaupuis
Chorey-lès-Beaune
21200 Beaune
☎ (80) 22 20 63
Open: daily 9am-7pm.

Alain Berthault TW
Cercot
71390 Moroges
☎ (85) 47 91 03
Open: by appointment.

Jean-Claude Biot TW
Chitry-le-Fort
89530 St-Bris-le-Vineux
☎ (86) 41 42 79
Open: by appointment.

Domaine Bouchard TW
and son
21200 Beaune
☎ (80) 22 14 41
Open: by appointment.

Claude Cornu TW
Magny-lès-Villers
21700 Nuits-St-Georges
☎ (80) 62 92 05
Open: by appointment.

Robert Defrance TW
rue du Four
89530 St-Bris-le-Vineux
☎ (86) 53 33 82
Open: by appointment.

Lucien Denizot TW
Les Moirots
Bissey-sous-Cruchaud
71390 Buxy
☎ (85) 42 15 92
Open: by appointment.

Roger Dessendre TW
St-Maurice-lès-Couches
71490 Couches
☎ (85) 49 67 60
Open: Monday to Saturday
9am-noon and 2-8pm.

Domaine Fribourg TW
Marcel and Bernard
Fribourg
Villers-la-Faye
21700 Nuits-St-Georges
☎ (80) 62 91 74
Open: by appointment.

T=tasting   E=English spoken   G=guided tours   C=château/building to visit

Gilles Gaudet   TW
St-Germain-du-Plain
71310 St-Germain-du-
   Plain
☎ (85) 49 62 12
Open: daily 9am-noon
and 2-8pm.

Caves des Hautes-Côtes TW
route de Pommard
21200 Beaune
☎ (80) 24 63 12
Open: by appointment.

L'Héritier-Guyot   TW
rue de Champ-aux-Prêtres
21006 Dijon
☎ (80) 72 16 14
Open: by appointment.

André l'Héritier-Guyot TW
blvd de la Liberté
71150 Chagny
☎ (85) 87 00 09
Open: by appointment.

Luc Sorin   TW
rue de Paris
89530 St-Bris-le-Vineux
☎ (86) 53 32 44
Open: by appointment.

Domaine Thevenot-
   Lebrun   TW
Marey-lès-Fussy
21700 Nuits-St-Georges
☎ (80) 62 91 64
Open: Monday to Saturday
8am-1pm and 2-7pm.

CHALONNAISE AND MACONNAIS TASTING CENTRES

Open permanently:

Les Vignerons du
   Caveau   TR
Mercurey
☎ (85) 47 16 53
July to September.

La Tour Rouge   TR
Buxy
☎ (85) 42 15 76

Caveau de la Cave
   Coopérative   TRW
Mancey
☎ (85) 51 00 83

Caveau St-Pierre   TRW
Lugny
☎ (85) 33 20 27

Le Baraban   TRW
Cluny
Union des Mâcon
July to September.

Caveau de la Cave
   Coopérative   TRW
Sologny
☎ (85) 36 60 64

Maison Mâconnaise
   des Vins   TRW
Mâcon
☎ (85) 38 36 70

Caveau du Pouilly-
   Vinzelles   TR
Vinzelles
☎ (85) 35 61 88
Closed Tuesday and
Wednesday.

Caveau de Chaintré   TR
☎ (85) 35 61 61
Closed Wednesday and
Thursday.

Maison de Dégustation
   du Moulin-à-Vent   TR
Romanèche-Thorins
☎ (85) 35 51 03
Closed during January and
every Wednesday.

Caveau du Pouilly-
   Fuissé   TW
Solutré
☎ (85) 37 80 06
Closed January and
February.

Caveau de la Cave
   Coopérative   TRW
Clessé
☎ (85) 36 93 88
Closed Sundays and public
holidays.

Caveau de la Cave
   Coopérative   TW
Chardonnay
☎ (85) 51 06 49

**Open weekends and
holidays:**

Caveau de la Cave
   Coopérative   TR
Bissey-sous-Cruchaud
☎ (85) 42 12 16
Closed Saturdays.

Le Vieux Logis   TR
St-Gengoux-de-Scissé
Closed Saturdays.

Le Virolis   TW
Virè
☎ (85) 33 10 57

Caveau d'Azé   TR
☎ (85) 33 30 42

Le Musée du Vin   TR
Igé
☎ (85) 33 33 56

Caveau de St-Amour   TR
☎ (85) 37 15 98

**Open at special
request:**

Caveau du Cru St-Véran
   au Relais Beaujolais-
   Mâconnais
Leynes
☎ (85) 37 18 66

R=red wine   W=white wine   P=rosé wine   S=sparkling wine

Chapter 4

BEAUJOLAIS

Old Wine Press
Beaujolais.

ALTHOUGH Beaujolais is part of Burgundy, the wines of this region are so different from other Burgundies that they deserve a section of their own.

Beaujolais is part of the Lyonnais and the inhabitants enjoy the good food that comes from this fertile region, which extends south into the northern Rhône. The Beaujolais vineyards start at the boundary with Mâcon, and run almost continuously to the Lyon suburbs, along the whole length of the motorways, the A6 and N6, yet by the time motorists reach Lyon, they usually have their foot hard down on the accelerator and are racing for the Mediterranean. Few tourists stop to visit this delightful part of the country-side with its good food, reasonably-priced hotels and marvellous wines. The Beaujolais, for all that, is still one of France's leading wine producers. There are about 9,500 growers producing an average 150 million bottles on 55,000 acres, and world-wide demand continues to grow unchecked.

The first records of Beaujolais date back to 1031 and Beraud, the first Lord of Beaujeu, who created the state. It was established to act as a buffer between the constantly-feuding states of Mâcon and Lyon. For four hundred years, Beaujeu remained the capital of the area, but then Villefranche took over as the commercial and political centre. Villefranche gained its charter in 1260, because it was already an important trading and staging centre. It handled agricultural produce from the surrounding fertile plains and was on the main route from the south coast to the north.

Although wine has certainly been grown in Beaujolais for hundreds of years, it was never very commercially significant because of the problems involved in moving it. The road network was not very good, although things improved in 1642 when the Canal de Briare was opened, with access to the Loire. Only in the last two hundred years, however, have the wines gained in popularity, partly because of the French Revolution and partly because of the demand for the lighter, fruitier style of wine that Beaujolais was able to produce.

Records show that before the Revolution, much of the land of Beaujolais was in the hands of a few very large agricultural estates. After the confis-cation of land, it was divided and this encouraged repopulation of the area.

The success of Beaujolais is that, in spite of its many vineyards and growers, it has just one product to sell, even though quality varies enor-mously. The staggering success of the Beaujolais Nouveau allows the grow-ers to dispose of their wine quickly. The better quality is kept for release the following year as Beaujolais Villages, and the best quality is reserved for the *Crus Beaujolais*.

Beaujolais is bounded on the east by the Saône, and in the west by the foothills of the Massif Central. The vineyards are planted on these slopes, sheltered from the worst of the weather by the Rigaud Massif, which rises to 3,350ft. These hills, the Monts de Beaujolais, protect the vineyards from the worst weather from the north and west, and help keep temperatures several degrees higher than in surrounding areas. This micro-climate rules out the very worst winter weather, except in freak years, and can push the summer temperatures up well over 100°F.

Vines grow everywhere, and even decorate the houses and their gardens.

You also become aware that you are approaching the Mediterranean because the houses are made of stone with red tile roofs — a familiar sight in southern France and northern Italy.

The different geology of the region is pronounced. The Mâconnais has a chalky soil which suits the Chardonnay grape so well, but the Beaujolais soil is mainly granite as far as Villefranche, and then limestone and clay further south.

The only grape variety allowed in Beaujolais is the Gamay, and all the nine *crus* are grown in the north of the region, on the granitic soil. This area is sometimes called the Haut-Beaujolais, and apart from all nine *crus*, contains all the villages entitled to the Beaujolais Villages *appellation*.

Although the soil is a major factor in the quality of the wine, the weather also plays a critical role, despite the protection afforded by the mountains. Hail can devastate the vineyards in minutes, and in 1975 about 5,000 acres of grapes were destroyed. The growers have tried many devices to try to beat the hail, and even use aircraft to sprinkle silver iodide filings into the clouds, to try to release their water content before they reach the vineyards.

A special method of fermentation has been developed to produce the special fruitiness of Beaujolais, and the Gamay grape needs to be handled carefully if its full potential is to be realised. Fermentation is similar to the system of carbonic maceration but takes place much more quickly, over five or six days. The temperature of the fermentation is also high because this draws out the full flavour, fruitiness and bouquet of the Gamay. A little white Beaujolais is made, from Chardonnay grapes, and there is also a little rosé, but the vast majority of the production is of red wine, which can appear under a number of *appellations*.

The straight Beaujolais *appellation* applies to wine with an alcohol content of 9°. If it has an alcohol strength of 10° or more it can call itself Beaujolais Supérieur. A wine needs a relatively high alcohol level to travel well, so almost all the Beaujolais exported is Supérieur. Beaujolais Nouveau and Primeur becomes available on 15 November each year, when the mad rush ensues to see which shipper can be first to bring it to England, New York or other major towns. It is perhaps the best example of marketing the world has ever seen. Although the Nouveau is perfectly drinkable, and fun to have, there is no doubt that it does improve with a little ageing. Yet up to a third of the entire harvest can be sold as Nouveau each year, relieving the growers of much expenditure on storage and further maturation.

The Nouveau is made by carbonic maceration. The grapes are not pressed, but placed in vats where the weight of grapes causes a little juice to be released, but fermentation starts inside the grape itself. This helps to trap the fruity flavour of the wine and produces the light style we associate with Beaujolais. A good Nouveau (and they can vary enormously), should have a fine red colour with just a tinge of purple, a warm, fruity nose and a taste that fills your mouth with fruit and flavour. Beaujolais is a very refreshing drink and even more so when served chilled.

The Nouveau is always released a few weeks after the harvest, while the Beaujolais Villages is not available until the following spring. About forty villages in the Haut-Beaujolais have the right to this *appellation* and they must meet certain rules. Yields must be under 45 hectolitres per hectare and there must be a natural alcohol content of 10°. Of the thirty-nine villages allowed the *appellation*, thirty-one are in the *départément* of the Rhône and the remainder in the Saône-et-Loire *départément*. Although the growers are allowed to sweeten their wines, they must not let the alcohol content rise above 14°.

The flagships of the Beaujolais are the nine *crus*: St-Amour, Juliénas, Chenas, Moulin-à-Vent, Fleurie, Chiroubles, Morgon, Brouilly and the Côte de Brouilly, the order in which the vineyards are met when driving south. The *crus* must have at least 10° of alcohol, but if the name of the vineyard is also on the label, the alcohol content must be 11°.

The Districts and Villages of Beaujolais

St-Amour

The village consists of the four hamlets Le Bourg, Le Plâtre-Durand, La Ville and Les Thévenins. It is unspoilt, and the church, with its frescoes, is worth a visit. Legend has it that a Roman soldier fell in love, married a local girl and settled here, and thus the name. That may be dubious, but it is a fact that the wines from the village age well in the bottle for a year or two, but they should not be kept more than four or five years. Production is now about 1,800,000 bottles a year.

Juliénas

Juliénas claims to get its name from Julius Caesar. Château de Juliénas is one of the best vineyards in the village, and the foundations of the house date back to the beginning of the fourteenth century when the Seigneur de Beaujeu ordered work to start. There is also a sixteenth-century toll house. There are a number of quite large vineyards in Juliénas, of 25 acres or so, but the majority of the 300 growers do not have their own facilities and belong to the village *coopérative*. This is housed in the Château du Bois de la Salle, which dates back to the sixteenth century. It has a modern tasting room which is very popular throughout the summer. There is a second tasting centre in the old church in the village, a new church having been consecrated in 1868. The wines of Juliénas are longer-lasting than those of St-Amour and require more bottle age.

Chenas

This is the smallest of the Beaujolais *cru* producers, and the wines in the past have often been used for blending with the grapes of the Côte d'Or, or they have been sent south and sold as Moulin-à-Vent. Chenas produces a full-bodied but light wine, with lots of fruit, that can be kept for some years.

The wines of the village can be tasted at the Cellier de Chenas, which also boasts a sculpture by Renoir showing woodcutters felling an oak tree (*chêne*) to clear the ground for a vineyard. The oak forests, long since gone, gave the village its name.

Moulin-à-Vent
This area in the comune of Chenas produces deep coloured, full, fruity and quite heavy wines which age better than any of the other *crus*. The growers produce about 4,250,000 bottles a year and the styles can be very different. There are many producers who prefer their wines to be drunk young so be sure you know what you have bought if you want to lay it down.

The commune used to be called Romanèche-Thorins, but the name was changed in 1936 to Moulin-à-Vent to salute the windmill which still stands, sailless, in the middle of the vineyards. The mill, the only one left in Beaujolais, is now a declared national monument. There are two tasting cellars in the village.

Fleurie
Fleurie produces light, elegant, flowery wines best drunk within two years of the vintage. The *cave coopérative* is run by the splendid Mme Marguérite Chabert, who took over as president when her father died in 1946; she still controls one of the finest wineries in Beaujolais. Wine can be tasted at either the *coopérative* or the *caveau*, and it is worth walking up to the chapel on the top of the hill overlooking the village for splendid views over the vineyards.

Chiroubles
This village has a wine history spanning back more than 1,000 years, and is the highest *cru* of Beaujolais in terms of altitude. The vines are planted very high on the hillsides, and had to be individually planted into holes dug out of the granite. Today there are about 400 growers in the village, mostly working on rented ground for which they agree to give the landlord part of the harvest. The wines produced are light both in colour and style. They have an intensity of colour, are very fruity and must be drunk young.

Morgon
This village is the largest of the *cru* producers, with Brouilly, its neighbour to the south. The wine is full, almost fat, and long-lasting, but it does not lose its youthfulness and freshness. Because of the sand and gravel soil, the wine of Beaujolais has a very distinctive taste of wild cherries. The wine can be tasted in the cellars of the fifteenth-century château, which attracts thousands of visitors every year.

Brouilly
Brouilly is special among the *crus* because it contains a number of estates producing very fine wines. The vineyards are around the five villages of St-Lager, Charentay, Odénas, Quincié and Cercié, at the foot of the mountains. It is the largest producer among the *crus*. There are two magnificent châteaux worth visiting, and the cellars of the Château de la Chaize are the largest in Beaujolais. Production amounts to almost 9,000,000 bottles a year and there are a number of styles, depending on the estate from which the wine comes. Generally the wine is light, with a very intense bouquet. It is best drunk

between one and two years old, but can go on a little longer with a good vintage.

Côte de Brouilly

This is the name given to the vineyards on the slopes of the hills above those of Brouilly. The wines are stronger, and the alcohol content can reach 14° because of the amount of sunshine on the grapes. The wines are big and powerful, fruity and with a hint of violets on the nose.

A Tour of the Beaujolais Region

The Beaujolais region is part of the Lyonnais and lies just to the south of Mâcon. It can be visited as part of an extended tour of Burgundy, or one can use either Belleville or Villefranche as a base for a longer stay.

There are a number of wine routes signposted, which lead through the winding lanes of this historic area. The vineyards run just to the west of the busy Autoroute 6 and Route Nationale 6, but motorists on these see little as they speed past, either on their way to or returning from the Mediterranean resorts.

The Route de Beaujolais is clearly signposted, both by name and by the symbol of a bunch of grapes on a red background. The best vineyards are to be found in the north, where the Beaujolais Villages produce the best of the wines — names such as Juliénas, Moulin-à-Vent, Fleurie, Chiroubles and the velvety, fruity Brouilly.

Two or three days are needed to visit the various vineyards properly, but by using either Belleville or Villefranche as a base, it is possible to tour the northern vineyards on the first day, and visit the southern ones on the second. This involves less than forty miles driving each day.

The history of Beaujolais stretches back more than 1,000 years, but it was in the tenth century that it came into its own, separating the warring states of Mâcon and Lyon. In 1031 it was known as *Bellijocum*, and its leader was Beraud, the first lord of Beaujeu.

The region has always been devoted to a mixture of agriculture and viticulture and much of it is still quaintly rural. In the sixteenth century, Villefranche became the capital of the region, and its agricultural produce and wine made Beaujolais famous throughout France. The completion of the Canal de Briare in 1642 meant that wine producers could ship their wines to Paris. Even though the journey, first by horse and cart, then by canal and river boat on the Loire, took a month, it was much cheaper than the overland route and the wine was not disturbed as much.

Beaujolais still retains a special charm, and a gentle pace of life. While there are few tourist attractions, the villages have hardly changed in hundreds of years, and almost everyone is involved in wine, either as a grower, a producer or a seller.

There are more than 5,000 vineyards in this small area, and at least 200 shippers. There are three main types of Beaujolais: the good honest wine drunk soon after the harvest; the wine from the designated villages which is at its best the following spring; and that from the north entitled to its own *appellation* which can go on improving for some years.

Beaujolais also has a deserved reputation for its gastronomy, which is not surprising considering the areas by which it is surrounded and the supplies from which it can draw. There is magnificent beef from Charollais to the northwest; Bresse to the east is famed for its dairy produce and cheeses; there are freshwater fish from the Saône and sheep and game from the mountains that form the backbone of Beaujolais.

With such a larder to draw on, and wines to wash the food down, it is not surprising that Beaujolais has more than its fair share of first class restaurants.

Whether you use Belleville or Villefranche as a base, the first day should be spent travelling north along the N6 leaving at Crêches-sur-Saône to start the tour. The route should cover St-Amour, Juliénas, Moulin-à-Vent, and Fleurie; with Chiroubles, Morgon and Brouilly after lunch. Including the Côte de Brouilly, these are the nine top producing communes, and the only ones allowed to use these names on their labels.

From Crêches it is easy to find the Route de Beaujolais, with its easily recognised symbol, and after that it is almost impossible to get lost because the route winds its way through the vineyards back to Villefranche. If your base is in Belleville, simply take the N6.

A tour of this nature is immensely rewarding, because it gives you the chance to sample the best wines of these nine communes and compare their different styles and characteristics.

Beaujolais is a place for the wine lover rather than the casual tourist. The most interesting buildings are those associated with wines — the farms, *chais* and cellars. Many of the farms are at least 200 years old, and in the eighteenth century there was a trend towards building massive outdoor cellars, or *chais*, away from the main farmhouse. Traditionally, the farms were always built with the cellars occupying the ground floor, and the family's accommodation above.

Tour of the Villages and Vineyards

The first port of call should be Le Plâtre-Durand, a small village clinging to the top of the hill overlooking St-Amour. Here there is an interesting little church and tasting cellar.

About a mile to the south-west of St-Amour is Juliénas. The wines of Juliénas are harder than those from St-Amour, with more tannin, so they take longer to mature, but the wait is worth it. The village tasting centre is in a former church, and Château du Bois de la Salle, now a wine co-operative, was formerly a priory.

Another mile south is Chenas, one of the prettiest villages of Beaujolais. The wines of Chenas cause endless battles among the wine experts. Some say they are among the richest in Beaujolais while others have described them as lacking charm. Much of the wine from the commune, however, goes to making Beaujolais sold under the Moulin-à-Vent label, named after the derelict windmill, now a national monument, which stands on top of the hill overlooking the tiny village of Les Thorins. (There is no village called Moulin-à-Vent.) The wines are big and fruity and are best after a little ageing.

Continuing south, cross into the commune of Fleurie, one of the biggest producers. The wine is soft and light and can be drunk either young or old. The most noted vineyard is Clos de la Roillette, considered by many to be the finest in the whole of Beaujolais. One of the great advantages of the Route de Beaujolais is that once on it, the distance between stops is never more than a mile or two, so most of the time can be spent tasting, or admiring the spectacular views, rather than travelling.

From Fleurie it is only a stone's throw to the small village of Chiroubles, a small commune whose wine is quickly snatched up after each vintage. The most celebrated vintage is that of Bel-Air. The wines are fresh and fruity and best drunk young. There is a monument in the town square to Victor Pulliat, the first winemaker in Beaujolais to realise the importance of grafting local vines on to disease-resistant American root stock to withstand the phylloxera outbreak at the end of last century.

The road now leads down to the commune producing the Morgon-Beaujolais — Villié-Morgon — and with Brouilly to the south, is the largest producing area.

The wines get their character from the shale on which the vines grow. They mature slowly, developing a rich, fruity nose and mouth-filling flavour. The whole of the area is dominated by the Mont de Brouilly, which rises to about 1,640ft and is capped by a chapel which acts as a landmark. From Crêches to Morgon the chapel should almost always be in sight ahead of you, and from Brouilly to Villefranche it should be behind.

Côte de Brouilly produces big powerful wines although supplies are limited. The wine comes from vineyards on the slopes of the mountain, while the vines on the plains surrounding it yield the grapes for Brouilly. Brouilly is much lighter, more subtle and fruitier than Côte de Brouilly, and production is about four times as great.

It is obviously foolish to drink too much, and out of the question if you are driving, but a modest tasting of each of these nine wines (even spitting it out if you must) will show just how different they can be.

Villefranche-sur-Saône does not have many sights of great interest, although many of the buildings are old. It does, however, have a good number of respectable hotels and restaurants considering its size. The Auberge Faisan-Doré, just outside the town by the Pont de Beauregard is the best place to dine, but there are a number of very good, much cheaper restaurants offering local cuisine and the region's wines. About six miles from Villefranche is Lacenas and the Château de Montauzan. It has a magnificent example of the huge eighteenth-century outdoor cellars, popular throughout the region. The château is also home of the *Confrérie des Compagnons du Beaujolais*.

Although not on the route, there is an interesting little wine museum in the Maison Raclet at Romanèche-Thorins.

Belleville is much smaller but again there is a choice of restaurants, although it is advisable to book a room at either of the two hotels, one near the station and the other a couple of kilometres north of the town. Having spent the first day visiting the *Crus Beaujolais*, the second should be spent around the Beaujolais Villages. There are thirty-nine communes and villages allowed to use this *appellation*. The nine *crus* are only allowed this *appellation* if production per acre is kept below a certain figure. If a grower (in Chenas for instance) prefers to exceed this limit, he is not allowed to use the name of the village by itself, but may call the wine Beaujolais Villages, or Beaujolais Chenas.

So, the thirty-nine Beaujolais Villages include the nine *crus* villages together with Jullié, Emeringes, Lancié, Villié-Morgon, Lantignié, Beaujeu, Régnié, Durette, Cercié, Quincié, St-Lager, Odénas, Charentay, St-Etienne-la-Varenne, Vaux, Le Perréon, St-Etienne-des-Ouillières, Blacé, Arbuissonas, Salles, St-Julien-en-Montmélas, Rivolet, Denicé, Les Ardillats, Marchampt and Vauxrenard, all of which are in the Rhône *département*, together with Leynes, St-Amour-Bellevue, La Chapelle-de-Guinchay, Romanèche, Pruzilly, Chânes, St-Vérand, and St-Symphorien-d'Ancelles, in the Saône-et-Loire *département*.

The second day can be spent visiting cellars and tasting centres either in the north or the south of the region. If you want to take the northern route, drive up again on the N6 to Crêches, and take the road to St-Amour.

Follow the route down to Chenas and then take the left-hand road to La Chapelle-de-Guinchay, where there is a pleasant tasting centre. Your route should then take you south to Romanèche-Thorins, through Lancié and back to Villié-Morgon. Both here and at Beaujeu, the next port of call, there are tasting centres. There is also a cooperage exhibition and local crafts museum in Beaujeu. The route should then take you to the tasting centre at Durette, and on to Odénas, St-Etienne-la-Varenne and Le Perréon, where there are both *coopérative* cellars and tasting centres to visit. Then head for Vaux-en-Beaujolais with its tasting centre, and Salles before driving back to Villefranche through Blacé and St-Julien-en-Montmélas.

For the southern circuit, take the Liergues road out of Villefranche. Here there are both *coopérative* cellars and tasting centres. Then drive to Theizé for a tasting via Pouilly-le-Monial. From Theizé head west for about a mile to St-Laurent-d'Oingt where there are two tasting centres, and then south to Le Bois d'Oingt. Here again there is both a *coopérative* and commune tasting cellar.

You should then return via Legny and Chessy, stopping off on the way to taste at St-Jean-des-Vignes, Lachassagne and Pommiers if you wish.

There are not many truly great buildings in Beaujolais, but two worth visiting are Château de Corcelles and Château de la Chaise. The first is at Corcelles-en-Beaujolais, north of Belleville and to the west of the N6. It was built in the fifteenth century, has recently been well restored and is now a national monument. Château de la Chaize is just to the west of Odénas, and was reputedly built by a nephew of the confessor to Louis XIV. It is now a private home, surrounded by vineyards.

PLACES OF INTEREST IN THE BEAUJOLAIS REGION

Corcelles-en-Beaujolais
Château de Corcelles, fifteenth-century castle, now a national monument.

Fleurie
Memorial to Victor Pulliat, the first man to root local wines on to disease-resistant American rootstock during the phylloxera outbreak.

Juliénas
Château du Bois de la Salle, former priory now a wine co-op.

Mont de Brouilly
Hill with fine views, capped with a chapel dedicated to wine.

Odénas
Château de la Chaize, fine building dating from the time of Louis XIV.

Le Plâtre-Durand
Near St-Amour; hill top village with fine views.

Les Thorins
Windmill overlooking the village, now a national monument.

Villefranche
Many old buildings.

Villié-Morgon
Museum of winemaking equipment.

The Gastronomy of Beaujolais

For gastronomic purposes Beaujolais is considered to be part of the Lyonnais, and there are many who would argue that it is the culinary capital of France. Certainly, Lyon boasts more than its fair share of starred restaurants, and just north of the city, slightly over the edge of Beaujolais country, is the Auberge Paul Bocuse, named after its patron chef, one of the finest in Europe.

The Lyonnais is a large area able to draw on the resources of many types of agricultural and horticultural enterprises. It is bordered to the north by the Mâconnais which offers a similar, but less accessible cuisine. To the east are the Jura and the Alps, the lower slopes of which are grazed by dairy cattle, the source of many fine cheeses. To the west is the Massif Central, and the foothills which are the home of the Charollais beef cattle, and to the south, there is the Rhône valley with its fish and access to the coast and the Mediterranean catches.

There is no distinct style of Lyonnais cuisine; rather, it is a collection of menus and dishes which vary according to the chef. Some dishes can be plain, while a neighbouring establishment will offer the same dish adorned with cream and truffles. The region also includes in the north-east the area of Bresse, noted for its special chickens, the only poultry in the world to have their own *appellation contrôlée*. The chickens are free range, fed on maize and buckwheat, and then plucked by hand so that only a ruff of feathers remains, the sign of a Bresse bird. The chicken is then soaked in milk which boosts the whiteness of the meat.

Bresse also harvests a host of other produce from its fertile land. Apart from vegetables, there are many dairy cattle, and these provide the milk for the world famous *Bresse Bleu*, or *Bleu de Bresse*, which is a strong flavoured creamy cheese.

Beaujolais itself makes fine tarts and the delicate white goat's cheese, *Chèvre*, although this is found in many other regions as well; the Saône and the Rhône provide the freshwater fish, including pike, used in many of the region's speciality dishes.

As with the rest of Burgundy, Beaujolais is not the place for the weak-hearted or those on a diet; the helpings are generous to say the least and many menus, even the more modestly-priced ones, expect you to eat your way through several courses.

In addition to many of the dishes mentioned in the Burgundy section, such as *coq au vin* and *boeuf Bourguignon,* you will find that lamb and pork also figure heavily on the menus of the Lyonnais. The lamb comes from the lush grass meadows of Beaujolais, and the pork from Lyon, which is famous for its *charcuterie*. There is also game from the Forez, the high, tree-covered hills between the Loire and the Massif Central.

The area is known for its frogs, and there are many different *grenouille* dishes. They can be served in butter, with a cream and herb sauce — *grenouilles à la Bressane* — or simply cooked in butter — *grenouilles sautées*. *Quenelle* is also a speciality; it is very a light, delicate poached mousse. *Quenelle de brochet* is pike, *quenelle de volaille* is chicken.

There are marvellous local soups, both fish and meat, and for many people they can be a meal in themselves. Especially, there is *potage à la jambe de bois*, a Lyonnais speciality. It is soup made from leg of beef on the bone as well as other meats and assorted vegetables.

A much lighter dish is *écrevisses à la crème*, crayfish from the Saône served in a cream sauce.

Lyonnais is also famed for its sweet pastry fritters called *bugne*, which are sometimes served decorated with acacia flowers.

Cardon is another name you might not have come across before. The English 'cardoon' looks like celery, is related to the thistle family and has a taste a little like that of a Jerusalem artichoke. In the Lyonnais it is baked with bone marrow to create *cardons à la moelle*, and it can be served with a cheese sauce.

Pork figures in many of the dishes, but especially sausages and hams. There is blood pudding cooked with apples, *boudin aux pommes de reinette*; a large pork sausage, similar to salami, called *rosette*; and *sabodet*, a sausage made from the pig's head and served hot in thick slices. There is also *cervelas*, a soft smooth pork sausage, similar to a Saveloy. It was originally made with brains, and is now lightly smoked, poached and can be eaten hot or cold. The Lyonnais style is *cervelas en brioche*, baked in a brioche dough.

Chapon de Bresse gros sel is a Bresse capon with sliced truffles under the skin, covered in rock salt and baked. Other Bresse poultry dishes include *poulet* (or *poularde* or *volaille*) *Célestine*, with tomatoes, mushrooms, wine and cream (and named after Napoléon III's chef); *poulet aux écrevisses*, with crayfish in a white wine and cream sauce; *poulet en vessie*, poached inside a pig's bladder; *poulet à la Mère Fillioux*, stuffed with sausage with sliced truffles, and served with a cream sauce, and *poulet au vinaigre*, a speciality, chicken served with shallots, tomatoes, white wine, vinegar and cream.

The presence of cattle is also felt with many ox, beef and calf dishes. *Gras-double à la Lyonnaise* is sliced ox tripe, fried with onions, vinegar and parsley; *saladier Lyonnaise* is a gargantuan salad of calf's head, pig's and sheep's trotters, sausage and ox muzzle (the nose and lips) all tossed in a vinaigrette and diced shallots. *Tablier de sapeur*, which literally means 'fireman's apron', originated in this region; it is a thick slice of ox tongue, coated in egg and breadcrumbs, grilled or fried, and served with a sauce, usually either tartare, mayonnaise or Béarnaise.

Jambon au foin used to mean ham cooked in fresh hay, in the same way that some cheeses are cured in it. Although the practice is still continued, it is more likely now to mean ham cooked in herbs.

Hare is a feature of Bresse cuisine, and *lièvre* (or *civet*) *de Diane de Châteaumorand* is stewed hare with red wine, mushrooms and onions. It is named after a seventeenth-century beauty who divorced her husband for his brother, and then ignored him and turned to her greyhounds for company. They, presumably, caught the hares.

Other speciality dishes are *pommes Lyonnaises*, sautéed sliced potatoes cooked with onions; *omelette à la Lyonnaise*, an omelette filled with onions and parsley; *civet à la Lyonnaise*, hare stewed with chestnuts; *galette Lyonnaise*, a cake of puréed potatoes and onions; and *saucisson à la Lyonnaise*, sausage served with a hot potato salad. The Lyonnais is also famed for its desserts and *pâtisserie*. There are *marrons à la Lyonnaise* (chestnut cake); *cocons* (marzipan sweets, often filled with liqueur in the shape of a cacoon); *pogne* (a brioche cake filled with fruit and jam) which is really a speciality of further south, but is now available here, and *tendresses* (flavoured nougat in a meringue case).

The most famous cheese is the *Bleu de Bresse*, a mild creamy blue cheese similar to a Gorgonzola; it is now almost all factory made. *Cervelle de Canut* (also called *Claqueret*), is a home-made mixture of curds, vinegar, white wine, oil and garlic. It means 'silk-weaver's brain' and was traditionally made by their families. *Fromage fort du Beaujolais* is a strong, firm cheese, often soaked in *marc*, and *Fourme de Montbrison* comes from the Forez foothills and is a firm cheese that is uncooked, unpressed and ripened for two months. It has a fruity taste, is lightly blue-veined and has its own *appellation*. *Rigotte de Condrieu* is a small, mild cheese made by the small dairies around Condrieu. It has a mild, milky taste and a reddish rind.

There are two goat's cheeses available locally; one comes from Bresse and the other from Forez. *Bressan*, also known as *Petit Bressan*, is a soft, small, mild goat's cheese still made on farms, with a slightly fruity taste. There is occasionally more than the hint of goat in the smell.

Brique du Forez, also known as *Chèvreton d'Ambert* and *Cabrion du Forez*, is named after its brick shape. It is a mild cheese with a nutty flavour, made on farms in the Ambert and Monts du Forez region.

HOTELS AND RESTAURANTS
OF THE BEAUJOLAIS REGION

LYON

Hotels and restaurants in and around Lyon have been included in this section, not only because there are so many good establishments here, but because it is an ideal base from which to tour.

(69000 Lyon)

Frantel
129 rue Servient
☎ (78) 62 94 12
A luxurious 245-room hotel, occupying the top 10 floors of the Credit Lyonnais tower giving marvellous views over the city. Air-conditioned, and the restaurant, L'Arc-en-Ciel, is a delight thanks to chef Jean Fleury.

Sofitel
20 quai Gailleton
☎ (78) 42 72 50
A near-perfect hotel, with faultless, unobtrusive service. Expensive, but the 190 rooms are modern, elegant, air-conditioned and very comfortable. The restaurant, Les Trois Dômes, offers a huge choice of fresh dishes daily, all supervised by Guy Girerd. The restaurant on the top floor offers superb views of Lyon, and there is also a Sofi-Shop offering snacks until the early hours.

Grand Hôtel Concorde
11 rue Grolée
☎ (78) 42 56 21

A 140-room, air-conditioned hotel, on the right bank of the Rhône. It has a four-star rating, merited by the comfort of the rooms, many of them recently completely refurbished. Good restaurant.

P.L.M. Terminus
12 cours de Verdun
☎ (78) 37 58 11
Near the Perrache railway station. A comfortable 140-room hotel in a nineteenth-century building, with an air of spaciousness. There is an airport shuttle bus every twenty minutes. No restaurant, but breakfast served.

Hôtel Bristol
28 cours de Verdun
☎ (78) 37 56 55
A comfortable 131-room hotel with reasonable rates. No restaurant but breakfast served.

Bordeaux et Parc
1 rue Béllier
☎ (78) 37 58 73
Another large hotel near the Perrache station. 87 rooms, no restaurant but breakfast served.

Royal
20 place Bellecour
☎ (78) 37 57 31
Very central 89-room hotel, next to the pedestrian precincts. Air-conditioned, well-equipped rooms, and the L'Oranger is reasonable and good.

Hôtel Carlton
4 rue Jussieu
☎ (78) 42 56 51
A friendly, quiet 90-room hotel with no restaurant, but breakfast served.

Parc Hôtel
4 rue du Prof. Calmette
☎ (78) 74 11 20
A large, modernised 70-room hotel with good restaurant, and patio for summer dining out.

Le Bistrot de Lyon
64 rue Mercière
☎ (78) 37 00 62
Not the best eating-place in Lyon but one of the liveliest. Good food in bustling surroundings. One of the very fashionable places, but worth it to mingle and sample the Lyonnais food.

Restaurant Orsi
3 place Kléber
☎ (78) 89 57 68
Run by Pierre Orsi, once a restaurateur in Chicago, and now patron of one of the best restaurants in Lyon. Marvellous food, excellent service, elegant surroundings and prices to match.

Christian Bourillot
8 place des Célestins
☎ (78) 37 38 64
The *patron chef* maintains a consistently high standard and never fails to delight. The food is always good, and it is an added pleasure to dine in an air-conditioned room.

Daniel and Denis
2 rue Turpin
☎ (78) 37 49 98
Another restaurant that
maintains a consistently
high standard, although
the menu does not change
quite as often as it should.
A very good wine list, and
another place to go 'to
see and be seen'.

Le Champier
10 rue des Fantasques
☎ (78) 28 41 33
A former silk-weaver's
premises, this restaurant
is run by Daniel Cantat,
who creates delicious light
dishes and excellent
sauces. Very reasonably
priced.

Dussaud
12 rue Pizay
☎ (78) 28 10 94
Run by Roger and Mon-
ique Dussaud; specialises
in the traditional Lyon-
nais meal, very good and
huge. Menus change
according to local market
supplies and prices are
very reasonable.

Chez Gervais
42 rue Pierre-Corneille
☎ (78) 52 19 13
A real Lyonnais treat. All
the local specialities are
to be found here; be guided in your choice by the
staff. The food is very
reasonable, the wine list
good but pricey.

Henry
27 rue de la Martinière
☎ (78) 28 26 08
Run by Pierre Balladone,
who specialises in very
light, stylish creations.
Very good value, the fixed-
price menu includes wine.

Léon de Lyon
1 rue Pléney
☎ (78) 28 11 33
Chef Jean-Paul Lacombe
offers a pleasant combin-
ation of Lyonnais cuisine
and the *nouvelle*, without
compromising either. His
fish dishes are wonderful,
and his Charollais some
of the best in Lyon.

La Mercière
56 rue Mercière
☎ (78) 37 67 35
Deserves a mention
because of the extra-
ordinary value for money
it offers at lunches.
Crowded in the evening,
when the frequently-
changing menu is equally
good value for money.
Best to book.

Nandron
26 quai Jean-Moulin
☎ (78) 42 10 26
An exciting, creative,
restaurant, with mar-
vellous wine list. Not for
those on a budget.

La Tour Rose
16 rue du Boeuf
☎ (78) 37 25 90
A lovely old restaurant in
the old town. The food
and service are excellent,
and the lunchtime prices a
bargain. Young chef
Philippe Chavent is
supremely in control.

Vettard
7 place Bellecour
☎ (78) 42 07 59
A super restaurant, again
mixing the best of the
Lyonnais tradition with
the best of the *nouvelle*. A
good but expensive wine
list.

**Hotels near the
airports**

Novotel
rue Lionel Terray
☎ (78) 26 97 48
196-room modern hotel
close to Bron airport.
Restaurant and pool.

Meridien
at Satolas airport, 16$\frac{1}{2}$
miles from Lyon on the
A43
☎ (78) 71 91 61
120 rooms, air-condition-
ing and restaurants.

Alain Chapel
12 miles north of Lyon
on the N83
☎ (78) 91 82 02
A family inn, run by
M. Chapel in Mionnay.
He is one of France's
greatest chefs, and deservedly so. The food is near-
perfect and you pay dearly
for the privilege of eating
it, but it is worth it. The
inn has 13 rooms, again
expensive and reserved
months ahead. Especially
recommended.

Paul Bocuse
Pont de Collonges
9km north of Lyon on the
N433 or D51 at
Collonges-au-Mont-d'Or.
☎ (78) 22 01 40
Tables here are sometimes
booked years ahead! He is
one of France's greatest
chefs, former president of
the *Nouvelle Cuisine Fran-
çaise* and winner of the
Gault Millau Best Meal of
the Year award. Nothing
more needs to be said,
except it is worth trying
to get a table to enjoy an
unforgettable experience.
Especially recommended.

BEAUJOLAIS

Belleville
(69330 Rhône)

Le Beaujolais
40 rue du Maréchal Foch
☎ (74) 66 05 31
Run by the Dalmaz
brothers, who serve very
good traditional local
cuisine and stock a fine
cellar. There are 10
reasonably-priced rooms.

Blaceret
(69830 Rhône)

Restaurant Le Beaujolais
On the N6, $5^1/2$ miles from
  Villefranche.
☎ (74) 67 54 75
A warm and friendly
restaurant, offering good
local cuisine and wine at
near bargain prices.

Chenas
(69840 Rhône)

Restaurant Robin
aux Deschamps
☎ (85) 36 72 67
Daniel Robin and his wife
run this delightful res-
taurant, set amidst the
vineyards. The food is
good, the views marvel-
lous and M. Robin senior
provides some of his own
wine from the nearby vineyards to augment a fine
list of local wines.

Fleurie
(69820 Fleurie)

Auberge du Cep
place de l'Eglise
☎ (74) 04 10 77
Chef Gérard Cortembert is
already a master in the
kitchen, having spent
three years at Alain

Chapel's. The dishes are
imaginative and always
good. It is necessary to
check opening times be-
cause the patron some-
times takes an unexpected
night off.

Juliénas
(69840 Rhône)

Chez la Rose
place du Marché
☎ (74) 04 41 20
A small comfortable hotel
with 12 very reasonably-
priced rooms, and a fair
restaurant specialising in
local cuisine.

Coq au Vin
place du Marché
☎ (74) 04 41 98
Also situated in the
marketplace in the middle
of the town. A rustic
restaurant with a lot of
charm.

Morgon
(69910 Rhône)

Le Relais des Caveaux
☎ (74) 04 21 77
Opposite the tasting
cellars, and a good place
to have a pleasant,
reasonably-priced lunch
before getting down to the
serious task of tasting.

**Quincié-en-
Beaujolais**
(69430 Beaujeu)

Auberge des Samsons
on the D37, 3 miles from
  Beaujeu
☎ (74) 04 32 09
A charming restaurant
with a style of its own.
The fine, light dishes,

prepared by Marcel Baïer,
are lovingly served by his
wife. A delightful place to
stop and one that will not
hurt your pocket.

Roanne
(42300 Roanne, Loire)

Troisgros
place de la Gare
☎ (77) 71 66 97
A 47-mile drive from
Villefranche and 55 miles
from Lyon, but worth it to
sample the delights of
Pierre and Jean Troisgros.
Although not on the wine
route, the detour is worth
it to taste the superb
cuisine. Very expensive
and advisable to book
well ahead.

Romanèche-Thorins
(71570 Saône-et-Loire)

Maritonnes
near the station
☎ (85) 35 51 70
A small, comfortable, 19-
room hotel with pleasant
restaurant specialising in
local cuisine. Try the
*Tournedos de Charollais
sauce Périgueux.*

Commerce
at the station
☎ (85) 35 51 82
A 15-room hotel, reason-
ably-priced, with a fair restaurant serving good hon-
est Beaujolais cooking.

**St-Georges-de-
Reneins**
(69830 Rhône)

Hostellerie de St-Georges
on the N6
☎ (74) 67 62 78

A charming lunchtime stop-over for good food, pleasantly priced.

Sables
by the Saône
☎ (74) 67 64 08
A modestly-priced 18 - room hotel, with pleasing restaurant.

St-Lager
(69220 Rhône)

Auberge de St-Lager
☎ (74) 66 16 08
A very reasonably-priced restaurant among the vineyards. Open for lunch only, but the fixed-price menu is a bargain.

Thoissey
(01140 Ain)

Au Chapon Fin
rue du Champ-de-Foire
☎ (74) 04 04 74
A very comfortable 25-room hotel, some rooms are in the old house and the rest in a new annexe, overlooking an attractive garden. The restaurant is excellent, the service efficient and friendly and the prices not too damaging.

Vaux-en-Beaujolais
(69460 Rhône)

Auberge de Clochemerle
rue Gabriel-Chevalier
☎ (74) 65 91 11
A rustic restaurant in a delightful setting, perfect for a lunchtime stop.

Villefranche-sur-Saône (69400 Rhône)

Hôtel Plaisance
96 ave. Libération
☎ (74) 65 33 52
A comfortable 68-room hotel with restaurant.

Hôtel Newport
ave. de l'Europe
☎ (74) 68 75 59
A reasonable 29-room hotel with restaurant

Auberge Faisan-Doré
au Pont de Beauregard
☎ (74) 65 01 66
A fine restaurant specialising in local cuisine.

Château de Chervinges
Chervinges-Gleizé, on the D34 or D38 1³⁄4 miles from Villefranche
☎ (74) 65 29 76
An elegant, quiet hotel with 11 rooms and 6 apartments, and a good restaurant.

Vonnas
(01540 Ain)

Georges Blanc
☎ (74) 50 00 10
A luxurious 30-room hotel, with superb restaurant. Patron Chef Georges Blanc received his third Michelin star in 1981, and deservedly so. Best to book, and save up.

THE VINEYARDS OF BEAUJOLAIS

BEAUJOLAIS VILLAGES

Paul Beaudet   TR
Pontanevaux
71570 La Chapelle-de-
  Guinchay
☎ (85) 36 72 76
Open: by appointment.

Jean-Pierre   TR
  Belleville
Les Bruyères
Régnié-Durette
69430 Beaujeu
☎ (74) 04 32 78
Visits: by appointment.

René Berrod   TR
69820 Fleurie
☎ (74) 04 13 63
Visits: by appointment.

Château du Carra   TR
Guy Durieu
69460 St-Etienne-des-
  Ouillières
☎ (74) 03 20 01
Open: by appointment.

Jean-Louis Chanay   TR
Le Trêve
69460 St-Etienne-des-
  Ouillières
☎ (74) 03 43 65
Open: by appointment.

Domaine du Chapitre   TR
blvd Emile Guyot
69830 St-Georges-de
  Reneins
☎ (74) 66 07 99
Open: by appointment.

Château de Châtelard   TR
Lancié
69220 Belleville
☎ (74) 04 12 99
Open: by appointment.

Louis Coillard   TR
69430 Beaujeu
☎ (74) 04 35 37
Open: by appointment.

Domaine du Crêt-des-
  Bruyères   TR
Régnié-Durette
69430 Beaujeu
☎ (74) 04 30 21
Open: by appointment.

Pierre Deshayes
  and son   TR
69460 Le Perréon
☎ (74) 03 21 31
Open: daily 9am-8pm.

Caveau des Deux
  Clochers   TR
Régnié-Durette
69430 Beaujeu
☎ (74) 04 36 50
Open: by appointment.

Joseph Drouhin   TR
rue d'Enfer
21200 Beaune
☎ (80) 22 06 80
Open: by appointment.

Georges Duboeuf   TR
Romanèche-Thorins
71570 La Chapelle-de-
  Guinchay
☎ (85) 35 51 13
Open: Monday to Saturday
8am-noon and 2-5pm;
closed in August.

Jean Durand   TR
Régnié-Durette
69430 Beaujeu
☎ (74) 04 30 97
Open: by appointment.

Paul Gauthier   TR
Blacé
69460 St-Etienne-des-
  Ouillières
☎ (74) 67 53 55
Open: by appointment.

Domaine de la
  Gérarde   TR
Régnié-Durette
69430 Beaujeu
☎ (74) 04 30 37
Open: by appointment.

Henri Grandjean   TR
Vallière
Régnié-Durette
69430 Beaujeu
☎ (74) 04 87 05
Open: by appointment.

Coopérative des
  Grands Vins   TR
Château du Bois de la
  Salle
69840 Juliénas
☎ (74) 04 42 61
Open: by appointment.

Château de Lacarelle   TR
69460 St-Etienne-des-
  Ouillières
☎ (74) 03 40 80
Open: by appointment.

Cave des Vignerons
  de Liergues   TR
Liergues
69400 Villefranche-sur-
  Saône
☎ (74) 68 07 94
Open: by appointment.

Bernard Mera   TR
Marchampt
69430 Beaujeu
☎ (74) 04 32 94
Open: by appointment.

T=tasting   E=English spoken   G=guided tours   C=château/building to visit

Domaine des Nugues   TR
Les Pasquiers
Lancié
69220 Belleville
☎ (74) 04 14 00
Open: by appointment.

Piat and son   TR
71570 La Chapelle-de-
Guinchay
☎ (85) 36 77 77
Open: by appointment.

Domaine du Py-de-   TR
Bulliat
Régnié-Durette
69430 Beaujeu
☎ (74) 04 20 17
Open: by appointment.

Domaine des
Quarante Ecus   TR
Les Vergers
Lantignié
69340 Beaujeu
☎ (74) 04 85 80
Open: by appointment.

Domaine des Rampaux   TR
Régnié-Durette
69430 Beaujeu
☎ (74) 04 35 68
Open: by appointment.

Joel Rochette   TR
Le Chalet
Régnié-Durette
69430 Beaujeu
☎ (74) 04 35 78
Open: by appointment.

Domaine de la Rouze   TR
Régnié-Durette
69430 Beaujeu
☎ (74) 04 30 48
Open: by appointment.

Jean-Michel Sauzon   TR
Les Grandes Bruyères
69460 St-Etienne-des-
Ouillières
☎ (74) 03 42 84
Open: by appointment.

Domaine de la Sorbière   TR
Quincié-en-Beaujolais
69430 Beaujeu
☎ (74) 04 30 32
Open: by appointment.

Domaine des Terres-
Dessus   TR
Lancié
69220 Belleville
☎ (74) 04 13 85
Open: daily 8am-8pm.

La Tour Bourdon   TR
GAEC de la Tour Bourdon
Régnié-Durette
69430 Beaujeu
☎ (74) 04 32 15
Visits: by appointment.

Gérard Trichard   TR
Bel Avenir
71570 La Chapelle-de-
Guinchay
☎ 36 77 54
Open: by appointment.

Brouilly

Vignobles de Bel-Air   TR
St-Jean-d'Ardières
69220 Belleville
☎ (74) 66 00 16
Open: by appointment.

Cave Béthu   TR
Pontanevaux
71570 La Chapelle-de-
Guinchay
☎ (85) 36 72 76
Open: by appointment.

Robert Condemine   TR
Les Bruyères
Cercié
69220 Belleville
☎ (74) 66 19 45
Open: by appointment.

Domaine Crêt des
Garanches   TR
Odénas
69460 St-Etienne-des-
Ouillières
☎ (74) 03 41 46
Open: by appointment.

Alain Michaud   TR
St-Lager
69220 Belleville
☎ (74) 66 29 49
Open: by appointment.

Jean-Paul Ruet   TR
Cercié
69220 Belleville
☎ (74) 66 35 45
Open: by appointment.

Domaine de Saburin   TR
Bouchard and son
21200 Beaune
☎ (80) 22 14 41
Open: by appointment.

Château des Tours   TR
St-Etienne-la-Varenne
69830 St-Georges-de-
Reneins
☎ (74) 03 40 86
Open: by appointment.

Chenas

Paul Beaudet   TR
Pontanevaux
71570 La Chapelle-de-
Guinchay
☎ (85) 36 72 76
Open: by appointment.

Château Bonnet   TR
71570 La Chapelle-de-
Guinchay
☎ (85) 36 70 41
Open: by appointment.

Georges Duboeuf   TR
71570 La Chapelle-de-
Guinchay
☎ (85) 35 51 13
Open: Monday to Friday
8am-noon and 2-5pm.

Les Gandelins   TR
71570 La Chapelle-de-
Guinchay
☎ (85) 36 74 89
Open: daily 9am-7pm.

R=red wine   W=white wine   P=rosé wine   S=sparkling wine

Mathelin TR
Châtillon-d'Azerques
69380 Lozanne
☎ (74) 84 39 42
Open: Monday to
Saturday.

Domaine des Pins TR
St-Jean-d'Ardières
69220 Belleville
☎ (74) 66 19 43
Open: by appointment.

Chiroubles

Collin and Bourisset TR
71680 Crêches-sur-Saône
☎ (85) 37 11 15
Open: by appointment.

Jacques Dépagneux TR
69400 Villefranche-sur-
Saône
☎ (74) 65 42 60
Open: by appointment.

Domaine du Moulin
69115 Chiroubles
☎ (74) 69 11 18
Open: by appointment.

Fleurie

René Berrod TR
69820 Fleurie
☎ (74) 04 13 63
Open: by appointment.

Domaine Bouchard
and son TR
21202 Beaune
☎ (80) 22 14 41
Open: by appointment.

Juliénas

Domaine de Beauvernay TR
71570 La Chapelle-de-
Guinchay
☎ (85) 36 77 77
Open: by appointment.

Mathelin TR
Châtillon-d'Azerques
69380 Lozanne
☎ (74) 84 39 24
Open: daily.

Domaine des Poupets TR
71570 La Chapelle-de-
Guinchay
☎ (85) 36 72 76
Open: by appointment.

Cellier de la Vieille
Eglise TR
69840 Juliénas
☎ (74) 04 41 43
Open: daily.

Morgon

Domaine de l'Ancienne TR
Curé
St-Jean-d'Ardières
69220 Belleville
☎ (74) 66 19 43
Open: by appointment.

Domaine Aucoeur TR
69910 Villié-Morgon
☎ (74) 04 22 10
Open: by appointment.

Collin and Bourisset TR
rue de la Gare
71680 Crêches-sur-Saône
☎ (85) 37 11 15
Open: by appointment.

Château Gaillard TR
69910 Villié-Morgon
☎ (74) 69 12 77
Open: by appointment.

Domaine de
Lathevieille TR
Charnay-lès-Mâcon
71000 Mâcon
☎ (85) 34 47 74
Open: by appointment.

Cellier des Samsons TR
Quincié-en-Beaujolais
69430 Beaujeu
☎ (74) 66 24 19
Open: by appointment.

Pierre Savoye TR
69910 Villié-Morgon
☎ (74) 04 21 92
Open: by appointment.

Caveau de Villié-
Morgon TR
Le Bourg
69910 Villié-Morgon
☎ (74) 04 20 99
Open: daily 9am-noon and
2-7pm.

Moulin-à-Vent

Château de Chénas TR
Chénas
69840 Juliénas
☎ (74) 04 11 91
Open: by appointment.

Gérard Lapierre TR
Chénas
69840 Juliénas
☎ (85) 36 70 74
Open: by appointment.

Maison Mâconnaise
des Vins TR
ave. de Lattre-de-Tassigny
71000 Mâcon
☎ (85) 38 36 70
Open: daily.

Jean Mortet TR
Romanèche-Thorins
71570 La Chapelle-de-
Guinchay
☎ (85) 22 22 60
Open: by appointment.

Clos du Tremblay
71720 Romanèche-
Thorins
☎ (85) 35 52 80
Open: by appointment.

St-Amour

Paul Beaudet TR
Pontanevaux
71570 La Chapelle-de-
Guinchay
☎ (85) 36 72 76
Open: by appointment.

Domaine Bouchard
and son TR
21202 Beaune
☎ (80) 22 14 41
Open: by appointment.

T=tasting   E=English spoken   G=guided tours   C=château/building to visit

Georges Duboeuf   TR
71720 Romanèche-
Thorins
☎ (85) 35 51 13
Open: daily 9am-noon and
2-5pm.

Jacques Duc   TR
St-Amour-Bellevue
71570 La Chapelle-de-
Guinchay
☎ (85) 37 10 08
Open: by appointment.

Mathelin   TR
Châtillon-d'Azerques
69380 Lozanne
☎ (74) 84 39 24
Open: Monday to Saturday
8.30am-noon and 2-7pm.

THE CAVES COOPERATIVES

La Cave Coopérative
 Beaujolais
Bully
69210 L'Arbresle
☎ (74) 01 27 77
Open: weekends and
public holidays 2-6pm and
every day between 1 July
and 31 August.

La Maison des Vignerons
Chiroubles
☎ (74) 04 20 47
Open: Monday to Saturday
10-11.45am and 2.30-
6.30pm, Sunday and
public holidays 2.30-
6.30pm.

La Cave du Château de
 Chénas
Chénas
☎ (74) 04 91 11
Open: daily.

Le Caveau de la Cave
 Coopérative
Le Bourg
69820 Fleurie
☎ (74) 04 11 70
Open: daily 9am-noon and
2-6pm.

La Cave Coopérative de
 Gleizé
Gleizé
☎ (74) 68 39 40

La Cave des Producteurs
 Juliénas
☎ (85) 04 42 61
Open: daily 8.15am-noon
and 2-6pm.

Cave Coopérative de
 Lachassagne
Lachassagne
☎ (74) 67 01 43
Open: Saturday only
8-11.30am and 2-5pm.

La Terrasse des Pierres
 Dorées
Le Bois d'Oingt
☎ (74) 70 62 81
Open: Monday to
Saturday.

La Cave Coopérative
 Perréon
Le Perréon
☎ (74) 03 22 83
Open: daily.

La Cave Coopérative
 Beaujolais
Létra
☎ (74) 71 30 52
Open: Monday to Friday
7.30am-noon and 1.30-
6pm; Saturday 8am-noon
and 2-5pm.

La Société Vinicole
 Beaujolais
Liergues
69400 Villefranche-sur-
 Saône
☎ (74) 68 07 94

La Cave Coopérative
 Beaujolais
Quincié
☎ (74) 04 32 54
Open: Monday to Friday.

La Cave Coopérative de
 St-Etienne-des-Ouillières
St-Etienne-des-Ouillières
☎ (74) 03 43 69
Open: daily.

La Cave de Bel-Air
St-Jean-d'Ardières
69220 Belleville
☎ (74) 66 00 16
Open: Monday to Saturday
8am-noon and 2-6pm.

La Cave Coopérative
 Beaujolais
St-Laurent d'Oingt
Open: Monday to Saturday
8am-noon and 2-6pm,
closed public holidays.

La Cave Coopérative de St-
 Vérand
St-Vérand
☎ (74) 71 73 19
Open: weekend afternoons
and public holidays.

La Cave Beaujolais du
 Beau-Vallon
Theizé
☎ (74) 71 75 97
Open: Saturday, Sunday
and public holidays.

R=red wine   W=white wine   P=rosé wine   S=sparkling wine

THE WINE-TASTING CELLARS OF BEAUJOLAIS

There are twenty-three wine-tasting cellars along the roads of the Beaujolais, which give trade visitors and a large number of tourists an opportunity of trying the region's products. These are:

Le Temple de Bacchus
69430 Beaujeu
☎ (74) 04 81 18

La Cadole du Char à
  Boeufs
69840 Chasselas
☎ (85) 35 11 99
Open: Friday to Monday 10am-noon and all other times by appointment.

Le Pavillon des Pierres
Dorées
69220 Châtillon-d'Azergues
☎ (74) 43 95 43
Open: Saturday 10am-noon and 3-6pm, Sunday 10am-noon.

Le Cellier du Babouin
69220 Chazay d'Azergues
Open: daily.

Le Caveau du Cru Chénas
69840 Chénas
☎ (74) 04 11 91
Open: daily 15 June-15 October, rest of year weekends only.

La Terrasse de Chiroubles
69220 Chiroubles
☎ (74) 04 20 79
Open: every afternoon.

Le Caveau des Voûtes
69400 Cogny
Open: daily.

Le Caveau de Dégustation
  des Viticulteurs
69820 Fleurie
Open: daily 10am-noon and 2.30-6.30pm.

Le Caveau de Gleizé
69400 Gleizé
☎ (74) 63 39 49
Open: Sundays and public holidays in summer, 2.30-8pm, rest of year 2.30-7pm.

Le Cellier de la Vieille
  Eglise
69840 Juliénas
Open: daily 9.45am-noon and 2.30-6.30pm.

Le Caveau de Jullié
69840 Jullié
Open: Sundays only.

Le Relais Beaujolais-
  Mâconnais
69840 Leynes
☎ (85) 35 11 29
Open: daily.

La Terrasse des Beaujolais
69400 Pommiers
☎ (74) 65 05 27
Tasting and restaurant; closed Tuesday afternoon and Wednesday.

Le Caveau des Deux-
  Clochers
69220 Régnié
☎ (74) 04 36 50
Open: Saturday and Sunday afternoon between Easter and 15 September.

Le Caveau de l'Union des
  Viticulteurs du Moulin-à-
  Vent
71570 Romanèche-Thorins
☎ (85) 35 51 03
Tasting and restaurant; cave open daily except Tuesday.

La Tassée du Chapitre
69460 Salles-en-Beaujolais
Open: daily May-October.

Le Caveau du Cru St-
  Amour
69840 St-Amour
☎ (85) 37 15 98

Open: daily.

La Maison des Beaujolais
69220 St-Jean-d'Ardières
☎ (74) 66 16 46
Tasting and restaurant; Closed Wednesday afternoon and Thursday.

Le Refuge des Pierres
  Dorées
69400 St-Jean-des-Vignes
Open: Sundays and public holidays 3-7pm.

Le Cuvage des Brouilly
69220 St-Lager
☎ (74) 66 18 34
Open: daily, except Tuesday, 10am-noon and 3-8pm.

Caveau de l'Union des
  Viticulteurs
69840 St-Vérand
☎ (74) 71 73 19
Open: daily.

Le Caveau de Clochemerle
69460 Vaux-en-Beaujolais
☎ 03 22 80
Museum.

Le Caveau des Morgen
Château de Foncrenne
69910 Villié-Morgan
☎ (74) 04 20 99
Park and small zoo.

Some wine-tasting cellars are to be found in the winegrowers' cooperatives, at Bully, Chiroubles, Fleurie, Gleizé, Juliénas, Lachassagne, Le Bois-d'Oingt, Létra, Le Perréon, St-Etienne-des-Oullières, St-Laurent-d'Oingt, St-Vérand and Theizé. These form the Association des Caveaux du Beaujolais, with offices at 210 Boulevard Vermorel, Villefranche. ☎ (74) 65 45 55

T=tasting   E=English spoken   G=guided tours   C=château/building to visit

Chapter 5
CHAMPAGNE

Montagne de Reims.
Champagne

THE WORD *Champagne* comes from the Latin word for a plain. Today the name is world-famous as the home of the greatest sparkling wine. Champagne is the 'Queen of Wines' and undisputed champion in the sparkling wine league. Because imitation is the sincerest form of flattery, it has been copied in most winemaking countries around the globe, but never truly equalled. Only in California are the *méthode Champenoise* wines worthy competitors.

Champagne is the most northerly major vineyard region in France, and although the province is really one large plain, 100 miles to the east of Paris, the vines are grown on gently-sloping hills which break up the landscape. The whole area was formerly the basin of a huge inland sea, and as fish and sea-creatures died and fell to the seabed, a huge stratum of chalk was built up; this forms the soil of Champagne, and is one of the reasons for its very special qualities.

The region is split by the river Marne, which runs from east to west through wooded hills. The hills are composed mainly of clay soils; in the river valley is to be found Epernay, the Champagne town, while on the plain is Reims, the Champagne capital.

The average annual temperature of Champagne is 50°F, about the lowest temperature at which vines can flourish, but the slight elevation of the vineyards on the gentle slopes protects them from all but the most severe spring frosts, when the worst damage can be done because the sap is rising. The chalk soil not only retains the heat of the sun which warms the roots, and reflects the sun's rays; it also keeps the soil well drained, and the nearby forests and woodlands help to regulate the humidity of the region. The chalk extends for many yards below ground, and it is not only suitable for vines; it has also allowed the growers to carve out the perfect cellars, and there are now 120 miles of tunnels and caves in the chalk.

Vines have certainly flourished in Champagne since Roman times. In 57BC Julius Caesar found himself in Champagne, having conquered Gaul. A Belgian tribe, the Remois, were already established in the province and they offered the emperor their allegiance. In gratitude, Julius ordered the building of a town, *Durocortorum*, 'the capital of Second Belgium', where eight major routes met. This town survived for nearly 500 years as a showplace, with its statues and theatres.

In AD92 the Emperor Domitian ordered the uprooting of half the vineyards in the Empire so that more land could be made available for growing grain. Vines were only to be grown in areas near to large military camps, so that wine could be produced for the soldiers. Champagne was one of the areas ordered to uproot its vines, but the edict from Rome was ignored by some growers, and wine has therefore been produced in Champagne almost continuously for some 2,000 years.

Reims has suffered through the centuries as a result of its situation in the north-east of France, close to the border. In the fifth century, when the Roman Empire was in decline and troops were withdrawn from Gaul, Reims was exposed to attack. The first invader was Attila the Hun. Reims was sacked and set on fire, as were the much smaller towns of Epernay and

Châlons. The powerful Archbishop of Reims managed to rally the inhabitants and restore order; indeed, so powerful were they that it was Archbishop St Rémi who baptised Clovis as the first Frankish king in Rheims Cathedral in 496. Rheims, incidentally, is not named after St Rémi, but after the Remois; but it was the Archbishop's coronation of Clovis which established the links between the city and the monarchy, and made his church the national cathedral.

Because of their links with royalty through Reims, the nobility of the province exercised immense power and influence in the French court. The Duke of Reims ruled his territory as a king, and the Count of Châlons was also Bishop of the diocese, commanding both spiritual and temporal loyalty. Great religious institutions, such as the abbeys of St Rémi, St Thierry, Hautvillers, Verzy and Orbais, were founded in the region. The monks introduced both learning and viticulture and founded hospices for the sick and travellers. Wine grew in importance, not only for the sacraments, but also because of the increasing numbers of visitors drawn to the region; as with beer in England, wine was often drunk because the water was not safe.

During the twelfth century, the Knights of Champagne played a prominent role in the First Crusade, and the Second Crusade was largely instigated by St Bernard at Châlons in 1147. Throughout this period, the wines of Champagne grew in popularity, and kings and emperors visited the province to taste them. Edward III of England besieged Reims because he wanted to be crowned there: he failed to take the town, but made off with many barrels of wine. In 1417, the Duke of Burgundy laid claim to Champagne, which led to one of the bloodiest and most famous periods of French history. The Burgundians were repulsed by Joan of Arc's army and Charles VII was crowned king in Reims Cathedral.

For the next 300 years the province flourished. The kings of France kept agents there to buy the best wines, the nobility built houses there and art and literature flourished. A school of sculpture was founded at Troyes and magnificent houses were built in Reims. In the eleventh century, the Steward's mansion was built in Châlons; it is now the Préfecture. Many of the abbeys were rebuilt, only to be destroyed again a century later during the Revolution.

Champagne became a bloody battleground again towards the end of the eighteenth century, when the country was thrown into war. The Battle of Valmy in 1792 marked the start of Napoléon I's wars, and the struggle ended in Champagne with the Battle of Reims, when the Russians invaded in 1814. They, incidentally, helped to coin the word *bistro*. They would enter inns and thump their hands down on the tables shouting *bystro*, the Russian word for quick. Thus bistros were created to serve food and drink quickly.

The Champagne area was not at peace for very long. The Prussians ruled Champagne for a time after Napoléon III's defeat at Sedan in 1870; the Germans invaded again in World War I and Champagne became a battlefield once more, the two battles of the Marne being the most costly. The second battle, in 1918, was decisive, however, in driving the Germans out. The cost was not only counted in lives; the vineyards were destroyed and the ground was scored with craters and trenches. Replanting was started, and in Reims, where four-fifths of the city had been destroyed, rebuilding commenced, and within a few years grapes were being grown again and wine made.

Hostilities in France at the beginning of World War II ended so abruptly that there were no long-drawn-out campaigns, and Champagne, though invaded, suffered little damage to its vineyards although Reims itself was very badly damaged.

Over the centuries Champagne has continued to produce wine, but originally this wine was a very different product to the one we know today, as it was still rather than sparkling. The growers soon realised that wines with a natural sparkle could be produced, but they had no means of trapping this sparkle in the bottle. Cloth pushed into the neck of the bottle and then covered with a wax seal did not form a very efficient stopper; another method, pouring a small quantity of oil on to the water so that it rested on the surface, was also not very effective.

The growers did not appreciate that after the initial fermentation following the harvest, the wine underwent a second fermentation in the spring, when temperatures again started to rise, and any remaining sugar and yeast started to react together. Consequently, they always bottled their wine after the first fermentation, and then the second would take place, blow out the cloth stoppers, and a large quantity of the harvest each year must have been ruined.

It was Pierre Pérignon, a young Benedictine monk from the Abbé de Hautvillers, who solved the problem and established his place in the history of Champagne. He was cellarmaster at the abbey, and was in charge of making wine, having been appointed in the late 1660s. He is reputed to have been the first person to make a totally still red wine; he was an expert at blending, and produced the first *cuvées*, the blending of wine from different villages. He also introduced corks to the district, although they had been in use in Spain, Portugal, southern France and England for some years before.

Using his scientific training, he also developed a method of controlling the fermentation so that the grapes produced a clear wine, instead of a cloudy one, which still retained its bubbles or *mousse*. Fermentation control led to another problem, however, because with a cork firmly in place, the bubbles could not escape. Eventually pressure built up and either the bottles exploded or the cork was shot out. Previously, although a sparkling wine was being produced, the stoppers were so ineffective that the gases escaped and so the end product was a still wine. Dom Pérignon developed a tougher glass able to withstand the build-up of pressure, and corks able to contain the gases, and so the first true sparkling Champagne was created.

Champagne soon became popular throughout the courts of Europe, and even the occupation of the province by the Russians helped to boost sales. The Russians developed a taste for the sparkling wine, and until their own revolution were Champagne's biggest customers.

The phylloxera which invaded Europe and destroyed the vineyards of France attacked Champagne later than other places, so the vineyards were able to go on producing wine long after Burgundy and Bordeaux had ceased production; this too boosted their popularity. At this time, most of the Champagne produced was sweet, varying from medium to very sweet. As tastes for drier wines developed, especially in Britain, the first dry Champagnes were produced. Also at this time, there was concern over the large quantity of Champagne being produced, and moves were made to introduce laws controlling the area of production, the types of grape to be used and so on. Until then, any grape had been allowed, and blenders were able to buy in grapes from a very large area, even outside Champagne, which at that time was much larger than it is now. This attempt to introduce controls led to the Champagne riots of 1910 and 1911, which followed the bad harvest of 1909. Buildings were broken into, and Champagne was tipped into the streets 'where it ran like rivers'. The next two harvests were good, and people once more concentrated on making Champagne.

The vineyards in Champagne now constitute one of the smallest vine-growing areas in France. They only cover one-fiftieth of France's total vineyard area, and run for 90 miles in belts of between 300yd and 1,200yd in width along the hillside slopes. The vines are squat and low-yielding and only three varieties are allowed: Chardonnay, a white, and Pinot Noir and Pinot Meunier, both red. About 75 per cent of the vineyards are planted with Pinot, one of the 'noble' grape families which give the wine body and backbone. The Chardonnay is also a 'noble' grape, and gives lightness, freshness and elegance.

After hand-picking, the grapes are pressed three times. The juice from the first pressing, the *vin de cuvée*, is used to produce the finest Champagnes; the juice from the second, *première taille*, and from the third, *deuxième taille*, are used in blending. The better the wine, the less *taille* used, is a good general rule. The Champagne laws are so strict that even the amount of juice to be extracted at each pressing is laid down. From 9,000lb of grapes, no more than 450 gallons of juice may be extracted at the first pressing, 90 gallons (enough to fill two casks) at the second, and 45 gallons (enough to fill one cask) from the third. A *cuve* is a vat, and *cuvée* is best described as a blend from various vats. After pressing, the juice is put into vats for about half a day so that impurities settle on the bottom. Fermentation has already started at this stage because of the action of the yeast on the sugar, and this is allowed to continue either in wooden vats or stainless steel fermentation tanks. As winter approaches and temperatures fall, the yeasts become less active and fermentation ends. To ensure that this happens, the cellar doors are often opened to let cold air in. During the winter, the wine is racked, usually three times. This means transferring it to another vat in such a way that the sediment is left behind. The winemaster also decides at this time which wines he is going to use for blends.

Before the spring, the wine is 'fined' by adding whipped egg-white which attracts any remaining sediment, filtered and then blended. A *dosage* or *liqueur de tirage*, is added to each bottle to feed the yeast to restart fermentation, and the amount added dictates how bubbly the wine will be. This *dosage* is cane sugar, dissolved in still wine, and 0.14g sugar produces about one atmosphere of pressure. The bottle is then capped, using a metal crown cork, able to withstand at least six atmospheres of pressure, which is necessary to withstand the pressure of the gases produced during secondary fermentation. The wine is then taken into the cellars and the bottles laid on their sides. Non-vintage wines must spend at least one year in the cellar, and vintage wines at least three years, although the best houses often far exceed this.

During secondary fermentation, sediment builds up in the bottle, and it was Mme Nicole-Barbe Veuve Clicquot who is credited with developing the system of *remuage* to remove it. The wines are placed in a rack called a *pupitre*. The bottles are placed, neck first, into holes which can be pointed towards the ground. Every day a *remueur* gives the bottle a twist and very gradually the bottle changes position until finally its neck points towards the ground. This is a very skilled job, and a *remueur* can turn up to 100,000 bottles in a day. The process takes a long time, however, sometimes as long as twelve weeks. Machines are now replacing the *remueur* and, once loaded, can do the same job round the clock, seven days a week. The process can take between one week and ten days using the machine, and many Champagne Houses have now started to use them.

Once the sediment has been shaken to the neck of the bottle, it is released. This is done by dipping the neck in a freezing solution, which solidifies the sediment. The cap is then removed and the frozen sediment shoots out because of the pressure behind it. Some wine is inevitably lost in the process, but this is topped up and a second *dosage* added, sometimes with a drop of added brandy. The sweetness of this *dosage* dictates the sweetness of the finished product. The bottle is then corked and wired, and is ready for despatch.

At present there are just over 59,000 acres of vineyards in Champagne; most are owned by the 17,000 or so growers, but about 7,500 acres are owned by shippers. Between them they produce a wide range of styles of Champagne, and it is always a little foolish when someone says that they once tried Champagne and did not like it, so have never tried again. There is, amongst the hundreds of Champagnes produced, something for everyone. Most Champagne sold is non-vintage, and the same house can produce several different styles. You will also see Buyer's Own Brands (BOB), which are blended to suit customers' demands, and may be produced for a hotel chain, supermarket or other client. Baron Philippe de Rothschild has his own Champagne, specially created for him.

Vintage Champagnes are only produced after the best harvests and are always dry, or *brut*. Although 80 per cent of the grapes must come from that year's pressing, up to 20 per cent can be blended from previous years to add style, or balance the wine. A good vintage wine will last for many years, but exactly how long depends on the maker. About ten years is a good rule, because it is best to drink wines on the way up to their peak, rather than on the way down. Some vintage wines, however, can be very old.

Pink or rosé Champagne became fashionable after World War II, when Princess Margaret took a liking to it. It can be made from Pinot Noir grapes, by allowing the juice to remain in contact with the grape skins long enough for it to take some of their colour, but the more usual way is to mix a local red wine with the Champagne just before bottling. The wine of Bouzy is widely used, but others include Ambonnay, Ay, Cumières, Dizy, Rilly, Verzenay and Villedommange.

Most Champagne is made from a blend of red and white grapes. If it is a result of using only white grapes, it is called a *Blanc de Blancs*, and if only red grapes are used, it is known as a *Blanc de Noirs*. Many of the Champagne Houses now offer *Cuvées de Prestige*, produced deliberately for special occasions. The wines are the finest which can be produced, and expense is no object. *Crémant* is the final category which is likely to be met. It has only half the pressure of normal Champagne and is therefore less gassy. It has become a very fashionable drink over the past few years.

Many of the best producers belong to the *Syndicat de Grandes Marques de Champagne*, and their wines are known as *Grandes Marques*, but like many of the unofficial listings, the *Syndicat* has one or two members who have allowed things to slip a little, while there are many eminently suitable candidates for membership waiting in the wings.

There are four main vineyard areas: the Montagne de Reims, the Vallée de la Marne, the Côte des Blancs (mostly Chardonnay) and the Aube in the south. The twelve best grape-producing communes are listed as *Grands Crus* and growers here receive the best prices. There are forty-one *Premiers Crus* where growers receive a slightly lower price, and in all other areas the growers get a lower price still.

In addition to sparkling wines, Champagne produces still wine; red, white and rosé under the Coteaux Champenois *appellation contrôlée*. The wine must be made only from the three grape varieties allowed in Champagne, and must follow all other conditions laid down by the Champagne AC.

In Champagne the maximum yield is 70,800lb per acre, and the quantity which may be used for the production of sparkling Champagne is fixed every year. The remainder can then be used for Coteaux Champenois. If growers want to boost the stocks of Champagne after a poor harvest, they will use most of the production for sparkling wines, so the quantity of Coteaux Champenois varies greatly from year to year. They tend to be very acidic wines, but can be very fine, and are worth drinking when visiting the area as most is consumed there, only just over a quarter of the production being exported.

Another wine well worth trying is Rosé des Riceys. It comes from the very south of the Champagne region, in the Aube, and is made only from the Pinot Noir grape. Only in certain years, when the grapes reach the correct ripeness, is it made. The grapes are not pressed initially, but put into a vat where their own weight squeezes the juice out. This juice, which is already fermenting, is then pumped over the whole grapes until the winemaker is happy that the colour is right. The juice is then run off and fermentation is allowed to continue in the normal way. The resulting wine has the most incredible colour, often described as a 'red sky at sunset' . It is austere with a flavour of gooseberries and is one of the rarest wines you can come across, and is therefore expensive.

Ratafia is made in Champagne, and is usually drunk as an apéritif. It is made by adding wine alcohol, usually Cognac, to freshly-pressed wine juice. It produces a sweet drink with between 18 and 22° of alcohol. There is also Marc de Champagne, a fiery spirit of 40° of alcohol and more, made from the *marc*, which is the pulp of grape skins, seeds and stalks left after the last pressing. The *marc* is pressed and the juice which is extracted is then distilled.

The Champagne Routes

Because the Champagne region attracts hundreds of thousands of visitors every year, a series of routes have been worked out for tourists to follow. These are known as the Champagne Routes, and there are three: Red, Green and Blue. They are so-called because each route can be followed by looking out for its colour on the signposts. The routes are well-marked, and provide an interesting way to see the region. The following description of the routes has been provided by the *Comité Interprofessionnel du Vin de Champagne*.

The Blue Route: The Mountain of Reims

The lovely slopes of the Mountain of Reims which overlook the Reims plain and the Vesle Valley to the north and east, and the Marne Valley and Epernay to the south and west, form not only one of the richest vine-growing areas of France, but also a much sought-after tourist centre.

The undulating land, with its sunny slopes over which the vines spread close to the ground, comes to an end at a short distance from the summit, where the forest caps it with a green and picturesque roof, a dense and in some spots, wild forest where good shooting is to be found.

The Mountain of Reims is shaped like a horseshoe, and the Blue Route that follows it abounds in gems of historical interest: scenes of outstanding historical events, mementoes of the past, glorious names renowned in the annals of Champagne wine.

From Reims to Montchenot: Leaving Reims by Route Nationale 31 (in the direction of Fismes and Soissons) take the D27 on the left at Thillois: you will pass by the grandstands and installations of the motor-racing circuit — one of the fastest in Europe — and enter Gueux, a favourite residential town for those who gain their livelihood in Reims, with a nine-hole golf course.

After Pargny, take the D26 and follow the flank of the Petite Montagne, where the vine already covers a vast area. The most famous growths are to be found, however, more to the east. Jouy and then Villedommange are next, with a fine twelfth and sixteenth-century church. A small detour can be made as far as the pilgrim centre of St-Lié (fifteenth-century chapel) where a magnificent view of the Reims plain, the skyline of the Mountain of Reims and the Tardenois woods can be enjoyed.

We next pass through Saâcy (twelfth-century church), Ecueil and Chamery, between vineyards and the 25,000 acres of forest which cover the whole of the plateau between the Vesle and the Marne. After Sermiers, we cross Route Nationale 51 (Reims to Epernay) at Montchenot (a fine terrace with a view of Reims and Laon).

From Montchenot to Villers-Marmery: Take Route Nationale 51 on the left, and continue for about 200yd and then turn right on the D26 via Villers-Allerand, where the Reims-Epernay railway is crossed at the foot of Mont Joly (900ft). Rilly-la-Montagne is a large village to which the people of Reims are always eager to come in the summer to sit under the greenleafed trees and patronise the welcome refreshment establishments. Chigny-les-Roses and Ludes-le-Coquet (fine twelfth-century church and Romanesque tower) are next. Here, vineyards cover more ground and the quality of their produce increases. Cross D9 which will bring you back to Reims or take you to Epernay through the Craon de Ludes pass (splendid views).

At Mailly, we find the first *Hors Classe* growths, then, after passing a windmill surrounded by vines (the only windmill remaining of a great number which used to be seen in the Champagne region) we come to Verzenay, noted for a very well-known wine of a high quality produced in quantity from a vineyard extending far into the plain, as far as Beaumont-sur-Vesle and Sillery. One of the Marquis de Sillery, beheaded in 1793, was the husband of the Comtesse de Genlis, governess to the future king, Louis Philippe d'Orléans.

The road now rises to a hillock surmounted by a beacon. From here, we get an open view of the vineyards and forest land with the town of Verzy, formerly the site of a large Benedictine abbey. On reaching the middle of this region, turn right into the D34. At the top of a hill, near a modern chapel and about 1km to the left, can be seen a strange freak growth: the so-called *faux* or twisted beeches with corkscrew branches. To the right, on the edge of the plateau, stands the Sinar observation post where General Gouraud prepared his offensives against the Champagne ridge in World War I.

Running down to Verzy, you now get back on to the D26.

From Villers-Marmery to Tours-sur-Marne and Ay: The ridge of hills now turns southwards, across the first quality vineyards of Villers-Marmery and Trépail, where black and white grapes grow side by side. Then, after Ambonnay, comes Bouzy, also famous for a *Hors Classe* vine from which are produced fragrant non-sparkling red wines.

From Bouzy one can either take the D19 to Tours-sur-Marne, with its old priory, or proceed north towards Louvois (twelfth-century church). Here, situated in a vast park, is the château formerly owned by Michel le Tellier, Chancellor of France and father of Louis XIV's minister after whom the estate was named. Only the outbuildings, gate and moats date back to pre-Revolution days.

From Louvois, D9 leads to Avenay, in the delightful Val d'Or (very interesting twelfth and sixteenth-century church); there was formerly a big Benedictine convent here, founded by St Bertha in 650.

The Ay road crosses the railway, after which a secondary road on the right runs into Mutigny, 2km ahead, a small village amid vines and forest from which there is a magnificent and far-sweeping view.

At Ay, we get back on to the Red Route (D1).

The Red Route: The Marne Valley

This is an itinerary through villages full of life and charm along the valley of the winding Marne. Graceful landscapes are glimpsed through a light haze which clears as it reaches the vine-laden hill-slopes, where work is taking place so that our most famous wine may always retain its reputation for clarity, coolness and unrivalled bouquet.

From Tours-sur-Marne to Cumières: On leaving the picturesque village of Tours-sur-Marne, continue westward along D1 to Bisseuil and then Mareuil-sur-Ay (twelfth-century church and a château which once belonged to Marshal Lannes de Montebello).

Ay, a busy little town with a population of 7,000, stands on the banks of the canal running alongside the Marne in the middle of a first-rate vineyard, in terrace formation, 900 acres or more in area, on the slopes of undulating ground in a particularly favoured position. The town was seriously damaged in the war but has preserved its large church, built in the Flamboyant style, and a few half-timbered houses, one of which is said to have been Henri IV's wine-harvest store.

Ay is close to Epernay (about 3km) which, like Reims, can be chosen as a starting point of a tour along the 'Champagne Road', where the Red and Green Routes meet.

Turning northwards, the N51 rises as it takes us through Dizy-Magenta, Champillon and its hill, towards Bellevue, 7km further on, where there is a splendid view of the Marne vineyards on the edge of the plateau. After Ste-Imoges and a stretch of D71 we come to Hautvillers on Route Nationale 386. 1km before this village, there is a very fine view.

Hautvillers can be reached, however, directly from Dizy-Magenta. There was formerly at Hautvillers a powerful Benedictine monastery where a cellarer, Dom Pierre Pérignon, in the seventeenth century, laid down the rules still practised today for the making of Champagne wine. The old abbey church contains, in addition to the tomb of Dom Pérignon, some richly-carved seventeenth and eighteenth-century stalls and panelling.

Only parts of the abbey have survived: the living quarters, with an arcaded gallery, an eighteenth-century monumental porch, and, in the grounds, a terrace overlooking the valley. Here open-air fêtes and folklore gatherings are held annually as a token of the gratitude of the Champenois villagers towards Dom Pérignon.

Next, down to Cumières, along a very picturesque road in the heart of the vineyards.

From Cumières to Dormans: Follow the right bank of the Marne along the D1 as far as Damery (fine twelfth, thirteenth and sixteenth-century church). The *Bon Roi Henri IV* used to come and stay here to escape the cares of war, accompanied by Anne du Puy, the *Belle Hôtesse*. Venteuil, Reuil, and Binson (old priory, with a twelfth-century chapel, restored after the war) are next.

Châtillon-sur-Marne has a colossal statue of Pope Urban II, a native of this town, who preached the Crusade in the eleventh century; there are also the remains of a feudal castle and a very striking view of the Marne.

From Verneuil, the D1 and Route Nationale 380 crossroads (Dormans to Reims) run through Vincelles to Dormans; a very old town, ravaged by every war, but retaining a beautiful church (partly thirteenth-century), a Louis XIII château with ancient turrets and a chapel commemorating the two Battles of the Marne, 1914 and 1918 (crypt and several modern works of art). If the return journey is made in the direction of Epernay, take Route Nationale 3 through Mareuil-le-Port which has an interesting church. If you wish to get an impression of the valley as a whole, on leaving Port-á-Binson take a road uphill on the right which runs on a higher level through Oeuilly, Boursault and Vauciennes and so on down to Epernay by Route Nationale 3.

The Green Route

As if by some intentional artifice on the part of nature, the Côte des Blancs follows, on the south side of the Marne, the line of a horseshoe almost symmetrical with that situated on the north of the Mountain of Reims.

The Green Route runs round it like a lasso so that tourists may see not only the vineyards which have become famous for the *Blanc de Blancs* they produce and the renowned Champenois centres such as Avize, Cramant, Le Mesnil and Vertus, but also the attractive but generally less well-known spots which, to the westward, present a rather unfamiliar aspect of the Champagne country.

One has only to look across from the heights of Avize or Le Mesnil to the vast expanse of the Catalaunian Fields and the infinite stretches of arid plains of the Champ de Châlons, to realise the great historical part which the Champagne country has played in the eastern region of France. In our times the crossroads of these great international highways welcome, more peacefully, a vast number of visitors to a country endowed with so great an abundance of gastronomic pleasures and glorified by the unrivalled quality of its wines.

From Epernay to Ablois or Oger: Leave Epernay by Route Nationale 51, which follows the valley of the Cubry to Pierry, at one time the home of Cazotte, author of *Le Diable Amoureux* and strange prophet of the Terror, then to Moussy, from which one should try to include the few miles to the tourist centre of St-Martin-d'Ablois. After returning to Moussy, take the D40 on the right and, by a hill-side road, reach Chavot with its old and well-situated church. Next, proceed down to Monthelon, standing on a fine projection overlooking the Cubry valley and Epernay. Then to Grauves, where it is proverbially said that 'the Holy Virgin of Grauves made more turns than she performed miracles', because the wooden screw of the wine-press is said to have been transformed into a statue of the Blessed Virgin. The road follows a deep ravine, on the left of which rises a steep and very picturesque rocky cliff, and then continues through the forest. 1,50yd before coming to Oger, there is a superb view of the Côte des Blancs and the Châlons plain.

From Oger to Bergères-les-Vertus or to Epernay: The D10 will bring us to Le Mesnil-sur-Oger, which produces an exceptionally famous *Blanc de Blancs,* so called because the wine is made exclusively from white grapes. The church contains some very fine seventeenth-century woodwork.

Vertus, birthplace of the poet Eustache Deschamps (fourteenth century) who sang the praises of his *'païs renommé'*, is an old fortified city, several times destroyed; there still remains a medieval gate and twelfth-century church, built over a crypt, at the foot of which a number of springs gush out to form a mirror-like pond. Between Vertus and Bergères-les-Vertus, black grapes are again seen, marking the end of the Côte des Blancs. Nearby is the isolated Mont Aima, where the sites of prehistoric dwellings, a Gallic *oppidum*, a Roman camp and a feudal castle can be found. Bergères-les-Vertus, a quaint name which highly amused the French soldiers of World War I, who used to sing, with the old Champenois:

Les pays de Bergères on elles ne sont plus guère
Le pays des vertus on elles n'en ont plus.

Turning back as far as Oger and continuing along D10, we come to Avize, and then Cramant, where the exclusive reign of the *Blancs* begins, two of the most glorious jewels in the Champagne crown. At Avize, there is an interesting church, the greater part in Romanesque style, (capitals and porch, twelfth-century; Flamboyant transept and choir). Above Avize, to the west, there is a picturesque road commanding a wonderful panoramic view of the surrounding country.

2km to the north of Cramant is the Château de Saran. Cuis, with its remarkable twelfth-century church, is the boundary of the black grape area; there is a fine view. Return to Epernay.

PLACES OF INTEREST IN CHAMPAGNE

TROYES

Churches:

St Peter's and St Paul's Cathedral, thirteenth and fifteenth centuries, one of the largest in France. Magnificent thirteenth-century stained-glass windows. *Ste Madeleine*, mid-twelfth century, Renaissance steeple, stone roodloft carved by Jean Gailde, famed stained-glass windows. *St Jean*, thirteenth-century church rebuilt in the sixteenth century; many works of art, octagonal clock-tower. *St Rémi*, started in the fourteenth century, still has fifteenth-century doorway and wooden portico. Steeple built in 1386 topped by a wooden spire. Many fine paintings, carvings and statues. *St Nicholas*, sixteenth-century church destroyed in 1524 and rebuilt over the next seventy years. Many fine paintings, statues and stained glass.

St Nizier, sixteenth-century Gothic-Renaissance cross. Roof has varnished tiles; many fine stained-glass windows. *St Martin*, built 1592; many statues and fine stained glass. *St Pantaléon*, built 1516, marvellous statues and stained-glass windows. *Basilisque St Urbain*, 'a gem of Gothic art', built on the site of the birthplace of Urban IV, who became Pope in 1261. Work on the church started the following year. Many fine statues and stained glass windows.

Museums:

Musée St-Loup, formerly an abbey, now a natural history and archaeological museum. *Pharmacie de l'Hôtel Dieu*, a traditional pharmacy.

Musée Historique, in a sixteenth-century building; museum of history, hosiery and sculpture.
Bibliothèque; marvellous old building housing thousands of old manuscripts.
Maison de l'Outil et de la Pensée Ouvrière; museum of handicrafts.
Musée d'Art Moderne Pierre Lavy; museum of Modern Art.

Interesting Buildings:
Hôtel de Ville; Louis XIII building started in 1620.

Hôtel de Marisy; started in 1528 with fine projecting corner decorated turret.
Hôtel de Chapelaines; unusual 1535 building retaining many original features.
Hôtel des Angoiselles; sixteenth-century, very picturesque building with unusual turrets.
Hôtel d'Autruy; built in 1560 in chequered brick and stonework.
Hôtel de l'Election; half-timbered house with painted porch gable.

EPERNAY

Musée de Champagne; history of the region.
Abbey of Hautvillers where Dom Pérignon discovered how to keep the bubbles in Champagne.
Cellars of Möet et Chandon.
Museum of Archaeology; all relics excavated locally.

REIMS

Cathedral; magnificent building which took 300 years to build and is France's most sacred building. Started in 1211, it was badly damaged in World War I, but rebuilt between 1927 and 1938.
University; founded in 1547.
Basilica of St Rémi; begun in the early eleventh century, incorporating tombs pre-dating it by 500 years.

Also worth seeing:
Palais du Tau;
The caves of the Champagne Houses;
Place Royale;
Porte Mars;
Hôtel de la Salle;
The ancient Jesuit college and library;
Chapelle Foujita;
Museum of St Rémi;
Museum in the Hôtel Le Vergeur;
Museum St Denis;
Motor Museum.

CHALONS-SUR-MARNE

Cathedral of St Etienne, consecrated in 1147.
Porte Ste Croix; a triumphal arch built for Marie Antoinette who visited the town in 1770 on the way to her marriage.

Châteaux:
Montmort, built in the sixteenth century of red brick and enclosed by moat.
Brugny, south of Epernay; two buildings connected by a crescent-shaped moat.
Mareuil; eighteenth-century with marvellous flower gardens.
Louvois, built in 1680 on the site of a ruined château; marvellous French gardens with six lakes, fountains and waterfalls.

The Gastronomy of Champagne

For centuries they have been eating well in Champagne. There are the *andouillettes* of Troyes, which is also famous for its *charcuteries* and stuffed tongues. There are *boudins*, brawn and hams from Reims and the neighbouring Ardennes, which also produces a fine array of game. Thrushes are a local delicacy, and there are excellent local meats and vegetables. The cooking in the region can range from the very rich to the more humble but equally enjoyable fare such as dandelion salad. Champagne also enjoys its desserts, such as meringues, macaroons and honeyed gingerbreads, and there is a marvellous selection of cheeses.

Champagne is, of course, used in cooking, for poaching the local freshwater fish, chicken, snails and meat, but the adventurous traveller who gets off the beaten track and away from the tourist circuit will best be rewarded by finding traditional cuisine. Pork and *charcuterie* is, as already mentioned, a speciality of the region. Perhaps the most famous dish is *pieds de porc à la St-Ménéhould*, which is pig's trotters slowly grilled and poached until the bones are so soft that they can be eaten. There is *jambon en croûte*, which is ham cooked in pastry, and smoked hams such as those from the Ardennes. *Andouilles* are made from a pig's large intestine stuffed with strips of chitterlings and tripe. *Andouillette* is a smaller version, but is usually grilled and served hot with a hot mustard sauce. *Andouillettes de mouton* are a speciality of Troyes; they are made from mutton and heavily spiced. Other sausages include *boudin noir*, which like English black pudding is made from blood, and *boudin blanc*, often made with chicken. *Boudin St-Ménéhould* is made from rabbit, which is the basis of many other local dishes. Both rabbit (*lapin*) and hare (*lièvre*) are to be found on menus. *Lapin Valenciennes* is rabbit stewed with prunes and raisins, with either wine or beer. *Civet de lièvre* is the French equivalent of jugged hare, and both rabbit and hare are used to produce delicious pâtés.

Other game brought in from the Ardennes includes wild boar and deer. Boar is *sanglier*, and *marcassin Ardennaise* is young boar (under a year old) roasted in red wine sauce with bacon, celeriac and juniper berries. Other meat dishes are *langue de Valenciennes Lucullus* (smoked tongue with *foie gras*), *hochepot* (a meat and vegetable stew), *carbonnade flamande* (beef braised in beer with onions) and *potée Champenoise*, which is a very filling stew of bacon, ham, sausage and cabbage.

Pigeons and thrushes which have gorged themselves on the grapes are also offered on menus. Often they come *en croûte*, but thrushes (*grives*) are also roasted and served whole on a bed of vine leaves. Other birds on the menu are likely to be quail (*caille*), pigeon and woodcock (*bécasse*). All make lovely pâtés. In addition to pâtés, there are terrines made from duck, rabbit, veal and chicken. *Potje flesh* or *potje vleesch*, although a Flanders dish, is served here and is a terrine of veal, chicken and rabbit. *Quenelles* too are popular and use either meat or fish. *Quenelles de brochet* are poached pike in a creamy sauce. *Pain à la reine* is fish mousse, which also includes pike, as does *cervelat de brochet*, a sort of pike sausage which is very light.

Other fish on the menu include: *carpe* (carp), *truite* (trout), *anguilles* (eels) and *barbillon* (barbel); the last is often stewed in Champagne. *Anguille au vert* is eel served in a herb and wine sauce, and *saterelles* may appear on menus instead of the more usual *crevettes* (both are shrimp).

There are good local snails (*escargots*) served either in Champagne sauce or with garlic butter. *Chou rouge à la flamande* is red cabbage stewed in vinegar with sugar and apples, and *ficelle picarde* is another succulent import, a ham and mushroom pancake with a white, buttery sauce. *Flamiche* is pumpkin or leek tart with cream, and *gougère* is a cheese-flavoured choux pastry ring, served cold. Another regional speciality is *salade de pissenlits au lard,* made from fresh dandelion leaves, cooked in pork fat with vinegar and served with diced bacon (*lardons*) and french bread or potatoes.

Champagne also has more than its fair share of desserts and confectionery. There is *anglois*, plum tart; *galopin*, bread pancakes sprinkled with sugar, and *gaufres*, waffles. There are the delicate *biscuits de Reims* which you can dunk in a glass of Champagne, and other macaroons. *Pain d'épices* is spiced gingerbread, often with honey, while *kokeboterom* comes originally from Flanders — it is the Dutch word for cake — and is a small raisin bun. You may also see either *talibur* or *rabote* on the menu; this is a whole apple cooked in a pastry case, a speciality of Champagne.

Because Champagne is surrounded by agricultural land, many of the cheeses it sells are really from outside the region, but it does have some of its own, and you are likely to be offered both the locals and the outsiders in a restaurant.

Barbery is a speciality Champenois cheese, also known as *Fromage de Troyes* or *Troyen Cendré* because it comes from the village of Barbery near Troyes. It is a soft cheese cured in wood ashes and shaped into rounds. It is made from cow's milk. *Chaource* is a very delicate cow's milk cheese with a fruity taste. It is soft and creamy, shaped into rounds, and is a speciality of Champagne with its own *appellation*. *Langres* is a strong Champagne cheese. It is made from cow's milk by small dairies; it is shaped into a cone, and is strong-smelling but not strong to taste. *Ervy-le-Châtel*, made round the town of the same name in Champagne, is a strong cow's-milk cheese, cone-shaped, and with a mushroomy smell. *Coulommiers* is really from the Ile-de-France but is widely available here, and some dairies have now started to make it. It is quite strong-smelling but has a *Brie* taste. *Caprice des Dieux* is a Champagne cheese, factory-made, pasteurised and very creamy. *Chaumont* too is a Champagne speciality, a strong-smelling, spicy cheese. *Carré de l'Est* comes from both Champagne and Lorraine, and is a white creamy cheese similar to *Camembert*.

HOTELS AND RESTAURANTS OF
THE CHAMPAGNE REGION

Beaumont-sur-Vesle
(51400 Marne)

La Maison du Champagne
2 rue du Port
☎ (26) 61 62 45
10 miles from Reims.
Closed 1 August to 15
October, and Wednesday
evenings and Sundays
from October to February.
A small, comfortable,
reasonably-priced 10-room
hotel and restaurant.

Berry-au-Bac
(02190 Aisne)

La Côte
☎ (26) 79 55 04
On the N44, 12 miles
from Reims. Closed Sun-
day evenings, Monday and
22 December to 21 Jan-
uary. A Michelin one-star
restaurant, specialising in
local cuisine and with a
fine selection of Coteaux
Champenois. Menu
changes with the seasons,
but worth trying for the
marvellous lamb with
garlic.

Châlons-sur-Marne
(51000 Marne)

Hôtel Angleterre
19 place Monseigneur-
Tissler
☎ (26) 68 21 51
Closed the last two weeks
of July, and over the
Christmas period. A good
18-room hotel, with a
very good restaurant,
Jacky Michel (closed Wed-
nesdays, except holidays).

Hôtel Bristol
77 ave. Pierre Sémard
☎ (26) 68 24 63
A comfortable, reasonably-
priced 24-room hotel,
without restaurant, but
breakfasts served.

Hôtel Pasteur
46 rue Pasteur
☎ (26) 68 10 00
28 rooms; budget prices;
no restaurant but breakfast
served. A seventeenth-
century building in an old
religious community; very
quiet.

Hostellerie aux Amies de
la Champagne
place de la Basilisque
☎ (26) 68 10 43
At l'Epine, 5¼ miles east
of Châlons on the N3. A
40-room, medium-price
hotel and a first-class restaurant of the same name,
sited next to the Gothic
Notre-Dame L'Epine
basilica. Chef Hughes
Houard does the most
marvellous things with
truffles, *foie gras*, snails
in Champagne, salmon
and lamb. A very good
fixed-price menu which
includes Champagne.

Châlons-sur-Vesle
(51140 Marne)

Restaurant l'Assiette
Champenoise
☎ (26) 49 34 94
On the D26, 6 miles from
Reims. Closed in Feb-
ruary, and on Sunday
evenings and Wednesdays.
Excellent fish and shell-
fish dishes, as well as
duck and a good selection
of local Bouzy wines.
Quite expensive. Highly
rated.

Cherville
(51150 Marne)

Relais de Cherville
1 rue de l'Eglise
☎ (26) 69 52 76
A relatively new
restaurant, but one with a

growing reputation. Good
regional cuisine, fairly
expensive.

Dormans
(51700 Marne)

Hostellerie Demoncy
☎ (26) 58 20 86
Closed 23 January to 1
March, Sunday evenings
and Mondays. A reason-
ably-priced, comfortable
10-room inn with
restaurant.

La Table Sourdet
☎ (26) 50 20 57
Very good food in this
reasonably-priced 14-room
inn.

Epernay
(51200 Marne)

Hôtel des Berceaux
13 rue des Berceaux
☎ (26) 55 28 84
Close to the town centre,
this 29-room hotel is run
by patron-chef Luc
Maillard and his English
wife. Restaurant good but
expensive. Tours arranged
to Champagne houses and
caves if requested.

Hôtel Champagne
30 rue Eugène-Mercier
☎ (26) 55 30 22
Modern hotel in the centre
of town. The 30 rooms are
very comfortable and
reasonable. No restaurant
but breakfast served.

Hôtel la Terrace
7 quai Marne
☎ (26) 55 26 05
Small, very comfortable 7-
room hotel by the river,
with very good restaurant.

Hôtel St-Pierre
14 ave. P-Chandon
☎ (26) 54 40 80
15 reasonably-priced
rooms, no restaurant but
breakfast.

Hôtel l'Europe
18 rue Porte-Lucas
☎ (26) 51 80 28
A very comfortable, if
slightly faded 26-room
hotel with a very good
restaurant. The fixed-price
menus are a bargain.
Closed Sunday evenings
and Mondays.

Hôtel Royal Champagne
Champillon
3¹/₂ miles north on the
N51
☎ (26) 51 11 51
One of the high spots of
the region in every sense.
The 25 delightful rooms
each have their own
terrace. The hotel is
surrounded by vineyards
on the top of a hill, with
marvellous views over the
Marne valley. Excellent
restaurant offering both
the traditional and the
creative. Expensive.

Le Chapon Fin
2 place Mendes-France
☎ (26) 55 40 03
Very good value fixed-
price menus.

Fère-en-Tardenois
(02130 Aisne)

Hostellerie du Château
route de Fisme, on D967
or N367 1³/₄ miles north
of Epernay
☎ (26) 82 21 13
A magnificent château and
restaurant next to the
thirteenth-century ruins of
the picturesque Château

d'Anne de Montmorency.
The Blot family have run
this marvellous hotel in
its own park for many
years. 8 suites and 15 magnificent rooms; service
and food all first-class.
Expensive. Closed January
and February.

La Ferté-sous-Jouarre
(77260 Seine-et-Marne)

Auberge de Condé
1 ave. Montmirail
☎ (26) 22 00 07
Closed Monday evenings
and Tuesdays except
holidays, and the last two
weeks of February and
August. Owned by Emile
Tingaud, but young chef
Yvon Le Moal now carries
on the marvellous culinary
traditions. Very good
menus, excellent wine-
list, especially the better
Champagnes, and prices
you might well expect.

Le Relais
4 ave. Franklin-Roosevelt
☎ (26) 22 02 03
Closed for most of
January, and Wednesday
evenings and Thursdays; a
quite acceptable restaurant
offering good food at very
reasonable prices.

Hautvillers
(51160 Marne)

Auberge de l'Abbaye
1 rue de la Croix
☎ (26) 59 40 37
4 miles from Epernay,
3¹/₂ miles from Ay.
A good restaurant set in
the vineyards, offering
traditional cuisine at
reasonable prices.

Le Mesnil-sur-Oger
(51190 Marne)

Le Mesnil
2 rue Pasteur
☎ (26) 50 95 57
About 8¹/₂ miles from
Epernay
Closed from 12 August to
5 September, Monday
evenings and Wednesdays
except holidays. A very
good, reasonably-priced
restaurant with an interesting wine-list.

Montchenot
(51500 Marne)

Auberge au Grand Cerf
On the N51 6¹/₂ miles from
Reims and 10 miles from
Epernay
☎ (26) 97 60 07
A very comfortable
restaurant with 10
reasonably-priced rooms.
Run by Alain Guichaoua
and his wife Françoise,
this delightful inn on the
slopes of the Mountain of
Reims offers excellent
food and a very good wine-
list, especially the still
wines of Bouzy and Saran.

Montmort
(51270 Marne)

Cheval Blanc
route de Sézanne, 11 miles
south of Epernay
☎ (26) 59 10 03
The 12 rooms in this
whitewashed inn are very
comfortable, the food is
simple but good, the
portions generous and the
prices more than accept-
able.

Les Petites-Loges
(51400 Marne)

Auberge de la Voute
1³/₄ miles south on the
N44 at Le Mont-de-Billy
☎ (26) 61 61 72

Very good regional cuisine, not expensive, and with a good wine-list.

Reims
(51100 Marne)

Novotel
route de Soissons
☎ (26) 08 11 61
Some way out of town, but a modern 125-room hotel ideal as a touring base, near the Paris auto-route. Restaurant for snacks only, but many good restaurants nearby.

Boyer les Crayères
64 blvd Vasnier
☎ (26) 82 80 80
Simply one of the best restaurants in France, and thoroughly deserving of its Michelin three stars. Having moved to the out-skirts of town, and being surrounded by the best Champagne cellars, Gérard and Elyane Boyer have continued to give faultless service. There are 16 luxur-ious rooms, and the res-taurant is near-perfect; superb seafish and exquis-ite desserts. Essential to book, and a healthy bank-balance is a must.

Hôtel la Paix
9 rue Buirette
☎ (26) 40 04 08
A modern 105-room hotel, 9 storeys, with swimming pool. The restaurant, Le Drouet, is good and not expensive.

Hôtel Frantel
31 blvd Paul-Doumer
☎ (26) 88 53 54
A modern 125-room hotel, air-conditioned, medium price range, with a very

good restaurant (Les Ombrages).

Hôtel Bristol
76 place Drouet-d'Edrion
☎ (26) 40 52 25
In the centre of town, a 39-room comfortable hotel, near the station. Reasonable prices, no restaurant but breakfast.

Le Florence
43 blvd Foch
☎ (26) 47 12 70
An elegant, rather 'fishy' restaurant run by Jean-Pierre and Denise Maillot. The friendliness of the service is matched by the excellence of the cooking, especially the sea fish. A very impressive wine-list, and more than reasonable prices.

Le Chardonnay
184 ave. d'Epernay
☎ (26) 06 08 60
Near the Hippodrome on the western outskirts of town. Owned by the Boyers and offering simpler, but still very good food at attractive prices.

Le Foch
37 blvd Foch
☎ (26) 47 48 22
Is worth a visit to sample the cuisine of Jacqueline Deschamps, especially her *salade Jacqueline* with home-made *foie gras*. A good wine-list, and you pay for quality.

Sept-Saulx
(51400 Marne)

Le Cheval Blanc
rue du Moulin
☎ (26) 61 60 27

An old coaching inn to the south-east of Reims. The inn almost straddles the main road, with motel-style bedrooms on one side and the inn and res-taurant on the other. The 25 rooms look out over an attractive garden, and the Vesle. Bernard Robert, the patron-chef, produces marvellous classical dishes, many with Cham-pagne. Moderately expensive.

Vailly-sur-Aisne
(02370 Aisne)

Cheval d'Or
☎ (26) 54 70 56
A rustic hotel with 21 rooms, just outside the Champagne region but ideal as a touring base. Good honest fare and budget prices.

Vertus
(51130 Marne)

Hostellerie de la Reine Blanche
18 ave. Louis Lenoir
☎ (26) 52 20 76
A very comfortable 23-room hotel in the middle of Champagne's white grape area. Good res-taurant and reasonable prices.

Vinay
(51200 Marne)

La Briqueterie
☎ (26) 54 11 22
A modern 42-room hotel, in its own gardens, 6km from Epernay. A good restaurant but fairly expensive.

THE VINEYARDS OF CHAMPAGNE

Abel Lepître   TSE
2 ave. du Gal Giraud
51100 Reims
☎ (26) 85 05 77
Open: Monday to Friday
by appointment. Closed
August.

Ayala   SE
2 blvd du Nord
51160 Ay
☎ (26) 50 13 40
Open: Monday to Friday
by appointment only.

Besserat de Bellefon TSE
allée du Vignoble
51100 Reims
☎ (26) 06 09 18
Open: Monday to Friday
9am-noon and 2-5pm.
Closed August.

Bollinger   TSE
16 rue Jules Lobet
51160 Ay
☎ (26) 50 12 34
Open: Monday to Friday
by appointment only.
Closed August.

Canard Duché TSE
Ludes
51500 Rilly-le-Montagne
☎ (26) 61 10 96
Open: daily by
appointment.

De Castellan   TSE
57 rue de Verdun
51200 Epernay
☎ (26) 55 15 33
Open: Monday to Friday
by appointment. Closed
August.

Charles Heidsieck TSE
3 place des Droits
 de l'Homme
51100 Reims
☎ (26) 85 03 27
Open: Monday to Thurs-
day by appointment.

Veuve Clicquot-
 Ponsardin   TSE
1 place des Droits de
 l'Homme
51100 Reims
☎ (26) 85 24 08
Open: January and 1
March to 10 April,
Monday to Friday 2.15-
4.30pm; Sundays and
public holidays 2.15-5pm.
11 April to 31 October,
Monday to Friday 9-11am
and 2 .15-5pm; Saturday
and Sunday 2.15-5pm.

Colléry   TS
2 place de la Libération
51160 Ay
☎ (26) 50 10 49
Open: Monday to Friday
8am-noon and 2-6pm.
Saturday and Sunday 8am-
noon.

Coopérative Vinicole de
 Mancy   TS
Mancy
51200 Epernay
☎ (26) 59 71 52
Open: Monday to Friday
9-11am and 2-5pm.
Closed August.

Deutz   TSE
16 rue Jeanson
51160 Ay
☎ (26) 55 15 11
Open: Monday to Friday,
by appointment.

George Goulet TSE
4 ave. du Gal Giraud
51100 Reims
☎ (26) 85 25 48
Open: Monday to Friday
by appointment.

Heidsieck &
 Monopole TSEG
83 rue Coquebert
51100 Reims
☎ (26) 07 39 34
Open: 10 April to 31
October, Monday to
Friday 9-11am and 2.30-
4.30pm. Public holidays
and weekends 2.30-
4.30pm. Closed 27 March
to 9 April and all August.

Henriot & Co   TSE
3 place des Droits de
 l'Homme
51100 Reims
☎ (26) 85 03 27
Open: Monday to Friday 8-
11.30am and 2-5.30pm.

Joseph Perrier, Son
 & Co   TSE
69 ave. de Paris
51000 Châlons-sur-Marne
☎ (26) 69 29 51
Open: Monday to Friday 9-
11am and 2.30-5pm, by
appointment. Closed
August.

Krug   TSE
5 rue Coquebert
51100 Reims
☎ (26) 47 28 15
Open: Monday to Friday
by appointment.
Closed July.

R=red wine W=white wine P=rosé wine S=sparkling wine

Lanson and son   TSE
12 blvd Lundy
51100 Reims
☎ (26) 40 36 26
Open: Monday to Friday,
by appointment.

Laurent Perrier   TSEG
ave. de Champagne
51150 Tours-sur-Marne
☎ (26) 59 91 22
Open: Monday to Friday,
by appointment. Closed
August.

Louis Roederer   TSE
21 blvd Lundy
51100 Reims
☎ (26) 40 42 11
Open: Monday to Friday,
by appointment. Closed
July.

Mercier   TSECG
73 ave. de Champagne
51200 Epernay
☎ (26) 54 71 11
Open: 15 January to 1
March and 15 November
to 23 December, Saturday
and Sunday 9-11am and
2-5pm. 1 March to 15
November, daily
9-11.30am and 2-5.30pm.

Moët et Chandon   TSEG
18 ave. de Champagne
51200 Epernay
☎ (26) 54 71 11
Open: 2 November to 12
March (closed New Year's
Day) Monday to Friday 9-
11.30am and 2-5pm.

G.H. Mumm   TSEG
34 rue du Champ de Mars
51100 Reims
☎ (26) 40 22 73
or (26) 88 29 27
Open: January and
February, Monday to
Friday 9-11am and 2-5pm.
1 June to 31 October,
daily 9am-5pm.

Perrier-Joet   TSE
26 ave .de Champagne
51200 Epernay
☎ (26) 55 20 53
Open: 1 May to 15 Sep-
tember, Monday to Friday
9am-noon and 2-5pm.

Philipponnat   TSE
13 rue du Pont
Mareuil-sur-Ay
51160 Ay
☎ (26) 50 60 43
Open: Monday to Friday
by appointment. Closed
August.

Piper-Heidsieck   TSCG
51 blvd Henri Vasnier
51100 Reims
☎ (26) 85 01 94
Open: 12 November to 2
April, Monday to Friday
9-11.30am and 2-5.30pm.
2 April to 11 November,
daily 9-11.30am and
2-5pm. Guided tour
through cellars by electric
train.

Pol Roger & Co   TS
1 rue Henri Lelarge
51200 Epernay
☎ (26) 55 41 95
Open: Monday to Friday
by appointment. Closed
August.

Pommery et Greno   TS
5 place Gal Gouraud
51100 Reims
☎ (26) 05 05 01
Open: Monday to Friday 9-
11.15am and 2-5.15pm.
Saturday, Sunday and
public holidays by
appointment.

Ruinart   TS
4 rue des Crayères
51100 Reims
☎ (26) 85 40 29
Open: Monday to Friday
9-11am and 2.30-4pm by
appointment.

Société des Producteurs   TS
Mailly Champagne
51500 Rilly-la-Montagne
☎ (26) 49 41 10
Open: by appointment
only.

Taittinger   TSG
9 place St-Nicaise
51100 Reims
☎ (26) 85 45 35
Open: daily 9-11am and
2-5pm.

T=tasting   E=English spoken   G=guided tours   C=château/building to visit

Chapter 6

<u>THE LOIRE</u>

Le Château De Nantes
Loire

THE LOIRE is France's longest river, flowing from the foothills of the Massif Central in the Ardèche to the Atlantic Ocean at Le Croisic, to the west of Nantes. It flows for almost 650 miles, first northwards, and then in a large sweep to begin its graceful westerly flow to the sea.

The beauty of the Loire is legendary, with its fairytale castles and walled towns. Its cuisine is magnificent and rich, and the banks and broadening valley of the river accommodate some of the country's most famous wines. Near its source are found the vineyards of Sancerre, Pouilly and the Coteaux du Giennois. Around the southern tributaries of the Loire are the vineyards of Reuilly and Quincy. To the east of Tours is Vouvray, and then the vineyards become more frequent and fan out more into the valley as we reach Chinon, Bourgueil, Saumur, Muscadet and many more smaller *appellations.*

The history of the Loire is more dramatic than almost anywhere else in France. For centuries the river provided one of the main traffic networks and the towns along its course prospered; for hundreds of years, Tours was one of the most important towns of France, far more significant than Paris. The prosperity of Tours grew in the fifth and sixth centuries, after the collapse of the Roman Empire. St Martin of Tours became the first patron saint of France while Gregory of Tours, also canonised, wrote the first history of the country.

In the ninth century, the Vikings used the Loire to raid deep inside France and many towns, including Tours, were sacked and burnt to the ground. In 1154, Henry Plantagenet became King of England, signalling another stormy period in the Loire's history. He was Count of Anjou and Duke of Normandy, and he married Eleanor of Aquitaine, thus vastly increasing his French possessions and leading to a murderous 301-year struggle between the French and the English. The French kings wished to free parts of their country from Plantagenet domination, and the English heirs of Henry Plantagenet wanted to extend their territory to include the whole of France.

During these centuries of war, the Loire was a frequent battlefield and to protect themselves from attack, the towns fortified themselves and castles were built. The battles ranged the whole length of the Loire, but some of the bloodiest were around Angers and Orléans. It was at the latter that Joan of Arc rallied the French army, raised the siege and won her place in history as the Maid of Orléans.

From the middle of the fifteenth century, when the English armies were finally defeated and driven from France, until the end of the seventeenth century, the Loire was one of the cultural centres of Europe. The French kings and their court moved into the Loire and used the materials from the defensive châteaux, which had been dismantled, to build the delightful castles we can still see today. The arts flourished, and Leonardo da Vinci was commissioned to work here, as was the sculptor Cellini. The Loire region reached its cultural peak during the reign of François I. He reigned from 1515 to 1547, and many of the finest châteaux were built in these years. He was responsible for the largest of them all, at Chambord. Although the châteaux of the Renaissance period were built as country homes for the nobility, there are still many reminders of the earlier troubled times. Fortified châteaux include those at Angers, Sully, Chinon, Loches and Montreuil-Bellay, and are in sharp contrast with those of Azay-le-Rideau, Châteaudun, Chaumont, Chenonceau, Ussé and Villandry, built during the Renaissance, all of which could grace a Walt Disney set.

Catherine de Medici is credited with introducing fine cuisine to the French court, and also the fork. She was the wife of Henry II, son of François, and she brought in chefs from Florence to pass on their skills. Another source of hostility which found expression in the Loire region was the religious wars between Huguenots and Catholics. Saumur, in the heart of the Loire, was one of France's main Protestant centres; another was at Sancerre, to the east. In the sixteenth century, many Huguenots made their way to the Loire, but there were several bloody battles until the Edict of Nantes was declared by Henry IV in 1598 which guaranteed all Frenchmen religious freedom. All went well for about a century, until the Edict was revoked by Louis XIV in 1685 and almost 400,000 Huguenots were forced to leave the country, many of them from the Loire Valley. This marked the commencement of the decline of the Loire region, and the introduction of the railway, and the gradual silting up of the waterway, added to its problems.

Today, the Loire is one of the most popular tourist regions in France. Visitors come to breathe in its history, and marvel at its architectural treasures, and to sample the food and drink. In addition to the wines, the Loire is a gourmet's paradise, having rich agricultural land on most sides as it does, and on the west being bordered by the Atlantic Ocean and its treasure-house of fish.

The Chenin Blanc is the main variety of white grape which is grown, especially in Touraine and Anjou. It is a very versatile grape, always high in acidity but producing very high sugar levels as well when ripe. Many people have been amazed at the wonderful dessert wines produced from it, and the decades for which they can survive. To the west of Anjou, the Muscadet grape is dominant, growing on squat vines, and with a low acidity, an essential quality of wines destined for early drinking. The third white variety is Sauvignon Blanc, to be found around Pouilly and Sancerre.

Of red varieties, the Cabernet Franc is undoubtedly the best, producing lovely wines in Chinon, Touraine and Anjou; although the Gamay is to be found virtually everywhere, and both reds are used in the rosé wines which are becoming more popular.

Other varieties are grown: the white Gros Plant in Muscadet; Pinot Noir for the red Sancerre; Chardonnay in Haut-Poitou; and Groslot, a red variety for the local rosé drunk in the cafés, which was imported from Armagnac.

Muscadet is the first vineyard area reached after driving in from Nantes, and it is a sensible place from which to start a tour of the Loire. There is an airport at Nantes to which one may fly from Paris and other French provincial cities as well as London.

As soon as you leave Nantes, the vineyards start to the north, east and south, but the best area is to the south-east of the city. The Muscadet grape originally came from Burgundy, and is still sometimes called the Melon de Bourgogne. Until the middle of the sixteenth century almost all the grapes grown were for red wines, but the Dutch, who traded in Nantes, wanted white wine for distilling, having been forced out of the Charente by high duties. Therefore, the vineyards were grubbed out and white grapes were planted over the next thirty years or so. The Muscadet was one of the varieties imported for this purpose. The Loire wines were not exported until the Dutch created a demand, and it was only after the turn of this century that they began to be sent to other parts of France. It is hard to believe that a wine that is now drunk all over the world was virtually unheard of outside France immediately after World War II. It is only in the last thirty years or so that large amounts have been exported.

The Muscadet grape does well here, because it is frost-resistant and ripens early. The grapes are normally ready to pick by the middle of September and often earlier. They then have to be gathered in quickly. Because of the low acidity of the Muscadet, it can easily oxidise if it comes into contact with the air, so the winemakers have developed a technique of fermenting the wine in large concrete tanks, in which it is then allowed to stay until the following spring, when it is carefully drawn off and bottled. Over the winter months, the wine remains in contact with the lees, dead yeasts and other sediment from fermentation, and this gives it extra body and flavour. During the winter, the gases are not all dispersed, and some carbon dioxide is generally to be found in the wine after bottling. This gives it a refreshing quality and accounts for the tingle on your tongue when you drink it. Because the wines are kept on the lees over the winter, you will see *sur lie* on many Muscadet labels.

There are three *appellations* within the region. The first to be awarded was for Muscadet de Sèvre et Maine, and Muscadet des Coteaux de la Loire, both in 1936. A year later Muscadet gained AC status.

The Vineyards of the Loire

Muscadet de Sèvre et Maine
Named after the two rivers flowing through the area, this is by far the biggest producer in the region, with an average output of more than four million cases a year. The acreage of Muscadet de Sèvre et Maine is still expanding and currently stands at about 20,000 acres. The Muscadet de Sèvre et Maine produces the best Muscadets of them all, and they need a little longer to age. All Muscadets, however, are light, fruity, crisp, refreshing wines which deserve to be drunk young. They are marvellously refreshing and the ideal accompaniment to many fish dishes. Muscadet is not allowed to be stronger than 12.3°.

The Coteaux de la Loire
To the east of Nantes, the vineyards here straddle both banks of the river. Production is tiny (about three million bottles a year), and Muscadet, which produces about twice that, is the third *appellation*, mostly to the south and south-west of Nantes. Muscadet de Sèvre et Maine easily outshines the other two *appellations*.

Gros Plant du Pays Nantais

The Dutch introduced the Gros Plant into Muscadet, and this now produces the Gros Plant du Pays Nantais which has VDQS status. 200 years ago, two-thirds of the vineyards were given over to the Gros Plant, but all were destroyed by phylloxera. Today there about 5,000 acres with yields restricted to 2,700 gallons an acre. It will never be a great wine, but it has high acidity and a special earthy quality.

Coteaux d'Ancenis

This is a small wine-producing area centred around Ancenis, the old fortified town about 25 miles to the east of Nantes on the Loire. It is also the capital for the Muscadet Coteaux de la Loire, but it is the reds grown here that are worth trying. The labels on the red wines will also carry the name of the grape used, either Gamay or Cabernet Sauvignon. There are about 300 growers working with the cooperative, *Les Vignerons de la Noëlle*, part of the massive *CANA* conglomerate, one of France's largest food companies. The wines are good, honest, everyday reds and rosés sold in the cafés and restaurants, always refreshing and good value for money; and occasionally you will come across a grower producing first-class wines.

Anjou

To the east of Ancenis, Anjou includes many of the prettiest scenes on the Loire. The gently rolling countryside is very fertile, and farmland and nurseries producing gorgeous arrays of flowers mingle with the vineyards, woodlands and orchards. The climate here is also very mild. Anjou enjoys more sunshine and hotter temperatures than Paris, less rainfall and very mild autumns, thus avoiding many of the harvesting problems growers in other regions face.

Angers is the capital of the province, although it is on the Maine, about 4^1/2 miles from where it joins the Loire. The town is still dominated by the fortress, from which there are magnificent views of the surrounding countryside and vineyards.

Many grape varieties are grown in Anjou, but the two most famous are Chenin Blanc for white, and Cabernet Franc for reds. The ever popular Rosé d'Anjou is made from a blend of Cabernet, Gamay and Groslot, although other varieties may be added as well. Grapes have always been grown in Anjou, and Charlemagne is recorded as having made the gift of a vineyard to the abbey of St-Aubin-des-Vignes in 769. In 1331 a law was passed banning the import of wines into Anjou for blending, to protect the quality of the local wines. The Anjou vineyards now extend to about 70,000 acres and produce about a quarter of all the Loire wines. Rosé wine still accounts for almost half of all production, and comes in many different styles to suit growing tastes, from dryish to very sweet. The Anjou scene is further complicated by the large number of *appellations* allowed, well over twenty. The best vineyards lie along the Layon River, to the south of Angers — the Coteaux du Layon. The wines are sweet, high in acidity and full of fruit but with a remarkable elegance. There are two *Grands Crus* — Quart de Chaume and Bonnezeaux. These wines show how versatile the Chenin Blanc is. The best wines of the Coteaux are rich, creamy and crisp, in many ways resembling a Sauternes, yet they can be bone dry with biting freshness and acidity.

Savennières

This commune, just outside Angers also produces fine wines. It also has two *Grands Crus*, La Roche aux Moines and La Coulée de Serrant. As young wines they have a biting acidity although full of fruit, but when aged for ten years or more they soften and mellow and their full honeyed potential is realised. Red wines are produced, but they are light and the best come from around Brissac. You may also find Vins de Thoursais VDQS wines to the south of Saumur. The red is made from the Gamay, and the white from Chenin.

Saumur

Perhaps the best sparkling wine of France after Champagne, it is made from the Chenin Blanc. The *méthode Champenoise* is used and the limestone rock, known locally as *tuff*, has been quarried to create huge complexes of corridors and cellars where the wines are still stored. The town of Saumur is the centre of the wine-producing region; it is dominated by its fourteenth-century château, and is famous internationally for its national riding school (formerly the *Cadre Noir*), whose emblem still figures on coats of arms and bottles throughout Saumur. Although Saumur does produce some rosé and red wines to the south, from Cabernet Franc and Pineau d'Aunis, sold as Saumur-Champigny, it is famous for its whites.

There are about ten companies producing Saumur wine, using their own grapes and buying in from more than 500 growers. Many of the Houses have connections with the famous names of Champagne. Saumur d'Origine, as it is now known, should be light and fresh, without either the great complexity of Champagne or its high price. Crémant de Loire is also produced and is a superior product, but it is not as yet widely available. Saumur also produces a bone-dry white, Saumur Blanc, which must have at least 11° of alcohol and a red, sold as Saumur Rouge, as opposed to Saumur-Champigny which is the better of the two.

Touraine

Touraine borders Anjou, and produces some of the Loire's best red wine. There are four main *appellations* — Chinon and Bourgueil for reds, and Vouvray and Montlouis for whites. The Cabernet Franc is mostly used for the reds, and is capable of producing very fine wines indeed with tremendous ageing potential. There are about 3,000 acres of vineyards on three major types of soil, all producing wines of different styles. The best Chinon is that from the slopes and hill tops of clay and lime and is the *vin de coteaux*. It has a glorious colour, a bouquet full of fruit and flowers, a smell of strawberries and violets, and a soft, elegant taste. The best vintages will last for fifteen years or more.

Bourgueil
The near-Mediterranean climate, because of its land-locked position, produces wines which vary enormously in quality. The best come from the steeply rising, south-east facing slopes which get plenty of sunshine. The clay, *tuff* and lime soil produces wines that can only be drunk when old, and which have a peppery taste, a hint of raspberries and a glorious roundness.

Vouvray
This village is just over five miles from Tours, on the north bank of the Loire, while the vineyards of Montlouis are on the south bank. Vouvray the village was given by Charlemagne to the abbey of St Martin in the eighth century. Since then it has been in and out of the Church's possession on a number of occasions. Although wine has been produced in and around Vouvray since Roman times, it was the monks who discovered the sites for the best vineyards and the right grapes to grow there. For almost 200 years the entire production was sold to the Dutch for blending with other wines, and because Vouvray was the most famous name in the region, almost all Touraine was sold under this label.

In 1936 the *appellation* of Vouvray was introduced, restricting production to eight communes. One of these has since been lost because of the expansion of Tours, and the remaining seven only plant Chenin Blanc.

The Vouvray produced can range from dry to sweet, and many growers now have a sparkling Vouvray to boost their lists. The *tuff* not only houses the cellars, homes have been carved into the rock and some are still occupied today. The grapes are always picked late in Vouvray, sometimes well into November. They have both acidity and sweetness, and it is their perfect balance that gives them marvellous ageing properties. No sweet Vouvray should be drunk young, and those from the finest vintages will go on maturing for several decades. They have very complex noses, full of flowers and fruit, and retain both long after a comparable wine from Sauternes will have lost its bouquet. The dry Vouvray is very high in acid, a mouth-puckering wine, and many growers leave their grapes as long as possible on the vine so that the acidity is reduced as sugar is created.

Montlouis
The vineyards here produce very similar wines to those of Vouvray although not as long-lasting. It gained its *appellation* in 1938, although production is still small. The sweet wines tend to lack the fullness of Vouvray, and the dry wines are less acidic because of the natural residual sugar.

Touraine-Azay-le-Rideau, Touraine-Amboise and Touraine-Mesland
Other vineyards of interest in the immediate area are Touraine-Azay-le-Rideau, famous for its magnificent Renaissance château, and its white and rosé wines; Touraine-Amboise, with its dominating castle, making both red and white wine; and Touraine-Mesland, noted for its full-bodied but still youthful reds and strong rosé, both made from the Gamay grape.

Jasnières, Coteaux du Loir and Coteaux du Vendômois

To the north of Tours are these lesser vineyards. Jasnières only produces white wine, both dry and sweet, and the latter can often be excellent, matching those of Vouvray, but, alas, production is still tiny. The Coteaux du Loir is made up of twenty-two communes on the river Loir, a tributary of the Loire. It makes red, white and rosé wine. The Coteaux du Vendômois produces a similar range, and similarly, the wines tend to be light and need to be drunk young.

Valençay

This small producing district, where about thirty-five growers produce red, white and rosé VDQS wines, borders Touraine in the south-east. The reds are pleasant to drink young, being fresh and fruity; the whites are uncomplicated, light and refreshing.

Cheverny and Cour-Cheverny

These vineyards on the south bank of the Loire around Blois, both carry the Cheverny *appellation*, granted in 1973. As with many of the other small *appellations* in the Loire, the growers face enormous competition from their better-known, larger neighbours. In Cheverny, the best wine is produced by the *Chai des Vignerons* at Chitenay, a consortium of a score of growers working together to vinify and market their wines.

Reuilly and Quincy

Between Valençay and Bourges are these two separate vineyards. Although classified as Loire wines, both vineyards are well south of the river. Reuilly consists of seven communes, all huddling around the town, and the wines gained AC status in 1937. The land is remarkably similar to that of Chablis; only white wine is produced and only from the Sauvignon Blanc. The wines are influenced by the chalk which gives a penetrating coolness, and they are fruity but often lack roundness. A very good rosé is made but only in very small quantities. Quincy is almost twice the size of its neighbour. It is just to the east, and gained its AC status in 1936, the second in France to do so. Over the years, the vineyards have suffered from the weather, thanks to both frosts and storms. Only white wine is produced, and it tends to be fuller and rounder than that from Reuilly.

Sancerre

As its wine increases in popularity both in France and abroad, Sancerre has more than doubled its production in the last ten years. The village is built on a hill which towers above the countryside. It is a natural defensive position, but even so, this failed to protect the inhabitants during the long and bloody Religious Wars. Sancerre was one of the centres of Protestantism in France, and was frequently attacked and overcome, but only after lengthy sieges. Today, the lush, vegetation-covered hills accommodate vineyards and a wide variety of other agriculture.

Traditionally the white wine came from the Chasselas grape but this has now been totally replaced by Sauvignon Blanc. There are fourteen communes entitled to the AC, and production of white wine can top 500,000 cases a year. Red and rosé is also produced but in much smaller quantities. The wines of Sancerre can vary from the soft to the austere, but all are fruity and dry and must be drunk very young.

More than a quarter of the 600 growers belong to the local cooperative and its Sancerre is now widely exported. The red Sancerre is becoming increasingly popular in English restaurants mostly because of its novelty value, but it is very light, and although it has a delicate nose and taste, there are many better reds from which to choose.

Menetou-Salon

To the south-west of Sancerre is this much smaller producing area which produces very similar style wines. It gained AC status in 1959 and consists of ten communes, growing Sauvignon Blanc and Pinot Noir. Many experts prefer the white Menetou-Salon to the Sancerre, because it lacks the attacking coolness that the chalk soils give to the Sancerre and has a more delicate bouquet. Generally, however, I think the Sancerre is the better white wine, and the reds and rosés from Menetou-Salon are superior.

Pouilly-Fumé

This is the last of the great producing areas of the Loire, on the eastern side of the river opposite Sancerre. The village is named after a Roman villa, and grapes have been grown since that time. From the eleventh century to the end of the eighteenth, the vineyards were in the hands of the Benedictine monastery at La Charité-sur-Loire and it was they who established the prestige of the wine. There are now about 1,500 acres of vineyards, mostly planted with Sauvignon, and seven communes are entitled to the *appellation*. The top three communes are Pouilly-sur-Loire, St-Andelain and Tracy-sur-Loire.

Pouilly-Fumé received its AC in 1937. It must only be made from the Sauvignon grape, have a minimum natural alcohol content of 11°, and production is limited to 990 gallons an acre, although this is often exceeded. The characteristics of Pouilly-Fumé smack of a classy wine. It has a greenish tint and a bouquet of asparagus, and a suggestion of flint that can also be spotted in the taste. Although dry, it is never thin, because it possesses natural glycerine which gives it body and a roundness. Most Pouilly is now produced by the Ladoucette family, headed by Baron Patrick. The wine produced at the Château du Nozet is the finest Pouilly available, well-balanced, elegant and expensive.

The region also produces Pouilly-sur-Loire, which is made from the Chasselas grape. It comes from the same communes, and in good years about 650,000 bottles are produced. It is not in the same class as the Fumé but still a very good, everyday quaffing wine.

The wines of Pouilly-Fuissé should not be confused. The latter come from Burgundy, and are made from the Chardonnay. Pouilly-Fumé also has nothing to do with smokiness, either in its colour, nose or taste. The term *fumé* comes from the grey colour of Sauvignon grapes as they ripen just before the vintage.

There are many other lesser vineyard areas in the Loire, notably around Orléans and Gien. These wines are honest drinking wines which can, and should be tasted locally, especially as they rarely leave the area.

A Tour of the Loire Region

The Loire is perhaps the most popular area of France with tourists and during the summer it is often possible to see more foreign car number plates than French. There are a number of reasons for this popularity, including the ease of getting there, and the attractions on arrival.

The Loire boasts so many fairy-tale châteaux that one is spoilt for choice. Coupled with the history and architecture, there is a wide range of cuisine to enjoy, from the marvellous seafood dishes around Nantes, to the rich stews and meats of Orléans. And, wherever you travel in the Loire, there is wine to be drunk.

For the most of the length of the River Loire, between the sea and Gien, it flows through a wide flood plain, lush and green and very fertile. This plain is surrounded by gently sloping hills which rarely reach any great height, and have changed little over the centuries. This green and pleasing landscape attracted the nobility who chose to build their fine châteaux along the banks of the Loire. No other region of France has such a large heritage of architectural wealth. In Alsace there are many beautifully-preserved villages, but in a compact area; in the Loire the glorious buildings stretch for mile after mile after mile. The Loire is easy to get to, especially from the Channel ports, and there is the added bonus of a leisurely drive through the prettier parts of northern France.

There are flights to Nantes from London and a number of internal airports in France, including Paris. The Loire also fits neatly into a larger itinerary, taking in other wine regions if you wish. If a tour is started at Nantes and finished at Gien, you are ideally placed to continue across to Burgundy. If Gien is the starting point and Nantes the finish, the obvious area to tour next is south into Cognac country and Bordeaux.

The Loire flows through twelve *départements* on its path to the sea, and there are good roads throughout the entire region. It is, however, one of the few areas in France where an itinerary using trains could be worked out. The French railways, SNCF, also offer a very good deal whereby cars can be hired at the bigger stations, so journeys from large town to large town can be made by train and then the vineyards may be explored by car.

Another excellent way of touring the Loire countryside is on a bicycle. A base at Nantes, Angers, Tours, Blois and Orléans ensures that there are thousands of vineyards within easy pedalling distance each day.

There are also quite good bus services run by the SNCF and a number of private companies, which allow travel out to the smaller towns and villages away from the Loire. If you choose this method of travel, however, buy the special visitor's ticket which gives unlimited travel for a given number of days.

The Loire, because of its length, has always been used as a transport system and there are many traces of very early settlements, dating back several thousand years BC. The flood plain was an ideal grazing area, and early man cultivated it and used it for rearing livestock at least 2,500 years before Christ. The stone and metal working skills of these early settlers can be seen at the museum in Le Grand Pressigny. The Romans under Julius Caesar invaded the area between 58 and 50BC. He led his troops against rebellious Celtic tribes at Bourges, and near Amboise he had boats built for his attack on Tours. The Romans improved agriculture, built roads, bridges and towns and created a measure of civilisation that has continued ever since. After 300 years of Roman rule and peace, during which Christianity was introduced, the legions withdrew and the invasions began, first the Huns, then the Childeric and the Franks. The young Frankish king, Clovis, brought peace to the area once more and he made Orléans his capital. His descendants were followed by Charlemagne, and the Loire entered its second great age of building with abbeys and castles, churches and fortified churches being constructed.

The wars after the death of Charlemagne led to many huge fortresses being built along the length of the Loire. For nearly 300 years, because of the marriage of Eleanor of Aquitaine with Henry, the English kings ruled over the territories that make up the Loire. Richard II was the last of the Plantagenet kings to rule northern France. However, for almost the next 200 years the ownership of the Loire and northern France was fiercely contested between England and France. It was the time of the Hundred Years War; the final defeat of the English deprived the crown of all its French possessions except Calais.

The French king could now truly call himself King of All France and he and his successors spent more of their time in the Loire. The third and greatest period of building began, spurred on by the arrival of the Italian Renaissance. Even Leonardo da Vinci was summoned to the French court at Amboise to assist in the building and decoration projects.

The Loire escaped the worst ravages of the French Revolution and the region prospered because of its agriculture and growing industrial strength around the cities. It even escaped the worst impact of World War I, but many towns, especially Orléans and Tours, were damaged by bombing during World War II. Fortunately much of the damage has been repaired and the buildings restored to their former glory.

PAYS NANTAIS

Tour of Nantes and the Surrounding Area

The tour starts in Nantes, which many guidebooks consider to be outside the Loire area. This, however, is the area of Muscadet, and most of the vineyards lie to the south of Nantes. The town itself stands at the confluence of the Loire and its tributary, the Erdre. It is a gateway to eastern Brittany and the

Loire Atlantique to the west. It was the seat of the Namnètes, a Gaul tribe, when the Romans arrived in 52BC. At that time it was already a busy commercial centre and port, exporting tin and other ores. Today there are many important old buildings to visit, and the museums house collections of relics from its Roman and Gallo-Roman periods.

Among the things to see include the Château des Ducs, open daily except Tuesday, a former thirteenth-century castle with the château built on its foundations. Nearby is the fourteenth-century keep from the Castel de la Tour. As different dukes ruled the area, they made their own architectural additions to the castle, so it is an amazing mixture of styles from the fourteenth to eighteenth centuries.

The cathedral dates from the fifteenth century and stands on the site of an earlier one, destroyed during a Viking invasion. It took more than 500 years to complete. The façade is important because of its five doors — most French cathedrals have only three. It has many fine sculptures, carvings, and tombs.

The Old Town can be explored through the narrow, winding streets. There are many half-timbered fifteenth-century buildings, especially in the rue Ste Croix, rue des Carmes and rue de la Juiverie.

Eglise Ste Croix is a seventeenth-century church in the heart of the Old Town. The interior represents many styles of architecture while the face is Jesuit style. La Psalette manor house dates from the fifteenth century, and is a perfectly-preserved medieval manor house. Today it is a fine museum. Near the museum, note the pebble stone wall, which dates from Roman times.

Porte-St-Pierre is a fifteenth-century gateway and the remains of the original city ramparts. Napoléon stayed at the Hôtel d'Aux, now a private house. Other places to see are the Hôtel Montaudoin, with its Greco-Roman architecture, and the monument to Louis XVI in the place Louis XVI.

The place du Commerce, now a commercial centre, used to be the port for Nantes, and the Palais de la Bourse was built at the end of the eighteenth century. So, too, was the place Royal with its marvellous fountain in the middle. The Grand Theatre is in the place Graslin, and dates from the seventeenth century, while the small café in the corner of the square, La Cigale, was built at the beginning of this century, but it has fine, colourful mosaics.

There are fine mansions on the Ile Feydau, where many of the rich merchants chose to live; most notable are the eight symmetrical mansions built in the early nineteenth century, around the place Mellinet.

The many museums include the marine museum, the Breton regional art museum, the decorative art museum, natural history museum, and Musée Dobrée, containing medieval and Renaissance sculptures and paintings and eighteenth-century tapestries. There is also a fine arts museum in rue Georges Clémenceau.

There is a *Route du Vin* signposted clearly for those wishing to tour the Muscadet region, the Gamay region and the Gros Plant. Villages worth visiting for tasting are Le Pellerin, Vertou, St-Fiacre, and, to the north of Nantes, Carquefou.

Ancenis is an ancient town which has always been important because of its defensive position over the river. It was here, in 1468, that Brittany ceded its independence to Louis XI of France. Today, only a tower remains from that original castle, but there are other buildings worth seeing from its more recent past, including some seventeenth-century pavilions. Ancenis' recent fame has been built on its wine, both Muscadet and Coteaux d'Ancenis. If the first day in the Nantes area is spent in exploring the town, the second day should be set aside for tasting the wines. The 'wine villages' include Ligné and Varades to the north, and Le Loroux-Bottereau, Mallet and Clisson to the south. There are, of course, many other villages to visit and those establishments offering tastings and visits can easily be seen.

ANJOU-SAUMUR

Tour of Angers

Angers is about thirty miles along the river from Ancenis and the castle dominates your approach. It has seventeen bastion towers, up to 164ft high. There is an outer and inner defensive wall, and a herd of fallow deer live in part of the moat, now dry. The first walls were built in the third century AD, and the wooden fortress was replaced by stone in the first half of the thirteenth century. Many works of arts and tapestries are displayed there. There are many other tapestries to be seen on display nearby, especially at the ancient Hôpital St Jean, founded in 1174 by Henry II as part of his penance for having Archbishop Thomas à Becket assassinated at Canterbury.

Other buildings which should be visited are the cathedral of St Maurice with its stained glass windows, Roman font and other treasures, and the Logis Barrault, a fifteenth-century mansion housing a fine arts collection. Nearby are the remains of Chapelle Toussaint, blown up in 1815 by accident while being used as an arsenal. The Tour St Aubin is a twelfth-century keep used by the monks of the Abbaye St Aubin, and the abbey, rebuilt in the seventeenth century, is now the Préfecture. During the day it is open to the public and the carved cloister and chapterhouse doorway should be inspected. There is a collection of Greek vases in the Renaissance Hôtel Pincé, and the collegiate church of St Martin, with its ninth-century interior and crypt.

Angers has many fine old buildings dating from the fifteenth century, with timbered and carved overhanging storeys which block out the sun in the narrow streets. Nearby there are many châteaux to visit, such as Le Plessis-Macé, originally a twelfth-century fortress, rebuilt in the fifteenth century; Bois-Mautboucher, Percher, Magnanne, St-Ouen and Le Plessis-Bourré near Mayenne. Serrant, to the west on the N23, has one of the finest châteaux in the Loire.

To the south of Angers there are many tasting centres, such as those at Savennières, Rochefort-sur-Loire, Brissac-Quincé, Gennes, Beaulieu-sur-Layon, Faye-d'Anjou, Thouarcé and Chemillé. The Saumur, Anjou, Savennières and Coteaux du Layon wines must be tried.

Tour of Saumur and the Surrounding Area

The château of Saumur dominates the town, which is the next stop upstream on the Loire. It was built at the end of the fifteenth century by Louis I of

Anjou. It has towers at each corner, and the bell turrets and ornate gable windows were added to give it a special charm. It stands on the site of an ancient fortress, and houses two museums, one for the decorative arts, the other tracing the history of the horse.

Other things to see in Saumur include the church of Notre-Dame-de-Nantilly dating from the twelfth century, with fifteenth-century tapestries and twelfth-century statues; the church of St Peter, with more sixteenth-century tapestries, Baroque organ loft and Angevin vaulting; and the Musée de la Cavalerie, which traces the history of cavalry and armour. Saumur is the home of the famous riding school (the *Cadre Noir*) founded by Louis XV and a horse's head features on many of the Saumur wine labels. The town hall is built around part of the city's defensive walls and contains fifteenth-century fireplaces. The Chapelle St Jean behind is thirteenth century, and the Notre-Dame-des-Ardilliers was once a major pilgrimage centre.

Just outside Saumur is St-Hilaire-St-Florent, which is the best place to taste the regional wine, and there is also a museum devoted to the mushroom. The national riding school is next door.

Other places to see nearby are Trèves, with its castle, Romanesque church and fifteenth-century keep; Dénezé-sous-Doué with its caves containing grotesque effigies, thought to have been carved in the sixteenth century, and eleventh-century church; and Rochmenier where there is an underground peasant museum showing how the troglodytes lived until quite recently.

At Montreuil-Bellay there is a charming château, the ruins of the Abbaye d'Asnières, the old wall and gateways and many old buildings.

South of Saumur is Champigny, famous for its wine, then Fontevraud l'Abbaye, an eleventh-century monastery in five parts — for monks, nuns, lepers, the infirm and repentant women. It houses the bones of both English and French monarchs and has now been beautifully restored after damage caused by the Revolution and Napoléon who turned it into a prison.

TOURAINE

Chinon, the next stop, is also famous for its own wine. Buildings of interest include the ruined Château St-Georges and the Château du Milieu, housing a Joan of Arc museum, the tenth-century Eglise St Mexme with frescoes, the twelfth-century Chapelle Ste Radegonde, built in rock and the Eglise St Maurice, built by Henry II, where Joan of Arc prayed. There is also a wine museum, a local art museum and the Caves Peintes, underground galleries where Rabelais got his inspiration for the *'Cave de la Dive Bouteille'* in *Gargantua*.

Tour of Tours and the Surrounding Area

Tours, the major population centre of the area, also offers the traveller a feast of beautiful buildings, good hotels and restaurants and an abundance of good local wine. Although damaged badly by bombing in the last war, the town has been carefully rebuilt. The cathedral of St Gatien took 300 years to construct so contains a number of carefully-blended styles. There are splendid views from the top of the south tower, which is open to the public. The fifteenth-century choir school is next door.

You should also see the remains of Henry II's Château Royal de Tours, of which two twelfth-century towers remain. They house a waxworks museum. The museum of fine arts, in the former archbishop's palace, also incorporates a section of the original Gallo-Roman town wall.

Other things to see near Tours include the eleventh-century priory of St Cosme, the Château de Plessis-lès-Tours, the Dolmen de Mettray, the Grange du Meslay and Abbaye de Marmoutier.

To the east of the town is Vouvray, famous for its wine, while Montlouis, with its tasting cellars, lies to the south.

Amboise must also be visited for its château, old buildings, fifteenth-century towers, and very good food shops. Already a town when Caesar invaded, it is said that the Romans stored their grain in the caves below the château. The present château, started in 1492, stands on the site of two earlier ones. Leonardo da Vinci was summoned there, and here he spent the last years of his life. Mary Queen of Scots was a guest at the château in 1560, when a Protestant uprising took place. The rioters were all killed at the château.

Nearby is the Clos-Lucé, where Leonardo stayed; it is now a museum dedicated to him, and has a delightful garden. The Porte des Lions is named after a pride of lions kept by François I in the dry moat. Also see the church of St Florentine with its flood marks, the tapestries in the old town hall, and the fifteenth-century chapel of St Hubert on the battlements said to contain the bones of Leonardo.

Blois is next, with the wines of Cheverny and Valençay. Blois itself was badly damaged by bombing and the cathedral, château and many old houses are being carefully restored. The château contains many exhibitions, museums and restored apartments. Also worth a visit is the Pavillon Anne de Bretagne, fifteenth century; the Houdini museum; the twelfth-century church of St Nicholas; the sixteenth-century cathedral of St Louis (with tenth-century crypt) and the Pont Gabriel. There are many fine buildings, fountains and statues as well.

Nearby is the massive château of Chambord with its six towers, 440 rooms and 365 chimneys. Its park is enclosed by a 20-mile-long wall, the longest in France. To the south is the equally famous château of Cheverny started in 1604, with its magnificent paintings. It also has a hunting museum. Further south still is Valençay, where the wine should be tasted and the château, which contains two museums and a spectacular formal garden, should be visited.

Because these Touraine wines are special, and many of them not widely exported, every opportunity should be taken to drink them.

ORLEANAIS

Tour of Orléans and the Surrounding Area

Orléans, the next suggested overnight stop, is in the centre of its own wine-producing area, and wines can be tasted in the city or at Cléry-St-André,

Olivet, Messas, Beaugency and Meung-sur-Loire. At Beaugency there is also the twelfth-century Eglise Notre-Dame, a tower from the medieval fortifications, an old town hall with tapestries and a fifteenth-century château with a museum of local culture. There is also a fine château at Meung. At Cléry-St-André there is a Gothic basilica which has long been a place of pilgrimage. Orléans has more than enough to keep the sightseer happy for several days, but in a short visit the main sights to see are the cathedral of Ste Croix, started in 1601, but with parts of the original, much earlier building; the old University library in rue de Bourgogne; the fifteenth-century church of St Aignan; museum of fine arts; history museum; natural history museum; and the very many fine old buildings in the old town, many of them dating from the sixteenth century.

It is also interesting to trace the links between Orléans and Joan of Arc, through the statues, her life history depicted in the cathedral's stained glass windows, the reconstructed house she stayed in during 1429 (Maison Jeanne d'Arc); and the Centre Jeanne d'Arc which has a collection of documents — and many more.

From Orléans the tour goes on to Gien, via the pilgrimage centre and church at St-Benoît. The Druids also believe St Benoît to be sacred and meet here. At Gien there is a fifteenth-century château, and the special wine of the area, the Coteaux du Giennois, should be tasted. Then it is south to two famous names in wines — Pouilly and Sancerre.

CENTRAL FRANCE

Pouilly derives its name from the Latin for 'the villa of Paulus' and dates from Roman times. It has always been prosperous because of its wines, the best whites in the Loire. Pouilly has a modest château, but the wine is the most important thing, and it can be tasted at the seven communes that make up the *appellation*.

On the other side of the river is Sancerre, also of Roman origin. Today, there are still many fine old houses, and some buildings date back to the eleventh and twelfth centuries. After a stroll around the village, again concentrate on the wine. While Sancerre is famous for its white wines, it also produces reds and rosés; all can be magnificent. To the south west of Sancerre is Menetou-Salon, which produces wines similar in style, although they are hardly known. It is worth trying them to make your own comparison, Menetou also has a glorious château, once owned by the richest man in France, Charles XII's minister of finance. It was completely restored in the last century.

Our last port of call is Bourges, which has many half-timbered Renaissance buildings, an archaeological museum and a fifteenth-century, partly-restored château. There is a museum depicting rural life in days gone by in the town hall, and a car museum. Among the churches worth seeing are Lanthenay, with its sixteenth-century paintings, and the Chapelle St Roch, erected after the plague which swept the town in 1584.

PLACES OF INTEREST IN THE LOIRE REGION

NANTES AND AREA

Nantes
Ancient, pre-Roman town; many old buildings; museums; thirteenth-century Château des Ducs; Castel de la Tour; fifteenth-century cathedral; Old Town; Eglise Ste Croix; La Psalette manor

house and museum; Porte-St-Pierre; Hôtel d'Aux, Hôtel Montaudoin; place du Commerce; place Royal; Grand Theatre; Ile Feydau; place Mellinet. Vineyards and tasting centres in most surrounding villages.

ANGERS AND AREA

Ancenis
Ancient town; remains of old castle; many fine buildings.

Angers
Château with museums; Cathédrale St Maurice (stained glass windows and treasury); Tour St Aubin; Logis Barrault; ruins of Chapelle Toussaint; Hôpital St Jean; church of St Serge (chancel vaulting); collegiate church of St Martin (ancient crypt); twelfth-century trinity church; reconstructed abbey of St Nicholas; many other fine buildings, museums, statues, and gardens.

Serrant
Magnificent Anjou château started in sixteenth century; moat, park and gardens.

Rochefort-sur-Loire
Old turreted houses, Romanesque church.

La Guimonnière
Château.

Ile-de-Béhuard
Island in Loire with tiny church of Notre-Dame built into the rock.

Gennes
Ruined church with twelfth-century tower and carvings.

Brissac-Quincé
Fine château, park, tapestries.

St-Barthélemy
Old mining town producing slate, shafts 1,312ft deep, château. Many wine villages and tasting centres.

SAUMUR AREA

Saumur
Château; horse museum; decorative arts museum (china collection); churches of Notre-Dame-de-Nantilly (twelfth-century) church of St Peter, sixteenth-century tapestries; cavalry museum; Hôtel de Ville with tapestries and fifteenth-century fireplaces; thirteenth-century Chapelle St Jean; pilgrimage church of Notre-Dame-des-Ardillières; many other old houses.

Trèves
Castle, Romanesque church, fifteenth-century keep.

Dénezé-sous-Doué
Caves containing grotesque sculptures, eleventh-century church.

Rochmenier
Troglodyte museum.

Montreuil-Bellay
Charming château, ruins of abbey of Asnières, old wall, old buildings.

Fontevraud l'Abbaye
Eleventh-century monastery, with tombs of many English kings and queens.

Champigny
Famous wine village.

TOURS AND AREA

Tours
Cathedral of St Gatien with south tower open to public, affording fine views; La

Psalette choir school (fifteenth-century); remains of Château Royal de Tours; waxworks museum; museum of fine arts;

Gallo-Roman remains; place Foire-le-Roi; medieval food market; Hôtel Babou de la Bourdaisière with fourteenth-century arches; museum of craft guilds; Beaune-Semblançay gardens with its fountains; glass museum; many fine old churches and other buildings.

Chinon
Famous wine centre, ruined château, Joan of Arc museum, tenth-century church, wine museum, local art museum, painted caves.

Priory of St Cosme
Ruined eleventh-century priory, twelfth-century refectory.

Plessis-lès-Tours
Fifteenth-century château.

Dolmen de Mettray
5,000-year-old historic site.

Parçay-Meslay
Romanesque church with frescoes.

Grange du Meslay
Near-perfect medieval tithe barn.

Abbaye de Marmoutier
Site of fourth-century abbey, now nunnery but caves open to public.

St-Cyr
Museum to Anatole France.

Montbazon
Remains of fortress.

Amboise
Château, fifteenth-century towers, caves under château, battlements, many old churches and other fine buildings, museums.

Clos-Lucé
Leonardo da Vinci museum.

Chambord
Massive château.

Cheverny
Château with collection of paintings by famous masters.

Valençay
Château, two museums, formal garden, wine tasting centre.

ORLEANS AND AREA

Blois
Old houses; cathedral and château (being restored) with museums, tapestries; Pavillon Anne de Bretagne, fifteenth century (now the Tourist Office); twelfth-century keep; Pont Gabriel 1717; many fine churches and museums.

Orléans
Cathedral of Ste Croix, Salles des Thèses; fifteenth-century church of St Aignan; fine arts museum; history and archaeological museum; natural science museum; many old buildings; Old Town; Joan of Arc memorials.

Châteauneuf-sur-Loire
English garden, château, museum of the Loire boatmen.

St-Benoît-sur-Loire
Pilgrimage centre, basilica, place of Druid worship.

Forêt d'Orléans
State forest with lovely walks, château, eleventh-century church.

Gien
Château, rebuilt in 1484; pottery works.

Lorris
Ancient royal town, church, Château de la Bussière, fishing museum, car museum, aquarium.

Bourges
Cathedral of St Etienne, started 1185, wonderful interior; Palais Jacques Coeur, fifteenth-century Gothic mansion; Hôtel Cujas, sixteenth-century house, now art museum; Hôtel Lallemant, Renaissance mansion now museum of decorative arts; fifteenth-century town hall.

Menetou-Salon
Château.

Gastronomy of the Loire

The larder of the Loire is one of the richest in France. There are marvellous seafish from the Atlantic, shellfish from the estuary, and freshwater fish available for much of the Loire's length. Touraine is famed as 'The Garden of France', Anjou has fruit (especially pears), there are apples and plums from Orléans, strawberries from Saumur, and even peaches and melons growing in the warm, landlocked centre of the region. On top of this there are marvellous vegetables, most notably asparagus. To the south of Orléans are woods and forests full of game, and to the east of the city, meadows and woodlands where a wide variety of wild mushrooms and fungi can be gathered.

Obviously, the cuisine of the region changes as you travel eastwards away from the sea, and fish dishes give way to meat and game in the far east, where the Loire area borders with the Ile de France.

Ever since the Italian chefs were introduced to the summer homes of the Royal Court in the Loire, the cuisine of the area has been classical rather than regional in style. There are still traditional local dishes to be found, but there are many great chefs specialising in the sort of cuisine for which France has become internationally famous.

Many of the towns are famous for one particular product, and these have been incorporated into special dishes which are worth trying. Tours is famous for prunes, Anjou for William pears; there are Reinette apples from Le Mans, strawberries from Saumur, and quince from Orléans. Because of the extensive orchards of both hard and soft fruit, desserts figure prominently on the menus, and there are mouthwatering tarts and the famous cherry *clafoutis*.

Freshwater fish offered on menus include lamprey and eels, pike, carp and shad. Meats include rabbit and hare, pork and excellent *charcuterie*, chicken and game birds such as partridge. Even larks are eaten, often in a pastry case. There are sheep in the Berry and cattle in Anjou, and many classical veal dishes originate from Orléans. Vegetables also figure prominently on menus. There is potato cake, cabbage stew and pumpkin pie. Finally, there are biscuits, macaroons and chocolates, especially from Blois, and a wide range of cheeses, made from both cow's and goat's milk.

As always, it is worth hunting out the small village restaurants, or making friends and, with any luck, being invited to someone's home to dine. There are some dishes special to the region which may only be tasted in this way.

There are many speciality dishes featuring fish such as *alose*, or *tanche à l'oseille*, grilled fish in a sorrel sauce. Usually shad, carp or tench is used. There is *chaudrée*, a speciality fish stew, often using conger eels and white fish cooked in garlic and white wine with potatoes. It gets its name from the large pot it was originally cooked in. *Bouilliture d'anguilles* is a freshwater fish stew, using locally caught eels, stewed in red wine, shallots, prunes and garlic.

Other fish dishes include *friture de la Loire*, small fish caught in the Loire and deep fried and served with lemon; *gravette*, a flat type of oyster (*huître*), served near the coast and the western parts of the Loire; and *lamproie*, an eel-like fish caught in the estuaries (*à la Chinonaise* means it is cooked in walnut oil). There is an excellent stew of different freshwater fish called *matelote*, to which is added onions, mushrooms and white wine. Eel, carp, pike, perch or barbel are normally used, and crayfish tails can be added. It is a speciality of the Loire, especially in Anjou and Touraine.

There are marvellous pork and tripe sausages called *andouilles*, which are served cold in thick slices as a first course; they are not be be confused with *andouillette*, which is a much smaller sausage, grilled and usually served hot with a strong mustard sauce. There are excellent white sausages, *boudin blanc*, made from the meat of chicken, pork or game but with no blood. These can be eaten as a starter, as can *cerneaux aux verjus*, a Touraine dish, consisting of unripe, green walnuts soaked in grape juice.

Stuffed cabbage, or *bardette*, is a traditional dish. The cabbage is usually stuffed with meats, especially hare. There are many variations on the stuffed cabbage theme, including *chouée*, from Anjou and Poitou, and *farci poitevin*. The first is boiled cabbage mixed with butter and served with boiled potatoes and sometimes cream, while the second is cabbage stuffed with herbs, pork, bacon and vegetables, cooked in a stock and eaten hot or cold. It is also sometimes called *far*. *Bouchelle à la Tourangelle* is a dish of veal kidneys and sweetbreads, with truffles and cream added: definitely not for the weight-conscious. Other *à la Tourangelle* (which means 'in the style of Touraine') dishes include a salad containing haricot and French beans. Normally dishes in this style also have prunes added. From Touraine and Anjou there is also *beurre blanc*, a reduction of shallots and Muscadet, or vinegar, whipped up with butter and served with many fish courses, especially pike.

One of the best local dishes is *fressure vendéen*, at its best when served in a private house, although it can be eaten in cafés and restaurants. It is pig's offal — heart, liver, lungs and spleen-cooked with blood and onions, and served cold with bread.

Blood and bits of pig figure in many dishes such as *gigorit*. It is also known as *tantouillet* in Poitou, where it consists of whole pig's head cooked in blood and red wine.

Berry is known among other things for *citrouillat*, or pumpkin pie, and there are many speciality pancakes, fritters and tarts made from maize flour and served as either savoury or desserts. *Millière* is a maize and rice porridge from Anjou, while *grapiau*, from Berry, is a thick pancake (also known as *sanciau*, and *matefaim*). As a savoury it is usually filled with potato, and it is sprinkled with sugar as a dessert.

Many dishes include game and poultry. There is *pâté de Chartres*, partridge in a pastry case, but many towns and districts have their own speciality *pâtés* and *foie gras*. *Pâté de Paques* from Poitou is made from pork, chicken or rabbit and hard boiled eggs; *pâté de vendéen* is made from rabbit. *Poulet en barbouille*, a Berry speciality, is chicken cooked in a red wine and cream sauce thickened with blood. Chicken can also be used to make mouth-watering light mousse, or *quenelles* (*de volaille*) although these are more usually made from pike (*de brochet*).

Pork is also a much-used meat. *Porc aux pruneaux* is a Tours dish with pork cooked in white wine (usually Vouvray), with cream and prunes. Pork can also be used for *rillettes*, a meat paste speciality of the Loire, although the ingredients vary from one area to another. Pork, rabbit, duck and goose can all be used. The meat is cooked with herbs in its own fat, and then beaten into a paste and put into earthen jars for storing. Different versions can be found in Amboise, Angers, Blois, Le Mans, Tours, Saumur and Vendôme. *Rillons*, also called *rillauds*, is another traditional Loire dish. The meat is prepared in the same way as for *rillettes*, but cooked more and served whole, not beaten into a paste. Vendôme is an Orléanais town noted for *rillettes*, and they sometimes appear under this name on local menus.

Potatoes, too, have their own dishes and a variety of local names. *Truche* is the Berry name for potato (*pomme de terre*) and *truffiat* is a potato cake or thick potato pancake. It can even mean potatoes in a pastry case, but this is more usually called *bourre-chrétien*.

The people of the Loire have a very sweet tooth and there are many dishes to choose from, apart from very good local cheeses. Many of the desserts use the first class local fruit, and tarts and pies are common.

Anjou is home of the *bourdaines*, baked apples stuffed with plum jam. In Berry there is *clafoutis*, a batter cake with cherries which used to be served to the pickers during the grape harvest. From Orléans, there is *cotignac*, a sweet made from quince paste, which is cut into squares. It is also known as *pâté de coings*. *Gâteau de Pithiviers* is named after a town in Orléanais, and is a rich puff pastry cake filled with a rum and almond flavoured cream. *Pâté de Pithiviers* is lark, often in pastry, so do not confuse the two.

There are many spellings of *gouéron* (*gouère* and *gouerre* being the most common). It can be either a cake or tart, but when it is offered around Berry, it is a goat's milk cheese cake.

Spiced gingerbread, called *nonnette*, or *pain d'épices*, is popular. It is often coated with honey or icing. Traditionally it was made by nuns, but now it is made commercially in factories. *Pêche à la royale* is a Touraine dish of peaches in a creamy sauce, while *poires tapées*, also from Touraine, are dried pears. Other desserts include *russerole*, from Touraine, a type of sweet pastry; and *tarte tatin*, an Orléanais speciality, a sort of upside-down apple cake.

Leading us into the cheeses of the region is the final dessert, *tourteau fromagé*, a traditional cheesecake from Poitou.

There are many cheeses worth trying made from goat's, sheep's and cow's milk. There is *Bondaroy au Foin*, also called *Pithiviers au Foin*, a soft cow's milk cheese with a tangy flavour, cured in hay. It is produced around Bondaroy and Pithiviers. *Caillebotte* is a soft curd cheese from Poitou, made from the milk of sheep, cow or goat; while *Chabichou Fermier*, from the same region, is a strong cone-shaped goat's cheese known by several other names including *Chaunay*, *Civray*, *Cajassous* and *Cabrichie*. *Couhé-Vérac* is another Poitou cheese, made from goat's milk. It has a nutty flavour, and is wrapped in chestnut leaves.

From Berry there is *Crottin de Chavignol*, an AC goat's milk cheese with a very strong taste. It is often served grilled, while *Crémet*, a mild and creamy cow's-milk cheese from Anjou and Nantes, is often eaten as a dessert with jam or fruit. *Frinot*, or *Frinault*, from Orléanais, is a soft, lightly-cured cheese, with quite a strong flavour. It is sometimes coated with ashes, when it is sold as *Frinault Cendré*. *Gien* is a nutty-flavoured cheese made from either cow's or goat's milk or a mixture. The cheese is cured in the leaves of the plane tree. Plane leaves are also used to wrap *Olivet Bleu*, a rich, blueish cow's-milk cheese from the Orléanais. It is very similar to *Vendôme Bleu*, while *Olivet Cendré* is a strong cow's milk cheese coated in ashes.

Mothe-St-Héray is a white, strong goat's milk cheese from Poitou, made in the dairy which gives it its name. It is also called *Chèvre à la Feuille*. *St-Benoît*, from Orléanais, is a round, soft, fruity cheese; while *St-Paulin*, also made from cow's milk, is quite hard, but mild. It comes from Anjou. Also worth trying are *Ste-Maure*, a tangy goat's milk cheese and *Selles-sur-Cher*, from Orléanais and Berry, a mild, soft, nutty-flavoured goat's cheese coated with charcoal. It is also called *Romorantin* The final cheese to seek out is *Valençay*, a pyramid-shaped goat's cheese with a mild, nutty flavour. Made around Berry and also known locally as *Pyramide*, the best is farm-made (*Valençay Fermier*).

HOTELS AND RESTAURANTS OF THE LOIRE REGION

Amboise
(37400 Indre-et-Loire)

Hostellerie du Château de Pray
☎ (47) 57 23 67
A beautiful thirteenth-century château north-east of the town on the D751. On top of a hill with fine views over the Loire, and is surrounded by its own parkland. 16 comfortable rooms and a delightful restaurant with a terrace by the river. Good value.

Hôtel Chanteloup
route de Blère
☎ (47) 57 10 90
A very comfortable hotel in town, with 25 rooms but no restaurant; breakfasts served.

Novotel
route de Chenonceaux
☎ (47) 57 42 07
A new 82-room hotel 1¼ miles out of town, with splendid view. Not expensive, and restaurant only offers basic snacks, grills.

Auberge du Mail
32 quai du Gén-de-Gaulle
☎ (47) 57 60 39
An exciting little restaurant, not expensive, and with a fine list. 15 comfortable, very reasonably-priced rooms.

Angers
(49000 Maine-et-Loire)

Hôtel Concorde
18 blvd Maréchal Foch
☎ (41) 87 37 20
A modern, very comfortable hotel in centre of town. There are 73 sound-proofed rooms. There is a quick brasserie, good for late-night snacks.

La Croix de Guerre
23 rue Château-Gontier
☎ (41) 88 66 59
A small 29-room hotel in the centre of town, offering simple accommodation at very reasonable prices. The restaurant is excellent and prices are very reasonable.

Hôtel Mercure
place Mendès-France
☎ (41) 60 34 81
A large and very comfortable 86-room hotel, expensive and with a good restaurant.

Hôtel d'Anjou
1 blvd du Maréchal Foch
☎ (41) 83 24 82
A very comfortable revamped 50-room hotel, near the flower market, not expensive. The restaurant, *Salamandre*, is good and reasonably-priced.

Hôtel Le Progrès
26 rue Denis-Papin
☎ (41) 88 10 14
A modern, comfortable 41-room hotel, no restaurant but breakfasts served.

Hôtel Iéna
27 rue Marceau
☎ (41) 87 52 40
A convenient, small, 25-room hotel, not too far from the city centre. Reasonable prices but no restaurant; breakfasts served.

Le Guéré
9 place du Ralliement
☎ (41) 87 64 94
A magnificent restaurant
in the hands of Paul Le
Guéré, very creative and
always good. Expensive,
with a fine wine list.

Restaurant Le Logis
17 rue St-Laud
☎ (41) 87 44 15
Very good little res-
taurant, specialising in
seafish and shellfish.

Restaurant Le Toussaint
7 rue Toussaint
☎ (41) 87 46 20
An excellent menu that
changes with the seasons.
The eels and *rillettes* are a
delight. Not over-expen-
sive, and with very fine
wines.

Azay-le-Rideau
(37190 Indre-et-Loire)

Le Grand Monarque
place de la République
☎ (47) 43 40 08
A charming small château
beside the river Indre
stands next to this 30-
room hotel in the centre
of town. A very warm
hotel, comfortable rooms
and a good restaurant with
many local fish special-
ities. Lots of pets always
in attendance.

Blois
(41000 Loir-et-Cher)

La Péniche
prom. du Mail
☎ (54) 74 37 23
A delightful floating
restaurant aboard a barge,
the *St Berthuin*, moored
on the northern bank of
the Loire. Very good
classical dishes at good
prices.

Hôtel Ibis
route Guignières, 1¹/4 miles
out of town on the A10
☎ (54) 74 60 60
A comfortable 40-room
hotel, with good res-
taurant; reasonable prices.

Hôtel St-Jacques
place Gare
☎ (54) 78 04 15
Very central 33-room
hotel, without restaurant,
but very reasonably-priced
rooms; breakfast served.

Novotel
at La Chaussée St-Victor,
2¹/2 miles out of town.
☎ (54) 78 33 57
A modern 116-room hotel
with every facility, including swimming pool.
Rooms not too expensive,
restaurant adequate for
snacks and quick meals
only.

Les Bezards
(45290 Loiret)

Auberge des Templiers
☎ (38) 31 80 01
The English food and
hotel critic Richard Binns
considers this the best-run
hotel in France, and cer-
tainly the Dépées leave
nothing to chance. The
service is warm and attentive, the 28 rooms com-
fortable and expensive,
and the local food marvellous. An experience worth
trying, but book.

Bourges
(18000 Cher)

Restaurant Jacques-Coeur
3 place Jacques-Coeur
☎ (48) 70 12 72
A marvellous establish-
ment under the direction
of André Quillerier. The
food matches the seasons,
and is always good. Many
of the best traditional
regional dishes found here
at reasonable prices.

Bourgueil
(37140 Indre-et-Loire)

Le Thouarsais
place Hublin
☎ (47) 97 72 05
A modest, comfortable
hotel in a quiet village;
ideal as a touring base, especially for budget travel.
30 rooms, no restaurant
but breakfast.

Germain
rue A. Chartier
☎ (47) 97 72 22
Closed October. Good,
local food at attractive
prices.

Brinon-sur-Sauldre
(18410 Argent-sur-Sauldre)

Auberge La Solognote
Grande Rue
☎ (48) 58 50 29
A homely, small, 10-room
inn run by André and Dom-
inique Girard. She does the
welcoming and he does
the cooking, and how!
Excellent, creative dishes.
Room rates reasonable,
fixed-price menu very
good value but the *à la
carte* is worth exploring.

Cande-sur-Beuvron
(41120 Loir-et-Cher)

Hostellerie Caillère
route Montils
☎ (54) 44 03 08
A marvellously scenic
country restaurant, set
among chestnut trees.
Very good food and wine
list.

Lion d'Or
☎ (54) 44 04 66
A 10-room, reasonably-
priced hotel with fair
restaurant.

Chaumont-sur-Tharonne
(41600 Loir-et-Cher)

La Croix Blanche
5 place Mottu
☎ (54) 88 55 12
A village inn for several hundred years, with 16 very comfortable rooms. Kitchens run by Madame Gisèle Crouzier, with an all female staff, and the food is magnificent. She is from Périgord, and now blends the cuisine of two of France's greatest gastronomic areas. An unforgettable experience.

Chaumont-sur-Loire
(41150 Loir-et-Cher)

Hostellerie Château
rue de Lattre-de-Tassigny
☎ (54) 20 98 04
A 15-room hotel, very comfortable, with swimming pool. Fair restaurant and reasonable prices all round.

Chenonceaux
(37150 Indre-et-Loire)

Le Bon Laboureur et Château
6 rue du Dr Bretonneau
☎ (47) 23 90 02
A delightful, olde-worlde 26-room hotel, and very good restaurant with good value for money fixed-price menus.

Chenehutte-lès-Tuffeaux
(49350 Maine-et-Loire)

Le Prieuré
☎ (41) 67 90 14
A marvellous 400-year-old house near the Loire, with marvellous parkland and woods behind. The 36 rooms are very comfortable and reasonable, the food good and modern.

Cour-Cheverny
(41700 Loir-et-Cher)

Trois Marchands
☎ (54) 79 96 44
A fine 40-room hotel, reasonably priced, with a fine restaurant with good speciality dishes.

Chinon
(37500 Indre-et-Loire)

Château de Marcay
A luxurious château 6 miles south of town on the D749 and D116.
☎ (47) 93 03 47
Parts of the house are 500 years old; the 34 bedrooms are large, ultra-comfortable and expensive. Restaurant good, although not great, but expensive. Still worth the experience, however.

Hôtel Diderot
rue Diderot
☎ (47) 93 18 87
A very friendly 22-room hotel for those on a budget. No restaurant, but breakfast served.

Clisson
(44190 Loire-Atlantique)

Auberge de la Cascade
at Gervaux
☎ (40) 78 02 41
A small, pleasing 10-room inn on the river Sèvre, with exceptionally good value fixed-price menus.

Hôtel Gare
place Gare
☎ (40) 36 16 55
Another inexpensive, but good value 35-room hotel, with good, homely restaurant fare.

La Bonne Auberge
1 rue O. de Clisson
☎ (40) 78 01 90
A delightful restaurant, offering very good value for money, and an open-air dinner is the ideal way to end a day of vineyard visiting.

Fontevraud l'Abbaye
(49590 Maine-et-Loire)

Abbaye
av Roches
☎ (41) 51 71 04
A delightful restaurant, just to the north of the village, offering the best bargain-priced food in the area. Other restaurants could learn from the quality of the fixed-price menu, and the price.

Croix Blanche
7 place Plantagenets
☎ (41) 51 71 11
A very reasonably-priced 19-room hotel, with fair restaurant. Great base for studying this historic region, especially its English links.

Gien
(45500 Loiret)

Hôtel Sanotel
21 quai Sully
☎ (38) 67 61 46
Comfortable 58-room hotel, moderately-priced but without restaurant; breakfast served.

Hôtel Rivage
1 quai Nice
☎ (38) 67 20 53

A 29-room hotel near the Loire with a fine restaurant featuring many dishes from fish offered up by the river. Rooms good value, restaurant expensive.

Langeais
(37130 Indre-et-Loire)

Hôtel Hosten
2 rue Gambetta
☎ (47) 96 82 12
A 12-room, reasonably-priced hotel, with a very good restaurant, *Le Langeais*.

Auberge de la Bonde,
3 miles from the village at St-Michel-sur-Loire
☎ (47) 96 83 13
A small, 13-room hotel, rooms simple but comfortable, and quite good restaurant.

Loches
(37600 Indre-et-Loire)

Hôtel de France
6 rue Picois
☎ (47) 59 00 32
A small, ancient town, packed with history, and a good base from which to explore. This comfortable 22-room hotel is typical of those in provincial France; it has additionally a very good restaurant with excellent fish. The fixed-price menu is a bargain.

Château
18 rue Château
☎ (47) 59 07 35
10 modest rooms, but very reasonably priced. No restaurant but breakfast served.

Luynes
(37230 Indre-et-Loire)

Domaine de Beauvois
2¹/2 miles to the west on the D49
☎ (47) 55 50 11
A beautiful 41-room hotel. Rooms are enormous and very comfortable, and very expensive. Set in own parkland with swimming pool and very good restaurant; both service and food are memorable.

Montbazon
(37250 Indre-et-Loir)

Château d'Artigny
on the D17, 1¹/4 miles from town
☎ (47) 26 24 24
Magnificent hotel built in 1915 to look like an eighteenth-century château. Stands on site of château built by Louis XV. 6 luxurious suites and 48 bedrooms. Set in own park and woodland, with heated swimming pool, tennis courts. Rooms are expensive, but you could spend as much on dinner in the atmospheric restaurant. Very popular so book.

Domaine de la Tortinière
1¹/4 miles north on the N10 and D287
☎ (47) 26 00 19
A delightful hotel in its own park. 14 rooms and 7 apartments, all expensive, and a good restaurant.

La Chancelière
1 place Marronniers
☎ (47) 26 00 67
Regional cuisine at its best. Reasonably priced. 4 comfortable rooms.

Montrichard
(41400 Loir-et-Cher)

Bellevue
quai du Cher
☎ (54) 32 06 17
Convenient, comfortable 30-room hotel, prices and restaurant reasonable.

Montreuil-Bellay
(49260 Maine-et-Loire)

Splendid et Relais du Bellay
rue Dr Gaudrez
☎ (41) 52 30 21
A very good restaurant; 26 rooms, reasonably priced, in new annexe. Also some rooms in main house.

Nantes
(44000 Loire-Atlantique)

Frantel
3 rue du Dr Zamenhof
☎ (40) 47 10 58
In the business part of town, this large 150-room hotel offers a high degree of comfort at reasonable prices. Le Tillac restaurant is now much improved.

Sofitel
rue A. Millerand
☎ (40) 47 61 03
Also in the business quarter, a comfortable 100-room hotel. A good restaurant, La Pêcherie, specialising in seafood, and the Café de Nantes, for less formal meals.

Hôtel Central
4 rue Couëdic
☎ (40) 20 09 35
A large, comfortable 143-room hotel, ranging from well-priced to expensive. Reasonable restaurant.

Domaine d'Orvault
at Orvault, 4^{1}/2 miles north-
west on the N137 and
D42, Chemin des Marais-
du-Cens
☎ (40) 76 84 02
10 minutes from Nantes,
set in a peaceful park. A
30-room, very comfort-
able hotel with very good,
but pricey restaurant.

Les Maraîchers
21 rue Fouré
☎ (40) 47 06 51
Run by Serge Pacreau and
his wife Marie, this very
popular, exciting res-
taurant offers excellent
food but it is expensive
and you should book.

La Cigogne
16 rue J-J. Rousseau
☎ (40) 89 12 64
Nantes' best bistro; the
shellfish are a must but all
the food is good and reasonably priced.

La Sirène
4 rue Kervégan
☎ (40) 47 00 17
A very good restaurant,
specialising in seafood
with a frequently changing
menu, according to the
seasons. Good wine list.

Mon Rêve
on the Divatte, at Basse-
  Goulaine, 5 miles away
  on the D751
☎ (40) 03 55 50
Gérard Ryngel has already
made his reputation and
his cooking is marvel-
lous. A very reasonable
fixed-price menu and an
adventurous *à la carte.*

Delphin
  at Pont de Bellevue,
  5^{1}/2 miles from Nantes
  on the D68 and D337

3 prom. de Bellevue
☎ (40) 49 04 13
One of the area's best
restaurants in the hands of
Joseph Delphin. Every-
thing excellent, especially
the fish and wine list.
Expensive but very good
value fixed-price menu.

La Lande-St-Martin
Haute-Goulaine, on the
  route de Poitiers, 6^{1}/2
  miles from Nantes.
☎ (40) 80 00 80
A comfortable 39-room
hotel, reasonably priced,
ideally suited as a touring
base.

Clémence
at La Chebuette, 10 miles
  from Nantes
☎ (40) 54 10 18
An interesting and varied
menu, reasonably priced.
The eels grilled over vine
leaves and *sandre* are two
of many specialities.

Manoir de la Comète
At St-Sébastien-sur-Loire
21 ave. Libération
☎ (40) 34 15 93
Very good fixed-price
menus during the week
lets you save up to splash
out at weekends. Christian
Thomas-Trophime is the
gifted patron chef.

Abbaye de Villeneuve
at Sorinières, 7^{1}/2 miles
  south on the N137 and
  D178, route des Sables-
  d'Olonne
☎ (40) 04 40 25
There are 16 very comfortable, expensive rooms to
retire to after sampling
the original cuisine in the
restaurant.

Nevers
(58000 Nièvre)

PLM Loire
quai de Médine
☎ (86) 61 50 92
A modern 60-room hotel,
by river but close to town
centre. Restaurant reasonable.

Hôtel Diane
38 rue Midi
☎ (86) 57 28 10
A very comfortable, cen-
tral 30-room hotel, close
to river.

Hôtel Magdalena
route de Paris
☎ (86) 57 21 41
A 38-room hotel, good
rates, just away from the
centre. No restaurant, but
breakfasts served.

Auberge Porte-du-Croux
17 rue de la Porte-du-
  Croux
☎ (86) 57 12 71
A very good restaurant
near the station, with
charming terrace and gar-
den. Good food, 3 rooms,
both reasonably priced.

La Renaissance
at Magny-Cours on the
  route Moulins, 7^{1}/2 miles
  south
☎ (86) 58 10 40
A marvellous restaurant
run by Jean-Claude Dray.
The food is always a de-
light, apart from the high
prices. 10 comfortable
rooms are much more
reasonably priced.

Nouan-le-Fuzelier
(41600 Loir-et-Cher)

Les Charmilles
route de Pierrefitte-s-
  Sauldre

☎ (54) 88 73 55
A peaceful, country house with 14 comfortable bedrooms, reasonably priced. No restaurant, but breakfasts served. Good garden.

Le Dahu
14 rue de la Mare
☎ (54) 88 72 88
Good local cuisine in a charming restaurant; one may also eat *al fresco*. Very good value menus.

Le Moulin de Villiers
route de Chaon, 1³/4 northeast on the D44
☎ (54) 88 72 27
A lovely country hotel in woodland, with its own lake. 20 comfortable, very reasonably-priced rooms and good, honest cooking. Very popular, so book.

Onzain
(41150 Loir-et-Cher)

Château des Tertres
A mile west of village in its own parkland off the D58
☎ (65) 20 83 88
Simple, but comfortable 14-room hotel, reasonably priced. No restaurant, but breakfast served.

Pont d'Ouchet
Grande Rue
☎ (65) 79 70 22
10 simple, budget rooms but good home cooking.

Domaine des Hauts de Loire
Luxury hotel and restaurant in huge parkland and private drive off the route de Mesland, 1³/4 miles from the village
☎ (65) 20 72 57

Warm and pampering service, marvellous food, good wine list, and everything is expensive, but the ideal place to pamper yourself.

Pouilly-sur-Loire
(58150 Nièvre)

L'Espérance
17 rue Réné-Couard
☎ (86) 39 10 68
Lovely restaurant specialising in fish. 4 reasonably-priced rooms.

Le Coq Hardi
ave. de la Tuilerie
☎ (86) 39 12 99
Very good restaurant and amazingly low prices. 9 comfortable rooms in the Relais Fleuri.

Bouteille d'Or
route Paris
☎ (86) 39 13 84
Comfortable 31-room hotel. Restaurant fair.

Romorantin-Lathenay
(41200 Loir-et-Cher)

Grand Hôtel Lion d'Or
69 rue Georges Clémenceau
☎ (54) 76 00 28
Marvellous restaurant, good speciality dishes, lots of game and chef Didier Clément an exponent of everything good about *nouvelle cuisine*. Not overexpensive. 10 good rooms, also reasonably priced. Gardens.

Les Rosiers-sur-Loire
(49350 Maine-et-Loire)

Jeanne de Laval
route Nationale
☎ (41) 51 80 17

Classical cuisine at its best (especially the salmon), in a delightful 13-room hotel, full of charm and friendly service. Reasonable prices. Some rooms in the quieter annexe. Excellent wine list.

Val de Loir
place Eglise
☎ (41) 51 80 30
Good 11-room hotel, with fair, but inexpensive food.

Sancerre
(18300 Cher)

Auberge Alphonse Mellot
16 place de la Halle
☎ (48) 54 20 53
Good local food and wine, and prices.

La Tasse d'Argent
18 Rempart des Augustins
☎ (48) 54 01 44
Very good, reasonably-priced menus and excellent wine list.

Panoramic
Rempart des Augustins
☎ (48) 54 22 44
Reasonable 59-room hotel, part of above.

L'Etoile
2 quai de Loire
at St Thibault, 3 miles east on the D4
☎ (48) 54 12 15
Fine views of the Loire, modest fare and 11 comfortable, inexpensive rooms.

Saché
(37190 Indre-et-Loire)

Auberge du XIIe Siècle
☎ (47) 26 86 58
Jean Louis Niqueux, the chef owner, prepares

marvellous fish dishes, but also try the *magret*. Very good wine list and not expensive.

Saumur
(49400 Maine-et-Loire)

Le Roi René
94 ave. Gén-de-Gaulle
☎ (41) 67 45 30
Very comfortable 28-room hotel, with good, inexpensive restaurant.

Anne d'Anjou
32 quai Mayaud
☎ (41) 67 30 30
Good 34-room hotel; no restaurant but breakfast.

St-Benoît-sur-Loire
(45730 Loiret)

Hôtel Labrador
☎ (38) 35 74 38
Small, simple, friendly 22-room hotel, reasonably priced; no restaurant.

St-Mathurin-sur-Loire
(49250 Beaufort-en-Vallée)

La Promenade
1 mile east of the village on the D952
☎ (41) 80 50 49
Jacques Morisan and his English wife Gillian run this attentive, friendly restaurant. Very reasonable.

Tours
(37000 Indre-et-Loire)

Méridien
292 ave. de Grammont
☎ (47) 28 00 80
A modern 125-room hotel with air conditioning, swimming pool, tennis and gardens. Reasonably expensive, with a good restaurant.

Le Bordeaux
3 place Maréchal Leclerc
☎ (47) 05 40 32
Close to the station, a 54-room hotel, reasonably-priced rooms, a good but inexpensive restaurant.

Les Cèdres
8 miles from Tours at Savonnières on D7
☎ (47) 53 00 28
Good, country hotel with swimming pool and 35 reasonably-priced rooms. Restaurant next door is separately owned.

Rôtisserie Tourangelle
23 rue Commerce
☎ (47) 05 71 21
Another of the gastronomic treats of Tours. Dine out on excellent regional food, not over-priced.

Hôtel Royal
65 ave. Grammont
☎ (47) 64 71 78
Very comfortable 35-room hotel, no restaurant.

Les Tuffeaux
19 rue Lavoisier
☎ (47) 47 19 89
Expensive but good restaurant in the old town; specialities include wonderful turbot.

Valençay
(36600 Indre)

Espagne
8 rue du Château
☎ (54) 00 00 02
Maurice Fourré, the chef, trained at the Ritz in London, and it shows; he and his brother Phillippe combine to make this a very good, and not too expensive restaurant. There are 17 rooms and apartments.

Vézelay
(89450 Yonne)

Poste et Lion d'Or
place du Champ-de-Foire
☎ (86) 33 21 23
A very comfortable 46-room hotel, with a fair restaurant.

L'Espérance
at St-Père-sous-Vézelay, 1³/₄ miles south-east on the D957
☎ (86) 33 20 45
Run by Marc Meneau. Exquisite is the word used by most guides to describe his cuisine, and I cannot better that. Expensive but worth it. There are 19 very comfortable, expensive rooms.

Vierzon
(18100 Cher)

Le Sologne
route Châteauroux
☎ (48) 75 15 20
A comfortable, quiet, 24-room hotel, no restaurant, but breakfasts. Very reasonably priced.

Villandry
(37300 Indre-et-Loir)

Le Cheval Rouge
☎ (47) 50 02 07
A marvellous restaurant with some superb creations. Not expensive. There are also 20 reasonably-priced rooms. A good touring base.

Vouvray
(37210 Indre-et-Loire)

Le Grand Vatel
8 rue Brûlé
☎ (47) 52 70 32
Inexpensive 7-room hotel with good restaurant.

L'Oubliette
Rochecorbon
☎ (47) 52 50 49
A very good little res-
taurant worth seeking out.
Good prices.

Les Fontaines
Rochecorbon
☎ (47) 52 52 86
Small 15-room hotel on
the N152. Comfortable,
reasonable but no
restaurant.

Le Val Joli
route Nationale
☎ (47) 52 70 18
Very good regional fare at
reasonable prices.

VINEYARDS OF THE LOIRE

ANJOU-SAUMUR

Anjou Rosé

Château Beaulieu   TP
Gratien et Meyerroute de
  Montsoreau
49100 Saumur
☎ (41) 51 01 54
Open: daily 9am-noon and
2-5pm.

Robert Lecomte-
  Girault   TP
Le Sablon
Faye-d'Anjou
49380 Thouarcé
☎ (41) 91 41 34
Open: by appointment.

Domaine des Quinze
  Deniers   TP
GAEC du Haut Coudray
Charcé-St-Ellier-Aubance
49320 Brissac-Quincé
☎ (41) 54 29 01
Open: by appointment.

Other Anjou Rosés

Aguilas-Gaudard   TP
La Brosse
49290 Chalonnes-sur-Loire
☎ (41) 78 10 68
Open: by appointment.

Domaine de Bablut   TP
Daviau brothers
49320 Brissac-Quincé
☎ (41) 91 22 59
Open: by appointment.

Domaine Cady   TP
Valette
St-Aubin-de-Luigné
49190 Rochefort-sur-Loire
☎ (41) 78 33 69
Open: daily 9am-8pm.

Domaine de la Croix-des-
  Loges   TP
Christian Bonnin
49540 Martigné-Briand
☎ (41) 59 43 66
Open: Monday to Saturday
9am-noon and 3-7pm.

Robert Lecomte-Girault TP
Le Sablon
Faye-d'Anjou
49380 Thouarcé
☎ (41) 91 41 34
Open: by appointment.

GAEC Longepe   TP
Les Brosses
49380 Champ-sur-Layon
☎ (41) 54 02 99
Open: by appointment.

Domaine des Maurières TP
Fernand Moron
St-Lambert-du-Lattay
49190 Rochefort-sur-Loire
☎ (41) 78 30 21
Open: by appointment.

GAEC du Petit
  Clocher   TRP
Denis and son
49560 Cléré-sur-Layon
☎ (41) (59 54 51
Open: by appointment.

Domaine Les Caves
  du Rocher   TRP
Baffet and son
St-Aubin-de-Luigné
49190 Rochefort-sur-Loire
☎ (41) 78 33 36
Open: by appointment.

Domaine de Ste-Anne TP
Henri Brault
St-Saturnin-sur-Loire
49320 Brissac-Quincé
☎ (41) 91 24 58
Open: Monday to Saturday
8am-noon and 2-7pm.

Bernard Sechet-Carret TP
Maligné
49540 Martigné-Briand
☎ (41) 59 43 40
Open: by appointment.

**Other Anjou
Vineyards**

Alain Arnault   TRW
Les Landes
Bouillé-Loretz
79290 Argenton-l'Eglise
☎ (49) 67 04 85
Open: by appointment.

Jacques Beaujeau   TRW
rue de l'Eglise
48380 Thouarcé
☎ (41) 91 41 17
Open: by appointment.

Domaine de Beillant TW
Jacques Peltier
Passavant-sur-Layon
49560 Nueil-sur-Layon

R=red wine   W=white wine   P=rosé wine   S=sparkling wine

☎ (41) 59 51 32
Open: by appointment.

Domaine des
Charbottières TR
Fillion brothers
Vauchrétien
49320 Brissac-Quincé
☎ (41) 91 22 87
Open: by appointment.

Clos de Coulaine TR
François Roussier
Coulaine
49170 St-Georges-sur-
Loire
☎ (41) 72 21 06
Open: Monday to Friday
10am-noon and 2-6pm,
Saturday 10am-noon.

Château de Fesles TR
Jacques Boivin
49380 Thouarcé
☎ (41) 91 40 40
Open: by appointment.

Domaine de Haute
Perche TR
Christian Papin
St-Mélaine-sur-Aubance
49320 Brissac-Quincé
☎ (41) 91 15 20
Open: by appointment.

Domaine des Hauts-
Perrays TRW
GAEC Fardeau-Robin
Chaudefonds-sur-Layon
49290 Chalonnes-sur-
Loire
☎ (41) 78 04 38

Joel Lhumeau TRW
Linières
Brigné-sur-Layon
49700 Doué-la-Fontaine
☎ (41) 59 30 51
Open: by appointment.

Les Caves de la Loire TR
49320 Brissac-Quincé
☎ (41) 91 22 71
Open: by appointment.

Château Montbenault TRW
Yves Leduc
Faye-d'Anjou
49380 Thouarcé
☎ (41) 78 31 14
Open: Monday to Saturday
9am-noon and 2-8pm.

Domaine de la Motte TR
André Sorin
49190 Rochefort-sur-Loire
☎ (41) 78 71 13
Open: Monday to Saturday
9am-noon and 2-7pm.

Domaine des Paragères TW
M. Aguilas-Gaudard
La Brosse
Chaudefonds-sur-Layon
49290 Chalonnes-sur-
Loire
☎ (41) 78 10 68
Open: by appointment.

Reveillère-Giraud TRW
La Gonorderie
49320 Brissac-Quincé
☎ (41) 91 22 80
Open: by appointment.

Domaine des Rochelles TR
M. Lebreton and son
St-Jean-des-Mauvrets
49320 Brissac-Quincé
☎ (41) 91 92 07
Open: by appointment.

Coteaux du Layon
(sweet white wines)

Clos de l'Aiglerie TW
Gousset and son
St-Aubin-de-Luigné
49190 Rochefort-sur-Loire
☎ (41) 78 33 05
Open: by appointment.

Jacques Beaujeau TW
49380 Thouarcé
☎ (41) 91 41 17
Open: by appointment.

Château du Breuil TW
Marc Morgat
Beaulieu-sur-Layon
49190 Rochefort-sur-Loire
☎ (41) 78 32 54
Open: Tuesday to Saturday
10am-noon and 3-7pm.

Domaine Cady TW
Valette
St-Aubin-de-Luigné
49190 Rochefort-sur-Loire
☎ (41) 78 33 69
Open: daily 9am-8pm.

Dhomme brothers TW
Le Petit Fort Girault
49290 Chalonnes-sur-
Loire
☎ (41) 78 24 27
Open: by appointment.

Logis du Prieuré TW
Jousset and son
Concourson-sur-Layon
49700 Doué-la-Fontaine
☎ (41) 59 11 66
Open: by appointment.

Domaine du Petit Val TW
Vincent Goizil
Chavagnes-les-Eaux
49380 Thouarcé
☎ (41) 91 43 09
Open: by appointment.

Saumur

Clos de l'Abbaye TRW
Henri Aupy
49269 Le Puy-Notre-Dame
☎ (41) 52 26 71
Open: by appointment.

Château de Beaulieu TW
49100 Saumur
☎ (41) 51 01 54
Open: daily 9am-noon and
2-5pm.

Bouvet-Ladubay TWS
St-Hilaire-St-Florent
49400 Saumur
☎ (41) 50 11 12
Open: by appointment.

T=tasting E=English spoken G=guided tours C=château/building to visit

Jean Douet TR
Les Rochettes
Concourson-sur-Layon
49700 Doué-la-Fontaine
☎ (41) 59 11 51
Open: by appointment.

Domaine des Nerleux TWS
Robert Néau
St-Cyr-en-Bourg
49260 Montreuil-Bellay
☎ (41) 51 61 04
Open: by appointment.

Noël Pinot TWS
Dampierre-sur-Loire
49460 Saumur
☎ (41) 51 14 35
Open: by appointment.

Château de St-Florent TRW
St-Hilaire-St-Florent
49416 Saumur
☎ (41) 50 28 14
Open: by appointment.

Cave de Vignerons
de Saumur TRWS
St-Cyr-en-Bourg
49260 Montreuil-Bellay
☎ (41) 51 61 09
Open: by appointment.

Michel Suire TW
Pouant-Berrie
86120 Trois-Moutiers
☎ (49) 22 92 61
Open: by appointment.

Château de Targe TR
Parnay
49730 Montsoreau
☎ (41) 38 11 50
Open: by appointment.

Château de Villeneuve TWR
Souzay-Champigny
49400 Saumur
☎ (41) 51 15 04
Open: by appointment.

Domaines des
Varinelles TRW
Claude Daheuiller
Varrains
49400 Saumur
☎ (41) 52 90 94
Open: by appointment.

CENTRAL FRANCE

Sancerre
(18300 Sancerre)

Jacques Auchères TW
Bué
☎ (48) 54 06 61
Open: by appointment.

Bailly-Reverdy TW
GAEC Bailly-Reverdy
and son
Bué
☎ (48) 54 18 38
Open: by appointment.

Domaine Balland-
Chapuis TWR
Bué
☎ (48) 54 06 67
Open: by appointment.

Cellier Croix-St-Ursin TW
Bué
☎ (48) 54 06 32
Open: Monday to Saturday
8am-noon and 1.30-7pm.

Gitton and son TRW
Ménétréol
☎ (48) 54 38 84
Open: by appointment.

Domaine de la
Mercy-Dieu TRWP
Bué
☎ (48) 54 18 38
Open: by appointment.

Domaine Paul Prieur
and son TRW
Verdigny
☎ (48) 54 20 28
Open: by appointment.

Bernard Reverdy
and son TWP
Chandoux-Verdigny
☎ (48) 54 26 13
Open: by appointment.

Domaine de St-Pierre TRWP
Verdigny
☎ (48) 54 08 45
Open: by appointment.

Christian Salmon TRW
Bué
☎ (48) 54 20 54
Open: by appointment.

Domaine des Trois-
Noyers TW
Roger Reverdy-Cadet
Chandoux-Verdigny
Open: by appointment.

Reuilly and Quincy

Domaine Henri
Beurdin TWR
Preuilly
18120 Lury-sur-Arnon
☎ (48) 51 30 78
Open: by appointment.

Claude Lafond TRWP
Bois-St-Denis
36260 Reuilly
☎ (54) 49 22 17
Open: daily 9am-7pm.

Guy Malbète TRWP
Bois-St-Denis
36260 Reuilly
☎ (54) 49 25 09
Open: by appointment.

Didier Martin TWP
route d'Issoudun
36260 Reuilly
☎ (54) 49 20 77
Open: by appointment.

Gérard Meunier-Lapha TW
Quincy
18120 Lury-sur-Arnon
☎ (48) 51 31 16
Open: by appointment.

R=red wine   W=white wine   P=rosé wine   S=sparkling wine

Raymond Pipet TW
Quincy
18120 Lury-sur-Arnon
☎ (48) 51 31 17
Open: daily 9am-noon and
2-6pm.

Gilbert Rousié TWP
36260 Reuilly
☎ (54) 49 20 15
Open: by appointment

Sorbe and son TP
La Quervée
Preuilly
18120 Lury-sur-Arnon
☎ (48) 51 03 07
Open: by appointment.

Pouilly-sur-Loire
(58150 Pouilly-sur-Loire)

Domaine des Coques TW
Patrick Coulbois
Les Berthiers
St-Andelain
☎ (86) 39 15 69
Open: by appointment.

Domaine Masson-
  Blondelet TW
Jean-Michel Masson
58150 Pouilly-sur-Loire
☎ (86) 39 00 34
Open: by appointment.

La Loge aux Moines TW
Patrice Moreaux
Les Loges
58150 Pouilly-sur-Loire
☎ (86) 39 00 52
Open: by appointment.

Les Moulins à Vent TW
Coopérative de Pouilly-sur-
  Loire
58150 Pouilly-sur-Loire
☎ (86) 39 10 00
Open: by appointment.

GAEC Roger Pabiot TW
  and son
Tracy-sur-Loire
58150 Pouilly-sur-Loire
☎ (86) 39 12 41
Open: by appointment.

Domaine Saget TW
Caves St-Vincent
58150 Pouilly-sur-Loire
☎ (86) 39 16 37
Open: daily 8am-noon and
2-6pm.

Château de Tracy TW
Alain Destutt d'Assay
58150 Pouilly-sur-Loire
☎ (86) 39 10 55
Open: by appointment.

TOURAINE

The wineries and vine-
yards are open to the
public for tasting. Most
have red and white wines.

Clos du Petit Mont TRW
Daniel Allias
37210 Vouvray
☎ (47) 52 74 95
or (47) 52 70 66

Marcel Aubourg TRW
2 rue de la Paix
Monthou-sur-Vièvre
41120 Les Montils
☎ (51) 44 04 74

Audebert and son TRW
  (Maison)
37140 Bourgueil
☎(47) 97 70 06

Jean-Claude
  Barbeillon TRW
Le Vieux Chai
Marcé Oisly
41700 Contres
☎ (54) 79 54 57

Maurice Barbou TRW
Les Corbillières
41700 Contres
☎ (54) 79 52 75

André Barc TRW
La Croix Marie Rivière
37500 Chinon
☎ (47) 93 02 24

Bartissol Cruse Diffusion
  'Blanc Foussy' TW
95 quai de la Loire
Rochecorbon
37210 Vouvray
☎ (47) 52 60 60

Berger brothers and
  son TRW
Les Liards
St-Martin-le-Beau
37270 Montlouis
☎ (47) 50 67 36

Besnard & Colin TRW
Commissionnaires en
  Vins
Chargé
47400 Amboise
☎ (47) 57 04 92

Jean-Pierre Boistard TRW
216 rue Neuve
Vernou
37210 Vouvray
☎ (47) 52 18 73

Jacques Bonnigal and
  son TRW
6 et 17 rue d'Enfer
Limeray
37400 Amboise
☎ (47) 30 11 02

Aimé Boucher TRW
279 route de Chambord
Huisseau-sur-Cosson
41350 Vineuil
☎ (54) 20 31 10

T=tasting E=English spoken G=guided tours C=château/building to visit

Georges Bouchet TRW
Caves St-Brice
37270 Montlouis
☎ (47) 50 80 41

Elie Bouges TRW
La Puannerie
St-Julien-de-Chedon
41400 Montrichard
☎ (54) 32 11 87

Domaine Guenault TRW
Jean-Claude Bougrier
Les Hauts Lieux
41400 St-Georges-
    sur-Cher
☎ (54) 32 34 62

Bougrier TRW
41400 St-Georges-
    sur-Cher
☎ (54) 32 31 36

Claude Boureau TRW
1 rue de la Résistance
37270 St-Martin-le-Beau
☎ (47) 50 61 39

André Boutet-Saulnier TRW
Vallée Chartier
37210 Vouvray
☎ (47) 52 60 07
or (47) 52 73 61

Gilbert Breuzin TRW
28 rue de Meuves
41150 Onzain
☎ (65) 20 71 50

Philippe Brossillon TRW
Mesland
42250 Onzain
☎ (65) 70 28 23

Yves Cadoux TRW
Les Cailloux
Soings-en-Sologne
41230 Mur-de-Sologne
☎ (54) 98 71 97

Cave Coopérative
    Agricole TRW
St-Romain-sur-Cher
41140 Noyers-sur-Cher
☎ (54) 29 91 22
or (54) 29 94 14

Cave Coopérative des
    Producteurs des Grands
    Vins de Vouvray TRW
Vallée Coquette
37210 Vouvray
☎ (47) 52 75 03

Cave du Moulin TRW
1 rue de l'Ecrévissière
41150 Onzain
☎ (65) 20 72 99

Cave des Viticulteurs
    du Vouvray TRW
Château de Vaudenuits
37210 Vouvray
☎ (47) 52 60 20

Cave Coopérative des
    Vignerons TRW
20 rue Gén-de-Gaulle
41400 St-Georges-sur-
    Cher
☎ (54) 32 30 46

Cave Coopérative des
    Producteurs de Vin
    de Montlouis TRW
2 route de St-Aignan
37270 Montlouis-sur-
    Loire
☎ (47) 50 80 98

Gilles Champion TRW
Vallée de Cousse
Vernou
37210 Vouvray
☎ (47) 52 02 38

Jacky Charbonier TRW
Le Biard
Angé-sur-Cher
41400 Montrichard
☎ (54) 32 10 06

Jean Chauveau TRW
19 rue de Tours
St-Martin-le-Beau
37270 Montlouis
☎ (47) 50 66 97

José Chollet TRW
23 rue de Rabelais
41150 Onzain
☎ (65) 20 79 50

Confrérie des Vignerons
    de Oisly et Thésée TRW
Cedex 112 Oisly
41700 Contres
☎ (54) 79 52 88

Couly Dutheil TRW
BP 234
12 rue Diderot
37502 Chinon Cedex
☎ (47) 93 05 84

Domaine de Peumen TRW
Pierre Dardouillet
Pouillé
41110 St-Aignan
☎ (54) 71 41 70

Débitant Tourangeau
    SAC TRW
26 rue Henri-Barbusse
37000 Tours
☎ (47) 61 50 82

Domaine des Sablons TRW
Jacques Delaunay
Pouillé
41110 St-Aignan
☎ (54) 71 44 25

Joël Delauney TRW
La Tesnière
Pouille
41110 St-Aignan
☎ (54) 71 45 69

Hubert Denay TRW
Le Breuil
37400 Amboise
☎ (47) 57 11 53

Maurice Desbourder TRW
Panzoult
37220 L'Ile-Bouchard
☎ (47) 58 53 03

Clos du Saut au Loup TRW
Dozon and son
Ligré
37500 Chinon
☎ (47) 93 26 38
or (47) 93 17 67

R=red wine   W=white wine   P=rosé wine   S=sparkling wine

Dutertre and son   TRW
Limeray
37400 Amboise
☎ (47) 30 10 69

Château de Ligré   TRW
Gatien Ferrand
37500 Chinon
☎ (47) 93 16 70

Ferrand   TRW
37120 Richelieu
☎ 58 10 37

Jean-Pierre Freslier   TRW
La Caillerie
37210 Vouvray
☎ (47) 52 76 61

Pierre Frissant   TRW
4 chemin Neuf
Mosnes
37400 Amboise
☎ (47) 57 23 18

Benoît Gautie   TRW
La Racauderie
Parçay-Meslay
27210 Vouvray
☎ (47) 51 30 47

GAEC Marteau-Cartier TRW
La Tesnière
Pouillé
41110 St-Aignan
☎ (54) 71 45 59

Girardot   TRW
Cave 801
41400 Chissay-en-
Touraine
☎ (54) 32 32 05

Domaine d'Artois   TRW
Château-Gaillard
Girault Artois
7 quai des Violettes
37400 Amboise
☎ (47) 50 07 71

René Gouron and son TRW
Cravant-les-Coteaux
37500 Chinon
☎ (47) 93 15 33

Paul Guertin   TRW
Le Carroi Raqueneau
Beaumont-en-Véron
37420 Avoine
☎ (47) 58 43 20

Guiraud   TRW
6 place Choiseul
37100 Tours
☎ (47) 54 54 27

Francis Haerty   TRW
Bertignolles
Savigny-en-Véron
37420 Avoine
☎ (47) 58 42 74

André Hogu   TRW
Chouzy-sur-Cisse
41150 Onzain
☎ (65) 20 47 77

Gaston Huet   TRW
Le Haut Lieu
37210 Vouvray
☎ (47) 52 78 87

Daniel Jarry   TRW
La Caillerie
route de la Vallée Coquette
37210 Vouvray
☎ (47) 52 78 75

Charles Joguet   TRW
Sazilly
37200 L'Ile-Bouchard
☎ (47) 58 55 53

Alain Joulin   TRW
2 rue Traversière
St-Martin-le-Beau
37270 Montlouis
☎ (47) 50 28 49

Domaine du Rin du
  Bois   TRW
Jean-Marie Jousselin
41230 Soings-en-Sologne
☎ (54) 98 71 87

Lame Delille Boucard TRW
Les Chesnaies
Ingrandes-de-Touraine
37140 Bourgueil
☎ (47) 96 98 54

François Leclair   TRW
La Rochette
Pouillé
41110 St-Aignan
☎ (54) 71 44 02

Hubert Lejeau   TRW
Monteaux
41150 Onzain
☎ (65) 70 25 20

Pierre Lothion   TRW
37 rue Gambetta
37210 Vouvray
☎ (47) 52 71 24

Jean Louet   TRW
3 rue de la Paix
Monthou-sur-Bièvre
41120 Les Montils
☎ (51) 44 04 54

Jacky Mandard   TRW
Bagneux
Mareuil-sur-Cher
41110 St-Aignan
☎ (54) 75 09 53

Marc Bredif   TRW
87 quai de la Loire
Rochecorbon
37210 Vouvray
☎ (47) 52 50 07

Château-Gaillard   TRW
Jean Marchandeau
Mesland
41150 Onzain
☎ (65) 70 28 36

Guy Mardon   TRW
Oisly
41700 Contres
☎ (54) 79 52 87

Domaine de la   TRW
  Charmoise
Henry Marionnet
Soings
41230 Mur-de-Sologne
☎ (54) 98 70 73

Joël Masse   TRW
Les Vaublins
41400 Bourré
☎ 32 09 03

T=tasting   E=English spoken   G=guided tours   C=château/building to visit

René Menard   TRW
Les Ribottières
37190 Azay-le-Rideau
☎ (47) 43 31 88

Robert Mesliand   TRW
15 bis, rue d'Enfer
Limeray
37400 Amboise
☎ (47) 30 11 15

Mirault (Maison)   TRW
15 ave. Brûlé
37210 Vouvray
☎ (47) 52 71 62

Daniel Mosny   TRW
Cangé
St-Martin-le-Beau
37270 Montlouis
☎ (47) 50 61 84

Moulin and son   TRW
5 route de Pocé
37400 Limeray
☎ (47) 30 10 47

Marc Mureau   TRW
Lossay
Restigne
37140 Bourgueil
☎ (47) 97 32 60

James Paget   TRW
Armentières
Rivarennes
37190 Azay-le-Rideau
☎ (47) 95 54 02

Gérard Paumier   TRW
Les Tassins
41110 Seigy
☎ (54) 75 08 08

René Paumier   TRW
Galeme
41110 Châteauvieux
☎ (54) 75 19 31

Domaine de la Prèsle   TRW
Jean-Marie Penet
41700 Oisly
☎ (54) 79 52 65

Marcel Percereau   TRW
and son
83 rue de Blois
37400 Limeray
☎ (47) 30 11 40

GAEC du Clouzeau   TRW
Pierre and Dominique
  Perceval
Cedex 343
Sassay
41700 Contres
☎ (54) 79 57 52

Château du Petit
  Thouars   TRW
Yves du Petit Thouars
St-Germain-sur-Vienne
37500 Chinon
☎ (47) 95 96 40

François Pironneau   TRW
Monteaux
41150 Onzain
☎ (65) 70 23 75

Plouzeau and son   TRW
54 Faubourg St-Jacques
37500 Chinon
☎ (47) 93 16 34

Jacky Preys   TRW
Bois Pontois
41130 Meusnes
☎ (54) 71 00 34

Jean-Maurice
  Raffault   TRW
Savigny-en-Véron
37420 Avoine
☎ (47) 58 42 50

Christian Ravenelle
  and son   TRW
Champdilly
41230 Soings-en-Sologne
☎ (54) 98 70 44

Bernard Regnard   TRW
La Picuse
Valaire
41120 Les Montils
☎ (51) 44 02 94

Georges Renou   TRW
Rue Basse
Restigné
37140 Bourgueil
☎ (47) 97 31 80

Etienne Saulguin   TRW
Nitray
Athée-sur-Cher
37270 Montlouis
☎ (47) 50 68 04

Hubert Sinson   TRW
Le Musa
Meusnes
41130 Selles-sur-Cher
☎ (54) 71 00 26

Sté des Vins Fins   TRW
13 rue Ledru-Rollin
37000 Tours
☎ (47) 20 63 93

Guy Trotignon   TRW
Angé
41400 Montrichard
☎ (54) 32 05 34

Vigneau-Chevreau   TRW
Vallée de Vaux
Chançay
37210 Vouvray
☎ (47) 52 93 22

**Chinon and
Bourgueil**

Clos de l'Abbaye   TR
GAEC de la Dime
ave. Jean Causeret
37140 Bourgueil
☎ (47) 97 76 30
Open: by appointment.

Marcel Audbert   TR
37410 Mestigue
☎ (47) 97 31 31
Open: by appointment.

Guy Caillé   TP
37500 Panzoult
☎ (47) 58 53 16
Open: by appointment.

R=red wine   W=white wine   P=rosé wine   S=sparkling wine

Domaine Hubert Callot-
Calbrun   TR
Benais
37140 Bourgueil
☎ (47) 97 30 59
Open: by appointment.

Domaine de la
Chanteleuserie   TR
Benais
37140 Bourgueil
☎ (47) 97 30 20
Open: by appointment.

Domaine René Couly   TR
rue Diderot
37502 Chinon
☎ (47) 93 05 84
Open: by appointment.

Marc Delaunay   TR
La Lande
37140 Bourgueil
☎ (47) 97 80 73
Open: by appointment.

Cave des Esvois   TR
Marc Mureau
Restigné
37140 Bourgueil
☎ (47) 97 32 60
Open: by appointment.

Domaine des Galluche   TR
Le Machet
Benais
37140 Bourgueil
☎ (47) 97 30 76
Open: by appointment.

Domaine du Grand Clos TR
MM. Audebert
ave. Jean Causeret
37140 Bourgueil
☎ (47) 97 70 06
Open: by appointment.

Domaine Hubert   TR
La Hurolaie
Benais
37140 Bourgueil
☎ (47) 97 30 59
Open: by appointment.

Régis Mureau   TR
La Gaucherie
Ingrandes-de-Touraine
37140 Bourgueil
☎ (47) 96 97 60
Open: by appointment.

Domaine de la
Noblaie   TRWP
Ligré
37500 Chinon
☎ (47) 93 10 96
Open: by appointment.

Domaine des Ouches   TR
Paul Gambier
Fontenay
Ingrandes-de-Touraine
37140 Bourgueil
☎ (47) 96 98 77
Open: by appointment.

Plouzeau   TR
Pierre Plouzeau
37120 Razinnes
☎ (47) 93 16 34
Open: by appointment.

Paul Poupineau   TR
Le Bourg
Benais
37140 Bourgueil
☎ (47) 97 30 30
Open: by appointment.

Domaine des Raguen-
ières   TR
SCEA Domaine des
Raguenières
Le Machet
Benais
37140 Bourgueil
☎ (47) 97 30 76
Open: by appointment.

Domaine du Raifault   TR
Savigny-en-Véron
37420 Avoine
☎ (47) 58 44 01
Open: by appointment.

Clos du Saut-au-Loup   TR
Jean-Marie Dozon
Ligré
37500 Chinon
☎ (47) 93 26 38
Open: by appointment.

Vouvray
(37210 Vouvray)

Bertier Pichot   TW
Coteau de la Biche
☎ (47) 52 16 64
Open: by appointment.

Château des Bidaudières TS
Bernard Avignon
☎ (47) 52 78 29
Open: by appointment.

Bernard Bongars   TS
Noizay
☎ (47) 52 11 64
Open: by appointment.

Clos du Bourg   TW
Domaine du Haut Lieu
☎ (47) 52 78 87
Open: by appointment.

Michel Brunet   TS
Alain Ferrand
Vernou-sur-Brenne
☎ (47) 52 14 78
Open: by appointment.

Chevreau-Vigneau   TWS
Chançay
☎ (47) 52 93 22
Open: by appointment.

Bernard Courson   TWS
Les Patys
☎ (47) 52 73 74
Open: by appointment.

Alain Ferrand   TWS
37210 Vouvray
☎ (47) 52 14 78
Open: by appointment.

André Fouquet   TW
rue Gambetta
☎ (47) 52 70 23
Open: by appointment.

Jean-Pierre Freslier   TWS
La Caillerie
☎ (47) 52 76 61
Open: Monday to Saturday
8.30am-8pm; Sunday
8.30am-noon.

T=tasting   E=English spoken   G=guided tours   C=château/building to visit

Sylvain Gaudron　　TWS
Vernou-sur-Brenne
☎ (47) 52 12 27
Open: by appointment.

Germain Gautier-
　Peltier　　　　TWS
Parçay-Meslay
☎ (47) 51 30 47
Open: daily 8am-9pm.

Le Haut-Lieu　　　TW
☎ (47) 52 78 87
Open: by appointment.

Jean-Pierre Laisement　TS
La Vallée Coquette
☎ (47) 52 74 47
Open: by appointment.

Pierre Lothion　　TW
rue Gambetta
☎ (47) 52 71 24
Open: by appointment.

Le Mont　　　　TW
Gaston Huet

Domaine du Haut-Lieu
☎ (47) 52 78 87
Open: by appointment.

Prince Poniatowski　TWS
Le Peu de la Moriette
☎ (47) 52 72 45
Open: by appointment.

Viticulteurs de Vouvray TS
☎ (47) 52 60 20
Open: by appointment.

PAYS NANTAIS

All are open to the public,
but as many are family
businesses an appoint-
ment made by telephone
is advisable.

Muscadet
and Gros-Plant

Domaine des
　Genaudières　　TWR
Augustin Athimon
44850 Le Cellier
☎ (40) 25 40 27

Gaby Aubron and son　TW
Les Rosiers
44330 Vallet
☎ (40) 36 36 12

GAEC Andouin brothers TW
La Momenière
44430 Le Landreau
☎ (40) 06 43 04

Château de l'Oiselinière　TW
Jean Aulanier
44190 Gorges
☎ (40) 06 91 59

Donatien Bahuaud　TW
La Loge B.P. No 1
44330 La Chapelle-Heulin
☎ (40) 06 70 05

Michel Bahuaud　　TW
2 rue du Grand Logis
44190 Clisson
☎ (40) 36 10 53

Barre brothers　　TWR
Beau Soleil
44190 Gorges
☎ (40) 06 90 70

Jean Beauquin　　TW
44330 La Chapelle-Heulin
☎ (40) 06 73 83

Henri and Michel　TW
　Bedouct
Le Pé-de-Sèvre
44330 Le Pallet
☎ (40) 26 40 81

Château de la Baslerie　TW
Philippe Besnard
44690 Château-Thébaud
☎ (40) 06 55 03

Alain Bire　　　　TW
Le Pé-de-Sèvre
44330 Le Pallet
☎ (40) 26 43 39

Claude Blanchard　TW
L'Imprévu au Quarteron
44190 Gorges
☎ (40) 78 07 82

Auguste Blanlœil　TW
La Huperie
44690 Monnières
☎ (40) 26 42 06

Constant Bochereau　TWR
route de Vallet
49270 Landemont
☎ (40) 98 72 14

Auguste Bonhomme　TW
rue de la Roche
44190 Gorges
☎ (40) 06 91 61

Pierre Bonnet　　TW
B.P. 13
44330 Vallet
☎ (40) 36 35 22

Domaine de la
　Levraudière　　TW
R. Bonnet-Huteau
44330 La Chapelle-Heulin
☎ (40) 06 73 87

Joseph Bosseau　　TW
12 rue des Vignes
44330 Le Pallet
☎ (40) 36 94 64

Laurent Bossis　　TW
Le Bourg
44690 St-Fiacre-sur-Maine
☎ (40) 36 94 64

Henri Bouchaud　　TW
Le Bois Joly
44330 Le Pallet
☎ (40) 26 40 83

Domaine des Dorices　TW
L. Boullault and son
La Touche
44330 Vallet
☎ (40) 33 95 30

R=red wine　　　W=white wine　　　P=rosé wine　　　S=sparkling wine

Jean Bouyer TW
49 rue d'Anjou
La Charouillère
44330 Vallet
☎ (40) 36 23 77

Claude Branger TW
La Févrie
44690 Maisdon-sur-Sèvre
☎ (40) 36 94 08

Michel Bregeon TW
Les Guisseaux
44190 Gorges
☎ (40) 06 93 19
& (40) 06 91 74

Jean-Daniel Bretaudeau TW
28 rue de la Poste
44690 Monnières
☎ (40) 26 40 55

GAEC Bretin and son TW
La Goulbaudière
44330 Vallet
☎ (40) 33 98 32
& (40) 36 36 07

Brochard brothers TW
La Grenaudière
44690 Maisdon-sur-Sèvre
☎ (40) 03 80 00

Domaine des Mortiers
Gobain TW
Robert Brosseau
La Rairie
44690 La Haye-Fouassière
☎ (40) 54 80 66

Anne-Marie Bureau-
Pineau TW
74 rue d'Anjou
44330 Vallet
☎ (40) 33 92 49

Marie-Josèphe Caille TW
La Pilotière
44330 La Chapelle-Heulin
☎ (40) 06 73 70
& (40) 06 72 59

Château de la TW
Malonnière
Germain Carbon
44430 Le Loroux-
Bottereau
☎ (40) 33 81 46

Castel brothers TW
412 route de Clisson
44120 Vertou
☎ (40) 34 01 64

Cave Coopérative des
Vignerons de la
Noëlle TWR
44150 Ancenis
☎ (40) 83 02 40

GAEC Charpentier
and son TW
La Guipière
44330 Vallet
☎ (40) 36 23 30

Roger Charpentier
and son TW
Les Aveneaux
44330 La Chapelle-Heulin
☎ (40) 06 74 40

Robert Chereau TW
Le Village Boucher
44690 Monnières
☎ (40) 26 45 49

Théophile Chereau
and son TW
34 rue de la Poste
44690 Monnières
☎ (40) 26 43 27

Domaine de Chasseloir TW
Chereau-Carre
44690 St-Fiacre-sur-Maine
☎ (40) 54 81 15

Michel Chiron TW
La Morandière
44330 Mouzillon
☎ (40) 26 41 43

Domaine des
Herbauges TW
Luc Choblet
44830 Bouaye
☎ (40) 65 44 92

Château de la
Jousselinière TW
Gilbert Chon
44450 St-Julien-de-
Concelles
☎ (40) 54 11 08

Les Cinq Vignerons TW
place de l'Eglise
44690 Monnières
☎ (40) 26 43 35

Michel Coraleau TW
La Bernardière
44330 La Chapelle-Heulin
☎ (40) 06 70 21

Château de la
Ragotière TW
Couillaud brothers
44330 La Regrippière
☎ (40) 33 60 56

Georges Dabin TW
La Bourchinière
44690 St-Fiacre-sur-Maine
☎ (40) 54 85 38

Jean Dabin TW
Le Bourg
44690 St-Fiacre-sur-Maine
☎ (40) 54 81 01

Bernard Derame TW
La Bourchinière
44690 St-Fiacre-sur-Maine
☎ (40) 54 83 80

Jean-Paul Doucet TW
La Roseraie
44330 La Chapelle-Heulin
☎ (40) 06 73 90

Jean Douillard TW
La Fruitière
44690 Château-Thébaud
☎ (40) 06 53 05

Philippe Douillard TW
La Champinjère
44330 Vallet
☎ (40) 36 61 77

Drouet brothers TW
6 rue Emile Gabory
44330 Vallet
☎ (40) 33 90 99

Domaine des Moulins TW
R.E. Dugast
44690 Monnières
☎ (40) 26 42 19
& (40) 20 07 83

T=tasting   E=English spoken   G=guided tours   C=château/building to visit

Henri Durance — TW
9 rue du Plessis Guéry
44330 Le Pallet
☎ (40) 26 48 59
& (40) 26 95 97

Château de la Roulière — TW
René Erraud
44310 St-Colomban
☎ (40) 05 80 24

Domaine des
Gautronnières — TW
Benjamin Fleurance
and son
44330 La Chapelle-Heulin
☎ (40) 06 74 06

Albert Forgeau and son — TW
La Rouaudière
44330 Mouzillon
☎ (40) 33 95 37

Alain Forget — TW
La Gautronnière
44330 La Chapelle-Heulin
☎ (40) 06 75 84

Jean Formon — TW
La Denillère
44120 Vertou
☎ (40) 34 36 58

Luc Fromont — TW
Le Pé-de-Sèvre
44330 Le Pallet
☎ (40) 26 46 85

Château de la
Mercredière — TW
Futeul brothers
Le Pallet B.P. 39
44690 La Haye-Fouassière
☎ (40) 54 80 10

Gadais brothers — TW
Le Côteau
44690 St-Fiacre-sur-Maine
☎ (40) 54 81 23

Alexandre Jean Gautier — TW
9 rue du Château
44115 Haute-Goulaine
☎ (40) 54 56 22

Gautier-Audas — TWR
7 rue du Château
44115 Haute-Goulaine
☎ (40) 54 56 22

André Gautreau — TW
La Heurnière
44190 Gorges
☎ (40) 36 11 81

Claude Giraud-
Guindon — TWR
Les Cossardières
44430 Le Landreau
☎ (40) 06 43 22

Domaine de Goulaine — TW
Comte G. de Goulaine
44115 Haute-Goulaine
☎ (40) 54 91 02
or (40) 61/62 74 09

Antoine Guilbaud — TW
Clos de Beauregard
44330 Mouzillon
☎ (40) 33 93 19

Marcel Guilbaud — TWR
Guilbaud brothers
Les Lilas. B.P. 1
44330 Mouzillon
☎ (40) 36 30 55

Domaine du Pin — TW
Maurice Guilbaud
44330 Mouzillon
☎ (40) 33 91 65

Guilbaud-Guérin — TW
La Villarnoult
44330 Vallet
☎ (40) 33 90 71

Jacques Guindon — TWR
La Couleuverdière
44150 St-Geréon
☎ (40) 83 18 96

Joseph Hallereau — TW
Les Chaboissières
44330 Vallet
☎ (40) 33 94 44

Domaine de la Grange — TW
GAEC Edmond Hardy
La Grange
44330 Mouzillon
☎ (40) 33 93 60

Jean-Louis Hervouet — TW
2 rue de la Margerie
44190 Gorges
☎ (40) 06 92 99

André Huchon — TW
La Charpenterie
44430 Le Landreau
☎ (40) 06 43 19

Domaine de la
Louveterie — TW
Pierre Landron and son
Les Brandières
44690 La Haye-Fouassière
☎ (40) 54 83 27

Clos des Rosiers — TW
Philippe Laure
44330 Vallet
☎ (40) 33 91 33

Jean Lebas — TW
La Rebourgère
44690 Maisdon-sur-Sèvre
☎ (40) 26 42 45

Lucien Lebas — TW
Haie-Trois-Sous
44690 Maisdon-sur-Sevre
☎ (40) 36 90 59

Michel Lebas — TW
38 rue de Bazoges
44330 Vallet
☎ (40) 36 38 97

Lesimple brothers — TW
La Brébionnière
44190 Clisson
☎ (40) 36 12 46

Château de la
Bourdinière — TW
Pierre Lieubeau
44690 Château-Thébaud
☎ (40) 06 54 81

R=red wine   W=white wine   P=rosé wine   S=sparkling wine

GAEC Germain and
Christian Luneau   TW
Bois Braud
44330 Vallet
☎ (40) 33 93 76

Domaine de la Grange TW
Pierre and Rémy Luneau
44430 Le Landreau
☎ (40) 06 43 90

Serge Luneau   TW
8 rue de la Tannerie
Chais: La Blanchetière
44430 Le Loroux-Bottereau
☎ (40) 33 82 14

Pierre Mabit   TW
Haute-Poëze
44430 Le Landreau
☎ (40) 06 43 88

Château La Noë   TW
Comte de Malestroit
44330 Vallet
☎ (40) 33 92 72

Jean-Claude Malidain TW
Le Petit Coin
44650 Corcoue-sur-Logne
☎ (40) 05 86 46

Clos de la Sablette   TW
Marcel Martin
44330 Mouzillon
☎ (40) 33 94 84

Domaine du Champ aux
Moines   TWR
Martin Jarry
44450 La Chapelle-Basse-
Mer
☎ (40) 03 68 00

Maurice Mary   TW
La Buronnerie
44120 Vertou
☎ (40) 34 72 98

Domaine de la
Minière   TW
André Menard-Gabory
44690 Monnières
☎ (40) 26 43 21

Domaine de la Haute-
Vrignais   TW
Loïc Molle
85660 St-Philbert-de-
Bouaine
☎ (40) 51/41 90 49
or (40) 51/58 19 74

GAEC Moreau brothers TW
La Petite Jaunaie
44690 Château-Thébaud
☎ (40) 06 63 50

Louis Nogue   TW
Château des Gillères
44690 La Haye-Fouassière
☎ (40) 34 02 57
or (40) 54 80 05

Jules Sarl Olivier   TWR
La Laize. B.P. 2
44115 Haute-Goulaine
☎ (40) 54 57 55

Ollivier and son   TW
La Grenaudière
44690 Maisdon-sur-Sèvre
☎ (40) 06 62 58

Louis-Marie Ordureau TW
rue du Grand-Pré
44680 St-Mars-de-Coutais
☎ (40) 04 85 14

GAEC Petiteau-Gaubert TW
La Tourlaudière
44330 Vallet
☎ (40) 36 24 86

Robert Pichaud   TW
Les Laures
44330 Vallet
☎ (40) 33 95 90

Domaine des Croix   TW
Bernard Pichon
44330 Vallet
☎ (40) 36 23 18

Raymond Pichon   TW
La Chevillardière
44330 Vallet
☎ (40) 06 74 29

Yves Provost   TW
Le Pigeon Blanc
44430 Le Landreau
☎ (40) 06 43 54

Yves Raude   TW
La Cordouère
44690 Monnières
☎ (40) 26 41 26

André Ripoche   TW
Le Pertunier
44430 Le Loroux-Bottereau
☎ (40) 33 83 69

Georges and Christian
Ripoche   TW
9 rue de la Sèvre
44690 La Haye-Fouassière
☎ (40) 54 80 37

Yves Ripoche   TW
Ste-Germaine
44690 La Haye-Fouassière
☎ (40) 54 84 46

Rolandeau   TW
La Frémonderie
49230 Tillières
☎ (40) 41/70 45 93

Rousseau   TW
21 rue du Progrès
44330 Vallet
☎ (40) 36 23 07
& (40) 33 93 50

Yves Samson   TW
La Mazure
44450 La Chapelle-b-Mer
☎ (40) 06 33 51

Domaine de
l'Hyvernière
Marcel Sautejeau   TW
44330 Le Pallet
☎ (40) 06 73 83

Château du Cléray   TW
Sauvion and son
44330 Vallet
☎ (40) 36 22 55

T=tasting   E=English spoken   G=guided tours   C=château/building to visit

Domaine de la Haute-
Maison   TW
Jean-Nicolas Schaeffer
44860 St-Aignan-de
Grand-Lieu
☎ (40) 31 01 83

Domaine de la Loge   TW
Secher and associates
44330 Vallet
☎ (40) 33 97 08

Benjamin Sourice   TWR
B.P. 6
49600 Geste
☎ (40) 41/56 64 61

Antoine Subileau   TWR
6 rue St-Vincent
44330 Vallet
☎ (40) 33 91 33

Gabriel Thébaud   TW
La Hautière
44690 St-Fiacre-sur-Maine
☎ (40) 54 81 13

Francis Viaud   TW
La Févrie
44690 Maisdon-sur-Sèvre
☎ (40) 54 81 17

André Vinet   TW
10 rue du Progrès
B.P. 6.
44330 Vallet
☎ (40) 36 31 22

Vinet   TW
La Quilla
44690 La Haye-Fouassière
☎ (40) 54 83 28

Sté des Vins Fins   TW
13 rue Ledru Rollin
B.P. 1615
37016 Tours Cedex
☎ (40) 47/37 60 52

R=red wine   W=white wine   P=rosé wine   S=sparkling wine

Chapter 7

ALSACE

Riquewihr
Alsace

ALSACE is sandwiched in the eastern corner of France, trapped between the Rhine in the east and the foothills of the Vosges in the west. To the south lies Switzerland, to the east north Germany, and to the west France. One glance at the map and it is easy to see why this province has been caught up in border disputes and wars over the centuries. It runs south for more than ninety miles encompassing a fertile plain, and the foothills beyond, on which most of the vineyards are planted. The region includes the two departments of *Haut-Rhin* and *Bas-Rhin*, and battles have raged here for more than 2,000 years. The first invaders were the Romans, then the Huns, and the Franks who restored some order to the war-torn country. For a short time, the province was ruled by the Dukes of Alsace, and then in the tenth century, it was absorbed into Germany. It remained a German province for the next 700 years. Because it was at the extreme edge of their territory, there were constant power struggles originated by the French, to wrest it from German rule, and so the fighting continued.

Despite all its problems, Alsace has continued to make some of the best wine in the world, grown in some of the prettiest vineyards. It was the Romans who persuaded the local growers to use wooden barrels in which to keep their wine, rather than clay jars. Because of the position of Strasbourg, wines were able to be shipped easily down the Rhine and they have enjoyed an international reputation for centuries.

Between the end of the thirteenth and the sixteenth century, Alsace was the scene of many outside attacks, and even internal rebellions as the peasants rose against their oppressive masters. There was a rising in 1525 when 20,000 peasants were killed after attempting to overthrow the Duke of Alsace. For a short time Alsace then prospered. It was part of the Holy Roman Empire and was rich in wine, food, timber and minerals. Artists and sculptors settled here, and many fine buildings were erected, a number of which are still intact today. But the Thirty Years' War shattered the peace of Alsace in 1618. Because of its frontier position, it was invaded time after time; mercenary armies plundered and murdered, crops were lost and there was famine. With resistance lowered, disease and plague spread through the province.

In 1648 at the Peace of Westphalia, which ended the Thirty Years' War, France regained control of Alsace and work started on rebuilding both the agriculture and the population of the area. Many settlers, especially Catholics, came from Switzerland, and there are still today striking resemblances between the national costume of the Swiss and the traditional Alsace costume. The Germans did attempt to regain control of Alsace but were decisively beaten at Turckheim in 1674. Seven years later, Strasbourg, previously independent in no man's land, became part of France.

Alsace's troubles started again in 1870 when Napoléon III declared war on Prussia. The Germans invaded Alsace with a huge army, and once more the people found themselves under the rule of the German Kaiser. Despite their troubled history and numerous masters, the Alsace people are fiercely French and patriotic, and it was in Strasbourg that the Marseillaise, the battle hymn of the Revolution was created. Under German rule, the locals were ordered to speak only German, and many of them left the province rather than remain under the control of the Kaiser. Alsace was part of the German Empire during World War I, and many of its young men were conscripted into the German army and sent to their deaths or to be captured on the Russian Front. During World War I, Alsace again became a battleground, but in the peace treaty it was given back to France and in 1919 became once again French territory. In World War II, many Alsace villages were again badly damaged in the fighting, but thankfully few scars remain today.

In fact, some of the villages are so fairy-like because they have remained unchanged for centuries, that it is difficult to imagine the troubled history of the province. Because of its links with Germany, the growers here adopted many of the techniques and grapes used by the vineyards on the Rhine. The French authorities recognised that the Alsace wines are unique and thankfully, while the controls are as rigorous as elsewhere in France, the wine laws for the Alsace *appellation* are very easy to follow. An Alsace wine must come from a clearly defined area, be made from a specific grape variety, and have eight per cent natural alcohol for the Alsace *appellation*, and eleven per cent for the *Grand Cru*. The *appellation* is different from anywhere else in France because while other AC's lay down grape varieties to be used, in Alsace the wine is sold under the name of the variety used.

There are seven varieties allowed. Chasselas is grown elsewhere in France as a dessert grape, but is grown here for wine; it is also called Flambeau d'Alsace. It produces a very fresh, light and elegant wine but the vineyard acreage is declining. Sylvaner is an ideal variety for Alsace because it is rot-resistant, and rot is one of the problems in parts of Alsace. It has been grown in Alsace for well over a hundred years, producing a wine similar to that from the Chasselas, but more elegant. It has high acidity, which gives it its refreshing quality, and often has a slight fizz. Pinot Blanc is also called Klevner and Clevner. It is grown widely elsewhere in France, notably in Burgundy. It produces well-balanced, elegant wines, which can be amazingly soft. Riesling, the noble wine of the Rhine, does as well in Alsace. It has been grown here since the 1750s at least and now accounts for just under twenty per cent of the vineyards. The vines do particularly well in the Alsace soil, and are sheltered by the mountains to the west. The Alsace Riesling is always dry with a fruity, flowery bouquet, and is rightly called the 'King of Alsace Wines'. Riesling made from grapes grown on light soil are best drunk young, but some, grown on limestone, age beautifully without losing their freshness. A 25-year-old Riesling, still pleasing to drink, is by no means unusual.

As all wines in Alsace are sold under the name of the grape used, it is important to learn a little about the growers because obviously standards vary, generally from good to outstanding. Most Riesling is simply sold as that, but growers can offer higher quality wine as Riesling Seléction Première, or Riesling Tradition, and the very best, as Riesling Réserve Personelle. In outstanding years, the growers may also add the term *vendange tardive* to show that the grapes have been late picked.

Muscat has been grown for the last 450 years, and until recently Alsace was the only place in France using it to make a dry wine. It is still an Alsatian speciality, a dry, fresh wine with the bouquet of freshly picked, sweet grapes. Almost all Muscat is blended from two varieties, Muscat Ottonel and Muscat d'Alsace, and only two out of five vintages produce really successful wines. Tokay d'Alsace, or Pinot Gris, is regarded as number three in the Alsace hierarchy, after Riesling and Gewürztraminer. The vine is reputed to have been brought back to Alsace by Lazare de Schwendi, a General who drove the Turks out of Hungary in the 1560s. He defeated the Turks and captured the fortified town of Tokay and with it 4,000 vats of Tokay wine. He liked it so much he introduced the vine to Alsace where it has grown ever since. It is a good story, but a myth, because Tokay is made in Hungary from the Furmint grape, although Pinot Gris does grow there. As with all grape varieties, there is intense controversy over whence they originated, and some claim the Pinot Gris was exported to Hungary from France and is really a relative of Pinot Noir. Whatever the truth, Tokay d'Alsace is a rich, full, heady wine that can last for many years. It is almost fat, and this masks the complexity of bouquet and taste. There is often a taste of smokiness, but the overwhelming impression is richness which is why it goes so well with *foie gras* and similar dishes.

Gewürztraminer is also special to Alsace. Although imitated in many countries, none can produce a wine to match the quality of the true Alsace Gewürztraminer. It is also the easiest grape variety in the world to recognise because of its spiciness and fruitiness. It is particularly popular in Britain and the United States although still not widely known outside the circles of wine experts. It is full, rounded and very fruity, with a biting freshness when young, typical of most Alsace wines. If allowed to age, it mellows beautifully, retains its roundness and develops a remarkable nose. It can last for many years.

Almost all the production of Alsace wine is white. Only the grapes mentioned on the label can be used, and because they are varietals there is a consistency of style even though quality can vary between producers.

The wine-producing region stretches for about seventy-five miles, but is nowhere more than two miles wide. The vineyard belt is generally between one and two miles wide, stretching up the foothills which rise to about 1,200ft. The vineyards are planted on the south and south-east facing slopes, which are well drained, and protected from the worst of the westerly weather by the mountains. The Vosges mountains also throw all Alsace into a rain shadow so it has one of the lowest rainfalls in France, less than twenty inches annually. Coupled with this are some of the best sunshine figures, and annual temperatures some degrees higher than those of its neighbours. In order to make best use of the sunshine, the grapes are picked as late as possible, usually between the middle of October and the middle of November.

All the conditions in Alsace are suitable for producing fine quality wines, and that is what the province is noted for: a quality which is guaranteed, and a price which is not too expensive.

There are more than 120 villages relying almost entirely on grapes or winemaking. About 30,000 people are directly involved in the growing or production in Alsace, and from the 30,000 acres of vineyards up to 20,000,000 gallons, or 150,000,000 bottles are produced of good vintages. And Alsace is still unique in that all Alsace AC wine must be bottled in the area of production.

Alsace is a relatively small province but it has more history packed into it than almost anywhere else in France, and several days are essential if you are to experience all its pleasures. Fortunately there is an excellent cuisine, fine wines and generous hospitality to ensure your stay is a memorable one. Apart from the white wines, there is a little red and some rosé from the Pinot Noir. The reds tend to be good, light quaffing wines, nothing out of the ordinary, but occasionally the rosés can reach great heights and subtlety. The Crémant d'Alsace has had its own *appellation* since 1976 and is made by the *méthode Champenoise*. It is clean and crisp, like all Alsace wines, but can be a bit too bubbly.

The other drink for which Alsace is famous is *eau-de-vie*. A wide range of fruits are individually fermented; the juice is then distilled and water added to reduce the alcohol strength to about 45°. The *eau-de-vie* is normally sold under the name of the fruit used, and the most popular are *framboise* (raspberry), *fraise* (strawberry), *poire* (pears), *cerise* (cherry), *mirabelle* (a small golden yellow plum), *prunes* (plums). Kirsch is made in almost the same way using small wild black cherries. Other fruits which can be used include rowanberries, blackberries, blackcurrants, sloe and even Gentian root.

A Tour of the Alsace Region

Alsace is one of the prettiest areas of France and one of the most unusual. Although very much part of France, it has spent long periods under occupation, especially by Germany. Being so close to the Rhine it has adopted a Rhine culture, with its own, almost Germanic dialect, and typically German architecture. Even the names of the towns and villages lead you to think that you may have strayed inadvertently across the border.

Today, Alsace is a thriving region with prosperous agriculture, fine wines and good food. There is little to remind you of the area's bloody past. However, Alsace has been a buffer state between France and its enemies since Roman times. The Rhine was easy to cross here, so the enemy armies tried to sneak through the back door of France using Alsace. Unfortunately, once across the river the invaders faced the rolling hills that dominate the landscape so most of the battles took place between the Rhine and this natural line of defence, on the wide plain.

Alsace today makes up the *départements* of Bas-Rhin and Haut-Rhin. The majority of vineyards are to be found on the slopes of the hills, the foothills of the Vosges Mountains. Over the centuries the area has been ruled by the Celts, the Romans, the Huns and the Franks, each in turn being conquered by a new invader. The Frankish king Clovis defeated the barbarians in AD496 and introduced a brief era of peace. Many of the towns and villages take their name from the Frankish language he introduced.

The Frankish kings were succeeded by the Merovingians, then by dukes, and in the tenth century, the province passed away from French control, staying away for 700 years.

The area has always had strong links with the Church, and in the sixth century there were forty abbeys in Alsace and the Bishops of Strasbourg had enormous influence and power. By the thirteenth century the number of abbeys had grown to more than 300. In the fourteenth century, the armies of Armagnac attacked and ravaged the countryside while the German rulers turned a blind eye. Less than a century later the peasants revolted, but the rebellion was crushed and more than 20,000 were slaughtered.

In the late sixteenth and seventeenth centuries, peace descended again on Alsace and it prospered. It was the richest part of the Holy Roman Empire, and many of the finest buildings still remaining date from this time. Between 1618 and 1648 Alsace again became a battleground, in the Thirty Years' War. When peace was signed, the province returned into the hands of France. The Germans tried to retake it in 1674 but were defeated by a small army. In 1870, however, when Napoléon III declared war on Prussia, the Germans annexed Alsace and it stayed in their hands until the end of World War I. Again in World War II the Germans overran Alsace, and in both wars the countryside became a battlefield, and many villages were virtually destroyed.

It is worth remembering their history as you travel through the region today. Perhaps it is a long tradition of turbulence that has given the Alsace people their zest for life, reflected in their festivals, food and behaviour.

Wine has been made in Alsace since before the Romans arrived. In fact the vines planted by the Romans were uprooted, and today the native grapes are preferred, producing the very distinctive wines, a distinction which has made them so popular among serious drinkers.

Tour of Strasbourg and the Surrounding Area

Any tour of Alsace must start in Strasbourg, not only because it is a marvellous city, but because it has so many good restaurants. Today, it is also a seat of the European Parliament, so for one week a month for most of the year, it is full of EEC officials enjoying the best food available, courtesy of their generous expense accounts. This has helped to push up prices, but it is still possible to eat very well and reasonably by avoiding the most fashionable restaurants.

Strasbourg is described as the Rhine gateway to France. The city was an independent state until 1681, and it was here that the Marseillaise was sung for the first time. A plaque still marks the house where Rouget de l'Isle composed the anthem in less than a day.

One could spend several days exploring Strasbourg and its surrounding area. If time is short, though, see the red-stoned Gothic cathedral, the Palais de la Musique, the opera house and the old universities. A stroll through the district known as La Petite France, along the canal banks is also recommended. Note the covered bridges and the marvellously-restored old warehouses, many of which have now been converted into excellent restaurants.

There are many old churches, such as St Pierre and St Thomas, the eighteenth-century château of the Cardinals de Rohan, the Prince Bishops of Strasbourg. There are also many good museums with displays of archaeology, fine art, history, Alsatian folklore and tradition, and modern art.

From Strasbourg, take the N4 to Marlenheim, (this is the most direct route, but as in all Alsace there are marvellous little lanes to follow that weave their way through the beautiful countryside.) Marlenheim marks the most northerly point of the winemaking region of Alsace, and in the area there are the wine-producing villages of Wangen, Westhoffen, Traenheim and Irmstett to visit. All the villages have their own charm and many are on the region's own wine route, which is signposted as from north to south through Alsace.

There are records of vines growing around Marlenheim in the sixth century; it was also the seat of one of the most beautiful palaces of that time in France, but nothing remains of that today. There are still some lovely old half-timbered houses in the old town, although the population is growing rapidly as it becomes a commuter town for Strasbourg.

Obernai to Kientzheim

To the south is Obernai, and on the way there, visit Rosheim, famous for its twelfth-century house, abbey church, fortifications and gateways. Obernai itself is a beautiful little town, with many lovely old buildings. Again it has many of the half-timbered houses that typify Alsace. There is a covered corn exchange, a six-bucket well, the thirteenth-century Kappelturm tower, a fine town hall and many good views from the village walls, around which it is possible to walk. Ste Odile was born here, and she founded the convent on the Mont Ste-Odile which towers above the town.

The journey south then continues to Barr, a centre for winemaking, again with many fine old houses, and a Romanesque bell tower. The small tortuous streets in the centre of this small town are worth exploring, as is the town hall built in 1640. Just to the south of Barr is Mittelbergheim. Wine-growing here can also be traced back more than 1,500 years. It is a lovely village and, by walking a few hundred yards from it and looking back, you will see a scene that cannot have changed for three or four hundred years. Many of the sixteenth and seventeenth-century ornately-timbered buildings remain, and a twelfth-century tower stands over them.

Andlau, just down the road, grew up around the Benedictine abbey founded by St Richarde in the ninth century. The church of St Richarde dates back to the eleventh century, and the doorway, crypt, and the frieze deserve close inspection, as do the choir stalls, which date from the fifteenth century. Nearby there is a ruined castle with two towers.

Other villages in the area, all producing wine, are Nothalten, Eichhoffen, Epfig with its eleventh-century chapel, and Stotzheim.

Dambach, the next port of call, is a Renaissance town with medieval town walls. It was fortified in 1333, when it became the property of the Bishops of Strasbourg. There are three gateways and many ancient houses and buildings. The chapel of St Sebastian, with its baroque altar, dates from

1696 and there is a fifteenth-century ossuary outside the walls. Nearby are the remains of the twelfth-century castle of Bernstein, with keep and Romanesque windows. The Hôtel de Ville dates from 1547 and its neighbour, the Hôtel de la Couronne, was built twenty-two years later. There are many leading Alsace winemakers and shippers in Dambach, and many places to taste the wine. Like many of these lovely old towns, however, the best way to explore is to park the car and travel on foot so that the narrow streets and alleys can be followed.

A visit to Haut-Kœnigsbourg is essential. It is a massive medieval fortress near Sélestat, standing proudly on top of a 2,500ft hill. It has a spectacular view over the surrounding countryside. It has been destroyed several times over the centuries but it was rebuilt between 1901 and 1903 by Kaiser Wilhelm II after the townspeople of Sélestat had donated it to him. The new castle is now a national monument — and a popular location for film makers.

Sélestat itself has many old houses, the Romanesque church of St Foy, an eleventh-century crypt and octagonal tower, the Gothic church of St Georges, and remains of the medieval fortifications. There is also a library containing many rare manuscripts and early printed works.

There are literally scores of wine villages along this route and all are worth visiting, but St-Hippolyte, enclosed behind its thirteenth-century walls is an essential stop. It is named after the Roman martyr whose remains were taken there in the eighth century. Nearby are the villages of Kintzheim, Orschwiller and Rorschwihr, which has a museum with Bronze Age and Roman remains found nearby. A little to the west is Ste-Marie-aux-Mines, a former silver and lead mine. You can see the tower of St-Pierre-sur-l'Hate, which was the fifteenth-century miners' church.

Back on the wine route, the tour takes us to Bergheim, with its medieval fortifications and gateway, and Gothic church. The lime tree growing just outside the walls is said to date from the thirteenth century. A statue which stood by the Porte-Haute, the remaining medieval gate, recalled a strange custom. Murderers who sought refuge in the town could not be prosecuted and this custom lasted for many years. The statue showed a man baring his bottom, and was eventually removed. Bergheim, too, has wine as its livelihood, and there are many opportunities to taste its produce.

Ribeauvillé, just off the N33, is a charming, well-preserved village. There is a fifteenth-century church, the thirteenth-century Butcher's tower, now a belfry, and the thirteenth-century castle of Guisberg, of which the keep and part of the round tower remain. There are many other remains of castles in the surrounding hills including that of St Ulrich, the largest. The Auberge du Soleil dates from the seventeenth century.

Just to the south are the villages of Riquewihr, Hunawihr and Mittelwihr. Riquewihr is now an enormous tourist attraction, thanks perhaps to an old saying, 'If you haven't seen Riquewihr, you haven't seen Alsace.' The village has hardly changed over the centuries with its old houses, fine carvings, statues and churches. There are even dungeons and the original wooden signs which have been used for almost 300 years.

Hunawihr is a small village with a fortified fourteenth-century church over-looking it. The church has some old paintings, and an unusual clock decor-ated with bunches of grapes. Mittelwihr is one of the oldest villages in Asace but was almost completely destroyed during the last war. It produces excellent wines because it is one of the hottest places in Alsace, having its own microclimate because it is protected on three sides by hills.

To the west on the N415 is Kaysersberg, birthplace of Dr Albert Schweit-zer. It has overhanging sixteenth-century timbered houses. The Holy Cross church has an interesting Romanesque west front and many art treasures, in-cluding a sixteenth-century carved altar-piece. The chapel of St Michael has an ossuary and there is a fifteenth-century fortified bridge with a castle over-looking the town. The castle has walls 13ft thick and affords excellent views.

The Alsace wine fraternity, the *Confrérie St Etienne*, meet at nearby Kientzheim, another small fortified town. There is a marvellous gateway and tower with a grotesque gargoyle. The church dates from the fifteenth century, and the château of the Knights of St Stephen is now the wine museum of Alsace.

Tour of Colmar and the Surrounding Area

Colmar has always been a wine town, and today it is at the heart of the Alsace wine trade. It is a medieval town that prospered during the Middle Ages and Renaissance, and this prosperity is reflected in the houses, foun-tains and statues. The Tanners' District has been declared a conservation sector. There are marvellous buildings such as the Pfister House, built in 1537, with its elaborate wooden gallery and carvings. There is also the Maison des Têtes, (1603) (called the 'House of Heads' because of the heads carved on the gable), and the canal district known as Little Venice. Churches to see include the thirteenth-century collegiate church of St Martin with its stained glass windows, the thirteenth-century church of the Dominicans, which contains Martin Schongauer's 'Madonna in the Rose Bower' (1473) and the Franciscans' church. The Unterlinden museum is said to attract more visitors than the Louvre. In short, every cultural and gastronomic need can be satisfied in Colmar very easily.

Outside Colmar are the wine villages of Katzenthal, with its new white church tower and remains of an eleventh-century château; and Neider-morschwihr, which has some nice old buildings but is rapidly becoming absorbed by the spread of Colmar.

Turckheim has three ancient gateways and many sixteenth and seven-teenth-century buildings, as well as a nightwatchman who does his rounds in the summer months every night at ten.

At Wettolsheim there is the site of a Roman settlement, and an exact replica of the grotto of Lourdes, while at Eguisheim there are more well-preserved buildings from the sixteenth and seventeenth centuries, and the ruins of three eleventh- and twelfth-century castles. There is also a ring of houses which constitute a sort of town wall, and a statue to Leo IX, the only Alsace bishop to become Pope.

Husseren-lès-Châteaux is the highest wine village in Alsace, with the vines virtually planted up to the maximum level at which they will grow — 1,300ft.

At Rouffach you can explore the Witches Tower, the Renaissance Town Hall and the many gabled half-timbered houses. Also of interest is the Church of Our Lady of the Assumption which dates from the eleventh century, and was then added to over the next 300 years; the Franciscans' church with its external pulpit, and the gabled corn exchange. There is also an enormous thirteenth-century grape press. A detour from here to the west, visits Munster, the home of one of the most famous cheeses in France.

Back on the wine tour, the next visit is to Guebwiller, with its twelfth-century Romanesque church of St Léger, and the Musée du Florival in the Dominican church which is also noted for its frescoes. The Hôtel de Ville is early sixteenth-century, and there are a number of old wells and fountains.

At Soultz there is a thirteenth-century church to St Maurice, and a town hall with a covered external staircase. Thann, the next place on the tour, is famous for its Gothic architecture. It is a busy town, with the famous Gothic collegiate church of St Thiébaut, built between the fourteenth and sixteenth centuries. There is also a Witches' Tower and the Storks' Tower.

The last port of call is to Mulhouse, south of the wine-growing region. It is a former fortified town, with the church of St Stephen noted for its stained glass windows, many old buildings and the former town hall with its sixteenth-century painted façade.

PLACES OF INTEREST IN THE ALSACE REGION

Altkirch
Gothic houses; eighteenth-century town hall; Sarcophagus of St Morand, twelfth-century.

Ammerschwihr
Sixteenth-century fountain; Tower of Knaves; fifteenth-century fortifications.

Andlau
Benedictine abbey of St Richarde (eleventh-century), ruined castle and tower.

Avolsheim
Tenth-century baptistry with murals; tenth-century Romanesque church.

Barr
Old houses, Romanesque bell tower.

Bergheim
Fourteenth-century Gothic church, medieval fortifications and gateway.

Birkenwald
Renaissance château.

Colmar
Medieval town, fountains, old buildings,
many old churches, museums.

Dambach
Renaissance city with town walls and gateways. Old houses, churches, twelfth-century castle remains.

Ebersmunster
Former Benedictine abbey founded in the seventh century. Baroque church.

Eguisheim
Old houses, three castles.

Ensisheim
Fine Gothic and Renaissance houses, sixteenth-century town hall, Jesuit church.

Geispolsheim
Former fortified town, eighteenth-century church, old houses.

Guebwiller
Twelfth-century Romanesque church, Dominican church and museum.

Haguenau
Eleventh-century town, twelfth-century church, old houses, museum.

Haut-Kœnigsbourg
Huge medieval fortress.

Hunawihr
Old houses, fifteenth-century church with frescoes, and unusual clock.

Kaysersberg
Old houses, Romanesque church, art treasures, fortified bridge, castle.

Kientzheim
Small fortified town, old houses, gateway and tower, château, museum, fifteenth-century church.

Kintzheim
One of best-preserved Gothic castles in Alsace.

Lautenbach
Romanesque church, sixteenth-century cloisters.

Marmoutier
Former abbey church, thirteenth-century nave.

Molsheim
Ancient town, former Jesuit church, old houses.

Mont-Ste-Odile
Convent, Romanesque chapels, ruins of many castles.

Mulhouse
Fortified town, fourteenth-century church with fine stained glass windows, old houses, town hall with sixteenth-century painted façade.

Murbach
Benedictine abbey, twelfth-century Romanesque church.

Neuf-Brisach
Citadel, museum.

Neuwiller-lès-Saverne
Abbey church, Romanesque choir stalls.

Obernai
Fortifications and bell tower, covered wheat market, old houses and famous well.

La Petite Pierre
Fortified château in regional park containing the ruins of many more castles.

Ribeauvillé
Fifteenth-century church, thirteenth-century Butcher's tower, castle, keeps and old houses.

Riquewihr
Traditional Alsatian village, with half-timbered houses and carvings.

Rosheim
Abbey church, ramparts and fortified gateways.

Rouffach
Historic town, old buildings, eleventh-century church, Witches' Tower.

Ste-Marie-aux-Mines
Former silver and lead mine, fifteenth-century church.

Saverne
Thirteenth-century château, twelfth-century Romanesque church, tapestries.

Sélestat
Romanesque church, old houses, medieval fortifications, library.

Strasbourg
Universities; Opera House; Palais de la Musique; Gothic cathedral; La Petite France; covered bridges; churches; museums.

Surbourg
Benedictine abbey, eleventh-century Romanesque church.

Thann
Gothic collegiate church, Witches' Tower, Storks' Tower.

Turckheim
Three old gateways and famous flowered fountain.

Wissembourg
Old town, ramparts, thirteenth-century church.

Gastronomy of Alsace

Alsace and its neighbour Lorraine share many specialist dishes, which often have a strong Germanic influence as one would expect. *Charcuterie* is very common and there are marvellous sausages, pâtés and potted meats. Strasbourg alone has many specialities, especially *foie gras* dishes and duck. The area has *choucroute*, the Alsace equivalent of sauerkraut, but read the menu carefully because it can be served either as a single dish or in helpings large enough to sustain you all day.

There are marvellous soups, game from the forests, and fish from the rivers and Mediterranean. There are quiches, originally from Lorraine, and many savoury tarts and sweet desserts. There are also good local cheeses and many wild mushrooms and fungi from the surrounding fields and woods. Fruit is plentiful and used in many dishes.

Beckenhoffe is one of the region's most famous specialities; it can be spelt in many different ways depending which town or village you are in. It can appear as *backenoffe*, *baeckaoffa* or *beckenoffe*. It is an Alsatian stew of beef, mutton and pork, steeped in local wine with potatoes and onions. It gets its name because it was traditionally cooked in a baker's oven.

Charcuterie includes *boudin blanc* and *boudin noir* (white and black puddings), *knockwurst*, a special small sausage from Alsace, and the famous *saucisse de Strasbourg*, smoked sausage which can be made of either pork or beef.

You may find *choucroute garnie*, which is pickled, fermented white cabbage served with peppercorns, ham and pork, Strasbourg sausage and boiled potatoes. It is cooked in wine, but it is best to drink beer with it (try one of the excellent local beers). This is a massive meal. Other cabbage dishes include *chou farci*, which is cabbage stuffed with pork and bacon usually.

The pigs which provide much of the meat for the *charcuterie* also yield excellent pork and this too figures heavily on the menus. *Civet de porc* is a pork stew in a thick, dark sauce; *chochon de lait à la gelée* is suckling pig served cold in jelly, while *porcelot rôti* is roast suckling pig, mouth-watering. There are rolled and smoked fillets of pork called *kassler*, and *porc à la Vosgienne*, which is pork cooked in wine, with vinegar, onions and plums. You will also find *schifela* on the menu, which is an ancient recipe consisting of hot, smoked shoulder of pork served with pickled turnips, or onion and potato salad. *Tourte à la Lorraine* is a pie with pork and veal, covered in cream or custard, and if you see *marcassin* on the menu, order it, because it is young boar, probably from the Vosges.

There are many fish dishes to choose from. Carp (*carpe*) is popular, especially *carpe à la juive*, braised carp served cold in a white wine and onion sauce. *Knopfe*, or *knepfle*, are *quenelles*, normally made of fish and usually fried, and not to be confused with *krapfen*, which are fritters stuffed with jam. *Tatelote Alsacienne* is a fish stew usually made with eels, but other freshwater fish, including pike, can be used.

Poultry too appears regularly on menus. *Coq au Riesling* is an Alsace speciality, chicken in a Riesling and cream sauce with onions and mushrooms. Goose and duck are also common, often reared for the *foie gras*, but none of the other meat is wasted. The *foie gras* is a great delicacy and can be cooked whole or sliced, and served either hot or cold. It can accompany many dishes or be eaten as a starter, and if so should be accompanied by a good, sweet wine. It is often served with truffles, a Strasbourg speciality. *Oie à l'Alsacienne* is a Strasbourg goose roasted, stuffed with local sausage meat and served with *choucroute*, while *magret* is breast of duck, usually lightly cooked.

Savoury flans and pastries are common. Look for *flammekuechea*, a bacon, cream and onion flan, sometimes with cheese; also known as *tarte flambée*, an Alsace speciality. There is *tarte à l'oignon Alsacienne*, an onion and cream tart, and *zewelmai* or *zewelwai*, an Alsace onion and cream flan, sometimes garnished with spring onions.

Other main course dishes you may come across are *leberknepfen*, or *leberknopflen*, dumplings made from calf's liver (although occasionally from pork) and *tourte aux grenouilles* (from Lorraine originally), frog's legs covered in egg custard in a pie. *Pfutters Alsacienne* are small fried potato squares, or potato puffs, while *spätsel*, *spätzel*, or *spaetzle*, is a noodle dumpling.

There are a number of soups such as *potage à l'Alsacienne*, made from local sausage, ham and potatoes. *Soupe aux grenouilles* is an Alsace speciality, frog's legs cooked with white wine and cream.

Other dishes you may discover are *salade de cervelas*, cold, white sausage, sliced and served with a vinaigrette sauce; and the delicious *waffelpasteta*, *foie gras* and truffles in pastry.

The people of the region have a sweet tooth, and this is reflected in the wide range of desserts. Try *berawecka*, or *bireweck*, a bread roll with dried prunes, pears, figs or dates, with added kirsch and spices. A cake can also be made using the same ingredients. There is *kaffenkrantz*, a *brioche* or rich cake, made with raisins, and usually eaten with coffee, and *kugelhopf*, or *kougelhopf*, a sweet *brioche* with almonds, raisins and currants, often soaked in Kirsch. *Tarte à l'Alsacienne* is an open tart often divided into sections, each with a different jam, while *tarte mougin*, sometimes au *m'gin*, *megin*, or *mengin*, is a Lorraine dish, a tart filled with cream and cream cheese.

All the cheeses of the area are made from cow's milk, and include *Carré-de-l'Est*, a white creamy cheese from Lorraine which is very mild, and *Gérardmer*, also known as *Gros Lorraine*, which is equally mild. *St-Rémy* is another smooth, strong cheese from Lorraine. There is *Géromé*, a smooth, strong-smelling, spicy cheese from Lorraine which can be eaten fresh or cured. It is also sometimes flavoured with fennel or caraway seeds.

Munster is Alsace's most famous cheese and there is even a '*route de fromage*' taking you round the twenty-eight villages making the cheese in the hills above Munster. It is a soft, supple cheese with a strong taste and smell. It has an orange rind and its own AC status. *Munster Laitier* is made by commercial dairies and is available all the year round, while *Munster Fermier* is made on farms and is best eaten in late summer and autumn. There is also *Munster au cumin*, flavoured with cumin or caraway seeds.

HOTELS AND RESTAURANTS OF THE ALSACE REGION

Ammerschwihr
(68770 Haut-Rhin)

Aux Armes de France
1 Grande-Rue
☎ (89) 47 10 12
Run by Pierre Gaertner,
who for the last 25 years
and more has created the
same classical cuisine, but
is now joined by son
Philippe, who practises
nouvelle, so an interesting
mixture is now develop-
ing. Food is always good,
the helpings are large, and
the wine list is except-
ional. Very popular, not
too expensive and the service is fast and good.
There are 8 very
reasonably-priced,
comfortable rooms, but
you must reserve.

A l'Arbre Vert
7 rue des Cigognes
☎ (89) 47 12 23
A very comfortable, friendly, 13-room hotel in the
village. Good and inexpensive restaurant serving
traditional Alsace cuisine.
Room prices ideal for
those on a budget, or want-
ing to save a few francs to
spend on more wine.

Andolsheim
(68600 Haut-Rhin)

Soleil
1 rue de Colmar
☎ (89) 71 40 53
3 miles from Colmar and a
good touring base. The 17
rooms are comfortable and
not expensive, the res-
taurant and wine list very
good.

Artzenheim
(68320 Haut-Rhin)

Auberge d'Artzenheim
rue du Sponneck
☎ (89) 71 60 51

A very friendly restaurant,
with 10 comfortable,
cheap rooms. Service
throughout is warm,
menus exciting and prices
reasonable.

Baldenheim
(67600 Bas-Rhin)

La Couronne
45 rue Sélestat
☎ (88) 85 32 22
A very good restaurant offering a mixture of classical and *nouvelle cuisine*,
but all modelled on traditional Alsace dishes.

Blaesheim
(67113 Bas-Rhin)

Restaurant au Boeuf
rue du Maréchal Foch
☎ (88) 68 81 31
A good Alsace restaurant
with many specialities and
very good local wines.
Not expensive.

Bas-Rupts
(88400 Vosges)

Hostellerie Bas-Rupts
2¹/₂ miles from Gérardmer
☎ (29) 63 09 25
A magnificent hotel and
restaurant high in the
hills. Modern cooking by
Michel Philippe which
regularly also scales the
heights, as does the bill.
There are 20 reasonably-
priced, very comfortable,
quiet rooms.

Belfort
(9000 Belfort)

Hostellerie du Château
  Servin
9 rue Gén Négrier
☎ (84) 21 41 85
10 attractive, not too
expensive rooms, a warm
welcome from Mme Lucie
Servin, and wonderfully
creative *nouvelle cuisine*

from young chef Domin-
ique Mathy. Restaurant
very pricey.

Grand Hôtel du Lion
2 rue G. Clémenceau
☎ (84) 21 17 00
Comfortable 82-room
hotel, reasonably-priced,
and good, inexpensive
restaurant.

Hôtel Américain
2 rue Pont Neuf
☎ (84) 21 57 01
A 40-room hotel,
modestly priced, no
restaurant, but breakfasts.

Le Sabot d'Annie
5 rue Aristide-Briand
☎ (84) 26 01 71
At Offemont 1³/₄ miles
north on the D13 and
D22. A very good
restaurant offering the
best from nature's larder
whether bought in the
market, or gathered in the
fields. Good prices.

Colmar
(68000 Haut-Rhin)

Terminus Bristol
7 place de la Gare
☎ (89) 23 59 59
A luxurious hotel in the
centre of town, opposite
the station (but the 70
spacious rooms are quiet).
Rooms are expensive, but
not so the marvellous restaurant, the *Rendez-vous
de Chasse* under the man-
agement of Richard and
Ilouka Riehm, and chef
Roger Muller. Very good
food and wine.

Hôtel Colbert
2 rue Trois-Epis
☎ (89) 41 31 05
50 very comfortable
rooms, reasonably-priced,
but no restaurant;
breakfast served.

Novotel
1¹/4 miles north near the
airfield, on the N83
☎ (89) 41 49 14
A modern, convenient 66-
room hotel, with swim-
ming pool. Restaurant for
snacks only.

Hôtel Le Champs de Mars
2 ave. de la Marne
☎ (89) 41 54 54
An attractive, modern, 75-
room hotel in the town
park, with two fair res-
taurants. Prices reasonable
for rooms and food.

Maison des Têtes
19 rue des Têtes
☎ (89) 24 43 43
Now back in business, and
one of the town's most
magnificent restaurants,
both for the grandeur of
its surroundings and its
cuisine. Super Alsace specialities and not expensive.

Au Fer Rouge
52 Grande-Rue
☎ (89) 41 37 24
A lovely house in the old
part of the city run by the
Fulgraff family. Son Pat-
rick is the chef and he is
destined for great things.

Restaurant Schillinger
16 rue Stanislas
☎ (89) 41 43 17
Marvellous restaurant,
expensive but worth it.
Advisable to book if you
want to enjoy the best
foie gras in town.

Auberge Père Floranc
9 rue Herzog
☎ (89) 41 39 14
At Wettolsheim, 2³/4 miles
south-west on the N417
and D1. Alsace food at its
best, created by René
Floranc, and not at all
expensive. Interesting
wine list and 13
reasonably-priced rooms.

Eguisheim
(68420 Haut-Rhin)

Caveau d'Eguisheim
3 place du Château St-Léon
☎ (89) 41 08 89
About 3 miles south-west.
Good food, very generous
portions, reasonable
prices and an excellent
wine list in this res-
taurant, tucked away in a
picturesque village.

Fougerolles
(70220 Haute-Saône)

Au Père Rota
8 Grande Rue
☎ (84) 49 12 11
Marvellous restaurant run
by Jean-Pierre and Chantal
Kuentz. Very good *nou-
velle cuisine* based on
Alsace dishes. Excellent
wine list and very reasonable prices. Last orders
taken quite early.

Illhaeusern
(68150 Haut-Rhin)

Auberge de l'Ill
rue de Collonges
☎ (89) 71 83 23
The Haeberlin brothers run
this restaurant, aware that
it is one of the great show-
pieces of French gastron-
omy, and the best in Al-
sace. Expensive, and it is
essential to reserve well
in advance, but everything
from service to food,
décor to wine is near
perfect.

La Clairière
route Guémar
☎ (89) 71 80 80
A quiet 24-room hotel, no
restaurant but breakfast.
Not expensive.

Kaysersberg
(68240 Haut-Rhin)

Chambard
9 rue du Gén-de-Gaulle
☎ (89) 47 10 17

A comfortable, 20-room,
fairly expensive hotel,
and a restaurant that is
still good but not as good
as it used to be.

Remparts
4 rue Flieh
☎ (89) 47 12 12
A small 30-room hotel
with friendly, attentive
service. No restaurant, but
breakfast served. Albert
Schweitzer was born just
down the road.

Arbre Vert
rue Haute-du-Rempart
☎ (89) 47 11 51
23 well-priced, comfort-
able rooms and a reason-
able restaurant.

Château
rue du Gén-de-Gaulle
☎ (89) 78 24 33
A small 12-room hotel,
very reasonably-priced and
popular, so book. Good
and cheap restaurant.

Hostellerie Abbaye
d'Alspach
☎ (89) 47 16 00
At Kientzheim, 1³/4 miles
east on the D28.
20 attractive, comfortable
rooms and a dinner-only
restaurant. Both rooms
and food good value.

Lapoutroie
(68650 Haut-Rhin)

Hôtel du Faudé
28 rue du Gén Duffieux
☎ (89) 47 50 35
An attractive, comfortable
hotel in the village, with
good views. Nice gardens
and a swimming pool, and
very good value res-
taurant.

Les Trois-Epis
(68410 Haut-Rhin)

Grand Hôtel
place de l'Eglise
☎ (89) 49 80 65
A glorious hotel with

spectacular views of both the mountains and over the Alsace plain. There are 49 rooms, luxurious and dear, and a marvellous restaurant, *Le Hohlandsbourg*, with chef Stephan François at the helm. Very good menus and very reasonably priced. Also indoor swimming pool and sauna.

Marchal
☎ (89) 49 81 61
Also has excellent views. 40 good rooms, not expensive, and a good, inexpensive restaurant. Very friendly.

Croix d'Or
☎ (89) 49 83 55
Comfortable 12-room hotel, with good value restaurant.

Marlenheim
(67520 Bas-Rhin)

Hostellerie du Cerf
30 rue du Gén-de-Gaulle
☎ (88) 87 73 73
A very comfortable 17-room hotel, recently modernised, and charging very reasonable rates. The father and son combination in the kitchen works very well and the restaurant is marvellous.

Muhlbach
(68380 Haut-Rhin)

Perle des Vosges
☎ (89) 77 61 34
A very comfortable, 25-room, friendly hotel with splendid views and fair restaurant. All good value.

Mulhouse
(68100 Haut-Rhin)

Sofitel
3³/4 miles north-east at Mulhouse-Sausheim, on the N422A
☎ (89) 44 75 75

Modern, comfortable hotel with 98 rooms. Air-conditioning, swimming pool, tennis, good restaurant and summer barbecues by pool. Rooms quite expensive, but worth it.

Frantel
4 place Charles de Gaulle
☎ (89) 46 01 23
A modern 96-room hotel in town centre, and near the station. Quite expensive. The restaurant, *L'Alsace*, is modern, comfortable and the food is very good, at very reasonable prices.

Le Vieux Paris
42 ave. R. Schumann
☎ (89) 45 42 70
The cuisine of Michel Finck changes according to what is available at the market that day, but is always good and reasonable.

Le Moulin du Kaegy
At Steinbrunn-le-Bas 5 miles south on the D21
☎ (89) 81 30 34
A very popular, if rather expensive, restaurant as the inventive cuisine of Bernard Bégat draws lovers of good food from many countries. Excellent wine list.

La Poste
7 rue du Gén-de-Gaulle
Riedisheim
☎ (89) 44 07 71
Has been in the Kiény family for many generations, and it shows in the marvellous service, welcome and cuisine. Amazingly good value.

Obernai
(67210 Bas-Rhin)

Le Parc
169 rue du Gén Gouraud
☎ (88) 95 50 08
A very roomy, elegant

hotel with 45 reasonably-priced rooms, and a good restaurant, not dear, with constantly changing, but always good menus.

Beau Site
1 rue Gén-de-Gaulle
At Ottrott-le-Haut, about 2¹/2 miles west on the N426.
☎ (88) 95 80 61
A very comfortable inn with 14 value-for-money rooms and a very good restaurant with fine wine list. Very good value. The red Ottrott wine should be tried.

Port-sur-Saône
(70170 Haut-Saône)

Château de Vauchoux
☎ (84) 91 53 55
A magnificent restaurant under Jean-Michel Turin, a very gifted, if as yet underrated chef. Food superb and a bargain.

Remiremont
(88200 Vosges)

Les Abbesses
93 rue Gén-de-Gaulle
☎ (29) 62 02 96
Jean-Claude Aiguier has already built up a deserved reputation for his wonderfully creative cuisine. Highly recommended and remarkable value for money. His wife Francine is the perfect hostess.

Ribeauvillé
(68150 Haut-Rhin)

Le Clos St-Vincent
route de Bergheim
☎ (89) 73 67 65
A marvellous hilltop inn, with 11 charming, good-value rooms always in demand (so reserve). Patron chef Bertrand Chapotin produces marvellous traditional dishes in his own creative way. Lunch is

particularly good value, but so are all the menus, even the most expensive. A delightful place to stop for a meal or to stay, if you are lucky enough to get a room.

Hostellerie des Seigneurs
de Ribeaupierre
11 rue du Château
☎ (89) 73 70 31
A delightful little hotel with 8 charming rooms. Not expensive, no restaurant, but breakfast.

Riquewihr
(68340 Haut-Rhin)

Le Riquewihr
route Ribeauvillé
☎ (89) 47 83 13
A new hotel on the edge of the old town. There are 49 rooms in Alsace rustic style, all very reasonably priced and with good views. No restaurant, but breakfast (and a bar that never seems to shut!).

Auberge du Schoenenbourg
2 rue de la Piscine
☎ (89) 47 92 28
Run by the Kiener family, this charming restaurant on a hill outside town is a tourist trap but the food is good and very well priced. Local wines, especially the Riesling, are magnificent, and try the marmite with crayfish (not what you might think).

Rouffach
(68250 Haut-Rhin)

Château d'Isenbourg
☎ (89) 49 63 53
About 9 miles from Colmar. A 200-year-old château with magnificent views over the Alsace plains. A luxurious, elegant hotel with 37 rooms and 3 apartments, all expensive, swimming

pool, tennis and attractive gardens. The restaurant, *Les Thomeries*, lives up to the high standards set by the rest of the establishment. Good food, some great wines, and not too expensive.

Strasbourg
(67000 Bas-Rhin)

Strasbourg is the principal city of Alsace, a mecca for tourists and also the home of the European Parliament, so it is often flooded with European Members of Parliament and Common Market officials. It is essential to book hotel accommodation well in advance, and even restaurants, if they are popular.

Hilton
ave. Herrenschmidt
☎ (88) 37 10 10
A luxurious 253-room, 5-apartment hotel, air-conditioned and close to centre of town. The restaurant, *Maison du Boeuf*, offers good value.

Hannong
15 rue du 22 Novembre
☎ (88) 32 16 22
A very comfortable, traditional hotel with 70 reasonably-priced rooms and all comforts, but no restaurant. Breakfasts served.

Hôtel des Rohan
17 rue Maroquin
☎ (88) 32 85 11
A small 36-room hotel, not too expensive, but family run, warm and friendly. No restaurant, but breakfasts served.

Nouvel Hôtel Maison
Rouge
4 rue des Francs-Bourgeois
☎ (88) 32 08 60
A medium-priced, 130-

room hotel in the centre of town. Efficient and friendly; no restaurant, but breakfast served.

Holiday Inn
20 place de Bordeaux
☎ (88) 35 70 00
A modern 168-room air-conditioned hotel, close to centre and near the *Palais de la Musique et des Congrès*. Swimming pool, sauna, disco and good restaurant.

Gutenberg
31 rue des Serruriers
☎ (88) 32 17 15
No restaurant but a charming 50-room hotel. Breakfast served.

Sofitel
place St-Pierre-le-Jeune
☎ (88) 32 99 30
An attractive, friendly hotel with 180 rooms, some rather small. The *Châteaubriand* restaurant is good, but pricey.

Terminus-Gruber
10 place Gare
☎ (88) 32 87 00
Large hotel with 78 sound-proofed rooms; it is opposite the station. The restaurant, *Cour de Rosemont*, is very good and there is a smaller restaurant, *La Brasserie*, and a café, *L'Auberge*. Rooms good value.

Novotel
quai Kléber,
☎ (88) 22 10 99
A convenient, modern 97-room hotel, reasonably priced and a restaurant for quick, inexpensive meals.

Novotel Strasbourg
6 miles south on the A35
rue de l'Ill
Illkirch
☎ (88) 66 21 56
Modern large hotel, with swimming pool. Room rates reasonable,

restaurant for snacks and grills.

Hôtel France
20 rue Jeu-des-Enfants
☎ (88) 32 37 12
A very central, 70-room hotel, not expensive, no restaurant but breakfasts served.

Monopole-Métropole
16 rue Kuhn
☎ (88) 32 11 94
Near the station. A 94-room, reasonably-priced hotel; no restaurant but breakfast available.

Grand Hôtel
12 place Gare
☎ (88) 32 46 90
94 rooms, not expensive, no restaurant, breakfast served.

Au Moulin
25 route de Strasbourg
☎ (88) 96 20 01
At Wantzenau, 8 miles north-east on the D468. A modern hotel built from an old mill. 20 very reasonably-priced rooms and a charming restaurant. The quality of the food is appreciated by the locals who flock here, especially on Sundays.

L'Ami Schutz
1 Ponts-Couverts
☎ (88) 32 76 98
Marvellous Alsatian food, many of the dishes rediscovered by chef Paul Schloesser. Food always exciting and good and very reasonably-priced.

Le Crocodile
10 rue de l'Outre
☎ (88) 32 13 02
Luxurious, expensive restaurant run by Emile Jüng and his wife. The food, however, is magnificent as are the wines, from one of the best restaurant wine cellars in France.

Buerehiesel
4 parc de l'Orangerie
☎ (88) 61 62 24
A lovely setting by the lake in the Parc de l'Orangerie, this delightful restaurant run by Antoine Westermann always impresses. The wine list is very good and the fixed price menu a bargain.

Maison des Tanneurs
42 rue Bain-aux-Plantes
☎ (88) 32 79 70
A very old building, dating back to 1572, but nothing dated about the cuisine. Good Alsace specialities with a lot of modern touches. Not expensive.

Maison Kammerzell
16 place de la Cathédrale
☎ (88) 32 42 14
Traditional Alsace cuisine in this very popular, old half-timbered building. Massive helpings but reasonable prices.

Zimmer
rue des Heros
At Wantzenau, 8 miles north-east on D468
☎ (88) 96 62 08

Another very popular restaurant which is crowded with locals at the weekend — always the best recommendation.

La Table Gourmande
43 route du Gén-de-Gaulle
☎ (88) 83 61 67
At Schiltigheim, 1^{3}/4 miles to the north. Alain Reix does have some Alsatian dishes but his repertoire is large and always fine. The food is light and delicate but prices have crept up lately.

Zimmer Sengel
8 rue du Temple-Neuf
☎ (88) 32 35 01
A delightful restaurant offering an alternative to Alsatian cuisine, but still very French. Very good value.

Valentin-Sorg
6 place Homme-de-Fer
☎ (88) 32 12 16
Very good restaurant with marvellous views over the city. Chef Roland Schmitt is very competent and his cuisine classical.

Strissel
place de la Grande-Boucherie
☎ (88) 32 14 73
A wonderful typical Alsatian restaurant, still firmly in the hands of the Schrodi family. All things Alsace served here and excellent value for money.

VINEYARDS OF ALSACE

AREA BETWEEN THANN AND COLMAR

Thann (68800)

Domaine Zind-
  Humbrecht   TW
Wintzenheim
☎ (89) 27 02 05
Open: daily.

Soultz (68360)

Cave Vinicole du Vieil
  Armand   TW
1 route de Cernay
☎ (89) 76 73 75
Open: Monday to Friday
8am-noon and 2-6pm;
weekends and public
holidays 10am-noon and
2-7pm.

Robert Roth and son   TW
38a route de Jungholtz
☎ (89) 76 80 45
Open: Monday to Saturday
8am-6pm; public holidays
2-5pm.

Louis Wintzer   TW
53 rue de Lattre
☎ (89) 76 80 79
Open: Monday to Saturday
8am-8pm; Sunday and
public holidays 9am-5pm.

Guebwiller (68500)

Domaine   TEW
  Schlumberger
100 rue Th. Deck
☎ (89) 74 27 00
Open: Monday to Friday
9am-5pm.

Orschwihr
(68500 Guebwiller)

Lucien Albrecht   TW
9 Grand Rue
☎ (89) 76 95 18
Open: Monday to Saturday
8am-5pm.

Materne Haegelin   TW
45-47 Grand Rue
☎ (89) 76 95 17
Open: Monday to Saturday
9am-6pm.

Vignobles P. Reinhart TW
7 rue du Printemps
☎ (89) 76 95 12
Open: Monday to Friday
9am-6pm; Sunday and
public holidays by
appointment.

Nicolas Rich   TW
20-22 rue de l'Eglise
☎ (89) 76 18 62
Open: Monday to Saturday
9am-6pm; closed end of
August and beginning of
September.

Soultzmatt (68570)

Château Wagenbourg   TW
Joseph Klein
25a rue de la Vallée
☎ (89) 47 01 41
Open: Monday to Friday
8am-noon and 2-6pm;
Saturday 8am-6pm; Sunday
and public holidays 8am-
noon and by appointment.

Camille Kubler and son TW
103 rue de la Vallée
☎ (89) 47 00 75
Open: Monday to Friday
10am-6pm; weekends and
public holidays 10am-
4pm, closed last two
weeks of August.

Seppi and Rita   TW
  Landmann-Ostholt
20 rue de la Vallée
☎ (89) 47 09 33
Open: Monday to Saturday
9am-6pm; Sunday and pub-
lic holidays 10am-6pm.

Westhalten (68111)

Cave Vinicole de
  Westhalten   TWE
route de Soultzmatt
☎ (89) 47 01 27
Open: Monday to Friday
9am-5pm, Saturday 9am-
noon; Sunday and public
holidays 10am-noon and 2-
7pm from Easter to mid-
December.

GAEC Diringer   TW
3 route de Rouffach
☎ (89) 47 01 06
Open: Monday to Saturday
8am-6pm.

Domaine du
  Bollenberg   TW
A. Meyer
☎ (89) 49 60 04
& (89) 49 62 47
Open: daily; food
available to 9pm.

Rouffach (68250)

GAEC Bannwarth
  and son   TE
19 rue du 4ᵉ Spahis
☎ (89) 49 62 37
Open: Monday to Friday
except public holidays.

Muré   TWE
(Clos-St-Landelin)
route Nationale 83
route du Vin
☎ (89) 49 62 19
Open: Monday to Saturday
8am-6pm; Sunday and
public holidays 10.30am-
6pm.

T=tasting   E=English spoken   G=guided tours   C=château/building to visit

Pfaffenheim (68250)

Cave Vinicole de
Pfaffenheim   TWE
route Nationale 83
☎ (89) 49 61 08
Open: Monday to Friday
8am-noon and 1.30-6pm;
Saturday 9am-noon and 2-
6pm; Sunday and public
holidays 10am-noon and
2-6pm.

GAEC J. Riefle and sonTW
11 place de la Mairie
☎ (89) 49 62 82
Open: Monday to Saturday
8am-7pm; Sunday and pub-
lic holidays 2-6pm from
April to December.

François Runner   TW
1 rue de la Liberté
☎ (89) 49 62 89
Open: Monday to Saturday
8am-6pm; Sunday and pub-
lic holidays by appoint-
ment.

Gueberschwihr
(68420 Herrlisheim)

Les Producteurs Réunis
d'Alsace   TW
route de Hattstatt
☎ (89) 49 61 08
Open: daily.

Caveau Corps de GardeTW
place de la Mairie
Open: daily July and
August 9am-noon and 2-
6pm; rest of year week-
ends only 10am-noon and
2-6pm.

Voegtlinshoffen
(68420 Herrlisheim)

Joseph Cattin and son   TW
18 rue R. Frémeaux
☎ (89) 49 30 21
Open: Monday to Saturday
8am-6pm; Sunday and pub-
lic holidays by appoint-
ment.

V. Immèle   TW
8 rue R. Frémeaux
☎ (89) 49 30 51
Open: Monday to Saturday
8am-7pm; Sunday 8am-
noon.

**Husseren-lès-
Châteaux**
(68420 Herrlisheim)

Edouard Colombain   TW
5 rue Jeanne d'Arc
☎ (89) 49 30 39
Open: Saturday only
1-7pm.

Kuentz-Bas   TWE
☎ (89) 49 30 24
Open: Monday to Friday
8am-noon and 2-6pm; Sat-
urday 8am-noon. Saturday
afternoon, Sunday and
public holidays by
appointment. Closed 20
August-15 September.

André Scherer   TW
12 route du Vin
☎ (89) 49 30 33
Open: Monday to Friday
8am-6pm; Saturday 9am-
noon; Sunday and public
holidays by appointment.

Eguisheim
(68420 Herrlisheim)

Emile Beyer   TW
7 place du Château
☎ (89) 41 40 45
Open: Monday to Saturday
8am-6pm; Sunday and pub-
lic holidays by appoint-
ment.

Léon Beyer   TWE
2 rue de la 1ᵉ Armée
☎ (89) 41 41 05
Open: by appointment.

Cave Vinicole   TWE
d'Eguisheim
☎ (89) 41 11 06
Open: daily 8am-noon and
2-6pm.

Bruno Hertz   TW
1 porte des Chevaliers
☎ (89) 41 81 61
Open: Monday to Saturday
8am-5pm; Sunday and pub-
lic holidays by appoint-
ment.

Bruno Sorg   TW
8 rue Monseigneur Stumpf
☎ (89) 41 80 85
Open: Monday to
Saturday; Sunday and pub-
lic holidays by appoint-
ment.

Wettolsheim
(68000 Colmar)

J-Louis Schoepfer   TW
35 rue Herzog
☎ (89) 41 41 29
Open: daily but closed 20
August-10 September.

J. Rémy Waller   TW
9 rue de la 5ᵉ DB
☎ (89) 41 50 98
Open: Monday to Friday
9am-8pm; Saturday, Sun-
day and public holidays
10am-8pm; closed first
two weeks of September.

Wunsch and Mann   TW
2 rue de Clefs
☎ (89) 41 89 68
Open: Monday to Friday
8am-noon and 2-6pm;
Saturday 8am-6pm; Sunday
3-6pm.

Wintzenheim
(68000 Colmar)

Josmeyer and son   TWE
76 rue Clémenceau
☎ (89) 27 01 57
Open: Monday to Friday 8-
11am and 2-5pm; Saturday
8.30-11am.

R=red wine   W=white wine   P=rosé wine   S=sparkling wine

Joseph Schaffar   TW
125 rue Clémenceau
☎ (89) 27 00 25
Open: Monday to Saturday
9am-noon and 1-6pm; Sunday and public holidays
by appointment.

Domaine Zind-
Humbrecht   TWE
34 rue Joffre
☎ (89) 27 02 05
Open: Monday to Friday
9am-5pm; Saturday by
appointment.

Turckheim (68230)

Cave Vinicole
de Turckheim   TW
16 rue des Tuileries
☎ (89) 27 06 25
Open: by appointment.

Charles Schleret   TW
1-3 route d'Ingersheim
☎ (89) 27 06 09
Open: Monday to Saturday
8am-6pm; Sunday and public holidays, 8am-noon.

Colmar (68000)

Domaine Viticole de la
Ville de Colmar   TW
2 rue du Stauffen
☎ (89) 79 11 87
Open: Monday to Friday
8am-8pm; Saturday, Sunday and public holidays
by appointment.

Martin Jund   TW
12 rue de l'Agne
☎ (89) 41 58 72
Open: Monday to Saturday
10am-8pm.

AREA BETWEEN COLMAR AND RIBEAUVILLE

Ingersheim
(68000 Colmar)

Cave Coopérative
d'Ingersheim   TW
1 rue G. Clémenceau
☎ (89) 27 05 96
Open: Monday to Friday
by appointment; Saturday
2.30-6.30pm; Sunday and
public holidays 10am-
6.30pm.

Dany Dietrich   TW
17-19 rue du Gén-Pau
☎ (89) 27 05 19
Open: daily 8am-8pm.

Niedermorschwihr
(68230 Turckheim)

Marcel Mullenbach   TW
12 rue des Trois-Epis
☎ (89) 27 04 13
Open: Monday to Saturday
2-6pm.

Katzenthal
(68230 Turckheim)

J. Marc Bernhard   TW
21 Grand Rue
☎ (89) 27 05 34
or (89) 27 25 42
Open: Monday to Friday
9am-6pm; Saturday 9am-
7pm; Sunday and public
holidays by appointment.

J. Paul Eckle   TW
29 Grand Rue
☎ (89) 27 09 41
Open: daily 8am-8pm.

Henri Klee   TW
11 Grand Rue
☎ (89) 27 03 81
Open: Saturday 2-6pm.

Ammerschwihr
(68770)

Les Caves Adam   TW
rue de l'Aigle
☎ (89) 78 23 21
Open: daily.

Félix Eppèle   TW
19 Grand Rue
Open: daily 9am-7pm.

Jérôme Geschickt
and son   TW
1 place de la Sinne
☎ (89) 47 12 54
Open: daily 9am-8pm.

Vins d'Alsace Kuehn   TW
3 Grand Rue
☎ (89) 78 23 16
Open: Monday to Friday
8am-noon and 2-5pm;
Saturday 9am-noon; Sunday and public holidays
by appointment.

GAEC André Wackenthaler
and son   TW
8 rue du Kaefferkopf
☎ (89) 78 23 76
Open: Monday to Saturday
10am-8pm; Sunday and
public holidays by
appointment.

Kientzheim
(68240 Kaysersberg)

GAEC Paul Blanck
and son   TW
(Domaine des Comtes de
Lupfen)
32 Grand Rue
☎ (89) 78 23 56
Open: Monday to Friday
9am-noon and 2-6pm; Saturday 9am-noon; Sunday
and public holidays by
appointment.

Kaysersberg (68240)

GAEC Victor Ancel
and son   TW
3 rue du Collège
☎ (89) 47 10 76
Open: daily.

Sigolsheim
(68240 Kaysersberg)

Meyer-Krumb   TW
5 rue Aspirant Girard
☎ (89) 47 36 02

T=tasting E=English spoken G=guided tours C=château/building to visit

Open: Monday to Friday 2-7pm; Saturday and public holidays 2-6pm.

Ringenbach-Moser   TW
12 rue du Vallon
☎ (89) 47 11 23
Open: Monday to Saturday 8am-noon and 1-6pm; Sunday and public holidays 9am-noon and 1-6pm.

Société Coopérative Vinicole de Sigolsheim et Environs   TWE
☎ (89) 47 12 55
Open: daily 9-11am and 2-5pm, from Easter to the start of the harvest.

Pierre Sparr and sons   TWE
rue de la 1ᵉ Armée
☎ (89) 78 24 22
Open: Monday to Friday 8am-noon and 2-6pm; Saturday 8am-noon.

Bennwihr
(68630 Bennwihr-Mittelwihr)

Les Caves Vinicoles de Bennwihr   TWE
3 rue de Gaulle
☎ (89) 47 90 27
Open: daily 9-11am and 2-5pm.

Mittelwihr
(68630 Bennwihr-Mittelwihr)

Frédéric Baltzinger   TW
20 route du Vin
☎ (89) 47 90 44
Open: Tuesday and Wednesday afternoon, closed September.

Frédéric Berger and son TW
8 rue de Riquewihr
☎ (89) 47 90 79
Open: Monday to Saturday 10am-7pm.

Edel brothers   TW
Domaine du Bouxhof
44 route du Vin
☎ (89) 47 90 34
Open: Monday to Friday 8am-8pm; Saturday, Sunday and public holidays 8am-6pm.

Horcher and son   TW
6 rue du Vignoble
☎ (89) 47 93 26
Open: Monday to Saturday 8am-6pm; Sunday and public holidays 9am-noon.

Edgard Schaller and son TW
1 rue du Château
☎ (89) 47 90 28
Open: Monday to Friday 8am-7pm; weekends and public holidays 9am-7pm.

Willy Wurtz   TW
6 rue du Bouxhof
☎ (89) 47 93 16
Open: weekends and public holidays 8am-7pm.

Beblenheim (68980)

Bott-Geyl   TW
1 rue du Petit Château
☎ (89) 47 90 04
Open: daily 8am-noon and 1-7pm; closed 10 August-10 September.

Cave Vinicole de Beblenheim   TW
14 rue de Hoen
☎ (89) 47 90 02
Open: daily 10am-noon and 2-6pm; closed mid-July to second week in August.

J. Paul Hartweg   TW
39 rue Jean Macé
☎ (89) 47 94 79
Open: Monday to Saturday 8am-6pm; Sunday and public holidays 8am-noon.

Riquewihr (68340)

Dopff au Moulin   TWE
Hostellerie au Moulin
☎ (89) 47 92 23
or (89) 47 93 13 (Hostellerie)
Open: Monday to Friday 8am-noon and 2-6pm from 1 April to 31 October; weekends and public holidays 9am-noon, 2-6pm.

Dopff-Irion   TWE
Château de Riquewihr
☎ (89) 47 92 51
Open: daily 9.30am-7pm; closed November to February.

Hugel and son   TWE
☎ (89) 47 92 15
Open: weekdays 9.30am-noon and 2-5pm, May to September; rest of year by appointment.

Preiss-Zimmer   TWE
42 rue de Gaulle
☎ (89) 47 92 58
Open: Monday to Friday 8am-5pm; weekends and public holidays, 9am-7pm.

Jean Lehmann and son TW
2-3 Chemin de Beblenheim
☎ (89) 47 82 99
Open: daily 10am-7pm.

Mittnacht-Klack   TW
8 rue des Tuileries
☎ (89) 47 92 54
Open: Monday to Friday 9-11.30am and 1-6pm; Saturday 10-11am and 1-5pm; Sunday and public holidays, 10am-noon.

Zellenberg
(68340 Riquewihr)

J. Becker   TWE
4 route d'Ostheim
☎ (89) 47 90 16
Open: daily 10am-4pm. Closed during the vintage.

R=red wine   W=white wine   P=rosé wine   S=sparkling wine

Eblin-Fuchs   TW
75 route du Vin
☎ (89) 47 91 14
Open: Monday to Saturday
8am-7pm; Sunday and
public holidays by
appointment. Closed 1-15
September.

Hunawihr
(68150 Ribeauvillé)

Cave Vinicole de
  Hunawihr   TW
☎ (89) 73 61 67
Open: Monday to Friday
9am-noon and 2-6pm from
Easter to 30 September;
weekends and public
holidays 10am-noon and
3-7pm.

David Ermel and son   TW
5 route de Ribeauvillé
☎ (89) 73 61 41
Open: Monday to Friday
8am-7pm; Saturday 9am-
7pm.

Frédéric Mallo and son TW
114 Grand Rue
☎ (89) 73 61 41
Open: Monday to Friday
9am-7pm; Saturday 9am-
5pm.

Ribeauvillé (68150)

Bott brothers   TW
13 ave. de Gaulle
☎ (89) 73 60 48
Open: Monday to Saturday
9am-noon and 2-6pm; Sun-
day by appointment 9am-
noon and 2-5pm.

Cave Coopérative
  de Ribeauvillé   TW
2 route de Colmar
☎ (89) 73 61 80
Open: daily except public
holidays, 9-11am and 2-
5pm.

Robert Fallet and son TW
36 Grand Rue
☎ (89) 73 60 47
Open: Monday to Saturday

8am-6pm; Sunday and pub-
lic holidays by appoint-
ment.

René Joggerst   TW
19 Grand Rue
☎ (89) 73 66 32
Open: daily; closed 15 January to 1 February.

Paul Schwach   TW
30-32 route de Bergheim
☎ (89) 73 62 73
Open: Monday to Friday
8am-noon and 1-7pm; Sat-
urday, Sunday and public
holidays, by appointment
between 2-6pm.

Jean Sipp   TW
60 rue de la Fraternité
☎ (89) 73 60 02
Open: daily 8am-noon and
2-6pm.

Louis Sipp   TWE
5 Grand Rue
☎ (89) 73 60 01
Open: Monday to Saturday
8am-6pm, Sunday and
public holidays 10am-6pm
Easter to September.

AREA BETWEEN RIBEAUVILLE AND BARR

Bergheim (68750)

-Robert Berger and son TW
20 rue des Vignerons
☎ (89) 73 68 22
Open: Monday to Saturday
8am-8pm; Sunday and pub-
lic holidays 9am-8pm.

GAEC Marcel Deiss   TW
15 route du Vin
☎ (89) 73 63 37
Open: Monday to Saturday
8am-noon and 2-6pm; Sun-
day and public holidays
by appointment.

Gustave Lorentz   TWE
35 Grand Rue
☎ (89) 73 63 08
Open: Monday to Friday
8am-5pm; Saturday 9am-
noon.

Rodern
(68590 St-Hippolyte)

Koeberle-Kreyer   TW
28 rue du Pinot Noir
☎ (89) 73 00 55
Open: daily 2-7pm.

Rorschwihr
(68590 St-Hippolyte)

Willy Rolli-Edel   TW
5 rue de l'Eglise
☎ (89) 73 63 26
Open: Monday to Saturday
8am-8pm; Sunday and pub-
lic holidays by appoint-
ment.

St-Hippolyte (68590)

GAEC René Klein   TW
  and son

3 rue Ch. Bléger
☎ (89) 73 00 41
Open: daily, July to
October 8am-7pm; rest of
year by appointment.

René Meyer   TW
14 route du Vin
☎ (89) 73 00 09
Open: daily; restaurant
closed Monday.

Orschwiller
(67600 Sélestat)

Louis Siffert   TW
16 route du Vin
☎ (88) 92 02 77
Open: daily 9am-noon and
2-7pm; closed January and
February.

T=tasting   E=English spoken   G=guided tours   C=château/building to visit

Châtenois (67730)

Désiré Hinterlang   TW
19 rue du Rhin
☎ (88) 82 07 28
Open: daily by appointment between 2-6pm.

Scherwiller (67750)

André Dussourt   TW
2 rue de Dambach
☎ (88) 92 10 27
Open: Monday to Friday 10am-6pm; Saturday 8am-noon, closed during the harvest.

Caveau Winstub
  à l'Ortenbourg   TW
88 rue de la Gare
☎ (88) 92 06 37
Open: daily except Monday 10am-9pm.

Frey-Sohler   TW
72 rue de l'Ortenbourg
☎ (88) 92 10 13
Open: daily 8am-8pm.

Dambach-la-Ville (67650)

Léon Beck   TW
4 rue Clémenceau
☎ (88) 92 43 17
Open: daily 10am-8pm.

Paul Beck and son   TW
1 rue Clémenceau
☎ (88) 92 40 17
Open: Wednesday to Friday 8am-4pm; Saturday 8am-6pm; Sunday and public holidays 2-6pm and by appointment. Closed January.

Cave Vinicole
  de Dambach-la-Ville   TW
☎ (88) 92 40 03
Open: daily 8am-noon and 2-6pm.

Willy Gisselbrecht   TW
and son
route du Vin
☎ (88) 92 41 02
Open: Monday to Friday 8am-6pm; Saturday 9am-5pm; Sunday and public holidays by appointment.

Louis Hauller   TW
Cave du Maître-Tonnellier
(88) 92 rue Foch
☎ (88) 92 41 19
Open: Monday to Friday 9am-noon and 1.30-7pm, and weekends 9am-noon and 2-6pm from 1 May to 30 September. Closed during the harvest.

GAEC Pernet   TW
20 rue de Gaulle
☎ (88) 92 42 17
Open: daily.

Robert Schaeffer   TW
3 place du Marché
☎ (88) 92 40 81
Open: daily; Sunday and public holidays by appointment.

Itterswiller (67140 Barr)

Gérard Sohler   TW
5 route du Vin
☎ (88) 85 51 60
Open: Monday to Saturday 8am-7pm, Sunday and public holidays by appointment.

Nothalten (67680 Epfig)

GAEC Geyer   TW
146 route du Vin
☎ (88) 92 41 80
& (88) 92 46 82
Open: Monday to Friday 11am-1.30pm and 5-8pm; Saturday 10am-8pm; Sunday and public holidays 10am-1pm.

Albe (67220 Ville)

Adrian brothers   TW
☎ (88) 57 12 87
Open: Monday to Friday 10am-7pm, Saturday 10am-6pm, Sunday and public holidays by appointment.

Epfig (67680)

Schmitt R. & G.   TW
299b rue Ste-Marguérite
☎ (88) 85 54 38
Open: Tuesday and Thursday 5-7pm; Saturday, Sunday and public holidays 8am-5pm. Closed during the harvest.

Gertwiller (67140 Barr)

Zeyssolf G. Sarl   TW
☎ (88) 08 90 08
Open: weekends 9am-6pm.

Andlau (67140 Barr)

Domaine Fernand   TW
Gresser-Kreydenweiss
12 rue Deharbe
☎ (88) 08 95 83
Open: daily, by appointment.

Marcel Schlosser   TW
7 rue des Forgerons
☎ (88) 08 03 26
Open: Monday to Saturday 9am-7pm; Sunday and public holidays by appointment.

Mittelbergheim (67140 Barr)

Emile Boeckel   TWE
2 rue de la Montagne
☎ (88) 08 91 02
Open: Monday to Friday 9am-noon and 2-5pm; Saturday 9am-noon; Sunday and public holidays by appointment.

R=red wine   W=white wine   P=rosé wine   S=sparkling wine

GAEC Armand Gilg
and son   TW
☎ (88) 08 92 76
Open: Monday to Friday
8am-noon and 1.30-6pm,
Saturday 8am-noon and
2-4pm.

André Rieffel   TW
11 rue Principale
☎ (88) 08 95 48
Open: Monday to Satur-
day.

Pierre Rietsch   TW
32 rue Principale
☎ (88) 08 00 64
Open: daily 8am-7pm.

A. Seltz and son   TWE
21 rue Principale

☎ (88) 08 91 77
Open: Monday to Friday
8am-6pm; weekends and
public holidays by
appointment.

Barr (67140)

Ed. Hering and son   TW
6 rue Sultzer
☎ (88) 08 90 07
Open: Monday to Friday
9am-7pm; Saturday 9am-
6pm.

Domaine Klipfel   TWE
6 ave. de la Gare
☎ (88) 08 94 85
Open: April-December
daily 10am-noon and
2-6pm; closed December
to March.

Caveau Lorentz-
  Klipfel   WTE
1 rue Rotland
☎ (88) 08 08 63
Open: 10am-noon and
2-6pm.

Charles Wantz   TWE
36 rue St-Marc
☎ (88) 08 90 44
Open: Monday to Friday
8am-6pm; Saturday 8am-
noon.

Alsace Willm   TWE
ave. du Dr-Sultzer
☎ (88) 08 19 11
Open: daily 8am-noon and
2-6pm.

AREA BETWEEN BARR AND MARLENHEIM

Obernai (67210)

C. Divinal   TWE
30 rue Leclerc
☎ (88) 95 61 18
Open: Monday to Thurs-
day 9am-4pm; Friday 9am-
3pm.

J. Paul Seilly   TWF
18 rue Gén. Gouraud
☎ (88) 95 55 80
Open: Monday to Friday
8am-noon and 2-6pm, or
by appointment; weekends
and public holidays by
appointment. Restaurant
open lunchtime and even-
ings daily except Monday.

Molsheim (67120)

GAEC Lucien Neumeyer
and son   TW
19 rue de Gaulle
☎ (88) 38 12 45
Open: Monday to Saturday
8.30am-6pm; Sunday and
public holidays 10am-
4pm.

Bernard Weber   TW
49 rue de Saverne
☎ (88) 38 52 67
Open: Monday to Friday 6-
9pm, Saturday 11am-6pm;
Sunday and public holi-
days by appointment.

Wolxheim
(67120 Molsheim)

J. Arbogast   TW
18 route de Soultz
☎ (88) 38 17 10
Open: Monday to Friday
9am-6pm; Saturday 9am-
5pm; Sunday 9-11am.
Closed for two weeks in
July.

Charles Dischler   TW
23 le Canal
☎ (88) 38 22 55
Open: daily 8am-8pm.

GAEC Muhlberger   TW
1 rue de Strasbourg
☎ (88) 38 10 33
Open: daily 9am-7pm.

Traenheim
(67310 Wasselonne)

Cave Vinicole de Traen-
  heim et environs   TW
☎ (88) 50 66 21
Open: Monday to Friday
9am-noon and 2-5pm; Sat-
urday, Sunday and public
holidays by appointment.

Frédéric Mochel   TW
56 rue Principale
☎ (88) 50 38 67
Open: Monday to Friday
8am-8pm, Saturday 8am-
6pm.

Charles Muller and son TW
42 Impasse de la Fontaine
☎ (88) 50 30 08
Open: Monday to Saturday
8am-6pm; Sunday 11am-
5pm.

Dahlenheim
(67310 Wasselonne)

J. Pierre Bechtold   TW
49 rue Principale
☎ (88) 50 66 57
Open: daily by
appointment.

T=tasting E=English spoken G=guided tours C=château/building to visit

Scharrachbergheim
(67310 Wasselonne)

G. Paul and son   TW
Open: Monday to Friday
9am-noon and 2-7pm.

Marlenheim (67520)

Michel Laugel   TWE
102 rue de Gaulle
☎ (88) 87 52 20

Open: Monday to Friday
9am-4pm.

GAEC Mosbach   TW
10 place Kaufhaus
☎ (88) 87 50 13
Open: Monday to Friday
8am-noon and 2-7pm;
Saturday 8am-noon and 2-
6pm; Sunday and public
holidays 9am-noon.

Cléebourg
(67160 Wissembourg)

Coopérative Viticole de
  Cléebourg et environs TW
BP 77
☎ (88) 94 50 33
Open: Monday to Saturday
8am-5pm; Sunday and
public holidays 9am-5pm.

R=red wine   W=white wine   P=rosé wine   S=sparkling wine

Chapter 8

<u>THE RHONE</u>

Above Tain
Rhône

THE VINEYARDS of the Rhône extend from just below Lyon as far south as Avignon. The vineyards straddle both sides of the river, but not continuously. In the north, the area under vine is a tight belt, rarely more than a few hundred yards wide, but in the south, when the river widens and the valley increases in size, the vineyards stretch themselves out.

The Rhône production area can be divided into two, the north and the south. For many years the north has been the more famous, producing some glorious wines, while the reputation of the south has been upheld by a handful of wines with most of the rest of the production going into heavy, strong reds of no great style. This is no longer the case. While the north still contains the same famous vineyards, the quality of the wine in the south has improved enormously with greater attention to vinification and viticulture.

The north vineyards are hot and rocky. The vines survive on terraces carved out of the steep hillsides. Syrah is the major grape under cultivation and almost all the red wines of the northern Rhône are produced from it. Vines have certainly been grown here since Roman times, and the Greeks, who traded at the mouth of the Rhône at least 2,500 years ago, could well have introduced them. The Greeks established the colony that was to become Marseille, and they planted grapes around the colony. Because of the prosperity of the Greek colony, it was frequently attacked by the Gauls, and a treaty was signed so that Marseille came under the patronage of Rome. The Romans named it Provincia, which gives us the name of Provence today.

Because Provincia was so close to the Roman Empire and the Rhône so navigable, many of the Romans came to settle here, and some of their greatest achievements can still be seen here. They built towns with amphitheatres, spectacular bridges and aqueducts, and roads that still form the framework for much of the travel in the area. The Romans were responsible for founding towns such as Arles, Avignon, Lyon, Orange, Nîmes, Valence and Vienne. You can marvel at the Pont du Gard and try to work out how it could have been built without machinery so many centuries ago.

For five centuries the region prospered under Roman rule until the Empire declined. Although wine production continued, its importance as a trading commodity decreased, and it was used mostly to satisfy local demand. Things looked up again in the ninth century when the influence of the Church began to be felt. As in Burgundy, the churches were given large parcels of vineyards as gifts, and they found themselves the owners of substantial properties in the Rhône.

Wine was not only needed for the sacraments, the monks soon realised that its sale was a valuable source of revenue to help with the upkeep of the monasteries and abbeys. For 600 years the Church and Christendom were to dominate the region. In the year 1305 Bertrand de Got was elected Pope Clément V by the College of Cardinals and he moved the Papal Seat from Rome to Avignon, and there it stayed for the next sixty-five years. During this time there was enormous building work undertaken, not just in Avignon but all around. A palace was built for the Pope, away from Avignon, to which he could retire in comfort, and it is still known today as the Pope's new *château*, Châteauneuf-du-Pape. Because the Papal seat was in Avignon, it was visited by royalty and princes from all over Europe and they drank the local wines. At this time, much of the land around Avignon was planted with vines and production was high. For the next 400 years the wines were shipped to other parts of France, but under a variety of names, often named after the vineyard, the grower, or the town near which they were produced. In 1731, however, some growers got together and decided to use the title 'Côtes du Rhône.' The growers all came from the Gard *département*, and for the next 150 years they marked their barrels with the initials 'CR'. In 1923 the growers in Châteauneuf-du-Pape formed their own rules, and in doing so set a precedent which was one of the major milestones in the history of French winemaking. Their rules about growing and winemaking were to form the basis for the *Appellation Contrôlée* system, and Châteauneuf-du-Pape was the first wine-growing area in France to be awarded this distinction.

Vineyards of the Northern Rhône

The Côte-Rôtie
This is the first vineyard area reached after Lyon. The region gets its name because the grapes are literally roasted in the scorching sun. Syrah is the predominant grape, but is blended with a little Viognier, a white grape widely grown throughout the Rhône. There are two types of soil found in the Côte-Rôtie, although both are mainly granite with chalk and the wine is usually made by blending grapes from both.

There are about 250 acres of vineyards starting just south of the old Roman town of Vienne and centred around five communes. The wines are noted for their rich, ruby colour and soft, fruity nose when mature. They age well and can go on for twenty years and more, and produce some of the best, if not the best wines of the Rhône.

Condrieu
This area is the start of the St-Josèph appellation which stretches southwards for about thirty miles. The vineyards are all on south-facing slopes on the eastern side of the river. Condrieu and its neighbour Château Grillet both make white wines from the Viognier. The wines have very powerful bouquets of fruit and flowers and a golden colour, but they do not travel. They should be drunk young and are an ideal accompaniment to fish and shellfish.

St-Josèph
Although it makes some white wines, St Josèph is more famous for its reds produced from the Syrah grape. They are firm tannic wines, needing three or four years to soften, and should ideally be drunk before they reach their fifth birthday. There are different styles, however, and some will last much longer, while others, being made with a fruitier taste, can be drunk between two and three years old. The St-Josèph *appellation* was only awarded in 1956 and the best wine comes from around the village of Mauves.

Hermitage

Hermitage is perhaps the most famous wine of the northern Rhône, although most drinkers are familiar only with its reds. In the last century, and well into this, however, it was white Hermitage that was sought after and which commanded very high prices. The wines have enormous ageing properties and there are whites from the 1930s that are still quite magnificent. The vineyards of Hermitage extend for 320 acres on the eastern side of the river, on southern-facing slopes, so that they get maximum sunlight. Most of the vineyards are planted with Syrah and the rest with Roussanne and Marsanne, two white grape varieties. The red wine is made mostly from the Syrah grape, with up to 15 per cent Marsanne and Roussanne, and it can be magnificent. It is rich ruby red, with a marvellous warming bouquet reminiscent of violets. It is strong in tannin which allows it to age well. When young the wine has a very dark colour, almost purply-black, and enormous fruit; most people drink the wines young but they are better for ageing. After five years they are good; after fifty, superb.

The white Hermitage is an elegant wine. The best is made only from the Roussanne grape, and the rest a blend of the two white varieties. They are dry and fruity when young but mature into full-bodied, powerful wines with complex bouquets and greatness.

The vineyards hug the hillsides on their terraces, which are too steep for any mechanisation, so all the work has to be carried out by hand. The terraces are retained by dry walls, many of them taller than a man, which date back for centuries. Some are said to date from the Roman times.

Crozes-Hermitage

Crozes-Hermitage is just to the north of Hermitage on the same side of the river, and has its own *appellation*. It grows the same grapes and makes its wine, both red and white, in exactly the same way; but they are not so long-lasting, and the reds lack the finesse of the Hermitages: They also lack the granite soil which is an important ingredient in the makeup of the Hermitage wines. The whites from Crozes-Hermitage can be excellent, however, and they, too, age well.

Cornas

On the west bank of the river is Cornas, about three miles from Hermitage on the opposite bank to Valence. The wine has become very popular in recent years and the acreage is now expanding. Cornas is a very powerful wine, similar to Hermitage, but not so complex or refined. It also needs years of ageing before it is at its best. The vineyards of Cornas mark the southern limit of red wine-making in the northern Rhône.

St-Péray

St-Péray which borders Cornas on the western bank of the Rhône, is noted for its white and sparkling wines. The sparkling wine is made from the Roussanne and Marsanne grapes, using the *méthode Champenoise*. It is a re-markable wine, full-bodied, with lots of fruit and a nutty flavour if allowed to age. The white of St-Péray is similar to those of Hermitage; a pale, almost straw-coloured wine with a refreshing acidity and fruity bouquet, again reminding one of violets. It can be drunk young, or allowed to age gracefully for a few years.

The Vineyards of the Southern Rhône

Châteauneuf-du-Pape
This is the most celebrated *appellation* within this huge grape-growing area which covers more than 82,000 acres between Montélimar in the north and Avignon in the south. Folklore has it that the first vines were planted on the stony ground around the château after Pope Clément took up residence at his new palace, but no-one really knows when viticulture began. There are records of the wines being drunk locally for centuries, but it was after the Napoleonic wars and the opening up of the country by canals and then railways, that the fame of the wines of Châteauneuf-du-Pape began to spread.

Unfortunately, because the wine became so popular in the first decades of this century, many other growers cashed in on its success by calling their own wines Châteauneuf-du-Pape. This forced the genuine growers of the wine to take action, and in 1923 they drew up rules to try to protect their wine and its reputation. These rules formed the framework on which the AC system was developed.

Châteauneuf-du-Pape must now come from a 7,400 acre area around the village, and the method of vine growing, pruning, harvesting, yields and wine-making are all strictly controlled. The vines are squat and surrounded by huge, flat stones to trap the heat from the sun during the day, and release it at night. Slightly unusual is the number of grape varieties allowed to be grown under the *appellation*. Up to thirteen varieties are allowed, and each grower has his own favourite blend, but Grenache is by far the most preferred variety, followed by Cinsault, Syrah, Mourvèdre and the white Clairette and Picpoul. A little white wine is produced, and some of this is now being made by the *macération carbonique* method but this is not typical. The white Châteauneuf is a powerful, full-bodied, dry wine.

White grapes are also added to the red wines, to rub off the rough edges, and the finished product, which legally must have at least 12.5° of natural alcohol, often has 14° and more — one reason why so many people think of Rhône wines as heady.

The typical Châteauneuf-du-Pape red is a big, powerful, warm fruity wine that needs years to develop fully. There is a new style of producing lighter wines, ready to drink earlier, but many of these are disappointing. The best reds go on for decades, but they are usually at their best between five and ten years old when they make the ideal accompaniment for red meats, game and many cheeses.

Côtes du Rhône-Villages
This comprises seventeen communes, and covers about 8,000 acres. The great mass of Côtes du Rhône wine is red or rosé; standards vary enor-

mously, although great efforts have, and are being made constantly to improve quality. The *appellation* was granted in 1967. The wines normally carry the village of origin, and if this is not on the label, the wine is blended from one of the other AC villages. The wines are deep ruby coloured, with a bouquet of fruit, spicy to taste, and full-bodied.

Gigondas
One of the first communes to act to get the Côtes du Rhône-Villages AC was Gigondas and it has since been given its own *appellation*. It produces wines of quality similar to the reds of Châteauneuf-du-Pape. It also makes rosé.

Tavel
This has the reputation of being the best rosé of France. It is made from a blend of up to ten varieties, but Grenache predominates, and can account for all. The wine is strong, often above 12°. Tavel can be drunk as an apéritif or with poultry, white meats, in fact a wide range of dishes. It is a full, fruity wine best drunk between three and five years old.

Lirac
The last *appellation* of the southern Rhône, producing both red, white and rosé. The reds can match those of the Côtes du Rhône-Villages, while the whites tend to lack zest.

Tour of the Rhône Valley

The Rhône valley is a marvellous place to spend a few days because it offers the tourist almost everything from excellent food and drink to spectacular scenery, from majestic castles and antiquities to cathedrals and museums. This tour starts in the northern Rhône, where some of the region's finest wines are to be found.

The wines of the Rhône have been famous for centuries, and the first vines were thought to have been planted by the Greeks who settled at the mouth of the great river in about 600BC. They founded a settlement called Massalia, which has continued to flourish and is today one of France's major ports and trading centres, although it is now known as Marseille.

The Greek vineyards gradually extended inland along the steep river banks. Hermitage and Côte-Rôtie wines have been grown for at least 2,000 years, while their neighbours St-Josèph and Cornas have pedigrees stretching back at least 1,000 years.

The great river was used throughout this time as the natural means of travel inland from the Mediterranean, and became an important trading route. As the Greeks' influence waned and they were forced to leave after attacks from the Gauls, the Romans took over. They named the region Provincia, the origin of Provence. They built most of the towns in Provence, and, especially along the river, they built bridges and fortifications.

Tour of the Northern Rhône

Vienne is the first of the towns south of Lyon. It is about twenty miles south of this great city, and has much to offer. There is the Cathédrale St Maurice, the Temple d'Auguste, Roman theatre, and many fine churches, buildings and museums, as well as sculptures everywhere.

Just across the river from Vienne is the village of Ampuis, famous as the home of one of the world's great red wines, Côte-Rôtie. The vines grow on the sun-drenched slopes of the hill above the village, and the wines are luscious and full, velvety, and with their characteristic bouquet of raspberries. As with most of the vineyards on this northern stretch of the Rhône, the plots are extremely steep and have to be worked by hand, as no machinery could cope with the gradients. A special system of training the vines has been introduced, the Guyot method, to support the plants on the slopes.

Two grapes are used to produce the Côte-Rôtie, the red Syrah, and the white Viognier. The wine is blended, and gets better with age. Many a bottle fifty years old and more has been drunk, still in perfect condition.

From Ampuis, travel to Condrieu, just to the south and at the foot of the hills. Originally the village was known as Coin du Ruisseau, literally 'corner of the river'. Here the river meanders gently past in its travels to the sea, and above the houses, on the hill slopes, are the vineyards producing the famous white wine, made from the Viognier grape, the only one allowed.

The wine has been made certainly since Roman times, although some say it was the Greeks who introduced this variety at least 600 years earlier. Whatever the origin, the Viognier produces a full-bodied, 'earthy' wine. It has a marvellous colour, and a rich, flowery bouquet. Almost all the production is of dry wine and as total yields are always less than one thousand cases a year do not miss the chance of sampling it here.

The next port of call should be to Château Grillet, which with only 7½ acres of vineyards, is the smallest *Appellation Contrôlée* in France. The vineyards are near the village of St-Michel-sur-Rhône, and its château dates back to the reign of Louis XIII when it was a hunting lodge. Since then much has been added. The façade is Renaissance, and some of the walls are three feet thick, showing that defence was an important consideration in this trouble-torn region.

Again, only the Viognier grape is allowed, and the wine spends about eighteen months in oak vats after two months or so on its lees after pressing. This length of time in the vats gives the wine its body, character and amazing colour (or lack of it, because it has virtually none).

Although some of the finest wines are produced in this area from very small vineyards, there is much other wine which is sold as honest to goodness Côtes du Rhône, and this should be sampled to see how it varies as you journey south.

Although Châteauneuf-du-Pape has an international reputation, the wines of Hermitage deservedly get more credit in wine circles. The vineyards are, again, on the very steep and rocky hillsides, and there is enormous rivalry between the growers. There are huge hoardings everywhere saying exactly which family owns which plot.

It is easiest to visit the vineyards of Hermitage and its neighbour Crozes-Hermitage from Valence, another spectacular old Roman town. Valence has many fine restaurants, including the *Pic* in the avenue Victor-Hugo with its three Michelin stars.

Also in Valence you should visit the cathedral with its magnificent interior, the Champ de Mars and the museums, including a motoring museum just outside town. The vineyards of Hermitage are just a few miles north of Valence and overlooking the town of Tain l'Hermitage which lies on the east bank of the Rhône. On the opposite bank is the town of Tournon.

The two largest producers of Hermitage are the families of Jaboulet and Chapoutier, and these two in particular battle it out to erect the biggest sign, or have their names painted in the largest letters on the walls that cut through the vineyards supporting the terraces.

Tain is the home of many of the *négociants*, and they continue a practice which has been conducted since Roman times when the commune was known as Tegna. The vineyards of Hermitage are certainly the oldest in France and were planted with the Syrah vines at least 600 years before Christ. How the wines got their name is not certain, but there is a story of a knight, Gaspard de Sterimberg, who, bored with the court of Castille, retired to live in seclusion on top of the hill above Tain. He built his hut at the summit of the 1,000ft-high hill on the site of an old Roman temple, and a small chapel still marks the spot today. Locals claim it was he who planted the Syrah vines, but while it is a nice story, it is not true.

Hermitage red is a marvellous full-bodied wine that changes its character as it ages. It can be drunk relatively young, after five years, but it will keep for decades, growing more elegant with age. Less well known are the Hermitage whites, which again have great staying power. They are big wines, full and fruity but with elegance.

While visitors are not looked upon too kindly during the harvest and in the early days of the winemaking, it is a fascinating place to visit at this time. Hermitage is one of the few places left where the grapes are still traditionally trodden by foot, at least in the first stages of pressing.

While Hermitage wines come from the hill, the Crozes-Hermitage wines are restricted to eleven villages around Tain. It is a useful experience being able to taste both the Hermitage and the Crozes-Hermitage within a short time to spot the difference between the two. While both *appellations* use the same grapes for their reds and whites, and the same method of winemaking, there is a difference; the Hermitage has a discernible class that its neighbour lacks.

While exploring this area, take a look at the bridge joining Tain and Tournon. Although no longer open to traffic, it has won its place in the history books because it was the world's first modern suspension bridge, built in 1826 by the French engineer Seguin. While Tain is busy and plain, Tournon is pretty and bubbly, with a sixteenth-century fort above it.

Around Tournon, on the west of the river, are the vineyards that make up the St-Josèph *appellation*, which was only awarded in 1956. Although the vineyards face those of Hermitage, the wines are different because the St-

Josèph red must be made wholly from Syrah. The St-Josèph vineyards are centred on Tournon and it is the village of Mauves, which produces the best wines. The whites are delicate and long-lasting, with a lovely fruity nose, while the reds are dark-coloured, but surprisingly light and fruity. They are not as long-lasting as their neighbours and should be drunk between two and seven or eight years old.

Two other *appellations* deserve a visit while exploring this part of the Rhône; these are Cornas and St-Péray. The villages lie side by side on the west bank of the Rhône opposite Valence. Cornas produces red wines entirely from the Syrah grape, while St-Péray is better known for its white wines, both still and sparkling.

Cornas is a charming, peaceful village, overshadowed by its neighbour Valence across the water. The Emperor Charlemagne visited Cornas in 840 and he is said to have been impressed by the wines. Today the red wines come from the grapes grown on the hill slopes behind the village. The slopes are very steep and because everything has to be done by hand, many of the vineyards have fallen into disrepair. Although there is the potential for extending the acreage under vine under the *appellation*, it appears that the labour is not available because people prefer either easier agricultural jobs on the fruit farms, or jobs in the towns. This is a shame, because the wine has many of the qualities of good Hermitage but at a fraction of the price. It is a wine for keeping and it develops into a big, full-bodied drink. The best vintages need to be kept at least ten years.

St-Péray is the most southerly of the northern Rhône vineyards. Its white wine was mentioned in the writings of two Roman historians, and in more recent times it has been praised by many celebrities including the young Napoléon Bonaparte (who discovered it while stationed as a cadet in Valence), Lamartine, Alphonse Daudet, Guy de Maupassant and Richard Wagner. The St-Péray sparkling wine is made by the *méthode Champenoise*, and even gets its yeasts sent down by train from Champagne. The sparkling wine usually has more body than Champagne, and a fruity, flowery style. It is much sought after, as is the still white, which is similar to the whites of Hermitage.

Tour of the Southern Rhône

The next stage of the tour takes us to the vineyards of the special Rasteau *vin doux naturel*, Beaumes-de-Venise, Gigondas and the spectacular town of Orange. The hillsides, which pressed in close to the river a few miles further north, have now been pushed back, and the Rhône now makes its way through a constantly widening plain.

In Orange there are a number of good hotels and many restaurants, and you should visit the Roman theatre and the impressive Arc de Triomphe. A short time should be allowed to explore the town before setting out for the vineyards, because while this section of the Rhône does not have the greatest wines, it does have some of the most interesting. About 12 miles north west of Orange on the N575 is Rasteau. It is noted for its *vin doux naturel*, made mostly from Grenache. Although it has its own *appellation* it is one of the least known of French wines, even inside France. It is a big, strong, grapey wine, which is very popular in the bars of the region. The wine is made in the same way as port, and is not to everyone's taste, but it should be tried and the visit to Rasteau is interesting, if only to see the communal wash-house where the women gather all day it seems, to scrub their family's laundry. Much of the area is planted with vineyards producing grapes for Côtes du Rhône-Villages wines. Rasteau is one of the seventeen villages allowed this *appellation*.

From the full-bodied reds of Rasteau and Cairanne, it is best to travel south to Beaumes-de-Venise, the home of one of France's best fortified sweet wines, and one that is becoming increasingly popular with British consumers. Because of its high alcoholic strength, about 21 per cent, the fortified wines are taxed more heavily abroad, but the vineyard area has increased over the last thirty years to meet growing demand which has helped maintain prices.

Beaumes is another Roman village, and became established early on as a spa centre because of the sulphur springs at Montmirail. There have been many archaeological digs in the area, uncovering Roman swimming pools and plumbing, and above the village a sculpture was discovered depicting winemaking and the treading of the grapes.

Beaumes is made from the Muscat grape and its chief characteristics are a mouth-filling lusciousness, lots of fruit and a long, lingering aftertaste. It has a glorious golden colour, great sweetness and bouquet and is in every way special. Just to the west is its neighbour Vacqueyras, and between the two is the church of Notre-Dame d'Aubune, overlooking the *cave coopérative* and built on the site where, in the eighth century, the Saracens were defeated by the Gauls. The surrounding hills are filled with caves, and the Saracens are said to have taken refuge in these for months after the battle. Beaumes actually gets its name from an old Provence word meaning grotto, and every year on 8 September there is a pilgrimage to the church to commemorate the victory.

Between Rasteau and Beaumes, close to Mont Ventoux, is Gigondas on the east bank of the river, and home of a very fine red wine. A derelict seventeenth-century château looks out over the sleepy village which is surrounded by vineyards. There is a café and tasting centre, and most of the private domaines are built on the sites of Roman villas. There are about thirty private estates, two large *négociants* and a good *cave coopérative*. The area is steeped in Roman history and it is thought that Roman officers chose Gigondas to retire to after seeing service in Orange.

Wine has been made through the centuries and the nuns at the abbey of St André by the River Ouvèze were producing the typical, deep, heavy reds when the Popes arrived in Avignon in the fourteenth century. The wines, heady and almost black, are complex and not for the casual drinker. There is also a very drinkable rosé.

Return to Orange and cross the river to Chusclan and Laudun, two villages producing good wines on the west banks. Chusclan is about seven miles from Orange and produces rosés. The winemaking tradition dates to Roman times, although Benedictine monks established many of the vineyards that now surround the village. The best rosé, the Cuvée de Marcoule, is named after the nearby atomic power station, but red wine production has massively overtaken it in recent years to cash in on the popularity of Côtes du Rhône wines abroad. The rosés are fruity, clean and dry and meant to be drunk young while the reds tend to be soft, fruity and warm and should be drunk in the first few years of their lives. There is some cold fermented wine, clean and fresh and very refreshing.

Laudun is one of the oldest Côtes du Rhône villages and earthen wine jars dating back to the third century BC have been found on the flat hilltop above it, known as the Plateau du Camp de César. There are now three *cave coopératives* producing red, white and rosé. The white is fresh and light and elegant, and one of the best to be found in this region, while the rosé can also be very good. The reds are warm, and fruity with a touch of spiciness and well balanced.

Although one has to detour to visit Laudun, it is worth the effort to see this old town, now spreading outwards as new houses are built to accommodate the workers who commute to Orange.

The next point of call is to Châteauneuf-du-Pape, probably the most widely known of all the Côtes du Rhône wines. This part of Provence came into its own in the year 1305, when Bertrand de Got was elected by the College of Cardinals as the new Pope — Pope Clément V. His first decision, to end the feuding in Rome, was to move the seat of the Papacy to his native France. Avignon became the new seat of power for the Roman Church, and for the next few decades there was feverish activity both in and around the city. New buildings, churches, and palaces were built, bridges were constructed and the vineyards prospered.

Because summer in Avignon was hot and oppressive, the Pope decided to build a summer palace. He chose a spot about ten miles upstream from Avignon, on a plateau overlooking the river, and as it was the Pope's new palace it was known as Châteauneuf-du-Pape. The palace was built on the site of a castle destroyed in 1248. It took fifteen years to build and was completed in 1333, a year before Pope John's death. Today, little remains of the Pope's summer palace, apart from a tower and some walls, but the village itself is fascinating, and there are many vineyards to visit and wines to taste.

Vines already grew in the area and it is not certain whether it was Pope Clément, or his successor John XXII, who developed the vineyards and discovered that the stony ground had the right properties for producing truly great wines. While the reign of the Popes in Avignon only lasted for sixty or so years, the vineyards have survived and prospered.

The production of Châteauneuf-du-Pape wines is strictly controlled. Two hundred years ago it was sold as *vin d'Avignon* and shipped all over the world, with good markets in both Britain and the United States. The wine started to be sold as Châteauneuf during the last century, and the growers, determined to improve standards and prevent imitators, drew up a set of rules in 1923 for growing and winemaking. In effect this was the first French area to receive an *appellation*, and when the national government decided in 1936 to set up its own wine controlling body, it modelled it on the rules laid down in Châteauneuf-du-Pape.

Most of the production is red, and these wines are full and powerful, with a sparkling red colour and strong violet-smelling nose. The best vintages can be drunk after a dozen years or more, but most of the reds should be drunk before this. There is also a white, which accounts for about 2 per cent of total production. It is exported but is not commonly found, so worth trying. The wines are fruity, with a yellow tint, dry but well-balanced, and they develop with age in the bottle.

To the west of Châteauneuf, and across the river using the N576 you will find Tavel, which produces one of the best rosés in France. Like Lirac, just to the north, which also produces rosés, Tavel is no more than a hamlet, a scattering of buildings in a rather austere landscape. The wines are anything but austere, however, and are light, fruity and full-bodied. At their best after two or three years, they are ideal for summer drinking and go well with buffets, barbecues and picnics.

There are two villages worth exploring while in the area. First is Roquemaure, named after a fort built by the Saracens which has long since vanished. History records that it was here that Hannibal floated his elephants across the Rhône on rafts.

The other village to seek out is Villeneuve-lès-Avignon which dates back to at least the thirteenth century. Many of the nobles attending the Papal court at Avignon chose to build their summer houses here. There are many fine old buildings as well as the imposing fort, the Fort St André, and several excellent eating establishments.

The last day should really be spent exploring the enormous treasures Avignon has to offer. Its wealth is overwhelming, from the splendour of the Popes' palace, the impressive city defences, the famous bridge, and the buildings. Among the things to be seen are: the Palais des Papes, Pont St Bénézet, the ramparts and fortifications, the palace gardens, the cathedral with its cupola, church of St Pierre, the frescoes in the church of St Didier and the museums of the Petit Palais, Calvet, Lapidaire and Louis Vouland.

PLACES OF INTEREST IN THE RHONE VALLEY

VIENNE TO VALENCE

Ampuis
Sixteenth-century château.

Annonay
César-Fihol Museum.

Condrieu
Maison de la Gaselle.

La Chapelle-Villars
Château, viewing point, regional natural history park.

Peaugrès
Safari park.

St-Cye-sur-Rhône
Château de Monlis

St-Michel
Picturesque village and viewing point.

St-Romain-en-Gal
Gallo-Roman excavations.

Serrières
Museum of batellerie.

Tain l'Hermitage
Roman ruins (Taurobole),

St Christopher's chapel, chapel of the Comtes de Larnage.

Tournon-sur-Rhône
Museum of the Rhône, Château de

Tournon, miniature railway.

Valence
Museum, St Apollinaire cathedral, Maison de Têtes, place des Clercs.

VALENCE TO BEAUMES-DE-VENISE

Beaumes-de-Venise
Ruins of the château and fortified walls, Grotte d'Ambrosi, necropolis.

Bollène
The troglodyte cave village of Barry, eleventh-century collegiate church of St Martin.

Bouchet
Abbaye du Bouchet.

Cairanne
Neolithic sites, Gallo-Roman excavations.

Gigondas
Fortifications.

Lagarde Paréol
Roman town.

Malaucène
Fourteenth-century church with old organ, belfry and chapel.

Mirabel-aux-Baronnies
Vantage point.

Mondragon
Château ruins, twelfth-century chapel.

Mornas
Château-fort-vantage point.

Nyons
Ancient city with château dating back to the seventh century.

Roaix
Neolithic site, traces of the Knights Templar's presence in the area.

Rochégude
Eighteenth-century château hotel.

Sablet
Ramparts, twelfth-century church, fourteenth-century chapel.

Ste-Cécile-les-Vignes
Ancient fortress, seventeenth-century cellars, Pont de l'Ouvèze (1647) Château d'Eau (1745), chapel of St Martin de Jussan, eleventh-century.

Séguret
Picturesque village.

Sérignan
Museum of national entomology.

Suze-la-Rousse
University of Wine, medieval château.

Vaison-la-Romaine
Medieval village and Gallo-Roman excavations.

NYONS TO AVIGNON

Avignon
Palais des Papes, ramparts, museums, churches, bridge of St Bénèzet, the Rhône.

Châteauneuf-du-Pape
Ancient village, ruins of the fourteenth-century Pope's palace.

Orange
Ancient Roman theatre, Arc de Triomphe (first-century).

Richerenches
Historic site, former home of the Knights Templars.

Sarrians
Eighteenth-century château. Seventeenth-century chapel.

Valréas
Old village with old château and church.

Visan
Notre-Dame des Vignes.

Gastronomy of the Rhône and Provence

Because of its geographical position, the northern Rhône valley below Lyon has little agriculture in the steeply sloping hills, although goats graze and olive trees grow. Where the valley broadens a little there are orchards, but the region, both north and south, relies heavily on its neighbours for much of its agricultural produce. In the north, the gastronomy is really an extension of that of Lyon, while in the south it is heavily influenced by the Provençale cuisine, although it has fine vegetables. There is, of course, the Rhône itself, and this provides a wide range of fish and allows access to the catches of the Mediterranean beyond.

In the northern part of the Rhône, the Lyonnais influence means rich foods, truffles and cream, excellent *charcuterie*, poultry and beef. In the south, where the river broadens out into the fertile Rhône valley, there are market gardens and orchards and citrus groves, although most of these are below Avignon and really in Provence.

The Greeks introduced the olive tree into the region, and it was widely planted outside their Marseille settlement. Even today, olive oil dominates the cuisine of the south, and the particularly succulent olives are used as an accompaniment to many dishes. The term *à la Provençale* means with tomatoes, garlic and olives.

Many of the shallow lakes of the Camargue, in the Rhône estuary, have been taken over for agricultural purposes and are now rice fields. This area of France is one of Europe's largest producers of rice, which also figures prominently in the cuisine of the southern Rhône.

The other major ingredient used in the south is fish, and there are marvellous soups, fish stews (*bouillabaise*) and a wide range of fish dishes offered on most menus. Garlic, too, figures heavily in the cuisine, and the farther east you travel, towards the Italian border, the more important the role of pasta becomes in cooking. In the northern Rhône, meals are large — many courses and big helpings.

Having already described the gastronomy of the Lyonnais (in the Beaujolais section) which accounts for many of the dishes of the northern Rhône, it is worth mentioning the mouthwatering *écrevisses*, crayfish or large freshwater prawns. They can be served in a host of ways but are always delicious. *Gratin de queues d'écrevisses* is one speciality, crayfish from the Rhône cooked in a sauce with cream and crayfish butter and then browned.

In the south, there are many regional dishes, mostly *à la Provençale*, and many use the herbs which abound. The lamb is excellent, and of course the fish. Also in the south of the Rhône you will find many dishes involving *aïgo*, which is garlic soup, usually poured over bread. There are many variations. *Aïgo bouido* is garlic soup with egg and oil and cubes of fried bread, and *aïgo à la ménagère* is a garlic soup with onion, leeks, tomatoes and poached egg. There is also *aïgo sau* (or *sou*), a fish and garlic stew served with potatoes.

Aïoli also figures prominently in the cuisine. It is a mayonnaise flavoured with garlic, to which can be added breadcrumbs and even cooked seaweed.

In Provence, it is often called *beurre de Provence*.

Fish dishes naturally figure prominently on menus. There are *anchois* (anchovies), which can be served either fresh or in brine, and *catigou*, a Camargue speciality of eels stewed in red wine with tomatoes and garlic. *Bouillabaisse* is the region's most famous dish, although it originated in Marseille. It is basically a fish stew although the recipe can vary enormously. It should contain conger eel and gurnard, and may contain John Dory, monkfish, red mullet, and many others. Often shellfish are added as well as garlic, saffron, herbs and sometimes orange peel. It is almost always served with *aïoli*, or another hot mix that can be added to the stew to taste. Exercise care, however, and add the paste sparingly; it can sometimes be very hot. There is a simpler version of this dish, appearing on menus as *bourride*. Other fish dishes include *boutargue*, a paste made from dried and salted roe, usually tuna or mullet; and *brandade de morue*, a Nîmes speciality of salt cod served with olive oil, garlic and cream. *Pissala* is an anchovy purée, and not to be confused with *pissaladière*, an onion, olive, anchovy and tomato tart. There is also *poupetan*, a creamy fish pâté, sometimes served with cheese; and *loup*, sea bass which is often grilled with fennel, or cooked over fennel twigs and then flambéed.

The region has many different styles of cooking, reflected in the 'à la' after many dishes. There is *à la Arlésienne*, which means cooked with tomatoes and onions, olives and potatoes or rice. *Salade Arlésienne* consists of potato, tomatoes, olives, artichokes and anchovies. *Soupe Arlésienne* is made with chick peas and spinach, with pasta and cheese.

There is a special type of artichoke (*artichaut*) grown in the southern Rhône and Provence, which is much longer than the normal variety. It also has a purplish colour. *Artichaut à la barigoule* is a traditional dish of artichokes stuffed with ham, onions, mushroom and garlic, and cooked in oil and wine.

Many dishes are cooked *à la Camarguaise*, which means with wine, tomatoes, garlic, herbs and black olives. Brandy and orange peel can also be added. There is also a special variety of small, sweet fig called *bargencote*, grown in Provence and added to many dishes.

Vegetable dishes include *aigrossade*, a dish of chick peas and other vegetables served with *aïoli*; while *anchoïade* is another anchovy paste with garlic and oil, usually served with toast or raw vegetables.

Meat is popular, although stews and casseroles are sensible choices as the beef can sometimes be tough. *Bedau* is the Provençale word for tripe, and can be delicious, as can *broufado*, a beef and onion stew with capers and anchovies. Meat dishes can be accompanied by *capouns*, cabbage stuffed with sausage, rice and cheese. It can also be eaten on its own, as can *ratatouille*, another Provence speciality, made from aubergine, tomato, onion, courgette and peppers all cooked together in oil.

Other meat dishes include *chacha*, the local name for a thrush. It is considered to be a delicacy, and can be used to make a pâté, casseroled, or braised and served whole. There is *pieds et paquets*, sheep's tripe and sheep's trotters in a white wine sauce with tomatoes, and *reguigneu*, fried uncured ham.

Many dishes are known by their local names which could cause confusion, so watch out for *claougeou*, the Provence name for squid; *clovisse*, a local name for clam; and *contar*, one of the many local names for snails. Other names for snails include *banarut*, *bajaina*, *limace* and *escourgol*. *Escargot à la sucarelle* is a dish of snails cooked with garlic, tomatoes, sausage and wine. Another local name is *esquinado à l'huile*, a dish of spider crab which is puréed and served cold.

Other dishes include *gargaméu*, tomato omelette, and *mesclun*, a mixed green salad of lettuce, dandelion leaves, chicory, fennel and other herbs. Special breads include *marette*, usually served with *bouillabaisse*, and *pan bagna*, a French loaf soaked in olive oil with a filling of anchovies, tomato, olives and onion.

To accompany the various dishes you might come across the following sauces: *rayte*, a red wine and tomato sauce with garlic and chopped nuts, usually served with fish, and *rouille*, a mayonnaise, pepper and garlic hot sauce sometimes served with fish instead of *aïoli*.

There are a number of cheeses of the region worth trying including *Annot*, a soft mild cheese made from either sheep's or goat's milk, also called *Tomme d'Annot*; and *Banon*, a mild cheese wrapped in chestnut leaves which can be made from the milk of cow, sheep or goat. Other cheeses include *Brousse*, an unsalted cream cheese from sheep or goat's milk, served with fruit; *Picodon*, small goat's milk cheese, delicate, made near Valréas; *Poivre d'Ane*, the same as *Banon* except that it is made with the herb savory, and *Tomme de Camargue* (also *Tomme Arlésienne*) a creamy, herby sheep's milk cheese.

HOTELS AND RESTAURANTS OF THE RHONE VALLEY

Les Angles
(30400 Gard)

Le Petit Manoir
chemin de la Pinède
☎ (90) 25 03 36
A comfortable, inexpensive hotel, with 40 pleasant rooms, good value restaurant, swimming pool, terrace.

Ermitage-Meissonnier
route de Nîmes, at
  Bellevue on the D900
☎ (90) 25 41 02
☎ (90) 25 41 68 (Restaurant)
A small, very comfortable 16-room hotel in delightful gardens. Excellent restaurant with many local specialities, quite expensive; a very fine wine list.

Arles
(13200 Bouches-du-Rhône)

Hôtel d'Arlatan
26 rue du Sauvage
☎ (90) 96 56 66
A 500-year-old building in old Arles, this 46-room medium-price hotel has a high reputation for its service and friendliness. Charming garden, no restaurant, but breakfast served.

La Roseraie
at Pont-de-Crau, 1¼ miles
  south-east on the N453
☎ (90) 96 06 58
A good base from which to tour. This modest 11-bedroom hotel in lovely gardens is comfortable and inexpensive. No restaurant, but breakfast.

Hôtel Jules César
blvd des Lices
☎ (90) 93 43 20
Very central, but secluded in its own garden, Arles' top hotel, a former convent, has 61 very comfortable, not too expensive rooms, and its restaurant, *Lou Marquès*, is rightly praised for its Provençale cuisine. Advisable to book in high season. Very good wine list.

Hôtel Mireille
place St Pierre
☎ (90) 93 70 74
A pleasant 35-room hotel
with swimming pool and
fair restaurant near the old
town. All prices reason-
able.

La Vaccarès
place du Forum
☎ (90) 96 06 17
A tremendous marriage of
very traditional Proven-
çale and *nouvelle cuisine*.
Good value.

Avignon
(84000 Vaucluse)

Hôtel d'Europe
12 place Crillon
☎ (90) 82 66 92
A 400-year-old hotel in
which Napoléon once
stayed. Inside the old city
walls, very central. Very
elegant hotel with 53
good, but fairly expensive
rooms. The restaurant, La
Vieille Fontaine, is charming and the food and wine
lists are good and not
expensive.

Bristol Terminus
44 cours Jean-Jaurès
☎ (90) 82 21 21A large
central hotel with 91
inexpensive rooms. No
restaurant, but breakfasts.

Sofitel
Pont d'Avignon
☎ (90) 85 91 23
3 miles out of town, a
modern 89-room hotel
with air conditioning,
swimming pool and good
views. The restaurant, Le
Majoral, is good, reason-
able and more adventurous
than most hotels.

Hôtel Mercure
route de Marseille
☎ (90) 88 91 10
Pool, 100 good rooms,
café for snacks.

Brunel
46 rue de la Balance
☎ (90) 85 24 83
Elegant restaurant, marvellous food, very good
prices.

Hiély
5 rue de la République
☎ (90) 86 17 07
Avignon's best restaurant,
very popular, so reserve.
Everything always of the
highest standard. Expen-
sive but excellent value.

Le Vernet
58 rue Josèph-Vernet
☎ (90) 86 64 53
A very elegant restaurant,
with two young but excit-
ing chefs. An exciting,
modern cuisine based on
traditional dishes and ingredients. Very reasonable
prices.

Baix (07210 Ardèche)

La Cardinale
on N86, 5 miles south of
the A7 Loriol exit
☎ (75) 85 80 40
A charming hotel in its
own grounds on the banks
of the Rhône, with an
annexe 1^1/4 miles down the
road. Swimming pool.
Altogether 15 rooms and
apartments, expensive but
luxurious. Very reasonably-
priced, good restaurant.

Les Baux-de-Provence
(13520 Bouches-du-Rhône)

Oustaù de Baumanière
☎ (90) 97 33 07
An exquisite restaurant

below the historic, atmospheric Les Baux. Very
expensive and booking is
essential, but worth it to
try one of France's best
restaurants. There are also
26 fairly expensive rooms
with swimming pool,
tennis and riding.

La Benvengudo
On the D78F 1^1/4 miles
south-west of village
☎ (90) 54 32 50
An old, large house with
18 very comfortable, but
well-priced rooms, and excellent value dinners. No
lunches served. Swimming
and tennis and attractive
gardens.

La Cabro d'Or
Val d'Enfer
☎ (90) 54 33 21
Very comfortable, medium-
priced 22-room hotel and
very good restaurant
owned by the Oustaù de
Baumanière people. Good
value.

La Riboto de Taven
☎ (90) 54 34 23
A delightful restaurant in a
super, shaded garden.
Quite expensive but a wonderful place for the many
specialities of the region.

Charmes-sur-Rhône
(07800 Ardèche)

La Vieille Auberge
on the N6
☎ (75) 60 80 10
A delightful inn with good
views. Good, reasonably-
priced restaurant, 7 rooms
also good value, and air
conditioning.

Châteaubourg
(07130 Ardèche)

Hostellerie du Château
6^1/4 miles north of Valence
☎ 40 33 28

A friendly, good restaurant with fine wine list, and not expensive.

Châteauneuf-du-Pape
(84230 Vaucluse)

La Mule du Pape
place de la Fontaine
☎ (90) 83 73 30
Marvellous local food. Menus very good value, wine list good but pricey.

Hostellerie des Fines
  Roches
on the D17 1¼ miles
  south-east
☎ (90) 83 70 23
A magnificent hotel on a hill overlooking the vineyards. 7 magnificent rooms, not at all expensive. The restaurant good and inexpensive; breakfast served on the terrace.

Condrieu (69420 Rhône)

Beau Rivage
2 rue du Beau-Rivage
☎ (74) 59 52 24
A lovely hotel by the Rhône with 24 large, comfortable, inexpensive rooms. Very good restaurant run by Mme Paulette Castaing, the owner, one of France's top woman chefs. Good wine list, and menu prices are good value.

Donzère
(26290 Drôme)

Roustan
about 7½ miles from
  Montélimar off the NA7
☎ (75) 51 61 27
An 11-room hotel by the river, very reasonably-priced, and with a good, inexpensive restaurant.

Fontvieille
(13900 Bouches-du-Rhône)

Valmajour
22 ave. d'Arles
☎ (90) 97 62 33
A large, comfortable, 32-room hotel, rates reasonable; no restaurant, but breakfast served.

La Regalido
rue Frédéric-Mistral
☎ (90) 97 60 22
A luxurious 13-room hotel, quite expensive but very comfortable. A very good brace of fixed-price menus; cuisine good and exciting but a little pricey.

La Peiriero
ave. des Baux
☎ (90) 97 76 10
Very comfortable new hotel with 40 rooms and lovely views. No restaurant, but breakfast served.

Le Patio
117 route du Nord
☎ (90) 97 73 10
A very good restaurant and creative menus not at all expensive. Many dishes cooked traditionally over vine cuttings.

Gigondas
(81490 Vaucluse)

Les Florets
☎ (90) 65 85 01
A charming 15-room hotel tucked away in the countryside almost a mile from the village. Very good, very cheap restaurant serving splendid local dishes.

Noves
(13550 Bouches-du-Rhône)

Auberge de Noves
2km north of Noves on
  the D28
☎ (90) 94 19 21
A large sprawling inn in its own grounds with tennis, swimming pool and terrace. 20 charming, comfortable and expensive rooms with a restaurant to match.

Orange
(84100 Vaucluse)

Hôtel Louvre et Terminus
89 ave. Frédéric Mistral
☎ (90) 34 10 08
A 34-room, reasonably-priced hotel, comfortable and with an inexpensive restaurant.

Hôtel Arène
place Langes
☎ (90) 34 10 95
No restaurant, but 30 well-priced rooms make this suitable as a touring base. Breakfast served.

Le Pigraillet
Colline St Eutrope
☎ (90) 34 44 25
A delightful restaurant, food excellent, wine list very good and a pool to relax by afterwards.

Orgon
(13660 Bouches-du-Rhône)

Relais Basque
route Nationale
☎ (90) 73 00 39
Closed mid-July to mid-August. Only open for lunch, but good food at reasonable prices.

Rochégude
(26130 Drôme)

Château de Rochégude
☎ (75) 04 81 88

The place to get spoiled.
A château in its own parkland, with heated pool,
tennis and 29 rooms and
apartments, all very expensive. The restaurant is
good and also pricey.

Roches-de-Condrieu
(38370 Isère)

Bellevue
1 quai du Rhône
☎ (74) 56 41 42
The food in the restaurant
in this 19-room hotel,
overlooking the river, is
marvellous and the prices
a bargain. Wine list is
good but expensive, and
the rooms are very reasonably-priced.

Roquemaure
(30150 Gard)

Château de Cubières
route d'Avignon
☎ (66) 50 14 28
   (66) 50 29 33 (res-
   taurant)
Lovely old house in its
own park. 19 very good
value rooms and a warm,
friendly and pleasing
restaurant that looks outside Provence for many of
its dishes.

St-Rémy-de-Provence
(13210 Bouches-du-Rhône)

Château de Roussan
on the Tarascon road, 1¹/₄
   miles out of town
☎ (90) 92 11 63
An eighteenth-century
château with 12 very com-
fortable rooms, expensive
and luxurious. No
restaurant but breakfast
served.

Soleil
ave. Pasteur
☎ (90) 92 00 63
A good base for touring,
15 comfortable, reason-
ably-priced rooms, no
restaurant, but breakfast.

Van Gogh
ave. J. Moulin
☎ (90) 92 14 02
Also recommended as a
touring base. Advisable to
book for one of the 18
comfortable, reasonably-
priced rooms. No
restaurant, but breakfast.

**Hostellerie du Vallon de
   Valrugues**
chemin de Canto Cigalo
☎ (90) 92 04 40
A very comfortable 34-
room hotel, quite
expensive but with fair
restaurant and heated pool.

Le Castelet des Alpilles
6 place Mireille
☎ (90) 92 07 21
The 19 rooms are large,
comfortable and well-
priced, and the restaurant
excellent value for money.
Eat on the terrace.

Château des Alpilles
on the D31, 1¹/₄ miles
   from St-Rémy
☎ (90) 92 03 33
A very peaceful 15-room
hotel in its own park.
Rooms expensive, no
restaurant but some light
meals available by the
pool.

Auberge de la Graio
12 blvd Mirabeau
☎ (90) 92 15 33
10 good rooms in the
centre of town, and a
reasonable restaurant.

Tain l'Hermitage
(26600 Drôme)

Le Commerce
1 ave. République
☎ (75) 08 65 00
A comfortable 48-room
hotel near the station.
Rooms reasonably-priced,
restaurant very reasonable.

Grappe d'Or
13 ave. Jean-Jaurès
☎ (75) 08 28 52
Pleasant restaurant with
terrace and reasonable
prices.

Tavel
(30126 Gard)

Auberge de Tavel
☎ (66) 50 03 41
Everything about this 11-
room hotel is pleasant;
the rooms are attractive
and not expensive, and
the restaurant under patron
chef Bernard Bonnevaux
produces delicious fare at
modest prices.

Hostellerie du Seigneur
place du Tavel
☎ (66) 50 04 26
7 very good value rooms
in this hotel restaurant,
run by Ange and Juliette
Bodo. Restaurant good and
exceptional value.

Valence
(26000 Drôme)

Hôtel 2000
ave. de Romans
☎ (75) 43 73 01
1¹/₄ miles out of town on
   the route Grenoble.
30 pleasant rooms in this
modern hotel, just outside
town. Not expensive; no
restaurant but breakfast
served.

Chabran
on the N7 at Pont de
l'Isère
☎ (75) 84 60 09
Michel Chabran constantly strives for new peaks of perfection in this magnificent restaurant, which is still incredibly good value. His wife Rose is the perfect hostess. There are also 12 delightful, modestly-priced rooms.

Château du Besset
at St-Romain-de-Lerps, 8
  miles to the north-west
☎ (75) 58 52 22
One of the finest hotels to be found anywhere. It oozes luxury and style. 10 rooms, hugely expensive; swimming pool, and marvellous grounds. The restaurant lives up to the high standards; exceptional wine list, immaculate and warm service.

Château de Châteaubourg
at Châteaubourg, 6¼ miles
  north-west on the D86
☎ (75) 40 33 28
Very good value in this ancient château; restaurant and dishes that cannot fail to please. Run by Jean-Marc and Danièle Reynaud; he cooks, she looks after a very fine wine list.

Pic
285 ave. Victor Hugo
☎ (75) 44 15 32
Jacques Pic is another of France's great chefs and his talents have earned him three stars from Michelin. The cooking is

heavenly and the prices deservedly high. There are 5 rooms, much sought-after and expensive.

Novotel
217 ave. de Provence
☎ (75) 42 20 15
A 107-room hotel, comfortable but quite expensive, no restaurant but café and breakfast served.

Vienne
(38200 Isère)

La Résidence de la
  Pyramide
41 quai Riondet
☎ (74) 53 16 46
A very comfortable, reasonably-priced 15-room hotel, no restaurant but breakfast served. If you can, eat at La Pyramide, a short drive away.

Chez Réné
at St-Romain-en-Gal, on
  the right bank of the
  Rhône on the N86
☎ (74) 53 19 72
Lovely classical menus at very good prices. The wine list is good and the restaurant air-conditioned.

La Pyramide
14 blvd Fernand Point
Another of the great names in French cuisine. The restaurant is now run by Mme Point, the widow of the great man. Still worthy of its Michelin two stars. Still an experience and essential to book.

Hostellerie Marais St Jean
at Chonas l'Amballan,
5½ miles away on the N7

☎ (74) 58 83 28
A very comfortable small hotel with 10 good rooms, not expensive, and a reasonable, inexpensive restaurant.

Mercure
at Chasse-sur-Rhône, 5
  miles north on the A7
☎ (78) 73 13 94
A large, very comfortable 115-room hotel. Rooms good but not expensive. Restaurant fair.

**Villeneuve-lès-
  Avignon**
(30400 Gard)

Le Prieuré
place du Chapitre
☎ (90) 25 18 20
An expensive 35-room hotel, with tennis, pool, and attractive gardens. Formerly a priory. Rooms and restaurant expensive.

La Magnaneraie
37 rue du Camp de Bataille
☎ (90) 25 11 11
Another very old house; some parts date back 600 years, with 20 very reasonably-priced rooms. Has terrace, swimming pool and tennis and a reasonable restaurant.

Résidence les Cèdres
39 blvd Pasteur
☎ (90) 25 43 92
A good touring base. A 25-room hotel in its own park. Rooms reasonably-priced, no restaurant but breakfasts. Some of the rooms are in 2 bungalows in the grounds, near the pool.

VINEYARDS OF THE COTES DU RHONE

THE AREA BETWEEN VIENNE AND VALENCE

Ampuis (69240)

Pierre Barge   TW
☎ (74) 56 10 80
Open: daily 9am-noon and
2-7pm.

Bernard Burgaud   TW
☎ (74) 56 11 86
Open: daily 8am-noon
and 2-6pm.

Albert Dervieux   TW
☎ (74) 53 37 75
Open: daily except Sunday
8am-noon and 2-7pm.

André & Louis Drevon TW
☎ (74) 56 11 38
Open: Monday to Saturday
8am-noon and 2-7pm;
Sundays and public
holidays by appointment.

Louis-Francis de
  Vallouit   TW
☎ (74) 56 12 33
Open: daily by
appointment.

Marius Gentaz   TW
☎ (74) 56 10 83
Open: daily by
appointment.

SA Guigal   TW
☎ (74) 56 10 22
Open: Monday to Friday,
except public holidays.

Vidal Fleiry   TW
☎ (74) 56 10 18
Open: Monday to Friday,
except public holidays.

Beaumont-Monteux
(26600)

Caves des Clairmonts   TR
Tain l'Hermitage
☎ (75) 84 61 91
Open: daily except Sunday
and public holidays.

Chavanay (42410)

Chol and son   TR
☎ (74) 59 10 53
Open: daily except
Monday.

Condrieu (69420)

Georges Vernay   TW
1 route Nationale
☎ (74) 59 52 22
Open: daily.

Cornas (07130)

Boissy-Delaygues   TR
quai du Gray St-Péray
☎ (75) 40 37 30
Open: Monday to Friday
except public holidays.

Auguste Clape   TR
St-Péray
☎ (75) 40 33 64
Open: daily.

André Fumat   TR
rue des Bouviers
☎ (75) 40 42 84
Open: daily 8am-8pm.

Marcel Juge   TR
place de la Salle-des-Fêtes
☎ (75) 40 36 68
Open: daily.

Noël Verset   TR
rue de la Couleyre
☎ (75) 40 36 66
Open: daily except Sunday
and public holidays.

Malleval (42410)

Le Caveau de Malleval TR
☎ (74) 59 21 80
Open: daily.

Mauves (07300)

Jean Chave   TR
☎ (75) 08 24 63
Open: daily by
appointment.

Coursodon   TRW
place du Marché
☎ (75) 08 29 27
or (75) 08 18 29
Open: daily.

Pierre Gonon   TR
rue des Launays
☎ (75) 08 07 95
Open: daily by
appointment.

Bernard Gripa   TR
route Nationale 86
☎ (75) 08 14 96
Open: daily except Sunday
and public holidays.

Mercurol (26600)

Cave Collonge   TR
Domaine La Négociale
☎ (75) 08 11 47
Open: daily.

Cave Michelas Robert   TR
Les Châssis Domaine
St-Jemms
☎ (75) 08 33 03
Open: daily.

Desmeure and son   TR
route des Romans
☎ (75) 08 10 56
Open: daily.

La Roche-de-Glun
(26600)

SA Paul Jaboulet   TR
Les Jalets
route Nationale 76
☎ (75) 84 68 93
Open: daily except Sunday
and public holidays.

T=tasting   E=English spoken   G=guided tours   C=château/building to visit

Ruoms (07120)

Vignerons Ardèchois
Ucova   TRP
'Chaussy'
☎ (75) 93 50 55
Open: daily.

St-Désirat (07340)

Cave Coopérative St-
Désirat Champagne TRW
☎ (75) 34 22 05
Open: daily.

St-Jean-de-Muzols
(07300)

Delas brothers   TRW
☎ (75) 08 60 30
Open: daily except Sunday
and public holidays.

St-Marcel-d'Ardèche
(07700)

Yves Terrasse   TR
Domaine du Roure
☎ (75) 04 67 67
Open: daily.

St-Péray (07130)

Jean-Francois Chaboud TS
21 rue Ferdinand-Malet
☎ (75) 40 31 63
Open: daily.

Cotte-Vergne and son   TS
☎ (75) 40 30 43
Open: daily by
appointment.

Darona and son   TS
Les Faures
☎ (75) 40 34 11
Open: daily except public
holidays.

Gilles and son   TS
☎ (75) 40 30 30
Open: Monday to Friday
and Saturday afternoons.

Jean Teysseire   TS
☎ (75) 40 41 36
Open: daily.

St-Pierre-de-Boeuf
(42410)

Alain Paret   TRW
place de l'Eglise
☎ (74) 87 12 09
Open: Friday and Saturday
only.

Tain l'Hermitage
(26600)

Cave Coopérative de TRW
Vins Fins
22 route de Larnage
☎ (75) 08 20 87
Open: daily.

Max Chapoutier   TRW
18 ave. de la République
☎ (75) 08 28 65
Open: Monday to Thurs-
day and Friday afternoon.

Henri Sorrel   TRW
ave. Jean-Jaurès
☎ (75) 08 29 45
Open: daily except public
holidays.

Maison Léon Révol   TRW
place du Taurabole
☎ (75) 08 22 21
Open: daily except week-
ends and public holidays.

Tournon-sur-Rhône
(07300)

Jean-Louis Grippat   TRW
☎ (79) 08 15 51
Open: daily by
appointment.

Vérin (42410)

Château Grillet   TW
Neyret-Gachet
☎ (74) 59 51 56
Open: daily.

THE AREA BETWEEN BOLLENE AND BEAUMES-DE-VENISE

Bouchet (26130)

Abbaye de Bouchet   TRW
☎ (75) 04 83 21
Open: daily, July and
August, closed Saturday
and Sunday for the rest of
year.

Domaine du Petit
Barbaras   TRW
SCEA Feschet and son
☎ (75) 04 80 02
Open: daily.

Beaumes-de-Venise
(84190)

Domaine Les
Bernardines   TRW
Maurin Castaud
quartier Ste-Anne
☎ (90) 62 94 13
Open: Monday to Saturday
except public holidays.

Cave des Vignerons   TRW
☎ (90) 62 94 45
Open: Monday to Saturday
except public holidays.

Domaine de
Coyeux   TRW
Yves Nativelle
☎ (90) 62 99 70
Open: Monday to Friday
except public holidays.

Bollène (84500)

Château de la Croix-
Chabrière   TRW
SCC J-M Gouyet
route de St-Restitut
☎ (90) 30 27 63
Open: Monday to Friday.

R=red wine   W=white wine   P=rosé wine   S=sparkling wine

Cairanne (84290)

Cave des Coteaux   TRPW
☎ (90) 30 82 05
Open: daily.

Domaine du Banvin   TRW
Cave Zanti-Cumino
☎ (90) 30 82 38
Open: Monday to
Saturday, and Sunday
afternoons.

Domaine Brusset   TRW
Caveau du Plan-de-Dieu
☎ (90) 70 91 60
Open: daily.

Domaine Le Bon-ClosTRW
Marcel Richaud
☎ (90) 30 85 25
Open: daily.

Domaine Le Plaisir   TRW
Gérard Pierrefeu
☎ (90) 30 82 04
Open: daily.

Rabasse-Charavin   TRW
Coteaux St-Martin
☎ (90) 30 82 27
Open: Monday to Saturday
and Sunday afternoon.

Société Civile
d'Exploitation Agricole TR
Domaine Rieu-Hérial
☎ (90) 30 82 02
Open: Monday to Friday.

Gigondas (84190)

Les Celliers Amadieu   TR
La Payouse
☎ (90) 65 84 08
Open: daily.

Domaine Raspail-Ay   TR
François Ay
☎ (90) 65 85 05
Open: Monday to Friday
and Saturday afternoon.

Domaine Gour de
Chaulé   TR
Beaumet
☎ (90) 65 85 62
Open: daily.

GAEC Domaine du
Pesquier   TR
R. Boutière and son
☎ (90) 65 86 38
Open: Monday to Saturday
and Sunday afternoon.

Domaine Les Goubert   TR
Jean-Pierre Cartier
☎ (90) 65 86 38
Open: daily.

Georges Faraud and son TR
Domaine du Cayron
☎ (90) 65 86 71
Open: daily.

GAEC Domaine
St-Gayan   TR
Jean Pierre and Roger
Meffre
☎ (90) 65 86 33
Open: daily.

Moulin de la Gardette
Caveau St-Vincent   TR
Laurent M. Meunier
☎ (90) 65 85 18
Open: Monday to Saturday
except public holidays.

La Cave des Vignerons
de Gigondas   TR
☎ (90) 65 86 27
Open: daily.

Château du Trignon   TR
SCEA Charles Roux
and sons
☎ (90) 36 40 27
Open: Monday to Friday
except public holidays.

Domaine Les Pallières   TR
SCEA Hilarion Roux
and sons
☎ (90) 65 85 07

Open: Monday to Friday
and Saturday afternoons,
except public holidays.

Lafare (84190)

Domaine de Cassan   TW
SCIA St-Christophe
☎ (90) 62 96 12
Open: daily.

**Mirabel-aux-
Baronnies** (26110)

GAEC Domaine de la
Taurelle   TRPW
Mme Claude Roux and son
☎ (75) 27 12 32
Open: daily.

Mondragon (84430)

Domaine de la
Guicharde   TR
François Biscarrat
Hameau de Derboux
☎ (90) 30 17 84
Open: Monday to Saturday
except public holidays.

Domaine Brun-Hypays TR
quartier le Grès
☎ (90) 30 15 42
Open: daily.

Cave des Vignerons   TR
route Nationale 7
☎ (90) 30 09 05
Open: Monday to Saturday
except public holidays.

Nyons (26110)

Coopérative Agricole
du Nyonsais   TRPW
place Ode-Serre
☎ (75) 26 03 44
Open: Monday to
Saturday.

Rochégude (26130)

Coopérative Vinicole   TR
☎ (75) 04 81 84
Open: daily.

T=tasting   E=English spoken   G=guided tours   C=château/building to visit

Piolenc (84420)

Domaine de Chanabas TRW
M. Robert Champ
☎ (90) 70 43 59
Open: Monday to Saturday
except public holidays.

Sablet (84100)

Caveau Le Gravillas   TR
☎ (90) 36 94 83
Open: Monday to Saturday
except public holidays.

Cellier des Voconces   TR
☎ (90) 36 93 24
Open: Monday to Friday
except public holidays.

Domaine de Verquière   TR
GAEC Chamfort brothers
☎ (90) 36 90 11
Open: daily.

Domaine du Pourra   TR
Chassagne Jean-Claude
☎ (90) 36 93 59
Open: Monday to Saturday
and Sunday afternoons.

**St-Maurice-sur-
Eygues** (26110)

Cave de Coteaux   TR
☎ (75) 27 63 44
Open: daily.

Ste-Cécile-lès-Vignes
(84290)

Max Ambert   TR
La Présidente
☎ (90) 30 80 34
Open: Monday to Saturday
except public holidays.

Domaine de la
  Grand'Ribe   TR
Abel Sahuc
☎ (90) 30 89 75
Open: daily.

Cave des Vignerons
  Réunis   TR
route de Tulette
☎ (90) 30 80 28
Open: Monday to Saturday
except public holidays.

**St-Pantaléon-lès
Vignes** (26770)

Cave Coopérative   TRP
☎ (75) 26 26 43
Open: Monday to
Saturday.

Sérignan-du-Comtat
(84830)

Domaine de la Renjarde TR
☎ (90) 70 00 15
Open: by appointment.

Henri Tezier   TR
route de Ste-Cécile
☎ (90) 70 01 60
Open: daily.

Suze-la-Rousse
(26130)

Coopérative Vinicole
  La Suzienne   TR
Open: daily.

Château de l'Estagnol   TR
Chambovet and son
route de Grignan D117
☎ (75) 04 81 38
Open: Monday to Friday
except public holidays.

Tulette (26130)

Cave Coopérative
  Costebelle   TR
☎ (75) 98 32 53
Open: daily.

Cave Costes Rousses   TR
☎ (75) 98 32 24
Open: daily.

Domaine Mazurd
  and son   TR
André Mazurd
☎ (75) 98 32 71
Open: daily.

Uchaux (84110)

Château St-Estève   TR
Français and son
☎ (90) 34 34 04
Open: Monday to Friday
and Saturday afternoon
except public holidays.

Vacqueyras (84190)

Le Vieux Clocher   TR
Arnoux and son
☎ (90) 65 84 18
Open: Monday to Friday
except public holidays.

Cave de Vignerons   TR
☎ (90) 65 84 54
Open: Monday to Saturday
except public holidays.

Château des Roques   TR
Dusser
☎ (90) 65 85 16
Open: Monday to Friday
except public holidays.

Château de Montmirail
  Archimbaud   TR
☎ (90) 65 86 72
Open: Monday to Saturday
except public holidays.

Domaine La Garrigue   TR
GAEC Bernard Albert
  and son
☎ (90) 65 84 60
Open: daily.

Domaine La Fourmone TR
GAEC Roger Combe
  and son
☎ (90) 65 86 05
Open: daily.

R=red wine   W=white wine   P=rosé wine   S=sparkling wine

GAEC Domaine des   TR
Lambertins
La Grande Fontaine
☎ (90) 65 85 54
Open: Monday to Saturday
and Sunday afternoons
except public holidays.

Domaine Les Cardelines TR
Jean-Pierre Guintrand
☎ (90) 65 86 74
Open: daily.

Mathieu Carlier   TR
☎ (90) 65 87 63
Open: Monday to Friday
except public holidays.

Archimbaud Vache   TR
Le Clos des Cazaux
☎ (90) 65 85 83

Open: Monday to Saturday
except public holidays.

Vaison-la-Romaine
(84110)

Domaine du Loug Serre TR
Bérard Lucien
route de Barbanot
☎ (90) 36 10 15
Open: Monday to Saturday
except public holidays.

Cave Coopérative de Vaison
et du Haut Comptat   TR
☎ (90) 36 00 43
Open: daily.

GAEC du Domaine
St-Claude   TR
C. Charasse & Associates

Le Palis
☎ (90) 36 23 68
Open: Monday to
Saturday.

Vinsobres (26110)

Cave Jaume   TRP
☎ (75) 27 61 01
Open: Monday to Saturday
except public holidays.

Domaine du Coriançon TRP
François Vallot
☎ (75) 26 03 24
Open: Monday to Saturday
except public holidays.

Domaine du Moulin   TRP
Jean Vinson
☎ (75) 27 60 47
Open: daily.

AREA BETWEEN NYONS AND AVIGNON
AND ORANGE AND VAISON-LA-ROMAINE

Bédarrides (84370)

Bérard and son   TR
☎ (90) 39 14 24
Open: Monday to Friday
9am-noon and 2-6pm,
except public holidays.

Domaine du Vieux
Télégraphe   TR
GAEC Henri Brunier
and son
route de Châteauneuf-
du-Pape
☎ (90) 39 01 19
Open: Monday to Friday
8am-noon and 2-6pm
except public holidays.

Domaine Font
de Michelle   TR
14 impasse des Vignerons
☎ (90) 39 00 87
Open: Monday to Friday
9am-noon and 2-5pm
except public holidays.

Camaret (84150)

Domaine du
Vieux-Chêne   TR
GAEC Jean-Claude and
Dominique Bouche
route d'Avignon
☎ (90) 37 21 58
Open: daily 8am-noon and
2-8pm.

Cohendy-Gonnet
and son   TR
La Berthète
route de Jonquières
☎ (90) 37 22 41
Open: Monday to Saturday
9am-noon and 2-6pm.

Caumont-Durance
(84510)

Cave Coopérative   TRW
Vinicole
☎ 22 40 09
Open: Monday to Friday
afternoons only, except
public holidays.

**Châteauneuf-en-
Gadagne** (84470)

Cave Clément   TRW
Domaine des Garriguettes
☎ (90) 22 50 10
Open: Monday to Friday
6-8pm; Saturday, Sunday
and public holidays, 9am-
noon and 6-8pm.

Cave des Vignerons   TRW
du Duché de Gadagne
☎ (90) 22 41 07
Open: Monday to Friday,
and Saturday afternoon.

Châteauneuf-du-Pape
(84230)

Domaine du'Clos de
l'Oratoire des Papes'   TRW
Léonce Amouroux
☎ (90) 39 70 19
Open: Monday to Friday
except public holidays.

T=tasting   E=English spoken   G=guided tours   C=château/building to visit

Paul Avril   TRW
Clos des Papes
13 route de Sorgues
☎ (90) 39 70 13
Open: Monday to Friday
9am-noon and 2-5.30pm.

Henri Boiron   TRW
route de Bédarrides
☎ (90) 83 73 37
Open: Monday to Saturday
and Sunday afternoon, and
public holiday afternoons
only.

Domaine le Bosquet des
  Papes   TRW
Maurice Boiron
☎ (90) 83 72 33
Open: Monday to Saturday
9am-noon and 2-7pm,
except public holidays.

Jean-Pierre Brotte   TRW
ave. Pierre-de-Luxembourg
☎ (90) 39 70 07
Open: daily 9am-noon and
2-6pm.

Caves Bressac   TRW
10 route d'Avignon
☎ (90) 39 70 02
Open: Monday to Friday
except public holidays.

Caves Reflets   TRW
chemin du Bois-de-la-Ville
☎ (90) 39 71 07
Open: Monday to Friday
and Saturday afternoons,
but all day Saturday in
July and August.

Caves St-Pierre   TRW
ave. Pierre-de-Luxembourg
☎ (90) 39 72 14
Open: Monday to Friday,
except public holidays.

Caveau Raymond   TRW
  Usseglio
route de Courthézon
☎ (90) 83 71 85
Open: daily 9am-7pm.

Domaine du Serre
  Rouge   TRW
☎ (75) 98 50 11
M. Brachet
Open: by appointment.

Château de la GardineTRW
Brunel and son
☎ (90) 83 73 20
Open: Monday to Friday
8.30am-noon and
1-5.30pm, except public
holidays.

Domaine de BeaurenardTRW
Paul Coulon and son
☎ (90) 39 71 79
Open: daily 8am-noon and
1-6pm.

Domaine du Vatican TRW
Diffonty and son
route de Courthézon
☎ (90) 39 70 51
Open: Monday to
Saturday, 9am-noon and 2-
7pm; Sunday and public
holidays by appointment.

Domaine de
  Montpertuis   TRW
Paul Jeune
7 ave. St-Josèph
☎ (90) 83 73 87
Open: daily 9am-noon and
3-8pm.

Domaine de la
  Roquette   TRW
René Laugier
☎ (90) 83 71 25
Open: daily 8am-noon and
2-7pm.

Domaine de Mont-
  Redon   TRW
☎ (90) 83 72 75
Open: daily.

GAEC Domaine
  Riché and son   TRW
27 ave. d'Avignon
☎ (90) 83 72 63

Open: Monday to Saturday
9am-noon and 1-7pm
except public holidays.

Domaine Roger
  Sabon and son   TRW
ave. Impériale
☎ (90) 83 71 72
Open: Monday to Saturday
except public holidays.

GAEC du Domaine
  Chante-Cigale   TRW
MM. Sabon-Favier
☎ (90) 39 70 57
Open: Monday to Saturday
8am-noon and 2-8pm.

GAEC du Clos
  Mont-Olivet   TRW
Joseph Sabon and sons
15 ave. St-Josèph
☎ (90) 39 72 46
Open: Monday to Friday
and Saturday afternoons
except public holidays.

Domaine Cuvée de
  Bois-Dauphin   TRW
Pierre Jacumin
☎ (90) 39 73 71
Open: daily 8am-noon and
1.30-7pm.

Jean Marchand   TRW
21 route d'Orange
☎ (90) 83 70 34
Open: Monday to Friday
8.30am-12.30pm and
1.30-6pm.

M. Anselme   TRW
Musée des Outils de
  Vignerons
☎ (90) 39 70 07
Open: daily 9am-noon and
2-6pm.

SCEA du Chantadu   TRW
7 ave. des Bosquets
☎ (90) 39 72 87
Open: Monday to Friday
8-11.30am and 2-6pm and
Saturday afternoon.

R=red wine   W=white wine   P=rosé wine   S=sparkling wine

SCEA du Domaine de Cabrières TRW
☎ (90) 39 73 58
or (90) 39 70 26
Open: Monday to Friday
8am-noon and 2-7pm;
Saturday 8am-noon and
2-4pm; Sunday by appointment.

SCEA Pierre Raynaud TRW
Domaine des Sénéchaux
1 rue de la Nouvelle-Poste
☎ (90) 83 73 52
Open: Monday to Friday
8am-noon and 1.30-7pm;
Saturday 1.30-7pm.

SCEA Jean Comte de
Lauzé TRW
7 ave. des Bosquets
☎ (90) 39 72 87
Open: Monday-Friday
8-11.30am and 2-6pm;
Saturday 2-6pm.

SCEA du Vieux
Lazaret TRW
ave. Baron-Le Roy
☎ (90) 83 73 55
Open: Monday to Friday
10am-6pm and public
holidays by appointment.

Courthézon (84350)

Berthet-Rayne
Christian TRW
route de Roquemaure
☎ (90) 70 74 14
Open: Monday to Saturday
8am-noon and 2-7pm,
except public holidays.

Château de Beaucastel TRW
Domaine de Beaucastel
☎ (90) 70 70 60
Open: Monday to Friday
8am-noon and 2-5.30pm,
except public holidays.

GAEC Hoirie Paul
Autard TRW
route de Châteauneuf-du-
Pape
☎ (90) 70 73 15
Open: Monday to Saturday
9am-8pm; Sunday by
appointment.

Le Cellier des Princes TRW
Coopérative Vinicole
route Nationale 7
☎ (90) 70 21 44
Open: daily.

Clos du Caillou TRW
Claude Pouizin
☎ (90) 70 73 05
Open: Monday to Friday
8am-noon and 2-7pm;
Saturday 8am-noon and 2-
4pm, closed public
holidays.

Aimé Sabon TRW
Domaine de la Janasse
☎ (90) 70 86 29
Open: Monday to Saturday
8am-noon and 1-7pm;
Sunday 1-7pm.

Domaine St-Laurent TRW
Robert Sinard
route St-Laurent
☎ (90) 70 87 92
or (90) 70 73 68
Open: Monday to Saturday
8am-noon and 3-7pm;
Sunday 3-7pm.

Société Jean-Paul
Jamet TRW
☎ (90) 70 72 78
Open: Monday to Saturday
8am-noon and 2-6pm,
except public holidays.

Jonquières (84150)

Domaine des
Calanges TRW
Biscarrat
route de Camaret
☎ (90) 70 60 67

Open: Monday to Friday
8am-noon and 3-6pm,
Saturday 3-6pm; closed
public holidays.

Domaine de
Grangeneuve TRW
H. & F. Martin
☎ (90) 70 62 62
Open: Monday to Friday
7am-noon and 2-8pm;
Saturday 2-8pm, closed
public holidays.

**Morières-lès-
Avignon** (84310)

Coopérative Vinicole TRW
rue Aristide-Briand
☎ (90) 22 45 45
Open: Monday to Friday
8am-noon and 2.30-
6.30pm; Saturday 2.30-
6.30pm, closed public
holidays.

Orange (84100)

Domaine Michel
Bernard TRW
La Serrière
☎ (90) 34 35 17
Open: daily Monday to
Friday, except public
holidays.

Domaine de
St-Suffrein TRW
Claude Chastan
route de Châteauneuf-
du-Pape
☎ (90) 34 49 85
Open: daily monday to Saturday 8am-12noon, 2-7pm.

Domaine Palestor TRW
Pierre Chastan
La Fagotière
☎ (90) 34 51 81
Open: Monday to Saturday
8am-noon and 2-7pm,
closed public holidays.

T=tasting E=English spoken G=guided tours C=château/building to visit

Domaine de Grand
Cyprès   TRW
G. Lindeperg
470 ave. Foch
☎ (90) 34 05 24
or (90) 34 01 82
Open: daily except public
holidays.

Puyméras (84110)

Cave Coopérative Comta-
dine Dauphinoise   TRW
☎ (90) 46 70 78
Open: daily Monday to
Saturday except public
holidays.

Domaine St-
Apollinaire   TRW
Frédéric Daumas
☎ (90) 46 41 09
Open: Monday to
Saturday, public holidays
by appointment.

Rasteau (84110)

Cave des Vignerons
de Rasteau   TRW
☎ (90) 46 10 43
Open: daily.

GAEC Charavin
Robert   TRW
Domaine des Coteaux des
Travers
☎ (90) 46 10 48
or (90) 46 13 69
Open: daily 8am-12.30pm
and 1-8pm.

Domaine de la
Garriguette   TRW
SC Caves Francis Vache
☎ (90) 46 10 41
Open: daily 8am-noon and
1-6pm.

Domaine de Beaurenard
la Ferme Pisan   TRW
Caveau Paul Coulon
☎ (90) 46 11 75

Open: daily except
Tuesday, 8am-noon and
1-6pm.

GAEC du Grand   TRW
JasDomaine des Nymphes
☎ (90) 46 14 13
Open: daily 8am-7pm.

Domaine la Soumade TRW
André Roméro
☎ (90) 46 11 26
Open: daily 8am-noon and
1-7pm.

Richerenches (84600)

Coopérative Vinicole de
Cellier des TempliersTRW
☎ (90) 35 05 09
Open: Monday to Saturday
except public holidays.

Roaix (84110)

Domaine Les
Peyrières   TRW
Florimond Lambert
☎ (90) 46 11 33
Open: daily except
Tuesday morning, 9am-
noon and 1.30-8pm;
Tuesday morning by
appointment.

Sarrians (84280)

Domaine Le Sang-des-
Cailloux   TRW
Jean Férigoule and Serge
Ricard
route de Vacqueyras
☎ (90) 65 85 67
Open: Monday to Saturday
8am-noon and 2-7pm.

Séguret (84110)

Cave Coopérative Vinicole
Les Coteaux-du-
Rhône   TRW

☎ (90) 70 04 22
Open: Monday to Saturday
8am-noon and 2-6.30pm,
except public holidays.

Sorgues (84700)

Domaine de BourdinesTRW
Gérard Baroux
☎ (90) 39 36 77
Open: Monday to Saturday
4-7pm, except public
holidays.

A. Ogier and son   TRW
Chemin du Fournalet
☎ (90) 39 18 31
Open: Monday to Friday 9-
11am and 2-5pm, except
public holidays.

Travaillan (84150)

SCEA Domaine Martin
Plan-de-Dieu
☎ 37 23 20
Open: Monday to Saturday
8am-noon and 2-7pm,
Sunday 2-7pm.

Domaine Les Routes Le
Plan-de-Dieu   TRW
Claude Maurizot
☎ (90) 37 20 51
Open: daily 8am-noon and
1-8pm.

Vedène (84270)

Frédéric Mitan   TRW
☎ (90) 31 07 12
or (90) 31 07 52
Open: Monday to Saturday
9am-noon and 2-6pm,
except public holidays.

Eric Daussant   TRW
Le Grand Plantier
☎ (90) 31 09 54
Open: Monday to Saturday
10am-noon and 1-8pm;
Sunday 1-8pm only.

R=red wine   W=white wine   P=rosé wine   S=sparkling wine

Valréas (84600)

Domaine du Val des
  Rois   TRW
Romain Bouchard
route de Vinsobres
☎ (90) 35 04 35
Open: daily 10am-
12.30pm and 3-7pm,
public holidays by
appointment.

Domaine de St-Chérin TRW
A. Gras and son
route de St-Pierre
☎ (90) 35 06 68
Open: Monday to Friday
2-7pm, except public
holidays.

La Verrière   TRW
Pierre Rosati
route du Pègue
☎ (90) 35 13 63
Open: daily 8am-noon and
1.30-7pm.

Union des Vignerons de
  l'Enclave des Papes TRW
Maison des Vins
11 ave. Gén-de-Gaulle
☎ (90) 37 36 74
Open: daily 8am-noon and
3-7pm except public
holidays and Sundays in
the winter.

Villedieu (84110)

Cave Coopérative   TRW
La Vigneronne

Villedieu-Buisson
☎ (90) 36 23 11
Open: daily from April to
September.

SCEA Domaine Les
  Aussellons   TRW
Benôit and Ezingeard
☎ (90) 36 23 42
Open: daily 8am-8pm.

Violes (84150)

Domaine des Favards TRW
Jean-Paul Barbaud
route d'Orange
Open: Monday to Saturday
10am-noon and 2-7pm,
except public holidays.

Vignoble de la Jasse TRW
Daniel Combe
☎ (90) 70 93 47
Visiting by appointment.

Domaine de la
  Damase   TRW
Serge Latour
route d'Orange
☎ (90) 70 91 01
Open: Monday to Saturday
8am-8pm, Sunday
afternoon and public
holidays by appointment.

Domaine de   TRW
  l'Espigouette
Edmond Latour
☎ (90) 70 92 55
Open: daily 8am-8pm.

Domaine des Richards
  Combe Pierre   TRW
route d'Avignon
☎ (90) 70 93 73
Open: daily 9am-8pm.

Domaine Tenon   TRW
Philippe Combe
☎ (90) 70 93 29
Open: daily 9am-noon and
2-7pm.

SCEA La Couran-
  çonne   TRW
☎ (90) 70 92 16
Open: daily 9am-8pm.

Domaine La Grangette
  St-Josèph   TRW
Monique Tramier
☎ (90) 70 92 12
Open: Monday to Saturday
8am-noon and 2-8pm,
except public holidays.

Visan (84820)

Coopérative Vinicole TRW
Les Coteaux
☎ (75) 30 91 12
Open: daily 8.30am-noon
and 2-6.30pm.

Domaine de la Cantharide
  Laget-Roux   TRW
☎ (75) 30 93 19
Open: daily during the
summer 9am-noon and
1-8pm

AREA BETWEEN BOURG-ST-ANDEOL AND COMPS

Aiguèze (30760)

Domaine Tour Paradis TRW
Georges Chabot
☎ (66) 82 18 80
Open: daily 9am-1pm and
3-8pm.

Bagnols-sur-Cèze
(30200)

Domaine de Signac   TRW
route d'Orsan
☎ (66) 89 58 47
Open: daily.

GAEC du Haut Castel TRW
M. Arène
☎ (66) 89 67 19
Open: Monday to Saturday
8am-8pm; Sunday by
appointment.

T=tasting   E=English spoken   G=guided tours   C=château/building to visit

Bourg-St-Andéol
(07700)

Cave Coopérative   TRW
☎ (75) 54 51 34
Open: Wednesday 8am-
noon and 2-6pm;
Saturdays 8am-noon.

Domaine de l'Olivet-
Goossens
☎ (75) 54 52 74
Open: Monday to Saturday
2-6.30pm.

Domaine des
Amoureuses   TRW
Alain Grangaud
☎ (75) 54 51 85
Visiting by appointment.

G. Herberigs   TRW
Château Rochecolombe
☎ (75) 04 50 47
Open: daily 8am-noon and
2-7pm, public holidays by
appointment.

Cadignac (30200)

Domaine de la
Réméjeanne   TRW
François Klein
☎ (66) 89 69 95
Open: daily 8am-noon and
1-7pm except public
holidays.

Chusclan (30200)

Cave des Vignerons   TRW
☎ (66) 89 63 03
Open: Monday to Saturday
8am-noon and 2-6.30pm
except public holidays.

Codolet (30200)

Cave Coopérative Les TRW
Côtes-du-Rhône
☎ (66) 89 08 71
Open: Monday to Friday,
and Saturday morning,
except public holidays.

Chevalier Brigand   TRW
☎ (66) 89 08 64
Open: Monday to Saturday
8am-noon and 2-7pm.

Colombier-Sabran
(30200)

Château de
Boussargues   TRW
☎ (66) 89 32 20
Open: daily 9am-7pm.

Domaine de Bruthel   TRW
Christian de Seresin
☎ (66) 79 96 24
or (66) 89 69 06
Open: Monday to Saturday
9am-noon and 2-7pm and
Sunday morning.

Moulin de Pourpré   TRW
Francis Simon
☎ (66) 89 73 98
Open: daily 8am-8pm.

Comps (30300)

Château de Farel   TRW
Pierre Silvestre
☎ (66) 74 50 83
Open: Saturday and Sunday
10am-noon and 2-4pm.

Domazan (30390)

Caveau du Château
de Domazan   TRW
place du Château
☎ (66) 57 03 18
or (66) 57 02 45
Open: daily 9am-noon and
2-6.30pm.

Aimé Esperandieu   TRW
☎ (66) 57 02 17
Open: Monday to Saturday
and Sunday morning.

Domaine des
Coccinelles   TRW
René Fabre
☎ (66) 57 03 07
Open: daily 9am-noon and
1-10pm.

Lucien Léotard   TRW
chemin des Jardins
Open: daily 8am-noon and
4-8pm.

Mas de Chantecler
Gérard Castan   TRW
Open: Monday to Saturday
8am-noon and 1-8pm;
Sunday 8am-noon.

Fournès (30210)

Cave Coopérative Les
Coteaux de Fournès TRW
☎ (66) 37 02 36
Open: Monday to Friday
except public holidays.

Caujac (30330)

Domaine de Marjolet TRW
Bernard Pontaud
☎ (66) 82 00 93
Open: Monday to Friday
9am-noon and 3-7pm;
Saturday 9-12noon.

Laudun (30290)

Cave des Quatre-
Chemins   TRW
Le Serre de Bernon
☎ (66) 82 00 22
Open: daily.

Cave des Vignerons   TRW
route de l'Ardoise
☎ (66) 79 49 97
Open: Monday to Saturday
except public holidays.

Lirac (30126)

Eugène Bayle   TRW
Caveau de la Fontaine
☎ (66) 50 10 53
Open: daily 9am-8pm.

Orsan (30200)

Cave des Vignerons   TRW
☎ (66) 89 62 05

R=red wine   W=white wine   P=rosé wine   S=sparkling wine

Open: Monday to Saturday, except public holidays.

Pont-St-Esprit (30130)

Cave Coopérative   TRW
☎ (66) 39 08 65
Open: Monday to Saturday except public holidays.

Pierre Coste   TRW
Domaine de Laplagnol
quartier Maconil
☎ (66) 39 12 50
Open: Monday to Saturday
8am-noon and 1.30-7pm,
except public holidays.

Pouzilhac (30210)

Domaine de
   Montargues   TRW
Laurent and son
route de Lyon
☎ (66) 37 14 39
Open: Monday 2-6pm;
Tuesday to Friday 10am-
noon and 2-6pm; Saturday
10am-noon. Closed public
holidays.

Remoulins (30210)

Cave Coopérative
   Vinicole   TRW
route d'Avignon
☎ (66) 37 14 51
Open: Monday to Friday
9am-noon and 2-6pm;
Saturday 9am-noon.
Closed public holidays.

Rochefort-du-Gard
(30650)

Domaine de la
   Rouette   TRW
Guigue and son
☎ 31 72 36 or 31 73 40
Open: by appointment,
Saturday 8am-noon and
2-7pm; Sunday 8am-noon.

Les Vignerons du
   Castelas   TRW
☎ (90) 31 72 10
Open: Monday to
Saturday, except public
holidays.

Roquemaure (30150)

Domaines des Garrigues et
   des Causses   TRW
Jean-Claude Assemat
☎ (66) 50 15 52
or (66) 50 29 76
Open: Monday to
Saturday, except public
holidays.

Château St-Roch   TRW
Verda and son
☎ (66) 50 12 59
Open: Monday to Saturday
8am-noon and 2-6.30pm,
except public holidays.

Coopérative Agricole de
   Vinification des
   Vignerons de
   Roquemaure   TRW
rue des Vignerons
☎ (66) 50 12 01
Open: Monday to
Saturday, except public
holidays.

Robert Degoul   TRW
Château de Bouchassy
☎ (66) 50 12 49
Open: Monday to Saturday
8am-1pm and 2-7pm,
except public holidays.

Robert Fuget   TRW
Château Boucarut
☎ (66) 50 16 91
Open: daily 9am-6pm.

Domaine de Castel
   Oualou   TRW
Pons Mure Marie
☎ (66) 50 12 64
or (66) 50 15 65

Open: Monday to
Saturday, except public
holidays.

Domaine de Maillac   TRW
Edmond Nataf and son
☎ (66) 50 34 00
Open: daily.

Sabran (30200)

Domaine de
   l'Amandier Carmes   TRW
Urbain Pages
☎ (66) 89 69 10
Open: daily 9am-noon and
2-8pm.

St-Alexandre (30130)

Domaine de
   Roquebrune   TRW
Pierre Rique
☎ (66) 39 23 03
or (66) 39 27 41
Open: daily 8am-noon and
1-7pm.

Domaine de l'Espéran TRW
Roger Sabatier
☎ (66) 39 18 64
Open: daily.

St-Etienne-des-Sorts
(30200)

Cave Coopérative   TRW
☎ (66) 89 64 05
Open: Monday to Friday
8am-noon and 1.30-
5.30pm, except public
holidays.

St-Gervais (30200)

Caveau des Vignerons
   de St-Gervais   TRW
Grand Rue
☎ (66) 89 35 67
Open: 15 June-15
September, daily 9am-
12.30pm and 2.30-7pm;
rest of year Wednesday
and Saturday 9am-
12.30pm and 2.30-7pm.

T=tasting   E=English spoken   G=guided tours   C=château/building to visit

Domaine Ste-Anne   TRW
Les Cellettes
☎ (66) 89 67 41
Open: Monday to Saturday
9-11am and 2-6.30pm,
except public holidays.

St-Hilaire-d'Ozilhan
(30210)

Cave Coopérative   TRW
☎ (66) 37 16 47
Open: Monday to
Saturday, except public
holidays.

St-Laurent-des-Arbres
(30126)

Cave Coopérative
  Lirac   TRW
☎ (66) 50 01 02
Open: daily 9am-noon and
3-7pm.

Domaine de la Tour   TRW
☎ (66) 50 01 19
Open: Monday to Friday
9am-noon and 2-6pm,
except public holidays.

Domaine Jean
  Duseigneur   TRW
route de St-Victor
☎ (66) 50 02 57
or (66) 50 25 01
Open: Monday to Friday
9am-12.30pm and 3-6pm,
except public holidays.

Domaine Rousseau   TRW
c/o Domaine de la Tour
☎ (66) 50 01 19
Open: Monday to Friday,
except public holidays.

GAEC Lombardo
  brothers   TRW
Domaine du Devoy
☎ (66) 50 01 23
Open: Monday to
Saturday.

St-Marcel-d'Ardèche
(07700)

Pierre Dumas   TRW
☎ (75) 04 63 92
Open: July and August
9am-1pm and 3-6pm, rest
of the year by
appointment.

St-Marcel-de-Careiret
(30330)

Cave Coopérative
☎ (66) 89 64 54
Open: Thursday 2-6pm.

St-Michel-d'Euzet
(30200)

Domaine des Riots   TRW
Riot brothers
☎ (66) 89 58 14
or (66) 79 91 10
Open: Monday to Friday
and Saturday morning.

St-Nazaire (30200)

Château du Bresquet   TRW
Juls Joël
☎ (66) 89 66 28
Open: Monday to Saturday
9am-12.30pm and
2-7.30pm.

St-Paulet-de-Caisson
(30130)

Chartreuse-de-
  Valbonne   TRW
☎ (66) 89 68 32
Open: Monday to Friday
9am-noon and 2-6pm,
except public holidays.

St-Victor-la-Coste
(30290)

Cave des Vignerons   TRW
☎ (66) 50 02 07
Open: Monday to Friday
and Saturday morning
except public holidays.

Domaine Estournel
  Rémy   TRW
☎ (66) 50 01 73
Open: daily 8am-noon and
1-7pm.

Domaine Pelaquie   TRW
☎ (66) 50 06 04
Open: Monday to Saturday
8am-noon and 1-7pm,
Sunday and public
holidays by appointment.

Louis Faraud and son TRW
Hameau de Palus
☎ (66) 50 04 20
Open: daily 8am-noon and
2-8pm, public holidays by
appointment.

Sauveterre (30150)

Cave Coopérative Pujaut-
  Sauveterre et Villeneuve-
  lès-Avignon   TRW
☎ (66) 82 53 53
Open: Monday to
Saturday, except public
holidays.

Saze (30650)

GAEC Valentin
  and Coste   TRW
Domaine de la Charité
☎ (90) 31 73 55
Open: Monday to Friday
6-7.30pm; Saturday
2-7.30pm, closed on
public holidays.

Domaine du Cabanon TRW
Achille Payan
5 place de la Fontaine
☎ (90) 31 70 74
Open: Monday to Saturday
10am-noon and 2-7pm,
except public holidays.

Domaine des Moulins TRW
André Payan
☎ (90) 31 70 43
Open: daily 8am-noon and
2-7pm.

R=red wine   W=white wine   P=rosé wine   S=sparkling wine

Tavel (30126)

Association de Producteurs
les Vignerons
de Tavel   TRWP
rue de la Commanderie
☎ (66) 50 03 57
Open: Monday to Friday
10am-noon and 2-7pm,
except public holidays.

Domaine Bernard   TRWP
Domaine de la Genestière
☎ (66) 50 07 03
Open: daily 8am-noon and
1.30-5.30pm.

Domaine des
Jonciers   TRWP
Pierre Roussel
rue de la Combe
☎ (66) 25 12 28
or (66) 50 27 70
Open: daily.

Domaine Maby   TRWP
☎ (66) 50 03 40
Open: Monday to
Saturday, except public
holidays.

Domaine de
Tourtouil   TRWP
Edouard Lefèvre
rue des Comeyres
☎ (66) 50 05 68
Open: daily 8am-8pm.

GAEC Charmasson-
Plantevin   TRWP
Domaine les Trois Logis
rue de Tourtouil
☎ (66) 50 05 34

Open: daily 8am-noon and
1-8pm.

GAEC Gabriel Roudiland
and Sons   TRWP
rue des Lavandières
☎ (66) 50 07 79
Open: daily.

Domaine de
Corne-Loup   TRWP
Jacques Lafont
☎ (66) 50 06 38
Open: Monday 2.30-6pm,
Tuesday to Friday 9am-
noon and 2.30-6pm,
Saturday 9am-noon, closed
public holidays.

Domaine de Roc
Epine   TRWP
J.P. and P.Lafond
route des Vignobles
☎ (66) 50 24 59
Open: Monday to Friday
9am-noon and 2-6pm,
except public holidays.

SCA Lévêque   TRWP
Seigneur de Vaucrose
route de Lirac
☎ (66) 50 04 37
Open: Monday to Friday
2-6pm, except public
holidays.

Société C.A.J.Oliver TRWP
Château d'Aqiéria
☎ (66) 50 04 56
Open: Monday to Saturday
8.30am-noon and 2-7pm,
except public holidays.

Tresques (30330)

Domaine de Fabre   TRW
Anne-Marie Lafont
☎ (66) 82 42 67
Open: Monday to
Saturday, except public
holidays.

Vénéjan (30200)

Cave Coopérative   TRW
☎ (66) 89 65 04
Open: Monday, Tuesday
and Thursday to Saturday,
except public holidays.

Domaine Nuit-des-
Dames   TRW
Richard Verdier
☎ (66) 79 20 54
Open: Monday to
Saturday, except public
holidays.

Domaine de St-
Georges   TRW
André Vignal
☎ (66) 89 73 14
Visits by appointment.

**Villeneuve-lès-
Avignon** (30400)

Domaine Blayrac   TRW
rue de la République
☎ (90) 25 66 68
Open: daily 9am-1pm and
5-8pm, closed Wednesday
afternoon.

THE COTEAUX DU TRICASTIN

Cellars open daily for
tasting:

Allan (26200)

Cave Almoric   TRW

Domaine des Sablas TRW
Monsieur Gianfaldoni

Roussas (26230)

Dom. de Grangeneuve TRW
Mme Bour

Valaurie (26230)

Dom. du Serre Rouge TRW
M. Brachet
☎ (75) 98 50 11

Caves Froment   TRW

Baume-de-Transit
(26130)

Ferme-St-Luc   TRW
M. Cornillon

Domaine du Bois Noir TRW
M. Estève
☎ (75) 98 11 02

T=tasting E=English spoken G=guided tours C=château/building to visit

Domaine de Raspail   TRW
M. Jalifier

Domaine du Célestin TRW
Mme Renée Roux

Terroirs St Rémy   TRW

Logis-de-Berre (26230)

Cave Vergobbi   TRW

Granges-Gontardes
(26290)

Domaine de la Tour
   d'Elysés   TRW
Cave Labeye

Château des Estubiers TRW
☎ (75) 98 53 86

Grignan (26230)

Tasting possible in the
wine museum and tourist
centre.

Malataverne (26230)

Domaine la Curate   TRW
M. Pommier

Clos Ste Agnes   TRW
M. Gaston Etienne

Mas des Sources   TRW
M. Truffaut

VINEYARDS OF COTEAUX DU TRICASTIN (SOUTH SECTION)

Syndicat des Vignerons
   des Coteaux du Tricastin
26130 Marie de St-Paul-
   Trois-Châteaux

Caves Coopératives open
to the public for tasting
and sale of wine. English
spoken.

Cave le Cellier des
   Templiers
84700 Richerenches

La Suzienne
26790 Suze-la-Rousse
☎ (75) 04 80 04

Le Cellier des Dauphins
26790 Tulette

Le Cellier de l'Enclave
84600 Valréas

Le Caveau de Dégustation
26230 Grignan

Le Caveau de Dégustation
26130 St-Paul-Trois-
   Châteaux

Le Domaine Bour
26230 Roussas

Le Cave des Estubiers
26290 Les Granges
   Gontardes

Domaine du Serre Rouge
26230 Valaurie
☎ (75) 98 50 11

Domaine Bauchière
84290 Cairanne

SICA Michel Bernard
La Servière
84100 Orange

Mas des Sources
26740 Malataverne

COTES DU VENTOUX REGION

Apt (84400)

Cave Coopérative   TRW
Le Vin de Sylla
☎ (90) 74 05 39
Open: Tuesday to Saturday
8am-noon and 2-6pm.

Aubignan (84810)

GAEC Rey   TRW
Domaine de St Sauveur
☎ (90) 62 60 39
Open: Monday to Saturday
8am-noon and 2-6pm,
except public holidays.

Beaumes-de-Venise
(84190)

Cave Coopérative   TRW
☎ (90) 62 94 45
Open: Monday to Saturday
8.30am-noon and 2-6pm,
except public holidays.

Beaumont-du-Ventoux
(84340)

Caveau de la Cave
   Coopérative   TRW
route de Carpentras
☎ (90) 65 11 78
Open: daily 9am-noon and
2.30-6.30pm.

Bedoin (84410)

Cave Coopérative des
   Vignerons du Mont-
   Ventoux   TRW
☎ (90) 65 60 03
Open: daily 8am-noon and
2-6pm; Sunday 9am-noon
and 2-6pm.

Bonnieux (84480)

Cave Coopérative   TRW
☎ (90) 75 80 03
Open: Monday to Saturday
8am-noon and 2-6pm,
except public holidays.

R=red wine   W=white wine   P=rosé wine   S=sparkling wine

Carpentras (84200)

Union des Vignerons des
  Côtes du Ventoux   TRW
route de Pernes
☎ (90) 60 24 66
Open: Tuesday to Saturday
9am-noon and 3-7pm.

Caveau des Vins   TRW
place du Théâtre
Open: daily throughout
the summer.

Domaine de la Sauve
  St-Ponchon   TRW
Raymonde and Marc
  Veyrier
☎ (90) 63 11 47
Open: Monday to Saturday
8am-noon and 2-6pm.

GAEC AymardlLes Galères
  Serres-Carpentras   TRW
☎ (90) 63 35 32
Open: Monday and Sunday
1-6pm and Tuesday to
Saturday 9am-noon and 1-
6pm.

GAEC Domaine Troussel
  Serres-Carpentras   TRW
☎ (90) 63 16 56
Open: Saturday 8am-noon
and 2-6pm, otherwise by
appointment.

Pascal and Giraud   TRW
route de Malaucène Serres-
  Carpentras
☎ (90) 63 00 85
Open: Monday to Saturday
8am-noon and 2-6pm,
except public holidays.

Caromb (84330)

Cave Coopérative
  St-Marc   TRW
☎ (90) 62 40 24
Open: daily 8am-noon and
2-6pm.

Augustin Ribas   TRW
☎ (90) 62 41 28
Open: Monday to Saturday
9am-noon and 2-6pm,
public holidays by
appointment.

Cabrières-d'Avignon
(84220)

Martial Marreau   TRW
La Bastidonne
Open: daily.

Châteauneuf-du-Pape
(84230)

Domaine du Vieux
  Lazaret   TRW
Jérôme Quiot
☎ (90) 39 73 55
Open: daily 9am-noon and
2-6pm.

Coustellet-Maubec
(84660)

Cave Coopérative
  Maubec-Gare   TRW
☎ (90) 71 90 01
Open: Monday to Saturday
8am-noon and 2-6pm,
except public holidays.

Cave Coopérative
  Maubec-Lubéron   TRW
☎ (90) 71 91 02
Open: Tuesday to Saturday
8am-noon and 2-6pm,
except public holidays.

Entrechaux (84340)

Domaine de Champ-
  Long   TRW
GAEC Gely and son
☎ (90) 36 17 64
Open: daily 8am-noon and
2-7pm.

Michel Mouret   TRW
Open: daily.

Gargas (84400)

Domaine la
  Coquillado   TRW
Percié du Sert-Cyprien
☎ (90) 74 11 05
Open: daily.

Gigondas (84190)

Pierre Amadieu   TRW
☎ (90) 65 84 08
Open: Monday to Friday
8am-noon and 2-6pm,
except public holidays.

Domaine St-André   TRW
André Rcy
Open: daily.

Goult (84220)

Cave Coopérative   TRW
☎ (90) 72 20 04
Open: Tuesday to Friday
8am-noon, Saturday 2-
6pm, except public
holidays.

Domaine la Verrière   TRW
Bernard Maubert
☎ (90) 72 20 88
Open: Monday to Saturday
8am-noon and 2-6pm,
except public holidays.

Le Barroux (84330)

Domaine Champaga   TRW
Phillippe d'Ollone
☎ (90) 62 33 09
Open: Monday to Saturday
8am-noon and 2-7pm.

Mazan (84380)

Cave des Vignerons
  de Canteperdrix   TRW
☎ (90) 69 70 31
Open: Monday to Saturday
8am-noon and 2-6.30pm
(Friday and Saturday 6pm).

T=tasting   E=English spoken   G=guided tours   C=château/building to visit

Mormoiron (84570)

Cave Coopérative Les
  Roches Blanches   TRW
☎ (90) 61 80 07
Open: Monday to Saturday
8am-noon and 2-6pm,
except public holidays.

Pernes-lès-Fontaines
(84210)

Cave Coopérative La
  Pernoise   TRW
☎ (90) 66 59 48
Open: Friday 8am-noon
and 2-6pm.

Les Eysserides   TRW
Michel Aquillon
☎ (90) 61 31 51
Open: Wednesday and
Saturday 2-7pm.

Puyméras (84110)

Cave Coopérative   TRW
☎ (90) 46 40 78
Open: Monday to Saturday
8am-noon and 2-6pm,
except public holidays.

Roussillon (84220)

A. Bonnelly   TRW
☎ (90) 75 61 40
Open: daily 8am-noon and
3-7pm.

Domaine Ste-Croix   TRW
Josèph Soulard
☎ 75 62 75
Open: daily except
Saturday afternoon from
8am-8pm.

St-Didier (84210)

Cave Coopérative
  La Courtoise   TRW
☎ (75) 66 01 15
Open: Monday to Friday
8am-noon and 2-6pm,
Saturday 8am-noon.

Vacqueyras (84190)

Aimé Arnoux   TRW
Le Vieux Clocher
☎ (90) 65 84 18
Open: Monday to Saturday
8am-noon and 2-6pm,
except public holidays.

André Devine   TRW
Open: daily.

Léopold Devine   TRW
Open: daily

Céline Cipolla   TRW
Chez Mme Saurel Gaston
Open: daily.

SEMA Pascal   TRW
Open: daily.

Vaison-la-Romaine
(84110)

Cave Coopérative   TRW
☎ (90) 36 00 43
Open: daily 9am-noon and
2-6pm.

Villes-sur-Auzon
(84570)

Cave Coopérative   TRW
  La Montagne Rouge
☎ (90) 61 82 08
Open: Monday to Saturday
8am-noon and 2-6pm,
except public holidays.

R=red wine   W=white wine   P=rosé wine   S=sparkling wine

Chapter 9

THE MIDI

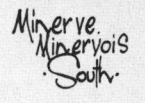

Minerve.
Minervois
South.

THE MIDI is the huge wine-producing region which stretches from the Rhône estuary westwards to the Spanish border. It includes Languedoc-Roussillon, Corbières, Minervois and a host of other smaller communes producing good, honest, everyday table wine. Every so often you can find a quite exceptional vineyard, and while the whole region produces vast quantities of wine, the standards throughout are improving by leaps and bounds because of improved cultivation, new and better varieties of grape, and investment in modern vinification techniques.

In the past this part of France has been responsible for much of the massive EEC wine surplus, at the time of writing large enough to fill 16,000 Olympic-size swimming pools. Now, things are changing. Thanks to improving quality, and the grubbing out of the worst vineyards, the wines have enormous potential, although most growers will still be content to produce good table wine.

This part of France also attracts millions of foreign tourists, and almost all discover during their stay the 'marvellous' wine of the local cooperative and wonder why it is not available when they return to their own countries. This is the area of cooperatives, and while most make good wine, and some very good wine, few make it in large enough quantities to consider exporting seriously, although this is changing. There are, however, some massive companies and Listel, with its thousands of acres of vineyards in the sand and some excellent *domaines*, is the best example. While much of Listel's huge holding, the largest in France, is planted along the coast, the best vineyards are to be found on the foothills rising a few miles inland. The vines stretch for as far as the eye can see in places, and run inland in belts up to sixty miles wide. The Midi can be divided into four principal areas — Roussillon, Languedoc, Corbières and Minervois.

LANGUEDOC-ROUSSILLON

Roussillon

Roussillon hugs the Mediterranean coast around the town of Perpignan. The vineyards produce red, white and rosé wines from mainly Grenache, Cinsault, Carignan and Mourvèdre grapes. There are also a number of sweet fortified wines, made chiefly from the Muscat grape. Huge quantities of this sweet wine is produced and most is drunk by the French.

Perpignan was, until the Middle Ages, the capital of Spanish Catalonia and this influence is still to be found everywhere, even in the language. In 1659, after more that 300 years of bouncing backwards and forwards between French and Spanish domination, it passed back into French hands with the signing of the Treaty of the Pyrénées.

Collioure

To the south of Perpignan is the small port of Collioure, close to the Spanish border, which produces a very individualistic wine, mostly from Grenache and Mourvèdre. This intense wine, full of hot sun, gained its AC status in 1949. Two other *appellations* exist at Caramany and Latour-de-France, about twenty miles inland from Perpignan. They acquired AC status in 1977.

Côtes de Roussillon

Generally, the wines of the Côtes de Roussillon are predominantly made from the Carignan grape. The AC Fitou wines must consist of at least 75 per cent Carignan and Grenache, and must remain in barrels for at least nine months. It is a strong, heady wine, but new vinification techniques have improved its quality no end and some fine Fitou wines can now be found. Many of the lighter Côtes de Roussillon wines are drunk young as *primeurs*, but because of their body and intense fruit, most benefit from ageing for a few years.

Corbières

The Corbières vineyards stretch from Narbonne in the north, inland as far as Carcassonne, and then south almost as far as Rivesaltes. In the north they merge with Minervois, in the south with the Côtes de Roussillon and in the west with the Blanquette de Limoux. The true potential of the Corbières wines has still to be realised, although some very good wines are already produced here, certainly rating more than their present VDQS status.

Total production for the region is well over seven million cases a year, and the Carignan is the main grape grown on the rolling limestone hills. Almost all the production is red but a little rosé and even less white is produced. The Corbières region is still the largest VDQS producing region of France. The wines are strong and heady with glorious deep colour when young, but they fade fast when made largely with the neutral Carignan grape. Attempts are now being made to blend with other varieties to give the wines more fruit and bouquet. Wines with higher alcoholic content are allowed to carry the title *Corbières Supérieur*.

Although most of the producers grow for the many cooperatives, there are some large estates as well as some fine château properties. Some of the best of these include Domaine de Villemajou in Boutenac where fine reds are made, using the *macération carbonique* technique following by ageing in wood. Good dry rosés are also produced. Domaine de Fontsainte also in Boutenac, makes some very good reds. The Corbières producing area centres around Bizanet, Boutenac, Camplong, Coustouge, Fabrezan, Gruissan, Lagrasse, Montseret, Ribaute, St-André-de-Cabrerisse, Tuchan and Villeneuve-lès-Corbières.

Blanquette de Limoux

To the west of Corbières is the Blanquette de Limoux, a region producing marvellous sparkling wines. The town of Limoux is due south of Carcassonne, and Blanquette is the local name for the Mauzac grape although the sparkling wine is usually made with the addition of a little Chardonnay. Most of the wine is made by the Limoux *coopérative* and a small quantity of still white is made, and sold as Vin de Blanquette. According to local growers, Limoux produced the first sparkling wine in France, at least 100 years before Champagne. The Blanquette grape gives the wine its zest, and its slightly cider-like aroma. Chenin Blanc can be added, but Chardonnay is used in the best *cuvées* which are made to the highest standards using the *méthode Champenoise*. The *coopérative* is responsible for more than three-quarters of all sparkling wine production. It was formed in 1946, and now has several hundred grower members and a deservedly high reputation. Apart from introducing very modern and closely monitored techniques, the *coopérative* has encouraged the planting of other classic grape varieties, not just the Chardonnay. Members are now producing good reds using Cabernet Sauvignon and Merlot.

Minervois
Minervois is another VDQS production region which really deserves a higher classification. It is centred around Peyriac-Minervois and the production region lies just north of the main Narbonne to Carcassonne road. The vineyards follow the line of the river Aude and occupy both the gravelly valley and quite steeply-rising hills to the north. The main grape is the Carignan, which in the valley produces a light red best drunk young, while in the hills and on the plateau produces a wine which benefits from ageing.

Clairette de Languedoc
Clairette de Languedoc is the region lying between Béziers and Montpellier, with the vineyards following the line of the river Hérault. It produces a white AC wine from the Clairette grape; much of it is fortified and sold as an apéritif. The wine is dry and high in alcohol, at least 13°. Quality varies enormously among producers, but some of it is very well produced.

Costières du Gard
Moving up the road to Nîmes takes us past the Costières du Gard which lies south of the main road and bordered in the east by the Rhône. It produces some very good red and rosé wines, with VDQS status. There is also a small production of white wine which has AC status and is produced under the name Clairette de Bellegarde. It is in this area that the most unusual wine company is to be found. For more than 100 years the Salins du Midi has been producing salt from the shallow lakes close to the sea by evaporating the water. Originally, cereals were planted in the sand dunes to try to prevent them drifting, but when phylloxera broke out in France and it was realised the disease could not travel through sand, vines were planted.

Today, the Domaines Viticoles des Salins du Midi, known as Listel, is France's largest wine producer, owning several thousand acres of vineyards. It produces very good quality table wines but also has the prestigious Domaines of Villeroy, de Jarras and du Bosquet among others. Much of their wine is produced in the 'Bardot' bottle, named after the French film actress because of its curved shape. The company has some of the most modern wineries in the world, and spends a fortune each year introducing the latest technology and replanting.

Coteaux du Languedoc
The Coteaux du Languedoc is the final wine-producing region in this stretch of coastline and runs in scattered communes between Narbonne and Mont-

pellier. The best producers are to be found in the hills to the north of Béziers. Here the Cévennes, the range of hills made famous by Robert Louis Stevenson, lose height as they approach the coastal plain. The villages of Cabrières, Faugères, St-Saturnin all produce good red and rosé wines. Altogether there are about a dozen villages of note including La Clape, at the mouth of the River Aude, which produces a fine white which improves considerably with a few years ageing. Although traditionally produced from local grapes, new varieties, including Chardonnay, are now being grown, to improve quality further.

As with the rest of the southern coast, the Muscat is used to produce a very sweet Muscat *vins doux naturels*. Biggest production comes from Frontignan, Lunel and Mireval.

Tour of the Midi

ARLES TO CARCASSONE

This mini-tour of the south of France, through Languedoc-Roussillon, takes the traveller to some of the most historic cities of France, rich in tradition and architecture. It is the part of the sun-drenched Midi favoured by the Romans, and there are still many spectacular monuments which recall their presence, including the areas at Arles and Nîmes, and the stunning Pont-du-Gard.

A journey through this region has many advantages, not just the wealth of history to be seen at almost every turn. This area produces more wine than any other in France, and has taken the greatest strides in recent years in improving quality. There are now many *domaines* producing excellent wines, reds, whites, rosés and sparkling wines. It is also the home of Listel, the largest vineyard owner in France, which started producing wine almost by accident. Their new multi-million pound winery near Sète is surrounded by thousands of acres of vines, many of them planted in the sand dunes. The vines were originally planted to prevent erosion of the sand dunes which surrounded massive salt pans. The parent company of Listel is Compagnie des Salons du Midi, and salt was its main business. Today, Listel is the largest wine company in France and it is pioneering new techniques in wine making all the time. It has also established a number of excellent *domaines* to produce very good AC wines.

There are, however, many other vineyards than can be visited all along the route, and if the sun is shining there is nothing nicer than to sit and enjoy a glass of wine, looking out towards the sea, with the promise of a fine meal to come at one of the many excellent restaurants and hotels along the coast.

Of course, another major attraction of this region is the Camargue, which while still a splendid wild area full of flamingoes, white horses and black bulls, is rapidly losing much of its traditional character. A relatively short time ago, it was possible to walk unhindered over huge tracts of land. Today, land has been fenced off to provide pseudo 'cowboy' riding ranches; some of the lakes have been drained for rice production, and barbed wire cordons off huge areas. It is still possible, however, to drive through this area and it is still a naturalist, botanist and birdwatcher's paradise.

It is perhaps the warm climate and the historic atmosphere which have attracted so many writers and artists to the region. It is the land of the poet Mistral; van Gogh immortalised many scenes around Arles in his paintings; Robert Louis Stevenson and Gauguin spent a lot of time in the area and Katherine Mansfield lived here for a time.

Travelling around this region has to be done in such a way as to be able to make all the necessary detours. One can fly in to Avignon, Nîmes, Montpellier or Béziers from Paris, and there are good rail links to and between these main towns and cities. There are also local bus services, but apart from touring in and around the towns, their timetables would be too restrictive.

There is evidence of the presence of early man dating back 300,000 years but most early settlements are now to be found west of the Rhône delta. The Greeks colonised the area around Marseille 600 years before Christ and spread both east and west, but the Romans had the greatest influence on the region, one that still remains today.

The Rhône was the natural transport system into the interior, and settlements were started along its bank which grew into great towns such as Arles and Avignon. As the Romans fanned out, Nîmes became a regional centre, as did Béziers, Carcassonne and Narbonne to the west. After the Romans left the area, the coastline in particular was attacked by pirates and then the Saracens, and these raids and incursions lasted for the next 500 years.

The eleventh to the thirteenth century was a period of religious fervour. It was the time of the Crusades and the seventh left the magnificent Aigues-Mortes in 1248. Splendid churches were built throughout the area, including the St Trophime at Arles, which can still be seen with its carved stone façade. The fourteenth century saw the growth of prosperity and culture of the area, as the Papal court moved to Avignon; 200 years later though the area was torn as Protestants and Catholics fought the bloody Wars of Religion, followed by religious persecution. As the area settled down and a period of prosperity appeared to be on the way, the plague struck and the population was decimated.

The prosperity of the region has developed in the last 250 years, mostly because of the growth of the major ports along the coast. Although agriculture still predominates, industries did develop, and manufactured goods needed to be exported together with farm produce and wine.

Today, this part of the Midi has a sleepy atmosphere, particularly during the summer when the sun beats fiercely down. Only the towns really bustle and even these seem to sleep, Spanish-style, during the afternoons, when it really is too hot to work.

Tour of Arles

The tour of Languedoc-Roussillon starts in Arles, and a day can easily be spent just walking around seeing its riches. Arles was the first real Roman settlement in Gaul. Almost everywhere you walk there is something of its past to be seen. There is a Roman obelisk in the place de la République made from Egyptian stone. It used to be just outside the centre in the middle of a chariot-racing arena. It is essential to visit this place, because it also houses the twelfth-century church of St Trophime with its famous façade, and the seventeenth-century Hôtel de Ville. The church is famed both for its antiquity and its carvings in stone. It was one of a string of pilgrimage churches built along the route to the shrine of St James of Compostela. The church is open to visitors and it has many treasures, including more carvings in both stone and wood, tapestries, and sarcophagi.

Also in the square is the tourist office, housed in what was once the archbishop's palace. Just an alley away is the place du Forum with its statue of Frédéric Mistral, perhaps the most famous son of the Camargue. He was not only the region's most outstanding poet, he gave his name to the fierce wind, that sweeps the area, and founded a splendid museum dedicated to all things Provençale.

You can also see, incorporated into the Hôtel Nord-Pinus, two Corinthian columns which, almost 2,000 years ago, formed part of a temple next to the Roman forum.

There are many other historic monuments to visit in Arles, the most important of which is the amphitheatre. All the Roman sites and museums are open to the public, and it is possible to buy a season ticket which allows you to visit them all at reduced prices.

The amphitheatre is still remarkably well-preserved, and is supposed to be the twelfth largest of the seventy known from the Roman world. It could hold up to 15,000 spectators. It was built in the first century on the site of an original wooden arena. It is still possible to walk down in the depths of the building through the cages where the animals and slaves were kept. During the Middle Ages it was used as a fortress, and two towers remain. It is used now regularly for bullfights, both the Spanish sort and the French. In the Spanish bullfight the animal is killed, while in the French version, young men try to capture rosettes draped over the bull's horns. The latter version is far more enjoyable.

In the rue du Cloître is the Roman theatre, built in the reign of Augustus. It has many well-preserved statues. It could seat 7,500 and it is still an excellent auditorium.

Other things to see are Les Alyscamps, a path lined with sarcophagi with a ruined Romanesque church; the St Trophime cloisters, dating from the twelfth century, around an enchanting garden; and the Roman baths of Trouille, said to date from the fourth century and part of Constantine's great palace. The water was carried 15 miles to the baths by aqueduct.

There are also many museums, such as the museum of Christian art (the finest collection of sarcophagi outside Rome); the museum of pagan art and the museum of fine arts in the rue du Grand Prieuré which includes a collection of old drawings by Picasso.

Nearby, and worth visiting, is St-Gilles, to the west of Arles, and another pilgrimage stop on the road to Compostela. It has a fine abbey church with carvings dating from the twelfth century depicting the life of Christ. In the crypt is the tomb of St Gilles, which dates from the eleventh century; there is a belfry to climb and a museum to be visited.

Tour of Nîmes

The next overnight stop is at the equally historic Nîmes. On the way it is worth making the detour to St-Rémy-de-Provence, birthplace of astrologer Nostradamus in 1503. His life is chronicled at the Musée Alpilles Pierre de Brun. The museum, in a sixteenth-century château, also has a collection of local art, and souvenirs of Mistral. His home is at Maillane, 4 miles away, where there is a museum. Also in St-Rémy is an archaeological museum housed in the Hôtel de Sade, once owned by the family of the notorious Marquis.

If you have time, visit the Roman excavations at Glanum, about a mile to the south. There is an archway from the second century BC, the oldest surviving in southern France, and an early mausoleum. Digs at Glanum uncover and show the presence of man as far back as Neolithic times.

Les Baux, some way to the west, attracts visitors in their hundreds of thousands, and the cliff-top fortress carved out of the stone, and its unspoilt village, are still appealing. There are many buildings from the fourteenth century, and the castle dates from the thirteenth. This area is so rich in history that one could spend days exploring, but in the short time available press on to Nîmes. As with Arles, it is possible to buy a season ticket giving access to all the main attractions, and saving quite a lot of money.

These attractions include the amphitheatre, not as large as the one in Arles but in much better order. It is used for French-style bullfights and throughout the summer, mock gladiator fights and chariot races are also staged for the tourists. In the blvd Hugo is the Maison Carrée, a temple built just before the birth of Christ, in Greek style. It is the finest remaining Roman temple of its type, and has a museum within the sanctum containing antiquities.

Try also to see the ornamental French gardens dating from the eighteenth century in the quai de la Fontaine. It also contains remains of Roman baths and the ruined Temple of Diana. Next to the gardens is the Tour Magne, an octagonal watchtower built in the first century BC: it is worth climbing up to the platform at the top for the views.

In the rue de la Lampèze there is a Roman collecting basin for water bought in from the Pont-du-Gard. From here it was distributed by ten canals to various parts of the city. The only other structure like it has been found at Pompeii. Also see the Porte d'Arles, a Roman gateway in the town walls dating from 16BC

Nîmes has some excellent museums; for instance the museum of old Nîmes, with its history of the town, as well as a history of bullfighting, the museum of archaeology, and the museum of fine arts.

Montpellier to Carcassonne

From Nîmes the trip runs south-west to Montpellier, which is a thriving town and university centre. It has many fine old buildings, but on the way a stop off at Aigues-Mortes is essential. It is a perfectly-preserved walled town. It is best to park outside between the canal and the Saracen's tower and to enter the town through the massive archway. Note how thick the walls are. The town is now a tourist trap full of souvenir shops and cafés, but one can still envisage what it was like 800 years ago when the armies start to assemble before setting sail on Crusade. There are magnificent views from the ramparts and you can walk right round the town along the walls.

While travelling from Nîmes, try also to spend some time in the Camargue. It is possible to cut down and use the coastal road which runs between the Etangs but be warned, the surface is extremely bad.

Montpellier is an old university town and capital of the Bas- (low) Languedoc region. It is still possible to walk round the roads that ring the old town, and these have been built on the site of the original fortified walls. One should walk down the promenade du Peyrou, with its seventeenth- and eighteenth-century mansions. The terraced walk also offers views of the Mediterranean. The botanical gardens, founded by Henry IV in 1593, are the oldest in France. Another essential visit is to the fourteenth-century Gothic cathedral, and the fabulous Fabre museum which houses one of the best collections of paintings in France. The university dates back to the eleventh century, when a school of medicine was founded. The law school dates from 1160, and the university proper was given its charter by Pope Nicholas IV in 1289.

Montpellier is also a good base from which to visit the many vineyards in the area, including Listel, which is just a short distance off the Montpellier to Béziers road.

Béziers is an agricultural and wine town, set in the heart of vineyards. It produces *vin ordinaire*, notably Muscat, the grape said to have been introduced by the Romans. As with Montpellier, after an hour or two's sightseeing in the town you should get out and visit the vineyards.

Béziers stands on a hill overlooking the River Orb. It was a former Roman town and there are still remains of an amphitheatre. It was fortified in the twelfth century by the Lords of Carcassonne, but this did not prevent a bloody massacre in 1209, when a force sent by the Pope killed all the inhabitants to stamp out heresy. The Roman-Gothic church of Ste La Madeleine was the scene of some of the bloodiest fighting. In the thirteenth century, the city walls were rebuilt, and at the same time the cathedral church of St Nazaire was constructed on the hill over the town. It is a fortified church and well worth visiting.

From Béziers, continue south-west to Narbonne. The journey proceeds through vineyards on the right and the Mediterranean on the left. You should take the trouble to stop at the occasional tasting centre to try the wines; these centres are all well-marked.

Narbonne was founded by the Romans in 118BC, although it then stood on the Mediterranean and became a flourishing port. When the Romans left in the fifth century, it was captured by the Visigoths who made it their capital. Their rule lasted for 300 years, until 719, when the Saracens invaded and took control. Then, the town was controlled by the Counts of Toulouse

PLACES OF INTEREST IN THE MIDI

ARLES AND AREA

Arles
Many Roman remains; amphitheatre; theatre; obelisks; church of St Trophime (twelfth-century); Hôtel de Ville; statue of Mistral; Hôtel Nord-Pinus; Les Alyscamps; Roman baths of Trouille; museums of Christian art, pagan art, fine arts.

St-Gilles
Abbey church, older crypt, museum, belfry.

NIMES AND AREA

Nîmes
Amphitheatre; Maison Carrée (Hellenic temple); French garden; Tour Magne; ruins of Temple of Diana; Roman baths; Porte d'Arles; museums; and old town.

St-Rémy-de-Provence
Birthplace of Nostradamus; Musée Alpilles Pierre de Brun, sixteenth-century château; archaeological museum.

Maillane
Home of Mistral; museum.

Glanum
Prehistoric and Roman excavations.

Les Baux
Hilltop fortress; many fourteenth-century buildings; churches; ancient hospital; old village; thirteenth-century castle.

Montpellier
Old town and university centre; promenade du Peyrou; seventeenth- and eighteenth-century mansions; botanical gardens (oldest in France); fourteenth-century Gothic cathedral; Fabre Museum.

Aigues-Mortes
Magnificent walled town, Saracen's tower, many old buildings.

Camargue
One of Europe's finest wild areas, ideal for birdwatchers and naturalists.

BEZIERS AND AREA

Béziers
Remains of Roman theatre, Roman-Gothic church of Ste La Madeleine; thirteenth-century city fortifications and walls; cathedral church of St Nazaire.

NARBONNE AND AREA

Narbonne
Thirteenth-century cathedral of St Just; twelfth-century basilica of St Paul-Serges; Palais des Archévêques; Gothic town hall; fine arts museum; history museum; old town.

Carcassonne
Cité; medieval fortifications; Basilique St Nazaire (eleventh-century); Château Comtal and museum; Porte Narbonnaise; church of St Vincent; cathedral of St Michel.

who ruled one half, and the bishops who ruled the other. It was not until the beginning of the sixteenth century that it was united under the French Crown. The thirteenth-century cathedral of St Just was never completed, but the 'choir' and two square towers can still be seen.

Additionally, the twelfth-century basilica of St Paul-Serge, and the three square towers of the fortified Palais des Archévêques are worth looking at. The Gothic-style town hall was added to the palace in the nineteenth century. The palace now houses two fine museums, one of art and history, and the other archaeological. It is also worth exploring the winding streets and alleys of the old town, with its many fine old buildings.

Narbonne is another wine town, specialising in Aude wines, and there are many opportunities to taste them both inside and around the town. There is also a wine centre.

The last port of call is Carcassonne, due west of Narbonne, the capital of the Aude *département*. The river Aude divides the town into town, the lower town, and the city (Ville, Ville-Bas and Cité). The Cité contains the finest remains of medieval fortifications in Europe, so is a must for any visitor to this region. The hill that comprises the Cité was certainly occupied in the fifth century BC by the Iberians, then by the Gallo-Romans. The inner ramparts were built in the late fifth century by Euric I, King of the Visigoths. The fortifications resisted all attempts to breech them for almost 300 years, until the Saracens stormed them successfully. Other things to be seen are the Basilique St Nazaire, from the eleventh century; the Château Comtal, incorporated into the fortifications in the twelfth century and now a museum; and the Porte Narbonnaise, surrounded by its twin towers, guarding the entrance to the Cité. When peace was restored to the region in the mid-seventeenth century, the fortifications were no longer needed and fell into disrepair. Work restoring them started in 1844 and continued for 120 years. Today, the city is a living museum to the past. In the Ville-Bas, see the church of St Vincent and the cathedral of St Michel, both from the thirteenth century.

Carcassonne is quite magnificent, and it has the additional pleasure of being primarily a wine town, so it is possible to sit in one of the shaded streets, sipping a glass of the local wine and drinking in the history at the same time.

Gastronomy of the Midi

The southern coast between the Rhône and the Spanish border plays host to a variety of cuisines, many of them reliant on garlic and olive oil, which grow in plenty throughout. The sea provides the ingredients for many traditional dishes, while there is lamb from Roussillon, beef from around Albi and Carcassonne, and the magnificent *cassoulet* originated in Toulouse can now be found, with interesting variations, throughout the Languedoc. *Cassoulet* is perhaps the region's most famous dish, traditionally made from mutton, pork, preserved goose, and any other meats that came to hand, together with haricot beans.

There are plentiful supplies of vegetables, especially tomatoes and aubergines which figure prominently in many dishes, and in the south-west, adjoining Gascony and the Dordogne, there are to be found much richer foods such as *foie gras*, duck, goose, truffles and so on.

Because of the poor pasture, much of the meat can be tough unless cooked slowly, but the people of the region have developed special slow cooking techniques, and casseroles and stews can be delicious. In the south-west small birds, especially thrushes, ortolans and quails are eaten, roasted whole, head and all, or served wrapped in pastry, or made into pâté. Snails, too, are frequently served, having been gathered fat from the vineyards.

There is excellent *charcuterie*, and the sausage of Toulouse is especially famous. Offal, including tripe, is favoured in the northern districts, up into the Cévennes foothills. Soups of all types, casseroles and stews figure prominently, while the south coast has excellent fish. Collioure is noted for its anchovies and sardines. Sète has its own famous offshore oyster beds, and Palava has created many speciality tuna dishes.

Because of the rice fields in the Rhône and the influence of Spanish cooking, rice is widely used to accompany dishes, but despite the closeness of the sea, many restaurants prefer to sell salted fish dishes rather than fresh. After *cassoulet*, the most famous dish is *brandade de morue*, a speciality of Nîmes. It is salt cod mixed with olive oil and pounded into a paste and served hot. In Roussillon, the Spanish influence is again seen in the cuisine. Bitter Seville oranges, tomatoes, aubergines and sweet peppers are often used, and always garlic.

Aïgo bouido is a traditional garlic soup with olive oil and eggs. It is slowly cooked with plenty of herbs, and served piping hot over cubes of fried bread. Other soups include *brou*, or *braou*, a Roussillon country soup made with cabbage and rice, and *cousina*, or *cousinat*, from the Cévennes and Vivarais, which is a chestnut soup, laced with cream, apples, and served with chunks of bread. This should not be confused with *cousinette*, which is a vegetable soup of sorrel, chicory and spinach. *Ouillade* comes from both Languedoc and Roussillon and is a soup made from cabbage and haricot beans, while *oulade* is a Languedoc cabbage and potato soup with added salt pork and sausage. You will also find *touron*, an onion and milk soup, usually poured over bread and served with cheese.

From Roussillon there is also *mayorquina*, a tomato and cabbage soup, and all the above may come with *millas*, a flat cake of maize flour often fried and eaten with soups and stews. It is also eaten as a dessert, however, when it is sprinkled with sugar. Another maize flour dish is *millassou*, which is a sweet flan offered as a dessert.

Bouillinade is the Roussillon version of *bouillabaisse*, and is a huge fish stew with added potatoes, onions, peppers and garlic. There are many dishes featuring *morue* (salt cod), and crayfish are also popular, especially *civet de langouste*, a Languedoc speciality of crayfish cooked in white wine with garlic, tomatoes and onions.

A lot of poultry is eaten, including duck and goose. *Alicot* is a speciality of the south-west, a duck or goose stew made from the wings and giblets with _cèpes_ and chestnuts from the Cévennes added. Other goose or duck dishes include _confit_. The birds are cooked in their own fats and then preserved in earthenware jars or bottles. Occasionally, pork and poultry is used and to add to the confusion, _confit_ can also be applied to a type of candied and crystallised fruit. _Magret_ is also worth sampling. It is the lightly-cooked breast of duck specially fattened for _foie gras_. It is usually grilled or gently fried but always served rare. Other birds are eaten and you will find ortolan, a small bunting which is usually fattened in cages before cooking. It is roasted on skewers, and when served _à la Landaise_ it has been stuffed and cooked in its own fat. _A la Brissac_ means with ham, truffles and mushrooms. The locals also serve _gobemouche_, the Languedoc name for the fig-pecker, a small bird which is usually grilled and served on a skewer.

Charcuterie is very common and there is excellent pork and sausage. _Coudenat_ or _coudenou_ is a large pork sausage served in thick slices and eaten hot. There is _galabart_, a large black pudding popular throughout the south of France, and _boutifare_, a Roussillon black pudding made from bacon and herbs. _Gratterons_ are cubes of pork and bacon, salted when hot and then eaten cold, and _marinoun_ is a very large pork sausage of the Languedoc. You will also come across _melsat_, a large white sausage which can be eaten either hot or cold, and _murcon_, a Languedoc sausage eaten hot.

Other rather more unusual meat dishes include _criadillas_, the Languedoc name for bull's testicles. They are a speciality of the Nîmes area, but generally are available only after a Spanish-type bullfight. _Fèche_ is dried and salted pig's liver, usually served with radishes, and there is _frappo_, a Languedoc speciality of stewed ox tripe.

Snails are popular and are served in many different ways. There is _escargots à la Arlésienne_ which means cooked in white wine, with ham and tomatoes. If they are offered _'lou cagaraulat'_ it means cooked with anchovies, nuts and tomatoes and is a Languedoc speciality. _A la Languedoc-ienne_ is with ham, anchovies, tomatoes and a piquant sauce, while _à la Narbonnaise_ means with bacon, anchovies, almonds and white wine, and sometimes with mayonnaise. _Cargolade_ is another speciality dish of Languedoc-Roussillon, of snails cooked in wine, or over charcoal.

Daube is the most famous stew, of either meat or fish cooked in wine, stock and vegetables. If it just says _daube_ on the menu, it usually means beef cooked in red wine. There is, however, _daube à la Béarnaise_, with ham and tomatoes, and _à l'Avignonnaise_, with lamb. _Escuedella_ is a Roussillon dish of beef boiled with eggs and served with pasta, and there is also _estouffade_ or _estouffat_, meat stew with wine, herbs and vegetables. This dish usually consists of one large chunk of meat. _Estouffade de haricots blanc_ is pork stewed with haricot beans and tomatoes.

There are many types of meat balls, including _boles de picoulat_, made from diced beef and pork, with eggs and garlic added. They are served with tomatoes and are a Roussillon speciality. _Caillettes_ are pork meatballs or faggots, often served with liver and spinach. Lamb and mutton dishes include _pétéran_, a Languedoc stew of sheep's trotters, tripe, ham and vegetables with wine; and there is _poitrine de mouton farcie à l'Ariègeoise_, mutton breast stuffed with ham and cooked in wine with vegetables.

Other meat dishes might include *gras double*, ox tripe stewed with ham, vegetables and herbs, or *Isard*, the local name for the Chamois, found in the Pyrénées. *Languette* is another Languedoc speciality, tongue; and there is *mongeto*, a local Languedoc name for haricot beans, so *mongetado* is stew of haricot beans with pork crackling. One of the most unusual dishes is *tripe de thon en daube*, which is to be found in the Languedoc; it is tuna tripe cooked in white wine with peppers and onions.

There are many sauces to accompany dishes including *Collioure*; the port gives its name to a mayonnaise sauce, flavoured with anchovy and garlic. *Feuillet* from Roussillon is a mixture of anchovies, olives, eggs and tomatoes, and *à la Languedocienne* means with *cèpes*, tomatoes, aubergines and garlic. You might also come across *foudjou*, from the Languedoc, which is goat's milk cheese mixed with brandy and garlic and eaten with potatoes.

Desserts include *cruchades*, fritters or pancakes made from maize flour, and *pescajou*, a sweet pancake from Languedoc. *Petit pâtés* are small sweet pastries, and *marrons glacés* are candied chestnuts. It is also worth looking for *pinu*, a small aniseed cake from Languedoc, and *touron*, an almond pastry with other nuts, marzipan and crystallised fruits.

Some of the cheeses of the region include *Bleu de Loudes*, a blue cheese from the Languedoc, made in the Velay region; it has little smell but quite a strong flavour; *Les Orrys*, a cow's milk cheese from the hills around Foix, on the River Ariège, to the north of Roussillon, which is strong and tangy. Then there is *Passé l'an*, really from Quercy, a hard, strong cheese, aged usually for at least two years, and *Pélardon des Cévennes*, a Languedoc soft cheese made from goat's milk, which has a nutty flavour. Finally, there is *Picodon*, goat's milk cheese made in Provence.

HOTELS AND RESTAURANTS OF THE MIDI

Agde
(34200 Hérault)

La Tamarisserie
quai Théophile-Cornu
2¹/₂ miles east on the D32
☎ (67) 94 20 87
A 30-room hotel, reasonably-priced, on the banks of the Grau d'Agde. The restaurant specialises in fresh fish from the Hérault estuary, as well as traditional Languedoc dishes.

Amélie-les-Bains-Palada (66110 Pyrénées-Orientales)

Castel Emeraude
route de la Corniche
☎ 39 02 83
A 31-room quiet hotel, to the west of the town overlooking the River Tech. Rooms reasonably-priced, and restaurant fair.

Arles-sur-Tech
(66150 Pyrénées-Orientales)

Glycines
rue Joc-de-Pilota
☎ 39 10 09
A very reasonably-priced 34-room *logis* and restaurant with attractive terrace.

Béziers
(34500 Hérault)

L'Olivier
12 rue Boïeldieu
☎ (67) 28 86 64
An excellent restaurant, run by William Druet and Michel Roque, the latter in charge of the kitchens and the marvellous cuisine. The menus are fairly expensive but worth it. A good idea to book.

Carcassonne
(11000 Aude)

Domaine d'Auriac
route de St Hilaire

☎ (68) 25 72 22
A very quiet 23-room hotel in its own parkland, 2¹/2 miles south east on the D104. Well-equipped with terrace, swimming pool, gardens, and tennis courts. The rooms are not expensive and the restaurant is reasonable.

Terminus
2 ave. Maréchal Joffre
☎ (68) 25 25 00
A reasonably-priced 112-room hotel near the station. No restaurant, but breakfast served.

Hôtel Montségur
27 allée d'Iéna
☎ (68) 25 31 41
A 21-room hotel, comfortable and not expensive. The restaurant at No 32 (☎ (68) 25 22 17) is good value.

Hôtel Cité,
place St-Nazaire
☎ (68) 25 03 34
A very comfortable, expensive 54-room hotel. A good, inexpensive restaurant during the summer season only.

Logis de Trencavel
290 ave. Général Leclerc
☎ (68) 71 09 53
A well-priced restaurant and 12 simple, inexpensive rooms.

Auberge Pont Levis
at the entrance to the city, near La Porte Narbonnaise
☎ (68) 25 55 23
A very good restaurant, offering local dishes at reasonable prices. Very good views.

Gignac
(34150 Hérault)

Restaurant Central Capion
3 blvd de l'Esplanade
☎ (67) 57 50 83
Good fare at reasonable prices, run by the Capion family.

Collioure
(66190 Pyrénées-Orientales)

Casa Païral
☎ (68) 82 05 81
A charming hotel from which to tour, 24 inexpensive rooms, no restaurant but breakfast served, and charming gardens.

Madeloc
rue R. Rolland
☎ (68) 82 07 56
Another good hotel to use as a base. There are 22 reasonably-priced rooms, no restaurant but breakfasts. Most rooms have balconies with views.

La Frégate
24 quai de l'Amirauté
☎ (68) 82 06 05
A very comfortable, recently renovated hotel with 25 inexpensive rooms, and a quite marvellous restaurant run by Yves Costa. The décor may not be much, but the food is magnificent and the wine list spectacular. Very good value.

La Bodega
6 rue de la République
☎ (68) 82 05 60
A very atmospheric restaurant in an old wine cellar. Good traditional local cuisine. Good inexpensive menus.

Lacaune (81230 Tarn)

Hôtel Fusiès
rue République
☎ (63) 37 02 03
A very friendly hotel just outside the area but a good touring base. There are 60 inexpensive rooms and a very reasonably-priced restaurant.

Château de Riell
☎ (63) 96 20 56
A rather grotesque château housing 20 very comfortable but expensive rooms, and a very good restaurant with chef René Serre producing delightful cuisine, a balance of traditional and modern. Expensive but very good, and a fine wine list.

Montpellier (34000 Hérault)

Hôtel de Noailles
2 rue des Ecoles Centrales
☎ (66) 60 49 80
In the heart of the old town. A 30-room, reasonably-priced hotel, no restaurant but breakfasts served. Parking is on the street and thefts from cars is a problem.

Hôtel Frantel
218 rue du Bastion-Ventandour
Le Polygone
☎ (66) 67 65 66
A modern, comfortable 116-room hotel, not expensive, with a good restaurant *Lou Pairol.*

La Demeure des Brousses
route des Vauguières
☎ (66) 65 77 66
2¹/2 miles east on the D172. An old converted farmhouse in its own

gardens, with 20 reasonably-priced rooms. The restaurant, L'Orangerie (☎ (66) 65 52 27) is fair.

Métropole
3 rue du Clos-René
☎ (66) 58 11 22
A large, comfortable, 84-room hotel with 4 apartments, not cheap but very good service. Restaurant good but also expensive.

Sofitel
allée Jules Milhaud
☎ (66) 54 04 04
A modern, very comfortable hotel with 98 quite expensive rooms, no restaurant, but breakfasts.

Le Chandelier
3 rue Leenhart
☎ (66) 92 61 62
A very good if somewhat expensive restaurant, with some marvellous ideas.

La Réserve Rimbaud
820 ave. de St-Maur
☎ (66) 72 52 53
A very good restaurant, with Jean Tarrit following his father's footsteps in the kitchen. Marvellous desserts, and a terrace for dining out in the summer overlooking the river. Expensive.

Les Frères Runel
27 rue Maguelone
☎ (66) 58 43 82
An excellent restaurant, run by the Runels, with marvellous fish dishes and tremendous game. Again expensive but worth it.

Mourèze
(34800 Herault)

Hauts de Mourèze
☎ (67) 96 04 84

10 very comfortable, inexpensive rooms, no restaurant but breakfast served.

Narbonne
(11100 Aude)

Réverbère
4 place Jacobins
☎ (68) 32 29 18
A truly magnificent restaurant run by Claude and Sabine Giraud. The food is creative but faithful to the locality, memorable, and excellent value.

La Résidence
6 rue du 1er-Mai
☎ (68) 32 19 41
A charming 26-room hotel near the cathedral. Very comfortable. Good value rooms; no restaurant, but breakfast served.

Novotel
1³/4 miles out of town
☎ (68) 41 59 52
A modern 96-room air-conditioned hotel. Rooms quite expensive, and cafeteria only available.

Hôtel Languedoc
22 blvd Gambetta
☎ (68) 65 14 74
A 45-room hotel near the centre of town, rooms not expensive, and a reasonable restaurant offering cheap meals.

Restaurant Alsace
2 ave. P. Semard
☎ (68) 65 10 24
Not expensive, and with some good fish dishes.

Le Floride
66 blvd Frédéric Mistral
☎ (68) 32 05 52
Alexis Lichine says he had his finest *cassoulet*

here, so what more need be said. Very reasonable prices.

Nîmes (30000 Gard)

Novotel
Périphérique Sud, D42
☎ (66) 84 60 20
Modern 96-room hotel, restaurant for snacks.

Sofitel
Périphérique Sud, D42
☎ (66) 84 40 44
Very comfortable, 98-room hotel. Dine in *Le Mazet* by the pool, or on the terrace. Reasonably priced.

Le Louvre
2 sq. de la Couronne
☎ (66) 67 22 75
A very comfortable 35-room hotel in a charming square. Good restaurant for local fare

Cheval Blanc et Arènes
1 place des Arènes
☎ (66) 67 20 03
Right opposite the arena, this comfortable 48-room hotel is friendly and inexpensive, like the restaurant.

Impérator
place Aristide Briand
☎ (66) 21 90 30
Restaurant: Enclos de la Fontaine
quai de la Fontaine
A luxury 62-room hotel in delightful gardens, and a good, if somewhat expensive, restaurant.

Restaurant Alexandre
Garons, 5 miles south on the D42
☎ (66) 70 08 99
Pierre Alexandre has the finest establishment in

town even if it is too close to the airport. The food is magical but the prices down to earth.

Perpignan
(66000 Pyrénées-Orientales)

Parc Hôtel
18 blvd Jean-Bourrat
☎ (68) 35 14 14
A reasonably-priced, very convenient 67-room hotel with air-conditioning. The restaurant, *Chapon Fin*, is good and improving.

Hôtel de la Loge
place de la Loge
☎ (68) 35 54 84
A charming, modernised 29-room hotel near the town hall. Very comfortable and reasonably-priced, no restaurant but breakfasts.

Hôtel Arcades
ave. d'Espagne
☎ (68) 85 11 11
A modern 128-room hotel, 1¼ miles south of the town on the N9. Fairly expensive, and a fair restaurant.

Novotel
☎ (68) 64 02 22
A modern 86-room hotel, 6 miles north off the N9. Comfortable, quite expensive, with cafeteria.

Les Antiquares
place Després
☎ (68) 34 06 58
Michel Aubailly, the patron chef, is another talented artist creating marvellous fish dishes and stylising traditional cuisine. Not expensive.

François Villon
1 rue Four St-Jean
☎ (68) 51 18 43
The cooking is very good, and the prices still very reasonable.

Le Vauban
29 quai Vauban
☎ (68) 51 05 10
Good traditional fare at super low prices.

St-Laurent-de-la-Salanque
(66250 Pyrénées-Orientales)

Auberge du Pin
route Perpignan
☎ (68) 28 01 62
A very comfortable, friendly 20-room hotel with very reasonably-priced rooms and an excellent value-for-money restaurant.

Hôtel Commerce
rue G. Péri
☎ (68) 28 02 21
Another good base hotel; 27 reasonably-priced rooms and cheap, but fairly good, restaurant.

St-Martin-de-Londres
(34380 Hérault)

La Crêche
route du Frouzet
☎ (67) 55 00 04
A charming small hotel and restaurant, 3 miles northwest on the D122. There are 7 very comfortable rooms, not expensive. The food is a delight, not cheap, but worth every franc.

St-Pons-de-Thomières
(34220 Hérault)

Château de Ponderach
just out of town on the route de Narbonne
☎ (67) 97 02 57
There are 11 charming rooms, not too expensive, in a very quiet setting, with marvellous food.

Sète (34200 Hérault)

Grand Hôtel
17 quai du Gal-de-Lattre-de-Tassigny
☎ (67) 74 71 77
A 51-room, very comfortable, modernised hotel; room rates reasonable, and the restaurant, *La Rotonde*, is good.

Impérial
1¼ miles out of town on the place E. Herriot
☎ (67) 53 28 32
Modern, very comfortable; 47 inexpensive rooms. No restaurant but breakfasts and cafeteria.

La Palangrotte
1 rampe Paul-Valéry
☎ (67) 74 80 35
A very good restaurant run by Alain Gémignani, specialising in marvellous fish dishes at very favourable prices.

Vernet-lès-Bains
(66500 Pyrénées-Orientales)

Résidence des Baüs et Mas Fleuri
blvd Clémenceau
☎ (68) 05 51 94
A charming 39-room hotel in this small spa town. Rooms comfortable and not expensive. No restaurant but breakfast served. Attractive gardens with swimming pool.

VINEYARDS OF COTEAUX DU LANGUEDOC

AREA AROUND MONTPELLIER

(All open daily for tasting
and visits)

Vérargues
Château de la Devèze TRW
M. Chevallier

St-Christol
M. Gabriel Martin   TRW

M. Facheris   TRW
Cave Coopérative

Langlade
M. Arnal   TRW

St-Génis-des Mourgues
Cave Coopérative   TRW
M. Orange

St-Drezery
Cave Coopérative   TRW
M. Gruvel

M. Spitaleri   TRW
Mas de Carrat

Fontaines
Domaine de la Roque TRW
M. Lauriol

Claret
Domaine de VilleneuveTRW
M. Florac

Cave Coopérative   TRW
M. Dumas

Corconne
Cave Coopérative   TRW

Lauret
Domaine de
   Cantafaroune   TRW
M. Haberer

Valflaunes
Cave Coopérative   TRW

St-Mathieu-de-Treviers
Cave Coopérative   TRW
M. Santanac

St-Gely-du-Fesc
Mas Puech de FourquesTRW
Mme Laliam

Montpeyroux
Domaine du Plô   TRW
M. Lonjon

Cave Coopérative   TRW

St-André-de-Sangonis
Domaine de Crès
   Ricards   TRW
M. Heulz

St-Saturnin
Cave Coopérative   TRW
M. Fenateu

St-Félix-de-Lodez
Cave Coopérative   TRW
M. Amador

Sallèles-du-Bosc
Domaine Vaillé
   Bernard   TRW

St-Jean-de-la-Blaquière
Cave Coopérative   TRW

Aspiran
Les Vignerons du
   Ceressou   TRW
M. Cambonie

Paulhan
Château de la Condamine
   Bertrand   TRW
M. Jany

Lézignan-la-Cèbe
Château d'Ormesson   TRW
M. d'Ormesson

Villeveyrac
Cave Coopérative   TRW
M. Pelissier

Abbaye de Valmagne TRW
Mme d'Aleine

St-Georges-d'Orques
Cave Coopérative   TRW
M. Cadène

Laverune
Château de l'Engarran TRW
Mme Grill

Loiras-du-Bosc
M. Jordy   TRW

Gignac
Maison des Vins de
   Gignac   TRW

Montpellier
Château de
   Flaugergues   TRW
M. de Colbert

La Costière   TRW
M. Teissier

Mauguio
Mas Combet   TRW
M. Gilles

St-Aunes
Mas de Calage   TRW
M. Delbez

AREA AROUND CABREROLLES

Pinet
Cave Coopérative   TRW

Nizas
Château de Nizas   TRW
M. Gaujal

Pézenas
M. Roux   TRW
Domaine de St-Jean-de-
   Bébian

R=red wine   W=white wine   P=rosé wine   S=sparkling wine

Cabrières
Cave Coopérative TRW
M. Courrenc

Gabian
Cave Coopérative
M. Jougla

Rouqessels
M. Benezech TRW

Fos
M. Ollier TRW

Faugères
Cave Coopérative TRW

M. Alquier TRW

Caussiniojouls
Château de la Gineste TRW

Guy Roque TRW

Cabrerolles
Château de la Liquière TRW
Jean Vidal

Bernard Vidal TRW

Domaine de Fabrègues TRW
M. Saur

Raymond Roque TRW

Christian Viguier TRW

P. Bitaillou/R. Coste TRW

Lentheric
Vidal Platelle TRW

M. Louison TRW

Laurens
Cave Coopérative TRW

Château de Greizan TRW
M. Lubac

Autignac
Domaine Curé TRW
M. Curé

Cave Coopérative TRW
J. Pons

St-Nazaire-de-Ladarez
Domaine J. and
  H. Madalle TRW
Libes-Cavaille

Causses et Veyran
Cave Coopérative TRW

Murviel-lès-Béziers
Château de Coujan TRW
François M. Guy

Cessenon
Domaine de
  Cazals-Viel TRW
M. Miquel

Puisserguier
Domaine de Milhau TRW
M. Lacugue

**Prades-sur-
Vernazobres**
M. Jougla TRW

Roquebrun
Cave Coopérative TRW

Berlou
Cave Coopérative TRW
M. Darde

St-Chinian
Maison des Vins TRW
M. Baro

Les Quatre Vents TRW
M. Simon

Cazedarnes
Domaine Fontcaude TRW

Domaine des Calmette
M. Calmette

Cébazan
Cave Coopérative TRW

Quarante
Château de Quarante TRW
Michel M. Py

AREA AROUND NARBONNET

Armissan
Domaine de Langel TRW
Alain M. Peyric

Domaine de Combe
  Longue TRW
Mm. Durand

Fleury d'Aude
Robert M. Boterro TRW

Domaine de St-Pierre-
  la-Garrigue TRW
Jacques M. Martinez

Domaine de Mire
  l'Etang TRW
M. Chamayrac

Domaine de Rivière
  le Haut TRW
Jean M. Segura

Narbonne
Domaine de
  l'Hospitalet TRW
M. Cools

Domaine de
  Complazens TRW
M. Egretier

Domaine de Ricardelle
  de la Clape TRW
M. Jousseaume

Domaine des Vires TRW
M. Lignères

M. Combastet TRW
Château de Ricardelle
  de la Clape

T=tasting   E=English spoken   G=guided tours   C=château/building to visit

Château de Capitoul TRW
M. Schaefer

M. Ortola TRW
Notre-Dame du Quatorze

Château de St-Charles du
Quatorze TRW

Gruissan
Château de Rouquette
sur Mer TRW
M. Boscary

Château de Moujan TRW
M. de Braquilanges

Salles d'Aude
M. Hue TRW

Château de Salles

Château du Pech TRW
de Celeyran
M. de St-Exupéry

Vinassan
Château de
Marmorières TRW
M. de Woillemont

MINERVOIS VINEYARDS

(Vineyards and cellars
open daily to the public.)

Ginestas
Celliers des Producteurs:

Argeliers TRW
11120 Ginestas
☎ (68) 46 11 14

Bize-Minervois TRW
11120 Ginestas
☎ (68) 46 10 20

Mailhac TRW
11120 Ginestas
☎ (68) 46 13 06

Pouzols-Minervois TRW
11120 Ginestas
☎ (68) 46 13 76

Roubia TRW
11200 Lézignan
☎ (67) 27 10 14

Montouliers TRW
34310 Capestang
☎ (68) 89 41 94

Artisans Vignerons:

MM. Ayraud-Pages TRW
Argens
11200 Lézignan
☎ (67) 91 21 43

Mme M.A. Sanconie TRW
11120 Ginestas
☎ (68) 46 22 52

M. Maurice Joyeux TRW
Montouliers
34310 Capestang
☎ (68) 89 41 92

Châteaux or Domaines:

M. Christian Bonnel TRW
Bize-Minervois
11120 Ginestas
☎ (68) 91 22 59

Mme Dominique
de Bertier TRW
Paraza
11200 Lézignan
☎ (67) 27 09 43

Mme Francine Gotti TRW
11120 Ginestas
☎ (68) 46 21 83

M. Pierre Fil TRW
Mailhac
11120 Ginestas
☎ (68) 46 13 09

M. Bernard Mazard TRW
11120 Ginestas
☎ (68) 46 12 01

M. Jacques
Meyzonnier TRW
Pouzols-Minervois
11120 Ginestas
☎ (68) 46 13 88

M. Guy Rancoule TRW
Mirepeisset
11120 Ginestas
☎ (68) 46 13 24

Peyriac-Minervois
Celliers des Producteurs:

Azille TRW
11700 Capendu
☎ (68) 91 40 29

Escales TRW
11200 Lézignan
☎ (67) 27 31 44

Homps TRW
11200 Lézignan
☎ (67) 91 22 14

Laure-Minervois TRW
11800 Trèbes
☎ (68) 78 12 12

Pepieux TRW
11700 Capendu
☎ (68) 91 41 04

Peyriac-Minervois
11160 Caunes-Minervois
☎ (68) 78 11 20

'La Grappe' Puicheric TRW
11700 Capendu
☎ (68) 43 70 01

'Le Progrès' Puicheric TRW
11700 Capendu
☎ (68) 43 70 23

Rieux-Minervois TRW
11160 Caunes-Minervois
☎ (68) 78 10 22

Tourouzelle TRW
11200 Lézignan
☎ (67) 91 23 29

R=red wine   W=white wine   P=rosé wine   S=sparkling wine

Artisan Vigneron:

M. Jean Biau   TRW
Tourouzelle
11200 Lézignan
☎ (67) 91 23 54

Châteaux or Domaines:

M. Jean Barthes   TRW
11800 Trèbes
☎ (68) 47 33 11

M. Jean-Baptiste
   Bonnet   TRW
Laure-Minervois
11800 Trèbes
☎ (68) 78 12 02

M. Cros
   Mayrevieille X   TRW
Laure-Minervois
11800 Trèbes
☎ (68) 78 14 64

M.Hélion de Beaulieu TRW
Tourouzelle
11200 Lézignan
☎ (67) 47 39 80

M. Bernard de Crozals TRW
Rieux-Minervois
11160 Caunes-Minervois
☎ (68) 78 10 51

M. Jean de Thelin   TRW
Blomac
11700 Capendu
☎ (68) 79 01 54

M. Aymar de Soos   TRW
Laure-Minervois
11800 Trèbes
☎ (68) 78 10 04

GFA La Boulandière TRW
Tourouzelle
11200 Lézignan
☎ (68) 27 06 27

GFA La Valseque   TRW
La Redorte
11700 Capendu
☎ (68) 43 70 12

M. Christian Ferret   TRW
Badens
11800 Trèbes
☎ (68) 79 15 25

M. Alfred Keim   TRW
Laure-Minervois
11800 Trèbes
☎ (68) 78 00 29

M. Roland Labène   TRW
Marseillette
11800 Trèbes
☎ (68) 79 00 19

M. Jean-Pierre
   Ormières   TRW
Laure-Minervois
11800 Trèbes
☎ (68) 78 17 82

M. Guy Panis   TRW
Bagnoles
11600 Conques-sur-Orbiel
☎ (68) 77 18 33

M. Jean-Yves Perret   TRW
Badens
11800 Trèbes
☎ (68) 79 18 37

Mme Madeleine
   Ramel   TRW
Tourouzelle
11200 Lézignan
☎ (67) 91 25 16

Mme Marie Remaury TRW
Azille
11700 Capendu
☎ (68) 91 40 22

Sté Mesnard-Bellissen TRW
11800 Trèbes
☎ (68) 47 37 33

Caunes-Minervois

Celliers des Producteurs:

Caunes-Minervois   TRW
11160 Caunes-Minervois
☎ (68) 78 00 98

Trausse-Minervois   TRW
11160 Caunes-Minervois
☎ (68) 78 01 15

Azillanet   TRW
34210 Olonzac
☎ (68) 91 22 61

Felines-Minervois   TRW
34210 Olonzac
☎ (68) 91 41 66

La Livinière   TRW
34210 Olonzac
☎ (68) 91 42 67

Siran 'La Siranaise'   TRW
34210 Olonzac
☎ (68) 91 42 17

Artisans Vignerons:

M. Charles Bacou   TRW
Cesseras
34210 Olonzac
☎ (68) 91 25 25

M. Jean Calvet   TRW
Azillanet
34210 Olonzac
☎ (68) 91 33 88

M. Jean-Claude
   Grasset   TRW
Beaufort
34210 Olonzac
☎ (68) 91 26 76

MM. Pierre and Robert
   Parisi   TRW
Cesseras
34210 Olonzac
☎ (68) 91 31 44

Châteaux or Domaines:

M. Daniel Domergue TRW
Trausse-Minervois
11160 Caunes-Minervois
☎ (68) 78 32 37

M. Marcel Julien   TRW
11160 Caunes-Minervois
☎ (68) 78 00 01

T=tasting   E=English spoken   G=guided tours   C=château/building to visit

MM. M. Moureau
and son   TRW
11160 Caunes-Minervois
☎ (68) 78 00 26

M. J.A. Tallavignes TRW
Trausse-Minervois
11160 Caunes-Minervois
☎ (68) 78 01 02

M. Gérard Blanc   TRW
La Livinière
34210 Olonzac
☎ (68) 91 42 87

Sté Gourgazaud   TRW
La Livinière
34210 Olonzac
☎ (68) 91 42 63

M. Jacques Maris   TRW
La Livinière
34210 Olonzac
☎ (68) 91 42 63

M. André Iche   TRW
Oupia
34210 Olonzac
☎ (68) 91 20 86

Mmes Mandeville
and Bardier   TRW
Siran
34210 Olonzac
☎ (68) 91 42 22

Mme Yvonne
Morbieu   TRW
11160 Caunes-Minervois
☎ (68) 78 00 02

M. Marc Remaury   TRW
Azillanet
34210 Olonzac
☎ (68) 91 22 66

Minerve

Celliers des Producteurs:

Agel   TRW
34210 Olonzac
☎ (68) 91 21 35

Aigne   TRW
34210 Olonzac
☎ (68) 91 22 44

Artisans Vignerons:

M. Antoine Abad   TRW
Minerve
34210 Olonzac
☎ (68) 91 22 94

M. Guy Cros   TRW
La Caunette
34210 Olonzac
☎ (68) 32 17 05

M. Pierre Derroja   TRW
La Caunette
34210 Olonzac
☎ (68) 91 23 04

Mme Jacqueline
Le Calvez   TRW
La Caunette
34210 Olonzac
☎ (68) 91 23 12

M. Roger Marcouire TRW
Minerve
34210 Olonzac
☎ (68) 91 26 81

M. Hervé Peyras   TRW
Minerve
34210 Olonzac
☎ (68) 91 25 49

M. Emile Rouanet   TRW
Minerve
34210 Olonzac
☎ (68) 91 30 37

M. Roger Rouquier   TRW
Aigne
34210 Olonzac

Châteaux or Domaines:

GFA Château   TRW
Agel
34210 Olonzac
☎ (68) 91 37 74

Mme Roselyne
Bourdiol   TRW
Aigne
34210 Olonzac
☎ (68) 91 22 54

M. Roland Fraisse   TRW
Minerve
34210 Olonzac
☎ (68) 91 30 66

M. René Maynadier TRW
Minerve
34210 Olonzac
☎ (68) 91 22 93

M. Jean Miquel   TRW
St-Jean
34360 St-Chinian
☎ (67) 38 07 56

M. André Tailhades
Minerve
34210 Olonzac
☎ (68) 91 26 77

Villeneuve-Minervois

Celliers des Producteurs:

Malves   TRW
11600 Conques-sur-Orbiel
☎ (68) 77 11 76

Villalier   TRW
11600 Conques-sur-Orbiel
☎ (68) 77 16 69

Villeneuve-Minervois TRW
11160 Caunes-Minervois
☎ (68) 26 16 02

Artisans Vignerons:

M. Camille Cabot   TRW
Villarzel-Cabardes
11600 Conques-sur-Orbiel
☎ (68) 77 12 07

Châteaux or Domaines:

MM. Poudou brothers TRW
Villeneuve-Minervois
11160 Caunes-Minervois
☎ (68) 26 17 86

R=red wine   W=white wine   P=rosé wine   S=sparkling wine

Coopératives:

Cave Coopérative de
  Vieillissement   TRW
Jouarres par Azille
11700 Capendu
☎ (68) 91 22 15

SICA 'Les Vignerons des
  Côteaux de Minerve' TRW
Route de Moussan
11100 Narbonne
☎ (68) 32 72 98

SARL 'Les Vignerons des
  Côteaux Occitans' TRW
RN 113
11200 Lézignan
☎ (67) 27 03 82

Union des Caves de
  Capendu   TRW
11700 Capendu
☎ (68) 79 00 76

SICA 'Vigneronne et
  Vinicole des Côteaux de
  Peyriac-Minervois' TRW
M. Michel Poudou
Rieux-Minervois
11160 Caunes-Minervois
☎ (68) 78 17 62

Union des Caves
  Coopératives de
  Peyriac-Minervois   TRW
M. Denis Jaumot
Laure-Minervois
11800 Trèbes
☎ (68) 78 17 57

UCTM Cave Coopérative
  'La Grappe'   TRW
Puicheric
11700 Capendu
☎ (68) 43 70 01

UCARO Union des Co-
  opérative Agricoles de la
  Région d'Olonzac   TRW
Maison du Minervois
34210 Olonzac
☎ (68) 91 35 74

Hauterives   TRW
Ornaison
11200 Lézignan
☎ (67) 27 09 06

VINEYARDS OF ROUSSILLON

Les Vignerons
  de Baixas   TR
66390 Baixas
☎ (68) 64 22 37
Open: by appointment.

Producteurs de la
  Barnède   TW
66670 Bages
☎ (68) 21 60 30
Open: Monday to Saturday
8am-noon and 2-7pm.

Moulin de Breuil   TW
Albert de Massia
Montesquieu
66740 St-Génis-des-
  Fontaines
☎ (68) 89 61 01
Open: by appointment.

Calvet-Marty   TR
36 ave. du Maréchal-Joffre
66300 Thuir
☎ (68) 53 42 62
Open: by appointment.

Domaine de Canterrane
Maurice Conte
Trouillas
66300 Thuir

☎ (68) 53 47 24
Open: Monday to Friday
9am-noon and 2-6pm,
Saturday 9am-noon.

Château Cap de Fouste   TR
Vignerons Catalans
route de Thuir
66011 Perpignan
☎ (68) 85 04 51
Open: by appointment.

Carbasse   TR
Fourques
66300 Thuir
☎ (68) 38 80 39
Open: by appointment.

Cazes brothers   TRWP
4 rue Francisco-Ferrer
66600 Rivesaltes
☎ (68) 64 08 26
Open: Monday to Saturday
8am-noon and 2-6pm.

Château l'Esparrou   TR
66140 Canet-en-
  Roussillon
☎ (68) 80 30 93
Open: Monday to Saturday
9am-noon and 2-5.30pm.

Illiberis   TR
Les Viticulteurs Réunis
route de Thuir
66011 Perpignan
☎ (68) 85 06 07
Open: by appointment.

Jaubert-Noury   TWP
rue des Artisans
St-Jean-Lasseille
66300 Thuir
☎ (68) 21 71 43
Open: July to September
daily 10am-noon and
4-8pm.

Château de Jau
Robert Doutres
Cases-de-Pène
66600 Rivesaltes
☎ (68) 64 11 38
Open: Monday to Saturday
9am-7pm.

Cave Coopérative
  Lesquerde   TR
St-Vincent-Lesquerde
66220 St-Paul-de-
  Fenouillet
☎ (68) 59 02 62

T=tasting   E=English spoken   G=guided tours   C=château/building to visit

Open: Monday to Saturday
8am-noon and 2-6pm.

Limouzy   TR
Henry Limouzy
Celliers du Taste-Vin
66000 Perpignan
☎ (68) 34 01 27
Open: by appointment.

Cave Coopérative de
  Montalba   TR
66130 Ille-sur-Têt
☎ (68) 84 76 53
Open: Monday to Friday
8am-noon and 2-6pm
(closes at 5pm on Fridays)

Coopérative de Pézilla-
  la-Rivière   TR
66370 Pézilla-la-Rivière
☎ (68) 92 00 09
Open: Monday to Saturday
9am-1pm and 3-7pm.

Coopérative de St-Paul-
  de-Fenouillet   TPW
ave. Jean-Moulin
66220 St-Paul-de-
  Fenouillet
☎ (68) 59 02 39
Open: by appointment.

Domaine Sarda-Malet   TR
ave. Victor Dalbiez
66000 Perpignan

☎ (68) 54 59 95
Open: by appointment.

Taichac   TW
Salvat and son
66610 Villeneuve-la-
  Rivière
☎ (68) 92 17 96
Open: by appointment.

Terrassous   TR
Les Vignerons de Terrats
66300 Thuir
☎ (68) 53 02 50
Open: Monday to Friday
8am-noon and 2-6pm,
weekends 8am-noon.

R=red wine   W=white wine   P=rosé wine   S=sparkling wine

Chapter 10

COGNAC AND ARMAGNAC

Hennessy's Museum
Cognac.

COGNAC

ALL COGNAC is brandy, but not all brandy is Cognac; and in fact all brandy does not have to be made from wine or the grape. As far as Cognac and Armagnac are concerned, however, they are the kings of the wine brandies, although one could argue for ever whether one deserves a higher place than the other.

There is no doubt that Cognac is the world's most famous brandy, although the area entitled to this *appellation* covers a small section of the south-west corner of France. To the south is the region producing Armagnac, and producers here claim that their pedigree is even longer and older than that of their neighbour.

All brandy is produced by distillation. Cognac is obtained by distilling wine so that the water evaporates and the essence of the almost pure alcohol is trapped. The word distillation derives from the Latin word *'destillare'* meaning to trickle down, and this is exactly what happens. The wine is heated in a still until it vaporizes, and then allowed to cool as it travels through the condenser. The alcohol content of the wine then trickles down the cooling chambers where it can be collected.

Cognac is produced in pot stills made of copper, and then allowed to mature in oak for many years before blending. The wine for Cognac must come from an area defined by law in 1919 covering almost 4,400 square miles. In 1938 the region was further divided into six zones of quality, with the best in the centre and the others radiating outwards in circles, rather like an archery target:

Grande Champagne
This area produces the grapes for the finest Cognacs. Just south of the town of Cognac, it consists of 31,600 acres of undulating, chalky countryside with a very mild climate. The Cognac is fruity and fragrant and very fine.

Petite Champagne
The Cognac produced in the 40,770 acres just to the south tends to be less elegant. The *appellation* 'Fine Champagne' means a blend of the two, although at least half must come from Grande Champagne.

The Borderies
A region covering only just over 10,375 acres, adjoining Grande Champagne in the north and Petite Champagne in the south. It is more clayey and woody, and the Cognac produced has a flowery bouquet and is full-bodied, which is why it is popular for blending.

Fins Bois
This area surrounds the previous three, and extends to more than 101,000 acres, although most of the land is used for other agriculture. The Cognac is light and quick to mature.

Bons Bois surrounds the above region, and covers 52,650 acres. The Cognac produced tends to be used for inexpensive blends.

The Bois Ordinaires

Most of the grapes from the coastal region of 12,000 acres are used to produce table wines, red, white and rosé. The wine that is distilled is used for blending with Cognac from the other zones.

The major grapes used for producing Cognac are all white; St-Emilion (known as Ugni Blanc in south France), Folle Blanche and Colombard. The vintage normally starts in the middle of October, is gathered by hand or machine, and the grapes are crushed in a horizontal press between three and five times. The wine is fermented for up to three weeks, and then distilled as soon as possible. Regulations decree that all distillation must be completed by the end of March following the harvest, but much of the wine spends some time on the lees, the sediment left after fermentation. The best wines for distillation are those which are high in acidity and low in alcohol.

The beautiful old copper pot stills of Cognac consist of a heating chamber, the still head, the swan's neck, a condenser and a container to receive the alcohol. Wood was used to fire the heating chamber, but oil or gas are now generally used. The still is not allowed to contain more than 550 gallons for the second distillation, although there are no restrictions on size of stills for the first distillation. The wine is put in the still, brought slowly to the boil and the vapours rise into the head of the still and then into the swan's neck, a long tube which carries it to the serpentine, the condenser, which is cooled by cold running water. As the vapours cool, they become liquid again, and are collected as the *broullis*, a milky-coloured spirit up to 30 per cent alcohol. The first liquid to emerge contains flavours which could taint the Cognac, so is discarded. This is known as the heads, while the tails, the last liquid to emerge, is also not used because the alcoholic strength has fallen too much.

It is the heart, the liquid collected between the heads and tails, which is then distilled a second time. Both distillations take about twelve hours and it is from the second that the Cognac is produced. Again the heads and tails are removed. The heads can be added to other distillations to extract as much Cognac as possible, but the tails are discarded. It takes about nine litres of wine to produce one litre of Cognac.

Cognac straight from the still is colourless, strong and fiery. Only after ageing in barrels made from Limousin oak does it get its colour, and is able to absorb tannin from the wood to mellow it and give it its bouquet. A barrel has a life of at least forty years but it takes about seven years before it is ideal for storing Cognac. Then, as the Cognac matures, it is switched to newer or older barrels depending on what characteristics it needs to gain or lose. The finest Cognac can stay in barrels maturing for many decades, but once bottled, the ageing process stops.

As the Cognac matures in the barrel, a small quantity is lost through evaporation every year. This loss, the equivalent of twenty million bottles annually, is known as the 'Angels' Share', and accounts for the black stains on the houses and buildings. The stain is really a black fungus. Even in barrel, great care has been taken to nurse the Cognac into maturity. Some barrels are stored in cellars below ground, and others in *chais*, which are really cellars above ground. Each cellar or *chai* affects the Cognac in a different way, so barrels may be moved from one to another if the blender thinks it will help.

Because Cognac is blended, huge stocks have to be kept, and most of the major Houses carry tens of thousands of barrels of Cognacs dating back for decades, some way back into last century. Unfortunately, these stocks also pose a massive fire risk, and in 1974 Martell lost 10,000 barrels of Cognac in one blaze. The various Houses now have their own fire-fighting teams.

There are many classifications of Cognac, and most Houses age for more than the legal minimum. The VSOP rating, Very Superior Old Pale, must be at least four years old; that means the youngest Cognac used in the blend must be that age. Up to eighty Cognacs can be used in a blend, and the oldest may be forty, or even sixty years old. In Britain, the best Three Star Cognacs will be at least four years old: VSOP, at least ten years old; and XO (Extra Old or Napoléon) can be twenty-five years old and in some cases very much older. In the United States, VSOP and Réserve must have four years in the wood; Extra, XO, Napoléon at least five, but most leading brands are aged for longer.

Although Cognac is now the most prestigious brandy in the world, the original reason for distillation was to sell more wines. Vines have been grown in the region certainly since the third century AD, but it was the rise of the port of La Rochelle, and the acquisition of Aquitaine by Henry II of England in 1152, that boosted exports of wine. At this time, wine was taxed by volume, not alcoholic strength, so merchants hit on the idea of distilling the wine and exporting only the 'concentrate' which could then be watered down again when it reached its destination. People of northern Europe, especially Britain, Denmark and Holland, had already started to distill wines, often because of the poor quality of the product after its sea journey, and so a taste grew for this fiery spirit which warmed the blood.

By accident, the merchants also discovered that the spirit improved by ageing in barrels. This came about during the War of the Spanish Succession, between 1701 and 1713, when the trade between Britain and France was interrupted and supplies had to be stockpiled. Cognac in those barrels which had been kept for many years was found to be much better than the recently-distilled brandy.

It was at about this time that some of the great Cognac Houses were founded. The first was Martell, established in 1715, followed nine years later by Rémy Martin, and then by Hennessy in 1765.

The trade in Cognac continued to flourish, despite occasional enforced stoppages caused by one war or another, until the phylloxera outbreak devastated the vineyards in the 1880s. By the early 1900s, however, much of the vineyards had been replanted and there was further expansion after the Second World War, as the export market grew rapidly. Today, almost 80 per cent of production is exported, with countries in the Far East climbing fast up the league table of importing nations.

A Tour of the Cognac Region

There are two well-signposted tours through Cognac country, and the time you have at your disposal dictates the one to choose. The first route starts in Cognac and leads in a rather erratic circle through Jarnac, Châteauneuf-sur-Charente, Barbezieux, Archiac, Segonzac and then back to Cognac. This tour is known as the 'red route' and will take three days.

The other tour, the 'white route', is also based on Cognac town, but takes you through Matha, St-Jean-d'Angély and Surgères to the historic town of La Rochelle on the Atlantic. You can stop over here, or make your way down the coast to Fouras, Marennes, La Tremblade and Royan before turning inland again and returning to Cognac, visiting Saujon and Saintes on the way. There is an added extension to the white route which from Saintes runs down to Pons and Jonzac, on the river Seugne, and through an area rich in Roman remains. A week or more could easily be spent on this second tour.

Whether you follow the red or the white route, signs with blue borders will be seen. These denote important historic buildings.

Cognac is, of course, the home of the world's most famous brandy. The town itself, in the heart of the region, attracts many thousands of visitors throughout the year. There are the cellars to visit and most of the major Houses have conducted tours with English-speaking guides. One of the first things you notice is the black staining on the walls and roofs of many of the buildings, caused by the steady evaporation from millions of barrels of maturing Cognac.

Wines were introduced to the region by the Romans and since then they have been exported to other parts of France and abroad, thanks mostly to the River Charente which flows through the region to the sea.

As the trade grew, so did the importance of La Rochelle, and many of the ports along the Charente. At one stage the river was navigable as far inland as Angoulême. For centuries the region shipped wines to England, Holland and Germany. When Henry II came to the English throne in 1154, English trade with Cognac increased dramatically, because it had become part of his kingdom thanks to his marriage to Eleanor of Aquitaine two years earlier.

During the sixteenth century there was a decline in the popularity of the region's wines, not helped by the religious wars which devastated many of the vineyards. It was during this time that the growers started to distil their wine into brandy. This was thanks to a law which levied heavy taxes on all freight shipped down the Charente. The taxes were charged on the volume of wine shipped, not on alcoholic strength, and it did not take long for the merchants to realise that it was much cheaper to send out distilled spirits. By the 1620s distillation was widespread throughout the region, and the second distillation had been introduced by Chevalier de la Croix Maron at La Brée, near Segonzac, which was quickly adopted by all. This second distillation gives Cognac its very special properties and makes it the finest brandy in the world.

In 1643 the firm of Augier was established, and today it is the oldest Cognac House. Other Houses followed such as Martell in 1715, Rémy Martin in

1724 and Hennessy in 1765. Many of these companies' original properties remain today, together with stills and equipment used then.

Although the trade has been disrupted on occasions, by the Napoleonic Wars for example, it has always been re-established quickly and today is as strong as ever, with exports to almost every country around the world.

The tours both start in Cognac because it is, and always has been, the heart of the region's success story. You can fly by small charter plane straight into Cognac's own airport, and there are commercial flights to Bordeaux where you can pick up a hire car. The most direct route from Bordeaux is by the A10 autoroute, leaving at Pons. There are also trains from Bordeaux to Cognac, and a day or two can be spent exploring the town on foot before hiring a vehicle.

Most of the larger Cognac Houses have guided tours throughout the year; others run them just during the peak season in the summer. All however, are proud of their product, and if you have a particular wish to visit a Cognac House that does not normally accept visitors, a letter sent in advance will often result in a private invitation. Augier, founded in 1643, is the oldest Cognac House still in existence, and visits can be arranged by appointment. Camus, established in 1863, has guided tours during weekday afternoons between June and September. Visiting at other times is by appointment. Hennessy, founded by an Irish officer in the army of Louis XIV, accepts visitors throughout the year, while Martell is open on weekdays only. Other Houses in Cognac accepting visitors are Cognac Otard, Prince Hubert de Polignac, Maison Prunier and Rémy Martin. Visiting by appointment is possible at Hardy, Monnet, Jules Robin and Salignac.

Houses outside Cognac are Bisquit, at Rouillac (appointment only); Courvoisier, open weekdays at Jarnac; Delamain and Hine, also at Jarnac (appointment only); and Denis-Mounié, part of the Distillers Company in Jarnac. At Aigre there is Cognac Gautier (appointment only), while Cognac A. Tesseron is at Châteauneuf-sur-Charente and the *Union Coopérative* is at Jonzac, both accepting visitors by appointment.

Tour of Cognac and La Rochelle

Things to see in Cognac town include the Château des Valois, by the bridge over the Charente, where the future François 1 was born in 1494. It is open to the public. There are many fine old buildings and quaint cobbled streets. The Tours de Porte St Jacques is the old town gate, and you should see the fourteenth-century Maison de la Lieutenance, half-timbered and the town's oldest building. There are pleasant walks around the town, a municipal museum featuring the history of Cognac (both the drink and the region), and there is a cooperage museum in the Hennessy grounds. The other essential visit is to the glassworks at St-Gobain, opened more than a century ago and now producing all the bottles for the region.

On the route between Cognac and Jarnac you will pass the fortified farm at St-Brice and spot the ruins of the abbey of Notre-Dame-de-Châtre. At Bourg-Charente there is a Romanesque church and Renaissance castle, Château de Bourg.

Many of the leading Cognac Houses which have developed outside Cognac are to be found in Jarnac but not much else. There is a Benedictine abbey and monastery, dating from the early eleventh century, but rebuilt about 250 years ago, at Bassac.

Barbezieux is the capital of the Petite Champagne area of Cognac and noted for the finesse of its brandy and the richness of its cuisine.

The journey back to Cognac then goes through the sleepy villages of Archiac, and Segonzac. Much of this area was settled by Huguenots in the sixteenth century, and because of the constant threat of attack from the surrounding Catholic regions, most of the farms were heavily fortified, and these defences can still be seen today. The area is also noted for its fine Romanesque churches with their statues and frescoes.

The white route allows you to see more of this very attractive part of rural France, with its mixture of vineyards and rich farming land, historic buildings, Roman relics and charming sea towns. Places worth visiting are Burie, with its stone wash-house built over a stream; Matha with its fine twelfth-century church, carvings and Hosanna cross; and the Renaissance castle built on an island in the river Boutonne at Dampierre.

At St-Jean-d'Angély there used to be a ninth-century abbey and the town was important as a stopping point for pilgrims making their way to Compostela in northern Spain.

At Surgères, there are the remains of an ancient castle, the ruined walls of which now surround a twelfth-century church, and then it is on to La Rochelle, a bustling and important sea port. For seventy-two years, from 1152, it was part of the land owned by the English Crown, and in the sixteenth century it was a stronghold of Protestantism. In 1568 it even declared itself an independent Protestant Republic. The town was besieged by Cardinal Richelieu and fell to Louis XIII's army in 1629; much of that period still remains. The port is protected by two huge towers, the Tour de la Chaine and the Tour St Nicholas. There is the former lighthouse, the Tour de la Lanterne, the town gateway, the Porte de la Grosse Horloge. Other things to see are the amazing array of different architectural styles in streets such as the rue du Mirage, des Merciers, du Palais and Chaudrier, and the highly ornate Hôtel de Ville. There are the museums of Lafaille, d'Orbigny and fine arts, many parks and pleasant walks. The Parc Charruyer includes some of the town's original fortifications.

South of La Rochelle are several attractive seaside towns, offering the chance for a few days' relaxation at any time of the year. Even in the spring and autumn it can be an invigorating place to be, walking across the sand with an Atlantic wind blowing around you. There are also many restaurants here specialising in sea-food. At Fouras, there is the regional museum, and opposite the town is the island of Ile-d'Aix where Napoléon stayed before being sent into exile on St Helena. There is a Napoléon museum in the well-preserved Commandant's House. There is the charming former naval base at Rochefort with its well-ordered streets and fine houses, and the fairytale castle of Roche-Courbon at St-Porchaire. At Brouage there is a well-preserved castle, fortified in the seventeenth century. At Marennes you should

PLACES OF INTEREST IN THE COGNAC REGION

Cognac
Cognac Houses, Charente, Château des Valois, Tours de Porte St, Jacques, Maison de la Lieutenance, municipal museum, glassworks of St-Gobain.

Jarnac
Cognac Houses, Benedictine abbey and monastery (at Bassac).

St-Brice
Fortified château of Garde-Epée, ruined abbey of Notre-Dame-de-Châtre.

Burie
Stone wash-house built over stream.

Matha
Fine twelfth-century church, carvings and Hosanna cross in graveyard.

Dampierre
Renaissance castle built on an island in the river Boutonne.

St-Jean-d'Angély
Site of ninth-century abbey.

Surgères
Remains of ancient castle around a twelfth-century church.

La Rochelle
Towers of Tour de la Chaine, and Tour St Nicholas: Tour de la Lanterne; town gateway, many old buildings, cobbled streets, museums.

Fouras
Regional museum.

Ile-d'Aix
Napoléon Museum.

Rochefort
Charming town with many fine buildings.

St-Porchaire
Beautiful castle.

Brouage
Castle with seventeenth-century fortifications.

Royan
New church shaped like a ship.

Saujon/Saintes
Roman ruins, first-century amphitheatre, arch of Germanicus, old town, cathedral of St Pierre, Abbaye aux Dames, church of St Eutrope with eleventh-century crypt, museum of fine arts.

Fenioux
Romanesque church.

Pons
Remains of twelfth-century castle.

enjoy the local oysters, and then drive over the toll bridge to Ile-d'Oleron. Much of Royan was destroyed during bombing in 1945, but there is a fine new church, built in concrete and shaped like a ship. At Saujon and Saintes there are Gallo-Roman remains including a first-century amphitheatre, and the arch of Germanicus. There is the old town with its cathedral of St Pierre and the church of St Eutrope, famous for its eleventh-century crypt. At Pons there are the remains of a twelfth-century castle and then it is back to Cognac.

Gastronomy of the Charente

One always eats well in the Charente, because in the west is the rich fish larder of the Atlantic, and to the north the fertile farmlands of the Loire. There is an abundance of vegetables and fruit from the Marais and the moist winds from the sea boost grass growth for grazing so that the cattle and sheep produce lean meat and plentiful milk for dairy products. There are many soups featured on menus, including *soupe aux fèves des Marais*, a thick vegetable soup of crushed broad beans, with bread and herbs, and *soupe de moules à la Rochelaise*, made from mussels and other shellfish with saffron, tomatoes, onions and red wine, and heaps of garlic.

Fish courses are plentiful, including the famous *bouilliture*, a freshwater eel stew, with red wine, shallots and prunes, and *casserons en matelote. Casseron* is the Charente name for cuttlefish and this dish is stewed in red wine with garlic. *Chaudrée Rochelaise* is a fish stew cooked in white wine with shallots, and *chevrettes,* the local name for shrimps. You will find *lamproie*, an eel-like sea-fish (lamprey) caught in the estuaries, and when served *à la Bordelaise*, it means cooked with red wine, blood and leeks. *Lumas* is the La Rochelle name for *cagouilles*, a particularly succulent snail from the Charente, often cooked in white wine with garlic and served as a starter.

Other first courses include *cèpes*, a fine mushroom of the boletus family, delicious by themselves or as an accompaniment. You may be offered *pibales*, or *piballes*, which are the local Charente and Bordelais names for very young eels, served fried, or *sourdons*, the Charente name for cockles. Fish courses could well include *pain de brochet d'Angoulême*, a pâté or terrine made from pike; and *migourée*, a Charente speciality. This is a fish stew with garlic and shallots cooked in white wine. There is also *mouclade*, another traditional local dish of mussels cooked in a wine sauce, with cream and egg yolks, and sometimes with *pineau des Charente*, a liqueur made from grape juice and Cognac.

Meat dishes include *agneau de prés-salés*, succulent lamb from the salt marshes, and *côte de mouton aux mojettes*, mutton chops with haricot beans. If meat is served *à la Charentaise* it means with white wine, shallots and mushrooms. *Crépinettes truffées*, are flat sausages, usually fried or grilled and often served with oysters as an hors d'oeuvre, and shouldn't be confused with *crêpes*, which are pancakes served as either a savoury or dessert. As a savoury they can come with a variety of meat or fish fillings, and as a dessert, they can be flambéed in Cognac and then served with sugar, jam or lemon juice, and even ice cream.

Entrecôte à la Charentaise is beef garnished with shallots and garlic, and there is *gigorit*, a Charente speciality, a whole pig's head cooked in red wine and blood.

Vegetables, especially cabbage, are used in cooking particularly for *farci*, which is stuffed cabbage. *Farci Poitevin* is cabbage stuffed with vegetables, pork, bacon and sausage and cooked in stock. *Farcidure* can either be a vegetable dumpling, sautéed or poached and sometimes served with cabbage soup, or it can be a sort of potato cake mixed with bacon, eggs and ham. It is usually the former on menus, however.

There is plentiful *foie gras* and duck and goose dishes. *Foie gras aux raisins* is duck or goose liver cooked with grapes, and *grillons Charentaise* is a pâté of goose and pork, usually offered as a starter.

There are many dessert dishes including tarts, flans, pancakes and fruit and *tartisseau*, which is a sweet fritter found in the Charente.

Much of the cheese is imported from neighbouring regions, but some goat's cheese is made such as *Chabichou*, and you will also find *Crottin Charentaise* made from cow's milk.

The people of Charente have a sweet tooth and you can find many fruits preserved in syrup and Cognac. These *fruits au Cognac* are excellent but quite expensive. They can be eaten alone at the end of a meal, or with ice cream. Cognac is also used as a filling for chocolates and there are many local makes available. You are likely to be served one or two with your coffee in the better restaurants.

Note: almost all of the wine produced in the Charente is for distilling, but there is a white Vin de Pays Charentaise, dry, crisp and refreshing and a good accompaniment for shellfish and local fish dishes.

ARMAGNAC

Armagnac is part of the ancient province of Gascony, the home of D'Artagnan, and is a corner of France that has only recently been fully opened up to the public. People would travel to Bordeaux to visit the vineyards, or travel through Gascony on their way to Spain, but few actually stopped to explore. Had they done so, they would have found a region steeped in history, of larger-than-life people whose generosity is matched only by the lavishness of their cuisine. It is a part of France where eating, and the enjoyment of food and drink, is taken very seriously, and it is not the place to dally if you have a plane to catch, or a boat to meet.

The region is now split between three *départements*, Lot-et-Garonne in the north, Landes in the west and Gers around Auch, the largest town. Condom in the north is also an important centre, especially for Armagnac, although Eauze is the capital of the region.

Armagnac is a very fertile region with rainfall from the Atlantic ensuring lush growing crops and grass for grazing. It is a very solidly agricultural region, with cereals, fruit and animal husbandry all competing with the vineyards. Like the Charente, the landscape is one of rolling hills with plenty of trees providing cover for game. The winters are normally cold and the summers hot, with the Atlantic responsible for the winds that sweep the area. The effects of the worst of the winds, however, are mitigated by the pine forests of the Landes in the west.

Armagnac is divided into three growing areas with Ténarèze in the centre, Bas-Armagnac on the western flank and Haut-Armagnac to the north, east and south. Wines have been grown here since Roman times at least, and there is a marvellous mosaic believed to date from the second century at an excavated Roman villa at Séviac. The local forests provided wood for barrels, and it is likely that the Gascons were the first in France to distil wine, having learnt the secret from the Moors across the border in Spain. Local monks could have been distilling the first Armagnac in the twelfth century, almost certainly preceding the first distillations in the Charente.

As with Cognac, the first Armagnac to be exported was destined to be added to other wines after shipping. It was cheaper to ship Armagnac because of the taxation which penalised wine exports. Tax was levied on volume not alcoholic strength. Gradually, however, the people of northern Europe, especially the Dutch, developed a taste for the fiery spirit and preferred to drink it by itself.

Although the Gascons have always been a warrior race and have hired out their military skills, it is only in the last 100 years or so that this southwest corner of France has been opened up. Previously Armagnac was taken by cart, barge and boat to Bordeaux for sale and shipping, but with the arrival of canals and then the railway, new export opportunities were created. In the middle of the last century there were more than 100,000 acres of vineyards, and all the wine was distilled using pot stills. In 1850, however, a new still was developed, the continuous or alambic still, and in 1936 it became compulsory for all Armagnac to be distilled using this. Since 1972, however, producers and distillers have been given the option of using either the Verdier still, named after the Montpellier chemist who developed it 122 years earlier, or the pot still. About 20 per cent of the wine produced in the region is distilled, the rest is sold as table wine or made into sparkling wine. There are about 30,000 acres under vine in the Armagnac region which covers about 2,300 sq miles.

Bas-Armagnac, a mixture of plain and forest, produces the best wine for Armagnac on its mostly clay soil; and the best of all comes from the villages carrying the unofficial *appellation* Grand Bas-Armagnac, in the extreme west. Ténarèze produces Armagnacs with a bouquet of violets. The vines grow on the low hill slopes on chalk, and produce grapes which make strong, lasting Armagnac, which can be either drunk as it is, or blended. Haut-Armagnac consists of chalky hills and is not really suited for wines for distillation. The grapes are used to provide distilled wine for blending.

Today, there are a dozen or so permitted white grape varieties: Folle Blanche, Folle Jaune, Picpoult, St-Emilion, Colombard, Jurançon, Blanquette, Mozac, Clairette, Meslier, Plant de Graisse and the disease-resistant hybrid Baco. After the harvest in October, a low-strength, high-acid wine is produced. The wine stays on the lees until distillation, and this, coupled with its low alcoholic strength, helps capture the brandy's bouquet.

Producing Armagnac still entails continuous distillation, rather than the two separate distillations of Cognac. In Armagnac, the wine is heated until it vaporizes and then it travels through a succession of pots during which it repeatedly cools down and vaporizes again, increasing in strength each time. The Armagnac is up to 55 per cent proof when it comes out of the still, and needs much more ageing in the special 88-gallon barrels to rub off its raw, harsh edges. There are still travelling stills, which go from vineyard to vineyard distilling the grower's grapes.

As with Cognac, all distillation must be completed by the end of March after the harvest. The brandy can go on maturing, mellowing and developing its colour for forty years or more, and then it is generally transferred to glass-lined vats for storage, where no further changes can take place. The Armagnac then depends on the skill of the blender for its quality. For sale in

Britain, Three Star Armagnac must be at least three years old, and two years for the United States, although in practice it is usually double this. There are very strict controls on the labelling of Armagnac, especially with regard to its age. Vintage Armagnac, from one year only, has to be fully authenticated before it is allowed to be sold.

There are more than 8,000 growers producing wine for distillation out of a total of 14,000 growers in the Armagnac region. Cooperatives account for almost half of all production of Armagnac. There are a number of wines with *vins de pays* and VDQS status produced in the Armagnac region, and several apéritifs and liqueurs with Armagnac as their base. Worth trying are Côtes du Condomois, Côtes de Montestruc, Vin de Pays des Côtes de Gascogne and Côtes de St-Mont. Floc de Gascogne is the most famous apéritif, a sweet drink made of fresh grape juice and Armagnac: and Armagnac is used, as in Cognac, together with syrup to preserve fruits, especially prunes.

A Tour of the Armagnac Region

Armagnac has always been the overshadowed 'younger brother' of Cognac. The region can trace its culture back as far as can Cognac, it produces a brandy that is steadily increasing its international reputation, and it is one of the finest places to dine in France.

Armagnac country is the home of the Gascons, whose most famous son was D'Artagnan. The countryside was for centuries embroiled in wars and feudal disputes and it has only recently become a centre for tourists.

Its drawback over the years has been that it lies tucked away in a sleepy corner of south-west France, about equi-distant from Bordeaux and Toulouse. There were no major rivers to provide easy navigation in the old days, and few main roads even today. The countryside is peaceful and undisturbed, strictly agricultural but with constant reminders of its troubled past in the fortified farms.

As with many country areas, travelling can be an adventure, roads are narrow and winding and place-names and signposts often non-existent. The great pleasure of Armagnac, however, is that because it was isolated from the rest of France for so long, it has retained a great deal of charm, and has borrowed the Spanish word '*mañana*'. There is no bustle or rush, everything will get done in time, and if you are invited as a guest to someone's home, do not make too many arrangements for afterwards. Luncheons often last for hours, and Gascon hosts, noted for their generosity, will always try to persuade you to have just one more glass of Armagnac before you leave.

Armagnac can be divided into three regions, each of which produces wines for distillation, having very different characteristics. These distillations are then blended to produce the finest Armagnacs, which although different from Cognac, can be as fine. The three regions are Bas-Armagnac, Ténarèze and Haut-Armagnac, and their three capital 'cities' — Eauze, Condom and Auch — form the basis of this triangular tour of the area.

Gascony has not really changed for many centuries. The people are fiercely patriotic, and families can trace their descent back in the same village for hundreds of years. The houses have survived and it is quite easy to visit some of the timber-housed hamlets and imagine what it must have been like two or three hundred years ago because so little has changed. Armagnac, which lies at the centre of Gascony, is still fiercely independent in many ways, and its very special brandy is produced by a number of small family concerns. But, as its fame spreads and its potential profitability increases, outsiders have taken an interest, and many of the Armagnac Houses now have outside shareholders, especially from Cognac.

It does not really matter where you start the trip, but Auch makes a pleasant beginning. This small town boasts many fine restaurants and two splendid ones. The Hôtel France, owned by M. Daguin, is in the place Libération and has an international reputation, and deservedly so. But across the square and down one of the narrow side-streets full of shops selling local wines, Armagnac and *pâté de foie gras*, there is another excellent restaurant which has not yet acquired the reputation it clearly deserves. This is the Claude Laffitte's establishment, which bears his name, in the rue Dessoles.

Apart from the Armagnac Houses and gastronomic shops, there is the cathedral of Ste Marie to visit, with its stained-glass windows and carved choir stalls. You can go up the sweeping stone steps to the place Salinis where the statue to D'Artagnan looks out over the town.

Some locals claim that Ténarèze, of which Condom is the capital, gets its name from the Latin for Caesar's Route, *Iter Caesaris*. There is no doubt that Roman legions used to cross this region on their way between the Spanish frontier and Bordeaux, preferring it because of the lack of rivers to cross.

One of the finest sites in Armagnac is to be seen at Séviac, where a second-century Roman villa has been carefully excavated. Its major attraction is a marvellous mosaic of vines growing, depicting a scene that has obviously been part of the way of life in Armagnac for at least 2,000 years.

Most of the Armagnac Houses only welcome visitors if an appointment has been made.

Armagnac also has many fine churches, and almost every village is worth a visit to see the richness of its architecture. You will also spot a number of keeps dotted around the countryside, relics of the region's warring past.

In Condom there is the sixteenth-century Gothic cathedral of St Pierre with its cloisters and episcopal palace. There are many old buildings in Condom, and one of the finest, the fourteenth-century Cordeliers monastery, is now the much-praised hotel, the Table des Cordeliers, with its excellent restaurant. There is also a museum of Armagnac in the town, above the cathedral cloisters. Nearby is the collegiate church of La Romieu and the Monluc vineyard and château at St-Puy. Also drive the few miles to Larressingle, a fortified village with imposing parts of the keep, church and ramparts still in evidence. The sixteenth-century château of Cassaigne, and a twelfth-century Cistercian abbey on the river Baïs at Flaran can also be found in this area.

At Vic-Fézensac there is a bull ring which practices the bullfights typical

PLACES OF INTEREST IN THE ARMAGNAC REGION

Auch
Armagnac Houses, cathedral of Ste Marie, with stained-glass windows and carved choir stalls, place Salinis, statue of D'Artagnan, museum.

Condom
Sixteenth-century cathedral, cloisters and episcopal palace, Table des Cordeliers, museum.

Séviac
Excavated Roman villa with magnificent mosaics.

St-Puy
Collegiate church of La Romieu, château.

Larressingle
Fortified village.

Flaran
Château Cassaigne and remains of twelfth-century Cistercian abbey.

Vic-Fézensac
Bull ring.

Termes-d'Armagnac
Keep.

Nogaro
Museum and Dartigalongue cellars.

Eauze
Gothic cathedral, many old buildings.

Cazaubon
Spa town

La-Bastide-de-l'Armagnac
Thirteenth-century fortified village, château, museum.

Fourcés
Fortified village.

Montréal
Fortified village.

Lupiac
Château de Castelmore, birthplace of D'Artagnan.

of the south of France. The bulls, and sometimes cows, have rosettes draped over their horns, and the brave young men of the region have to pluck these from the animal's charging head.

Other places worth visiting are Termes-d'Armagnac, with a splendid keep over the river, the Dartigalongue museum and cellars at Nogaro, and Eauze with its Gothic cathedral and many old buildings. Just to the west is the spa town of Cazaubon which also has several good hotels and restaurants.

There is a thirteenth-century fortified village at La Bastide-de-l'Armagnac, and another museum of Armagnac at the nearby Château Garreau. Two other thirteenth-century fortified villages are at Fourcés and Montréal. Finally, one should visit the village of Lupiac and the Château de Castelmore which dominates it, as it is famous as the home of D'Artagnan.

Gastronomy of Gascony

The cuisine of Gascony is greatly influenced by its neighbours, Bordeaux to the north, Roussillon to the east and the Pyrénées and Spain to the south, but it has many of its own specialities. There is excellent poultry, goose and duck, *foie gras*, *charcuterie* like *galabart* and *coudenat*, the first a large black pudding, and the second a large pork sausage eaten hot in thick slices. There is Gascony ham, a host of game from the forests of Landes; and goose fat and Armagnac figure prominently in the preparation of many dishes. Goose and duck in every form figure on the menus. *Magret de canard* is breast of duck specially fattened for the *foie gras*; *confit d'oie* is goose cooked and preserved in its own fat; *oie fumé* is smoked goose eaten raw; *rillettes d'oie*, goose pâté; *cou d'oie farci*, stuffed goose neck; *coeurs de canard* (or *oie*) *en brochettes*, duck's or goose's heart grilled on skewers; *grattons* are small pieces of salted cooked duck or goose fat, served cold, and *foie aux raisins* is liver of goose or duck cooked in white wine with grapes. Other goose and duck dishes include *alicuits de volaille*, giblets and wings of duck or goose, cooked in a wine sauce with *cèpes* and mushrooms; and *foie gras* figures in a variety of ways, either as a starter or as an ingredient in more complex dishes.

Soups include *cousinette*, a vegetable soup with spinach, sorrel and chicory, and *garbure*, a Gascony speciality. It is a vegetable soup with cabbage, beans, garlics and chunks of duck, goose, pork or turkey. It is often served as a starter but is a meal in itself. *Salda* is a soup with cabbage and haricot beans, bacon, ham and sausage; and *tourins à l'ail* is garlic soup, but the stock can also be flavoured with tomatoes or onions. You may also be offered *millas* with your soup. These are flat cakes of maize flour served with soups and stews and not to be confused with *millassou*, which is a sweet maize flour flan.

Perhaps the most famous dish of the region, however, is *poule au pot*, which is said to have been created for Henri IV of France. It is chicken breast, stuffed with ham and liver and cooked in wine. It was named after the king because one day after eating it he said it was his hope that every family in France would be able to enjoy a chicken for their Sunday lunch.

Many small birds are eaten in the region including pigeon, ortolans and thrushes. *Salmis des palombes*, is a dish in which pigeons are part-roasted and then stewed in red wine with onions, ham and mushrooms. Ortolans are usually roasted and served on a skewer.

Other meat dishes might include *chorizo*, a very spicy sausage originally from Spain; *civet de lapin*, rabbit cooked in wine; and *daube à la Béarnaise*, beef cooked in wine with ham and tomatoes. *Estouffat* is beef cooked in wine with herbs, usually with Armagnac and shallots added, while *Gasconnade* is a regional speciality — leg of lamb roasted with anchovies and garlic. *A la Gasconne* usually means with ham and garlic. There is also *poitrine de veau farcie*, veal breast stuffed with sausage and herbs and cooked with vegetables.

The most famous dessert is *croustade*, paper thin pastry, several layers high with apples, mouth-watering and very special. There are also *cruchades*, pancakes made from maize flour; and *pastis Landaise*, a sort of *croustade* but with a prune rather than an apple filling. *Glacé aux pruneaux* is ice cream with chopped prunes and Armagnac, and, as in Cognac, there are many fruits preserved in syrup and Armagnac to eat by themselves or with ice cream.

Most cheeses are imported from surrounding regions but there is *Amou*, a strong sheep's milk cheese, named after the town near which it is made.

HOTELS AND RESTAURANTS OF COGNAC AND ARMAGNAC

COGNAC

Angoulême
(16000 Charente)

Hostellerie du Moulin
du Maine Brun about 6
miles out of town on the
Cognac road
☎ (45) 96 92 62
A luxury, very comfor-
table, very expensive
quiet 20-room hotel in its
own gardens. Very good
restaurant, also expensive
but worth it, with a fine
wine list. Formerly a mill-
house.

Hôtel France
1 place Halles
☎ (45) 95 47 95
Very central 61-room
hotel, comfortable and not
too expensive. A reason-
ably-priced restaurant.

Novotel
3¾ miles north on the
N10 at Champniers
☎ (45) 68 53 22
Large modern 100-room
hotel, air-conditioned and
soundproofed. Swimming
pool and cafeteria.
Reasonably-priced rooms.

La Chamade
13 rampe d'Aguesseau
☎ (45) 38 41 33
The best restaurant in the
area, marvellous stylish
modern cuisine, and still
very reasonably-priced.

Barbezieux
(16300 Charente)

La Boule d'Or
9 blvd Gambetta
☎ (45) 78 22 72

A small, friendly, comfortable 28-room hotel; very
good value for money
menus.

Vieille Auberge
5 blvd Gambetta
☎ (45) 78 02 61
Small inn with 6 rooms,
all simple but very good
value; good, inexpensive
food and pleasant terrace.

Bourcefranc
(17560 Charente-
Maritime)

Les Claires
rue William Bertran
☎ (45) 85 08 01
Named after the oysters
that figure prominently on
the menus, together with
marvellous fish dishes
prepared by Michel Suire.
Good food and prices, as
well as 20 comfortable,
inexpensive rooms.

Cierzac
(16660 Charente)

Le Moulin de Cierzac
about 8 miles south on
the D731
☎ (45) 83 61 32
A small, quiet, 10-room,
inexpensive hotel and
restaurant, in its own
grounds beside the river.

Cognac
(16100 Charente)

Le Valois
35 rue 14-Juillet
☎ (45) 82 76 00
A very comfortable 27-
room hotel, close to the

centre, not expensive, no
restaurant, but breakfast.

Le François 1er
3 place François 1er
☎ (45) 32 07 18
Also very central; a
29-room comfortable
hotel, but no restaurant,
breakfast served.

Hôtel Moderne
24 rue Elysée-Mousnier
☎ (45) 82 19 53
A pleasant, 40-room,
cheap hotel, no restaurant,
but breakfast served.

Les Pigeons Blanc
110 rue Jules-Brisson
☎ (45) 82 16 36
A very reasonably-priced
restaurant, and 6 modest,
but very reasonable
rooms.

Logis de Beaulieu
at St-Laurent-de-Cognac,
3¾ miles to the east on
the N141
☎ (45) 82 30 50
A very reasonably-priced,
good restaurant, and 21
rooms from reasonable to
expensive.

La Flotte
(17630 Charente-
Maritime)

Richelieu
on the Ile-de-Ré
☎ (46) 09 60 70
A little out of the way but
worth it for peace, relaxation and excellent food.
Restaurant is expensive
and good; the 30 rooms
are very expensive. Some

of the accommodation is in bungalows in the grounds.

Jarnac
(15200 Charente)

Domaine de Fleurac
at Fleurac, 6 miles north-east on the D157 or N141
☎ (45) 81 78 22
A very comfortable, friendly château; both the restaurant and the rooms are reasonably-priced.

Château
place Château
☎ (45) 81 07 17
Very good food, reasonably-priced and good wines.

La Ribaudière
at Bourg-Charente, 3 miles away on the N141
☎ (45) 81 30 54
Pleasant restaurant on the river, inexpensive and attractive terrace.

Marennes
(17320 Charente-Maritime)

Terminus
au port du Chapus
☎ (46) 85 02 42
A 10-room, pleasant hotel, inexpensive rooms, and cheap but good restaurant.

Nieuil
(16270 Charente)

Château de Nieuil
☎ (45) 71 36 38
To the east on the D739
A marvellous château hotel in its own, expensive grounds. 10 rooms and 3 apartments, all expensive, but a very good value restaurant in the hands of Mme Luce Bodinaud, a talented creative cuisinière mixing old and new.

La Rochelle
(17000 Charente-Maritime)

Les Brises
Chemin de la Digue-Richelieu
☎ (46) 43 89 37
A very comfortable, not expensive 46-room hotel by the sea, no restaurant, but breakfasts served.

Le Champlain
20 rue Rambaud
☎ (46) 41 23 99
Very comfortable 36-rooms and apartments, not expensive, no restaurant but breakfast served.

France-Angleterre
22 rue Gargoulleau
☎ (46) 41 34 66
Modern hotel with 76 rooms, good value, and very good restaurant, *Le Richelieu*, with wonderful fish dishes.

Saintes
(17100 Charente-Maritime)

Relais du Bois St-Georges
rue de Royan
☎ (46) 93 50 99
A comfortable, modern, inexpensive 21-room hotel, very reasonably-priced restaurant, with home grown vegetables.

Hôtel Commerce Mancini
rue des Messageries
☎ (46) 93 06 61
A very comfortable 46-room hotel, rates reasonable, and a good restaurant with some very unusual dishes.

ARMAGNAC

Auch
(32000 Gers)

Hôtel de France
place de la Libération
☎ (62) 05 00 44
Magnificent hotel and restaurant in the centre of town. André Daguin is internationally renowned, and rightly so, for his magnificent creations. The 30 rooms are grand and some are very expensive. The restaurant is expensive, but excellent value.

Claude Laffitte
38 rue Dessoles
☎ (62) 05 04 18
One of the most underrated French restaurants I know. Patron chef Claude Laffitte, fiercely proud of his Gascon cuisine, is marvellously creative with regional dishes, especially *magret*, *foie gras*, and fish. His set menus are a bargain and he deserves much more serious recognition from the gastron-

omic guides. (My best meal ever in France was at one of M. Laffitte's tables). Excellent wines of Cahors and Madiran.

Barbotan-lès-Thermes
(32150 Gers)

Château Bellevue
at Cazaubon, 1³/4 miles away on the D626
☎ (62) 09 51 95
A very comfortable 27-

room hotel in its own park; room rates reasonable, and good, well priced-restaurant.

Château de Bégué
at Cazaubon, on the D656
☎ (62) 69 50 08
A quiet hotel in its own grounds with swimming pool. 32 inexpensive rooms and fair restaurant.

La Bastide Gasconne
☎ (62) 69 52 09
Charming, elegant hotel with food influenced by Michel Guérard. The 49 rooms are not expensive, and the restaurant is excellent value for money.

Eugénie-lès-Bains
(40320 Landes)

Les Prés d'Eugénie
☎ (58) 51 19 01
Run by Christine and Michel Guérard, this excellent 35-room hotel is only surpassed by the world-wide reputation of its restaurant. M. Guérard is a master, and his pupils, thankfully, are spreading the word in kitchens around the globe. A gastronomic experience that will not be forgotten. Expensive, but worth it, and one must book. Rooms exquisite and expensive. A near perfect place to eat and stay.

Luppé-Violles
(32110 Gers)

Relais de l'Armagnac
☎ (62) 08 95 22
Roger Duffour is another of the great chefs of France, and ardent advocate of Gascon cuisine. The food is always a treat and not over-expensive, while the 10 rooms are equally well priced.

Plaisance
(32160 Gers)

La Ripa Alta
place de l'Eglise
☎ (62) 69 30 43
A simple 15-room hotel, very reasonably-priced, to allow you to spend more in the magnificent restaurant of Maurice Coscuella. The menus are still amazingly good value, the food exciting and creative, and the wine list, especially the Armagnacs, tremendous.

Poudenas
(47170 Lot-et-Garonne)

La Belle Gasconne
☎ (53) 65 71 58
Spectacular restaurant run by Marie-Claude Gracia and husband Richard. The welcome and service is warm and the regional specialities outstanding although the menus

remain exceptionally good value. The number of covers is limited so it is essential to reserve.

Riscle
(32400 Gers)

Paix
☎ (62) 69 70 14
An inexpensive 16-room hotel, with very good value restaurant, specialising in regional dishes, especially *foie gras*, duck and goose.

Villeneuve-de-Marsan
(40190 Landes)

Hôtel Europe
☎ (58) 45 20 08
A simple, inexpensive 18-room hotel, but another quite stunning restaurant, this time run by Robert Garrapit, a highly creative, innovative chef, a lover of all Gascon dishes which he shapes into masterpieces. Dining here is still a very affordable pleasure.

Darroze
☎ (58) 45 20 07
A 35-room inexpensive hotel in the hands of the Darroze brothers who run a splendid restaurant, with some quite exceptional dishes. Bargain prices and good wines.

DISTILLERIES AND VINEYARDS OF COGNAC AND ARMAGNAC

COGNAC

The Cognac Houses
English is spoken by almost all the establishments.

Augier brothers   TE
place de la Salle Verte
PO Box 48
Cognac 16102
☎ (45) 82 00 01
Visits by appointment with Barton and Guestier, Bordeaux Cognac's oldest shipper.
(☎ (56) 35 84 41)

Bisquit   TE
Domaine de Lignères
route Nationale 736
16170 Rouillac
☎ (45) 96 55 11
Visits by appointment: modern computerised distillery and largest vineyards in Charente.

Camus La Grande
  Marque   TEG
29 rue Marguérite de Navarre
BP 19
16100 Cognac
☎ (45) 32 28 28
Open: Monday to Friday 2.15-3.45pm between June and September; rest of year by appointment.

Courvoisier   TEGC
place du Château
BP 59
16200 Jarnac
☎ (45) 81 04 11
Open: Monday to Friday 8.30-11.45am and 2-4.45pm

Delamain and Co   TE
5-7 rue J & R Delamain
16200 Jarnac
☎ (45) 82 14 26
Open: by appointment.

Cognac Denis Mounié   TE
Souillac
16200 Jarnac
☎ (45) 81 05 38
Open: by appointment.

Cognac Gautier   TE
BP 3
28 rue des Ponts
16140 Aigre
☎ (45) 96 10 02
Open: by appointment.

A. Hardy   TE
BP 27
16100 Cognac
☎ (45) 82 59 55
Open: by appointment.

Société Jas Hennessy TEGC
1 rue de la Richonne
16101 Cognac
☎ (45) 82 52 22
Open: 1 October-31 May, Monday to Friday 8.30-11am and 1.45-4.30pm. 1 June-30 September, Monday to Saturday 8.30am-5pm except public holidays.The house contains a museum and guides speaking English.

Cognac Hine   TE
16 quai d'Orangerie
16200 Jarnac
☎ (45) 83 00 08
Open: by appointment.

Martell and Co   TEGC
place Eduard Martell
BP 21
16101 Cognac
☎ (45) 82 44 44
Open: 1 October-31 May, Monday to Friday 8.30-11am; June and Sep-

tember, Monday to Friday 8.30am-5pm; July and August Monday to Saturday 8.30am-5pm.

J. G. Monnet and Co   TE
BP 22
52 ave. Paul Firino Martell
16100 Cognac
☎ (45) 35 13 40
Open: by appointment.

Cognac Otard   TEG
Château de Cognac
BP 3
16101 Cognac
☎ (45) 82 40 40
Open: 1 October-31 March, Monday to Friday, on the hours of 10, 11, and 2-5pm; 1 April-30 September, daily.

Cognac Prince Hubert de
  Polignac   TE
49 rue Lohmeyer
BP 35
16102 Cognac
☎ (45) 82 45 77
Open: 1 April-30 June and 15-30 September, Monday, Tuesday, Thursday 3-5pm; Friday 10am-noon and 2.30-6pm; 1 July to 15 September 9am-7pm daily. Guided tours at 10am, 11am, 2pm.

Maison Prunier   TE
7 ave. Général Leclerc
16102 Cognac
☎ (45) 82 01 36
Open: 15 June-15 September, Monday to Saturday by appointment.

T=tasting   E=English spoken   G=guided tours   C=château/building to visit

Rémy Martin and Co   TE
20 rue de la Société
  Vinicole
16100 Cognac
☎ (45) 82 41 11
Open: by appointment.

Cognac Jules Robin   TE
36 rue Gabriel Jaulin
BP 68
16103 Cognac
☎ (45) 82 17 23
Open: by appointment.

L. de Salignac and Co   TE
Domaine de Breuil
rue Robert Daugas
16101 Cognac
☎ (45) 81 04 11
Open: by appointment.

Cognac A. Tesseron   TE
blvd Pelisse
16120 Châteauneuf-sur-
  Charente
☎ (45) 62 52 61
Open: by appointment.

Union de Coopérative de
  la Région Délimitée du
  Cognac et du Pineau   TE
route de Cognac
17500 Jonzac
☎ (45) 48 10 99
Open: by appointment.

Musée du Cognac   EC
blvd Denfert Rochereau
16103 Cognac
Open: 1 June-30
September, daily except
Tuesday, 10am-noon and 2-
6pm; rest of year open
daily except Tuesday, 2-
5.30pm

**Producers of Pineau
and Cognac**

Château de Dampierre sur
  Boutonne   TEGC
Charente-Maritime

17470 Aulnay-de-
  Saintonge
☎ (45) 38 82 24
Open: 1 June to 30 Sep-
tember daily, 9.30am-
noon and 2.30-7pm; 1
October - 31 May, Sun-
days and public holidays
10am-noon and 2-5pm, or
by appointment. English
spoken.

Rémy Couillebaud   TGC
141 Malvieille
Moulidars
16290 Hiersac
☎ (45) 96 91 27
Open: daily
Museum of old distilling
equipment.

M. Philippon   TW
Le Logis Mosnac
16120 Châteauneuf-sur-
  Charente
☎ (45) 62 53 79
Open: daily.

G. Antoine   T
16370 St-Sulpice-de-Cognac
☎ (45) 83 85 85
Open: daily.

Château de
  Didonne   TWRGC
route de Bordeaux
Semussac
17120 Cozes
☎ (46) 05 05 91
or (46) 05 55 95
Open: daily.
Château in beautiful parkland; agricultural museum,
arboretum and restaurant.

Château Chesnel   TGC
Cherves Richemont
16370 Cognac
☎ (45) 83 28 11
Open: daily.
Audio-visual presentation
and tours.

Pierre Landreau   TC
Salles d'Angles
16310 Segonzac
☎ (45) 83 71 96
Chai and distillery open
weekends.

Domaine de la Grolette TGC
J. Ordonneau and son
16370 Cherves-de-Cognac
☎ (45) 83 24 69
House, *chai* and distillery.

Guillon-Painturaud   T
Biard
16130 Segonzac
☎ (45) 83 41 95
Open: daily.

Francis Gacon   T
Les Touches-de-Périgny
17160 Matha
☎ (46) 58 53 27
Open: daily.

Cognac de Laroche   T
BP 67
16103 Cognac
☎ (45) 32 09 11
Open: daily.

Maison Gombert   TWP
Javrezac
16100 Cognac
☎ (45) 82 15 07
Open: daily, Pineau and
white and rosé wines.

Logis de Brissac   TC
Veuve Baron and son
16370 Cherves-de-Cognac
☎ (45) 82 22 68
Open: daily. Speciality
liqueur chocolates also.

A.M. Pinaud   TGC
La Chaumière
17160 Dampierre-sur-
  Charente
☎ (46) 91 01 06
Open: daily.

R=red wine   W=white wine   P=rosé wine   S=sparkling wine

G. Rousteau and son   TWP
GAEC JY Crois
16370 Bréville
☎ (45) 80 86 74
Open: daily. Also white
and rosé wine.

Gérard Vollaud   TC
Boursac
16130 Ars
☎ (45) 82 01 01
Open: daily. Also camp-
site, accommodation and
restaurant.

Brard Blanchard   T
Boutiers
16100 Cognac
☎ (45) 32 19 58
Open: daily.

Cartais Lamaure   T
La Grange du Bois
Bourg-Charente
16200 Jarnac
☎ (45) 81 10 17
Open: daily.

Maurice Lascaux   TEG
Logis de Renfermis
16720 St-Même
Open: daily. English
guided tours.

Paul Boussuet   TG
Logis de Folle Blanche
Senouches
17610 Chaniers
☎ (46) 91 51 90
Open: daily.

Domaine de Chadeville T
Gourry de Chadeville
16130 Segonzac
☎ 83 40 54
Open: daily.

Chez Sabourin   TC
Jeannine & Guy Chainier
Arthenac
17520 Archiac
☎ (46) 49 14 18

Open: daily. Also
camping, accommodation
and restaurant.

Michel Forgeron   T
Chez Richon
16130 Segonzac
☎ (45) 83 43 05
Open: daily.

Bureau National
Interprofessionnel du
Cognac   E
3 allées de la Concorde
16101 Cognac
☎ (45) 82 66 70
Open: daily.

Office du Tourism   E
16 rue du 14-Juillet
16100 Cognac
☎ (45) 82 06 71
Open: daily.

ARMAGNAC

Armagnac Vve
Goudoulin   T
Domaine de Bigor-
Courrenssan
32330 Gondrin
☎ (62) 06 35 02
Open: by appointment.

Armagnac Lafontan   T
Distillerie des Coteaux de
Gascogne
32440 Castelnau-d'Auzan
☎ (62) 29 23 80
Open: Monday, Tuesday,
Wednesday, Friday and
Sunday, 9am-noon and 2-
6pm.

Armagnac Marquis de
Terraube   T
Terraube
32700 Lectoure
☎ (62) 06 10 03
Open: Saturday afternoon
and by appointment.

Binelli-Mesthe   T
29 rue Thierry Cazes
32500-Fleurance
☎ (62) 06 10 10
Open: Monday, Tuesday
and Thursday to Saturday,
9am-noon and 2-7pm.

Cave Coopérative de
Condom   T
ave. des Mousquetaires
32100 Condom
☎ (62) 28 12 16
Open: Monday to Friday
8.30am-noon and 2-6pm.
Weekends by appoint-
ment.

Cave brothers   T
Lannepax
32190 Vic-Fézensac
☎ (62) 06 36 01
Open: Wednesday 4-6pm.

Cave des Producteurs
Réunis   T
32110 Nogaro
☎ (62) 09 01 79
Open: Monday to Friday
9am-noon and 2-6pm.

Compagnie Viticole des
Grands Armagnacs   T
route de Bordeaux
40190 Villeneuve-de-
Marsan
☎ (58) 45 21 76
Open: Monday to Friday
8am-noon and 1.30-5pm.

Daguin   T
rue Guynemer
32000 Auch
☎ (62) 05 00 45
Open: daily 8am-noon and
2-6pm.

T=tasting   E=English spoken   G=guided tours   C=château/building to visit

Dartigalongue and son T
32110 Nogaro
☎ (62) 09 03 01
Open: daily 8am-noon and
2-6pm.

Distillerie Carrère T
36 rue des Alliés
32500 Fleurance
☎ (62) 06 11 06
Open: Monday to Friday
2-6pm.

Esquerre-Bounourre T
place des Maures
32000 Auch
☎ (62) 05 20 71
Open: daily except
Thursday, 8am-noon and 2-
6pm.

SARL Henri Faget
and family T
Château de Cassaigne
Cassaigne
32100 Condom
☎ (62) 28 04 02
Open: daily 9am-noon and
2-7pm.

Gelas and son T
ave. Bergès
32190 Vic-Fézensac
☎ (62) 06 30 11
Open: Monday to Friday
2-5pm.

Ets Papelorey T
Rue des Carmes
32100 Condom
☎ (62) 28 15 33
Open: Monday to Friday
10am-noon and 2-5pm.

Charles Garreau
and family TC
Château Garreau
40240 La Bastide
de l'Armagnac
☎ (58) 44 81 08
or (58) 44 84 03
Open: daily 9am-noon and
2-6pm for visiting the
Armagnac Museum.
Visiting caves on Tuesday
and Wednesday, and Satur-
day by appointment.

SARL Jacques Ryst T
25 rue de la République
32100 Condom
☎ (62) 28 08 08
or (62) 28 13 32
Open: Monday to Friday
9am-noon and 2-6pm.

SA Janneau sons T
50 ave. d'Aquitaine
32100 Condom
☎ (62) 28 24 77
Open: Monday to Saturday
10am-noon and 3-6pm,
1 July-15 September.

SA Marquis de Caussade T
ave. de l'Armagnac
32800 Eauze
☎ (62) 09 94 22
Open: Monday to Friday
10-11am and 2-3pm.

SA Sempé T
Aignan 32290
☎ 09 24 24
Open: Monday to Saturday
11am-noon and 5-6pm,
1 May to 1 September.

Domaine de Cassanel T
SA Pallas
47600 Nerac

☎ (56) 65 01 51
Open: Monday to Friday
2-5pm.

Société des Produits T
d'Armagnac
route de Cazaubon
32800 Eauze
☎ (62) 09 82 13
Open: by appointment.

Société Fermière du
Château de Malliac T
Château de Malliac
32250 Montréal-de-Gers
☎ (62) 28 44 87
Open: Monday to Friday,
8.30-12noon and 1-5pm.

Trepout T
Château Notre-Dame
32190 Vic-Fézensac
☎ (62) 06 33 83
Open: Monday to Friday
9am-noon and 2-6pm,
Saturday 9am-noon. Satur-
day afternoon and Sunday
by appointment.

Sté Delord T
Lannepax
32190 Vic-Fézensac
☎ (62) 06 36 07
Open: Monday to Friday
8am-noon and 2-6pm.

Armagnac Samalens
Société VEVA T
Laujuzan
32110 Nogaro
☎ (62) 09 14 88
Open: Monday to Saturday
9am-1pm and 3-7pm, or
by appointment.

R=red wine   W=white wine   P=rosé wine   S=sparkling wine

Chapter 11

NORMANDY AND
CALVADOS

Le Manoir de Courteille
St-Fraimbault-Normandy

ALTHOUGH not made from the grape, Calvados deserves a mention because it is the third great brandy of France. Coming from Normandy, it has been made in the same way for centuries, although its name is believed to stem from a Spanish ship wrecked off the coast during the Armada. This galleon, the *El Salvador*, was one of the ships sent by Philip II of Spain to crush England in 1588. The ship was wrecked on the rocks off the Normandy coast and almost all hands were lost. The locals named the rocks Calvados, and eventually this became the name for the *département* as well.

Even in the dawn of French history, apple trees grew wild all over the north, and the Gauls who inhabited what was to become Normandy and Brittany made cider from the juice of the fruit. When the Romans invaded, the chroniclers noted the abundance of the apple trees which thrived in the damp, mild climate, but the cider which was produced by allowing the apples to ferment was nothing like the drink made today. The Normans, and then the Britons, picked the apples when they were green to make their cider, and the resulting drink was bitter and highly acidic. During the reign of Charlemagne, in about 800, the first rules of cider-making were laid down as attempts were being made to cultivate the trees and establish the first orchards.

The first mention of apple brandy is in 1553, in a document prepared by Gilles de Gouberville, a Normandy farmer who was distilling his own cider, although the drink had been made for centuries before that.

During the reign of Henri IV, the Normandy apple brandy distillers formed themselves into a corporation and strict rules were laid down about its production. Today, there are strict controls over the production of apple brandy and Calvados. Although apple brandy is produced in Brittany, Normandy, the Loire and Maine, only a very small area is allowed to call it Calvados. Three *appellations* are applied to Calvados, and these are geographical zones in which various other factors also play an important part. Quality is determined by the soil, the manner of distillation and the period of ageing in oak barrels. The *appellations* were established in 1942.

The very finest Calvados comes from the heart of Normandy, the Pays d'Auge, and it carries the *appellation* Calvados du Pays d'Auge AC. It is of the finest quality and has a subtle bouquet, intense fragrance, and a smooth, lingering flavour.

The next *appellation* is Appellation d'Origine Réglementée and covers the districts surrounding the Pays d'Auge, namely Cotentin, Calvados, Pays de Bray, Pays de la Risle, Perche, Pays de Merlerault, Vallée de l'Orne, Domfrontais and Mortainais. These are normally blends of Calvados originating from different soils.

The final *appellation* is Eaux-de-Vie de Cidre and covers much of Brittany, Maine, Haute-Normandie and Seine-Maritime. The brandy has less of a ripe apple flavour, is less refined in taste and does not linger on the palate.

Calvados is made by producing cider from special cider apples (of which there are at least forty-eight varieties), distilling it, ageing and blending. All three *appellations* have to conform to the same rules laid down for the making of cider. The cider must be made by pulping or crushing the fruit, and allowing the juice to drain off. Fermentation must take place naturally and must last at least one month and the minimum alcohol content must be at least 4°. It takes two-and-a-half tonnes of cider apples to produce twenty-two gallons of pure alcohol in the form of apple brandy and Calvados. Most growers use about two-thirds of their apples for cider to be drunk — either still or sparkling — and about one third for cider to be distilled. The cider distillation normally starts in March the year after the apples were harvested and must be completed by the end of September.

In the Calvados du Pays d'Auge, the cider is distilled in exactly the same way as Cognac, in Charente-type stills so that the heads and tails can be removed and only the finest brandy produced from the heart. As in Cognac, the Calvados has a strength of about 70° after the second distillation. In the *Appellation d'Origine Réglementée*, a continuous still can be used although the flow rate is restricted to 5,500 gallons of cider in a 24-hour period, and the heads and tails are still drawn off.

Calvados must be aged for at least two years before being sold, and the *Bureau National du Calvados* monitors and authenticates age claims by producers. Most Calvados, about 70 per cent is drunk young (after two years' ageing), while the rest is aged for six years or more. For storage the producers use oak casks, but for ageing they use new oak barrels so that the brandy can extract the tannin from the wood. During this ageing process the Calvados develops its colour, the alcoholic strength drops and the brandy is mellowed ready for the final blending.

The blending is the most important stage and relies entirely on the skill and experience of the cellar master. Blending has two purposes, to produce the best possible balanced brandy, and to give the product its distinctive qualities so that it can be recognised as coming from a particular house. Once the Calvados has been blended it goes back into barrels so that the various brandies can marry together before being bottled at which time all ageing ceases, and the spirit stabilizes.

The production of Calvados each year obviously depends on the size of the apple harvest, but in a good year about 17,500,000 bottles of Calvados can be produced, of which 3,500,000 are AC and 14 million AOR.

The label of Calvados must carry its *appellation* although the age of the brandy is not given. Three Star normally means at least two years ageing in wood; Vieux or Réserve, is ageing for three years; VO or Vieille Réserve, for four years; VSOP for five years; Extra, Napoléon, Hors d'Age, Age Inconnu, six years and over.

A Tour of Normandy and the Calvados Département

Normandy is one of the most popular regions of France with British tourists because it is so close across the Channel. In fact, it is quite possible to take a ferry across and spend a very rewarding week in this historic part of France. Apart from Calvados, a stay in Normandy will introduce you to their marvellous cider and some of the best food to be had in France. One can dine out at scores of seafood restaurants.

Normandy is a large region, and weeks could be spent exploring it, but the route suggested here takes about a week and travels through the heart of the Calvados country, which overlaps in places with the 'cider trail'. It also takes in some of the more historic towns of Normandy, and places known for their gastronomy.

Getting to Normandy could not be easier, and those on a larger tour of France could include this tour either at the beginning or the end of an itinerary. There are regular flights to Caen airport from London, Rennes and Cherbourg. There are flights to Cherbourg from Alderney, Guernsey and Jersey in the Channel Islands, and Southampton and Bournemouth. There are also flights from London to Deauville.

By train there are regular services from Paris St-Lazare to Rouen, Dieppe, Le Havre and Fécamp, and to Evreux, Lisieux, Caen, Cherbourg and St-Lô. From Paris Montparnasse there are services to Alençon and Granville, and from Paris Nord to Le Tréport. It is also possible to get cross-country services to Normandy calling at Tours, Le Mans, Alençon, Caen, Rouen, Lille and Amiens.

You can drive from Paris by the Normandy Motorway (A13) to Evreux, Rouen or Caen. It is 150 miles from Paris to Caen, 175 miles from Nantes, 433 miles from Lyon, 348 miles from Bordeaux and 628 miles from Marseille. You can also drive on the RN12 to Nonancourt. From northern France, Belgium or Holland, use the RN29 to Aumale, and from Brittany take the RN176 to Avranches or the RN12 to Alençon. From southern or western France use the RN138 to Alençon or Rouen.

Most British visitors, however, are likely to come straight across the Channel. There are car ferry connections from Britain between Newhaven and Dieppe, Southampton and Portsmouth to Le Havre, and Southampton, Portsmouth and Weymouth to Cherbourg. There are also connections from Eire with sailings from Rosslare to either Le Havre or Cherbourg. Passenger-only ferries also sail between the Channel Islands and Carteret, Portbail and Granville.

The region is named after the Norsemen, the Vikings, who settled in the tenth century, although they had been raiding this coastline for many years before. Today the region is divided into five *départements*: the Eure and Seine Maritime which form Upper Normandy, with Calvados, Manche and Orne, making up Lower Normandy.

There are many marvellous beaches, and there is an obvious interest for those who served in World War II, from both sides of the Atlantic, in the D-Day invasion beach-heads. There are 375 miles of coastline from Le Tréport in the east to the spectacular Mont-St-Michel in the west.

Inland, Normandy is one of the richest larders of France's agriculture. There are orchards and lush pastures feeding the dairy cattle providing cheeses, cream and rich milk, and to the south, the forests with their pleasant walks and nature conservation parks.

A car is the best way to explore the region, and there are more than a score of motoring routes to follow, all clearly signposted. These take in some of the most famous cheesemaking areas, or the areas where the pear is made into perry (*poiré*). There is also a Calvados route and a cider trail to follow.

Bayeux to Deauville and the Coast

This route starts at the historic town of Bayeux and then follows a weaving course through the countryside to Caen and Lisieux before heading north to Pont-l'Evêque, world-famous for its cheese, and to the scenic coastal town of Honfleur which has been immortalised by many great painters. From Honfleur the route follows the coast through Trouville and Deauville. It also takes in some of the most famous beach-heads of World War II ending at Omaha beach, just to the west of Abbaye Ste-Marie, before turning inland again and driving the short distance back to Bayeux.

While most of the other tours in this guide are designed to give the visitor as great a view of the vines and wines as possible, this tour is designed as a relaxer, either before the start of a strenuous, even though enjoyable trip, or at the end of one.

The Calvados *département* dominates the centre of Normandy and our tour takes us through the northern part of it. It is the area considered by many to produce the finest Calvados. It also includes the official cider route, so offering the chance to taste all the drinks apples can produce, from the non-alcoholic refreshing fruit juice, to a wide range of ciders, sparkling, strong or sweet, to Calvados itself which can range from a fiery spirit to a brandy of great refinement.

Bayeux is home of the famous eleventh-century tapestry which depicts the Norman invasion of England and their success at the Battle of Hastings.

There is also the cathedral, a fine arts museum and a memorial museum of the Battle of Normandy. One of the great pleasures of this town, however, is the large number of marvellously preserved old buildings, many of them dating back to the fifteenth and sixteenth centuries.

Places in the area to visit are Brécey, 10km to the south-east, with a fine château open to the public. It also has charming gardens. To the south there is the forest of Cerisy, and just below it, another fine château to visit at Balleroy. There is a museum at Le Molay-Littry, just to the south of the town, and interesting churches at Tour-en-Bessin to the west and St-Gabriel to the east. There is also the Abbaye de Mondaye to the south-east.

From Bayeux with its many fine hotels and restaurants (especially the Relais Château d'Audrieu in its own park on the D158), Caen is the next stop. On the way, the ruins of the Abbaye d'Ardenne are passed just before you get to Caen, and to the north are Thaon and Secqueville with churches worth visiting.

Caen itself is almost an historic monument in its own right. There is a medieval castle housing a museum of fine arts. There is a museum of Normandy, the Abbaye-aux-Hommes and Abbaye-aux-Dames, many well-preserved old buildings, the churches of St Peter, St John, St Michael and Notre-Dame. Caen has its own university and many of its finest and oldest buildings are to be found in the rue Pierre. Caen also boasts many good hotels to suit all tastes and pockets.

To the south of the town is Gouvix with a château open to the public, and there is also a château, although not open, and interesting church at St-Laurent-de-Condel. There is a riding school and stables here as well if you would like to do some riding through woodland and along the banks of the River Orne.

The road from Caen to Lisieux takes you past Château Canon at Mézidon, and there is a museum just to the north at Crèvecoeur-en-Auge, and Château Victot at Victot-Pontfol.

It is worth a small detour here to include the cider route, which lies to the north of the N13 and the parallel D50, just before you get to Lisieux. The route, which is clearly marked *La Route du Cidre* with an apple symbol, takes you through winding lanes connecting the small towns of Cambremer, Beuvron-en-Auge, Bonnebosq and Beaufour-Druval.

For a real taste of Normandy hospitality, stay overnight in some of the farmhouses. Those that accept visitors for tours and tastings display a sign saying *Cru de Cambremer*. Many of these farms also produce Calvados, and you can inspect the cellars, see the presses and taste the products. As some of the farms are a little off the beaten track, and despite the good sign-posting it may be necessary to stop at times to ask for directions, a small knowledge of French will be useful.

Points of interest to see on this mini-tour are: the view from the chapel of Clermont, the château and stud at Victot, Cambremer church, Grandouet church, the abbey remains at Val Richer, the château of Roque Baignard, the church at Druval, and the Schlumberger museum at Crèvecoeur-en-Auge.

Both the cider and the Calvados from the Pays d'Auge is considered by many to be the finest, but it can vary enormously even from one farm to the next. The pleasure of this trip is that it offers the chance to taste a wide range of both ciders and Calvados. These drinks are, however, very potent, and for those who are touring by car, it is vital to nominate a driver and let him or her stick to non-alcoholic apple juice. The driver can always buy a bottle or two of the alcoholic kind to try at leisure and in safety, later on.

Lisieux is another ancient town, famous for its pilgrimages to the shrine of Ste Thérèse. There is the cathedral of St Pierre in the centre of town, the church of Ste Thérèse and a Carmelite convent chapel, and two museums, one of the history of the town, and other of marine creatures. Just to the south is the château of St-Germain-de-Livet which is open to the public. There are also a number of Roman ruins and excavations in the area.

Another detour worth making is the few miles east to Bernay, another historic town on the Charentonne. There are a number of churches, including the eleventh-century abbey church, which is another religious and pilgrimage centre. There are many well-preserved old houses and two museums, a municipal museum and one devoted to local folklore traditions.

After returning to Lisieux, the route heads north to Pont-l'Evêque, home of one of the world's most famous cheeses, and many Calvados and cider producers. Just outside town on the Deauville road there is the Musée de

Calvados, which traces the history of Calvados-making, including displays of tools and distilling equipment. There are many old houses and the area is fast developing into a popular inland tourist spot with lake, boating and other amenities.

From Pont-l'Evêque, take the Honfleur road past the château at St André d'Hebertot and the old church at Beuzeville. There is another fine church and museum at Pont-Audemer, before we turn north and head for Honfleur and the coast.

Honfleur is still as picturesque as ever, which is why it still attracts painters by the score as it has done for almost 200 years. It is a busy fishing port and marina, with a seventeenth-century dock and sixteenth-century governor's residence. Other things to see are the salt stores, the churches of Ste Cathérine, with its belltower, and St Léonard; the local history museum and the museum Eugène Boudin, and the nearby beauty spot of Côte-de-Grâce with its chapel. Again there are many old buildings in the town and a wide choice of hotels and restaurants.

The route now leads to Trouville, a fashionable resort with fine promenade, walks and cliffs. There are museums, aquariums and a casino. Its neighbour Deauville, which has always overshadowed it, attracts visitors from all over the world. It retains its fashionableness with excellent sporting facilities including golf courses, horse racing and motor circuits and casinos. There are many first-class hotels but prices can vary enormously.

The journey back along the coast to Arromanches goes through many charming little seaside resorts such as Houlgate, Cabourg and Vers. All these, and many other resorts have fine beaches.

As mentioned earlier, this stretch of coastline was the one chosen for the Allies' D-Day landings. Much of the coastline took an enormous pounding so most of the buildings had to be rebuilt. The Normandy invasion has not been forgotten, and apart from the beautifully-kept war cemeteries, there are many museums of the landings and other reminders of it. The landings started on 6 June 1944 and part of the American invasion force was given the task of establishing a beach-head at Vierville-St-Laurent on the Omaha beach. Caen was taken after fierce fighting on 9 July, and the peninsula was effectively secured when Cherbourg fell on 26 June, when the German 7th Army was isolated. There was still fierce fighting, however, and battles were fought at St-Lô, Alençon and Falaise. Today, there are war museums at Aigle, Arromanches, Bayeux, Benouville, Cherbourg, Dieppe, Ouistreham-Riva-Bella, Ste-Marie-du-Mont and Ste-Mère-l'Eglise.

Apart from the coastal resorts and beach-heads, other things to seeinclude the churches at St-Pierre-Azif, Fontaine-Henry and Abbaye-Ste-Marie. There are châteaux open to the public at Fontaine-Henry and Creully.

There are many other areas of Normandy worth exploring, but this one is special because of its historical links. It also produces the best Calvados and after a day spent touring, exploring and breathing in the sea air, there is no better way of relaxing after a good meal, than with a glass of fine old Calvados.

PLACES OF INTEREST IN NORMANDY AND CALVADOS

Arromanches
Seaside resort, Normandy landings museum, fortified harbour.

Beuvron-en-Auge
Old cider village, old houses, covered market, craft shops.

Cabourg
Seaside resort associated with Marcel Proust.

Caen
Ancient town with many old buildings; medieval castle, museums; Abbaye-aux-Hommes, Abbaye-aux-Dames, churches, university.

Clermont
Beauty spot and chapel.

Courseulles-sur-Mer
Seaside resort, marina, famous for its oysters.

Deauville
Fashionable resort, marina, horse-racing, motor-racing, casinos.

Falaise
Birthplace of William the Conqueror, eleventh-century castle, old churches, fountain, wash-house, ramparts and gateways.

Honfleur
Pretty fishing village and seaside resort, old docks and houses, churches and museums.

Houlgate
Seaside town and spa with excellent beaches.

Isigny-sur-Mer
Traditional fishing village.

Lisieux
Shrine of Ste Thérèse, cathedral, convent chapel, museums.

Luc-sur-Mer
Seaside resort on the 'Mother of Pearl' coast.

Ouistreham-Riva-Bella
Seaside resort, marina, twelfth-century church, museum.

Pont-l'Evêque
Cheese and Calvados town, museums, old buildings. The Musée du Calvados is worth a visit. Open daily, free entry.

Suisse-Normande
Outdoor activity among the ravines, gorges and woods surrounding the valleys of the River Orne and its tributaries.

Trouville
Seaside resort, promenades, aquariums, museums, casino.

Vierville-sur-Mer
Seaside resort with some remains of the Atlantic Wall defences. Allied landings memorial, old buildings and church.

Vire
Ancient city with fifteenth-century clock-tower and gateway, church of Notre-Dame, museum, fine vantage point.

Invasion Beaches
British sector:
   Sword Beach,Hermanville-Colleville
   Juno Beach, Bernières-Courseulles,
   Gold Beach, around Asnelles.
American sector:
   Omaha Beach, Colleville-St-Laurent,
   Utah Beach, La Madeleine.

Gastronomy of Normandy and Calvados

Normandy is known for its apples, its cattle and dairy products and the size of the helpings. Sour cream figures in many dishes, and is used for *sauce Normande*. The dairy cattle provide the milk for a galaxy of cheeses, *Pont-l'Evêque*, *Livarot* and *Camembert* being the most famous. Cider is also widely used in cooking, as is Calvados; and the region is able to draw on the sea to the north and the rich pastures all round for its cuisine.

Normandy is rich in pigs and poultry. The sausages of Caen are famous, as is its tripe. Sheep from the salt marshes south of Cherbourg give marvellous lamb, while the cattle give beef, and milk for butter and cheese.

The cuisine of Normandy changes the farther you travel inland. Obviously, along the coast, fish and shellfish predominate, while inland traditional country fare is to be had. Although helpings are large in the coastal restaurants, they get positively mountainous as you travel south.

Before you start your meal try a glass of *pommeau*, which for many years has been drunk on festive occasions in country farms. It used to be made just for family use, but it is now a popular apéritif, made from a mixture of unfermented apple juice and Calvados. The mixture is allowed to stand in oak barrels for up to two years during which time it develops a rich amber colour and a marvellous bouquet. Served cool it is a marvellous way to start a meal.

Thick vegetable soups figure on the menu and the most famous is *potage Normande*, made from potatoes and leeks. There is also a wide range of *charcuterie* and offal, such as *andouilles de Vire*, lovely tripe sausages, usually served cold as a first course; and *boudin blanc*, a white pudding made from either pork or poultry.

The whole region is noted for its tripe. It can be served *à la mode de Caen*, which means stewed with onions, carrots, leeks, herbs, garlic, pig's trotters, cider and Calvados, or *de la Ferté-Macé*, which is small pieces of tripe cooked on skewers.

Fish dishes often involve cider as a cooking ingredient, and there is *barbue au cidre* which is brill cooked in cider. You will also discover *matelote à la Normande*, a fish stew, usually made with sole, conger eel, cream, cider and Calvados. Other fish dishes include *barbue à l'oseille*, which is brill cooked in a sorrel sauce; and *colin à la Granvillaise*, hake marinated and then fried with shrimps. *Marmite Dieppoise* is a stew containing fish and shellfish with leeks, cream and white wine, and there are *moules à la Normande*, mussels cooked in a cream and white wine sauce.

If the menu mentions *à la mode de cocherel*, it normally means with onions, potatoes and artichokes. *Alose* (shad) is often cooked this way, wrapped in bacon and then grilled. *A la Deauvillaise* means poached with onions and cream, and is a local way of presenting sole.

Demoiselle is a Normandy word for *langoustine*, caught off the Cherbourg peninsula, and another traditional dish is *vras à la Cherbourgeoise*, wrasse stuffed with a smaller one and cooked in cider. Finally, there is *sole Normande*, which is sole poached in cider and cream, as opposed to *sole au glui*, an old Normandy recipe in which the fish is grilled with straw.

There are a number of rich salad courses, the most famous of which is *salade Normande*, also called *salade cauchoise*. It includes potato, ham, celery and cream. *Cauchoise* is also used to describe a sauce with apple, cream and Calvados. Non-meat courses include *ficelle Normande*, pancakes stuffed with cream and cheese, with ham and mushrooms added, and there is omelette *à la Mère Poulard*, a simple, light and fluffy omelette named after its creator who owned the Hôtel Poulard in Mont-St-Michel early this century. Done properly it is magnificent, but it is difficult to imitate. *Omelette Normande* means filled with mushrooms, shrimps and sometimes with cream and Calvados. When a dish has *sauce Normande* attached, it means made from cider and sour cream and it can be served with meat, fish or vegetables.

Duck is highly regarded and you will find *caneton à la Rouennaise*, which means that it is stuffed with its own liver, lightly roasted and then pressed, to squeeze out the blood to thicken the sauce. *Duclair* is a type of duck raised round the town bearing that name. *Poulet Vallée d'Auge* is a famous chicken dish, although veal can sometimes be used. The meat is cooked in cider, with apples and cream and then flambéed with Calvados.

In the meat section of the menu you will find *escalope Normande*, although it can also be referred to as *escalope Calvados*, or *Vallée d'Auge*. It usually means veal flambéed in Calvados and served with apples and cream. Escalope normally refers to veal but it can be applied to other meats and occasionally to fish. You will find *graisse Normande*, beef and pork fat, cooked with vegetables and herbs and then pressed into jars. It is used in the cooking of many local dishes and there is *soupe à la graisse*, with potatoes and vegetables and *graisse Normande* added. It is more of a stew than a soup. There is *pieds de mouton à la Rouennaise*, which are stuffed sheep's trotters, and *à la Cherbourgeoise*, which means served with onions and carrots.

For those with a sweet tooth there is a wide range of desserts to choose from. There are *bordelots*, baked apples in pastry, similar to *douillon*, a Normandy speciality, which can be either whole apple or pear in a pastry case. *Mirliton* is a small sweet tart, and *panachée mirliton* means a mixed fruit tart. You will also find *sablé*, a shortbread thought to come originally from Sablé-sur-Sarthe in Maine. There is also *sucre de pommes*, sugared apples, sometimes served on a stick, and *tergoule*, or *tord-goule*, a Normandy speciality of rice pudding and cinnamon.

There are many fine cheeses in Normandy because of the abundance of dairy cattle. The most famous are *Bondon de Neufchâtel*, also called *Bondard*, which is soft and creamy; *La Bouille*, also creamy but with a fruity taste and strong smell, and *Bricquebec*, a mild cheese made by the monks at the abbey of the same name. *Brillat-Savarin* is soft, mild and creamy, and of course there is *Camembert*, again mild and creamy and world famous. Unfortunately, traditional farm-made *Camembert* is now rare. Other soft cheeses include *Carré de Bray*, with a mushroom smell; *Coeur de Bray*, with a heart shape and fruity tasting; and *Demi-Sel*, a mild slightly salted cheese. *Excelsior*, *Fin de Siècle*, also known as *Parfait*, and *Gournay* are all small, soft, creamy cheeses, while *Livarot* is strong and spicy, rich-tasting with an orange rind. Finally there is *Monsieur*, firm, fruity and strong smelling, *Pavé d'Auge*, a firm, almost spicy cheese with a yellow rind, and *Pont-l'Evêque*, made since the thirteenth century and now world famous. It is a soft cheese with a strong taste and used to be known as *Augelot* because it was made on farms in Auge.

HOTELS AND RESTAURANTS OF
THE NORMANDY REGION

Bagnoles-de-l'Orne
(61140 Orne)

Hôtel Bois-Joli
☎ (33) 37 92 77
Friendly, comfortable and inexpensive 19-room hotel, with a good restaurant specialising in Normandy food.

Cabourg
(14390 Calvados)

Grand Hôtel
promenade Marcel Proust
☎ (31) 91 01 79
Expensive, very comfortable 70-room hotel, good restaurant, which is not as expensive.

Hôtel Paris
39 ave. Mer
☎ (31) 91 31 34
Inexpensive 24-room hotel, no restaurant, but breakfast.

Hostellerie Moulin-du-Pré
Charming inn 4¹/₂ miles away on the route to Gonneville
☎ (31) 78 83 68
A delightful restaurant, good food at reasonable prices, 10 inexpensive rooms.

Caen
(14000 Calvados)

Le Relais des Gourmets
15 rue de Geôle
☎ (31) 86 06 01
A good regional restaurant and 32 comfortable, inexpensive rooms.

Le Manoir d'Hastings
At Bénouville, 6 miles to the east
☎ (31) 44 62 43
A former priory, now run by Claude Scaviner, by many fêted as Normandy's top chef; not expensive.

Novotel
outside Caen on the road to Doubres
☎ (31) 93 05 88
Big, comfortable, not expensive hotel, cafeteria-style restaurant. 126 rooms.

Caudebec-en-Caux
(76490 Seine-Maritime)

Marine
quai Guilbaud
☎ (35) 96 20 11
Good, comfortable, inexpensive 33-room hotel with similar restaurant.

Manoir de Rétival
rue St Clair
☎ (35) 96 11 22
A small, quiet hotel with a dozen reasonably-priced rooms, no restaurant, but breakfast served.

Conteville
(27210 Eure)

Auberge Vieux Logis
☎ (32) 57 60 16
Worth a visit (if you can afford it) to sample the works of Yves Louet, one of France's great chefs. The food is always excellent but the prices have risen in line with his reputation.

Coutances
(50200 Manche)

Grand Hôtel
place Gare
☎ (33) 45 06 55
Comfortable, inexpensive 25 rooms, and adequate, good value restaurant.

Hôtel Moderne
25 blvd Alsace-Lorraine
☎ 45 13 77
Small 17-room hotel, reasonable restaurant; both rooms and food cheap and a good base for touring for budget trips.

Domfront
(61700 Orne)

Hôtel Poste
rue Foch
☎ (33) 38 51 00
Comfortable, inexpensive 28-room hotel, and modest, good value restaurant.

Falaise
(14700 Calvados)

Normandie
4 rue Admiral-Courbet
☎ (31) 90 18 26

Comfortable 30-room hotel, with very reasonable rates and cheap menus, good for touring base and budget trippers.

Flers
(61100 Orne)

Auberge Relais Fleuri
115 rue Schnetz
☎ (33) 65 23 89
Good regional fare at reasonable prices.

Honfleur
(14600 Calvados)

La Ferme St-Siméon
route A. Marais
☎ (31) 89 23 61
A very comfortable, very expensive 19-room hotel, with views across the Seine estuary; the restaurant is highly praised for its cuisine, but prices are high and one must book.

Léry
(27690 Eure)

Beauséjour
2 place de l'Eglise
☎ (31) 59 05 28

A very fine restaurant and affordable.

Lisieux
(14100 Calvados)

Restaurant Le Parc
21 blvd Herbert Fournet
☎ (31) 62 08 11
Very good value and some excellent fish dishes.

Mortain
(50140 Manche)

Hôtel Poste
place des Arcades
☎ (33) 59 00 05
There are 29 comfortable, inexpensive rooms and a modest, but good value restaurant.

Pont-Audemer
(27500 Eure)

Le Vieux Puits
6 rue Notre-Dame du Pré
☎ (32) 41 01 48
Excellent, traditional regional fare and warm, pleasant service. Not expensive, and 14 good value rooms.

Le Petit Coq au Champs at Campigny, 6 miles south on the D810 and D29
☎ (32) 41 04 19
An exquisite 10-room hotel with excellent traditional Normandy cooking. Eating and staying there are both hugely expensive, but memorable, and why not be pampered.

Saint Lô
(50000 Manche)

La Crémaillerie
27 rue du Belle
☎ 57 14 68
Good regional fare at very good prices and 12 comfortable, inexpensive rooms.

Vire
(14500 Calvados)

Le Cheval Blanc
2 place du 6 Juin 1944
☎ (31) 68 00 21
Excellent value restaurant and hotel. There are 22 inexpensive, comfortable rooms and warm and friendly service.

PRODUCERS OF CALVADOS, CIDER, POMMEAU AND PERRY

The following farms and establishments make, sell and give tastings of Calvados, cider and *pommeau*. All are open daily. A number of producers have been selected by the Calvados Tourist Office as 'special', because they can give detailed explanations of Calvados- and cider-making. These establishments can be recognised by the sign *Cru de Cambremer*, and are all found around Cambremer.

Albert Biron   *Ci Ca P*
Beaufour-Druval
☎ (31) 64 86 55

Philippe Bouvard   *Ci P*
Léaupartie
☎ (31) 63 02 93

René de la Brière   *Ci*
Beuvron-en-Auge
☎ (31) 79 23 81

Marcel-Jean
   David   *Ci Ca P*
Beuvron-en-Auge
☎ (31) 79 23 05

Mme L. Dupont   *Ci Ca P*
Victot-Pontfol
☎ (31) 63 03 75

René Elie   *Ca*
Gerrots
☎ (31) 79 26 77

André Elie   *Ci Ca*
Léaupartie
☎ (31) 63 02 41

Paul Grandval   *Ci*
Cambremer
☎ (31) 63 01 74

Yvon Grandval   *Ci Ca*
Grandouet
☎ (31) 63 01 80

Mme Emile Hardy   *Ca*
Victot-Pontfol

François Hélie   *Ci Ca*
Rumesnil
☎ (31) 63 03 18

Gérard Desvoye   *Ci*
St-Aubin-Lebizay
☎ (31) 64 86 92

Michel Lesufleur   *Ci*
St-Ouen-le-Pin
☎ (31) 31 02 29

Bernard Montais   *Ci Ca*
Rumesnil
☎ (31) 63 02 01

Robert Turmel   *Ci Ca*
St-Laurent-du-Mont
☎ (31) 63 04 74

Charles Foucher   *Ci Ca*
Cambremer
☎ (31) 63 01 71

Roger Giard   *Ca P*
Grandouet
☎ (31) 63 02 40

Jean-Pierre Floquet   *Ci Ca*
Drubec
☎ (31) 64 85 31

Louis Lemoine   *Ca Ci P*
N.D. d'Estrées
☎ (31) 63 00 94

There is a cider trail, and producers on it are:

Anée   *Ci*
27 rue du Perré
61120 Vimoutiers
☎ (33) 39 00 40

Michel Boissel   *Ci*
Ferme de la Garenne
St-André-d'Hébertot
14130 Pont-l'Evêque
☎ (44) 64 13 91

Jean-Luc Coulombier   *Ci*
GAEC de l'Hermitage
50320 St-Jean-des-
   Champs
☎ (31) 61 31 51

Léon Desfrieches   *Ci*
route de Divés
St-Désir-de-Lisieux
14100 Lisieux
☎ (31) 31 17 53

Duché de Longueville   *Ci*
Anneville-sur-Scie
76590 Longueville-sur-
   Scie
☎ (31) 83 32 64

Etienne Dupont   *Ci*
Victot-Pontfol
14430 Dozulé
☎ (31) 63 03 75

Elle-et-Vire   *Ci*
50890 Condé-sur-Vire
☎ (31) 57 20 14

Michel Hamel   *Ci*
Les Petits Bois
St-Josèph
50700 Valognes
☎ (31) 40 17 12

Jean Lemonier   *Ci*
Soumon-St-Quentin
14420 Potigny
☎ (31) 90 88 18

Gérard Marlet   *Ci*
Le Friche Menuet
St-Germain-de-Livet
14100 Lisieux
☎ (31) 31 18 24

T=tasting   E=English spoken   G=guided tours   C=château/building to visit

The pear route runs from Domfront in a circle through Barenton, Mantilly, St-Fraimbault, Ceaucé, Sept-Forges, Beaulandais and St-Brice. Many of the producers also make cider and Calvados as well as perry (*poiré*). They are:

Adrien Boisgontier *Ca Po*
Les Martellières
61330 Sept-Forges

Maurice Boisgontier *Ci Po*
Le Haut Thibois
61330 La Baroche-sous-Lucé

Emile Bouvet *Ca Po*
La Noë Rousse
61350 Passais-la-Conception

Auguste Brodin *Ci Po*
La Chatrie
61350 St-Fraimbault

Chais du Verger
Normand *Ca Po*
61700 Domfront

Albert Demeslay *Ci Po*
Les Roseaux
61350 St-Fraimbault

Emile Drolon *Po*
La Champinière
61350 Mantilly

Roland Goussin *Ci Ca Po*
rue Abbé Joly
61350 St-Fraimbault

Maurice Havard *Po*
Meslay
50720 Barenton

Victor Havard *Ci Po*
Bas-Meslay
61350 St-Fraimbault

Mme Marie Heuzé *Ca Po*
37 rue de Maréchal Foch
61700 Domfront

Bernard Ledezert *Po*
Les Bissons
61350 St-Roch-sur-Egrenne

Claude Lemercier *Po*
La Goulvandière
61350 Mantilly

Daniel Lemercier *Po*
Les Vallées
61350 Mantilly

Isidore Lemorton *Ca Po*
La Baillée Fêtu
61350 Mantilly

Louis Lemorton *Ci Ca Po*
La Fouquerie
50640 Le Teilleul

Roger Lemorton *Po*
Beauregard
61350 Mantilly

Gérard Leroyer *Ci Ca Po*
La Duretière
53110 Melleray-la-Vallée

Roger Leroyer *Po*
Le Ronceray
61350 St-Roch-sur-Egrenne

André Mauger *Ci Po*
Les Rivières
61700 Beaulandais

Maurice Olivier *Ci Ca Po*
St-Auvieu
61350 Passais-la-Conception

Claude Pacory *Ca Po*
Les Grimaux
61350 Mantilly

Léon Perouin *Ci Ca Po*
rue des Tisserands
61350 St-Fraimbault

Isidore Sallard *Ci Ca Po*
Le Champ de la Vallée
61600 La Ferté-Macé

Armand Suvigny *Ci Ca Po*
Chenilly
50140 St-Jean-du-Corail

Other major producers of Calvados, cider, *pommeau* and *poiré*:

Pennedepie (14600)

Etienne Lebey *Ca*
Ferme de la Bouillette
route d'Honfleur
☎ (31) 89 01 65
Open: daily.

Claude Brize *Ca*
Ferme d'Appréval
☎ (31) 89 11 71
Open: daily.

La Rivière-St-Sauveur
(14650)

Didier Alleaume *Ca Po*
☎ (31) 89 04 48
Open: daily 9am-7pm.

Distillerie des Fiefs
Ste-Anne *Ca*
Gonneville-sur-Honfleur
☎ (31) 89 14 22
Open: Monday to Saturday 2-6pm.

Pierre Lecesne *Ca Ci*
RN 175
St-Benoît-d'Hébertot
☎ (31) 64 03 47
Open: daily.

Jules Hommet *Ca, Ci*
St-Julien-sur-Calonne
☎ (31) 64 08 26
Open: daily.

Bonneville-la-Louvet
Association
d'Agriculteurs *Ca Ci P Po*
chez Ernest Maudet
☎ (31) 64 75 11
Open: daily, July-September, weekends only rest of year.

Ci=cider	Ca=Calvados	P=Pommeau	Po=Poiré(perry)

Annebault (14430)

Groupement des
  Agriculteurs de la Côte
  Fleurie   *Ci Ca P*
RN 175
☎ (31) 4 82 16
Open: at weekends and the
summer holiday season.

Jean-Pierre Floquet   *Ci Ca*
D16 at Drubec
☎ (31) 64 85 81
Open: daily.

Cresseveuille (14430)

Emile Mercher   *Ca*
La Forge-Moisy
☎ (31) 79 21 45
Open: daily.

**St-Philbert-des-
Champs** (14130)

Jacques Letellier   *Ci*
☎ (31) 64 72 84
Open: daily.

Coquainvilliers
(14130)

Régis Chrétien   *Ci*
☎ (31) 62 29 77
Open: daily July and
August, weekends only
rest of the year.

Beuvron-en-Auge
(14430)

Marcel David   *Ci Ca P*
Manoir de Sens
☎ (31) 79 23 05
Open: daily.

Bures-sur-Dives
(14670)

Groupement
  d'Agriculteurs *Ca Ci P Po*
chez Thomine
route des Marais
☎ (31) 23 21 53
Open: every afternoon.

St-Désir-de-Lisieux
(14100)

Le Père Jules   *Ca Ci*
Léon Desfrieches
D45
Clos de la Pommeraye
☎ (31) 31 17 53
Open: daily.

Notre-Dame d'Estrées
(14340)

Germaine and
  Robert Bastard   *C Ca*
La Pature
☎ (31) 63 01 78
Open: daily.

Le Mesnil-Simon
(14140)

Les Douaires   *Ci*
Bruno Gondouin
on D511
☎ (31) 63 80 25
Open: daily.

St-Julien-le-Faucon
(14140)

René Ouin   *Ca*
rue de la Baronnerie
☎ (31) 63 81 46
Open: Monday to Saturday
and Sunday afternoon.

Prêtreville (14140)

Régis Courtemanche   *Ci*
Manoir de Querville
☎ (31) 32 31 88
Open: daily.

St-Germain-de-Livet
(14100)

Gérard Marlet   *Ci*
☎ (31) 31 18 24
Open: daily 10am-noon
and 2.30-6pm; closed
Tuesday in July and
August.

Vieux-Pont-en-Auge
(14140)

Pierre Rade   *Ci*
☎ (31) 63 81 19
Open: Monday to Saturday
9am-8pm.

Michel Touze   *Ci*
☎ (31) 20 78 67
Open: mornings, Monday
to Saturday.

Michel Fernagut   *Ci*
☎ (31) 20 73 00
Open: daily.

Lisores (14140)

Maurice Conan   *Ci Ca P*
route Livarot-Vimoutiers
☎ (31) 63 53 22
Open: Monday to Saturday
and Sunday morning.

Jacques Lecourt   *Ci Ca P*
Ste-Foy-de-Montgommery
☎ (31) 63 54 17
Open: daily.

**Ste-Foy-de-
Montgommery**
(14140)

Marc de Lesdain   *Ca Ci P*
route Livarot-Vimoutiers
☎ (31) 63 53 07
Open: daily.

The following are
producers of *pommeau*:

André Aubree   *P*
Amaye-sur-Seulles
14310 Villers-Bocage

Roger Bazin   *P*
Ecots
14170 St-Pierre/Dives

Albert Biron   *P*
Beaufour-Druval
14340 Cambremer

T=tasting   E=English spoken   G=guided tours   C=château/building to visit

Michel Boissel   P
St-André-d'Hébertot
14130 Pont-l'Evêque

Elfried Bouvard   P
Léaupartie
14340 Cambremer

Fernand Cadot   P
Cormolain
14240 Caumont-l'Evente

Cidrerie de Montgommery P
Ste-Foy-de-Montgommery
14140 Livarot

Cidreries du Calvados   P
14140 Livarot

Paul Chanu   P
St-Martin-de-Sallen
14220 Thury-Harcourt

Jean Chapron   P
Fontaine-le-Pin
14190 Grainville-
  Langannerie

Maurice Conan   P
Lisores
14140 Livarot

Michel Clouet-Letac   P
Bonneville-la-Louvet
14130 Pont-l'Evêque

Marcel David   P
Beuvron-en-Auge
14430 Dozulé

Philippe Daufresne   P
Ouilly-Le-Vicomte
14100 Lisieux

Arthur Mme Delacour   P
'le Château'
Tréprel
14690 Pont-d'Ouilly

Serge Desfrieches   P
Ouilly-le-Vicomte
14100 Lisieux

Léon Desfrieches   P
St-Désir
14100 Lisieux

Daniel Dupont   P
'La Mérouzière'
14110 Condé/Noireau

Etienne Dupont   P
Victot-Pontfol
14430 Dozulé

Distillerie du Houley   P
Ouilly-du-Houley
14590 Moyaux

Alain Geffroy-Lemoine   P
Laize-la-Ville
14320 May/Orne

Roger Giard   P
Grandouet
14340 Cambremer

Jean-Pierre Hardy   P
Lisores
14140 Livarot

Jules Hommet   P
St-Julien/Calonne
14130 Pont-l'Evêque

Pierre Huet   P
14340 Cambremer

Michel Jean   P
St-Germain-le-Vasson
14190 Grainville-
  Langannerie

Marc de Lesdain   P
Ste-Foy-de-Montgommery
14140 Livarot

Jacques Lecourt   P
Lisores
14140 Livarot

André Leboucher   P
Le Vey
14570 Clécy

Louis Lemoine   P
Notre-Dame-d'Estrées
14340 Cambremer

Jean Lemonnier   P
Soumont-St-Quentin
14190 Grainville-
  Langannerie

André Noppe   P
14340 Canbremer

Yves Pellerin   P
Lecompte
route de Paris
14100 Lisieux

Daniel Requier   P
Monteille
14340 Cambremer

Robert Turmel   P
St-Laurent-du-Mont
14340 Cambremer

Ci=cider   Ca=Calvados   P=Pommeau   Po=Poiré(perry)

Chapter 12

SAVOIE AND JURA

Village of Château-Chalon
Jura

SAVOIE

CLOSE to the Swiss border, the vineyards of Savoie produce mostly white wines, and Seyssel is a very good sparkling wine made by the *méthode Champenoise*. The vineyards, some of the prettiest in France, are the most northerly of the Rhône valley, and produce light reds and rosés as well.

The 3,000 acres of vineyards hug the lower slopes of the Alps south of Lake Geneva, and run south to Lac du Bourget and beyond to Chambéry and Myans. As the vineyards are scattered because of the terrain, a number of separate *appellations* have been created, although much of the wine of the region is sold under the Vin de Savoie *appellation.*

Haute-Savoie is the area immediately below Lake Geneva (Lac Léman in French) and the white Chasselas grape is the most widely planted. It is the grape that produces Fendant just across the border in Switzerland. The Chasselas wine must be drunk young, and is an ideal accompaniment for the fresh-water fish caught locally. The best comes from Crépy whose vineyards run between Geneva and Evian. There are about fifteen villages and communes allowed to add their name to the Vin de Savoie *appellation.* Some of the best are Ayze, Marignan, Marin and Ripaille, Apremont, Abymes and Chignin, although they use different grape varieties.

Crépy is one of the three special *appellations* in Savoie, the others being Seyssel and Roussette. Seyssel, in the *départements* of Savoie and Ain, produces its sparkling wines from the Roussette and Molette grapes. The *méthode Champenoise Seyssel* has become so popular that producers have expanded and now import grapes, although wines from outside the region are sold as Blanc de Blancs Mousseaux. Roussette is the other special Savoie wine, named after the grape which produces a full-bodied but delicate wine. Although the Roussette grape is used, others can be added if the producing commune's name is not added to the label. Among the other grapes used are Chardonnay and Mondeuse. Roussette de Savoie has the AC title, but there is also Roussette de Bugey (VDQS) and Vin de Bugey.

The Mondeuse grape is used to make the best red wines, and the best of these come from Chignin and Montmélian. These two, together with Chautagne, south of Seyssel which is made from the Gamay grape, are the only reds to carry the AC Vin de Savoie.

THE JURA

Château-Chalon is the flagship of the Jura, which gets its name from the limestone mountains on the French-Swiss border. The vineyards of the Jura cover about 3,000 acres (the same as Savoie) and sprawl along the slopes of the mountains, which stretch for more than 225 miles. They start on the plain of the river Saône between Lyon and Grenoble, and extend almost as far as Basel. The vineyard belt, known as the Côtes du Jura, runs from just north of Arbois, through Pupillin, Poligny, Château-Chalon and Cousance.

The *appellation* Côtes du Jura covers all the wines produced in the region, except Vin Jaune. There are reds, whites, rosés and sparkling wines, and the most unusual Vin de Paille, named because the grapes used to be dried on straw which imparts very special characteristics. There are some other AC titles allowed, mostly for higher strength wines.

Arbois is considered the heart of the best wine-making district in the Jura and carries its own *appellation* when the wines have a higher alcoholic content. The white wines are normally made from Chardonnay or Savagnin, a local variety of the Traminer, and used exclusively for the Vin Jaune.

The vineyards are almost all on western facing slopes looking out over the Burgundy plain. The western facing slopes attract heavy rainfall, and are also prone to hailstorms, but the harvest normally takes place during traditionally sunny, warm autumns. The Chardonnay produces delicate, light wines, and much of it is used for sparkling wine production. The Savagnin ripens late but produces wines powerful in alcohol and flavour, which can be added to the Chardonnay to improve the finished product. It comes in to its own in the incredible Vin Jaune, however. How this winemaking method came to be adopted has been forgotten in the mists of time, but the system is a little similar to that used in sherry production.

The grapes ripen late and are picked and crushed, and then placed in old barrels where they must lie for at least six years. The barrels are never completely filled, and a special yeast, living on the inside of the wood, quickly grows to cover the whole surface of the liquid. Although the yeast grows on oxygen, it prevents the wine being exposed to the air and after a number of years a miraculous transformation takes place. The wine has attracted colour from the wood and should be a glorious golden colour, and have a slightly oxidised bouquet and nutty flavour. The wines are incredibly long-lasting, and still drink well after fifty years; people who have tried bottles 100 years old are still impressed. The best Vin Jaune comes from Château-Chalon with its own AC, but there are other good producers around Arbois. It is inevitably expensive because of its long production method.

The growers are especially proud of the rosé wines, made from the Poulsard grape, and this is also used, together with Trousseau and Pinot Noir, for the light style reds.

The other unique wine produced by the Jura is Vin de Paille, named because it has the colour of straw, and the grapes were traditionally spread over straw to dry before crushing, to concentrate the sugar content and therefore their sweetness. Today, the grapes are usually hung up to dry for a statutory minimum of two months before being made into lush, rich wines which can still display extraordinary youth after some decades. They are now quite rare, however, and very expensive.

The final district of the Jura worth noting is L'Etoile, particularly for its sparkling wines made by the *méthode Champenoise*.

A Tour of the Jura

The Jura is another of those tucked-away corners of France which although rich in history and tradition — and wine-making — has not been popular with tourists until recently. It is part of Franche-Comté, a province lying between Alsace and Lyon, for centuries the buffer state between Burgundy and Switzerland. Because of its strategic position it was frequently in the front line and the Jura, a range of mountains, provided a natural defence. To-day, the mountain slopes are planted with the vineyards for which the area is noted. The main vine areas are around Arbois, Château-Chalon and L'Etoile and red, white and rosé wine is produced.

It is still possible to stop off and taste the wine as you tour the area, but there are many other things to see and do. Apart from its historical re-minders, the Jura is a place to enjoy being in the countryside, and especially the mountains. There is a galaxy of sporting activities available, with spa towns, excellent hotels and restaurants to accommodate your needs.

St-Claude to Poligny

A good starting point for a tour of the Jura is at St-Claude in the south, one of the first towns reached on entering the region from Savoie. St-Claude is a small industrial town at the junction of the rivers Bienne and Taçon. There is the cathedral of St Pierre, which was once a fortified refuge, with carved wooden stalls depicting scenes from the fifteenth century. The altar-piece was given to the church in 1553 by Pierre de la Baume, Bishop of Geneva. Other things to see are the church of Sacré-Coeur, the 164ft-high bridge, and the viaduct and bridge over the Bienne. There are also museums, one for pipes which are made in the town, and the other for diamonds. Diamond-cutting is one of many industries in St-Claude; others include fancy goods and woodworking.

To the west of the town, beyond the lake and dam of Vouglans, is St-Amour, a summer holiday resort with marble-quarries and sawmills in the sur-rounding hills. There is a collegiate church rebuilt in the seventeenth cen-tury, and the Promenade de la Chevalerie.

North of St-Claude is Orgelet, famed for its fifteenth-century church of Notre-Dame-de-Merlia and its rampart remains. Many of the buildings are from the sixteenth and seventeenth centuries. There is a former Bernardine convent built in 1708, and a hospital dating from 1292.

After leaving the D470 beyond Orgelet and joining the N78 you arrive at Conliège. This is a typical vine-growing village with a thirteenth-century church, enlarged in the seventeenth century. It has a fine wrought-iron gate and richly-carved pulpit, installed in the eighteenth century. Nearby at Rev-igny there is a seventeenth-century church.

Lons-le-Saunier is a spa town with light industry. It is an ideal centre for an outdoor activity holiday — with plenty of wine-tasting to revive you in the evening. The town nestles in the foothills of the Jura, surrounded by vineyards which grow both on the slopes and on the plateau above. The town produces cheese, chocolate, toys and clocks and is famous as the birth-place of Rouget de Lisle, author of 'La Marseillaise'. The arcaded rue de Com-merce dates back to the sixteenth century, and the church of St Désiré is built over an eleventh-century crypt. Other things to see are the restored Cor-deliers church, the tombs of the Chalon family, the eighteenth-century Préfecture and the Promenade de la Chevalerie, the former training ground of the Chevaliers de l'Arquebuse. The museum houses relics found nearby, many from the Gallo-Roman age.

Worth visiting nearby are the Cirque de Baume-lès-Messieurs, Château-du-Pin, Arlay with its ruined twelfth-century castle, and Montmorot.

Champagnole, east on the D411, is at the foot of Mont Rivel (2,788ft). Nearby is the state forest of La Joux with giant conifers dating back to the time when the Spanish ruled the province. In the area is the Palladian-style château at Syam, with its old mill and nineteenth-century forge, Pont de la Chaux, and at Sirod, the twelfth-century church with thirteenth-century vaulting and partly Romanesque nave. If you prefer, Syam can be visited on the return journey to St-Claude.

Sellières is the next port of call, with its ancient monuments, including the fifteenth-century gateway and rampart remains. Worth visiting are the Hôtel de Ville, the church and the Cloîtres des Cordeliers.

Poligny is just up the road on the N33. Here there is the collegiate church of St-Hippolyte which dates from the fifteenth century, and its seventeenth-century doorway. There is also a thirteenth-century church of the Dominicans and the remains of a Romanesque church containing sculptures and altarpieces. The fifteenth-century convent of the order of Ste Clare has seventeenth-century cloisters, and the town hall dates from the seventeenth and eighteenth centuries. Other sights are in the seventeenth-century hospital with its dispensary, almost as it was originally, and many fine buildings including Renaissance mansions. The town is also the home of a National Dairy College.

Arbois to Morez

From Poligny it is a short drive past the Grottes Planches to Arbois, in the heart of the main vine-growing belt. Several of the winemakers welcome visitors, and there are tasting cellars as well. Apart from wine, Arbois was the home of Louis Pasteur and many of his experiments were performed here. His home is open to the public, and there is a statue of him in the town. Things to see include the twelfth-century church of St Just, the Capucins bridge, the Tour de la Gloriette, dating from the thirteenth century, and large sections of the ramparts and towers. There are many fine old houses, including some built in the seventeenth century which form an arcade at street level. There is a wine-making museum, and both Château Pecauld and Château Bontemps are worth a visit. In the first week of September there is a wine harvest festival in the town. Arbois is a delightful centre with many good hotels and restaurants, and offers the best opportunity to taste the better wines of the region.

From Arbois, drive north along the D469 and N5 to Dole, which used to be the chief city of Franche-Comté. There are many examples of fifteenth, sixteenth and seventeenth-century architecture, and while Pasteur carried out his experiments in Arbois, he was actually born here, so there is an opportunity to visit his birthplace. There is the sixteenth-century collegiate church of Notre-Dame with its 243ft-high belfry, a museum housing painters of the French school, the Law Courts and the former convent of Cordeliers.

The seventeenth-century hospital, now the Pasteur hospital, has a two-storey cloister and dispensary worth seeing. Nearby is Mont Roland, Plumot, Château de St-Ylie, Chaux and the La Serre forests.

The next call is Salins-lès-Bains, and there is a pleasant drive through the forests around Port-Lesney and Mouchard. At the former there are the ruins of a fifteenth-century castle and an eighteenth-century chapel, while the latter is the home of the National Forestry School. Salins is a former capital of the Earldom of Burgundy, and is now noted as a spa town. Remains of the ramparts and defence towers are still visible, and there are tours of the old salt works. Visit the seventeenth-century Hôtel Dieu with its dispensary, wood panelling and collection of earthenware; the eighteenth-century town hall, and thirteenth-century church of St Anatole. The church of St Maurice also dates from the thirteenth century, while the Notre-Dame-Libératrice chapel was started in the seventeenth century. Look out for the eighteenth-century monumental fountain and the old houses with their round and square towers.

The tour now travels north on the N33 through Quingey with its ruined medieval castle, passing Chenecey just off on the right, with its old castle ruins, old forges and caves.

Although Besançon is not in the Jura, but in Doubs, it is worth a visit because it is such an old town. It is almost enclosed by hills and dominated by the citadel which is regarded as Vauban's masterpiece. There are Roman remains, including a triumphal arch, and the cathedral of St John dating from the eleventh century, with its clock showing both the months and seasons as well. The church of Notre Dame also dates from the eleventh century, and there are many ancient buildings. The town hall was built in the sixteenth century, while the law courts and Renaissance Palais Granvelle date from the seventeenth century. The fountain is more than 400 years old. Other things to see include the almshouses, with their sixteenth-century carved wooden arcade; Carmes convent: St François church; Hôpital St Jacques; library, and the churches of St Pierre, St Maurice, and Ste Madeleine. Also look out for the Banque de France, the Préfecture and the mansions dating from the sixteenth and seventeenth centuries. There is a sculptured wooden gallery at the old Hospice du St Esprit and many fountains and statues.

Besançon was also the birthplace of Victor Hugo, the Lumière brothers, Charles Fourier and Proudhon. There is a fine arts museum and museums of natural history, clock-making, local folk arts and the French Resistance movement. There are numerous hotels and restaurants and many bracing walks in and around the town.

Besançon marks the most northerly point of this tour, and the route now drops south to Ornans on the D67. Ornans, too, is the birthplace of many famous people, including Nicolas Perrenot, chancellor of the Emperor Charles V, the mathematician Pierre Vernier and the painter Gustave Courbet, whose home is now a museum. It is a charming old town on the River Loue, and many of the oldest houses are floodlit during the season. Things to see include the twelfth-century church which contains a marble bust of Christ, and seventeenth-century wrought-iron communion rails, as well as an eighteenth-century high altar. The St Louis hospital dates from the eighteenth century, and you should also see the old Minimes church.

There are a number of delightful walks around this town, which is a country resort, and some of the most engaging promenades are along the river where you can see how the old houses overhang the river.

The journey then continues south-east on the D67 to Lods, home of the painter Lancrenon, which is a small town on the banks of the Loue. There is a sawmill, a small sixteenth-century château and some interesting caves. There is a very old forge and a museum of winemaking and the 'La Loi' rock. The area is surrounded by vineyards, and it is another good place to taste the local wines.

South of Lods is Pontarlier, another ancient town built where the valleys of the Doubs and Drugeon meet. Things to see should include the eighteenth-century triumphal arch, the former portal of the order of Annonciades dating from the sixteenth century, the town hall and the church of St Bénigne. There are also many recreational facilities available. Nearby is Joux castle, at La Cluse-et-Mijoux, which is open to the public; the Entre-Portes gorge; Grand Taureau (4,339ft), Montbenoît Abbey, and St-Point lake.

The D471 will take you through Nozeroy, an ancient country town with ruins of a twelfth-century castle, and old ramparts and gateways. It is an old feudal township and the castle was built by Jean de Chalon l'Antique. The gateways are the Porte de l'Horloge and Porte de Nods. The fifteenth-century church has a plaited straw altarpiece dating from the seventeenth century.

The tour has to run back to Champagnole before it heads south on the N5 to the last port of call, Morez, where there is a strange group of viaducts. Morez is a small industrial town manufacturing enamel plate, watches and ski equipment, and because of its altitude (2,394ft), it is also a popular winter holiday resort. The best view of the town is from the Roche-au-Dade belvedere, and you should also visit the museum.

PLACES OF INTEREST IN THE JURA

Acey
Abbey founded in 1136 by Cistercian nuns, now occupied by Trappists.

Andelot-en-Montagne
Fourteenth-century church, La Joux state forest.

Arbois
Wine cellars, house of Pasteur, churches, Capucins bridge, ramparts, towers and gateways, houses from fifteenth century, museum.

Arinthod
Twelfth-century church, old fountain, old cross.

Arlay
Ancient town, castle ruins, eighteenth-century castle open to public.

Baume-lès-Messieurs
Sixth-century abbey founded by St Colomban, an Irish monk. Provided the monks who started Cluny. Twelfth-century abbey church, museum.

Bellefontaine
Summer walking and winter skiing resort.

Besançon
Ancient town, many old buildings and churches, ramparts, citadel, ancient town hall and law courts, statues, fountains, museums.

Les Bouchoux
Old church.

Cerniebaud
Cross-country skiing resort.

Chalain
A natural amphitheatre among the rocks; beauty spot.

Champagnole
Summer holiday centre.

Château-Chalon
Fortified since Roman times; famous wine-producing centre. Site of Benedictine abbey founded in the seventh century.

Clairvaux-lès-Lacs
Church with fifteenth-century stalls.

Conliège
Wine-producing village. Thirteenth-century church, carved pulpit.

Dole
Ancient town, many old houses, birthplace of Pasteur, fine churches and museums.

Doucier
Holiday resort in summer.

Foncine-le-Haut
Sixteenth-century church, skiing resort.

Foncine-le-Bas
Holiday resort and spa.

Lods
Sixteenth-century château, caves, home of painter Lancrenon.

Lons-le-Saunier
Spa town, many sixteenth-century buildings, rue de Commerce, old churches, museums.

Moirans-en-Montagne
Sixteenth-century church, twelfth-century manor.

Morez
Winter sports town, viaducts.

Mouchard
National Timber School.

Nozeroy
Old feudal town, castle ruins, gateways and towers, fifteenth-century church.

Orgelet
Fifteenth-century church, rampart and tower remains, old convent and hospital.

La Pesse
Cross-country skiing resort.

Poligny
Fifteenth-century church, thirteenth-century Jacobin church, old convent, many old buildings, town hall, museum, Renaissance mansions.

Port-Lesney
Old bridge, ruins of fifteenth-century castle, old abbey remains, eighteenth-century chapel, summer riverside resort.

Prémanon
Reindeer valley, skiing resort.

St-Amour
Seventeenth-century church, summer holiday resort.

St-Claude
St Pierre cathedral, tall bridges and viaducts, museums.

St-Hymetière
Twelfth-century church.

St-Laurent-en-Grandvaux
Site of monastery founded in 523, country holiday resort.

St-Lothian
Eleventh-century church built over earlier crypt. Interesting houses.

St-Maurice-Crillat
Gothic church, ruins of dungeon and keep.

Salins-lès-Bains
Spa town and resort, remains of ramparts and towers, old saltworks, many old churches, seventeenth-century hospital, fountains, museums, town hall.

Sellières
Ancient monuments, fifteenth-century gateway, rampart remains, old church.

Syam
Old mill and forge, and Palladian-style château.

Vers-en-Montagne
Ruined fifteenth-century castle.

Villers-Farlay
Site of Roman camp, fifteenth-century church.

Vouglans
Massive dam and lake.

Gastronomy of Savoie and the Jura

Excellent cheeses are one of the highlights of Savoie cuisine, and cheese is used in many of the traditional dishes. Cheese and potatoes is another favourite mix, and has given rise to such creations as *gratin Dauphinois* and *gratin Savoyara*.

The mountain lakes provide excellent fresh fish, especially trout, and pike and freshwater crayfish are other specialities. From the lower areas come poultry and pigs; hams and sausages are another feature of the cuisine of both Savoie and the Jura. There are plentiful supplies of fresh fruit and vegetables. Game abounds in the woods and forests on the higher slopes. The forests also provide a wide range of wild mushrooms, fungi and truffles.

The cuisine of both regions is typical country fare and one does eat well. Portions are also quite large, because presumably it is important at most times of the year to stock up well with food to keep the cold out. This also explains why there is so much *charcuterie*, because the locals have had to keep food stored over the winter months as many of the higher-altitude villages were cut off by the snow. The area is also famous for its nuts and is the largest producer of walnuts in France.

There are many types of nourishing, filling soups featuring vegetables. *Soupe à la Franc-Comtoise*, is made from potato, turnip and milk, and *potée à la Franc-Comtoise*, *is* a cabbage and potato soup with pork and sausage added. *Soupe aux grenouilles* is a creamy soup made from frog's legs and white wine, and *soupe Savoyarde* is a thick soup with potatoes, vegetables and cheese. The most unusual soup is *soupe aux cerises*, made from cherries.

Fish dishes are plentiful and menus can be confusing if local names are used. *Féro* is a highly-prized type of salmon found in the lakes of Savoie although, alas, it is now quite rare. *Lavaret* is another salmon-type fish found in the lakes, while *omble-chevalier* is char, also known as *ombre-chevalier*. *Pochouse* is a freshwater fish stew, cooked in wine, and *quenelles* are mousses made from fish, usually pike (*de brochet*). A delicious sauce is *sauce Nantua*, made with truffles and freshwater crayfish tails.

There are many different meats served in a number of ways. *Brési* is smoked and salted beef or veal, dried and served in thin slices, while *brochettes* are usually pieces of meat served on a skewer. *Brochette Jurassienne* is cheese wrapped in ham and fried in oil and served skewered. *Civet de marmotte* is a rich stew of wine, vegetables and marmot, the ground squirrel found living in burrows in the Alps. It is not commonly offered, though you are likely to see *défarde*, from Dauphiné, a stew of lamb's trotters and tripe. *Faisan à la Chartreuse* is pheasant cooked slowly with vegetables, bacon and sausage and laced with the liqueur which comes from the

Carthusian monastery founded in Dauphiné in the eleventh century.

Caion is a Savoie name for pig or pork, while *cardon* is a sort of coarse celery cooked and served under a layer of grilled, grated cheese. There are a number of different types of cheese dishes, including *croustades Jurassiennes*, cheese pastries, or sometimes presented as a toasted sandwich with a cheese and ham filling.

There are many sorts of sausage including *diot* from Savoie made from pork and vegetables and cooked in white wine. In Dauphiné *farçon* is a large sausage, while in Savoie it is a dish of potatoes cooked with egg, milk, raisins and prunes and served as a dessert. It is also called *farcement*, and it is easy to see why people can easily order the wrong dish.

Escalope de veau belle Comtoise is a Jura speciality, and consists of thin slices of veal in breadcrumbs and baked with ham and cheese. Another Jura speciality is *fechun*, cabbage stuffed with bacon and vegetables, and *fondue*, usually Gruyère cheese melted in white wine and kirsch into which bread or pieces of meat are dipped. *Fondue de Franche-Comté* is the same as above except that eggs replace the kirsch.

Other dishes to look for are *frérottes*, potatoes and onions cooked in lard, *jésu* which is smoked pork liver sausage from the Jura and *Jésus de Morteau*, which is the same sausage smoked over juniper twigs. A delicious recipe is *langues fourrées* which is stuffed tongues from the Jura, but also try *gratin savoyard*, thin slices of potato baked with cheese and a beef stock. There is also *longeole*, a Savoie sausage, and *omelette Savoyarde*, usually an omelette filled with sautéed or fried potatoes and cheese. *Ramequin* is a special type of Jura fondue, cheese with red wine, mustard and garlic; while *pormonier* is a pork and herb sausage from Savoie. When a dish is followed by *à la Savoyarde*, it usually means with cheese and potatoes. Finally in the meat courses, look out for *poulet au Vin Jaune*, a Jura speciality of chicken cooked in the special wine of the region.

There are many fine desserts to choose from including *biscuit de Savoie*, a very light sponge cake with nuts; *gâteau Grenoblois*, a walnut sponge or pastry case; and *gougère*, puff pastry rings, sometimes flavoured with cheese as a savoury. *Laitiat* is a special Jura drink made from wild fruits and the whey of milk, while *malakoff* is an almond pastry from the same area. *Mont Blanc* can be something of a gargantuan experience. It is meringue covered in chestnut purée and whipped cream. In the south of the region you may be offered *pogne*, a brioche cake filled with pumpkin or ham, or *raviole*, a pastry made with goat's milk. There is also *sèche*, a sweet tart from the Jura.

There are many cheeses to be found throughout Savoie and the Jura. Most of those from the Savoie are made from cow's milk and include *Abondance*, a firm, mild smooth cheese, and *Beaufort*, a hard, almost salty cheese like *Gruyère* without the holes. It is strong and fruity. There is also *Beaumont*, mild and creamy with a yellow rind, *Bleu de St-Foy* and *Bleu de Tignes*: blue veined, creamy and strong tasting. *Bleu de Sassenge* is also blue veined but milder. The monks at the abbey of Chambarand make a mild and creamy cheese, named after them while *Colobière* is a small, mild, round cheese.

Other Savoie cheeses worth trying are *Fondu aux Raisin*, a processed cheese, mild and coated with grape seeds, and *Reblochon*, a quite hard, but mild and creamy cheese. There is also *St-Marcellin*, a small, mild cheese originally made from goat's milk, but now made commercially from cow's milk. *Tamié* is a very silky cheese, smooth tasting and made by the monks from the abbey of the same name.

Of the goat's milk cheeses found in the Savoie look out for *Chèvrotin des Aravis*, a mild smelling and tasting cheese made in the mountains; *Persillé des Aravis*, a blue veined tangy cheese from the same district; and *Tomme de Savoie*, a mild cheese often sold by the name of the village in which it is produced.

In the Jura there are also to be found cheeses made from both cow's milk and goat's milk. The cow's milk cheeses include *Bleu de Gex*, blue veined, strong tasting and very similar to *Bleu de Septmoncel*. There is *Cancoillotte*, a fruity-tasting cheese spread, often eaten warm on toast, and *Comté*, a hard cheese with small holes, a Jura version of *Gruyère*. The French also make their own version of *Emmental*, known as *Emmental Français*. It is a hard, tangy cheese made in huge rounds. Other Jura cow's milk cheeses include *Mamirolle*, made at the famous National Dairy College. It is strong and firm; *Morbier* has a similar texture with a black streak running through it, and *Vacherin Mont d'Or* is a mild, creamy product, best eaten when fully ripe and runny.

Cheeses made from goat's milk include *Chèvret*, of which there are many types throughout the region. They range in strength from mild to strong and are sold under a variety of names including *Tomme des Allues, de Beaufort, de Courcheval, de Combovin, de Corps, de Crest, de Pelvoux, de Belley* and *Tomme de Chèvre*.

HOTELS AND RESTAURANTS OF SAVOIE AND JURA

SAVOIE

Aix-lès-Bains
(73100 Savoie)

Le Manoir
rue Georges Ier
☎ (79) 61 44 00
A very comfortable, central 72-room hotel, reasonable rates and a good, inexpensive restaurant.

Les Iles Britanniques
place Etablissement
  Thermal
☎ (79) 61 03 77
Comfortable, inexpensive 88-room hotel, with fairly good, budget-priced restaurant.

Annecy
(74000 Haute-Savoie)

Auberge de Savoie
1 place St François
☎ (50) 45 03 05
Very good food at very reasonable prices.

Artemare
(01260 Ain)

Vieux Tilleul
At Luthézieu, 5 miles
  north on the D31 and D8
☎ (79) 87 64 51
Charming little hotel with very good local fare. 10 inexpensive but comfort-

able rooms and a good, inexpensive restaurant.

Belley
(01300 Ain)

Pernollet
9 place de la Victoire
☎ (79) 81 06 18
20 very comfortable, inexpensive rooms, and a good, but slightly more expensive restaurant; but the food is good and the wines better.

Le Bourget-du-Lac
(73370 Savoie)

Ombremont
2 miles north overlooking
the lake
☎ (79) 25 00 23
Very comfortable 18-room
hotel which prides itself
on its cuisine, although
both quite expensive.

Bateau Ivré
☎ (79) 25 02 66
Run by Jean Jacob, this
first class restaurant offers
marvellous fish dishes on
top of a comprehensive,
but ever-changing menu.
Very reasonably-priced.

Eloise
(01200 Ain)

Le Fartoret
3 miles from Bellegarde-
sur-Valserine
☎ (50) 48 07 18
A good base for touring,
from this 40-room,
inexpensive hotel. Very
good value restaurant,
specialising in local fare.

Evian-lès-Bains
(74500 Haute-Savoie)

Royal
☎ (50) 75 14 00
A luxury hotel on the
southern shores of Lake
Geneva (Lac Léman). The
200 quite expensive
rooms are ultra-comfort-
able, and the restaurant,
the Café Royal, is vast
but still manages to
maintain high standards.

La Verniaz
route d'Abondance
☎ (50) 75 04 90
Another luxury hotel with
35 rooms, and 5 secluded
chalets in the grounds.
Restaurant good, and
neither it nor the rooms
are expensive.

Bourgogne
73 rue Nationale
☎ (50) 75 01 05
Traditional fare very well
presented and not expen-
sive. There are also a
number of comfortable
rooms, equally reasonably-
priced.

St-Alban-de-Montbel
(73610 Savoie)

St-Alban-Plage
☎ (79) 36 02 05
A quiet 16-room hotel,
reasonably-priced, no
restaurant but breakfast.

St-Julien-en-Génèvois
(74160 Haute-Savoie)

La Diligence et la Taverne
du Postillon
ave. du Génève
☎ (50) 49 07 55
An excellent traditional
restaurant, very good
cooking at very
reasonable prices.

Abbaye de Pomier
5 miles south on the
N201
☎ (50) 04 40 64
A charming restaurant
with a creative, constantly-
changing menu of
excellent dishes very
sensibly-priced.

Le Soli
rue Mgr Paget
☎ (50) 49 11 31
Small, but comfortable,
25-room hotel, not
expensive, no restaurant
but breakfasts served.

Hôtel Rey
at Col du Mont Sion,
about 5^1/2 miles south
☎ (50) 44 13 29
A pleasant 31-room hotel,
inexpensive; with a

restaurant, separately
owned, close by.

**St-Pierre-de-
Chartreuse** (38380 Isère)

Beau Site
☎ (76) 88 61 34
A very comfortable
34-room hotel, rates
reasonable, and a good
cheap restaurant.

Auberge Atre Fleuri
1^3/4 miles south on the
D512
☎ (76) 88 60 21
An inn providing comfort-
able and friendly service.
8 inexpensive rooms, and
good traditional food in
the restaurant.

Seyssel
(01420 Ain)

Rhône
by the river
☎ (50) 59 20 30
A pleasant 15-room hotel,
rooms inexpensive and
restaurant good, special-
ising in fish from the
river.

Talloires
(74290 Haute-Savoie)

Auberge du Père Bise
beside the lake
☎ (50) 60 72 01
A super luxurious 34-room
hotel, rightly expensive,
but the guests lack for
nothing. Restaurant good,
but pricey.

L'Abbaye
route du port
☎ (79) 67 77 33
Another luxury hotel, with
31 quite expensive rooms,
and a wonderful restaurant
in this former abbey; good
food at sensible prices.

THE JURA

Arbois
(39600 Jura)

Le Paris
9 rue de l'Hôtel-de-Ville
☎ (84) 66 05 67
A very friendly restaurant, offering specialities of the region at reasonable prices. 18 comfortable rooms, also well priced.

Messageries
2 rue Courcelles
☎ (84) 66 15 45
Comfortable 26-room hotel, inexpensive, no restaurant but breakfast served.

Châtillon
(39130 Jura)

Chez Yvonne
1¼ miles east on the D39
☎ (84) 25 70 82
Very friendly 8-room hotel, good for a base. Reasonable room prices and very good, inexpensive regional fare.

Courlans
(39750 Jura)

Auberge de Chavannes
3¾ miles from Lons-le-Saunier
☎ (84) 47 05 52
Very good restaurant with regional specialities, still reasonably-priced despite its popularity.

Crissier
(1023 Crissier—Switzerland)

Girardet
1 rue d'Yverdon
☎ 34 15 14
Girardet, considered by many to be the best restaurant in the world, so a must for anyone with an interest in food. Frédy Girardet is certainly one of the best chefs in the world, if not the best. The whole experience is heavenly (at least, as I imagine heaven to be) The food is perfect, as is the service, the décor, the wines, the warmth and the staff. Obviously it is expensive but who cares; and book well in advance, everyone else does.

Divonne-lès-Bains
(01220 Ain)

Château de Divonne
route de Gex
☎ (50) 20 00 32
Beautiful hotel in own grounds with magnificent views. 28 luxury rooms and a very good restaurant, but everything expensive.

Les Grands Hôtels
☎ (50) 20 06 63
A luxury grouping of hotels with more than 140 rooms, all for full board letting only, expensive but the restaurant is good and reasonably-priced.

Mont Blanc-Favre
route Grilly
☎ (50) 20 12 54
Comfortable, 18-room, very reasonably-priced hotel, with modest restaurant.

Coccinelles
route Lausanne
☎ (50) 20 06 96
Small comfortable 18-room hotel, inexpensive rooms, no restaurant but breakfasts served.

Dole
(39100 Jura)

Grand Hôtel Chandioux
place Grévy
☎ (84) 79 00 66
Comfortable hotel, with reasonable rates and good, inexpensive restaurant.

Malbuisson
(25160 Doubs)

Le Lac
Grande Rue
☎ (81) 89 34 80
A very comfortable 55-room hotel, reasonably-priced with a good, traditional, inexpensive restaurant.

Poligny
(39800 Jura)

Hostellerie Monts de Vaux
2½ miles away on the Génève road
☎ (84) 37 12 50
10 inexpensive rooms and a good, value-for-money restaurant.

Salins-lès-Bains
(39110 Jura)

Auberge le Val d'Héry
☎ (84) 73 06 54
Modest 7-room, inexpensive inn with restaurant.

VINEYARDS OF SAVOIE AND JURA

SAVOIE

Coopératives open daily:

Société Coopérative des
Vins de Chautagne   TRW
73310 Ruffieux
☎ (79) 63 27 12

Coopérative de Vente des
Vins Fins de
Savoie   TRWPS
73800 Montmélian
☎ (79) 84 04 86

Coopérative des
Vins Fins   TRWPS
73300 Cruet
☎ (79) 84 28 52

Coopérative Le   TRWP
Vigneron Savoyard
73190 Apremont
☎ (79) 28 33 23

Vineyards and Wineries open daily:

Domaine de Termont   TWS
Dominique Allion
73800 Les Marches
☎ (79) 28 10 38

Maurice Bal   TW
73800 Les Marches
☎ (79) 28 14 15

Claudius Barlet and
son   TRWP
73170 Jongieux
☎ (79) 36 82 08

Joseph Barlet   TRW
Barcontian
73170 Jongieux
☎ (79) 36 82 44

GAEC La Cave du
Prieuré   TRW
Raymond Barlet and son
73170 Jongieux
☎ (79) 36 82 22

René Bernard   TW
73190 Apremont
☎ (79) 28 33 30

Les Rocailles   TRWPS
Pierre Boniface
73800 St-André-lès-Marches
☎ (79) 28 14 50

La Chètraz   TRW
Alain Bosson
73310 Serrières-en-
Chautagne
☎ (79) 63 70 32

La Tour de Marignan   TW
Canelli-Suchet
74140 Sciez
☎ (52) 72 60 65

Le Château   TRW
Michel Cartier
38530 St-André
Chapareillan
☎ (79) 45 21 26

Le Gaz   TW
Georges and Jean Chapot
73190 Apremont
☎ (79) 28 33 69

Alain Chautemps   TW
38530 St-André
Chapareillan
☎ (76) 45 22 51

Domaine des Granges
Longes   TRW
Denise Cochet
73800 Les Marches
☎ (79) 28 10 78

Claude Delalex   TW
74200 Marin
☎ (50) 71 45 82

Louis Droguet   TW
73190 Apremont
☎ (79) 28 31 80

Noël Dupasquier   TRWP
Aimavigne
73170 Jongieux
☎ (79) 36 82 23

Marcel Fert   TW
74130 Marignier
☎ (50) 90 67 23

Daniel Fustinoni   TRWP
73800 Les Marches
☎ (79) 28 13 30
or (79) 28 10 53

Maurice Gandy & son   TW
73800 St-André-lès-
Marches
☎ (79) 28 10 57

Mme Vve Josèph
Girard   TRW
Château de Monterminod
73230 St-Alban-Lyesse
☎ (79) 33 01 24

Jean-François Girard-
Madoux   TRW
Torméry
73800 Chignin
☎ (79) 28 11 76

Edmond Jacquin   TRWP
73170 Jongieux
☎ (79) 36 82 35

Château La Marre   TRW
Henri Jeandet
73170 Jongieux
☎ (79) 36 82 17

André Magne   TRW
38530 St-André-
Chapareillan
☎ (79) 28 10 86

Louis Magnin   TRW
73800 Arbin
☎ (79) 84 29 05

Jean Masson   TW
73190 Apremont
☎ (79) 28 33 57

GAEC de Miribel   TRWP
Masson brothers
73170 Jongieux
☎ (79) 36 83 68

Gaston Maurin   TW
73800 Les Marches
☎ (79) 28 12 97

R=red wine   W=white wine   P=rosé wine   S=sparkling wine

Grande Cave de Crépy TW
Claude Françoise,
  Jacqueline Mercier
74140 Loisin
☎ (50) 94 01 23

Michel Million   TRWP
  Rousseau
Monthoux
73170 St-Jean-de-Chevelu
☎ (79) 36 83 93
or (79) 36 80 08

Jean Neyroud
  and son   TRW
74270 Designy
☎ (50) 77 22 73

Gérard Ollivier   TW
564 Chemin de Jacob
73000 Chambéry
☎ (79) 69 50 65

Perceval brothers   TRW
73800 Les Marches
☎ (79) 28 11 18

Caveau de
  Dégustation   TRWPSC
Jean-Claude Perret
73800 St-André-les
  Marches
☎ (79) 28 13 32
or (79) 28 05 08

Philippe Fernand   TRWP
73170 Billième
☎ (79) 36 73 96

Jean-Pierre Quenard   TRW
La Tour
73800 Chignin
☎ (79) 28 13 39

André Quenard and son TRW
Torméry
73800 Chignin
☎ (79) 28 12 75

Claude Quenard   TRW
Le Villard
73800 Chignin
☎ (79) 28 12 04

Raymond Quenard   TRW
73800 Chignin
☎ (79) 28 01 46

Le Cellier des Tours TRWP
Mme René Quenard and son
73800 Chignin
☎ (79) 28 01 15
or (79) 28 13 77

Bernard Rey   TRWP
Chevigneux
73310 Chandrieux
☎ (79) 63 27 58

Bernard Richel   TW
73190 St-Baldolph
☎ (79) 28 31 42

André Tiollier   TRW
St-Laurent
73800 Cruet
☎ (79) 84 30 58

Jean Baptiste Veyron
  and son   TRW
73190 Apremont
☎ (79) 28 33 58

Jean Vullien   TRW
73250 Fréterive
☎ (79) 28 61 58

Négociants

Jean Cavaille   TRW
ave. du Petit Port
73100 Aix-lès-Bains
☎ (79) 61 04 90

Caves du Châtelet   TRWP
18 rue Marc-Courriard
74100 Annemasse
☎ (79) 92 08 45

Distillerie Routin   TRWP
rue Emile-Romanet
73000 Bissy-Chambéry
☎ (79) 62 33 91

Dolin Sté   TRW
ave. du Grand-Ariétaz
73000 Chambéry
☎ (79) 69 59 09

Jacal Sté   TRW
ave. de La Motte-Servolex
73000 Chambéry
☎ (79) 62 30 44

S.A. Perrier and son TRWP
73800 St André-les Marches
☎ (79) 28 11 45

S.A. Perret   TRW
73170 Billième
☎ (79) 36 83 54

Maison Adrien
  Vacher   TRWP
73800 Les Marches
☎ (79) 28 11 48

Varichon and Clerc TRWS
01420 Seyssel
☎ (50) 59 23 15

Vittet Dupraz   TRW
73170 Billième
☎ (79) 36 83 53

THE JURA

Arbois
(39600)

Fruitière Vinicole
  d'Arbois   TRWP
2 rue des Fossés
☎ (84) 66 11 67
Open: by appointment only.

Lucien Aviet   TRW
Montigny-lès-Arsures
☎ (84) 66 11 02

Pierre and Georges
  Bouilleret   TP
Pupillin
☎ (84) 66 20 05
Open: by appointment only.

Maurice Chassot   TWP
15 route de Lyon
☎ (84) 66 15 36
Open: by appointment only.

Domaine de la Croix
  d'Argis   TR
Henri Maire
Château Montfort

T=tasting   E=English spoken   G=guided tours   C=château/building to visit

☎ (84) 66 12 34
Open: by appointment only.

Jacques Forêt   TRWP
44 rue de la Faïëncerie
☎ (84) 66 11 37
Open: by appointment only.

Jean-Claude Gallois   TRW
☎ (84) 66 12 87
Open: Monday to Friday
9am-noon and 2-6pm.

Domaine de la
  Grange Grillard   TW
Henri Maire
Château Montfort
☎ (84) 66 12 34
Open: by appointment only.

Roger Lornet   TRWP
Montigny-lès-Arsures

☎ (84) 66 09 40
Open: by appointment only.

Jean François Nevers   TR
4 rue du Lycée
☎ (84) 66 01 73
Open: by appointment.

Overnoy-Crinquand   TWP
Pupillin
☎ (84) 66 01 45
Open: by appointment.

Désiré Petit and son TRWP
Pupillin
☎ (84) 66 01 20
Open: by appointment.

Rolet and son   TRWP
Montigny
☎ (84) 66 00 05
Open: by appointment.

Abbaye de St-Laurent   TR
Jean-Marie Dole
Montigny-lès-Arsures
☎ (84) 66 22 99
Open: by appointment.

Domaine du Sorbief   TP
Henri Maire
Château Montfort
☎ (84) 66 12 34
Open: by appointment.

André & Mireille
  Tissot   TRWP
Quartier Bernard
Montigny-lès-Arsures
☎ (84) 66 08 27
Open: by appointment

COTES DU JURA

Château d'Arlay   TRW
Renaud de Laguiche
Arlay
39140 Bletterans
☎ (84) 85 04 22
Open: by appointment.

Bernard Badoz   TW
15 rue du Collège
39800 Poligny
☎ (84) 37 11 98
Open: by appointment.

Baud and son   TWP
GAEC Baud and son
Le Vernois
39210 Voiteur
☎ (84) 25 31 41
Open: by appointment.

Jean Bourdy   TR
Arlay
39140 Bletterans
☎ (84) 85 03 70
Open: by appointment.

Emile Bourguignon   TWS
Vincelles
39190 Beaufort
☎ (84) 25 03 03
Open: by appointment.

Chantemerle   TRWS
Joseph & Xavier Reverchon
4 rue du Clos
39800 Poligny
☎ (84) 37 16 78
Open: by appointment.

Chartreux de Vaucluse TW
Pierre Pignier
Montaigu
39570 Lons-le-Saunier
☎ (84) 24 24 30
Open: by appointment.

Bernard Clerc   TW
Mantrey
39230 Sellières
☎ (84) 85 58 37
Open: by appointment.

Gabriel Clerc   TRWPS
Mantrey
39230 Sellières
☎ (84) 85 50 98
Open: by appointment.

Grand brothers   TRWS
GAEC Grand brothers
Passenans
39230 Sellières
☎ (84) 85 28 88
Open: daily 9am-noon and
1.30-7pm

Château Gréa   TWS
Pierre de Boissie
Rotalier
39190 Beaufort
☎ (84) 25 05 07
Open: Monday to Saturday
9am-noon and 2-7pm

Caveau des Jacobins   TR
Fruitière Vinicole de
  Poligny
39800 Poligny
☎ (84) 37 14 58
Open: by appointment.

Paul Pavet   TRW
Domblans
39210 Voiteur
☎ (84) 44 61 92
Open: by appointment.

Pierre Richard   TWS
Le Vernois
39210 Voiteur
☎ (84) 25 33 27
Open: by appointment.

Rolet and son   TW
Montigny
39600 Arbois
☎ (84) 66 00 05
Open: by appointment.

R=red wine   W=white wine   P=rosé wine   S=sparkling wine

Chapter 13
PROVENCE

Ollières,
Côte De Provence

PROVENCE is the region running from the east of the Rhône estuary, along the coast to Nice. It has always produced a lot of wine, red, white and rosé; but the sun has always been its great enemy. In the past, the baking summer Mediterranean sun has produced grapes which are made into wines high in alcohol, which have not really been able to match rivals further west, from the Rhône or Languedoc-Roussillon. There have been isolated areas producing good wines, and thanks to a great effort in recent years there have been enormous improvements in the quality of wines throughout Provence.

The vineyards run from Marseille to Nice and inland from Arles, from Aix-en-Provence and Draguignan. There are five separate ACs within the Côtes de Provence, small areas of excellent wines: Cassis, Bandol, Bellet de Nice, and Palette d'Aix, as well as the VDQS Coteaux d'Aix-en-Provence. Vins de Pays include: des Coteaux Varois, les Maures and le Caume, all from the Var, Petite-Crau (Bouches-du-Rhône) and des Sables du Golfe du Lion.

Only in 1977 did Côtes de Provence achieve AC status, which shows how recent the change to improved techniques has been.

Wine-producing Areas of Provence

Bandol
Bandol is on the coast to the west of Toulon, and the vineyards stretch for about ten miles producing red, white and rosé wines. The reds are by far the best, with enough tannin to give longevity. They should not be drunk before they are two years old, and certainly improve for some years after this. They are made from blends of Mourvèdre, Cinsault and Grenache, which must account for 60 per cent of the *cépage* or blend of grapes. They are full-bodied, firm wines with good bouquets (thanks to the Mourvèdre grape) and they must spend at least eighteen months in barrel. Bandol as a producing district, and indeed all the most famous wine areas of coastal Provence, are unusual in that winemaking is not the principal occupation. Fishing and tourism still predominate in the area, and in Bandol there are only about 200 wine-producers scattered through the sun-baked hillsides.

Cassis
To the west of Bandol is the even smaller *appellation* of Cassis, again making all three types of wine, although here the whites are predominant and they are the best in Provence. There are less than 400 acres of vineyards hugging the hillsides around the town. The white is made from a blend of (predominantly) Clairette, Marsanne, and Ugni Blanc, and is dry and fruity, with a refreshing acidity. It is highly popular as an accompaniment to fish, especially in neighbouring Marseille.

Bellet
This is an even smaller production area in the hills behind Nice making white, red and rosé wine, much of which is drunk locally on the Côte d'Azur.

Coteaux d'Aix-en-Provence

Around Aix-en-Provence is the huge production area allowed to use the VDQS Coteaux d'Aix-en-Provence label. Here enormous sums of money have been and are being spent on improving standards, both in the vineyards and the wineries. There is already one tiny area with its own AC (Palette) and it will not be long before others earn this accolade; some deserve it already.

Palette

Palette is to the south of Aix-en-Provence and produces red and white wines. Red wine comes from the grapes which do so well in the Rhône, Grenache, Cinsault and Mourvèdre. They are big, full-bodied wines, with glorious colour, bouquet and longevity. The whites, made from the Clairette, are fruity and well balanced, and something of a rarity outside the region. There are also some sparkling wines made, and some producers use the *méthode Champenoise*.

A Tour of Provence

Wines have been produced in this sun-drenched part of France for more than 2,500 years, but they are still not widely known outside France. The wines of Bandol, to the west of Toulon, have been available in Britain for some time, and now the producers of Provence are trying to promote sales of the other wines of the region throughout Europe and North America. At present, this area of France is much more widely known as the summer playground of the rich and famous with Monte Carlo, Cannes and Nice on the coast.

This tour, however, starts just outside Toulon, France's largest naval base, and follows a large circle, through most of the wine producers of Côtes de Provence. There is an official *Route des Vins*, and this route crosses it several times, but allows the chance to taste all the various styles of wine and enjoy the countryside as well.

This part of France, colonised by the Greeks in about 600BC, is typical Mediterranean countryside. The rocky soil affords scrub vegetation and olive trees but little else, except in those small patches where vines can be grown. The best time to visit the area is in the late spring, when the rains have passed and the plants and flowers are out. It is really the only time of the year when the countryside can be said to look pretty. As the sun rises higher in the sky during the summer, the plants die away, the grass turns to hay and the earth is baked hard. In the summer, temperatures on the rocky coastal plain can rise to unbearable levels, so this route never goes more than a few miles from the sea, to take advantage of a gentle breeze, and a refreshing chilled glass of local wine.

Although the Greeks established Marseille and planted the vines, little remains of their presence today. It was the Romans who built the great towns which now dominate the region, but most of these are in the west: Avignon, Arles, and the like. This part of the countryside is really for relaxing in, for a leisurely exploration of vineyards, eating some fine food and drinking some very agreeable wines.

Tour of Hyères and the Surrounding Area

The tour should start at Hyères to the east of Toulon, just north of the airport into which you can fly from Paris. Drivers may take the N7 or the toll Autoroute de Provence. Trains run to Marseille or Toulon, where car hire is available. Local transport is also available, but not to be relied on for reaching some of the wine areas which are a little off the beaten track.

Hyères is the oldest resort on the Riviera; Cathérine de Medici planned to build a summer palace there in the sixteenth century, but the plan came to nothing. Queen Victoria visited it regularly, and novelist Robert Louis Stevenson lived there for a time. The town is a few miles inland from the coast, and there are palm tree-lined avenues and well-irrigated flower gardens. There are the ruins of a castle on the hill overlooking the town, and a municipal museum with many remains from both the Greek and Roman occupations.

The townspeople are proud of their parks and gardens and you should visit these, especially the Jardins Olbius Riquier and Parc St-Bernard. Other things to see are the place St-Paul and the chapel of Notre-Dame de Consolation. There are many good hotels and restaurants both in and around the town, and it is a pleasant place to make a base.

The beaches are found about 7km to the south at the end of a peninsula. The drive down the Route du Sel goes past the salt pans at Les Pesquiers to La Tour-Fondue. From here, the islands of Ile de Porquerolles, Ile de Port-Cros and Ile du Levant are offshore. Together the islands are known as the Iles d'Hyères and can be reached by a fifteen-minute boat crossing from La Tour-Fondue. The peninsula on which the beaches are situated used to be another island in this chain, but it became landlocked many centuries ago.

Severe storms still occasionally sweep the area in winter, and in 1811 a fierce storm actually forced a channel through the peninsula, separating it again from the mainland briefly, but the sands quickly returned. Even today, if the weather is very bad, this road can be closed.

There are vineyards on Ile de Porquerolles, and many charming walks on all three islands, although the Ile du Levant is in part occupied by the French Navy and much of the land is restricted.

From Hyères, take the N98 to Le Lavandou, which is named after the lavender fields cultivated along the banks of the river Batailler; it is a charming little fishing port. There are good beaches along the coastline here, and inland the Massif des Maures dominates the landscape and does so until Fréjus is reached. The coastline is known here as the Côte des Maures, which is named after the hills, which in turn were named after the dark-coloured pine trees on their slopes. The densely-wooded hill slopes have some marvellous walks, and the villagers from the many hamlets in the Massif still earn their income in part from gathering sweet chestnuts and bark from the cork trees.

Just north of Le Lavandou is the hilltop village of Bormes-lès-Mimosas, which is worth a visit. There is a sixteenth-century chapel to St Francis, and in front of it there is a statue to Francesco di Paola, who is said to have saved the village from the plague in 1481. The village, with its large tree-lined square and old houses, has been little changed by the tourists who now visit it in growing numbers.

Circular Tour from St-Tropez to Toulon

From Bormes, the next stop is St-Tropez. Either take the coastal road through some marvellous little resorts with splendid beaches, or the higher road a little way inland, through Cogolin. On the lower route, there are the beaches where the Allies landed in 1944; and if the high road is chosen, you can do a little tasting along the way. There are cellar and tasting centres at Bormes, La Môle, La Croix-Valmer and Cogolin.

St-Tropez, of course, is one of the most famous resorts in the world, bursting with fine hotels and restaurants. It has always attracted artists because of the perfect light and many of their works of art are now housed in the town's museum of modern art. There is also a maritime museum in the citadel with many exhibits from the old town. It was only eighty years ago that St-Tropez got its first real road into the town; before then people used the narrow gauge railway, or the ferry from St-Raphaël.

The harbour at St-Tropez still houses the traditional fishing boats, but they are now dwarfed by the luxury yachts of the rich, while the quays are packed with artists dashing out oil paintings to sell to the tourists.

The main sights to see are the sixteenth-century chapel of Ste-Anne, just outside town; and also the statue of the French Admiral Bailli de Suffren, who with a tiny fleet of five ships managed to harass the Royal Navy around the globe in the mid-eighteenth century. His home was Château Suffren, in the old town, near the town hall.

St-Tropez is surrounded by huge beaches, and the new marina-holiday complex of Port Grimaud. Cars are not allowed, and it is a little like a mini-Venice, to be visited only on foot or by boat, with conducted tours available through the maze of canals.

Continuing along the N98, the family resort of Ste-Maxime is popular throughout the year with lively evening entertainment and many sporting facilities. It also has many good restaurants, and a fine reputation for its food. Detours are also possible from here into the hills, to sample more of the local wine around Plan-de-la-Tour and La Garde-Freinet.

Fréjus, once a Roman harbour, is now a couple of kilometres inland, and there are some fine ruins, including the remains of a fifth-century baptistry. There is an incomplete Roman theatre to the north of the town, now used for bullfights, and there are guided tours of the thirteenth-century cathedral and cloisters of Notre-Dame-de-Victoire in the town centre. There is a museum containing antiquities found in the area.

St-Raphaël, Fréjus' neighbour, has a twelfth-century church of the Knights Templar and a fine archaeological museum.

From Fréjus and St-Raphaël the route turns inland, away from the beaches and into the hills and the vineyards. Draguignan, a small town with a reputation for good food, both in its restaurants and its shops, is the first main town. It has many fine old buildings and fountains, and the centre is dominated by the seventeenth-century Tour d'Horloge, There is a medieval gateway and the façade of a thirteenth-century synagogue in the rue de la Juiverie. A museum is housed in the eighteenth-century former summer palace of the

Bishops of Fréjus. Nearby is the spectacular area of gorges and plunging waterfalls known as the Verdon Gorges. There are wine-tasting cellars in Draguignan and in many of the villages on our road to Brignoles, especially Les Arcs, Vidauban and Le Luc.

Brignoles is another market town and agricultural centre, famous for its museum, which houses, amongst other things, the oldest Gaulish Christian sarcophagus, dating from the third century. Just south of Brignoles is Besse, the home of Gaspard de Besse, a sort of eighteenth-century French Robin Hood. He was finally captured and executed at Aix-en-Provence. There is also a beautiful Cistercian abbey at Le Thoronet, and many of the original twelfth-century buildings have been restored to their austere splendour.

Other places to visit in the area are Salernes with its thirteenth-century castle ruins; Entrecasteaux, a medieval village with château and fortified Gothic church; and Tourtour.

From Brignoles, drive in a sweeping curve back down to the coast using the N560 and taking in La Roquebrussanne, and a small detour off to La Ste-Baume, where legend has it that Mary Magdalene lived in retreat in a cave for the last thirty years of her life. The cave, Grotte de St Pilon, can be reached on foot from the D80.

Continue on the D80 down to Gémenos, with its eighteenth-century château and nearby chapel of St Jean de Garguier, with its collection of religious paintings dating back for the last 500 years, and then on to La Ciotat, on the coast, a former Greek settlement. The Musée Tauroentum, built on the site of a Roman villa, and housing many of the Roman finds made nearby should be visited. Then it is just a short drive to Bandol.

Bandol is the home of one of the region's most famous wines, and you can sit out at one of the many beach cafés and sample it at leisure. Just off the coast is the Ile Bendor, now a tourist trap with art gallery, museum, zoo and the World Museum of Wines and Spirits.

The final point of call before returning to Hyères should be to Toulon, a bustling, crowded city, with few attractions surviving the heavy bombardments during the last war. There are some good restaurants, however, and the fish and vegetable markets are worth visiting, as are the maritime and archaeological museums.

PLACES OF INTEREST IN PROVENCE

AROUND HYERES

Hyères
Castle ruins, many fine buildings,
museum, parks and gardens.

Iles d'Hyères
Walks, vineyards.

Le Lavandou
Charming fishing village, lavender fields.

Bormes-lès-Mimosas
Pretty hilltop town.

Chartreuse-de-la-Verne
Monastery.

Grimaud
Ruined castle, Knights Templar church.

ST-TROPEZ AND FREJUS AREA

St-Tropez
Modern art museum; maritime museum; citadel; sixteenth-century chapel of Ste Anne, statue of de Suffren.

Port Grimaud
Modern holiday complex and marina, no roads — just canals.

La Garde-Freinet
Wine-tasting centres.

Fréjus
Fifth-century baptistry, Roman theatre, thirteenth-century cathedral, museum and many Roman antiquities, Buddhist pagoda, zoo, safari park.

St-Raphaël
Twelfth-century church of the Knights Templar, archaeological museum.

DRAGUIGNAN AREA

Draguignan
Tour d'Horloge; fountains; old buildings; thirteenth-century synagogue; medieval gateway. Verdon Gorges (nearby); prehistoric dolmen.

Montferrat
Ruined castle, chapel.

Canjuers
Caves

Comps-sur-Artuby
Thirteenth-century church.

Bargème
Castle ramparts, highest village in Var (3,588ft).

Bargemon
Old buildings, castle, fortified gateways.

BRIGNOLES AREA

Brignoles
Market town; museum with sarcophagi.

Besse
Home of Gaspard de Besse.

Le Thoronet
Cistercian abbey.

Salernes
Thirteenth-century castle ruins.

Entrecasteaux
Medieval village, château, fortified Gothic church.

La Ste-Baume
Sacred grotto.

BANDOL AREA

Bandol
Wine centre and resort.

Ile Bendor
Tourist island with zoo, museum, art gallery and wine museum.

Gémenos
Eighteenth-century château and chapel.

La Ciotat
Former Greek settlement, shipbuilding centre, museum.

Gastronomy of Provence

In many respects the gastronomy of Provence is similar to that of the southern Rhône, with seafish predominating along the coast. Olive groves hug the hillsides and provide the basic cooking oil, and there are plentiful supplies of vegetables. There are many salads to accompany fish and meat courses, and the people of Provence like strong, fiery tastes which is why garlic, peppers and raw onions are all used in dishes. Marseille is said to have been the home of *bouillabaisse*, and stews of fish and meat abound.

Garlic is extensively used, both as an ingredient and to make soups and sauces. As one moves nearer the Italian border, the food changes, and there are many pasta dishes, especially around Nice. There is *canelloni*, *ravioli* and *gnocchi*, and a French version of pizza called *pissaladière*.

There is a little game, some venison, hare and rabbit, and the beef, which tends to be locally reared, needs long, slow cooking in stews or *daubes* to be at its best.

Garlic soup is naturally offered everywhere. There is *aïgo*, a straightforward garlic soup usually poured over bread, and *aïgo bouido*, with olive oil and eggs added together with cubes of fried bread. *Aïgo à la ménagère* is garlic soup with onion, leek, tomatoes and poached egg, and *aïgo saou*, or *sou*, is garlic soup with fish, and sometimes potatoes. Other soups include *soupe d'épautre* made with mutton, vegetables and garlic, and you will often find *méjanels* added; this is a thick pasta made in Provence and added to both soups and stews. Accompanying soups you may well find *aïoli*, a mayonnaise sauce flavoured with garlic and sometimes with breadcrumbs.

Fish dishes can include *anchoyade*, or *anchoïade* which are simply anchovies, or they can be served as *anchois à la Suédoise*, when they are presented cold with an apple and beetroot salad. *Bouillabaisse* is universally popular and is a fish stew of conger eel, gurnard, and many other species, cooked with saffron, garlic, onions, tomatoes, oil and wine. Other frequently offered fish courses are *bézuque*, the Provence name for sea bream and *blade*, the local name for saddled bream. You may find *boutargue*, a paste made from dried and salted tuna roe, or *capoum*, the local name for scorpion fish. Eels are popular and there is a very good dish, *catigot d'anguilles*, of eels cooked in red wine and tomatoes and garlic. Another local fish name is *claougeou* for squid, and you may find *tarte aux blettes*, a flan with sardines, not to be confused with *tarte aux épinards*, which is filled with sweet spinach.

There is *loup grillé au fenouil*, sea bass cooked with fennel, or over fennel twigs and normally flambéed with Pernod. Try *moules nautile*, mussels with tomatoes, onions, and saffron in white wine, or *à la Niçoise*, with tomatoes, anchovies, olives, garlic and capers. There is *nonat*, a dish of small fish, deep fried, or used in soups and omelettes, and *rouille*, a hot pepper and garlic mayonnaise, served with fish. *Stocaficado* is also worth trying. It is dried cod stewed with tomatoes, potatoes, garlic and olives.

There are a host of meat and vegetable dishes, mostly in stews and casseroles. There is the famous *daube*, a meat, or sometimes fish stew, as opposed to *daube de muscardins*, which is cuttlefish cooked in red wine.

Dishes which come à la Arlésienne, originally from Arles, are cooked with tomatoes, onions, potatoes, aubergines and olives. Provence produces its own rather long, purplish artichoke (artichaut), and when served à la Barigoule comes stuffed with mushrooms, ham and onions, and cooked in wine and oil. Artichaut à la Provençale means cooked in oil, with herbs and garlic.

Snails are popular and there are many local names including bajaina and banarut. Cantareux are small snails cooked in a tomato sauce, and escargots à la sucarelle means snails with tomatoes, sausage, and garlic in white wine.

Barbouillade is a stew made from artichokes and broad beans, while broufado is a meat stew, usually beef, with onions, capers, anchovies and vinegar. Other meat dishes might include porchetta, a suckling pig, stuffed and spit roasted, and pieds et paquets, a Provence speciality of sheep's tripe and trotters, cooked with tomatoes in white wine.

Non-meat main courses include berlingueto, hard boiled eggs on a bed of chopped spinach, and boursotto, a pastry stuffed with vegetables, anchovies, rice and cheese. There is capoun which is cabbage stuffed with rice and sausage meat, and sometimes cheese, and gargaméu, omelette with tomatoes. If dishes are à la Marseillaise, it means with tomatoes, anchovies, onions, olives and garlic. Mesclun is a green salad with lettuce, chicory, endive, dandelion leaves and other greenery, while nureio is a salad of lettuce, anchovies and sliced hard boiled eggs. Other dishes might include missoun, small sausages, sliced and sometimes added to soups, pan bagna, a Provence sandwich in which the bread is soaked in olive oil and then filled with olives, anchovies, onions, tomatoes and sometimes sliced hard boiled eggs. Papetons are fried aubergines, while pascado is a bacon omelette. There is ratatouille, a mix of aubergines, tomatoes, courgettes, onions and peppers cooked in oil, and salade Niçoise, made from tomatoes, onions, broad beans, lettuce, olives, tuna, anchovies and hard boiled eggs.

Sauces include rouille, a hot pepper and mayonnaise sauce; raito, a tomato, garlic and nut sauce in red wine to accompany fish; and pistou, a basil, garlic and olive oil sauce. Soupe au pistou is a vegetable soup with pistou added, and not to be confused with pissalot, an anchovy sauce served cold. A la Provençale means with tomatoes, garlic, olive oil and onion.

Desserts include brigne, a sweet fritter; calisson, or canissoun, marzipan sweets; and chichi frégi, another sort of sweet fritter. Crenchente is a raisin cake while fougassette is a cake flavoured with orange, and in season, orange blossom.

There are a number of mild cheeses made from both goat's and sheep's milk and these include Annot, Banon, which is usually wrapped in chestnut leaves, and Brousse de la Vesubie, a soft, very mild cheese often served with fruit. There is also Picodon de Valréas, a small, mild goat's milk cheese, and Poivre d'Ane, which is similar to Banon but with the herb savory added. Finally there is Tomme Arlésienne, a mild creamy sheep's milk cheese with a herby taste.

HOTELS AND RESTAURANTS OF PROVENCE

(See also southern Rhône section)

Aix-en-Provence
(13100 Bouches-du-Rhône)

Hôtel Paul Cézanne
40 ave. Victor Hugo
☎ (42) 26 34 73
A very comfortable, attentive 44-room hotel, not expensive; no restaurant, but breakfast served.

Le Pigonnet
ave. du Pigonnet
☎ (42) 59 02 90
A very comfortable hotel with 50 not expensive rooms and a good, well-priced restaurant.

Le Nègre-Coste
33 cours Mirabeau
☎ (42) 27 74 22
Very good value 36-room hotel, the oldest in the town; no restaurant but breakfast served.

Caravelle
29 blvd Roy-René
☎ (42) 21 53 05
Comfortable, inexpensive 30-room hotel; no restaurant but breakfast served.

Mas d'Entremont
montée d'Avignon
1³/4 miles away on the N7 at Celony
☎ (42) 23 45 32
Charming hotel with 9 rooms and 7 bungalows in the grounds. Rooms and restaurant good value.

Novotel Aix Est
Résidence Beaumanoir
off the A8
☎ (42) 27 47 50
Air-conditioned 102-room hotel, not expensive, caféteria-style meals.

Caves Henry IV
32 rue Espariat
☎ (42) 23 70 71
An atmospheric cellars restaurant, with an innovative, constantly-changing menu, using the best and freshest local produce; good value.

Charvet
9 rue de Lacépède
☎ (42) 38 43 82
Henri Charvet is a young chef, and many of the gastronomic guides consider this the best restaurant for miles around. The food is always good, and brother Gérard oversees the charming restaurant.

Bandol
(83150 Var)

Auberge du Port
9 allée Jean Moulin
☎ (94) 29 42 63
Very good fish and shellfish with local wines, but a little expensive.

Ile Rousse
blvd Louis Lumière
☎ (94) 29 46 86
Modern, very comfortable hotel, rooms expensive, restaurant good value and service impeccable.

La Ker Mocotte
rue Raimu
☎ (94) 29 46 53
Comfortable 19-room hotel by the sea, room rates reasonable and inexpensive restaurant good value.

Beaurecueil
(13100 Bouches-du-Rhône)

Relais Ste-Victoire
☎ (42) 28 94 98
A comfortable, not expensive inn with 8 rooms and a very good restaurant.

Bormes-lès-Mimosas
(83230 Var)

Paradis
Mont des Roses
☎ (94) 71 06 85
Very comfortable, inexpensive 20-room hotel, no restaurant, but breakfast served.

Safari
route du Stade
☎ (94)71 09 83
Very comfortable 33-room hotel, with marvellous views. Rooms good value and restaurant reasonable, but only dinner served.

Brignoles
(83170 Var)

Mas la Cascade
1¹/4 miles away on the D554 Toulon road
☎ (94) 69 01 4910
comfortable, well-priced rooms and a good, inexpensive restaurant.

L'Abbaye de la Celle
at La Celle, on the D554 and D405
☎ (94) 69 08 44
Comfortable 33-room hotel in its own park, not expensive, and a reasonable restaurant.

Le Brusc (83140 Var)

St Pierre
Montée Citadelle
☎ (88) 25 02 52
Good, not expensive local fare.

Mt-Salva
chemin Mt-Salva
☎ (88) 25 03 93
Good, inexpensive, with
Provençale specialities.

Canadel-sur-Mer
(83240 Var)

Le Roitelet
☎ (94) 05 61 39
Comfortable, friendly 7-
room hotel, inexpensive,
and a good restaurant with
nice terrace.

Karlina
☎ (94) 05 61 65
Very comfortable, 11 rooms
from cheap to expensive,
good restaurant.

Cavalière
(83980 Var)

Le Club
by the beach
☎ (94) 05 80 14
Luxury throughout; one of
the best hotels in the area.
32 rooms, very expensive
and half-board only in the
high season; restaurant
good and one must book.

Surplage
☎ (94) 05 80 19
Very comfortable, 63
good rooms, not over-
expensive, restaurant good
and reasonably-priced.

Cavalaire-sur-Mer
(83240 Var): not to be
confused with the above.

Calanque
rue Calanque
☎ (94) 64 04 27
A very comfortable 35-
room hotel, quite
expensive, but a good
inexpensive restaurant.

Pergola
ave. Port
☎ (94) 64 06 86
Comfortable 32 rooms,
reasonably-priced, good
inexpensive restaurant.

Hôtel Raymond
☎ (94) 64 07 32
A comfortable 35-room,
inexpensive hotel with a
very good fish restaurant,
Le Mistral.

Cotignac
(83570 Var)

Lou Calen
1 cours Gambetta
☎ (94) 04 60 40
A charming 16-room inn
and restaurant with very
friendly service. Rooms
good value, and the
restaurant even better
value, dine by the pool.

Draguignan
(83300 Vars)

Col de l'Ange
☎ (94) 68 23 01
Very comfortable 30-room
hotel, 1³/4 miles out of
town on the D557. Rooms
inexpensive, and restaurant
good and well priced.

La Calèche
7 blvd Gabriel-Péri
☎ (94) 68 13 97
Good food at very
reasonable prices.

Hyères
(83400 Var)

Pins d'Argent
At Hyères Plage, 3 miles
to the south-east
☎ (94) 57 63 60
Pleasant 20-room hotel,
not expensive, no res-
taurant but breakfast served.

Le Vieux Puits
At La Bayorre, 1³/4 miles
to the east
☎ (94) 65 01 05
Good food at good prices.

Le Tison d'Or
1 rue Galliéni
☎ (94) 65 01 37
Good food and good value
fixed-price menus.

La Québécoise
At Costebelle, 1³/4 miles
south
☎ (94) 57 69 24
Very nice restaurant, well
priced, and 10 inexpensive
but comfortable rooms.

Vieille Auberge St Nicholas
At Salins d'Hyères, 3¹/2
miles east on the N90
☎ (94) 66 40 01
Very comfortable, attentive
inn. 11 good-value rooms,
fine restaurant and very
good wine list.

Le Lavandou
(83980 Var)

L'Orangeraie
plage de St-Clair
On the N559
☎ (94) 71 04 25
A modern, 18-room, not
expensive hotel; no res-
taurant, but breakfast served.

Au Vieux Port
quai Gabriel-Péri
☎ (94) 71 00 21
Owned by the above; good
fish dishes in a delightful
setting, but expensive.

La Bouée
2 ave. Charles Cazin
☎ (94) 71 11 88
Good, inexpensive fare;
eat outside if you can.

Nans-lès-Pins
(83860 Var)

Domaine de Châteauneuf
On N560 1³/4 miles out of
town
☎ (94) 78 90 06
Charming 32-room hotel
in delightful surroundings,
expensive but luxurious.
Good Provençale restaurant,
also dear.

Ramatuelle
(83350 Var)

Auberge des Vieux Moulins
route des Plages
☎ (94) 97 17 22
Good food but a little
expensive, 7 comfortable,
reasonably-priced rooms.

Hostellerie Le Baou
☎ (94) 79 20 48
Comfortable and friendly
16-room hotel, rooms
good and quite expensive;
restaurant, good and
reasonably-priced.

Salon-de-Provence
(13300 Bouches-du-
Rhône)

L'Abbaye de Ste-Croix
3 miles north-east on the
Val-de-Cuech road

☎ (90) 56 24 55
A marvellous twelfth-
century abbey with 24
expensive rooms, and a
much improved restaurant,
also expensive.

Mercuré
5¹/2 miles south-east on A7
☎ (90) 53 90 70
Modern, 100 moderately-
priced rooms, and modest
dinner-only restaurant;
good base hotel.

Francis Robin
1 blvd Georges Clémenceau
☎ (90) 56 06 53
Very good restaurant and
not over expensive.

St-Tropez
(83990 Var)

Byblos
ave. Paul Signac
☎ (94) 97 00 04
Marvellous 70-room, very
expensive hotel, and a
good restaurant with
exciting dishes at reasonable prices. Lovely to eat
by the pool.

Résidence de la Pinède
on the Bouillabaisse
beach
☎ (94) 97 04 21
Very large, ultra comfortable hotel with 40 rooms

and apartments, air-
conditioned and expen-
sive. Restaurant good but
also expensive.

La Mandarine
route de Tahiti
☎ (94) 97 21 00
Modern 40-room hotel,
very attractive and with
its own beach. Expensive,
but restaurant is good and
reasonably-priced.

Mas de Chastelas
1³/4 miles away on the
route de Gassin
☎ (94) 56 09 11
Charming 31 rooms and
apartments, all expensive,
like the restaurant, but
very friendly and attentive.

Leï Mouscardins
In the port
☎ (94) 97 01 53
Good restaurant, popular
and not too expensive.

Les Santons
At Grimaud, 6 miles away
☎ (94) 43 21 02
Very good restaurant run
by Claude Girard, always
popular, essential to book
well in advance. The cuisine
is always good and innov-
ative, and criticisms that
it is not are unjustified.

VINEYARDS OF COTES DE PROVENCE

All vineyards are open by appointment.

AREA AROUND LE THORONET

Gonfaron
(83340 Var)

Cave Coopérative   TRW
Vinicole
Open: Tuesday to Saturday.

Domaine de l'Esparron TRW
MM. Migliore
☎ (94) 78 32 23
Open: daily.

Domaine des Serres   TRW
Alain Olivier
☎ (94) 78 32 89
Open: Wednesday and
Friday afternoons only.

Domaine Le Val   TRW
d'Amrieu
Open: Monday to Saturday
in July and August;
Wednesday, Friday and
Saturday rest of the year.

Le Luc
(83340 Var)

Domaine de la
Bemarde   TRW
☎ (94) 60 71 31
Open: Monday to Friday,
weekends by appointment.

Cave Les Vignerons
du Luc   TRW
rue de l'Ormeau
☎ (94) 60 70 25
Open: Monday to Saturday.

Domaine de la CaronneTRW
Denis Baccino
☎ (94) 60 71 28
Open: daily.

Domaine de la
Grande Lauzade   TRW
Open: daily.

Domaine de la LauzadeTRW
Open: daily.

Domaine de la
Mascaronne   TRW
Leon Frizet
☎ (94) 60 71 32
Open: Monday, Thursday
and Saturday.

Domaine de Paradis   TRW
M. B. Dellasalle
☎ (94) 60 70 71
Open: Monday to Friday.

Domaine de la
Pardiguière   TRW
Jean Bianco
☎ (94) 60 72 54
Open: Monday to Saturday.

Domaine de Brigue   TRW
Roger Brun
☎ (94) 60 74 38
Open: daily.

Flassans-sur-Issole
(83340 Var)

Commanderie de
Peyrassol   TRW
Yves Rigord
☎ (94) 69 71 02
Open: Tuesday to Sunday;
Monday by appointment.

Domaine de St-BaillonTRW
Hervé Goudard
☎ (94) 69 74 60
Open: daily.

Domaine de la
Seigneurie   TRW
Open: Monday,
Wednesday and Friday.

Coopérative Vinicole TRW
Open: daily.

Domaine du Petit
Campdumy   TRW
Open: daily except Friday.

Cabasse
(83340 Var)

Coopérative Vinicole TRW
La Matavonienne
Open: daily (except
Sunday afternoon).

Domaine de la Plaine TRW
Open: daily 10am-7pm.

Domaine des Pomplés TRW
Open: Saturday; all other
times by appointment.

SCA Château de
Réquier   TRW
Open: Monday to Saturday.

Domaine du Grand
Campdumy   TRW
Open: Monday to
Saturday.

Le Thoronet
(83340 Var)

Coopérative La
Thoronéène   TRW
Open: daily except Satur-
day and Sunday afternoons.

Domaine de Ste-CroixTRW
Open: Monday to Saturday.

Domaine de la PugetteTRW
Open: daily.

Prieuré Ste-Marie
Vieille   TRW
Open: daily.

Carcès
(83570 Var)

Domaine St-Jean   TRW
Mme Maille
☎ (94) 04 50 97
Open: daily.

T=tasting   E=English spoken   G=guided tours   C=château/building to visit

Coopérative La
  Carçoise   TRW
Open: daily except Satur-
day afternoon and Sunday.

Coopérative Les
  Coteaux   TRW
Open: Monday, Tuesday,
Thursday and Friday.

Marcel Foussenq   TRW
Open: Monday to Saturday.

Jassaud   TRW
Open: daily.

SCI du Grand Cros   TRW
Open: daily.

Correns
(83570 Var)

Domaine des Aspras TRW
Lisa Latz
☎ (94) 59 59 70
Open: daily.

Coopérative La
  Corrensoise   TRW
☎ (94) 59 59 46
Open: Saturday only.

Domaine de Miraval TRW
Open: daily.

Domaine de Réal
  Martin   TRW
Open: Monday to Saturday.

Montfort
(83340 Var)

Domaine de
  Castellamare   TRW
Jean-Patrick Croisy
☎ (94) 59 51 88
Open: daily.

Coopérative Vinicole TRW
☎ (94) 59 59 02
Open: Monday and
Wednesday to Saturday.

Château Robernier   TRW
☎ (94) 59 59 11
Open: daily.

Cotignac (83570 Var)

Coopérative de
  Vignerons   TRW
☎ (94) 04 60 04
Open: Monday to Saturday.

Domaine des Muets   TRW
Open: Monday,
Wednesday and Friday.

Domaine de Nestuby TRW
Jean Roubaud
☎ (94) 04 60 02
Open: Monday to Saturday.

Entrecasteaux
(83570 Var)

Coopérative Vinicole TRW
☎ (94) 04 42 68
Open: Monday to Saturday.

St-Antonin
(83510 Var)

Coopérative La
  St-Antonaise   TRW
☎ (94) 04 42 79
Open: Monday to Saturday.

Château Mentonne   TRW
Mme Perrot de Gasquet
☎ (94) 04 42 00
Open: daily.

Lorgues
(83510 Var)

Château de Berne   TRW
Open: Monday to Saturday.

Castel Roubine   TRW
☎ (94) 73 71 55
Open: daily.

Coopérative La
  Lorguaise   TRW
☎ (94) 73 70 10
Open: Monday to Saturday.

Domaine des Aumèdes TRW
M. J. Normand
☎ (94) 73 70 32
Open: daily.

Flayosc
(83300 Var)

Coopérative La
  Flayoscaise   TRW
☎ (94) 69 74 60
Open: Monday afternoon
to Saturday morning.

AREA AROUND HYERES

Hyères (83400 Var)

Domaine de
  Mauvanne   TRW
☎ (94) 66 40 25
Open: Monday to Saturday.

Domaine des Fouques TRW
☎ (94) 57 21 84
Open: daily.

Domaine de Ste-Eulalie TRW
☎ (94) 57 21 24
Open: Monday to Saturday
morning.

Domaine de la
  Jeannette   TRW
Mouette brothers
☎ (94) 57 24 44
Open: Monday to Saturday.

Domaine de la Grand
  Bastide   TRW
Laure Hairs
☎ (94) 28 20 49
Open: Monday to Saturday.

Le Pradet
(83220 Var)

Clos Cibonne   TRW
André Roux

R=red wine   W=white wine   P=rosé wine   S=sparkling wine

384

☎ (94) 21 70 55
Open: Monday to Saturday
afternoons only.

SGIA La Navicelle   TRW
Elisabeth Saurin
☎ (94) 98 43 54
Open: Monday to Saturday.

Domaine de l'Artaude TRW
Georges Lemarchand
☎ (94) 98 43 22
Open: Monday to Saturday.

La Valette
(83000 Var)

Château Redon   TRW
Marc Tortel
☎ (94) 75 05 25
Open: Saturday only.

Hugues   TRW
Open: Monday to Saturday
afternoon.

La Farlède
(83400 Var)

Coopérative Vinicole TRW
☎ (94) 48 41 61
Open: Saturday morning
only.

La Crau
(83400 Var)

Domaine de la
Castille   TRW
☎ (94) 66 71 48
Open: Monday to Saturday
morning.

Domaine de la
Navarre   TRW
☎ (94) 66 70 01
Open: Monday to Saturday
and Sunday afternoon.

Vignoble Gaspérini   TRW
☎ (94) 66 40 25
Open: Monday to Saturday.

Domaine de la   TRW
Grassettée

Gérard Bresson
☎ (94) 66 70 03
Open: Monday to Saturday.

Coopérative Vinicole TRW
La Travailleuse
☎ (94) 66 73 03
Open: Wednesday,
Thursday and Saturday.

Solliès-Pont
(83210 Var)

Domaine de Landué TRW
Germain Arnaud
☎ (94) 28 94 87
Open: Saturday only.

Domaine de la
Tousque   TRW
Open: Monday, Friday and
Saturday morning.

Pierrefeu
(83390 Var)

Domaine de
l'Aumerade   TRW
☎ (94) 28 20 32
or (94) 28 20 37
Open: Monday to Saturday.

Domaine des Baux   TRW
Open: daily.

Coopérative Les Vig-
nerons de Pierrefeu TRW
☎ (94) 28 20 09
Open: Tuesday to Saturday.

Caves Rochebois   TRW
Open: daily.

Château La Gordonne TRW
☎ (94) 66 81 46
Open: Monday to Saturday.

Château Montaud   TRW
☎ (94) 28 20 30
Open: Monday to Saturday
morning.

Domaine Les
Marroniers   TRW
☎ (94) 28 21 15
Open: Monday to Saturday.

Collobrières
(83400 Var)

Coopérative des
Vignerons   TRW
☎ (94) 04 50 97
Open: Tuesday to Saturday.

Cuers (83400 Var)

Cave Coopérative
l'Amicale   TRW
☎ (94) 28 60 72
Open: Monday to Saturday
morning.

Cave de Vinification
St-Roch-lès-Vignes   TRW
☎ (94) 28 60 60
Open: Monday to Saturday
morning.

Bagnis   TRW
Open: Monday to Friday.

Château de Gairoird   TRW
Deydier de Pierrefeu
☎ (94) 48 50 60
Open: daily.

Puget-Ville
(06260 Alpes-Maritime)

Coopérative La
Pugetoise   TRW
☎ (94) 48 31 05
Open: Monday to Saturday.

Mme Hermitte   TRW
Open: Monday to Saturday
morning.

GAEC Château du
Puget   TRW
☎ (94) 48 31 07
Open: daily.

Mas du Haut Rayol   TRW
☎ (94) 48 34 09
Open: daily.

Domaine de Grand-Pré TRW
Emmanuel Plauchut
☎ (94) 48 32 16
Open: daily.

T=tasting   E=English spoken   G=guided tours   C=château/building to visit

Carnoules
(06260 Alpes-Maritime)

Coopérative La
  Laborieuse   TRW
Open: Tuesday to
Saturday.

Domaine du Deffends TRW
Mme Michel Donon
☎ (94) 28 33 12
Open: daily.

Pignans
(06260 Alpes-Maritime)

Domaine de RimauresqTRW
☎ (94) 48 80 45
Open: Monday to Saturday.

Domaine de Valcros   TRW
Open: daily.

La Garde
(04120 Alpes-de-Haute-
Provence)

Coopérative Vinicole TRW
Chai de l'Union des Caves
  des Maures et de l'Estérel
Open: daily.

La Londe
(83250 Var)

Domaine du Bastidon TRW
☎ (94) 66 80 15
Open: Monday to Saturday.

Domaine des
  Bormettes   TRW
☎ (94) 66 81 35
Open: Wednesday morning
and Saturday morning.

Domaine du CarrubierTRW
☎ (94) 66 82 82
Open: Monday to Saturday.

Cave Coopérative   TRW
☎ (94) 66 80 26
Open: Monday to Saturday
8am-noon.

Clos Mireille   TRW
Domaine Ott
☎ (94) 66 40 25
Open: Monday, Tuesday,
Thursday and Friday.

Domaine du Galoupet TRW
☎ (94) 66 40 07
Open: Monday to Saturday.

Domaine du Gros Pin TRW
Open: Monday to Saturday
morning.

Domaine de la
  Cheylanne   TRW
Open: Saturday morning.

Domaine de la Vieille
  Londe   TRW
Open: Tuesday to Saturday.

Domaine de la Source
  Ste-Marguérite   TRW
J.R. Fayard
☎ (94) 66 81 46
Open: Monday to Saturday.

Domaine St-André-de-
  Figuière   TRW
André Connesson
☎ (94) 66 92 10
Open: Tuesday to Saturday.

Domaine des Myrtes TRW
☎ (94) 66 83 00
Open: Monday to Saturday.

Mas des Borrels   TRW
Charles-André
☎ (94) 57 32 45
Open: Monday to Saturday.

Domaine du Jasson   TRW
Open: Monday to Saturday.

Domaine de
  Maravenne   TRW
Open: daily.

AREA AROUND DRAGUIGNAN

Draguignan
(83300 Var)

Coopérative la
  Dracénoise   TRW
☎ (94) 68 04 60
Open: Tuesday to Saturday.

Domaine Christiane
  Rabiega   TRW
M. & Mme Lengagne-
  Rabiega
☎ (94) 68 44 22
Open: daily.

Domaine du Dragon TRW
Paul Garro
☎ (94) 68 00 34
Open: daily.

Figanières
(83300 Var)

Coopérative La
  Figaniéroise   TRW
☎ (94) 67 94 65
Open: Tuesday to Friday.

GIE Hermitage
  St-Pons   TRW
☎ (94) 67 90 28
Open: Monday to Saturday.

Trans
(83720 Var)

Coopérative La
  Transiane   TRW
☎ (94) 70 80 18
Open: Monday to Saturday.

Clos Cassivet   TRW
Open: daily.

La Motte
(83920 Var)

Coopérative La
  Mottoise   TRW
☎ (94) 70 25 68
Open: Monday to Saturday.

R=red wine   W=white wine   P=rosé wine   S=sparkling wine

Domaine de Clastron TRW
☎ (94) 70 24 57
Open: Monday to Saturday.

Domaine Les
Demoiselles TRW
☎ (94) 70 24 60
Open: daily.

Château d'Esclans TRW
☎ (94) 70 24 04
Open: Monday to Saturday.

Domaine des Grands
Esclans TRW
☎ (94) 70 26 08
Open: Monday to Saturday.

Domaine Jas
d'Esclans TRW
M. and Mme Lorgues-
Lapouge
☎ (91) 70 27 86
Open: Monday to Saturday.

Domaine de St-Romain
d'Esclans TRW
☎ (94) 70 24 92
Open: daily.

Domaine de
Valbourgès TRW
☎ (94) 70 24 69
Open: Monday to Saturday.

Bagnols-en-Forêt
(83440 Var)

Coopérative Vinicole TRW
☎ (94) 40 60 13
Open: Tuesday to Saturday.

Le Muy
(83490 Var)

Coopérative
l'Ancienne TRW
☎ (94) 45 10 42
Open: Monday to Saturday.

Domaine de la
Péguière TRW
Open: Monday to Saturday
and Sunday afternoon.

Château du Rouët TRW
Bernard Savatier
☎ (94) 45 16 00
Open: Monday to Saturday
and Sunday afternoon.

Fréjus
(83600 Var)

Coopérative La
Fréjusienne TRW
☎ (94) 51 01 81
Open: Monday to Saturday.

Domaine de
Curebéasse TRW
Jean Paquette
☎ (94) 52 10 17
Open: Monday to Saturday.

Puget-sur-Argens
(83600 Var)

Coopérative La
Pugétoise TRW
☎ (94) 45 50 33
Open: Tuesday, Thursday
and Saturday morning.

Château de
Vaucouleurs TRW
☎ (94) 45 20 27
Open: Wednesday and
Saturday mornings.

Cave Audéemar TRW
☎ (94) 45 51 70
Open: Saturday.

**Roquebrune-sur-
Argens** (83600 Var)

Domaine de
Marchandise TRW
Open: daily.

Domaine de la
Garonne TRW
Open: Monday to Saturday.

Domaine des Planes TRW
C. and I. Rieder
☎ (94) 45 70 49
Open: Monday to Saturday.

Les Arcs
(83460 Var)

Château Ste-Roseline TRW
Baron Louis de Rasque de
Laval
☎ (94) 73 32 57
Open: Monday to Saturday
in summer, Monday to
Friday rest of year.

Coopérative l'Arçoise TRW
☎ (94) 73 30 29
Open: Monday to Saturday
11.45am-5.45pm.

Domaine des Hauts
de St-Jean TRW
☎ (94) 73 31 09
Open: Tuesday to Saturday
9am-noon and 4-7pm,
Sunday 9am-noon.

Domaine des Clarettes TRW
☎ (94) 73 31 51
Open: Monday, Thursday
and Saturday.

Taradeau
(83460 Var)

Coopérative La
Taradoise TRW
☎ (94) 73 02 03
Open: Monday to Saturday.

Château St-Martin TRW
☎ (94) 73 02 01
Open: Monday to Friday.

Château de Selle TRW
Domaine Ott
☎ (94) 68 86 86
Open: daily.

Vidauban
(83550 Var)

Coopérative La
Vidaubanaise TRW
☎ (94) 73 00 12
Open: Monday to Saturday.

T=tasting E=English spoken G=guided tours C=château/building to visit

Vieux Château
d'Astros   TRW
☎ (94) 73 02 56
Open: daily.

Château d'Astros   TRW
☎ (94) 73 00 25
Open: Monday to Saturday.

Domaine des Blais   TRW
☎ (94) 73 06 53
Open: Monday to Saturday.

Domaine des
Espérifets   TRW
Open: Monday to Saturday.

Domaine des Féraud TRW
☎ (94) 73 03 12
Open: Monday to Saturday
morning.

Domaine de Peisonnel TRW
Pierre Lemaître
☎ (94) 73 02 96
Open: daily.

GAEC Clos St-Luc   TRW
☎ (94) 73 03 04
Open: Monday to Saturday.

Camp Romain   TRW
Open: Monday to Friday.

Château de St-Julien
d'Aille   TRW
☎ (94) 73 02 89
Open: Monday to Saturday.

AREA AROUND ST-TROPEZ

Le Cannet-des-Maures
(83340 Var)

Domaine de la
Bastide Neuve   TRW
☎ (94) 60 73 30
Open: daily.

Domaine des Bertrands TRW
☎ (94) 73 02 94
Open: Monday to Saturday
morning.

Coopérative La
Cannetoise   TRW
Open: Monday to Saturday.

Domaine de Colbert TRW
☎ (94) 60 77 66
Open: Monday to Saturday
morning.

Domaine de la Faïsse
Noire   TRW
☎ (94) 60 73 82
Open: Monday to Sunday
morning.

Domaine de l'Hoste TRW
☎ (94) 60 73 37
Open: Monday to Friday.

Domaine de Reillanne TRW
☎ (94) 60 73 31
Open: Monday to Saturday;
Sunday by appointment.

Domaine de Roux   TRW
Elisabeth Giraud

☎ (94) 60 73 10
Open: Monday to Saturday.

Domaine de la Grand
Pièce   TRW
☎ (94) 73 02 87
Open: daily.

La Garde-Freinet
(83310 Var)

Coopérative Les Fouleurs
de St-Pons   TRW
Open: Friday and Saturday.

Grimaud
(83360 Var)

Coopérative Vinicole TRW
☎ (94) 43 20 14
Open: Monday to Saturday.

Domaine de la Tourre TRW
☎ (94) 43 27 78
Open: Tuesday and Thursday.

Gassin
(83990 Var)

Domaine de Bertaud TRW
Yves Lemaître
☎ (94) 50 16 13
Open: Monday to Saturday.

Château Minuty   TRW
Jean Farnet
☎ (94) 56 12 09
Open: Monday to Saturday.

Les Maîtres Vignerons de
la Presqu'ile St-Tropez TRW
☎ (94) 56 32 04
Open: Monday to Saturday
in summer, Monday to
Friday rest of year.

Domaine de la
Rouillère   TRW
☎ (94) 79 20 26
Open: daily.

St-Tropez
(83990 Var)

Coopérative du Golfe de
St-Tropez   TRW
☎ (94) 97 01 60
Open: Tuesday to Saturday.

Domaine de
St-Antoine   TRW
☎ (94) 97 05 61
Open: by appointment.

Ramatuelle
(83350 Var)

Coopérative Vinicole TRW
☎ (94) 79 23 60
Open: Tuesday to Saturday.

Domaine de la Bastide
Blanche   TRW
Open: Monday to Friday 9-
11.30am and 3-6pm,
Saturday 9-11.30am.

R=red wine   W=white wine   P=rosé wine   S=sparkling wine

Domaine de ValdérianTRW
Open: daily.

La Croix-Valmer
(83420 Var)

Domaine de la Croix TRW
☎ (94) 79 60 02
Open: Monday to Saturday
morning.

Domaine des
  Palmeraies   TRW
Open: daily.

Cogolin
(83310 Var)

Cave Coopérative   TRW
☎ (94) 54 40 54
Open: Monday to Saturday
morning.

Domaine des
  Garcinières   TRW

☎ (94) 56 02 85
Open: Monday to Saturday.

Domaine de St-Maur TRW
☎ (94) 56 09 25
Open: Monday to Saturday.

Bormes
(83230 Var)

Domaine de
  l'Angueiroun   TRW
☎ (94) 71 11 39
Open: Monday to Saturday,
except public holidays.

Domaine des CampauxTRW
☎ (94) 49 57 09
Open: Monday to Saturday.

Cave Coopérative   TRW
☎ (94) 71 27 36

Open: Monday to Saturday
morning.

Domaine de Léoubes
☎ (94) 64 80 03
Open: Monday to Saturday
morning.

Domaine de la
  Malherbe   TRW
S. Ferrari
☎ (94) 64 80 40
Open: Monday to Saturday
morning.

Domaine de Ste-MarieTRW
☎ (94) 49 57 15
Open: daily.

Domaine du Grand
  Noyer   TRW
Daniel Guerin
☎ (94) 71 18 52
Open: Monday to Saturday.

COTEAUX D'AIX-EN-PROVENCE

Les Milles (13290)

Château La SemencièreTRW
Mme Rodrigues-Ely
quartier Mont-Robert
☎ (42) 24 20 05
Open: Saturdays.

Puyricard (13540)

Château du Seuil   TRW
Mme Carreau-Gaschereau
☎ (42) 24 45 99
Open: daily for visits and
tastings.

Aurons (13121)

Domaine Le Petit
  Sonnaillet   TRW
☎ (90) 57 36 05
Open: Saturday for tastings.

Les-Baux-de-Provence
(13520)

M. David   TRW
Mas Ste-Berthe
☎ (90) 97 34 01
Open: daily for tastings.

SF du Mas de la Dame TRW
☎ (90) 97 32 24
Open: daily for tastings.

Coopérative Vinicole
  du Val-d'Enfer   TRW
Cave de Sarragan
☎ (90) 97 33 58
Open: daily for tastings.

Berre (13130)

Vins Sardou   TRW
Domaine de Castillon
ave. de Sylvanes
☎ (42) 85 40 02
Open: Monday to Friday 2-
7pm; Saturday 8-12noon
and 2-7pm.

Coudoux (13111)

Cave du Domaine de St-
  Hilaire   TRW
Max Lapierre
chemin de la Croix
☎ (42) 28 84 03
Open: Thursday, Friday
and Saturday.

Eguilles (13510)

Coopérative Vinicole TRW
1 place Lucien-Fauchier
☎ (42) 24 61 12
Open: daily except Sun-
days and public holidays.

La Fare-lès-Oliviers
(13580)

Coopérative Vinicole TRW
route de Roquefavour
☎ (90) 57 61 47
Open: daily except Sun-
days and public holidays.

T=tasting   E=English spoken   G=guided tours   C=château/building to visit

Fontvieille (13990)

MM. Lombrage   TRW
Château d'Estoublon
☎ (90) 97 70 23
Open: daily for tasting.

Gignac-la-Nerthe
(13700 Marignane)

Vins Sardou   TRW
Château Vignerolles
☎ (42) 88 55 15
Open: daily except Sunday
and Monday 2-7pm. Satur-
day 8am-noon and 2-7pm.

Istrés (13140 Miramas)

SCA du Domaine de   TRW
   Sulauze
☎ (90) 58 02 02
Open: daily except Sunday.

Jouques (13490)

SICA Bordonado   TRW
Domaine de la Grande
   Séouve
☎ (42) 57 82 44
Open: daily.

Gabriel Adaoust   TRW
Notre-Dame des Bèdes
☎ (42) 57 82 93
Open: daily 8am-8pm,
except Saturday 8am-2pm.

Château Revelette   TRW
Domaine de Revelette
☎ (42) 57 82 82
Visiting by appointment.

Lambesc (13410)

Audibert brothers
   and sister   TRW
Cave du Lion-d'Or
12 ave. de Badonviller
☎ (42) 28 05 40
Open: Monday to Friday
mornings; all day Saturday.

GAEC de Bonrecueil TRW
Domaine de Bonrecueil
route de Salon
☎ (90) 55 05 65
Open: Monday to Saturday.

Cave Coopérative
   Vinicole   TRW
Boulevard des Coopératives
☎ (42) 28 00 20
Open: daily except Sun-
days and public holidays.

Lançon-de-Provence
(13680)

Domaine de Gigery   TRW
Mme Yvonne Chaleyer
route de Lançon à
   Pélissanne
☎ (90) 57 70 04
Open: Monday and Satur-
day and Wednesday after-
noons.

SCA La Durancole   TRW
Domaine de Calissanne
on D10 between St-
   Chamas and La Fare-lès-
   Oliviers
☎ (90) 57 63 03
Open: daily except Sunday.

Coopérative Vinicole TRW
place du Champs de Mars
☎ (90) 57 71 09
Open: Tuesday to Saturday.

Martigues (13500)

Coopérative Vinicole de St-
   Julien-lès Martigues   TRW
between Martigues and
   Sausset-lès-Pins
☎ (42) 80 33 93
Open: Tuesday to Saturday.

Mouriès 13890

Domaine de Lauzières TRW
Joseph Boyer daughters
☎ (42) 04 70 39
Open: daily except Sunday.

Mas de Gourgonnier   TRW
Le Destet
route de Maussane D78
☎ (90) 97 50 45
Open: daily.

Pélissanne (13330)

Domaine des Crottes et de
   la Bidoussanne   TRW
Magnan
route d'Eguilles
☎ (90) 55 05 62
Open: Wednesday after-
noons, and all day Satur-
day and Monday.

Cave Coopérative
   Vinicole   TRW
13 ave. Fréderic-Mistral
☎ (90) 55 04 66
Open: daily except Sunday
and public holidays.

Port-de-Bouc (13110)

Mas de Roseron   TRW
Christian Martini
route de Port-de-Bouc at St-
   Mître-lès-Remparts
quartier Plan Fossan
☎ (42) 80 98 64
Open: Monday to Saturday
8am-12noon and 2-7pm,
Sunday mornings.

Vins Sardou   TRW
Mas de l'Hôpital
☎ (42) 06 20 99
Open: Monday to Friday
2-7pm, Saturdays 8am-
noon and 2-7pm.

Le Puy-Ste-Reparade
(13610)

SICA Bordonado   TRW
Château La Coste
☎ (42) 28 60 28
Open: daily.

R=red wine   W=white wine   P=rosé wine   S=sparkling wine

SCA Fonscolombe   TRW
Château de Fonscolombe
☎ (42) 28 60 05
Open: Monday to Friday
8am-noon and 2-6pm,
Saturday 8am-noon.

Domaine Les Bastides TRW
Salen
St-Cannadet
☎ (42) 28 62 66
Open: daily.

Rians 83560

Château Vignelaure   TRW
M. Georges Brunet
☎ (42) 57 83 15
or (42) 57 85 27

Château Pigoudet   TRW
route de Jouques
☎ (94) 80 31 78
Open: Monday to Saturday.

Coopérative Vinicole TRW
quartier St-Esprit
☎ (94) 80 33 78
Open: Saturday morning.

Rognes 13840

Château Barbebelle   TRW
M. Brise Herbeau
☎ (42) 50 22 12
Open: daily.

Château de Beaulieu TRW
D14C, 5km before Rognes
☎ (42) 28 23 22
Open: Monday to Saturday.

Coopérative Vinicole TRW
place de la Coopérative
(42) 28 23 05
Open: Monday,
Wednesday and Saturday,
8am-noon and 2-6pm.

St-Cannat (13760)

SCMM Commanderie
de la Bargemone   TRW
route Nationale 7
☎ (42) 28 22 44
Open: Monday to Saturday
8am-noon and 2-6pm. Sun-
day 10am-noon and 2-6pm.

Château de Beaupré TRW
route Nationale 7
☎ (42) 28 23 83
or (42) 28 20 03
Open: daily.

Coopérative Agricole
et Vinicole   TRW
☎ (42) 28 20 17
Open: daily except Sun-
days and public holidays.

St-Chamas (13250)

Joseph Merlin   TRW
Domaine de Suriane
☎ (91) 93 91 91
Open: daily.

St-Etienne-du-Grès
(13150)

GAEC Trevallon   TRW
vieux chemin d'Arles
☎ (90) 91 26 00
Open: daily.

St-Rémy-de-Provence
(13210)

Terres Blanches   TRW
Noël Michelin
on D99 between St-Rémy
and Plan-d'Orgon
Open: Monday to Friday
2-6pm, Saturday 8am-
noon and 2-6pm.

Domaine de la
Vallongue   TRW
Ph. Paul-Cavalier
13810 Eygalières
on D24 between the D99
and Mouriès
☎ (90) 95 91 70
Open: daily except Sun-
days and public holidays.

Sénas 13560

Société Coopérative
Vinicole   TRW
quartier de la Gare
☎ (90) 57 20 25
Open: daily except Sun-
days and public holidays.

Velaux (13880)

Coopérative Vinicole TRW
☎ (42) 87 92 09
Open: daily except Sun-
days and public holidays.

Vernegues (13116)

Domaine de
Château-Bas   TRW
Cazan
☎ (90) 57 43 16
Open: daily.

T=tasting   E=English spoken   G=guided tours   C=château/building to visit

Chapter 14

THE SOUTH-WEST

Cahors
South-West

IF WE EXCLUDE the Bordelais, Cognac and Armagnac, there is still a massive area of south-west France producing wine, stretching from Bergerac and Cahors to the Spanish border and the Jurançon. There is the famous 'black' wine of Cahors, the soft wines of Frontonnais, and the refreshing, slightly sparkling white of Gaillac.

The Vineyards of the South-West

CAHORS

Cahors has been made for almost 2,000 years, and has been exported to Britain for the last 800 years. There are records of it being produced during the reign of Emperor Domitian in AD96, and the local poet Clément Marot praised its qualities. François I preferred it above all other wines and is reputed to have planted a Cahors vine in the grounds of Fontainebleau. The Russian Orthodox Church also chose Cahors as its communion wine, and Tsar Peter the Great swore that Cahors wine cured his stomach ulcers.

The red wine vines of Cahors grow either along the valley of the river Lot, or on the slopes rising from it. The valley is mostly chalk, and fertile from alluvial deposits, while the hill slopes are limestone, and each area yields totally different wines. The main grape variety is the Malbec or Cot Noir, known locally as Auxerrois. It must account for at least 70 per cent of the total stock of vines, and gives the wine its tannin, deep colour and ability to age. Other varieties include Merlot, for roundness, mellowness and bouquet, and the Tannat, for backbone. A little Jurançon Noir is also grown to go into the blend, but it is gradually being replaced by the other two varieties. Auxerrois must also comprise at least 70 per cent of the wine, and the other varieties can be added to it as the individual grower directs. A tiny quantity of white is made for local use.

The best wines are said to come from the slopes, although most are now blends of the two. The wines are dark red, very tannic, and full. They improve with age, and some Cahors wines have still been drinking well after many decades. The wines produced on the slopes are usually more tannic and longer-lasting than those from the valley, but the style today is to produce lighter, earlier-to-drink wines which accounts for the blending.

The Cahors wines gained *appellation* status in 1971 and constant efforts are being made by the growers to improve overall standards. Young Cahors wines, fairly tannic, are excellent with *foie gras*, meat dishes in sauces and delicatessen meat while an old Cahors, fully matured with a marvellous bouquet, goes well with red meat, game and cheeses. They should be drunk slightly below room temperature.

BERGERAC

This area lies on the Dordogne, just fifty miles to the east of Bordeaux, and the river has been the key to its fortunes over the years. Grapes were being gathered here in Roman times. Bergerac has almost all the qualities of Bordcaux; the same soils, the same climate and the same vines, but the wines have always been overshadowed by their more prestigious neighbour, and often penalised financially. The exception is Monbazillac, just to the south of the town of Bergerac, which produces fine, although rarely great, sweet white wines.

The vines spread out on either side of the Dordogne although the soils vary considerably, from alluvial silt to chalk, and clay with chalk. There are 27,500 acres of vineyards which have traditionally produced mainly whites, both dry and sweet, and some red and rosé. In the last twenty years, red wines have become more popular and now account for about half of production. The AC titles are Bergerac, Côtes de Bergerac, and Côtes de Saussignac.

For Bergerac and Côtes de Bergerac reds, the Cabernet Sauvignon, Cabernet Franc, Merlot and Malbec are preferred. The Côtes de Bergerac and Côtes de Saussignac sweet whites are made from Sémillon, Sauvignon and Muscadelle, while the dry white uses a blend of the three above as well as up to 25 per cent of Ugni Blanc as long as there is an equal quantity of Sauvignon.

The red wines of Bergerac are very similar to claret and cost less. Some areas, however, such as Pécharmant, produce much stronger, deeper-coloured wines. The Côtes de Bergerac reds have more body and the rosés are noted for their delicate bouquet and fruit. The dry whites of Bergerac are light and fruity with a lot of fragrance because of the Sauvignon grape. The sweet whites are rich, sweet and elegant; and, while not a match for Sauternes, compare favourably with many of the more expensive sweet wines of Bordeaux.

Red Bergerac should be drunk young, while the Côtes de Bergerac, with more body, are best after three or four years. The dry whites and rosés are also made for quick drinking while the sweet whites are stayers and improve with bottle ageing.

Monbazillac

The vineyards of Monbazillac have been exporting their sweet wines for 500 years, and the Dutch were particularly fond of them, even though the Bordelais tried to ruin the trade by imposing taxes on their export. The vineyards cover about 6,250 acres around Monbazillac, which lies between the river Dordogne and a small stream called La Gardonette. The wine is special because it comes from a small valley enjoying its own microclimate, similar to that in Sauternes, as it encourages the growth of 'Noble Rot'. This rot attacks the juice and converts it to sugar, and the grapes are picked in stages only when they are fully ripe.

Only Sémillon, Sauvignon and Muscadelle are allowed for the wine, which must have an alcoholic strength of at least 12°. It has a perfume of wild flowers and honey and needs many years to mature. It should not be drunk before it is five years old, when it should have reached an amber colour, although great vintages need fifteen years of ageing and more.

Montravel

This is a small vineyard area lying near Castillon-la-Bataille, producing mostly dry white wines which carry their own ACs. The wines can be found with labels bearing the words, Montravel, Côtes de Montravel, and Haut-Montravel. For the sweet whites of Haut-Montravel and Côtes de Montravel, only Sémillon, Sauvignon and Muscadelle can be used. For the dry whites, up to 25 per cent of Ugni Blanc can be added, provided that a similar quantity of Sauvignon is used.

Montravel is a dry wine with a lot of fruit and a certain acidity because of the Ugni Blanc grapes, which compliments the Sauvignon-produced bouquet. The sweet wines have fruit and pronounced bouquet. The dry whites must be drunk young, to appreciate their freshness, while the sweet wines need at least five years ageing in the bottle.

Pécharmant

This is a red wine named after the area of gravelly slopes on the right bank of the Dordogne. The vines are south-facing, and cover about 425 acres. This is the region which used to produce Rosette, although now only a small quantity is made. Cabernet Franc, Cabernet Sauvignon, Merlot and Malbec are used to produce a full-bodied red wine, well rounded with a ruby colour. It ages well, and should be kept for at least five years.

COTES DE BUZET

Côtes de Buzet is a new *appellation*, about sixty miles south of Bergerac. It gained its title in 1973, having been excluded by the strict designation of the Bordeaux region, which restricted grapes for production to the *département* of Gironde only. For many years, grapes from the Côtes de Buzet had travelled north to be added to claret. Good red wine is produced on the chalky, gravelly soils and the *coopérative* at Damazan is the leading producer. The wines are as good as lower growth clarets, and have a certain novelty in Britain at the moment, possibly because of their names.

COTES DE DURAS

This region was hit in the same way as the Côtes de Buzet when the Gironde-only ruling was drawn up for Bordeaux. There are about 1,000 acres of vines around the town of Duras, which lies about twenty-eight miles south of Bergerac. About a third of the production is red wine, mostly made from Cabernet Sauvignon, while the rest is white wine made from a number of varieties including Sauvignon, Sémillon, Ugni Blanc, Colombard and Mauzac. The wines are overshadowed by those from both Bordeaux and the Côtes de Buzet.

GAILLAC

Gaillac is a large producing area spread around the town which bears its name, and to the east of Albi, the *département* capital for Tarn. The region lies about fifty miles south of Cahors. There are more than 12,000 acres of vines planted on the hillsides overlooking the river Tarn. Red grape varieties include Gamay, Syrah, Duras and Négrette, and the wines are noted for their long life and ability to travel. The same grapes are used for rosé. The region has many grape varieties very rarely found elsewhere, and records show they have been planted for centuries so this little enclave could well have been one of the first in this part of France to be planted with vines. White wines are made chiefly from Mauzac, Muscadelle, Sémillon and Len de l'El, another of the unusual local varieties. Both still and sparkling whites are made and they tend to be sweetish.

Mauzac wines are slightly sparkling, low in acidity, but this is balanced by fruit. They should be drunk young. Sparkling wines are made by a sort of *méthode Champenoise*, but instead of disgorging all the sediment, as in Champagne, some sugar is left in the bottle to go on fermenting. The finished wine can still be bone dry, and crisp, but it has a sediment. This variation is known as *méthode rurale*. The style of the sparkling wine has been improved enormously in recent years and newly-introduced varieties are now being used to add elegance, especially Sauvignon.

MADIRAN

To the south of Armagnac country, Madiran is in the foothills of the Pyrénées and produces powerful, long-living reds. A few years ago there were only a handful of vineyards left, but now there are about 2,000 acres and the wines are certainly the best in the south-west and a match for many a good claret. It can be a wonderfully soft wine, well-balanced, fruity and lingering. It is produced from traditional, local grapes such as Tannat, Courbu, Bouchy and Pinenc, but classic varieties such as Cabernet Sauvignon are now being used to add distinction. The vineyards in the Vic-Bilh hills are also the home of Pacherenc, the white wine of the region. It is a blend of a number of grapes and is made both sweet and dry.

JURANÇON

This is another area where traditional local grapes are grown to produce strong white wines. The wine is made from a blend of Courbu and Manseng. The dry whites are strong in alcohol, firm, and full of aromas, while the sweet is spicy and aromatic, with a remarkable golden colour. The growers do try to pick the grapes for the sweet wines after they have attracted Noble Rot and after fermentation they are kept in barrels usually for two years.

IROULEGUY

The Irouléguy wine region is to the east of Jurançon, and just to the south in the slightly steeper Pyrénées foothills, very close to the Spanish border. It produces red, white and rosé wines and the red, similar in style to the Madiran, is the best of the three.

BEARN

Béarn lies to the north of Basque country, and the wines have their own *appellation*, AC Béarn. Most of the production is red and rosé, and almost all is produced by *coopératives*.

COTES DU FRONTONNAIS

The small Côtes du Frontonnais vineyard region is about fifteen miles north of Toulouse, and is centred on the town of Fronton. It produces mainly red and rosé wine from the local grape, the Négrette, related to the Auxerrois of Cahors. The wines are light and fruity.

A Tour of the South-West

The Dordogne is another region of France beloved of the English because of its history, scenery, culture, wines, and its food. Other regions are famous for their cuisine, but the Dordogne outshines them all. It is the land of Cyrano de Bergerac, truffles and *foie gras*. It is the area where you can spend a week walking through vineyards producing some of France's lesser-known wines, and return home weighing pounds more than when you left.

The Dordogne river runs through the south of the region, but there are many other beautiful rivers to be explored. A lunch on the terrace of a little inn overlooking the Dordogne or Lot can be an unforgettable experience.

It is about 500 miles from the French channel coast to the Dordogne, and while the journey can be done within a day using the excellent autoroutes, it is very tiring to do so; it is much better to drive down in a leisurely way and enjoy the scenery on the way, unless you put the car on the train and travel overnight to Bordeaux or Toulouse. There is also a reasonable train service between the major towns of the Dordogne, although travel from the stations into the countryside is more difficult without your own transport. It is possible to get cheap rail passes which give unlimited travel over a certain number of days, and there are also rail and drive facilities, which allow hire of a vehicle at a number of given destinations. Equally, if you want to work off all the rich meals, hire a bicycle — but there are some fairly steep hills.

There are flights into Bordeaux, Clermont-Ferrand or Toulouse, but from there hired cars are virtually essential.

The Dordogne also makes an ideal stop-over as part of a much longer holiday. It is midway between Bordeaux and Toulouse, so ideally placed for trips to the other wine regions, or to the south and the Mediterranean.

The *département* of Dordogne includes most of Périgord and Quercy, the two gastronomic hearts of France. Périgueux, the capital lies in the heart of the *département*, and both it and the many other towns in the area are worth visiting, not only for their food but also for the richness of their past.

Early man is known to have populated this region because the flat-topped hills afforded good defensive positions, and the rivers provided water and transport. There are traces of their occupation here dating back at least 30,000 years. Most notable are the famous cave paintings at Lascaux, now closed, unfortunately, to protect them, although there is a very good replica to be seen.

The area was governed by the Romans for 300 years; on their withdrawal to Italy, the Visigoths moved in. Then the Saracens swept in from the south, uniting the disparate Christian kingdoms. Charlemagne founded the Holy Roman Empire and the region enjoyed an all-too-brief period of peace.

For almost three hundred years, the region was a battlefield between the English and the French. It changed hands constantly, especially during the Hundred Years' War. At Castillon in the Dordogne in 1453 the fate of the English armies was sealed when they were roundly beaten by the French army. The Dordogne was then caught up in the religious wars which tore France apart for another hundred years, and as one of the main centres for the Huguenots it was the scene of much bloody fighting.

As with other parts of France, the region was in the hands of powerful dukes and lords, and they exerted a formidable power, which is still reflected in the castles and châteaux that pepper the countryside. Today, these castles are the only reminder of a troubled past. As the tourists drive through the countryside now, all they see is a fertile region with a rich agriculture. The sheep are grazed on the hills to provide marvellous lamb and mutton, and the areas of vineyards produce marvellous wines from big, powerful reds, to delicious sweet whites.

Bergerac wines are now gaining a deserved reputation abroad, mostly because of the increasing prices of Bordeaux, while the wines of Cahors have been known outside France for a long time.

Apart from grapes, the region is also noted for its fruit trees, chestnuts, walnuts, tobacco, and above all, its truffles. These delicacies are now so valuable that spores are being planted commercially among the roots of young oaks and apples. The truffle commands more per pound than any other agricultural product harvested, and huge areas are being planted both in the Dordogne and in the south of France to exploit this marvellous crop.

The thousands of small farms also have their geese, and the *pâté de foie gras* is the best in France, especially the most expensive which has a truffle in its heart.

There are inns, hotels and campsites throughout the region, but in the summer months it is very popular, so it is advisable to book accommodation well in advance.

Tour of Limoges and the Surrounding Area

The tour of the Dordogne starts in Limoges, just outside the Dordogne, which has a vast array of hotels, restaurants and inns. Of special note is the excellent La Chapelle-St-Martin, 7 miles out of town on the N147 and D35.

Limoges is the capital of the former province of Limousin, a city full of history and well worth a visit. It stands on the river Vienne, has a fine Gothic cathedral, and many other old buildings and churches. It was sacked by the Black Prince; even then it was famous for its enamels. Today, it is noted for its porcelain, and there is a huge collection in the Musée Adrien Dubouché. You should also visit the local museum of folklore, and the church of St Michel-des-Lions.

It is possible to make many detours from Limoges to see places of interest and these include Oradour, about 10 miles north-west of Limoges.

There are the ruined remains of a village destroyed by the SS in 1944, still today as it was when the Germans left after killing 642 men, women and children. At Châlus there is a castle on the hilltop where Richard Lionheart was fatally wounded in 1199. Parts of the wall and a tower still remain. Near Châlus is the twelfth-century moated Château de Montbrun, and the thirteenth-century castle at Jumilhac-le-Grand.

About twenty miles north and east of Limoges is Bourganeuf with its Tour de la Zimzim, and town hall containing many fine tapestries. A Turkish prince was kept captive in the town at a castle owned by the Knights Templar.

South of Limoges, which is by far the largest city in the region, is Uzerche, with its church to Ste Eulalie. Next is Brive-la-Gaillarde, scene of many sieges in the past. One can take the train from Uzerche to Brive-la-Gaillarde, first along the river Vézère and then past the Saillant Gorges.

In Brive you can walk along the boulevard Lachaud, which encircles the old town. This marks the line of the original fortifications, which have long since disappeared. In the centre of the old town is the church of St Martin and all the town's roads radiate from it. There are also many old buildings to be explored around the church.

There is Arnac-Pompadour nearby with its castle, and very loose ties with Madame de Pompadour, and Ségur-le-Château, home of one of the oldest military families in France. The village has many old houses and the ruined castle dates from the twelfth century. To the north is St-Yrieix-la-Perche with many medieval buildings, and to the south-west is the seventeenth-century Château Hautefort, a fortified château built on the site of a medieval castle. It was burnt down in 1968 but has now been well restored. The magnificent castle is set in gardens, and there is a drawbridge and dry moat.

South to Cahors

After an overnight stay in Brive the route goes to Souillac and Cahors, home of the 'black' wine, as it was known in Britain for centuries because of its dark colour. Although it is not a long drive, there are again plenty of detours to be made to see some of the more interesting sites.

A little way to the west of the route is 'castle country'. This area, around Domme, has some beautiful castles, all commanding picturesque views over the meandering river. At Trémolat there is a fortified church, while nearby at St-Cyprien there is the sixteenth-century Château de Fages on the hill, overlooking the castle at Berbiguières on the opposite bank of the Dordogne.

Near Beynac is the fifteenth-century château at Les Milandes, where the exotic dancer Miss Josephine Baker retired, with the children she adopted; and the fortified Château de Fayrac, home of one of Henry of Navarre's captains. Beynac is a medieval town, and once a Huguenot stronghold. It is defended by the castle of Castelnaud built in the twelfth century (1,000ft above the valley floor), and its own spectacular castle with incredible views, on top of the hill dominating the town.

Nearby is La Roque-Gageac, another medieval fortress, while to the north is Sarlat-la-Canéda, birthplace of Etienne de la Boétie, who was Montaigne's closest friend. His mid-fifteenth-century home can still be seen, and there are many other fine houses, the cathedral, place des Oies and the nearby Château de Puymartin, which are all worth visiting.

Domme is a fortress town perched on top of the hill, and a delight to visit. You enter through a tiny archway and there are many tiny, twisting alleys to explore; walk along the castle ramparts which afford marvellous views, and there are caves in the limestone to be visited.

There are also a number of things to see from Brive to Cahors. There are the incredible underground caves at Padirac, which are an essential visit, and where you can even take a boat trip; the fortress at Castelnau (not to be confused with Castelnaud); and the sixteenth-century Château de Montal, which are both open to the public. Another place well worth a visit is the marvellous thirteenth-century castle at Montfort, perched on the cliffs.

Between Montfort and Souillac is Fénelon, with its impressive walled castle built in the fifteenth century. The writer, François de Salignac was born here. Souillac is actually in Quercy, and is famous for its ancient Romanesque church with its carvings. There is also an impressive clock tower and many fine old buildings. Nearby, and worth a visit if there is time, are the medieval castle at La Treyne, and Gourdon with its Cordeliers church, fortified gateway, caves and the Salle des Colonnes.

Rocamadour is reputedly the second most beautiful town in France, a place of pilgrimage balanced precariously on the cliff side. It is a well-preserved medieval town; one enters through the old gate with its old buildings, chapels and churches and chapel to the Virgin de Notre-Dame-de-Rocamadour at the top of the Staircase of the King.

Cahors is the most southerly point of the tour, and apart from old buildings, the cathedral, north gate, cloisters and fortifications with towers, a visit to the nearby Pont Valentré, a towered bridge crossing the river Lot is essential. Our purpose in coming to Cahors, however, is to taste the wine, and there is a vineyard route to the south encompassing the vineyards and a large number of tasting stops; it is not advisable to stop at them all. The Cahors wine has been made in the same way for centuries, and is long-lasting. Most of the producers sell bottles and magnums, and the latter store and keep better.

Périgueux, Bergerac and Libourne

From Cahors the next place to visit is north-west; the capital of the region, Périgueux, famous for its food. The town is surrounded by farms producing *foie gras*, and the shops are full of it. Things to see include the cathedral of St Front, the church of St Etienne, the Pont des Barris and the museum of Périgord. The cathedral is named after St Front, an apostle sent by St Peter to convert the people of the region. The huge cathedral is a mass of domes and minarets, and has a vast interior. Surrounding it is the old town, with many medieval houses huddled together in narrow streets. Near the church of St Etienne, once the cathedral, is what was once the remains of a Roman amphitheatre, although only the domed gateways remain.

Just to the north is Brantôme, with its twelfth-century abbey, cloisters and refectory. Another place to visit is Bourdeilles, a thirteenth-century village with imposing castle, and old mill. The castle tower offers fine views over the river and surrounding countryside.

Having eaten one's fill in Périgueux it is time to travel south again for wine country and Bergerac. There are three wine areas to visit: the vineyards of Bergerac, St-Emilion and Monbazillac. Bergerac wines have long been overshadowed by those of Bordeaux, but are now becoming more widely known. The wines are good, but rarely great. In the case of the sweet, white wines, from Monbazillac just to the south, they do not have the same quality as a good Sauternes or Barsac, but they are fine wines, and are drunk locally as an apéritif.

Bergerac is the home of Cyrano de Bergerac, an actual historical character, and is another former Huguenot stronghold. Much of the town was destroyed during the religious wars, but the church of Notre-Dame survived. Other things to see are the tobacco museum (Bergerac is the centre for the tobacco trade) the fortified church and the local market. Nearby, there is the fifteenth-century château at Monbazillac, and very many small fortified towns or *bastides*. You can see these at Villefranche-du-Périgord, Villeréal, Eymet, Beaumont, Monpazier and Monflanquin. Most of these *bastides* are still very well preserved, the best being Eymet with its arcaded main square and the remains of its medieval castle.

At Villeréal there is an ancient covered market and fortified church. To the south of Monpazier is the huge, impressive castle of Biron which dominates the landscape for miles. The castle dates from the fifteenth century, and there is a Renaissance church and house below it. The *bastide* at Monpazier was started in 1267, but is still well preserved with many of its ancient features. At Cadouin there is a Cistercian monastery with Romanesque abbey church. It was famous as the home of the Holy Shroud until 200 years ago, when experts decided that the Shroud dated from the eleventh century not the first, and could not be authentic.

The final visit overlaps with the tour of Bordeaux. Libourne stands on the northern banks of the Dordogne, looking out over the vineyards that make up Entre-Deux-Mers with their Bordeaux *appellation*.

Libourne was founded by an Englishman, Roger de Leybourne, and still has some of its medieval fortifications, including some towers. From Libourne, travel east to visit the wine region of St-Emilion, which is in Bordeaux, while its neighbour Bergerac is not. St-Emilion is an ancient town; there was a Gallic hill fort there at least 2,000 years ago. Today, there are many reminders of this ancient history. You should see the church carved out of the rocks, the cloisters in the collegiate church, the twelfth-century Château du Roi, and the hillfort site.

Other nearby places to visit are Castillon-la-Bataille, site of the battle at which the French beat the English to end the Hundred Years' War; the Château de Montaigne; the abbey of Blasimon with its Romanesque abbey church, and the ancient village of La Réole.

Around Libourne is the river port of Vaynes, with its château once owned by Henry of Navarre; the prehistoric cave drawings at Grotto-de-Pair-non-Pair; the Château de Breuilh and the fortified church at St-Jean-de-Blaignac.

PLACES OF INTEREST IN THE SOUTH-WEST

LIMOGES AND AREA

Limoges
Gothic cathedral; porcelain museum; old buildings and churches, folklore museum; church of St Michel-des-Lions.

Uzerche
Church of Ste Eulalie.

Brive-la-Gaillarde
Old town centre, church of St Martin, many old buildings.

Oradour-sur-Glane
Ruined village destroyed by SS in 1944.

Châlus
Hilltop castle where Richard Lionheart was fatally wounded.

Bourganeuf
Tour de la Zimzim, town hall with tapestries.

Montbrun
Moated twelfth-century château.

Jumilhac-le-Grand
Thirteenth-century castle.

Arnac-Pompadour
Ancient village and castle linked with Madame de Pompadour.

Ségur-le-Château
Ancient village, ruined twelfth-century castle.

Hautefort
Magnificent fortified seventeenth-century château, gardens.

AREA AROUND SOUILLAC

Domme
Fortress town, castle ramparts, fine views, caves.

Trémolat
Fortified church.

St-Cyprien
Sixteenth-century château.

Berbiguières
Hilltop castle.

Les Milandes
Fifteenth-century château near Beynac.

Fayrac
Fortified château.

Beynac
Medieval fortified town, castle.

La Roque-Cageac
Medieval fortress.

Sarlat-la-Canéda
Historic town; many old houses; birthplace of Etienne de la Boétie; cathedral; château.

Padirac
Underground caves and grottos, an essential visit.

Castelnau
Fortress-château.

Montfort
Thirteenth-century castle.

Fenélon
Fifteenth-century castle.

Souillac
Romanesque church (carvings); clock tower; nearby medieval castle of La Treyne.

Gourdon
Cordeliers church, caves, Salle des Colonnes.

Rocamadour
Pilgrimage town, chapels, old buildings, beauty spot.

Cahors
Cathedral; north gate; old buildings and fortifications; towers; Pont Valentré.

AREA AROUND PERIGUEUX

Périgueux
Cathédrale St Front; church of
St Etienne; Pont des Barris; museum;
food shops; Roman remains.

Brantôme
Twelfth-century abbey, cloisters and
refectory.

Bourdeilles
Old village, thirteenth-century castle,
walls, mill.

BERGERAC AREA

Bergerac
Old Huguenot stronghold; church of Notre-
Dame; fortified church; tobacco museum;
local market.

Monbazillac
Fifteenth-century château, wine tasting.

Bastide towns
Villefranche-du-Périgord, Villeréal,

Eymet, Beaumont, Monpazier,
Monflanquin.

Biron
Imposing huge castle, Renaissance
houses and church.

Cadouin
Cistercian monastery and Romanesque
abbey church.

LIBOURNE AREA

Libourne
Ancient town with medieval
fortifications, towers.

St-Emilion
Wine town; Gallic hill fort; collegiate
church; 'cave' church; twelfth-century
château.

Castillon-la-Bataille
Scene of the final English defeat by the
French, ending the Hundred Years' War.

Montaigne
Château.

Blasimon
Abbey, Romanesque church.

La Réole
Ancient village.

Vaynes
Ancient river port, château.

Grotto-de-Pair-non-Pair
Prehistoric cave drawings.

Breuilh
Château.

St-Jean-de-Blaignac
Fortified church.

The Gastronomy of South-West France

The gastronomy of the south-west corner of France is rightly famous
worldwide. There is no doubt than one can eat as well in this part of France
as anywhere else in the country, and in some areas, even better. Périgord and
Quercy, home of Cahors wine, are internationally regarded for their food and
the goose and *foie gras* is legendary. There is a massive array of *charcuterie*
with hot sausages, pâtés and hams, and even spicier versions as you travel
south into the Basque country and Béarn.

Again, the influence of neighbouring Spain is reflected in many of the
dishes with tomatoes, sweet peppers, garlic and onions figuring heavily.

The Pyrénées are home to a wide range of game and freshwater fish abound in the clear streams and rivers. Basque cooking features many fish dishes and there is excellent fresh tuna, sardine and shellfish. In the north, cattle predominate, while in the south sheep graze the lower slopes of the Pyrénées. Throughout the south-west of France, stews and casseroles are popular.

Périgord and Quercy are also famed for their truffles, and these feature in many dishes, as do *cèpes* and other fungi found wild. The cuisine of these two *départements*, however, is not for the faint-hearted nor for the figure conscious. It is rich and oppulent and no-one bothers to count calories.

The region is also rich in fruit and vegetables, and there is an abundance of nuts, especially walnuts which are pressed for their oil. The people of the south-west also have a sweet tooth so there is a wide range of desserts, pastries and chocolates — and, of course, there is a huge range of wines, something to suit every dish.

The cold mountain nights must have been responsible for many of the thick soups which are popular. There is *bougras*, a vegetable soup using the stock in which black pudding has been cooked; *cousinette*, from Pays Basque, a soup made from spinach, sorrel and chicory; and *elzekaira*, also from Pays Basque, a cabbage, haricot beans and garlic soup. *Garbure* is a thick vegetable soup with pieces of pork, sausage and preserved duck or goose, while *ouillade* is another cabbage and haricot bean soup. You will also find *sobronade* from the Périgord, a soup of pork and ham with vegetables and haricot beans, and *tourin Périgourdin*, an onion and milk soup, poured over bread and sometimes with grated cheese added.

With the soup, or meat stews, you might be offered *millas*, a maize flour cake eaten like bread with soups; but sometimes it is sprinkled with sugar and eaten as a dessert. When in France, do as the French do, so adopt the custom of *chabrot*, the practice of pouring a little wine into the last of your soup after all the solids have been eaten, swilling it around to capture all remaining drops of liquid, and then drinking it.

Fish courses are numerous. There is *alose*, which is shad, and when served *à l'Adour*, it means stuffed with sorrel and cooked with ham. *Anguillettes* are baby eels (a Pays Basque local name), and *besugo* is another Pays Basque dish, sea bream cooked with garlic and peppers. *Carpe à la Neuvic* is carp stuffed with truffles and *foie gras*, while *chipirones* is the Pays Basque name for squid, and *à l'encre* means stewed with tomatoes in its own ink. *Lamproie*, an eel-like fish, is common and you will certainly come across *ttoro*, a Pays Basque fish stew made with tomatoes, garlic and onions.

There are obviously many different styles of cooking, and if the dish is followed by *à la Basquaise*, it usually means with tomatoes, rice and peppers, while *à l'échirlète* is from the Périgord and means cooked with goose fat and garlic. It is a popular way of presenting potatoes. *A la Périgourdine* usually means with truffles and *foie gras*, while *à la Neuvic* indicates a dish stuffed with *foie gras*, truffles and cooked in white wine.

Duck and goose dominate the menus. There is *alicot*, a concoction of giblets and wings of duck or goose, cooked with *cèpes*, chestnuts and wine, and *magret*, the breast of duck specially fattened for *foie gras*. It is usually lightly grilled and always served rare. *Canard* is duck, while *canard sauvage* is wild duck. *Confit* is preserved duck or goose, usually made from the rest of the bird after the liver has been removed, while *foie gras* appears in many forms, either cooked or cold, as a starter, main course or as a rich accompaniment. *Foie aux raisins* is *foie gras* cooked with grapes in white wine. *Lou trébuc* is another name for *confit* or other preserved meats, and is one of many speciality dishes in the wide range of *charcuterie* that is available. *Boudin blanc Quercynoise* is a speciality white pudding made from pork or poultry; there is *chorizo*, a hot spicy sausage from Pays Basque; and *coudenat*, a large sausage made with pork and eaten hot in thick slices. *Galabart* is a black pudding while *loukinka* is a spicy sausage with garlic from the Pays Basque, often eaten with oysters. There is also *tripotchka*, another spicy black pudding from Pays Basque.

Other poultry dishes might include wild birds such as ortolans, small buntings usually roasted and served on skewers. They are fattened before slaughter and stuffed. *Palombe* is wild pigeon, and when served *à la Périgourdine* is stuffed with truffles and *foie gras*. *Pintade pharaonne* is a Quercy speciality, guinea fowl stuffed with truffles, and flambéed. It is usually served on fried bread with *foie gras*. *Cou d'oie farci*, from Périgord, is a goose neck stuffed with *foie gras* and truffles and cooked in its own fat. It is often served cold. There is also *poule au pot*, chicken stuffed with liver and ham and cooked in wine. *Salamis des palombes* are wood pigeons cooked in red wine with onions, mushrooms and ham, and *dodines de volaille* are chicken pieces stuffed and braised. *Tourtière*, from the Périgord, is a pie with chicken and salsify.

Meat dishes, including game, are *ballotine de lièvre à la Périgourdine*, boned hare stuffed with meats and truffles and rolled into a packet. There is also *cargolade*, snails cooked in wine. *Cassoulet* is a meat and haricot bean stew, often served with stuffed goose neck in Périgord, while *daube* is a beef stew with added ham, onions and tomatoes all cooked in wine. *Estouffade* is another meat stew with vegetables and wine. *Isard* is the local name for Chamois, found in the Pyrénées, but now quite rare on menus, while you may well be offered *lièvre à la Périgourdine*, which is stuffed hare, cooked in red wine and brandy, with *foie gras* and truffles. Other meat dishes include *mouton à la Catalane* which is mutton cooked in white wine with garlic, ham and vegetables, and *poule rouilleuse*, chicken cooked in a white wine sauce thickened with its own blood. There is also *poule farci à la mode de Sorges*, from Périgord, which is chicken stuffed with vegetables and poached.

Other main course dishes could include *cèpes à la Périgourdine,* which means cooked with bacon and herbs in grape juice, *chou farci*, cabbage stuffed with meats, sausage and vegetables, and popular throughout the south west, and *friand*, small pastries served as savouries, or with almonds as a dessert. *Friand de Bergerac* is a potato cake. *Fricassée Périgourdine* is a vegetable and bacon mixture, often added to soups and stews, while *jambon de Bayonne*, is a very mild ham eaten at the start of the meal, or with salad.

Egg dishes include *oeufs en cocotte Périgourdine* which means eggs cooked in a Madeira and truffle sauce, and there is also *omelette aux truffes* (stuffed with truffles), and *pipérade*, which is a Pays Basque omelette with tomatoes, ham, onions and peppers.

Speciality truffle dishes include *tourte de truffes à la Périgourdine*. This is a tart with truffles, *foie gras* and brandy, and there is also *truffes sous la cendre*, which is a dish of truffles, wrapped in bacon and then pastry and baked.

Maize flour cakes, dumplings and fritters are common and can be served as an accompaniment to soup, stews or desserts. *Rimottes* is a sweet maize flour porridge, while *rousette* is a pancake or fritter made from sweet maize flour. *Crispés* are fried dumplings from the Périgord, and *cruchardes* are pancakes made from maize. *Gougnettes* are large fritters from Quercy, usually sweet, while *merveille* is a sweet fritter from Périgord, and *millassou* is a sweet maize flour cake. *Miques* are dumplings from the Périgord which can be served either as a savoury or dessert.

Other dishes which can be tried before you attack the desserts are *salda*, a cabbage and bacon stew with haricot beans; *saucisse à la Catalane*, sausage fried with orange peel, herbs and sometimes sweet peppers; and *hachue*, a Pays Basque ham cooked with onions and peppers. Two very good potato dishes are *pommes Basque*, baked potatoes stuffed with tomatoes, ham, peppers and garlic, and *pomme de terre à la Sarladaise*, layers of thin potato slices and truffles baked.

Apart from the numerous sweet fritters and pancakes for dessert, try *cajasse*, a sweet pastry found in Périgord, and *gâteau Basque*, a tart filled with custard or fruit. There is also *jacque,* an apple pancake from Périgord.

Finally, there are many cheeses to choose from. The cow's milk cheeses include *Bethmale*, *Bleu de Quercy*, and *Les Orrys*. They are all strong and tangy and the Quercy cheese is blue veined. Goat's milk is used to make *Cabécou*, from Périgord, which is soft with a nutty flavour, and *Picadou*, which is wrapped in leaves and aged in jars. There are also many cheeses made from sheep's milk, apart from *Roquefort* types, and these include *Ardigasna* and *Iraty* from Pays Basque, and *Laruns* from Béarn.

HOTELS AND RESTAURANTS OF THE SOUTH-WEST

(see also restaurant and hotel sections in Cognac, Armagnac, and Roussillon)

Aire-sur-l'Adour
(40800 Landes)

Domaine de Bassibé
at Ségos, 5 1/2 miles south
 west on N134
☎ (58) 09 46 71
A very comfortable, not-
too-expensive hotel with
9 good rooms and an

excellent restaurant, a
little pricey with very
good wines.

La Commerce
3 rue Labeyrie
☎ (58) 76 60 06
Good restaurant with local
specialities; fixed menus
excellent value, 22
comfortable, inexpensive
rooms.

Albi
(81000 Tarn)

La Réserve
at Fonvialane 1 3/4 miles
 north-west on the route
 de Cordes
☎ (63) 60 79 79
Very comfortable 20-room
hotel, not too expensive,
lovely setting by the river
Tarn. Good restaurant and
reasonable prices.

Hostellerie St-Antoine
17 rue St-Antoine
☎ (63) 54 04 04
Comfortable 56-room
hotel; good value rooms
and a very good, well-
priced restaurant.

Chiffre
50 rue Séré-de-Rivières
☎ (63) 54 04 60
Comfortable 39-room
hotel, with good, inexpensive restaurant.

Bergerac
(24100 Dordogne)

La Flambée
route Périgueux
1³/4 miles out of town
☎ (53) 57 52 33
Comfortable 21-room
hotel, not expensive, with
a reasonable, inexpensive
restaurant.

Le Cyrano
2 blvd Montaigne
☎ (53) 57 02 76
Very good restaurant, very
rich food and very reasonable prices, especially the
fixed-price menus. 10
simple, inexpensive rooms.

Cahors
(46000 Lot)

Hôtel France
252 ave. Jean Jaurès
☎ (65) 35 16 76
A modern 77-room hotel,
inexpensive and a good
touring base; no restaurant
but breakfast served.

La Taverne
41 rue J.B. Delpech
☎ (65) 35 28 66
Very good restaurant;
superb local dishes at extremely good prices, good
local wine list as well.

Restaurant Marco
at Lamagdelaine, 4 miles
  away
☎ (65) 35 30 64
Good regional food at low
prices.

Les Templiers
at Montat, 5 miles away
  on the D47
☎ (65) 21 01 23
Good food and good prices.

Caillac
(46140 Lot)

Relais des Champs
☎ (65) 30 92 35
An attractive hotel in
pleasant gardens, 22 small
rooms, but inexpensive
and a good restaurant offering regional specialities.

Catus
(46150 Lot)

Gindreau
☎ (65) 36 22 27
At St-Médard-Catus, 3
miles away, very good
regional food, very
reasonably-priced.

Damazan
(47160 Lot et Garonne)

Hôtel du Canal
☎ (53) 79 42 84
A small 21-room hotel;
reasonably-priced and
inexpensive restaurant.

Duras
(47120 Lot et Garonne)

Hostellerie des Ducs
☎ (53) 83 74 58
Comfortable, with 15 inexpensive rooms and pleasant,
good value restaurant.

Duravel
(46000 Lot)

Auberge du Baran
Comfortable, friendly inn
run by an English couple,
Roger and Trisha Wash-
bourne. Very good tradi-
tional local fare at good
prices. Rooms inexpensive.

Eugénie-lès-Bains
(40320 Landes)

Les Prés d'Eugénie
☎ (58) 51 19 01
Run by the internationally-
acclaimed Michel Guérard
with his wife Christine.
Magnificent, luxurious
hotel; service impeccable,
food perfect. The 35
rooms and apartments are
very expensive and
heavily in demand. The
restaurant has only a
limited number of covers,
so book early. The food is
expensive, but worth it.

Eymet
(24500 Dordogne)

Château
rue Couvent
☎ (53) 23 81 35
Simple, inexpensive 10-
room hotel, with modest,
inexpensive restaurant.

Les Eyzies-de-Tayac
(24620 Dordogne)

Centenaire
☎ (53) 06 97 18
Very good restaurant, with
excellent, creative dishes
at affordable prices; there
are 32 very comfortable,
not too expensive rooms
and apartments in an
annexe a short drive away.

Cro-Magnon
☎ (53) 06 97 06
Very good restaurant with
Périgord dishes, but a

blend of old and new styles. Restaurant prices very reasonable, and there are 27 inexpensive rooms.

Gaillac
(81600 Tarn)

Occitan
place de la Gare
☎ (63) 57 11 52
Central 13-room, inexpensive hotel, no restaurant but breakfast served.

Le Vigneron
3/4 mile out on the N88
☎ (63) 57 07 20
Good food at very reasonable prices.

Goujounac
(46250 Lot)

Hostellerie de Goujounac
☎ (65) 36 68 67
Good food, many traditional regional dishes and amazingly low prices. There are also 5 simple, very inexpensive rooms.

Luppé-Violles
(32110 Gers)

Relais de l'Armagnac
☎ (62) 09 04 54
Super restaurant. The food is always excellent, and the set price menus are tremendous value for money. There are also 10 comfortable, inexpensive rooms.

Pau
(64000 Pyrénées-Atlantiques)

Continental
2 rue Maréchal Foch
☎ (59) 27 69 31

A comfortable 110-room hotel, reasonably-priced with a good, inexpensive restaurant, Le Conti.

Paris
80 rue E. Garet
☎ (59) 27 34 39
Comfortable 41-room, not expensive hotel, no restaurant but breakfast served.

Bilaa
at Lescar 4 miles away
☎ (59) 81 03 00
Modern, comfortable and friendly 80-room hotel, not expensive; no restaurant but breakfast served.

Domaine du Beau Manoir
about 33/4 miles south-east
of Pau on the D209
☎ (59) 06 17 30
Very comfortable, modern hotel with 32 well-priced rooms, and a good inexpensive restaurant. Good views.

Pierre
16 rue L. Barthou
☎ (59) 27 76 86
Very friendly, very good restaurant and very reasonable. Good local wines.

Patrick Jourdan
14 rue Latapie
☎ (59) 27 68 70
Specialist traditional dishes, very good value.

Plaisance
(32160 Gers)

La Ripa Alta
place de l'Eglise
☎ (53) 69 30 43
Excellent restaurant, run by Maurice Coscuella, a

marvellously creative chef. Menus very good value, and there are 15 comfortable, inexpensive rooms.

Poudenas
(47170 Lot et Garonne)

La Belle Gasconne
☎ (53) 65 71 58
Run by the marvellous Mme Marie Claude Gracia, one of the best mistresses of the kitchen in France. Marvellous food, and very good value. Must book.

Puymirol
(47270 Lot et Garonne)

L'Aubergade
52 rue Royale
☎ (53) 95 31 46
Lovely old restaurant run by Michel Trama, a marvellous, magical chef. Lovely food, very good value, and good wine list.

St-Etienne-de-Baïgorry
(64430 Pyrénées-Atlantique)

Arcé
☎ (59) 37 40 14
Lovely, comfortable 24-room hotel; not expensive and a very good restaurant; a good base for visiting the Irouléguy vineyards.

Ségos
(32400 Gers)

Domaine du Bassibé
☎ (58) 09 46 71
Very good, quite expensive restaurant, run by the Capelles, and 6 ultra-comfortable, expensive rooms.

VINEYARDS OF THE SOUTH-WEST

FRONTONNAIS

NB: All vineyards produce rosé and red wine

Appellation Château

Château Bellevue
la Forêt   TRP
SCEA Bellevue la Forêt
31620 Fronton
☎ (61) 82 43 21

Château Clos-
Mignon   TRP
Muzart brothers
31620 Villeneuve-lès-
Bouloc
☎ (61) 82 10 89

Château Flotis   TRP
Kuntz and son
31620 Castenau
d'Estrétéfonds
☎ (61) 35 12 04
or (61) 35 10 03

Château La Palme   TRP
SA du Domaine de la Palme
31340 Villemur-sur-Tarn
☎ (61) 09 02 82

Château Les Peyreaux TRP
Linant-de-Bellefonds-
Vovette
31340 Villematier
☎ (61) 35 36 48

Château Cransac   TRP
Cave Les Côtes de Fronton
31620 Fronton
☎ (61) 82 41 27

Château Montauriol   TRP
UPV Villaudric
31620 Villaudric
☎ (61) 82 44 14

Appellation Domaine

Domaine du Dèves   TRP
André Abart
31620 Castelnau
d'Estrétéfonds
☎ (61) 82 14 97

Domaine de Coutinel TRP
Manoêlle Arbeau
82370 Labastide-St-Pierre
☎ (63) 64 01 80

Domaine de Bel Air   TRP
Bonhomme and son
31620 Fronton
☎ (61) 82 45 75

Domaine de la
Colombière   TRP
Baron de Driesen
31620 Villaudric
☎ (61) 82 44 05

Domaine de Laurou   TRP
Campillo-Perry
31620 Fronton
☎ (61) 82 40 88

Domaine de Matabiau TRP
Jean-Louis Delmas
31620 Fronton
☎ (61) 82 45 42
Michel Lugou   TRP

Domaine de Tembouret
31620 Fronton
☎ (61) 82 93 29
or (61) 82 42 71

Domaine Caze   TRP
Maurice Rougevin-Baville
31620 Villaudric
☎ (61) 82 90 30

Domaine de Baudare   TRP
Claude Vigouroux
82370 Campsas
☎ (63) 30 51 33

Domaine de Faouquet TRP
Robert Béringuier
31620 Bouloc
☎ (61) 82 06 66

Domaine de Joliet   TRP
François Daubert
31620 Fronton
☎ (61) 82 46 02

Other Producers

Urbain Blancal   TRP
Les Bêtirats
31620 Villaudric
☎ (61) 82 44 09

GAEC Les Dauban   TRP
Escaoudomillas
31620 Fronton
☎ (61) 82 45 43

GAEC de Cahuzac   TRP
Les Peyronnets
82170 Fabas
☎ (61) 64 10 18
or (61) 30 30 58

Serge Galvani   TRP
Aux Banguis
31620 Bouloc
☎ (61) 82 04 27

Sté Lacaze and son   TRP
Le Parc
82170 Dieupentale
☎ (63) 02 52 38

André Dejean   TRP
Croix Peyrat
82370 Campsas
☎ (63) 30 55 68

Robert Tregan   TRP
Bois Huguet
82370 Campsas
☎ (63) 64 02 31

T=tasting   E=English spoken   G=guided tours   C=château/building to visit

BERGERAC

(All open Monday to
Saturday for visits and
tastings unless stated.)

Bergerac (24100)

Château Champarel-
  Pécharmant   R
Bouché
☎ (53) 57 34 76

Raymond Bourges   R
Aux Costes
☎ (53) 57 59 89

Christian Boyer   WR
Le Brandal
☎ (53) 57 26 58

Ginette Calfour   R
Pécharmant
☎ (53) 57 94 45

Cave Coopérative   WR
Boulevard de l'Entrepôt
☎ (53) 57 16 27

Château de Corbiac   R
B. Durand de Corbiac
Pécharmant
☎ (53) 57 20 75

Chartreuse de
  Peyrelevade   R
Gilbert Dusseau
Pécharmant
☎ (53) 57 44 27

Château Puypezat   WR
GAEC Puypezat
Rosette
☎ (53) 57 27 69

Clos Peyrelevade   R
Edith Giradet
Pécharmant
☎ (53) 57 43 30

MM. Guilhon   WR
6 blvd de Monbazillac
☎ (53) 57 05 20

Gérard Lacroix   WR
Les Costes
☎ (53) 57 64 49

Gérard Lajonie   WR
St-Christophe
☎ (53) 58 30 02
or (53) 57 17 96

Robert Marty   WR
Les Renards
☎ (53) 57 34 87

Château de Planque De
  Meslon   WR
☎ (53) 58 30 18

Paul Pomar   WR
St-Christophe
☎ (53) 57 71 62

Domaine du Haut-
  Pécharmant   R
André Roches
☎ (53) 57 29 50

Francis Roman   R
Les Galinoux
☎ (53) 57 97 88

Jean-Pierre Yot   WR
St-Christophe
☎ (53) 57 50 22

Boisse
(24560 Issigeac)

Denuel   R
Le Plantou
☎ (53) 58 71 58

Jean-Louis Molle   R
Moulins de Boisse
☎ (53) 58 71 18

Bonneville
(24230 Vélines)

Château de Bloy   WR
Guillemier brothers
☎ (53) 27 50 91
or (53) 27 50 59

Carsac-de-Gurson
(24610 Villefranche-de-
Lonchat)

Cave Coopérative de
  Carsac et St Martin de
  Gurson   WR
La Grappe de Gurson
☎ (53) 80 78 84

Domaine des Peyrières WR
Jean Grenier
☎ (53) 80 74 51

Colombier
(24560 Issigeac)

Jean Revol   WR
La Rayre
☎ (53) 58 32 17

Pierre Roche   WR
☎ (53) 58 32 28

Domaine La Verdaugie WR
Lucien Roux
☎ (53) 58 32 71

Château La Jaubertie WR
Henri Ryman
☎ (53) 58 32 11

Conne-de-Labarde
(24560 Issigeac)

Jean-Guy Fourtout   WR
Les Verdots
☎ (53) 58 34 31

GAEC du Bois de
  Pourquie   WR
☎ (53) 58 30 61

Creysse
(24100 Bergerac)

Coll   W
☎ (53) 57 67 81

Domaine des Bertranoux WR
Guy Pecou
☎ (53) 57 28 62

R=red wine   W=white wine   P=rosé wine   S=sparkling wine

Société d'Exploitation du
Château de Tiregand   WR
☎ (53) 23 21 08

Cunèges
(24240 Sigoules)

Domaine du Meyrand   WR
GAEC Lorenzon
☎ (53) 58 46 32

Eymet (24500)

Marcel Murer   WR
☎ (53) 23 81 38

Flaugeac
(24240 Sigoules)

GAEC Clos Bellevue   WR
M. Royère Blanchard
☎ (53) 58 40 23

Domaine du Moulin de
Peytirat   WR
Robert Guibert
☎ (53) 58 41 91

Le Fleix
(24130 La Force)

Cave Coopérative   WR
☎ (57) 46 20 15

Fonroque
(24500 Eymet)

Lucien Farjout   WR
Au Petit Lac
☎ (53) 23 90 50

Fougueyrolles
(33220 Ste-Foy-la-Grande)

Château de Masburel   WR
Roland Bartoux
☎ (57) 46 15 78

Domaine Roque-Peyre   WR
MM. Valette and son
☎ (57) 46 23 05

Château de Berneries   WR
Jacques Dubernet
☎ (57) 46 23 08

Marty and son   WR
Conterie
☎ (57) 46 22 43
or (57) 46 37 04

Château Péchaurieux   WR
Comte de Peyrelongue
☎ (57) 46 23 12

Jean Claude Samuel   WR
☎ (57) 46 22 20

Fermage Château de
Bonnières   WR
M.C. Ubald Bocquet
☎ (57) 46 01 98

Gageac-Rouillac
(24240 Sigoules)

Château de Peytirat   WR
Jean Régis Guibert
☎ (53) 58 45 08

Château de Perrou
A. de Madaillan
☎ (53) 27 92 81

Raymond Merillier   WR
La Ferrière
☎ (53) 27 92 91

Jean Louis Metifet   WR
Cuvée de nos Ancêtres
☎ (53) 27 92 99

De la Verrie de Vivans   WR
☎ (53) 27 92 82
or (53) 27 92 82

Gardonne
(24130 La Force)

Pierre Briau   WR
☎ (53) 27 88 47

Maurice Renou   WR
Aux Mouthes
☎ (53) 27 91 08

Ginestet
(24130 La Force)

Domaine du Lac   WR
Guy Gaudy
☎ (53) 57 45 27

Lamonzie-St-Martin
(24130 La Force)

Jean Louis Constant   WR
Castang
☎ (53) 24 07 08

Christian Pauty   R
☎ (53) 24 07 58

Lamothe-Montravel
(24230 Vélines)

Francis Guillot   R
Les Auvergnats
☎ (53) 58 65 96

Domaine de la
Roche-Marot   WR
Pierre Parizel
☎ (53) 58 60 58

Guy Reverdy   WR
Fonladan
☎ (57) 40 22 66

Lembras
(24100 Bergerac)

Georges Baudry   R
Grand Jaure
☎ (53) 57 35 65

Minzac
(24160 Villefranche-de-
Lonchat)

Château La Plante   WR
Jacques Mornaud
☎ (53) 80 77 43

SCA Domaine de la
Rogère   WR
☎ (53) 80 78 43

Monbazillac
(24240 Sigoules)

T=tasting   E=English spoken   G=guided tours   C=château/building to visit

Jean-André Alary WR
La Gueylardie
☎ (53) 58 34 99

Domaine de Combet WR
Robert Alexis
☎ (53) 58 34 21

Roger Auche W
Le Bourg
☎ (53) 58 33 34

Alberte Bardin WR
Repaire du Haut-Theulet
☎ (53) 58 30 30

Château Pintouka WR
Georges Beaudoin
☎ (53) 57 00 84

Domaine du Haut
 Bernasse WR
Jacques Blair
☎ (53) 58 36 22

Jean Borderie WR
La Haute Brie
☎ (53) 58 30 08

Jean Camus WR
☎ (53) 58 30 45

Château de Thenoux WR
Pierre Carrère
☎ (53) 58 38 53

Cave Coopérative de
 Monbazillac
B.P. 2
☎ (53) 57 06 38

Jean Ceglarek WR
La Fonrousse
☎ (53) 57 10 39

Serge Chabrol W
☎ (53) 58 33 10

Château de Monbazillac W
☎ (53) 57 06 38
or (53) 58 30 27
Open: Monday-Sunday in
September.

Clos Fontindoule W
Gilles Cros
☎ (53) 58 30 36

Domaine La Truffière et
 Tirecul WR
Yves Feytout
☎ (53) 58 30 23

GAEC Ganfard WR
Haute-Fonrousse
Géraud and son
☎ (53) 58 30 28

GAEC de Malfourat WR
Château de Malfourat
MM. Christian and
 Patrick Chabrol
☎ (53) 58 30 63

GAEC La Sabatière WR
MM. Martinet and son
☎ (53) 58 30 39

GAEC de Sigala WR
MM. Sutel and son
Sigala
☎ (53) 58 30 05

Jean Genéste WR
Petit Paris
☎ (53) 58 30 41

GFA des Vignobles de
 Poulvère et des Barses WR
☎ (53) 58 30 25

Labasse-Gazzini WR
☎ (53) 58 30 01

Domaine de Bernasse WR
Laffitte
☎ (53) 58 36 10

Château Péroudier WR
Charles Loisy
☎ (53) 58 30 04

Marcel Monbouche WR
☎ (53) 57 07 07

René Monbouche WR
Le Marsalet
☎ (53) 57 94 36

Henri Morguet WR
☎ (53) 58 38 00

Château Theulet WR
SCEA Alard
☎ (53) 57 30 43

SCEA Pouljol WR
Les Moulinières
☎ (53) 58 33 49

Domaine de la Maroutie WR
Mme Veuve René Serieis
☎ (53) 58 30 38

Société Civile de la
 Borderie WR
Château La Borderie
☎ (53) 57 00 36

Roger Sutel WR
La Truffière-Thibaut
☎ (53) 57 00 15

Unidor WR
B.P. 1
route de Mont de Marsan
☎ (53) 57 40 44

Christian Verdier WR
Moulin de Malfourat
☎ (53) 58 34 30

Dominique Vidal WR
La Haute-Borie
☎ (53) 27 20 32

Château Treuil de
 Nailhac WR
Hurmic Vidal
☎ (53) 57 00 36

Château de la Fonvieille WR
Violet Quemin
☎ (53) 58 30 07

Domaine Cabaroque WR
Paul Yourassovski
☎ (53) 58 34 48

Monestier
(24240 Sigoules)

Andreola brothers WR
La Malaise
☎ (53) 58 41 31

Michel Baron WR
La Bastide
☎ (53) 58 46 65

R=red wine   W=white wine   P=rosé wine   S=sparkling wine

Domaine Les
 Auvergnats WR
Patrick Bertrandie
☎ (53) 58 80 52

Michel Brouilleaud WR
La Croix Blanche
☎ (53) 58 45 82

Cuisset - GAEC des
 Eyssards WR
Le Bourg
☎ (53) 58 45 48

GAEC des Terrasses WR
MM. Cuisset
☎ (53) 58 44 36
or (53) 58 46 63

Domaine Tourmentine WR
Pierre Grenier
La Bastide
☎ (53) 58 42 63

Domaine du Bost WR
Eric Héraud
☎ (53) 58 41 01

Domaine Le Pigeonnier WR
Jean Labreigne
☎ (53) 58 41 22

Société de la Font
 du Roc WR
Les Vigiers
☎ (53) 27 92 72

Monfaucon
(24130 La Force)

Fernand Biau WR
La Mallevieille
☎ (57) 46 23 20

Monsaguel
(24560 Issigeac)

Jean Gardeau R
Le Terme
☎ (53) 58 72 98

Montazeau
(24230 Vélines)

Château Les Grimards WR
Paul Joyeux
☎ (53) 27 51 85

Château de Ségur WR
André Peytureau
☎ (53) 27 51 89

Montcaret
(24230 Vélines)

Claude Ledeme WR
☎ (53) 58 61 08

Philippe Poivey WR
Montravel
☎ (53) 58 66 93

Château Le Grand
 Chemin R
Claude Reichert
☎ (53) 58 62 31

Montpeyroux
(24610 Villefranche-de-
Lonchat)

Château du Berny WR
Cyrille Montels
☎ (53) 80 77 99

Domaine de Fonfrède WR
Jean Rautou
☎ (53) 80 77 16

Montpon (24700)

Domaine de Garrauty R
M. Leconte
☎ (53) 80 31 74

Nastringues
(24230 Vélines)

Jean-Claude Banizette WR
Libarde
☎ (57) 46 11 25

Pineulh
(33220 Ste-Foy-la-Grande)

Pierre Sabloux WR
73 Ave. Clémenceau
☎ (57) 46 01 34

Plaisance
(24560 Issigeac)

Jean Guiraud R
Les Valades
☎ (53) 58 72 85

Pomport
(24240 Sigoules)

J.C. Alary WR
La Fontpudière
☎ (53) 57 47 27

Beigner-Gagnard WR
Le Chrisly
☎ (53) 58 42 35

Château Belingard WR
Comte de Bosredon
☎ (53) 57 05 01

Charles Charrut WR
Le Malveyrin
☎ (53) 58 42 33

Château Les Olivoux WR
Jean-Jacques Dailliat
☎ (53) 58 41 94

Dupas and son WR
GAEC Chantalouette
☎ (53) 58 42 36

Château du
 Haut-Malveyrin WR
Gérard Durand
Le Galinou
☎ (53) 58 42 41

Nadine Fauche WR
Gaffou
☎ (53) 58 42 17

GAEC du Barouillet WR
Le Barouillet
☎ (53) 58 42 20

GAEC de Grange
 Neuve WR
MM. Castaing
Grangeneuve
☎ (53) 58 42 23

T=tasting   E=English spoken   G=guided tours   C=château/building to visit

GAEC Quatre Châteaux
Réunis WR
Association Carrére
☎ (53) 58 30 67

Pierre Gaspard WR
Le Bourg
☎ (53) 58 43 94

Château Le Fagé WR
François Gérardin
☎ (53) 58 32 55

Château Le Reyssac WR
Jean Gouy
☎ (53) 58 42 08

Laurent Grima WR
Château Roc de Caillevel
☎ (53) 58 42 16

Gilbert Guilhon WR
☎ (53) 58 42 12

Jean Labaye W
Pécoula
☎ (53) 58 41 89

Château Caillevel WR
Marc Lacoste
☎ (53) 58 43 30

Michel Lagrange WR
La Calevie
☎ (53) 58 42 24

Louis Lambert WR
Montlong
☎ (53) 58 44 10

Claude Larrue WR
Bélingard
☎ (53) 58 30 79

Marcel Massy WR
Le Grand Chemin
☎ (53) 58 30 81

Albert Monbouche WR
Bélingard
☎ (53) 58 30 57

Bertrand de Passemar WR
Sanxet
☎ (53) 58 37 46

Rousserie brothers WR
Monlong
☎ (53) 58 80 29

Château Le Garry WR
Jean Russac
☎ (53) 58 42 04

Domaine du
Haut-Montlong WR
René Sergenton
☎ (53) 58 81 60
or (53) 58 44 88

Mme Vilate and son WR
Le Malveyrin
☎ (53) 58 42 29

Ponchapt
(33220 Ste-Foy-la-Grande)

Jean Bertrand WR
Golse
☎ (57) 46 22 53

Marc Chavant WR
☎ (57) 46 22 59

Port-Ste-Foy
(33220 Ste-Foy-la-Grande)

Jean Rebeyrolle WR
La Ressaudie
☎ (57) 46 03 35

SICA Viticole des
Coteaux de Ste-Foy WR
Château Puyservain
Paul Hecquet
☎ (57) 46 11 46
or (57) 46 00 84

Union des Viticulteurs
de Port-Ste-Foy WR
☎ (57) 46 02 37

Prigonrieux
(24130 La Force)

Château Monplaisir R
Jean-Louis Blanc
☎ (53) 58 91 86

Raymond Desplanchcs WR
Franchemont
☎ (53) 58 02 14

René Girou WR
Combrillac
☎ (53) 58 02 06

Château de Simondie R
Jallain
☎ (53) 58 02 21

Domaine de Latour WR
Louis Marché
☎ (53) 58 00 02
or (53) 63 12 12

Château Combrillac WR
Jean Priou
☎ (53) 58 91 67

Puyguilhem
(24240 Sigoules)

Jean-Louis Piazetta WR
Les Brandeaux
☎ (53) 58 41 50

Razac-de-Saussignac
(24240 Sigoules)

GAEC du Castellat WR
Lescure and son
Le Castellat
☎ (53) 27 93 66

GAEC de la Combe WR
La Combe
☎ (53) 27 86 51

Christian Mespoulède WR
La Maurigne
☎ (53) 27 83 82
or (53) 27 81 60

Francis Pialat WR
Les Picots
☎ (53) 27 93 37

Domaine Les Frétillères R
Bernard Rigal
☎ (53) 27 92 69

Domaine du Cantonnet WR
Jean-Paul Rigal
☎ (53) 27 88 63

R=red wine   W=white wine   P=rosé wine   S=sparkling wine

Château Court
Les Mûts WR
Pierre Sadoux
☎ (53) 27 92 17

Rouffignac-de-Sigoules
(24240 Sigoules)

Domaine La Guillonie WR
Pierre Autran
☎ (53) 58 43 27

Christian Beigner WR
La Selmonie
☎ (53) 58 43 40

Louis Borderie WR
Les Cailloux
☎ (53) 58 84 14

Albert Couture WR
Maye de Bouye
☎ (53) 58 36 76

Pierre Eymery WR
Château Le Caillou
☎ (53) 58 43 03

Claude Lenéveu WR
Treuil de Rabot
☎ (53) 58 44 98

Domaine de la Barde WR
Christian Monbouche
☎ (53) 58 43 19

Mme Veuve Vergnol WR
Les Saintes
☎ (53) 58 43 24

St-Antoine-de-Breuilh
(24230 Vélines)

Domaine du Champ
de Mars WR
L. Eboto and son
☎ (57) 46 21 39

GAEC du Rival WR
MM. Marceteau
Le Mayne
☎ (57) 46 21 12

Clos des Gottes WR
Jacques Pervieux
☎ (57) 46 25 84

St-Aubin-de-Cadelech
(24500 Eymet)

GAEC du domaine du
Siorac WR
A. Landat and son
☎ (53) 23 82 93

Pierrette Marti and son R
☎ (53) 23 84 86

St-Avit-St-Nazaire
(33220 Ste-Foy-la-Grande)

Société Civile
d'Exploitation WR
Agricole du Bru
☎ (57) 46 12 71

St-Laurent-des-Vignes
(24100 Bergerac)

Domaine des Grands
Champs WR
André Cathal
☎ (53) 57 42 57

Pierre Cathal WR
Clos Le Petit Marsalet
☎ (53) 57 53 36

Domaine La Marche WR
Chaussade
☎ (53) 57 30 91

Domaine du Poncet WR
Chevalier
Le Poncet
☎ (53) 57 30 98

GAEC du Grand
Marsalet WR
MM. Nadal-Ode
☎ (53) 57 30 59

Clos des Cabanes WR
Jacky Melet
☎ (53) 57 35 53

André and Bernard
Sergenton WR
Les Doris
☎ (53) 57 47 28

SICA Producta WR
(Union de Viticulteurs)
☎ (53) 57 40 44

St-Martin-de-Gurson
(24610 Villefranche de
Lonchat)

Guy Arnaud and son WR
La Font de Barbu
☎ (53) 80 76 97

GAEC du Priorat WR
☎ (53) 80 76 06

Maurice Lansade WR
Le Couleaud
Le Vin du Beau Père
☎ (53) 80 78 16

Georges Mondary WR
Couderc
☎ (53) 80 77 40

St-Méard-de-Gurson
(24610 Villefranche-de-
Lonchat)

Château Laulerie WR
Argivier and son
☎ (53) 82 48 17
or (53) 82 47 61

Jean-Claude Campesato WR
L'Houme
☎ (53) 82 49 68

Domaine du Gouyat WR
☎ (53) 82 45 26
or (53) 82 46 30

Exploitation Familiale WR
M. Salien
Jolibois
☎ (53) 82 48 55
or (53) 82 47 02

Château Le Ras WR
GAEC du Maine
M. Barde
☎ (53) 82 48 41

T=tasting   E=English spoken   G=guided tours   C=château/building to visit

Domaine de Barradis WR
Raoul Michel
☎ (53) 82 49 34

Christian Prioleau WR
Moulins des Poutières
☎ (53) 82 46 03

**St-Michel-de-
Montaigne**
(24230 Vélines)

Jean Bernard Basset WR
☎ (53) 58 64 53

Château Perreau WR
Jacques Benoist
☎ (53) 58 63 16

Château Michel de
 Montaigne WR
Mme Malher-Besse
☎ (53) 58 60 56
Closed: Mondays.

Jean-Yves Reynou WR
Perreau
☎ (53) 58 60 55

St-Nexans
(24520 Mouleydier)

Georges Dupré WR
Les Blanchiers
☎ (53) 58 36 11

Josèph Favareille WR
Les Donats
☎ (53) 58 34 15

Dénis Lafaurille WR
☎ (53) 58 32 95

René Lafon WR
Grande Borie
☎ (53) 58 32 84

Domaine Les Hauts-
 Perrots WR
Jean Moulinier
☎ (53) 58 37 37

St Perdoux
(24560 Issigeac)

Château Le Paradis R
Roger Chambaud
☎ (53) 58 36 69

St-Pierre-d'Eyraud
(24130 La Force)

Jacques Chadeau R
Le Sautier
☎ (53) 58 05 73

**St-Sauveur
(24520 Mouleydier)**

Maxime Leyx R
La Réfrénie
☎ (53) 23 26 04

St-Seurin-de-Prats
(24230 Vélines)

Guy Pointet R
☎ (53) 58 62 66

St-Vivien
(24230 Vélines)

Michel Bonneaud WR
Le Rigalot
☎ (53) 27 52 35

Cave Coopérative
 Vinicole WR
St-Vivien et Bonneville
☎ (53) 27 52 22

Saussignac
(24240 Sigoules)

Château La Garrigue WR
Jean-Pierre Battistella
☎ (53) 27 92 46

Château Les Cavailles WR
Mme M. Biaussat
☎ (53) 27 92 28

Caille
☎ (53) 27 87 52

Pierre Chaumont WR
La Bachonne
☎ (53) 27 84 66

Clary WR
☎ (53) 58 38 13

Max Cousinet WR
Rudel
☎ (53) 27 92 44

Irénée Festal WR
Les Ganfards
☎ (53) 27 81 04

GAEC Ganfard Haute
 Fon-Rousse WR
Ganfard
☎ (53) 27 92 18
or (53) 58 30 28

Jean Gazziola WR
Les Plaguettes
☎ (53) 27 93 17

Château de Fayolles WR
GFA Henri de Dietricht
☎ (53) 27 93 28

Victor Gianduzzo WR
☎ (53) 27 86 03

Domaine de Garrou WR
Didier Hemery
☎ (53) 58 10 07

Domaine Les
 Plaguettes WR
Gilbert Mallet
☎ (53) 27 92 23

Daniel Richard WR
La Prade
☎ (53) 27 93 34

Sigoules
(24240 Sigoules)

Cave Coopérative de la
 Région de Sigoules WR
☎ (53) 58 40 18

Les Vignobles du
 Mayne WR
Ch. Martrenchard and son
Le Mayne
☎ (53) 58 40 01

R=red wine   W=white wine   P=rosé wine   S=sparkling wine

Domaine de Perthus WR
Elie Prevost
☎ (53) 58 40 38

Michel Prouillac WR
Le Mayne
☎ (53) 58 40 92

Thenac
(24240 Sigoules)

Bellanger WR
Biran
☎ (53) 58 43 37

Domaine du Félix WR
Louis Beylat
☎ (53) 58 41 84

Josèph Daroda WR
Caillevet
☎ (53) 58 44 73

Château Gaillevet WR
Daniel Dumez
☎ (53) 58 80 71

GAEC Château Panisseau WR
Panisseau
☎ (53) 58 40 03

GAEC Domaine de
Capulle WR
MM. Migot
☎ (53) 58 43 67
or (53) 58 42 67

Domaine du Cauffour WR
Raymond Girol
☎ (53) 58 43 68

Guy Rey WR
Bois Martin
☎ (53) 58 45 76

Vélines
(24230 Vélines)

Alain Garcia WR
Le Pointet
☎ (53) 27 51 53

Château La Rayre WR
Itey de Peironin
☎ (53) 27 50 14

**Villefranche-de-
Lonchat**
(24610 Villefranche-de-
Lonchat)

Cave Coopérative de Villefranche et Minzac WR
☎ (53) 80 77 37

Jean Lovato WR
Puygrenier
☎ (53) 80 77 45

Château Montarut WR
Jean Moreau
☎ (53) 80 78 59

Domaine de
Beauregard WR
Jean-Marie Teillet
☎ (53) 80 76 34

GAILLAC

Domaine Les Rives TR
Jenne Aakster
Montans
81600 Gaillac
☎ (63) 40 44 37

Domaine de
Pialentou TRWP
Jean-Louis Ailloud
81600 Gaillac
☎ (63) 57 17 99

Domaine de
Labarthe TRWPS
Jean Albert
Castanet
81150 Marssac-sur-Tarn
☎ (63) 56 80 14

Château de
Frausseilles TRWP
Jean Almon
Frausseilles
81170 Cordes
☎ (63) 56 06 28

Mas de Grouze TRW
Francis Alquier
81800 Rabastens
☎ (63) 33 80 70

Jean-Claude Arbeau TW
Négociant en Vins
chemin des Flouriès
81600 Gaillac
☎ (63) 57 01 09

Pennesalvié TRWP
Albert Arnaud
81140 Castelnau-de-
Montmiral
☎ (63) 33 90 38

GAEC de Boissel
Rhodes TRWPS
René Assie
Château de Rhodes
81600 Gaillac
☎ (63) 57 06 02

Mas de Pignou TRW
Jacques Auque
81600 Gaillac
☎ (63) 57 10 04

Château de Terride TRP
Henrich Bauser
81140 Castelnau-de-
Montmiral
☎ (63) 33 11 38

La Croix des
Marchands TR
Jean-Marie Bezios
Le Rivet
Montans
81600 Gaillac
☎ (63) 57 19 71

Brousse TRP
Roland Boissel
Cahuzac-sur-Vère
81140 Castelnau-de-
Montmiral
☎ (63) 33 91 02

Domaine de
Lasbordes TRWP
Maurice Bou
Lagrave
81150 Marssac-sur-Tarn
☎ (63) 57 05 91

T=tasting E=English spoken G=guided tours C=château/building to visit

GAEC de Gradille   TRW
Alfred Bousbacher
81310 Lisle-sur-Tarn
☎ (63) 57 14 89

Al Couderc   TRW
Michel Bousquet
Labastide de Levis
81150 Marssac-sur-Tarn
☎ (63) 55 41 37

Domaine de Mazou TRWPS
E. Boyals and son
81310 Lisle-sur-Tarn
☎ (63) 33 37 80

Au Payssel   TRW
Louis Brun
Frausseilles
81170 Cordes
☎ (63) 57 09 16

Château de Saurs   TRW
Marie-Paule Burrus
Saurs
81310 Lisle-sur-Tarn
☎ (63) 57 23 11

Balagès   TR
Félix Candia
Lagrave
81150 Marssac-sur-Tarn
☎ (63) 57 74 48

Cave de Vinification de
  Labastide de
  Levis   TRWPS
81150 Marssac sur Tarn
☎ (63) 55 41 83

Cave de Vinification de
  Labastide de
  Levis   TRWPS
RN 88
81600 Gaillac
☎ (63) 57 01 30

Cave de Vinification
  de Labastide de
  Levis   TRWPS
Plazolles
D99 Cunac
81000 Albi
☎ (63) 54 56 62

Cave de Tecou   TRWPS
Tecou
81600 Gaillac
☎ (63) 33 00 80

Cave Les Trois
  Clochers   TRWPS
St-Salvy
81310 Lisle-sur-Tarn
☎ (63) 57 34 04

Les Terrisses   TRWP
Joseph Cazottes
St-Laurent
81600 Gaillac
☎ (63) 57 09 15
or (63) 57 16 80

Château de
  Clarès   TRWPS
Pierre Clarès
81150 Marssac-sur-Tarn
☎ (63) 55 40 12

Domaine de la
  Jonquière
Jeanine Couderc
81300 Grauhlet
☎ (63) 34 58 76

Domaine de Graddé   TRW
Etienne Coursières
Campagnac
81140 Castelnau-de-
  Montmiral
☎ (63) 33 12 61

Mas des Vignes   TRWPS
GAEC Jean Cros & son
81140 Cahuzac-sur-Veere
☎ (63) 33 92 62

Domaine de Bertrand TRWP
Henri Cunnac and son
Donnazac
81170 Cordes
☎ (63) 56 06 52

Domaine Clément
  Termes   TRWP
GAEC Jean David and son
Les Fortis
81310 Lisle-sur-Tarn
☎ (63) 57 23 19

Château de Lastours TRWP
GAEC J.H.F. de Faramond
81310 Lisle-sur-Tarn
☎ (63) 57 07 09

Domaine de Lacroux TRWP
GAEC Derrieux and son
Lincarque
81150 Cestayrols
☎ (63) 56 81 67

Domaine de la
  Tour   TRWPS
Claude Fiault
Boissel
81600 Gaillac
☎ (63) 57 06 05

Mas Mathieu   TRW
Camille Gasquet
Vors
81600 Gaillac
☎ (63) 57 10 36

Mayragues   TR
Alain Geddes
81140 Castelnau-de-
  Montmiral
☎ (63) 33 94 08

Beaudinecq   TS
Bernard Guilhabert
Campagnac
81140 Castelnau-de-
  Montmiral
☎ (63) 33 15 03

Pagats   TRPW
Alain Guiraud
Andillac
81140 Castelnau-de-
  Montmiral
☎ (63) 33 90 87

Château d'Escabès   TRW
Colette Hauchard
St-Salvy
81310 Lisle-sur-Tarn
☎ (63) 40 42 93

GAEC Hirissou   TWS
Brens
81600 Gaillac
☎ (63) 57 07 27

R=red wine   W=white wine   P=rosé wine   S=sparkling wine

Domaine de la
 Ramaye   TRWPS
Maurice Issaly
Ste-Cécile-d'Avès
81600 Gaillac
☎ (63) 57 06 64

La Petite Cave   TRWPS
94 rue Josèph Rigal
(face place St-Jean)
81600 Gaillac
☎ (63) 57 57 70

GAEC de Boissel-
 Rhodes   TRWPS
Guy Laborie
81600 Gaillac
☎ (63) 57 36 48

Mas d'Oustry   TRW
Robert Larroque
81600 Gaillac
☎ (63) 57 06 13

Laubarel   TRWPS
Yvan Lavernhe
81600 Gaillac
☎ (63) 57 06 82

Matens   TW
Thierry Lecomte
81600 Gaillac
☎ (63) 57 43 96

St-Eugène   TRW
René Leduc
Broze
81600 Gaillac
☎ (63) 57 10 39

St-Laurent   TS
Edmond Malle
81600 Gaillac
☎ (63) 57 13 49

Mas de Boudac   TRW
Jacques Marty
81600 Gaillac
☎ (63) 57 51 66

Domaine de Lécusse TRWP
Pierre-Ange Mattei
81600 Gaillac
☎ (63) 33 90 09

Domaine de
 Bouscaillous   TRWP
Yvon Maurel
Montels
81140 Castelnau-de-
 Montmiral
☎ (63) 57 10 16

Domaine de Moussens TRP
Alain Monestie
Cestayrols
81150 Marssac-sur-Tarn
☎ (63) 56 81 66

Domaine des Issards TRWP
Claude Montels
Amarens
81170 Cordes
☎ (63) 56 08 03

GAEC Château de
 Tauziès   TRWP
81600 Gaillac
☎ (63) 57 06 06

La Pierre Plantée   TRW
Frédéric Pascal
81140 Castelnau-de-
 Montmiral
☎ (63) 57 10 24

Domaine de Saurs   TRWP
Yves Pages
Saurs
81310 Lisle-sur-Tarn
☎ (63) 57 23 34

Jean-Paul Pezet   TRWP
Bernac
81150 Marssac-sur-Tarn
☎ (63) 55 42 53

Domaine des Très
 Cantous   TRWP
Robert Plageoles
81140 Cahuzac-sur-Vère
☎ (63) 33 90 40

Manoir de
 l'Emmeillé   TRWPS
Charles Poussou
Campagnac
81140 Castelnau-de-
 Montmiral
☎ (63) 33 12 80

Condomines   TRW
Claude Ramond
Andillac
81140 Castelnau-de-
 Montmiral
☎ (63) 33 91 95

(SNR) Société Négoce
 Représentation   TRWPS
Renaud
53 ave. Lattre de Tassigny
81600 Gaillac
☎ (63) 51 71 76

Mas d'Aurel   TRWP
Albert Ribot
Donnazac
81170 Cordes
☎ (63) 56 06 39

Jean-Louis Ribot   TRW
chemin de Balitrands
81600 Gaillac
☎ (63) 57 06 53

GAEC de Boissel-
 Rhodes   TRWPS
81600 Gaillac
☎ (63) 57 06 07

Mas de Donat   TRWP
Yves Robert
81600 Gaillac
☎ (63) 57 06 88

Négociant   TRWPS
Georges Rolland
36 rue de la Marne
81600 Gaillac
☎ (63) 57 01 37

Mas de Picary   TRWP
Roger Rouquie
Broze
81600 Gaillac
☎ (63) 57 07 93

Château Labastidié
 Blanche   TR
Madeleine Roux
81150 Florentin
☎ (63) 55 40 12

Monsieur Henri
 Socovins   TRW
8 allée des Pervenches
81600 Gaillac
☎ (63) 57 19 19

T=tasting   E=English spoken   G=guided tours   C=château/building to visit

Téoulct TS
Jean Thomas
81600 Gaillac
☎ (63) 57 40 73

La Salvetat TRWP
Claude Thouy
Livers-Cazelles
81170 Cordes
☎ (63) 56 05 06

Union Vinicole
Coopérative TRW
101 ave. Foch

81600 Gaillac
☎ (63) 57 22 07

Laborie TRWS
Jacques Vayssette
81600 Gaillac
☎ (63) 57 31 95

Busque TS
André Vaissières
81300 Graulhet
☎ (63) 34 59 06

Domaine de Bosc
Long TRW
Ludwig Willemborg
81140 Cahuzac-sur-Vère
☎ (63) 33 94 45

Château de Salettes TRW
Hildegard Willemborg
91140 Cahuzac-sur-Vère
☎ (63) 33 94 45

MADIRAN

Château d'Aydie TR
GAEC Vignobles Laplace
64330 Garlin
☎ (59) 04 01 17
Open: Monday-Saturday,
8am-1pm and 2-8pm.

Domaine Barrejat TR
Maurice Capmartin
32400 Maumusson
☎ (62) 69 74 92
Open: Monday to Saturday
8am-noon and 2-8pm.

Domaine du Crampilh TR
Lucien Oulié
Aurion-Idernes
64350 Lembeye
Open: by appointment only.

Château de Gayon TR
Vignerons Réunis du
Vic-Bilh Madiran
Crouseilles

64350 Lembeye
☎ (59) 68 10 93
Open: Monday to Saturday
8.30am-1.30pm and
2-4.30pm.

Domaine de Maouries RW
André Dufau and son
Labarthète
32400 Riscle
☎ (62) 69 80 36
Open: by appointment only.

Château Montus TR
Alain Brumont
Maumusson
32400 Riscle
☎ (62) 69 74 67
Open: by appointment only.

Domaine Pichard TR
Auguste Vigneau
Soublecause
65700 Maubourguet

☎ (62) 96 35 73
Open: by appointment only.

Producteurs de Plaimont TR
32400 St-Mont
☎ (62) 69 78 87
Open: by appointment.

Domaine de Teston TR
Lafitte and son
32400 Maumasson
☎ (62) 69 74 54
Open: daily 8am-noon and
2-7pm.

Vignerons Réunis
du Vic-Bilh TR
Crouseilles
64350 Lembeye
☎ (62) 68 10 93
Open: Monday to Saturday
8.30am-12.30pm and 2-
4.30pm.

BEARN AND IROULEGUY

Febus Aban TW
Coopérative Vinicole de
Bellocq
64270 Salies-de-Béarn

☎ (59) 38 00 30
Open: by appointment only.

Cave Coopérative
d'Irouléguy TR

64430 St-Etienne-de-
Baïgorry
☎ (59) 37 41 33
Open: by appointment only.

R=red wine   W=white wine   P=rosé wine   S=sparkling wine

CAHORS

Domaine de la Bergerie TR
Les Côtes d'Olt
Parnac
46140 Luzech
☎ (65) 30 71 86
Open: by appointment only.

Domaine de la Caminade TR
L. Resses
Parnac
46140 Luzech
☎ (65) 30 73 05
Open: Monday to Saturday
8am-noon and 2-7pm.

Domaine de Caunezil TR
Les Côtes d'Olt
Parnac
46140 Luzech
☎ (65) 30 71 86
Open: by appointment only.

Château du Cayrou
Jean Jouffreau
Clos de Gamot
46220 Prayssac
☎ (65) 22 40 26
Open: daily 9am-1pm and
2-8pm.

Château de Chambert TR
Floressas
46700 Puy l'Evêque
☎ (65) 87 24 58
Open: by appointment.

Les Côtes d'Olt
Parnac
46140 Luzech
☎ (65) 30 71 86
Open: by appointment.

Clos La Coutale TR
Bernède and son
Vire-sur-Lot
46700 Puy l'Evêque
☎ (65) 36 51 47
Open: by appointment.

Domaine de Dauliac TR
Les Côtes d'Olt
Parnac
46140 Luzech
☎ (65) 30 71 86
Open: by appointment.

Domaine Eugénie TR
Jean Couture
Rivière-Haute
46140 Albas
☎ (65) 30 73 51
Open: by appointment.

Clos de Gamot TR
Jean Jouffreau
46220 Prayssac
☎ (65) 22 40 26
Open: daily 9am-8pm.

Domaine de Gaudou TR
Durou and son
Vire-sur-Lot
46700 Puy l'Evêque
☎ (65) 36 52 93
Open: by appointment only.

Domaine de Grauzils TR
Pontie and son
Gamot
46220 Prayssac
☎ (65) 30 65 44
Open: by appointment only.

Château de Haute-Serre TR
Georges Vigouroux
Cieurac
46230 Lalbenque
☎ (65) 38 70 30
Open: daily 10am-noon
and 3-6pm.

Domaine Labarrade TR
Les Côtes d'Olt
Parnac
46140 Luzech
☎ (65) 30 71 86
Open: by appointment only.

Château Lacapelle-
Cabanac TR
Alex Denjean
46700 Puy l'Evêque
☎ (65) 36 51 92
Open: by appointment only.

Domaine des Landes TR
Les Côtes d'Olt
Parnac
46140 Luzech
☎ (65) 30 71 86
Open: by appointment only.

Domaine Lou-Camp-
Del-Saltre TR
Roland Delbru and son
46220 Prayssac
☎ (65) 22 42 40
Open: by appointment only.

Domaine de Massabie TR
Les Côtes d'Olt
Parnac
46140 Luzech
☎ (65) 30 71 86
Open: by appointment only.

Domaine de Paillas TR
SCEA de St-Robert
46700 Puy l'Evêque
☎ (65) 21 34 42
Open: by appointment.

Château Parnac
Les Côtes d'Olt
Parnac
46140 Luzech
☎ (65) 30 71 86
Open: by appointment.

Domaine du Pech-
de-Clary TR
Antonia Valette-Clary
Lamagdelaine
46090 Cahors
☎ (65) 35 37 08
Open: daily 9am-8pm.

Domaine du Pic TR
José Roucanières
Douelle
46140 Luzech
☎ (65) 20 04 48
Open: by appointment only.

T=tasting E=English spoken G=guided tours C=château/building to visit

Domaine de la Pineraie TR
M. Burc and son
Peygues
46700 Puy l'Evêque
☎ (65) 30 82 07
Open: Monday to Saturday
7am-noon and 2-8pm,
closed bank holidays.

Clos Triguedina TR
Baldès and son
46700 Puy l'Evêque
☎ (65) 21 30 81
Open: by appointment only.

Domaine de Verdou TR
Emile Arnaudet
Douelle
46140 Luzech

☎ (65) 30 91 34
Open: by appointment only.

Domaine de Vignals TR
Les Côtes d'Olt
Parnac
46140 Luzech
☎ (65) 30 71 86
Open: by appointment only.

R=red wine   W=white wine   P=rosé wine   S=sparkling wine

APPENDIX

The Wine Club: Buying Your Wine

THERE are many reasons why it makes sense to buy wines direct from the wine-maker, or a *négociant*, although the most important reason is the money that you can save. At present you can buy your wine straight from the shelf of your local supermarket, wine store or other outlet, but this is limited in that what you can buy depends on what they choose to sell. Buying yourself allows much greater insight into the world of wine.

Because of the very complicated United States import regulations, the need to have all wine labels checked and approved before wines can be brought into the country, and the various confusing state laws, the task of the individual wine importer is made much more difficult than in Europe and Britain. In Britain, the best way to buy wine is either direct from the cellars in France or from a wine shipper (who arranges for it to be shipped across to the UK, and handles the tax and customs formalities on your behalf).

Anyone can set up a wine club; there are no formal rules governing their operation. Obviously, the more people within the club, the larger the orders will be and a proportionately higher discount will be obtainable. All you need to form a wine club is a few like-minded friends. They must have roughly the same tastes in wine as yourself to enable you to buy in bulk, and a yen to be a little adventurous.

A wine club can buy direct from a shipper or wholesaler (if they will do business with you) or direct from the winemaker in France. Most wine shippers will do business if they are assured that the club is a serious buyer, and their credit rating is good. Most will require bankers' references and possibly trade references before accepting your first order; but if that order is large enough there should not be any great difficulty in placing it.

The easiest way of setting up a club is to approach people who like wine, and appreciate the advantages of bulk buying. Then wine merchants, shippers and so on can be asked for their lists and, if large quantities are being ordered, their wholesale price list can be obtained as well.

The organisation and formalities of a wine club should be kept to a minimum. It may hold its own events to sample different wines, but when buying it is best to keep the orders simple. In the beginning, members might be offered just one red and one white wine. The organiser, and perhaps a small tasting panel, should sample the wine first; if the club evinces genuine interest, a tasting should be arranged for you by the merchant or shipper. Initially it is a good idea to insist that orders from members are accompanied by a cheque. This means that the master order, together with the full sum, can be placed. This is a very good way of establishing a working relationship with a supplier, as he will be delighted to get his money so promptly.

Most suppliers will start to offer discounts on purchases above ten cases, with the discount increasing as the order increases. Most have a ceiling on discounts, say for 50 or 100 cases, but few clubs are likely to be ordering in these quantities.

It is possible to place orders for mixed cases, and some shippers specialise in this, but it does make life difficult for both the organiser and the supplier. It is also advisable if at all possible to have orders delivered to one address. Most shippers will deliver large orders to a single address without charge. The shipper would rather have a single drop because it reduces his costs, and if all the members live within a small area, this should not cause any problems. If the members are scattered, individual deliveries may be the answer, but the cost of this has to be added to the final bill.

It is possible to arrange your own transport and collect wine from the supplier, and it may be cost-effective to hire a van and do this. Some offer extra discounts if you collect the wine, and of course it is the best way if you are buying direct from the cellars in France and only having to carry it back to Britain. Again there are shippers, notably the cross-channel ferry operators, who will arrange to transport wine from France, but normally the consignment must be collected from their warehouses on the UK channel coast.

In the United States you can also approach leading shippers, merchants and even wine stores to negotiate special terms for large orders. If your club gets a reputation for reliability and big orders, the wine merchants themselves will start to approach you with offers of tasting in a bid to get you to buy from them. Most have facilities for staging tastings, with food, at a very modest price.

Anyone can go to France and buy wine. The very best wines, from Burgundy and Bordeaux, may be in short supply, and you may not be able to buy by the case, but the price which is charged will be considerably less than the price asked by a wine merchant at home.

After the vintage each year, some regions of France do offer a small proportion of their wine for sale *en primeur*. This is one way of testing demand, because if there is a rush to buy, the wine growers know that they had better adjust their prices upwards. This is always a good time to buy, especially during excellent and very good vintages, because the price is relatively low. The customer gets the chance of a bargain, because the wine may not be suitable for drinking for many years, so there is always the element of risk, but the customer has to store the wine until it is ready for drinking, thus reducing the grower's storage costs and releasing much needed cellarage.

Often prices can double between the *en primeur* price and the next offering, just a few months later. After a few years, the price can have increased tenfold and more. This leads us to another interesting problem. When one buys wine, the main aim should always be to lay down good drinking stocks for the future, but one should never forget that wine is a valuable commodity, and the commercial possibilities of future re-sale should never be overlooked. It is possible, by balancing the two elements, future drinking stocks and potential re-sale wine, to cut the costs of your own wine-drinking considerably.

Wine bought now is not likely to have much of a profitable re-sale value for a number of years; but after five years or more it can often be sold privately or through auction for substantial profits. If money is no object, then you can hang on to wine and enjoy drinking it, but if you discover that you have four cases of a particularly good wine in the cellar which has risen considerably in price, it makes sense to keep two to enjoy, and sell two for a large profit which can finance new purchases.

There are many examples that I could give, but a 1964 Château Cheval-Blanc which was selling for £40-£50 a case in 1971 was realising £230 a case in 1980, £290 in 1981, £440 in 1983, and £600 early in 1985. Château Latour 1962 cost about £55 a case in 1971 and £330 in 1981 but was fetching almost £550 in auction just two years later, and £600 by 1985.

Although these are both very fine wines, it does illustrate that although the price continues to increase, there is a period of initial modest growth before a surge. In later years, the price of wine at auction can literally double in a year, and the decision that has to be made is whether to sell, and when. By getting the timing right, and realising several hundred dollars or pounds, it is possible to make fresh investments, and it is also possible to drink free wine after a few years, by realising profits on popular wines, and using that money to re-stock. I am not sure that I am in wholehearted agreement with this policy, because the main aim of buying wine must be to enjoy it yourself and with friends. It does seem to make sense, however, to sell wines that are either not to your taste after a few years, or seem to be becoming so expensive that it is madness not to dispose of a case or two. There is no reason at all why the esoteric pleasures of wine, and the commercial world of market forces should not be blended harmoniously to your advantage. And, as it is possible to sell some of your wine at auction, it is also possible to buy it there as well.

If we look at the various methods of buying wine it is easy to see why there are advantages in doing it yourself. You can cut out the middleman and his profits, the retailer's profits and his costs in running a store, and you have total freedom to buy exactly what you want.

Fine wine stores still have a role to play, and will often try to secure particular wines for you even if they do not stock them generally. Wine Shippers sometimes make special offers available to the public and there are wine clubs specialising in buying direct from the growers, in bulk, which gets them large discounts. In all these cases, however, costs have to be met and these have to be passed on to the customer in higher prices.

For people living in Britain and Northern Europe, the most pleasurable way of buying wine is to visit France and the wine growers' cellars and to choose and negotiate your own supplies. If you are just buying half a dozen bottles there is no problem, because they will not even have to be declared at Customs and there will be no duty to pay. If you are buying several cases either for your own use, or for friends who have formed themselves into a club, there are various formalities to complete, but none are daunting, and the end result is that you have the wine of your choice at a price very much lower than if you had bought it in a shop. It is possible to organise buying trips and enjoy a few days of good eating and drinking into the bargain.

If you are buying in France and taking the cases back with you to Britain, you will have to pay duty at Customs by going through the Red 'something to declare' channel. You will have to pay the current excise duty depending on what you have bought (the duty on light wine is less than that for fortified wines), and you will also have to pay Value Added Tax, although this can be claimed back if you have a VAT number and a legitimate reason for claiming exemption. You must also get a VAT ticket from the seller exempting you from paying it when you leave the country. It is also possible to hire containers which can be Customs-sealed, and this can save a lot of paperwork, but it is only really worth it if you are bringing in very large consignments, and if that is the case it might be best to employ a professional shipper.

Many of the cross-Channel ferry companies operate a wine shipping service, provided that the consignment is of reasonable size. Not only do they guarantee its shipment, they also cover it for breakages *en route*. Most of them, like P&O Townsend Thoresen, Brittany Ferries and Sealink, require you to pick up the wine once it is in Britain, but special arrangements can be made to have it forwarded to you at a price.

If you are just travelling around exploring the vineyards, you will have no trouble in buying a few bottles or a small number of cases. If you are on a big buying trip, make an appointment with the wine grower or co-operative so they can have things ready for you. It is always the case that the more interest you show in a wine-grower's produce, the more he will be encouraged to delve deeper into his cellars. If the pleasure expressed is genuine, there is no finer way of passing a few hours than tasting your way through the owner's private stock. It brings us back to the question of whether wine should be bought as an investment. I think that it can and at times, should be, but it can never make up for the delight in drinking good wine with others who appreciate it as much.

If you travel round France regularly you will discover wines made by small cooperatives, and wonder why they are not on sale back home, but perhaps they are not geared up to export, or their output is not big enough to cope even if they could win the orders. They are, however, more willing to sell to visitors, so if you do find a particularly good producer, buy, tell your friends, but do not try to set up an importing agency, as not only is it hard work, but you will find his prices shooting up. Shop around, however, and taste the wines from several producers before making a choice.

Everyone has their preference for a particular style of wine, and if you are trying to negotiate a price direct with a grower-producer, or through an agent, it is best to handle only one or two wines at a time, one red and one white for instance.

Even an agent in Britain or the United States will be prepared to handle orders from individuals and wine clubs if the volume is right. Loads of forty or fifty cases will attract discounts, reducing the price per bottle considerably.

Normally, after the introduction to an agent or shipper, you will have to present details of your bank, and two commercial references, before an order is placed. For the first two or three deals, the shipper is likely to want cash with the order, or cash on delivery, but after a business relationship has been established, you should be able to get credit, with a further discount if you do pay immediately. It is always worth building up a rapport with growers and shippers, not just because they are generally charming people, but because the wine trade, like everything else, relies very heavily on the old friends' network. Friends tell each other when they discover a magnificent new wine, or when they hear of some old bottles that have been discovered tucked away at the back of a cellar. Friends will often give you first option to buy. Above all, it is much more pleasant doing business with friends.

So, if you discover that you have friends who share your interest in wine, you can plan what you need to buy, over a bottle or two, of course. While *Vin de Table* is cheap in France, it does not make much sense to go all that way to buy something which you could buy for just a little more back home. When you are buying, look for the bargain always, look for good wines to drink currently, and look for wines to lay down to build up your cellar. And always pay as much as you can afford, because you will benefit later on. If you are thinking of laying down a cellar, even if you intend buying direct, I recommend *Webster's Wine Price Guide*, by Oz Clarke and Rosemary George.

The alcohol and spirit laws in the United States are designed to confuse the unsuspecting traveller; in some states, the regulations are being revised. Although US Customs enforces the law of the state in which you arrive, the onus is on you to know what your allowance is before you return home. This is especially so in those states where the import of larger quantities, even though duty is paid at the airport, is prohibited. The US Customs Service does issue a leaflet, 'Know Before You Go', which sets out the regulations as they apply state by state. If you want to import wine in bulk for friends, the procedure is extremely complicated. It is possible to set up a wine club if the state allows the importation of approved wines, but it is perhaps best to seek the aid of a specialist shipper and enlist his support and advice. Again, by buying direct through him, especially if you place sizeable orders, it is possible to obtain big discounts.

Storing and Serving

HAVING spent hard-earned money buying wine, it is essential to store it properly before drinking it. The ideal storage space is, of course, an old-fashioned cellar where the air temperature is constant, but modern architecture and modern living, often in high rise flats, means that few of us have this luxury.

I was fortunate enough recently to have my garden landscaped, and a wine-cellar was a central feature. It is well below ground level, entered by steps, and it enjoys a constant temperature of about 59°F (15°C) and humidity of about 65 per cent. These conditions are ideal for the storage of wine, and allow it to age slowly and correctly. The main rule, however, in choosing storage space is to find somewhere where the temperature does not fluctuate. Wine can withstand cold, but it cannot cope with constantly changing temperatures. There is a lot of nonsense talked about wine storage and correct temperatures, but obviously a basement next to the central heating boiler is not suitable, nor is a space in the attic where the heat from the sun can raise temperatures many degrees each day, before they plunge back during the night. It is usually possible, however, to find somewhere in the house where wine can be stored correctly. A cupboard under the stairs may be suitable, or a cupboard in an unheated spare bedroom. It is possible to use insulating materials such as foam blocks or polystyrene, and there are even commercial cabinets, electrically cooled, to ensure the wine is kept at the correct temperature.

If you are storing a lot of wine, it is worth the effort of preparing a special room for it. If you have a basement or cellar, and it is well aired, that is fine, but if not, it might be possible to have part of your roof space converted, or wine racks concealed in a cupboard in a hallway or room. It is essential though to check that when the work is completed, the temperature is constant, and the humidity normal. It is possible to buy both thermometers and humidity gauges very cheaply so that you can keep a constant check on the conditions.

Wine should always be stored on its side, in a room which has a gentle air flow, and which is free from damp. The bottles need to be laid down on their sides to keep the corks moist. If the cork dries out, it shrinks, and this allows air to enter and the wine oxidises and eventually turns to vinegar. If the room is too moist, mould will develop and while this may look very attractive, it is not good for the wine and is a positive nuisance. Damp will also cause the labels on the bottles to come off, and this can lead to all sorts of confusion.

How you store your wine in your chosen storage space is not important, provided you know what you have got and where. It is possible to have a carpenter build a complicated, expensive, system of bins and racks; or you can simply store the bottles in the cases in which they arrive. The best way, I think, is to have some sort of shelving system, so that you can scan the bottles easily. I use stainless steel filing cabinets designed for office use. They are relatively cheap to buy, and each cubbyhole holds exactly a dozen bottles. Each hole is numbered, and each number has a page in my cellar book so that I know what wine is where. I make a note of when the wine was bought, from whom, its price, vintage and pedigree. I make notes about each bottle drunk, how it is drinking, and how I think it will drink in the future. This sort of cellar book *cum* diary makes very interesting reading as you look back at some of the vintages drunk, and the comments made about them at the time.

Having the luxury of a cellar, I now have two places in which to store wine. I keep bottles for immediate, everyday use in a large cupboard in a corner of the dining room. This holds about 100 bottles, but is rarely full, and we use this supply for normal drinking through the week. For special occasions we rely on the cellar, and it is almost as much fun deciding what wine to choose with a particular dish as actually drinking the wine.

Wine does not like to be disturbed too much, so it should be moved as little as possible. There is no doubt that the finest wines are those from the cellars of the best châteaux which have simply been taken straight from the bottling line to their underground home directly below. Even fairly modest wines can drink beautifully when consumed at source. The more a wine is moved, the more it is disturbed, which is why you should never contemplate drinking a really good old wine for several weeks after buying it. It needs time to settle.

When you have decided what wine to present at a dinner party, you should collect it from the cellar at least twelve hours, and ideally a day, before it is needed. This allows it time to warm up and it should be stood upright, away from direct heat or sunshine, to allow any sediment to settle. Most wines do not require decanting and the corks can be removed only minutes before pouring. Red wines do improve if they are allowed to breathe a little, and fine old reds need to be handled with great care, especially if they require decanting. The aim of decanting, however, is to remove sediment from the bottle so that the diner is not offered cloudy wine. It is not necessary to decant old bottles, but the process of carefully pouring from the bottle at the dinner table is so laborious, that it makes sense to see to this chore beforehand. Besides, an accidental nudge at the table could mean one guest getting a sudden splash of sediment which would not be appreciated.

For normal reds I open the bottle thirty minutes to one hour before serving. Rosés, whites and Champagnes are left to the last minute, while fine old reds, and old ports which need decanting, receive attention two or three hours before the wine needs to be poured. There is no skill required to decant, just a steady hand, and a good strong light behind the bottle so that you can see the sediment inside. The wine must have been allowed to settle after being brought up from the cellar, and ideally, the cork should have been pulled some time before, again giving the wine time to settle down. There are elaborate frames and racks to assist with decanting, but these are expensive and not really necessary. You need a good, clean decanter, and a funnel because it makes pouring easier. Check that the neck of the bottle is clean and start to pour. The secret of decanting is a steady hand and a smooth motion. Once you have started to pour, carry on, until you can see the sediment rising up to the neck of the bottle. Do not allow this to leave the bottle. At this point gently lower the bottle and remove the decanter to the dining room.

Most fine old Bordeaux and Burgundy wines benefit from decanting, although it is one subject which provokes fierce debate. In Burgundy for instance, it is very unusual to decant old bottles, but it is a simple procedure and it does guarantee maximum pleasure. Vintage port also needs decanting and I must say, the age-old custom of using a strong carving knife, or similar, to crack off the neck of the bottle, cork and all, still fills me with apprehension. Port tongs can be used and these are heated and then applied to the neck of the bottle. The sudden application of intense heat to the neck of the bottle causes the glass to crack neatly. It is possible to extract the cork in quite recently-bottled ports using conventional corkscrews, but great care should be taken not to disturb the crust on the wine. If the crust is not disturbed it is usually possible to decant normally without having to resort to filtering. If the cork cracks in two as you attempt to remove it, pull out the top part, and push the remainder carefully into the bottle. If the crust is disturbed a fine cloth, such as muslin or linen, or a filter pad can be used during the decanting.

Good wine deserves good glass. Crystal is fine, but it can interfere with your perception and appreciation of the colour of the wine, so I prefer clean, clear and large glasses. There is nothing worse than being offered wine in a small glass. It makes the task of the host more difficult because he is constantly having to replenish glasses, and wine is best enjoyed in glasses which allow the wine to develop to best advantage.

Again, there is much argument about the correct temperatures at which wine should be served. As a general rule, lighter-style reds, such as Beaujolais, should be served slightly chilled while the big, gutsy, more alcoholic wines, such as those from the Rhône, drink better a little above room temperature. The extra degree or two seems to soften any rough edges the wine may have. Everyday Bordeaux should be drunk at room temperature, while older clarets should be drunk just a little cooler, and generally, red Burgundies cooler still. Most whites and rosés should be served well chilled, as should non-vintage Champagne. That means an hour or two in the fridge and then the wine should be kept cool using an ice bucket, or similar cooling device. Fine white Burgundy and vintage Champagne, and some of the better full-bodied whites from other parts of the world, Australian Chardonnay for example, require less chilling, and should only be put in the fridge for thirty minutes or so. These big, full bodied whites then have the chance to warm up in the glass releasing their bouquets.

It may be a heresy, and it is certainly not good practice, but if guests suddenly arrive without warning with good news and you want to open a bottle of Champagne, you can stick it in the freezer or the ice box for ten or fifteen minutes.

Some sherry, Madeira and port also benefits from being served chilled. Fino sherry and Manzanilla should be served well chilled and white port should be served cold. When it comes down to it, however, as with all matters to do with wine, you should do what you prefer, and ignore the experts!

Visiting a Vineyard or Cellar

MOST of the vineyards mentioned in this book are open during the week to members of the public. If an appointment is requested, this usually means that the vineyard is family-run and that the family will be out tending the vines, or in the winery. The appointment can usually be made a day or so in advance, and they will be very pleased to welcome you. It is quite common for vineyards to close their doors to visitors, or at least to ask for advance notice of callers, during the harvest and initial winemaking stages, which follow it. This is, of course, the winemakers' busiest time of year. If a vineyard advertises that it is open for tasting, one can normally arrive unannounced. Most large establishments have reception areas and the biggest, which can get hundreds of thousands of visitors a year, will have hostesses to greet guests, and to conduct them on guided tours in a number of different languages. Most small winemakers will not speak English, and no matter how bad your French, it is best to try to speak it a little because it is appreciated. If your French host sees that you are making an effort, then his English, if any, might surface as well. There is no doubt, however, that a little wine does help the conversation along.

It must be said that growers only offer tasting facilities because they expect you to buy their wine. Not everyone does, of course, and there is no compunction to do so, but the aim of tasting wine is to find something you like enough to buy.

If you visit a small vineyard, you will probably be offered a small glass of just one or two wines. It should be tasted properly, but that does not mean making some of the strange faces comics make when they imitate wine tasting. You can spit the wine out if you wish, but if you are only sampling one or two, it does not really matter. It all depends on how many vineyards you plan to visit that day, and whether you are driving.

There are large tasting centres catering for tourists where you can taste many wines, and a number of the wine growing areas have set up their own tasting establishments and these are mentioned in the book where relevant.

In a proper tasting room there will be facilities for spitting with tubs filled with sawdust or similar receptacle. In a cellar it is quite in order to spit out wine on to the floor.

Having tried the wines (and do not be afraid to ask for something you have not been offered but especially want to taste) decide whether you want to buy. If so, ask for the price list and start to negotiate. The prices of the wines will be written down. Reductions cannot usually be obtained if you are buying a bottle or two only. For one or more cases, though, try to get a discount. Most vineyards, and virtually all the smaller ones, will not accept credit cards and many will not accept cheques even supported by cash cards, so make sure to carry enough francs.

It is true that drinking wine creates friendships. If the winery is not busy, it is possible to spend several hours tasting and talking to the owner. The more interest and appreciation you show in the wines, the more samples are likely to appear. If it is clear that you are knowledgeable and discerning, it is surprising what rare vintages can be offered in special instances.

There is nothing daunting about visiting a cellar, winery or tasting centre. It is meant to be a pleasurable experience. The idea is, obviously, not to quaff huge quantities of wine by the glassful; it is the nicest way to learn about wine from the people who know most about it, the winemakers themselves.

GLOSSARY

AOC: *Appellation d'Origine Contrôlée*, a system of quality control introduced by the French in 1935, with strict rules governing the growing, production and sale of specific wines. In many areas, however, the AOC, or AC as it is known in the UK and USA, is little more than a guarantee of area of origin, rather than quality. There are many AC wines which do not merit the title when compared to neighbouring VDQS wines, which do.

Assemblage: the blending of wines for a specific wine.

Bin: a container, usually in a cellar, for storing bottles on their sides so that the corks remain in contact with the wine and do not dry out. An end of bin sale is literally the disposal of odd bottles of wine left in the bin. These bottles may sometimes have been overlooked for years, and tremendous bargains can be found.

Blanc de Blancs: white wine made from white grapes.

Blanc de Noir: white wine made from red grapes.

Blend: almost all wines are blended to improve quality. This blending can be from grapes in another part of the same vineyard, or from another region completely. The blending is controlled by the quality designation held by the wine.

Botrytis cinerea: also known as *pourriture noble*, or Noble Rot. The fungus which attacks some grapes if harvesting is delayed. The grapes shrivel as the juice is converted into sugar. These late-picked, rot-attacked grapes are used to produce naturally sweet wines, such as Sauternes. The grapes are often individually picked.

Bottles: many different sizes and shapes of bottle are used for the wines of France, but in the AC areas only certain bottles may be used. The situation is complicated by the import regulations of various countries. The United States insists that French wines must be bottled in 75cl flasks (25.36 US ounces) and half bottles which hold 37.5 cl. (12.65 US ounces). The EEC now insists all wines are bottled in 75cl bottles, but vintages preceding the directive can still be sold in other bottles. In Britain, most wines from the Rhône, Burgundy, and Bordeaux come in 75cl bottles, old bottles from Alsace hold 71-73cl, and bottles of Champagne about 80cl. A magnum is generally 1.5 litres, or two bottles. In Champagne the bottle sizes increase as follows: Magnum, 2 bottles; Jeroboam, 4 bottles; Rehoboam, 6 bottles; Methusaleh, 8 bottles; Salmanazar, 12 bottles; Balthazar, 16 bottles; Nebuchadnezzar, 20 bottles.

Bottle age: the time a wine spends in the bottle. With some wines, this can be useful because the wine continues to age and improve; with most, however, the wines are stabilised before bottling so no further action takes place.

Bottle stink: an unpleasant smell from the neck of the bottle immediately the cork has been withdrawn. In almost all cases this will vanish, as the musty air escapes and the wine can be drunk. It is not the same as bad wine, or corked wine, although is often mistaken as such.

Brut: means dry and is usually applied to sparkling wines and Champagne.

Carbonic maceration: a system developed in the Rhône vineyards more than fifty years ago, but now widely used to improve the quality of ordinary wines. The grapes are allowed to soak in their own juices before the fermentation takes place. It produces a much fruitier, light style of wine.

Cépage: is the different varieties used in a blend.

Chai: an above ground 'cellar' for storing wine.

Chaptalisation: the addition of sugar to the grape juice to assist fermentation. This addition is quite legal, does not sweeten the wine, and there are strict rules as to exactly when it should be added.

Classified wines: usually refers to those fine wines of Bordeaux which have been graded into *crus*, or growths. The classification system is urgently in need of revision.

Commune: a village or parish producing wine.

Consumé: the wine or spirit lost through evaporation; in Cognac known as the 'angel's share'.

Corked: a fault in a bottle of wine caused either by a bad cork, or by air getting inside and oxidising the wine. In either case the wine smells 'off' although the smell can vary in degrees of unpleasantness. In a restaurant, it should be sent back; at a friend's dinner table, one should exercise great tact! A corky wine is one that actually smells of cork, and is usually a sign of a poor cork, or infestation by a cork weevil. A really bad corked wine can be detected from several yards away.

Côte (or *coteaux*) literally means 'slope'. Grapes grown on the sides of hills are generally better than those from the valley or the tops of the hills.

Crémant: generally, sparkling wines bottled at a slightly lower pressure than those for full sparkling wines. In Champagne, the wine is normally bottled with about five to six atmospheres of pressure, whereas a *crémant* would usually have between three to four.

Cuvé, or *cuvée:* generally the contents from one vat after blending. In Champagne it can mean the juice from the first pressing which goes into the first ten casks.

Cuve close: a system for producing sparkling wines which differs from *méthode Champenoise* in that the second fermentation takes place in steel tanks, and the wine is pumped under pressure for bottling.

Deposit: most old wines leave a sediment or deposit in the bottom of the bottle, and great care should be taken when pouring them. Decanting is important, especially with port and old claret.

Esters: are compounds found in wine and formed by the reaction of alcohol on acid. They contribute to the bouquet of the wine, and once in the blood may be a contributory factor in hangovers.

Filtration: the removal of all deposits from the wine before bottling; this not only prevents impurities which may taint the wine, but enhances the colour.

Fining: is a technique by which deposits in the wine can be removed, usually by the addition of egg white. The egg white attracts the deposits, and then sinks to the bottom of the vat or tank, so that the pure wine can be drawn off. A number of other substances are allowed for fining including ox blood; the most common is now bentonite.

Fortified wines: wines that have a higher alcoholic content because they have been strengthened by the addition of a '*dosage*' usually brandy made from distilled wine.

Lees: the sediment left in the vat or tank after the wine has been drawn off.

Liqueur de dosage: not to be confused with *dosage*. This is the sweet liquid used to top up sparkling wines, especially Champagne, after disgorgement and before bottling.

Méthode Champenoise: the two fermentations necessary to produce Champagne and other good sparkling wines. The second fermentation must take place in the bottle.

Mis en bouteille: an indication of the bottler.

Mousseux: French term for a full sparkling wine, apart from Champagne.

Must: the crushed grapes, or grape juice before fermentation.

Négociant: a merchant buying, storing and selling wines.

Nose: the wine's smell or bouquet. Smell alone should tell you whether the wine is drinkable.

Oenology: the study of wine. Oenologists are usually the winemakers.

Oxidation: the action of oxygen in the air on wine, usually through a bad cork. The wine can develop a bad smell, and will eventually turn to vinegar. Ironically, most wines should be opened in good time, however, so they have time to breathe and improve by being exposed to air.

Pasteurisation: heating the wine to kill off yeasts or bacteria.

Phylloxera: the louse that spread through Europe in the 1870s to 1890s, devastating most of the vineyards. Phylloxera-resistant American root stock is now used to withstand the pest, although there are now sprays which can be applied.

Pétillant: a slightly sparkling wine, often naturally produced by the grape variety used.

Racking: the process of moving wine from one barrel or cask to another leaving the lees or sediment behind.

Sec: French word for 'dry', applied to still wines.

Tannin: an element in wine that assists longevity, and which is particularly noticeable in young red wines. Tannin comes from the grape skins and stems, and some is also absorbed from the oak of the barrels in which it rests. In young wines, tannin makes the mouth pucker, because it is astringent and dries out the roof of the mouth. Tannin is usually an asset in older wines because it assists long life. As the wine ages, however, the astringency of the tannin is lost and in very old wines is often deposited as part of the sediment in the bottom of the bottle.

Tartrates: are often found in both red and white wines. They appear as small crystals and are frequently mistaken for bits of broken glass. They are formed for a number of reasons, but usually because of a sudden change in temperature. They are often to be found in the small bottles of wine served by airlines in flight. They are, however, completely safe to drink and are usually an indication of a better than average wine, one that has not been over-filtered.

Ullage: topping up of barrels whose levels have fallen due to evaporation.

Vin de Pays: slightly better than *vin de table*, and both are at the bottom of the quality ladder although there are many that are very good, drinkable wines.

VDQS: *Vins Délimités de Qualité Supérieure*, a wine striving hard for AC status but in most cases, with a little way still to go.

Vintage: either the harvest each year, or the wines made from the grapes of a designated year.

Further Reading

Wines:

Wine Companion, by Hugh Johnson
(Mitchell Beazley)

Pocket Wine Book, by Hugh
Johnson (Mitchell Beazley)

French Fine Wines, by Stephen
Spurrier (Collins Willow)

French Country Wines, by Stephen
Spurrier (Collins Willow)

Bordeaux, by David Peppercorn
(Faber & Faber)

Burgundy, by Anthony Hanson
(Faber & Faber)

The Wines of the Rhône, by John
Livingstone-Learmonth and
Melvyn C.H. Master (Faber &
Faber)

*Guide to the Wines and Vineyards of
France; The Great Wine Châteaux
of Bordeaux; The Good Wines of
Bordeaux; The Great Wines of
Burgundy; The Wines of Loire,
Alsace and Champagne*
all by Hubrecht Duijker (Mitchell
Beazley)

Chablis, by Rosemary Collins
(Sothebys)

*The Century Companion to the
Wines of Bordeaux,* by Pamela
Vandyke Price (Century)

*The Century Companion to the
Wines of Burgundy,* by Graham
Chidgey (Century)

*The Century Companion to Cognac
and other Brandies,* by James
Long (Century)

Champagne, by Patrick Forbes
(Gollancz)

Webster's Wine Price Guide, edited
by Oz Clarke (Mitchell Beazley)

Champagne, by Tom Stevenson
(Sothebys)

Food, Hotels and Restaurants

*The Pocket Guide to French Food
and Wine,* by Tessa Youell and
George Kimball (Xanadu)

French Leave 3, by Richard Binns
(Chiltern House)

The Taste of France, by Fay
Sharman (Macmillan Papermac)

The Gault Millau Guide to France
(Mitchell Beazley in UK and
Knapp in USA)

Michelin Guide to France (Michelin)

*The Good Hotel Guide (Britain and
Western Europe)* (UK Consumers'
Association)

INDEX